MINDSTYLES / LIFESTYLES

...the universe begins to look
more like a great thought
than like a great machine

sir jasper jeans

Corita

MINDSTYLES
LIFESTYLES

BY NATHANIEL LANDE

**A COMPREHENSIVE
OVERVIEW OF TODAY'S
LIFE-CHANGING PHILOSOPHIES**

INTRODUCTION: DR. HANS SELYE
CONCLUSION: R. BUCKMINSTER FULLER
COLOR ILLUSTRATIONS: CORITA KENT

THE ANALYSTS ○ THE SCIENTISTS ○ THE GROUPS ○
THE PHYSICIANS ○ THE PSYCHICS ○ THE HEALERS ○
THE MEDITATORS ○ THE PREACHERS ○ THE GURUS
○ THE MOVERS ○ THE SHAKERS ○ THE ACTIVISTS ○

PRICE/STERN/SLOAN
Publishers, Inc., Los Angeles

For Andrew:

It's not always where you're going –
It's also where you're coming from . . .

GRAPHIC DESIGN / ED POWERS

Published by Price/Stern/Sloan Publishers, Inc.
410 North La Cienega Boulevard, Los Angeles, California 90048
Printed in the United States of America.
Library of Congress Catalog Card No.: 76-10562
ISBN: 0-8431-0409-0

acknowledgments

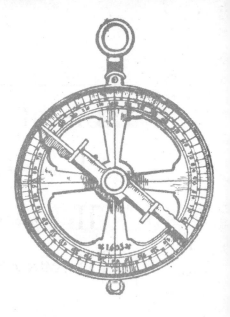

The writing of a book of such range and detail has occupied many months spent in research and writing, and the discussion and selection that are such an important part of the editing process. Almost as much again has been discarded as has been included, though this may seem hard to believe.

My gratitude is due to all those who have given so generously of their time in talking to me, working with me, and generally facilitating the appearance of the book in its final form. For space reasons, I can only list them in alphabetical order and hope each will accept this as a token of my thanks for a unique and invaluable contribution.

For support and advice:

Joan Fulton, Joan Hackett, Hans Holzer, Marge and Michael Levee, Toni Lilly, Cynthia Lindsay, David Mendelsohn, Barbara Pallenberg, Gabriel and Ruth Perle, Roger Price, Barbara Roberts, Allegra Snyder, Jaime Snyder.

For research and writing:

Steven Bush, Jackie Davidson, Lisa Degens, Fern Fadness, Rodger Fadness, Lindsay Gilliland, Barbara Goldman, Leslie Hall, Stephen Mann, James Pickett, David Schulke, Patt Schwab, David Sentence, Christopher Spurrell, Eva Welsh, and Gloria Wetzel. And a special thanks to Art Kunkin for his excellent research and writing on Scientology and est.

This book could never have been without the efforts of Afton Slade, an old friend and graceful writer, whose work has embellished many of its pages. The industry and creativity of Jean Atcheson, my editor, imposed order on an unruly mass of material — the final form of the book is the result of much stimulating discussion with her and Larry Sloan, my publisher. Auriel Douglas, Chuck Gates, and Ed Powers added their outstanding editorial and artistic expertise to our endeavors.

I could not have been more pleased to publish my first book with Hans Selye and Buckminster Fuller serving as my "bookends." To them both, my grateful thanks; I could not be in better company.

Lastly, I must thank Corita Kent, whose gorgeous paintings raise my book to the level of an art work, and all the other contributors who graciously allowed me to interview them or make use of their work. I asked each for his or her help because they represented the very best in their fields and were prepared to be forthright and candid.

So, to Dick Atcheson, Stewart Brand, Sidney Cohen, Stewart Emery, Heinz Von Foerster, Buckminster Fuller, Elmer and Alyce Green, Robert Greenblatt, Hans Holzer, Madeline Hunter, Nathan Kline, Lester Kirkendall, Bill Kroger, Geoff Languedoc, John and Toni Lilly, Ernie Lykissas, Eleanor Macklin, Rollo May, Andrea McNichol, Gerard O'Neill, J. B. Rhine, Hans Selye, George Serban, Allegra Snyder, Tom Vinetz. . .

Thank you! The quality of your responses has enriched both my book and my life.

Nathaniel Lande
Beverly Hills, California
September 1976

table of contents

PART A: The Mind Masters and Their Therapies

PART B: Theories in Action

V SEX STYLES 207-232

the way things are

"Three passions, simple but overwhelmingly strong,
have governed my life: the longing for love, the search
for knowledge, and unbearable pity for the suffering of
mankind. These passions, like great winds, have blown me
hither and thither, in a wayward course, over a deep ocean
of anguish, reaching to the very verge of despair.

I have sought love, first, because it brings ecstasy —
ecstasy so great that I would often have sacrificed all
the rest of life for a few hours of this joy. I have sought
it, next, because it relieves loneliness — that terrible
loneliness in which one shivering consciousness looks over
the rim of the world into the cold unfathomable lifeless
abyss. I have sought it, finally, because in the union
of love I have seen, in a mystic miniature, the prefiguring
vision of the heaven that saints and poets have imagined.
This is what I sought, and though it might seem too good
for human life, this is what — at last — I have found.

With equal passion I have sought knowledge. I have
wished to understand the hearts of men. I have wished
to know why the stars shine. And I have tried to apprehend
the Pythagorean power by which number holds sway above the
flux. A little of this, but not much, I have achieved.

Love and knowledge, so far as they were possible, led
upward toward the heavens. But always pity brought me back
to earth. Echoes of cries of pain reverberate in my heart.
Children in famine, victims tortured by oppressors, helpless
old people a hated burden to their sons, and the whole world
of loneliness, poverty, and pain make a mockery of what
human life should be. I long to alleviate the evil, but
I cannot, and I too suffer.

This has been my life. I have found it worth living,
and would gladly live it again if the chance were offered me."

—Bertrand Russell, *Autobiography*

YESTERDAYS

There was a time when life was simple. Sure, there were problems. But we could always go to our family, our priest, our fellow villagers, our associates, or our close friends and talk them out. Even if they didn't know how to deal with the problems any better than we did, it was at least a chance to let off steam. Our journeys away from home seldom involved more than a few miles. We didn't have the barrage of media to occupy us, so we spent our evenings in conversation or in solitude, thinking — and the only news we heard was news that somehow involved us.

The Mass Age

Then came the Mass Age — with its mass technology, mass communications, mass advertising, mass production, mass emotion. Not only were we assaulted daily with more news than we cared to hear; we also began to feel guilty about our very existence through constant reminders that there was a "population explosion." There was so much talk about too many people and too few jobs that we began to feel as if we had better hang on to whatever work we could find, whether we liked it or not.

War came and went, and came again — and while war used to be a distant faraway activity in that outside world where other people had to deal with it, now it became a terrifyingly real series of images flickering into our living rooms. Exposure became a way of life; we began to learn things we never really wanted to know. The foods we had been eating for years were suddenly instigators of disease, and the tobacco we had enjoyed since the Indians first shared it with us was hazardous to our health.

How does it look from here? Not so good. Apathy is settling over the land like a moldy mantle; inflation and unemployment are uncontrolled. Medical schools turn out eager young doctors who are more interested in being able to pay their malpractice premiums than in treating human beings; by the time engineers have mastered the current body of knowledge it is apt to be out of date; lawyers have priced themselves and their skills almost out of the market, and there are few openings for newcomers at the bar.

Educational Surplus

There is a surplus of teachers, yet it would appear we need to re-examine our educational system. Educational test scores at every level are going down across the country. Colleges complain that the majority of the entering freshmen do not read effectively and cannot write coherently. Ph.D.s, particularly in the humanities, cannot find work. The jobs are simply not there waiting for the June graduates. We are training people in skills they will not be able to find opportunities to use,

14

breeding massive frustration. Overqualified in many areas of professional and technical training, our society is emotionally, physically, and psychologically underqualified for survival.

Perhaps we are morally underqualified as well. To maintain lavish incomes, the legal profession opposes no-fault insurance, commissions to screen medical malpractice claims — moves that might lessen litigation or promote real justice are fought and frequently killed by legislatures made up mostly of lawyers. It has come to seem as if nothing is sacred save the fee and the interests of the client. A sense of deep moral commitment or responsibility? Irrelevant . . . outmoded. Not only were most of the cast who played out that sordid Watergate drama, lawyers; a survey taken of law students at the time revealed that most couldn't understand what the Watergate participants had done that was so wrong.

Mass Thinking

And the lawyers are not alone. Whipped by the demands of organized technology, organized labor, mass production, mass thinking, we are beginning to grow numb to feeling individual responsibility. Six men at three national networks control television programming across the country — and apparently equate the lowest program quality with the highest potential quantity of viewers. Television, like the country, has its roots founded in violence and profit. Is it quality or quantity? There is little validation for the network theory, but there is no one near their peaks of power to challenge them. "The Incredible Machine," a well-made documentary about the human body that was turned down by all three networks, was finally shown on the public broadcasting channels to one of the largest audiences in viewing history.

The Declaration of Independence tells us we are all entitled to the pursuit of happiness, and pursue it we do, frantically. But where is the pursuit of excellence? Where are the heroes, the stalwarts who care about justice and honesty and commitment? In a world of frustration and stress, our creative power is not being used to solve our real, most deeply felt problems.

A New Age Yet Unborn?

We may be, as Rollo May suggests in *The Courage to Create,* "living at a time when one age is dying and the new age is not yet born." Faced with the frightening possibility of change, some people are paralyzed into inaction and apathy. Others pursue old goals, believe in old truisms long after they have ceased to be valid. When apathy becomes the principal characteristic of a society, that society capitulates to the forces of history. For the new age, when all is said and done, will be forthcoming with or without our consent. Whether the future is forged by sensitive and aware individuals, or simply exists as some limbo inhabited by robot men, depends upon our courage to participate in its evolution.

As an example, the energy crisis was a crisis of priorities, of unintelligent planning, of misrepresentation. An intelligence crisis, to be sure. The argument raging over the safety and advisability of nuclear energy is fast becoming academic — the increasing cost of construction and the rapidly dwindling supply of uranium will soon cancel each other out. If we invested a portion of the billions proposed for nuclear facilities in solar energy, we could solve the problem with a permanent, nonpolluting source. But this would require an alteration of all our habitual ways of thinking. Decisions have to be made in the best interests of all society, feeding into the computer other criteria than profit and protection of monopoly. There has to be a way of breaking out of the box.

Maybe we are. We are at least beginning to question our belief systems. There is a sense of re-evaluation, re-awakening, a renewed search — a consciousness revolution. We must solve our inner as well as our outer problems if man is to survive, or, as Faulkner put it, not only endure, but prevail.

We are in a very real crisis. The written Chinese word for crisis is a combination of the symbols for danger and opportunity. The purpose of this anthology is to provide a means of investigating a variety of concepts, at least in brief outline. Meanwhile, what's happening?

> On February 29 at 9:30 a.m., Frederick LeBoyer delivered his 10,000th baby. In the warm, darkened delivery room he used his supremely simple technique for easing the birth trauma, caressing the child and helping him start life without pain, confusion, and fear.

> A young man working his way through medical school by playing drums in a rock band reported to his therapist that in all his years he had reached only three peaks of perfection when suddenly he felt like a great drummer.

> Gregge Tiffin conducted an Astral Projection Workshop, assigning an astrological guide to each participant.

> Stephen Gaskin admitted another new member to his self-sustaining agricultural commune.

Phil Butler altered his state of consciousness in the Lilly Tank. Completely suspended in darkness, silence and water for a period of four hours, he hallucinated without the aid of drugs.

A group of Swamis led several hundred people in silent meditation on a football field while children and dogs frolicked around them.

Reverend Ike delivered a sermon on how to acquire wealth on every level.

Arthur Janov heard his 2,000th primal scream.

The recorded voice of Moshe Feldenkrais echoed through a roomful of leotard-clad ladies in Berkeley.

Lonnie Barbach conducted her third seminar on human sexuality and orgasm to a group of women.

Judith and Al Richard packed to go on a marriage encounter weekend.

Phyllis Longbach felt instant enlightenment and joyously decided to devote her life to the Majaraj-Ji and his Divine Light Mission.

An editor brought a ping-pong table into the new New York offices of her magazine and was fired for blurring the line between work and play.

A group of shaven-headed men squared off around a table at the Synanon Center in Santa Monica, California, to play The Game.

In Seattle, Joanie Lusk wept in convulsive sobs, soothed and patted by a circle of her peers in Re-evaluation Counseling, discharging the pain of her rejection by a girls' sorority in the seventh grade.

At 9:45, having just completed his manuscript on current psychological disciplines, Dr. Jerry Morrow realized in one blinding flash why schools do not enhance wisdom, governments cannot maintain order, courts do not dispense justice, prosperity fails to produce happiness, Utopian plans never generate Utopias — and at 9:46, he shot himself.

Every age has its symbol, some figure or object that seems to freeze for all time what life was like. In the '20s it was the flapper with the champagne glass. The effervescent view of life went flat with the hard economic conditions of the '30s, and the Great Depression is remembered by black and white photographs of lonely victims standing on street corners. The complexities and deep divisions of life in the '60s require a map of Vietnam.

Now, midway through the '70s, it is a feeling rather than a figure that best characterizes the life of many people — the terrible feeling of tension. Stress has been called the emotional virus of the '70s.

○ *More than 100 million Americans take tranquilizers.*

○ *At least 100 million Americans support an $80 million astrology industry.*

○ *Americans spend more than $1 billion each year on various forms of psychotherapy.*

Whether the current situation presages our downfall or the exciting emergence of a new awareness, it's very likely you are not familiar with all the concepts at your disposal. New approaches, old disciplines — they're right here in our own time. The very fact that they exist tells me you should know more about them. You should have a choice.

How to find your own place, your domain — a mathematical concept, an entity, a housing center in your mind? Here we present some pathways, some routes to the domains now existing. Some are Band-Aids, some delusions, a few offer real breakthroughs, dramatic new ways to look at self and society, new ways to think and to be.

At the very end of this book, after Buckminster Fuller's *Conclusions,* are some *Afterthoughts* of my own, drawn from experiences that affected me during the writing of the book. They really form part of this introduction — the two are complementaries that mirror each other.

Back in November 1972, Joyce Carol Oates envisioned the future in a powerful article in *Saturday Review.* One thing she said I particularly like and think I see already happening:

> *"Instead of hiding our most amazing, mysterious, and inexplicable experiences, we will learn to articulate and share them; instead of insisting upon rigid academic or intellectual categories . . . we will see how naturally they flow into one another, supporting and explaining each other. Yesterday's wildly ornate, obscure, poetic prophecies evolve into today's calm statements of fact."*

— *Nathaniel Lande*

preface/ON STRESS

BY HANS SELYE, M.D.

Hans Selye, M.D., Ph.D., D.Sc., F.R.S., is the world-famous endocrinologist whose concept of stress was acclaimed at the World Congress of Medical Psychology as "breathtaking in its scope. It has permeated medical thinking and influenced medical research in every land, probably more rapidly and more intensely than any other theory of disease ever proposed." Born in Vienna, Dr. Selye obtained his Ph.D. and M.D. degrees from the German University in Prague; since 1945 he has been at the University of Montreal, where he is currently professor of experimental medicine and surgery. The General Adaptation Syndrome which he outlines in this article on stress, he modestly does not mention as being his own discovery — and the basis for his worldwide renown. Fortunately for the general public, Dr. Selye's open, informal way of writing has made his views on this important topic available to a far wider circle of readers than those in his own specialized field. I am indeed grateful to him for this contribution in the form of a Preface to my book.

It was with the greatest pleasure that I accepted the invitation to write an introduction to this book.

Nathaniel Lande's investigation into the incredibly diverse ways of living and thinking that characterize America today is both exhaustive and objective. His years of experience in many widely different domains furnish the personal background and contacts, without which the writing of a book of such encyclopedic scope as this could not even be contemplated.

These days every aspect of society is being evaluated and challenged, and as traditional values fall into disrespect, it becomes more and more difficult for an individual to choose, and to defend, any one pathway.

During 40 years of research on stress, I have found no single situation in our lives that is more damaging, more stressful, than that of being faced with a number of alternatives and the necessity of choosing amongst them, but of having no solid criteria upon which to base the decision.

The Concept of Stress

The word *stress*, like the words *success*, *failure*, or *happiness*, means different things to different people. It would seem that no single definition can be agreed upon, although the word has become increasingly part of our daily vocabulary.

There is an important conceptual and semantic distinction, however, which must be drawn in order to make some sense out of this confusion. Most people think of themselves as undergoing conditions of stress, to which their reaction is tension, joy, or anxiety, as may be appropriate. In fact, the situation is quite the reverse.

In physiological terms, stress is the *nonspecific response* of the body to any demand made upon it. Thus, when an organism is called upon to readjust or adapt in order to maintain normal functioning, it is under stress. Interestingly, it is completely irrelevant whether the agent or situation provoking the stress is pleasant or unpleasant; the signs are the same. Sorrow, joy, heat, cold, worry, pain, trauma — all can induce the same physiological manifestations of stress in the body. A *stressor*, then, is any stimulus which is intense enough and/or brought to bear for long enough to induce the reaction of stress. To speak of emotional stress or physical stress is incorrect, for these terms actually refer to stressors, all of which are different, but all of which give rise to the same bodily reaction: the demand for adaptation. It is the intensity of this demand and how long it continues that matter in drawing a distinction between stress and *distress*.

Stress is, in fact, the spice of life; as is clear from the definition, there is no way of avoiding it. No matter what you do or what happens to you, you are constantly being challenged to maintain life and to resist and adapt to changing external influences. Even while fully relaxed and asleep you are under some stress: your heart must continue to pump blood, your intestines to digest last night's dinner, your muscles to move your chest to permit respiration. Even your brain is not at complete rest while you are dreaming.

Nor is stress simply nervous tension; stress reactions occur in lower animals, which have no nervous system, and even in plants. Stress is not the nonspecific result of damage. We have seen that it is immaterial whether an agent is pleasant or unpleasant; its stressor effect depends merely on the intensity of the demand made upon the adaptive work of the body. Normal activities — a game of tennis or even a passionate kiss — can produce considerable stress without causing conspicuous damage.

Three Stages

The concept of stress is very old. It must have occurred even to prehistoric man that the loss of vigor and feeling of exhaustion that overcame him during hard labor, prolonged exposure to cold or heat, loss of blood, agonizing fear, or any kind of disease had some elements in common. He might also have noticed that whenever he was faced with a prolonged and unaccustomed strenuous task — swimming in cold water, lifting rocks, or going without food — he would pass through three stages.

First, he would experience hardship, then he would get used to it, and finally he would not be able to stand it any longer. Primitive man, if he took the time to identify this three-phase response, certainly did not think of it as a general law regulating the behavior of living beings faced with an exacting task. The immediate necessities of finding food and shelter kept him far too busy to worry about such concepts. Yet the vague outlines were there, ready to be analyzed and translated from indistinct feelings into the precise terms of science.

GAS

The name "General Adaptation Syndrome" or GAS was coined to describe the response of any living thing to a stressor. The GAS is composed of three distinct phases: the alarm reaction, the stage of resistance, and the stage of exhaustion.

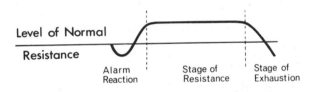

The alarm reaction represents a "call to arms" of the body's defenses, and is activated when an organism first encounters a stimulus strong enough to necessitate adaptation. Think of the shock of your first dive into a cold lake — even colloquially, it's quite "alarming."

But after a few minutes, the water will feel less cold; you might remark to a less enthusiastic friend that the temperature was really quite pleasant once you got accustomed to it. The stage of resistance has been reached, and how long it can last depends upon such factors as the actual temperature of the water, your physical condition, your metabolic rate (e.g., how quickly your body can produce the

heat necessary to maintain normal temperature), and so on.

But sooner or later, you will probably notice that you are again cold and beginning to shiver; the stage of resistance, the acquired adaptation to cold, is wearing off, and the stage of exhaustion is imminent. Physically, you can no longer produce enough heat to offset its loss to the water; in your muscles, the wastes from each cell are beginning to accumulate, resulting in tiredness and aching. A cramp could ensue now, just as it could during the shock of your first exposure to the cold.

Severe Stress

Only the most severe stress leads rapidly to the stage of exhaustion and death. Most of the physical and mental stressors which act during a limited period produce changes corresponding only to the first and second GAS stages: at first they may upset and alarm us, but then we get used to them. In the course of a normal human life, everybody goes through the first two stages many, many times; otherwise we could never become adapted to perform all the activities and face all the demands which are man's lot.

For instance, a foot race produces a stress situation, mainly in our muscles and cardiovascular system. To cope with this we first have to warm up and get these organs ready for the task at hand (by doing this, we can avoid the physical extremes of the alarm reaction). Then for a while we will be at the height of efficiency in running; but, eventually, exhaustion will set in. This could be compared with an alarm reaction, a stage of resistance, and a stage of exhaustion, all limited primarily to the muscular and cardiovascular systems. But such an exhaustion is largely reversible; after a good rest we will be back to virtually normal again.

It is only when the whole organism is exhausted and hopelessly encumbered by the accumulated wastes of life that it enters into the terminal stage of exhaustion of the GAS. This happens in senility at the end of a normal life span, or through the accelerated aging caused by excessive stress. Only when all our adaptability is used up will irreversible, general exhaustion set in, to be followed by death.

GAS and Aging

There seems to be a close interrelation between the GAS and aging. People can become used to a number of things (cold, heavy muscular work, worries) which at first had a very alarming effect upon them. Yet, after prolonged exposure, sooner or later, all resistance breaks down and exhaustion sets in. It is as though something were lost or used up during the work of adaptation. Although we have a term for this phenomenon, *adaptation energy*, we still have no precise concept of what this energy might be. It would seem that at birth, each of us inherits a certain amount of adaptation energy, the magnitude of which is determined by our individual genetic background. We can draw upon this capital thriftily for a long but monotonous, uneventful existence, or spend it lavishly in the course of a stressful, intense, but perhaps more colorful and exciting life. In any case, there is just so much of it, and we must budget accordingly.

Absolute freedom from stress is death. Contrary to public opinion we must not — and indeed cannot — avoid stress. But we can meet it efficiently and enjoy it by learning more about its mechanism and by adjusting our philosophy of life accordingly.

Man has always tried to identify and neutralize those stressors which could be considered negative, and maximize those which are pleasant. Vast strides have been made in the alleviation of stressors which cause physical discomfort. Much of the world's population is now clothed, housed, fed, and vaccinated. It is natural that in the more affluent West, the main concern of many investigators in this latter half of the century is to resolve the social and emotional problems with which we are now confronted. The proliferation of alternative mindstyles and lifestyles bears witness to the depth of this concern, with the lay person as well as the professional.

Alternatives

It seems that the most common source of mental or emotional distress is also the oldest: the duty to choose amongst alternatives. As the existentialists say, "Man is condemned to be free." One of the advantages of this book is that it offers information about a wide range of systems of belief and ways of being which have enabled their adherents to define more clearly their chosen pathways through life, and to face the dilemmas that are an inevitable hazard along the way: Of course, for many individuals, the moral choices have already been made and all that is needed is a framework within which to fit them. Other readers, generally dissatisfied with their lives, may be looking for a new orientation, a fresh approach. Whichever is the case, this book will surely be of help in this regard, presenting as it does a myriad of thought-provoking philosophies and ideas.

Once an individual's philosophical and moral position is settled, probably his next choice is that of a lifestyle in harmony with it. Once again, within these pages can be found accounts of many widely disparate ways of life, outlined with an objectivity and thoroughness that will surely be appreciated by those in quest of an alternative way of living. Of course, the most important, and perhaps the most difficult choice is always the first one. But almost any direction is better than none at all; as Montaigne put it, echoing the words of Seneca some 1,500 years earlier, "No wind blows in favor of the ship without a port of destination."

When we say someone is under stress, we actually mean under excessive stress, i.e., distress — just as the statement "He is running a temperature" refers to an abnormally high temperature, raised above the regular heat production essential for life.

Each one of us has an optimal stress level. To keep stress from becoming distress, we must have not only the right amount but the right kind for the right duration. Distress often results from prolonged or unvaried stress, or from frustration.

Even the experts do not know why the stress of frustration rather than that of excessive muscular work is much more likely to produce disease, such as peptic ulcers, migraine, high blood pressure, or even a simple "pain in the neck." In fact, physical exercise can even relax us and help us withstand mental frustration. Often a voluntary change of activity is as good as or even better than rest, when completing a particular task becomes impossible. Substituting demands on our musculature for those previously made on the intellect not only gives our brain a rest but helps us to avoid worrying about the frustrating interruption. Stress on one system can help to relax another.

Work is a basic biological need of man. The question is not whether we should or should not work, but what kind of work best suits each individual. In order to function normally, man needs work as he needs air, food, sleep, social contacts, or sex. Few people would enthusiastically welcome the discovery of test-tube babies making sex superfluous. Let us not look forward with eager anticipation to the days when automation will make all labor redundant.

Many therapeutic techniques help us indirectly by improving our physical and mental fitness. Among these, the counsel most commonly given is to relax and refrain from any but the most unavoidable activities, or to seek diversion in leisure and play. However, this kind of advice is more easily given than followed, because active people are particularly dependent upon finding outlets for their pent-up energy, and cannot relax or play without continuously suffering from the feeling that they are wasting their time.

For people with an irrepressible drive to seek stress, some comparatively unexacting diversionary activity seems infinitely preferable to doing nothing. But because the so-called leisure occupations have in many cases become not occasions to relax but highly goal-oriented competitive efforts at outstanding achievement in sports, social, educational, and civic events, they represent a poor antidote to the emotional stressors of daily work.

This problem is particularly important for those who are approaching or have reached the retirement age and simply cannot go on utilizing their energy in the way to which they have become accustomed. As the progress of technology increasingly shortens work hours for most standard occupations, semiretirement will be possible almost as soon as a career begins. Not everyone wants to be a sportsman, or knows how to occupy additional leisure time with the more passive enjoyment of music, painting, sculpture, travel, or spectator sports. Hence, many people seek to release energy through such dangerous outlets as drugs, excessive drinking, violence, and other forms of destructive behavior. We may be able to solve our age-old problem of having to live by the sweat of our brow, but the fatal enemy of all utopias is boredom.

Homo Faber

Why should we work so hard to avoid work? The French philosopher Henri Bergson justly points out that it would be more appropriate to call our species *homo faber*, "the making man," rather than *homo sapiens*, "the knowing man," for the characteristic feature of man is not his wisdom but his constant urge to work on improving his environment and himself.

The most important aim of man cannot be to work as little as possible. For the full enjoyment of leisure, you have to be tired first, just as for the full enjoyment of food the best cook is hunger.

Don't listen to the cherished slogans of the agitators who keep repeating that "There is more to life than just work" or that "You should work to live, not live to work." These sound pretty convincing, but are they really? Our aim should rather be not to avoid work but to find the kind of occupation which, for us, is closest to play. The best way of avoiding undue stress is to select an environment (spouse, boss, social group) which is in line with our innate preferences, and to find an activity which we like and respect. Only thus can we eliminate the need for constant

adaptation that is the major cause of stress.

Among the procedures we use to protect ourselves against the damaging effects of distress, some are activities employed by the individual as a means of diversion from daily routine while others are more formal techniques or therapies. Some of these treatments are described in *Mindstyles* and in *Body Styles.*

Just as muscular exercise, hot baths, saunas, and the like appear to be of some help in combatting the distress caused by the regular occurrences of everyday life, a number of psychological methods also enjoy considerable popularity. Although most of these techniques seem to have beneficial effects upon general well-being and mental performance, the reasons why they work cannot yet be fully explained in medical terms. Great progress has been made, however, in understanding the biochemical changes that accompany the refreshing relaxation induced by such different indirect means of improving well-being as participating in athletics, spending time in relaxed meditation, drinking a cup of coffee, or ingesting psychologically active drugs, such as tranquilizers. We need also to bear in mind that excessive or inappropriate use of any of these techniques can cause considerable damage, so until we know more about their mechanisms of action, we should proceed with caution.

Ethical Decision-Making

One of the main causes of distress in modern society arises from the need to make decisions about ethical problems. This has always been a troublesome area, full of pitfalls and hidden occasions of stress. But the situation has become particularly acute with the dwindling credibility and popularity of those traditional bastions of ethical codes, the organized religions. Many individuals now seriously question the relevance of many of the basic tenets on which they have formulated their lives, and consequently have begun to look elsewhere for a moral philosophy that more accurately represents them. (This is detailed in *Alternate Lifestyles* and in *Godstyles*.)

The instinct for survival and self-preservation is as characteristic of man as it is of other animals, and is just as powerful. The principal teaching of the Christian and many other religions, to respect the rights and wishes of one's fellow man as fully as one's own, is a worthwhile ideal but a practical impossibility, because it is not consonant with this basic instinct.

It is a scientifically established fact that man has an inescapable natural urge to work egoistically for things that can be stored up in order to strengthen his own well-being in the unpredictable situations with which life may confront him. This is not an instinct we should combat or be ashamed of. We can do nothing about having been built to work, and to work primarily for our own good. Every living being looks out for itself first of all. There is no example in nature of a creature guided exclusively by altruism and the desire to protect others. Hoarding is a vitally important biological instinct that we share with all animals, such as ants, bees, squirrels, and beavers.

However, "Earn thy neighbor's love," unlike love on command, *is* compatible with man's nature. It is based on the philosophy of altruistic egoism, which advocates the creation of personal capital, in the form of the feelings of accomplishment and security

we derive from actions that make others think well of us. Who can blame someone who wants to assure his own happiness and security by accumulating the treasure of other people's benevolence toward him? Practice of such a philosophy, in fact, can make you virtually unassailable, for none of us wants to attack and destroy those upon whom we depend.

I have spent 40 years of my life in the attempt to elucidate the mechanisms of stress and to apply these findings to everyday life. My experience has led me to some conclusions which may help others:

It is not sufficient to help only when asked. You must overcome your shyness in approaching people who may need your assistance, but — as usually happens — are too timid or too proud to ask for it.

Course of Goodwill

Before each major decision, take time to ask yourself which course will earn you more goodwill. Almost all actions give and take some of it. To give something to one (even if it is only your time and attention) necessarily deprives another. To offer major assistance that will really be appreciated throughout a person's life, you may have to expose a good friend to, what momentarily would seem senseless or purely egotistic behavior. And when you have to communicate an unpleasant decision, the benevolent tone of tact is usually more effective than the cold logic of tactics.

When faced with a task which is painful, yet indispensable to the achievement of your aim, don't procrastinate. Doctors cut right into an abscess to eliminate the pain; they don't prolong it by gently rubbing the surface.

Nothing paralyzes your efficiency more than frustration; nothing helps it more than success. Even after the greatest defeats, you can best combat the depressing thought of being a failure by taking stock of all the past achievements which no one can deny you. Such conscious stock-taking is most effective in re-establishing the self-confidence necessary for future success — you would be surprised how much this can help when everything seems hopeless.

Realize that men are not created equal, although they should all have a birthright to equal opportunities. In a free society, their performance ought to determine their progress. There will always be leaders and followers, but the leaders are worth keeping only as long as they can serve the followers by acquiring their love, respect, and gratitude.

Success Formulas

Finally, do not forget that there is no ready-made success formula which would suit everybody. We are all different and so are our problems. The only thing we have in common is our subordination to those fundamental biological laws which govern all living beings, including man. No previous code of ethics — religious, philosophical, or political — has provided specific prescriptions for each possible event we may meet in life. Each individual must meet a situation in his own way, on the basis of his unique genetic background, previous experiences, or state of health. Neither Christianity, communism, nor patriotism can tell you precisely what to do in each specific situation. Many times, in fact, you should not "do unto others as you would like them to do unto you," because their requirements may not be the same as yours. The decision on how to be most useful to the different individuals in your life must remain a problem for your own ingenuity to solve.

The study of the disparate solutions to the stressors in life is profoundly interesting in itself. The mere number of mindstyles and lifestyles so conveniently collected in this book is proof that no single solution is appropriate to all people. However, to have a basis for choosing one's own individual pathway, a few fundamental, scientifically founded and verifiable criteria can be of help.

Hans Selye
Montreal, 1976

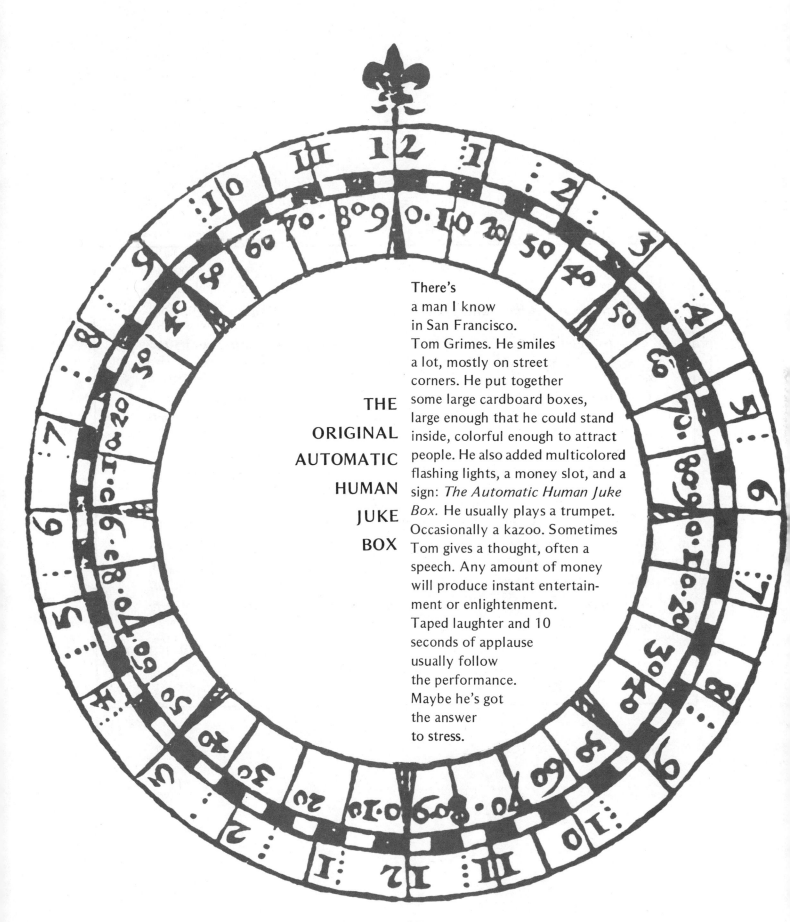

THE

ORIGINAL

AUTOMATIC

HUMAN

JUKE

BOX

There's
a man I know
in San Francisco.
Tom Grimes. He smiles
a lot, mostly on street
corners. He put together
some large cardboard boxes,
large enough that he could stand
inside, colorful enough to attract
people. He also added multicolored
flashing lights, a money slot, and a
sign: *The Automatic Human Juke
Box.* He usually plays a trumpet.
Occasionally a kazoo. Sometimes
Tom gives a thought, often a
speech. Any amount of money
will produce instant entertainment or enlightenment.
Taped laughter and 10
seconds of applause
usually follow
the performance.
Maybe he's got
the answer
to stress.

"I and many others, known and unknown to me, call upon you:

— to celebrate our joint power to provide all human beings with the food, clothing, and shelter they need to delight in living;

— to discover, together with us, what we must do to use mankind's power to create the humanity, the dignity, and the joyfulness of each one of us;

— to be responsibly aware of your personal ability to express your true feelings and to gather us together in their expression.

"We can only live these changes: we cannot think our way to humanity. Every one of us, and every group with which we live and work, must become the model of the era which we desire to create. The many models which will develop should give each one of us an environment in which we can celebrate our potential — and discover the way into a more human world."

Ivan Illich

THE MIND MASTERS

Psychology has always had an identity crisis. As an outgrowth of philosophy it struggled as a science. It was in need of the security of medicine and physics.

From medicine it took the model of pathology; from physics it took the idea of the parts and not the whole.

Man was thought of as a bundle of responses to stimuli. Behavior was no more than segments, experiences and experiments that could be managed and controlled.

Today there is a new approach, a focus on the intrinsic complexity of the individual and his richness and power of mind and consciousness. There is a new belief in man and his built-in capacities for growth and self-actualization.

There are new paths to bring about change, to search and understand and to heal. No longer are mind and body divided. There is a regard for completeness and fullness. Scientists are investigating feeling and its relationship to memory, and how this combination sets off electrical charges in the brain which activate changes in body chemistry.

Logic and rationality once dominated man's thinking rather than emotions and feelings. We are no longer rebelling against guilt and repression. There is interest in the will and in responsibility for self as a positive, natural, liberating force. This part looks at those Mind Masters who helped bring it all together.

THE ORIGINS OF PSYCHOTHERAPY

The Dark Ages represent a ponderous weight of darkness, gloom, ignorance, suspicion, and fear of the unknown, which reduced man and his psyche to a mere shadow of the self that had once been perceived by the classic philosophers. Through the Middle Ages philosophy and reason, the true parents of psychology and psychotherapy, were ousted by credulity and conjecture. The freedom to examine and question, to explore and discuss, to doubt and disagree, to feel and show love openly — these were dangers to be chained up, manacled by the dark, obsessive thought structure that permeated Christian society. Open discussion and private talks, an occasional dialogue were the stuff of conspiracy, heresy, the work of the nonbeliever, the devil within — fit material for the racks and bonfires of the Inquisition.

Possession by the Devil

To the primitive mind it seemed evident that evil, the devil and his demonic forces were the causative agents in all forms of mental disorders. The extreme religious beliefs and suspicions of the medieval period simply changed the objects of attention. The mission of the early forefathers of psychopathology in the late 15th and 16th centuries was clearly the necessary extermination of witches and witchcraft. All nervous disorders and other "possession by the devil" were equally targets to be eliminated and physically destroyed.

Slight progress can be seen later in the 16th century with the establishment of the first hospitals for the mentally ill: the Bethlehem Royal Hospital (Bedlam) in London in 1547; the Santa Maria della Pieta in Rome in 1548. Now those sick or "possessed" could easily be removed from society — an appropriate signature on a piece of paper and the unfortunate could be committed by a knowing family or helpful friend, and his associate disorders dealt with, far from the eyes and ears of society, save for those who came to stare and snigger at the antics of the "moonstruck." Patients were chained, beaten, bled, and immersed in. ice-water baths — typical cures for such afflictions as melancholia, hysteria, and other nervous disorders.

Humane Treatment as Breakthrough

One of the first genuine breakthroughs in the humane treatment of these illnesses occurred in Paris at the mental hospitals of Bicetre and Salpetriere, where the physician Philippe Pinel (1745-1826) took over as administrative head and reformed them completely. He was horrified by the existing conditions and changed them radically: chains and fetters were removed, warm, comfortable, sleep-inducing baths replaced dousings with ice-water, bleedings were abolished, and fresh air and more freedom were seen as essential ingredients in restoring health.

Finally, conditions became more favorable and the idea of psychotherapy began to emerge. Its development coincided with the discovery and use of hypnosis, which can be attributed somewhat indirectly to the work of a Viennese holder of three doctorates, Franz Anton Mesmer (1734-1815). Mesmer's work in Paris with "animal magnetism" or "mesmerism" later developed into hypnosis; Mesmer received no recognition for his work, however, and was forced to leave Paris as a result of charges that he was a charlatan. A committee headed by no less a free thinker than Benjamin Franklin, then American ambassador to France, issued a statement denying the existence of animal magnetism and its purported cures.

Charcot and Hypnotism

Hostilities, fears, doubts, and anxieties continued to be projected onto hypnotism by the medical community until Freud's famous teacher, Jean Martin Charcot (1825-1893) finally brought hypnosis the recognition it deserved. Charcot, a distinguished neurologist at the Hospital Salpetriere, did not need to concern himself with the views of his skeptical peers, for he was already highly regarded for his many medical achievements. At that time Charcot mistakenly thought hypnosis itself was a nerve disorder similar to if not identical with hysteria. He believed that only "hysteria neurotics" could be hypnotized, and thus concluded that the two conditions were of similar origin. He also traced hysteria to the uterus, hypothesizing that disorders of the womb were the source of neurosis and hypnosis. Do we perhaps glimpse here an early trace of Freud's theory of sexual psychology?

There were two schools of hypnosis in France at that time: Charcot's in Paris and the followers of Bernheim and Liebault at Nancy who viewed hypnosis as a condition of ordinary sleep, induced by suggestibility. Later the Paris school discovered that hysteria was not confined to females and that the state of hypnosis was not pathological; even before that, however, Charcot had achieved the feat of freeing hypnosis from the realm of the occult and gaining acceptance for it in the world of medicine.

Freud on Hypnosis

Hypnosis continued to be used as a major tool in psychotherapy. It eased explorations into the unconscious and the emotive complexes of the past. It relieved or abated many of the disturbing symptoms of neurosis and could be used to suggest alternative behavior. However, its results did not last very long, because the patient was not compelled to use his own mind or reasoning faculties to work through his problems. Instead of urging recollection back through the "resistances," as Freud called them, hypnosis temporarily eased the mind around them. They were still there "dammed up" and not understood, waiting to return at some future date. As Freud said, "The results were capricious and not permanent; therefore I gave up hypnotism. And then I understood that no comprehension of the dynamics of these afflictions was possible as long as hypnosis was employed."

For these reasons, Freud abandoned hypnosis, and a new therapy based on understanding was born. "True psychoanalysis only began," he wrote, "when the help of hypnosis was discarded."

To the extent that the therapies, their techniques, and their methods of analysis have the power to dispel the veils of man's ignorance, to loosen and free us from the bonds of our beliefs and the patterns of our neuroses, our behavior can be altered permanently through understanding, and we can be more open . . . more ourselves.

PSYCHOANALYSIS / SIGMUND FREUD (1856-1939)

Born in Freiberg, Moravia, on May 6, 1856, Freud was the oldest in a family of seven. After obtaining his M.D. from the University of Vienna in 1881, he became professor of neuropathology at the University and remained there until the last year of his life when he was compelled to flee a Nazi-dominated Vienna.

A number of thinkers were significant in guiding and directing Freud's development. The first of these was Jean Charcot of the famous Hospital Salpetriere in Paris, with whom Freud studied from 1885 to 1886. With Charcot, Freud cultivated and developed his interests in the areas of hypnosis, hysteria, and sexuality as a possible basis of neurosis. Charcot's other famous pupil, Pierre Janet (1859-1947), with whom Jung was later to study, shared Freud's views about hypnosis, hysteric neurosis, and the unconscious, but never gained either the recognition or the following that Freud did. Instead Janet went on to develop a "psychology of dissociation" and became the last in • the line of distinguished Salpetriere psychiatrists.

Three years after his stay with Charcot, Freud returned to France in order to pursue his interest in hypnosis at the other famous French school, at Nancy. Here he studied with Bernheim and Liebault, who had formed the hypothesis that hypnosis was not a disease but rather a state of induced sleep.

In the 1890s Freud joined forces with yet another major thinker in his development, Josef Breuer (1842-1925), a colleague at the University of Vienna. With Breuer he explored hypnosis as a treatment of what was then known as "hysteria neurosis." Ideally, they found, hypnosis led to catharsis, the intense emotive release of an unconscious complex as it is brought to the surface.

In 1895 Freud and Breuer coauthored a work, *Studies in Hysteria*, based on a case study of one of Breuer's patients, which pointed the way to Freud's particular form of psychotherapy — psychoanalysis. However, because of personal differences, the two never worked together again.

In 1900 Freud published his definitive work, *The Interpretation of Dreams*, which demonstrated his idea that the major function of dreams was to relieve emotive tensions, and that "dream censorship," the source of distortion in dreams, came from the same source as the mechanism of repression.

Freud's idea of sex as being the underlying causal factor in neurosis finally emerged in his book *Three Essays on the Theory of Sexuality*, published in 1905. This thought became the cornerstone of his theories and beliefs for the remainder of his life.

The Psyche or Structure of Personality

The components of the psyche or personality entity are the *id,* the *ego,* and the *superego.* The id is defined by Freud as the source of instinctual drives and is the repository of hereditary influences, the source of all psychic energy. It is the oldest element and is dominated by the pleasure principle *(eros).* The id is governed by the ego, whose function is reality testing and reconciling the id with the outside world. The ego represses all unacceptable impulses, through sublimation, and is guided in its work by the superego. The superego, in turn, is influenced primarily by others, such as parents and society; it produces the phenomenon of conscience.

Freud divided the mind into the *unconscious,* the *preconscious,* and the *conscious.* He likened the structure of the mind to an iceberg. What can be seen on the surface as the smaller part is the conscious, the larger submerged part he designated as the unconscious, and between them, screening them from each other, is the preconscious. As Freud said, "Everything unconscious that can easily exchange the unconscious condition for the conscious one is better described as 'capable of entering consciousness,' or as preconscious." It is through the preconscious that the id reaches the ego. Considerable portions of the ego and superego are also unconscious; it is as though they were roots extending upward from the submerged unconscious into the upper or conscious part of the psyche.

Stages of Psychosexual Development

On its birth the infant's *libido* is at full current. This psychosexual source of energy develops through the following stages:

1. The *oral stage* — here the erotogenic zone is the mouth and it continues to be so from approximately two to four years of age.

2. The *anal stage* — here pleasurable attention is directed to the excretion process. Freud thought that the child wished to achieve an unassisted bowel movement as a way of pleasing the parents.

3. The *phallic stage* — here, from three to seven, the child anticipates the genital stage by deriving pleasure from fondling the genitals. Also during the phallic stage the male

child experiences a conflict caused by his incestuous desire for his mother, which is accompanied by a sense of guilt and a fear of castration by the father — in other words, the Oedipus conflict. During the "normal" course of personality development the conflict will be resolved when the boy begins to identify with his father and therefore is drawn away from the unconscious thought of having intercourse with his mother. Similarly, the girl turns toward her mother once thoughts of seducing her father (the Electra complex) dissolve, or diminish.

4. The *latency stage* — here the child from six to 11 identifies with the parent of the same sex, plays and associates with members of its own sex and represses the hostile and aggressive feelings of the prior stage.

5. The *genital stage* — here the child awakens to intimate and affectionate feelings of sexuality for the opposite sex.

If a person becomes "fixated" or not fully developed at any of these stages this contributes to mental maladjustment in adulthood, and whenever a problem occurs in later life, there will be a regression to the particular stage where development was arrested. This theory of libidinal development was introduced by Freud in 1905 with the publication of his *Three Essays on the Theory of Sexuality.*

Instincts

Recognizing there were an indeterminate number of instincts, Freud insisted that only two, *eros* and *thanatos,* were fundamental to human behavior. He defined eros as the pleasurable or productive life-giving instinct and thanatos as death, the destructive instinct. It is the tension between these two polarities, otherwise known as *libido,* or psychosexual energy, which generates action in the individual. This action is again governed by the three forms of mental activity: the id, the ego, and superego.

It is this arrangement of forces and faculties and the background within which they struggle for a stage of balance or equilibrium that for Freud constituted the human psyche. Given this definition, he claimed that the individual who proved incapable of resolving the warring factions was out of balance and internal proportion and consequently suffering from a neurosis: "A person only falls ill of a neurosis when the ego loses its capacity to deal in some way or other with the libido." He further claimed that the stronger the ego, the more easily it can handle the libido. Furthermore, "every weakening of the ego, from whatever cause, must have the same effect as an increase in the demands of the libido; that is, make a neurosis possible."

Anxiety

In each example of neurosis a certain amount of anxiety is present. Anxiety that is not released builds and is repeated; it "yields to a symptom-formation, which enables the anxiety to be 'bound.' "

Another source of neurosis is contributed by the commands and demands of a remorseful superego, the repetitious "shoulds" and "shouldn'ts," "don'ts" and "ought not tos" which tend to drain and shrink the ego's life forces, sapping the energy needed for other, more immediate activities.

In some cases these conditions can become so severe, and the ego is in such a state of disorganization, that a person's relationship to the real or outside world is severed. As Freud put it, "When the ego is detached from the reality of the external world, then, under the influence of the internal world, it slips down into psychosis."

Psychoanalytic Therapy

When a patient's ego is "weakened" and fallen, it becomes the task and challenge for the psychoanalyst to uncover the causes of the malignant conditions. He primarily draws upon the technique of "free association" or "talking out," where the patient is compelled to express everything that comes into his head, even if it is disagreeable to say it, even if it seems unimportant or positively meaningless. This method is also applied to the patient's dreams in order to gain further insight into the problem. The analyst probes into the past and the unconscious for repressed experiences primarily of a sexual nature, since to Freud all causes of the psychic imbalance were sexual in origin, stemming from unresolved conflicts in childhood.

To Freud patients often gave the impression that they were " 'fixed' to a particular point in their past, that they do not know how to release themselves from it, and are consequently alienated from both the present and the future." These fetters of "fixations" must be broken and understood, otherwise as Freud put it, the patients remain "marooned in their illness, as it were."

Usually, when probing for these points of fixation, resistances of all sorts emerge, which must be faced and worked through by both analyst and patient. The energy or motivating force for the breakthrough or breakdown of resistances springs from the "transference" relationship — the intense interpersonal relationship that develops between analyst and analysand. To Freud this transference is "something necessarily demanded," and it can be either negative or positive. If negative, the

34

In psychology, physiology and medicine, wherever a debate between the mystics and the scientists has been once for all decided, it it is the mystics who have usually proved to be right about the facts, while the scientists had the better of it in respect to theories. wm. james patient will exhibit a hostile attitude toward the analyst, which often gets in the way of further development. If it is positive, however, it will become the true motivating force for the patient's development. Through it the weak ego becomes strong, and the patient finds himself able to achieve things that would otherwise be beyond his power — "his symptoms disappear and he seems to have recovered — all of this simply out of love for his analyst."

·Psychoanalysis Now and Then

The psychoanalytical techniques utilized by today's therapists have been considerably broadened in scope since the day Freud first tried his therapy sessions. Meanwhile, the philosophy of psychoanalysis still offers a view of happiness based on the twin poles of love and work.

This homeostasis or balance is made possible by the isolation of the causes of anxiety, a process which is achieved by making the unconscious conscious in a patient. Technically, this means strengthening the ego, reducing the control of the superego, while at the same time expanding the awareness of the id.

Such manipulation of the triad is not a simple matter, especially as the process of psychoanalysis is often accompanied by a sense of shame at the extent and intimacy of personal revelation, which can hinder the process of recovery.

However, the standard techniques of psychoanalysis, which Freud had established by 1914, are designed to cope with the onset of shame. Such techniques are most clearly viewed in terms of goals, in which transference and resistance to transference form the basic polarities of interchange. Toward the end of a course of therapy (which

can last for several years), the working through becomes the most important part of the healing process. This is the time during which old anxieties are played out and the healthy structure of the mind rehabilitated.

Ideally, the analyst should exude warmth and be nonjudgmental. Such a combination of qualities will reassure the patient to such an extent that little tension is generated in the ongoing interaction. If, however, the psychoanalyst finds that comments made about him by the patient during the process of transference are true, then he is ethically bound to submit himself for further analysis. Genuine dislike felt by the psychoanalyst for the patient cannot be allowed to exist during the psychoanalytical relationship either, because it naturally reduces the possibilities of offering constructive comment.

Treatment usually lasts for anywhere from one to five hours a week, each session lasting 45 minutes. Beginning analysis, then, can be regarded as a substantial commitment both in time and in financial resources.

Modifications

Recent modifications to Freudian theory have resulted in less emphasis being placed on the process of catharsis than in the past — a development arrived at during Freud's lifetime, when he began to regard insight and correct judgmental technique as more fundamental in reorganizing the character structure.

Most recently, Freudian analytical techniques have been utilized more often with schizophrenic patients — although the greatest attention is still paid to neurosis. In the final assessment, however, it would be erroneous to view Freudian psychoanalysis as only useful for those who are trapped in poorly resolved sexual hangups. It is still the most utilized of all therapeutic techniques.

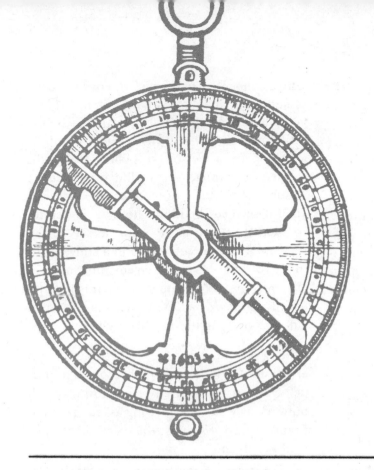

JUNGIAN ANALYSIS
CARL GUSTAV JUNG (1875-1961)

Born in Kesswil, Switzerland, the son of a liberal Protestant clergyman who had cultivated a deep interest in Oriental thought, Jung was brought up in Basel, where he later attended the University and received his M.D. degree in 1902. He became deeply interested in hypnosis after joining the staff of the Burgholzli Hospital in Zurich in 1900. At the time, Jung had read Freud's *The Interpretation of Dreams,* and his interest in the hysteria-hypnosis phenomenon led him to France in 1902 where he, like Freud before him, studied in the Paris school of hypnosis. The school was being run by Pierre Janet, Charcot's prize pupil and Freud's fellow student. As a consequence of his exposure to Janet's work, Jung's first research focused on the much-disputed phenomenon of psychic dissociation, the case where a split-off complex manifests itself as a voice, as if the complex itself had consciousness. Jung's doctoral dissertation, *On the Psychology and Pathology of So-called Occult Phenomena,* stands out as the main area of his interest during this stage of his development. At the time dissociation was thought of as "cultic" and highly unscientific, yet to Jung it was an area where spiritual and scientific knowledge intersect and become unified.

His next period of development, from 1904 to 1907, was localized around more strictly scientific interests, while he followed the teachings of the association school and developed his own word association test. Jung's interest in the human psyche as a whole again brought him into conflict with the traditional thinkers in the field; the usual association tests were designed to gather information about perceptions of isolated sense organs, whereas Jung's word association test was intended to gain access to and reveal insight into the inner life of the subject or patient. The test was composed of 100 common words which were read to a patient, who was told to respond with the first word that came to mind. When there was a delay, repetition, or no response at all, Jung discerned that a complex, a repressed feeling pattern, was in operation. Such complexes, he surmised, were dominating and unconsciously motivating the individual.

In 1907 Jung returned to the patients at Burgholzli in order to discover what "actually takes place inside the mentally ill." The next four years of pursuing this question with psychotic patients were extremely trying ones, and there were times, during his deeper probes into the psychotic world, when Jung feared for his own sanity, and even thought he had lost it.

The Freud-Jung Controversy

During this time Jung thought a great deal about Freud's controversial theories of sexuality. Freud was still viewed with distaste by the academic world, and although Jung agreed with some of his ideas he feared his career might be threatened if he too fully identified himself with Freud's thought.

However, in 1906 he daringly wrote a paper on *Freud's Theory of Hysteria*, and in the following year Freud invited Jung to visit him and the two talked intensely for 13 hours. Jung was now more impressed by Freud's sexuality theory, although he still had reservations, which he tried to advance on several occasions. Each time, however, Freud would emphasize his naivete and lack of experience. Jung could not decide to what extent Freud's strong emphasis on sexuality

was connected to his own subjective prejudices, and to what extent it was verifiable. He also deeply questioned Freud's attitude toward the spirit. Freud insisted that anything in a person or work of art that seemed to express some kind of spirituality was in fact evidence of repressed sexuality. To Jung it seemed Freud was holding desperately to sexuality, as if it were a self-defined religion. This was confirmed in a conversation in 1910 when Freud begged Jung never to abandon the sexual theory: "That is the most essential thing of all. You see, we must make a dogma of it, an unshakable bulwark."

Jung wrote that he said this with the emotion of a father telling his son to promise he will go to church every Sunday. "A bulwark against what?" Jung asked. To which Freud replied, "Against the black tide of mud — of occultism."

This alarmed Jung, to whom it demonstrated that Freud no longer was reasoning in a scientific way, but had become caught up with his own personal power drive. This struck at the heart of their friendship, for Jung knew he could never accept such an attitude.

He was left with grave questions about the limits of Freud's understanding. He had often noticed the eruption of unconscious religious data in Freud's dreams, questions which were originally raised when the two men traveled to America together in 1909, to lecture and receive honorary degrees at Clark University in Worcester, Massachusetts. On that journey they spent seven weeks talking together and analyzing each other's dreams daily. Jung felt Freud was not dealing adequately with his dreams, and on one occasion when Freud had had a dream that Jung felt needed additional details from his personal life, Freud replied, with a suspicious look, "But I cannot risk my authority!"

Jung was stunned, as he said: "That sentence burned itself into my memory; and in it the end of our relationship was already foreshadowed. Freud was placing personal authority above truth."

Questions from these conversations stayed with Jung and grew; his interest in the unconscious, its nature, and the structure of the psyche deepened. So intensely did he wrestle with these questions that his life became chaotic as he tried desperately to bring them to conclusion. As he pondered, it was as if the doors of the unconscious suddenly opened and expanded, and awareness of the realm of universal opposites flooded in on him, rich in imagery and universal symbols, a flood of content from what Jung subsequently defined as the "collective unconscious." This was quite different from the personal unconscious that Freud had explored. It was not just a reservoir of repressed conscious thoughts, but opened up an infinite realm of material common to all mankind.

Inspired by this discovery, Jung attempted systematically to define the elements in his vision of the structure of man's mind, a task which occupied him until 1921.

Jung's Structure of the Mind

Jung defined the *anima* as the personification of the feminine nature of man's unconscious, whereas the *animus* was the corresponding masculine side of the female. Anima and animus usually manifest themselves in dreams and fantasies. They are the symbolic expressions of the undeveloped side of the individual. Jung named the outer side, the face we present to society, the *persona.*

Jung agreed with Freud in his definition of ego as the center of consciousness; however, the unifying core of human personality Jung called the *self.* Likewise with the idea of the libido. Jung felt the libido should be seen in a more general setting; it is not strictly sexual energy, but rather psychic energy, of which sexuality is a substate.

Jung defined the *collective unconscious* as the reservoir of thoughts and images of all mankind, a sort of agglomeration of the *archetypes.* Archetypes "are unconscious, pre-existent forms that seem to be a part of the inherited structure of the psyche and can manifest themselves anywhere, at any time."

They . . . "might be compared to the axial system of a crystal, which, as it were, preforms the crystalline structure in the mother liquid, although it has no material existence of its own." In itself, the archetype is empty and "purely formal."

Jung distinguished between the *personal*

unconscious, which is made up of "contents which have at one time been conscious but which have disappeared from consciousness through having been forgotten or repressed," and the collective unconscious, the contents of which "have never been in consciousness, and have therefore never been individually acquired, but owe their existence exclusively to heredity."

To Jung consciousness produced certain conscious attitudes that distinguish differing "types" of individuals, which he named the *introvert* and the *extrovert*. Each of these types has four functions: thinking, feeling, sensation, and intuition, which represent four aspects of conscious orientation. In each individual they are present in varying proportions; it is as if the psyche were a four-sectioned circle of awareness, and as the individual grows, the four sections are gradually filled with content from the unconscious. The filling in of these sections Jung named *the individuation process*, because at some point in the process the individual suddenly has an insight into his true self.

This system and its structural definitions were first published in 1912 in Jung's great work, *The Psychology of the Unconscious*.

Refining the Individuation Process

This period of theoretical structuring seemed to restrict Jung's wider interests, and he now turned to more social applications of these discoveries. This social interest lasted from 1922 to 1928, and ranged from the art of poetry to educational theories, to the love problems of his students and patients.

In 1929 Jung again abandoned more general problems and returned to further development of the individual. It was as if he had realized that before one can solve major social problems one must solve individual ones. In order to gain deeper insight into individuation, he studied the ancient philosophical systems of both East and West.

For Jung the dream was the beginning, middle, and end of the individuation process. It is the starting point because it manifests "the unconscious side," which needs to be brought to consciousness, both directly and symbolically. Once the analyst has discussed the analysand's first dreams with him the whole problem takes on a new perspective. Jung discovered his patients dreamed in sequences, that the dreams formed a series of related themes which eventually culminated in a "great dream," which expressed mythological and divine images that arise from the collective unconscious. Through these great dreams the self was expressed in symbols whose meaning and content transcended themselves.

Although Jung had long been deeply interested in mythology and Eastern philosophy, which he conceived as ideal systems for understanding man's unconscious thought, he felt more immediate help could be found in the psychophilosophic systems of the West. Medieval alchemy stood out as the most promising system built on a European semiscientific foundation. With typical thoroughness Jung plunged into alchemy in such depth that he remains today one of its few modern authorities. For the next 20 years he pursued questions in this field. It fascinated him, because in it he found preserved a philosophical and psychological tradition that would have been lost had the medieval Church ever realized that it existed. To the materialistic Church fathers these scientists were endeavoring to achieve the praiseworthy goal of changing lead into gold. In fact, as Jung has shown us, these alchemists were practicing exercises in analogical reasoning which were teaching them means of transforming *lead-mass-body* into *gold-spirit-light* — in effect, turning ignorance and darkness into knowledge and light.

Analytical Psychology

Throughout all the stages in the development of Jung's thought, his attention continued to center on understanding transference, the intimate and deeply significant relationship that arises between analyst and patient. Through the years Jung abandoned both hypnosis and word association as methods of gaining insight into the psyche in favor of trying to understand the person more directly in the moment.

Jungian analysis can in effect be seen as anticipating logotherapy or existential analysis. All three are more philosophical than biological in character; it is not surprising, therefore, to discover that Jung's therapeutic techniques are not clearly defined. He was much more intent on liberating the archetypal forces within each individual psyche; thus, his respect for the infinite varieties of potentiality existing within each dictated the need for as flexible an approach as possible.

Therapy

Therapy begins with a probing series of interviews in which the patient's conscious state is discerned. This delineation of the outline of consciousness is important, as it is a sort of funnel into the workings of the unconscious, that sea of potentialities which, like all fertile sources, is subject to foreign growth. If the variety of compensations which have been forced into the unconscious can be discerned on the surface of the conscious being, then there is a greater likelihood that the educational process of the individual can be more incisively oriented by the therapist, to the point where, hopefully, the foreign growth will be flushed out of the unconscious sea of potentiality.

One of the differences between the Freudian analyst and the Jungian is that the Freudian classically sits behind the patient, who lies on a couch while the analyst takes notes. The Jungian faces the individual more directly so they can look into each other's eyes and read each other's facial expressions. This to Jung was a more natural setting for the exploration to occur. Possibly it was also both more threatening and more intimate, an appropriate blend for a man who saw infinite potential within the nature of man.

"Learn your theories as well as you can," Jung wrote, "then put them aside when you touch the living miracle of the human soul."

INDIVIDUAL PSYCHOLOGY/ ALFRED ADLER (1870-1937)

Born near Vienna, Adler was greatly influenced by a childhood bout with pneumonia, which he contracted at the age of five. After this encounter he decided to become a doctor, and received his M.D. in 1895 from the University of Vienna. In 1906 he met Freud, and soon became a member of the inner circle. Within five years, however, he parted with the Freudians on theoretical grounds — he disagreed with Freud's interpretation of dreams and the principles of sex trauma as the root cause of mental disorders — and started his own school of Individual Psychology. He rapidly gained adherents, and together he and his followers established several clinics for the guidance of children.

In 1927 Adler came to the United States to teach at Columbia University, and in 1935 he occupied the first chair of medical psychology to be established in this country, at Long Island University. He died in the streets of Aberdeen, Scotland, while he was giving a lecture series at Aberdeen University.

Superiority Drive

The main shift in Adler's theory for understanding the workings of neurosis was the instinctual striving for superiority. When this drive was thwarted, the subsequent tension that built up in the psyche because of the accompanying loss of fulfillment might be sufficient, Adler believed, to cause neurosis through "overcompensation." "Every neurosis," Adler asserted, "can be understood as an attempt to free oneself from a feeling of inferiority in order to gain a feeling of superiority." The healthy individual should be able to make his neurosis work for society. In other words, a person would be successful if he made the relevant "adjustments" that kept him in alignment with the part of society in which he functioned. This adjustment was made possible by the process of "compensation," the shock absorber which mediated conflict between the individual's striving for superiority and his constitutional inferiority.

This conflict, carried on as it was within the milieu of society, led Adler to focus special attention on the relationships between mother and child and between child and sibling. For Adler, it made all the difference to the child's future adjustment within society whether the individual was the only, first, or last child born into a family, because this would affect the degree of attention he received — whether he was pampered as a child or not. If neglected, the child might grow up with a vengeful attitude toward society, owing to the loss of opportunities in which his confidence might have been built up. In modern sociological terms, the child would be described as suffering from lack of "socialization skills." Similarly, if a person had been spoiled during childhood, he would be likely to demand more from society as a means of satisfying his selfish whims.

Reality Principle

It was 1927 when Adler arrived in America, and these ideas speedily caught on among child educators here. At that time, however, they had gained little backing from actual research. An interest has recently been shown in Adler's formulation of the "reality principle," the will to modify the egocentric drives of infancy into alignment with society. This adjustment ability was conceived of as existing universally in the human psyche, and seemed as plausible as the universalistic claims made on behalf of Freud's Oedipus complex. Adler did, however, accept Freud's designation of the ego — the only part of Freud's three-part division of the psyche that Adler did not dispute. To Adler the ego represented the sum of one's wholeness or personality.

Individual Psychology

Adler called his system Individual Psychology — a name that heralded his intention to treat the patient as an individual worth listening to, rather than as an impersonal problem. This atmosphere was captured in the term *empathetic understanding,* which had previously been associated with other psychotherapeutic techniques but was now more fully delineated by Adler.

Focus now was directed to building up the patient's ego through an understanding of his innate potential. Adler called this potentiality "social interest," which was another way of stating that individuals are goal-oriented. In the process of striving for their goals, they develop a "sense of life," the courage to judge themselves realistically, and the common sense to confront the social and physical environment constructively. This was an ideal formula rather than an explicit one for a therapy that aimed at developing social adequacy. Along with such concepts as sibling rivalry and empathetic understanding, it served as a base for the development of some group therapy ideals that have become very popular since Adler's day.

We can discern in Adler some of the first signs of humanistic psychology: the individual who comes to the therapy session is viewed as a person with a problem rather than a patient with an illness. The norm is still an external one, however, and the client is still expected to base his behavior on what society anticipates from him.

Adler viewed the individual, not as a battlefield with ego, superego, and id constantly in conflict, but as a unity or totality. "Very early in my work," he wrote on the theory of personality, "I found him to be a unity! The foremost task of Individual Psychology is to prove this unity in each individual . . . ."

Adlerian Therapy

Adler was an advocate of the multiple-analyst approach to therapy. It allowed the patient to interact with two or more different personalities, thereby reducing the possibility of psychotherapeutic impasses. There was the added advantage that any patient who was not getting on particularly well with one of his therapists might easily pursue therapy with one of the other therapists dealing with the case. In this way the possibility of trauma, which a change of analyst might bring about under the Freudian system, was greatly reduced.

The important thing to Adler was the individual client's lifestyle — his own system of subjective convictions about himself.

Consequently, Adler, like Jung, found it hard to think of neurosis as a disease. Not surprisingly, Adler was one of the first psychoanalysts to treat schizophrenics. He was able to do this with more ease because his system placed less emphasis on the concept of transference than that of Freud or Jung.

An important idea in Adler's therapy is the

need to examine the patient's concept of "reality" because psychotic problems are viewed as being caused by an inferiority complex of some sort. Thus the prime function of the Adlerian therapist is the building up of image and optimism, and the future rather than as a means of delineating repressions within the subconscious. Throughout the therapeutic process, in fact, the emphasis of Adlerian therapy is on the enhancement of a sympathetic atmosphere. A sense of humor is useful in establishing such an atmosphere — a joke showing that life was not so bad, for instance, might defuse a **patient's** morbid inclinations toward death.

Dreams, as in Freudian and Jungian therapies, are used during the interpretative stage of analysis, although Adler regarded dreams as a problem-solving activity for the future. The past is only referred to when it might illuminate the continued existence of maladaptive lifestyle. In such circumstances, additional techniques for bringing home the unrealistic basis of the patient's lifestyle might be used. Here Adler thought early recollections had special significance, for they reveal the style of a person's life in its origins. The first memory reveals the individual's fundamental view of life, the first crystallization of the attitude that is uniquely his.

THE NEO-FREUDIANS

KAREN HORNEY (1885-1952)

Born in Hamburg, Germany, Karen Horney received her M.D. from Berlin University. Later, she was trained in psychoanalysis by Karl Abraham, a close friend of Freud's, and in 1920 became an instructor at the Berlin Institute for Psychoanalysis. In 1932 she came to the United States, at the invitation of Franz Alexander, to become associate director of the Chicago Institute for Psychoanalysis, and two years later, left to teach at the New School for Social Research in New York. She was greatly influenced by the work of anthropologists Ruth Benedict and Margaret Mead, whose findings she adapted to psychoanalysis. The concomitant fact that she rejected such basic Freudian tenets as penis envy and the libido theory eventually led to her ejection from the New York Psychoanalytic Society. Consequently she founded the American Institute for Psychoanalysis and headed it until her death in 1952.

In her most popular book, *New Ways in Psychoanalysis*, Horney stated that "psychoanalysis should outgrow the limitations set by its being instinctive and genetic psychology." This statement, made in 1939, expressed her initial remolding of the Freudian psychoanalytic model, a system of thought she had criticized ever since she first found herself at odds with Freud's views on the role of women, in 1917. In consequence, Horney has become something of a feminist heroine in psychology.

Aware of the cultural differences between America and Germany, she was shocked by the emphasis Americans placed on success, a concept which she pointed out inevitably meant that a majority of people would feel they had "failed" in life. She saw human relationships as contaminated by rivalry, making it almost impossible to allow genuine warmth and security. This was disastrous, she felt, for the development of a healthy, free personality, because the need for security in a potentially hostile world is a basic dynamic in the formation of character. Her system is similar to Adler's, especially in relation to the drive for superiority. Unlike Adler, however, she explained personality as being molded by the mind in its constant sifting through of the wealth of values that exist in each specific culture.

To her the core of neurosis lay in human relations, which were brought about by the conditions of the culture rather than erotic instinctual energy. Certain types of cultural conditions obstructed the child's development, thwarting his confidence in himself and others. This resulted in a "basic anxiety," which she defined as a "feeling of being isolated and helpless toward a world potentially hostile." The child, wishing to keep this anxiety to a minimum, changes his natural, spontaneous relationships to others and the movement toward or away from other people then becomes artificial, compulsive, and binding. Such compulsive, artificial movements clash, collide, and develop into "basic conflicts" or knots of anxiety, which form the neurosis.

As a consequence of this cultural derivation for neurosis, Horney saw a great need for reassurance implanted in early childhood.

Children born into loveless surroundings, who did not receive proper reassurance or recognition, she believed, would surely develop such anxiety complexes.

The Pride System

To counter such feelings, the individual would set up a defense mechanism, which Horney called the "pride system," a facade that would give the appearance of normality although he might be at odds with himself behind it. She defined *face* as the personality's need to appear integrated despite an essential rift in character. Distortion, improper channeling of the innate drive for wholeness and real experience, resulted in an *idealized image of the self*. The neurotic person would build a set of selected status symbols from the particular culture into a goal, which would almost invariably remain unachieved, thereby compounding his basic contempt for himself.

Such narrow visions of one's place in life Horney was bent on curing through a therapy aimed at self-realization, overcoming the dichotomy between a person's real experience and abilities and his idealized view of himself. Such an "adjustment" would enable him eventually to live more comfortably with the true picture of the self. The word "adjustment," however, belies the pain involved in the process of stripping away the false self-esteem — and Hornian therapists were, and are, trained to expect violence on both mental and physical levels. Once this stripping process has taken place, however, the therapist can concentrate on building up the client's true integrity, through encouragement interspersed with honest appraisal. This process, known as the *supportive technique*, has proved very popular, as demonstrated by the voluntary

funding of a Karen Horney clinic in New York — which is unusual in that the fees paid by the patients are directly related to their economic resources.

In retrospect, Horney had a significant effect upon the Freudian "orthodoxy." She was the only woman psychoanalyst with sufficient stature to enter into controversy with Freud, and one of the first psychoanalytical theorists to propose that tensions generated by a culture could be the cause of neurosis.

Harry Stack Sullivan (1892-1949)

An American who obtained his M.D. from the Chicago College of Medicine and Surgery in 1917, Sullivan defined psychiatry as equivalent to social psychology. After working with schizophrenics in Chicago, he joined the staff of St. Elizabeth's Hospital in Washington, D.C., where he was exposed to a revised form of psychoanalytic theory by William Alanson White. In 1936 he helped plan and develop the Washington School of Psychiatry. Three years later, he joined Karen Horney as a dissenter from Freudian orthodoxy, and the two founded the Zodiac Club and the Association for the Advancement of Psychoanalysis. By 1943, however, both were working separately, Horney continuing her exploration of the *real self* — "that central inner force, common to all human beings and yet unique in each, which is the deep source of growth" — while Sullivan investigated the individual's many relationships to his society. He also turned his attention to behavior disorders, and in 1940 published *The Study of Interpersonal Relations*.

Sullivan's concept of personality arose from his work and observations with schizophrenic patients at St. Elizabeth's Hospital. He defined *personality* as "the relatively enduring pattern of recurrent interpersonal situations which characterize a human life." However, in working with the patients he noticed something of deeper significance — that they often used language as a defense barrier rather than a common ground for communication. This "verbal shield" he diagnosed as being caused by low self-esteem, which resulted in anxiety, which he defined as a physiological and psychological reaction learned in early childhood.

As the generally destructive effects of anxiety became increasingly evident to Sullivan, both in the commonness with which they occurred in everyday life and in the connections between anxiety and the conditions of being "normal" or "abnormal," he began to concentrate on understanding the patterning of behavior to which the individual was subjected within society. Once he had discerned what he thought were the fundamental types of patterning, he set about finding ways to diminish anxiety, both in the individual and in the society that created the original tension. In the year before his death, he was instrumental in setting up the World Federation of Mental Health, and at the same time was involved in the UNESCO committee investigating the causes of tension among a variety of cultures.

Otto Rank (1884-1939)

Another member of the Freudian circle, Rank propounded the theory of birth trauma as the basis for his therapeutic ideas. His theories caused a falling out with Freud, which resulted in his ousting from the group.

In his book on birth trauma, published in 1924, Rank suggested that the infant's sudden separation from the warm security of the womb was a physiological and psychological shock which left him — and every one of us — with a burden of primal anxiety. (Janov's primal therapy, page 66, stems directly from this, as does the LeBoyer method of easing the birth trauma, page 109.) To compensate for this Rank developed "rapid therapy" techniques in which the rapid interchange of speech and analytical comment between patient and therapist was designed to speed up the process of transference.

Once the patient's primal anxiety (known as "life fear") was uncovered, the analyst was free to concentrate on helping him to look forward to the process of separation by gently and gradually undoing the patient's reliance on him. The aim of this separation was to inspire the successive stages of what Rank called "the wills of life," which would enable the patient to become a fully integrated personality. This emphasis on "wills" has led to Rank's theory of neurosis becoming known as "will therapy." It is a system which, like those of Jung and Adler, directs attention to present functioning potential as opposed to the Freudian emphasis on the unconscious past.

Rank also departed from Freud in emphasizing love as a healthy instinct to be encouraged — people must be taught to love and respect themselves. The idea of the need for love reinforcement was considerably overexposed in the early days of "flower power," but it is proving of value in some of today's therapy groups.

Sandor Ferenczi (1873-1932)

One of the inner Freudian circle, Ferenczi spent many years in clinical work and focused particularly on evolving techniques for psychoanalytic cure. In the introduction to his *Theory and Technique of Psychoanalysis,* however, he stressed his loyalty to the master by stating explicitly that his "technical innovations should only be applied occasionally as (a means) of reinforcing Freudian methods."

Unlike Freud, however, Ferenczi found himself less remote from involvement with his patients, and on at least one occasion wrote to Freud about his willingness to consummate the psychoanalytic relationship. For the most part, however, he confined his expressions of affection for various patients to the simple exchange of gifts and dining out. This "love" for patients nonetheless led Ferenczi to reappraise the role of the analyst during the process of psychoanalysis, and to move toward a more active involvement that would more directly reflect the sympathy he felt. The whole process of the interview was made more flexible, and Ferenczi also employed the idea of bringing about a more rapid transference — that critical moment when the patient is finally prepared to tell all.

For his time, Ferenczi's ideas were considered quite bold, and they proved a fertile source for other therapists.

Melanie Klein (1882-1960)

Born in Germany, Melanie Klein received her training from Karl Abraham in Berlin, after having studied psychoanalysis under Ferenczi in Budapest. By 1919 she had become the first analyst to treat children under six years of age. This forced a breakaway from the standard Freudian techniques of analyzing patients through free association, a procedure that depends upon the ability of the analysand to string sentences together — a rare quality in the very young child. Klein's solution to the communication problem was the evolution of

a "play-analysis technique" in which the psychoanalyst gave the child various objects and watched how he manipulated them. By 1930, Klein had moved to London, where she continued her practice.

The Klein system of therapy was based on the assumption that the child's play symbolized the problems being experienced in the home situation. These were not restricted to the simple interaction between the child, his parents, or his siblings, but also included relationships with parts of the body, such as, for example, the mother's breast. If the experiences of these were "good," Klein labeled them "happy objects"; if the reverse, they became "bad objects." Both good and bad objects were preserved so vividly in the child's unconscious that the imprints left by such childhood memories remained for the rest of life. There was a close resemblance, Klein found, between the temporary reactions of the child to the loss of a loved object and the more permanent adult reactions that are diagnosed as depression or similar psychoses.

From such observations, she deduced that the roots of all neurosis are formed before the child entered the genital stage, as defined by Freud. In this pregenital phase the child's automatic reaction was to put objects in the mouth, which she saw as a possible explanation for why the neurotic tried to incorporate all manner of objects into the unconscious which had failed to satisfy him during infancy.

Until Klein's work, little attention had been paid to a means of eliciting information from the patient out of the moment, beyond a reapplication of Freudian technique. She can be viewed as having done more to shape child psychoanalysis technique than Adler, through the countless child clinics that are based on her discoveries.

Theodore Reik

Reik came to the United States in 1938 after a long and close association with the Freudian circle in Vienna. He originally decided to work in psychoanalysis on the advice of Freud in 1913 and was deeply moved by his master's death in 1939. Near the beginning of his book, *The Search Within*, Reik clarifies his relationship and debt to Freud when saying that, "One is not 'intimate' with a genius, however familiarly he may speak to you as a friend."

This comment sets the tone for Reikian analysis which, of all the offshoots among a variety of psychoanalytic "systems," remained closest to the orthodox Freudian style. Even so, Reik differed with Freud over the cause of neurosis, which he saw as stemming from the pre-Oedipal stage of the individual's life. This belief led Reik to focus on the infant stage of human growth, and to particularly emphasize collaborative effort between patient and analyst in order to do so, because he viewed "lack of mothering" as the cause of neurosis. Reik identified three components: lack of mothering, quality of mothering, and quantity of mothering. All three were crucial to the development of the "adjusted" person, but he saw the quality of mothering as most important. An insensitive or lazy mother, for instance, was less likely to comprehend the range of a child's nonverbal communicative gestures, with the probable result that the infant's imagination and conceptual ability would be retarded and it would be forced to communicate and conceptualize on the obvious, concrete level.

Similarly, intensity of mothering was vital in the child's adjustment to life. Overprotection might turn a son into a "sissy," or perhaps ultimately a homosexual (which Reik considered as not a disease but a condition caused by a surfeit of womanly protective instincts). Alternatively, a son might have an obsessive fear of involvement with any woman other than his mother. In either case, Reik referred to this spectrum of maladjustment as the *Jocasta complex.*

Erik Erikson

Born in Denmark, Erikson trained in psychoanalysis under Anna Freud in the 1920s and became one of the first post-Freudians to specialize in child analysis. He later lectured at Harvard and Yale before retiring to California.

In Erikson's seminal work *Childhood and Society*, published in 1950, he speaks of an *identity crisis* in adolescence as the motivating force in the development of personality. When this crisis is reached, the individual finds it necessary to align his character with the values that prevail within his particular society. This extended Freud's theory of infantile sexuality, which stressed the identity conflict as being between the id and the ego, to an age beyond puberty. Consequently, to Erikson, the motivating energy of the individual was not solely psychosexual but also psychosocial. He claims also that the "will" of each individual is capable of resolving contradictions or conflicts within itself, and is not strictly susceptible to the "slings and arrows of the irrational id," as Freud would say.

More generally speaking, Erikson built upon and further extended Freud's five stages of libidinal or psychosexual development. They became eight stages, each with its own particular crisis, and in each of them Erikson defined various strengths that indicated healthy development. To define them, Freud's (1) oral, (2) anal, (3) phallic, (4) latency, and (5) genital stages become for Erikson:

1. Oral-sensory (trust vs. mistrust; strengths: drive and hope)

2. Muscular-anal (autonomy vs. shame and doubt; strengths: self-control and will power)

3. Locomotor-genital (initiative vs. guilt; strengths: direction and purpose)

4. Latency (industry vs. inferiority; strengths: method and competence)

5. Puberty and adolescence (identity vs. role confusion; strengths: devotion and fidelity)

6. Young adulthood (intimacy vs. isolation; strengths: affiliation and love)

7. Adulthood (generativity vs. stagnation; strengths: production and care)

8. Maturity (ego integrity vs. despair; strengths: renunciation and wisdom)

Erich Fromm

Born in Frankfurt, Germany, Fromm graduated with a Ph.D. in psychology and sociology from the University of Heidelberg in 1922, and subsequently studied at the Psychoanalytic Institute in Berlin. He emigrated to the United States in 1933, and took a teaching post at Columbia University the following year; from 1941 to 1950 he taught at Bennington College in Vermont, and then moved on to a professorship at the National University of Mexico, holding a concurrent position at Michigan State from 1957 to 1961. In 1962 he accepted the position of professor of psychiatry at Columbia University.

According to Fromm, one of the easiest ways of dealing with fears of loneliness is to hand over control of one's "self" to external institutions. He defined this process as "authoritarianism," or the development of "symbiotic relationships." However, he felt deeply that it was the resourcefulness of the individual that should be regarded as the spring of personal fulfillment, which would eventually break off and release the feelings and thoughts repressed by authoritarianism.

The individual's ability to produce is key in Fromm's system of development. Those who lacked self-fulfillment would be more susceptible to the formation of a *pseudo-self*, rather similar to Horney's idealized image. But unlike Horney, Fromm paid little attention to the dynamics of the pseudo-self image, which he describes as "essentially a reflex of other people's expectation."

Fromm as Humanist

Here we see Fromm emerging as a humanist, warning man against giving up the courage to individuate, which is the source of his contentment through the personal fulfillment it offers him. This courage allows the individual to face the unknown more directly, to go through the "uncertainty" of life. Because, to Fromm, "Uncertainty is the very condition to impel man to unfold his powers. If he faces the truth without panic, he will recognize that there is no meaning to life except the meaning man gives his life by the unfolding of his powers."

More importantly, Fromm stressed the eventual despising of the self, the stage when the individual was made aware of his insecure existence. The cure for such distortion, or neurotic behavior, was the idea of "relatedness" or the intimacy of love, both of the self and of others in society. Thus the whole of the society within which the individual is nurtured from infancy to maturity is bound to affect in some way his ability to give of the self. The giving itself is viewed as a courageous act, one which is at the very basis of the individuation process.

His therapy for the neurotic was based simply upon the instilling of confidence into the individual who had lost courage. All the techniques of psychoanalysis were drawn upon in order to uncover the exact reason for the loss; further, once the reason had been discovered, Fromm believed that the individual had to be convinced that society itself must develop this courage. In a "healthy" society, in fact, everyone must share the burden of responsibility to face the unknown, to go through uncertainty and yet maintain the ability to produce and unfold themselves. That kind of courage is indeed the very foundation of society's own well-being.

Franz Alexander (1891-1964)

Originally from Hungary, Alexander formulated most of his theories while working at the Chicago Institute of Psychoanalysis, which he founded during the 1920s. Karen Horney worked with him there for a few years but found herself at increasing variance with Alexander's orthodox Freudianism. He concentrated chiefly on refining this orthodoxy, distinguishing between the sexual and nonsexual impulses comprising the libido. He saw the id as buying indulgence for gratification of impulses through prior agreement with the superego to accept punishment for any excesses committed while the id was "unleashed" from its control.

Such periods of "release" (more commonly recognized by society as lapses into criminality) could be justified as essential for the release of surplus energy. Not all lapses need lead to criminality, however, for there were many ways in which excess energy could be disposed of — through play, for example, innocent or erotic.

Building on these insights, Alexander saw the analyst as taking over the role of the patient's superego during the process of therapy. His assuming the role once played by the patient's parents enabled the patient to relive past relationships in the present, which brought the analyst in turn an opportunity to teach the patient to be aware of his drives. He could then learn to accept or renounce them in accordance with his own individual conscious judgment.

This concept of making the patient re-expose under more favorable circumstances emotional situations he had not been able to handle in the past was Alexander's main contribution to the therapeutic process.

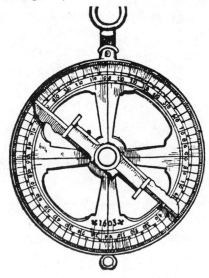

BEHAVIOR MODIFICATION
B. F. SKINNER

Skinner showed early promise as a lucid writer and powerful thinker, qualities which have made him the premier representative of the behaviorist school in America today. He received his Ph.D. from Harvard in 1951 under Edwin G. Boring, with a doctoral dissertation that concerned reflex and its behavioristic orientation. He migrated to the University of Minnesota, then to Indiana, and finally back again to Harvard in 1948, where he is still teaching and writing. His *Walden Two* and *Beyond Freedom and Dignity* have become classics in a far wider field than that of behaviorist psychology.

The Radical Behaviorist

Skinner describes himself as a radical behaviorist, as opposed to earlier behaviorists such as John B. Watson, whom Skinner claims was too extreme in his position that no distinction whatever existed between animal and human psychology. Skinner's own radical behaviorism assumes that behavior is the only legitimate concern of psychology. Behavior can be seen, predicted, and measured — and is open, therefore, to empirical, scientific investigation. Indeed, Skinner would like to see psychology become as empirical and systematic as the "hard" sciences such as physics.

Radical behaviorism does not deny the existence of internal states. These inner states can have some value, Skinner admits, and no account of human behavior would be complete without studying introspection. He believes, though, that what can be seen by introspection is not consciousness or mind but rather the person's body. And he does not think that feelings or other objects of introspection are causes of behavior.

To find the causes of behavior, Skinner looks to the environment that immediately precedes the behavior in question. The environment is extremely important in determining behavior, for before behavior can be changed, the environment itself must alter. In *Beyond Freedom and Dignity,* published in 1973, Skinner maintains that we will have to change the cultural environment before we are able to change the human behavior that results from it, and that this is the only solution for such problems as overpopulation and pollution. He proposes using a *technology of behavior* in order to change behavior on a massive scale. We have sufficient knowledge to change our culture in this way, but people are unwilling to use it. Indeed, Skinner himself is often attacked as promoting tyranny and Big Brother tactics. A reading of *Beyond Freedom and Dignity* will show otherwise.

Operant Conditioning

An important part of Skinner's theory of human learning and behavior is *operant conditioning.* According to him, there are certain things such as food, sexual contact, and so on, which contribute essentially to our survival. When we are successful in seeking out these things, the behavior which brought this about is "reinforced." That behavior, consequently, is made stronger. When our behavior successfully reduces an undesirable condition, that behavior also is reinforced and strengthened. These principles are used extensively in behavior modification therapy to induce new, more desirable behavior and to extinguish undesirable behavior.

Behavior Modification Therapy

Behavior modification therapy bases its methodology on the belief that neurosis results from learning unadaptive behavior through normal learning processes. The goal of this form of therapy is to help the client "unlearn" his problem-producing responses to internal and external stimuli. A characteristic which sets this apart from many other forms of therapy is its reliance on scientific methods to examine the therapeutic results.

In treatment, emphasis is placed on dealing with the symptomatic behavior as it presently exists in current situations, rather than exploring earlier causes for it. Although causes are not extensively dealt with, behavioral therapy is rooted in determinism, the belief that all behavior is determined by prior experiences. Behavior is a set of responses to stimulation, and all responses are learned. The work of the therapist is based on the application of techniques from learning theory. These methods are aimed at reversing unadaptive learning and providing new, adaptive learning experiences. The task of the therapist is to discover which specific responses are maladaptive and under what circumstances they occur.

There are several preparatory steps in this process. First, it is necessary to establish a good working relationship between therapist and client that is founded on trust and a commitment to certain behavioral goals for the client. Once rapport is established, history-taking begins. The therapist then attempts to provide the client with as much understanding as possible about the nature of the behavior, the forces instrumental in producing it, and the unadaptive learning processes at work.

Treatment may take several different forms, including the following: (1) *Systematic desensitization*, reducing anxiety through techniques of relaxation, then approaching the anxiety or fear-provoking stimuli in gradual steps. (2) *Assertion training*, one of the most successful and widely used behavioristic techniques. It is based on the assumption that each individual has the right to voice his feelings. Attention is paid to specific details, and the client keeps an account of the exact conditions under which he feels fearful of expressing his feelings. The specific situations are then worked on, often in the form of role playing. (3) *Flooding*, a method in which fear-provoking stimuli are presented in imagination or in real life, with the therapist attempting to maintain the client's anxiety until he reaches a point where he is able to respond to the stimuli in a nonanxious way — usually within 20 to 40 minutes. (4) *Aversive techniques*, such as electric shock. This is undoubtedly the most unfavorably popularized method, with the result that behavior therapy is sometimes identified exclusively with it. In actuality, aversive techniques are seldom used.

Emphasis on Therapy Form

To a very large degree, then, behavior therapy makes greater use of the scientific model than other types of therapy. Although it does include preliminary history-taking, the discovery of the reasons for destructive behavior is definitely secondary to the step-by-step tackling of the behavior itself through programmed techniques. In this sense, emphasis is put on the therapy form itself rather than on the client-therapist relationship. Through the discovery of better and better techniques, it is believed that a successful therapy outcome is increasingly assured.

REALITY THERAPY/WILLIAM GLASSER

A practicing psychiatrist in Los Angeles since 1957, William Glasser serves as consultant for both the Ventura School for Girls of the California Youth Authority and the Los Angeles Orthopedic Hospital. In addition he teaches the methods of Reality Therapy at the University of California, Los Angeles. He developed the theory along with his last teacher and present colleague, Dr. G. L. Harrington.

New Ways to Fulfill Needs

Essentially, Reality Therapy tries to help the individual become more closely in touch with the real world about him; it provides him with assistance in learning new ways of fulfilling his needs in real-life situations. The obvious fact is that we depend primarily on involvement with other people to fulfill our needs, and the difficulty is that we are associated with them on varying levels as we live out our lives.

To the reality therapist, the two basic needs of man are to love and be loved and to feel that we are worthwhile to ourselves and to others. Glasser claims that we all have similar needs, but that we vary in our ability to fulfill them. To be worthwhile, we must maintain a satisfactory standard of behavior, and for this reason the reality therapist includes morals, standards, values, and right-and-wrong behavior in his treatment.

Responsibility is another basic tenet of reality therapy, where it is defined as the ability to fulfill one's needs and to do so in a way that does not deprive others of the ability to fulfill theirs.

There are three parts to reality therapy, the first of which is involvement. The therapist must become intimately involved with his patient to help him face the reality around him and see how his behavior is contrary to it. The second part consists of the therapist rejecting the unrealistic behavior while still accepting the patient himself, while the third is one in which the therapist must suggest and teach the patient better ways of fulfilling his needs in relationship to the world around him.

The therapy is basically a form of behavior modification where the individual is treated not as a patient sick with a disease stemming from some past crisis, but rather as someone needing guidance in facing the present conditions of his reality. Attention is directed to both present and future behavior. What the patient may have done in the past is not relevant — if it had been acceptable, Glasser points out, that person would not be in therapy. The principles of reality therapy are extremely straightforward and easy to understand; Glasser makes the point that it can be applied equally effectively to daily living by people who are not sick, and that there is no need for prolonged, specific training "other than the application of effort, sensitivity, and common sense."

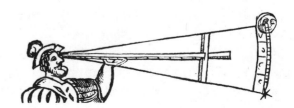

TRANSACTIONAL ANALYSIS/ ERIC BERNE (1910-1970)

Berne was trained in Freudian psychoanalysis, but developed his own therapy techniques during World War II while working in a military hospital with groups of soldiers. He was a leading exponent of the theory of Transactional Analysis, or TA.

According to Berne, just as infants need physical stimulation in order to feel good, so too adults need psychological *strokes* showing recognition and attention from others. Berne terms this need *recognition hunger.* Interestingly, the strokes do not have to be what would normally be considered positive in order to provide the recognition we crave; seemingly negative or painful interactions are equally effective in satisfying our recognition hunger. An exchange of strokes becomes a transaction and transactions may be linked together to form complex patterns of behavior. Games are made up of these complex patterns.

Adult Games

These patterns or games are taught to the child by his family (or substitute family) very early in life. As children, each of us learns precisely what behavior, at what time, will elicit the psychological strokes that we need. The lesson is learned so well that we go on playing the same games as adults. These family games go back through previous generations and unless a person can struggle free from them, they are taught to his children and the legacy continues.

The problem with these games is that the person is "programmed" into old and fixed behavior which limits his view of reality. A family game predetermines one's relationships, feelings, pursuits and occupation. Also, people tend to associate with others who play the same games and consequently both friendships and marriages are often bound to complementary roles in the same game.

Ego States

The concept of *ego states* is important in Berne's theory. An ego state consists of a system of feelings and behaviors. He distinguishes three ego states in his personality theory. The first is an ego state like that of the parents. This is called *Parent*, and when a person is in this ego state, he feels and acts as his parents did. The second ego state, *Child*, consists of old feelings and behaviors which were learned as a child. The third ego state, *Adult*, is when the person is not unconsciously behaving, thinking, or feeling like his parents or like he did as a child. He is directly confronting the reality of the present situation. We all have these states within us and we shift from one to another. Each has a value and a function in the psyche. The aim of transactional analysis is not to eliminate any of these ego states, but rather, to put them in the proper balance.

In his book *Games People Play*, Berne describes a game called "If It Weren't For You." In the case he outlines, the wife blames her husband for being too domineering and not allowing her to do things on her own, such as take dancing lessons. In this relationship the husband is mostly in the Parent ego state and the wife in the Child. In reality, she is allowing him to dominate her because she has a fear of dancing which she does not want to face.

Therapy in transactional analysis exposes the games in which a person is entrapped and encourages more Adult interaction. Therapy usually begins with a preliminary period of individual diagnosis and treatment; once the therapist thinks he is ready, the patient usually goes into group therapy. The group generally consists of eight to 10 adult patients and a trained psychotherapist. The fact that the interaction between them is primarily verbal distinguishes a transactional analysis group from other groups which make extensive use of physical techniques. Ideally, each person's games are played out in the group and discussed. According to Berne, the therapist should not be merely a technician.

He recommends taking time before each group session to spend a few minutes focusing on important principles. This acts as a sort of meditation where the therapist tries to put himself into an open, clear state of mind.

Adult Autonomy

The goal of this therapy is what Berne calls *Adult autonomy*, which involves the qualities of awareness, spontaneity, and intimacy. When a person is freed from his games, he can see things more truly as they are. This has the pleasant result that he becomes more aware of the world around him, more spontaneous in his actions and feelings, and more intimate in his relationships with others.

REICHIAN THERAPY
WILHELM REICH (1897-1957)

Reich entered the Vienna inner circle as a promising young man studying under Freud. He proved a most able pupil and subsequently received a post as director of a seminar investigating case histories of stalemates and analytic failures. From this work he developed his theory of resistance, analyzing it as a compact defense mechanism, which he called *character armor*. He expressed these ideas in his now-famous book *Character Analysis,* published in 1933, shortly before Reich emigrated to the United States as a consequence of Hitler's rise to power.

Reich parted from Freud, however, in the sexual implications he developed from Freud's theories. Freud believed that the awareness of instincts and complexes gave the power to control them, and that the sexual desires should be controlled for the good of

society. Reich, on the other hand, suggested that these desires must be released by transferring them to some realistic sex object before the neurosis can be cured. Thus, he encouraged sexual relations for problem adolescents and extramarital sex for troubled marriages. At these "excesses" Freud broke with Reich both personally and professionally.

"Good Orgasms"

Reich further postulated that man was only at harmony with himself once he had drained all excess sexual energy from his body. The draining of this energy was not simply a release, it took on the scope of an art form. The orgasm was the gate to happiness, something which could be worked on and improved through techniques learned in therapy sessions. Similarly, "good orgasms" were the keystone of a successful society, because they removed the discontent of its citizens.

According to Reich, sex is the primary human drive and sexual energy is the human manifestation of the fundamental energy of the universe. He believed that this sexual or life energy, which he called the *orgone*, could be isolated, and in 1939 he started building and selling *orgone accumulators*, which achieved some public popularity in the United States, where Reich was living and teaching. The Food and Drug Administration prevented Reich's marketing of his orgone accumulators in 1957. The psychiatrist's subsequent dispute with the FDA resulted in his being imprisoned, and he died in jail the same year.

Most neo-Reichian therapists of today give Reich credit for discovering a correlation between sexual energy and universal energy.

Present-day Reichian therapists stress the working through of psychological and interpersonal feelings which arise in the process of releasing certain muscular tensions and dealing directly with one's body. Reichian methods are now often used in conjunction with a variety of interpersonal therapeutic techniques in the attempt to deal with a person on all his levels of experience.

Among the therapies directly derived from Reichian theory and techniques are Alexander Lowen's Bioenergetics and Ida Rolf's Structural Integration (Rolfing), both of which are discussed in *Body Styles.*

RATIONAL EMOTIVE THERAPY/ ALBERT ELLIS

Born in Pittsburgh, Ellis grew up in New York City, where he studied at the College of New York and at Columbia University. He is now a fellow of the American Psychological Association and president of the Society for the Scientific Study of Sex. As director of the Institute of Rational Living and director of clinical services of the Institute of Advanced Study in Rational Psychotherapy in New York, he has been instrumental in developing the concepts of Rational Emotive Therapy.

In his work as a marriage and family counselor, Ellis observed that people were gaining much insight by means of traditional psychotherapeutic methods, but were not making enough headway in actually being able to solve their problems. With this dilemma in mind, he formulated a therapy based on the premise that emotional problems are primarily caused by irrational attitudes and beliefs about oneself, others, and the world at large. Rational Emotive Therapy (R.E.T.) is an attempt to focus clearly on these specific irrational patterns of thought and subsequent disturbing behavior. Clients are taught to become aware of their irrationalities and discard them, in order to be able to confront difficulties in a logical way and increase the chance of living a productive and pleasurable life.

R.E.T. has been borne out by some studies showing its effectiveness over other therapies. Progress can be startling, and is further encouraged, where necessary, by the use of unconditional positive regard on the part of the therapist.

Root Causes

Understandably, most clients have a hard time trying to change their fundamental views of life, but Ellis works in the belief that everyone is capable of readjusting his views. Those few who are already in a condition to experiment with a new set of postulates are given a more or less immediate opportunity of release from the state of chronic anxiety which accompanies most kinds of neurosis. Despite the clear-cut R.E.T. theory, each individual therapy session may require different techniques as the actual cause of the anxiety is sought. As Ellis says in his book *Growth Through Reason*, the emphasis is on getting to the root causes as quickly as possible, so that the individual can "accept reality, desist from condemning himself and others," and then "actively persist at making himself as happy as he can be in a world that is far from ideal."

Self-Acceptance

R.E.T. concentrates on helping the client by offering practical suggestions on how to relate better to people, rather than teaching him to relate well in order to convince himself of his own value as a human being. The logical extension of the view marks R.E.T. as a unique therapy because, at the moment, it is the only one that encourages the individual to fully accept himself outside the context of others who are extremely successful in a given society. As Ellis says, R.E.T. clearly distinguishes between a client's preference and his need to be accepted and achieving; it teaches him specifically that he does not have to judge himself. Consequently, it offers a radical solution to the ego problem by simply eliminating any suggestion that the client needs a "healthy ego." Instead, by accepting his own uniqueness, he feels sufficiently secure and resilient to be able to deal with his everyday life. As Ellis puts it in *Growth Through Reason*, "instead of feeling depressed, anxious, or hostile, (he) will now tend to feel only disappointed, sad, and frustrated."

Rational Emotive Therapy emphasizes that people are responsible for creating their own disturbing emotions, and that consequently they are capable of rearranging their lives in more satisfying ways. Action-oriented, it makes use of many scientifically based procedures that work toward the practical aim of creating significant philosophic, emotional, and behavioral changes. The aim of R.E.T. is to help individuals integrate their intellectual and experiential processes, to enhance their growth and creativity, and to rid themselves of unproductive and self-defeating habits.

THE DOUBLE BIND THEORY

Gregory Bateson

Gregory Bateson was greatly influenced by the linguistic and mathematical premises of Alfred Korzybski; both came to recognize neurosis and psychosis as stages of deterioration in communication. This idea became the basis for Bateson's theory of the *double bind*.

The double bind is a state of immobility of thought and emotion that occurs when an individual (child) is forced to respond to another (parent) on a level of communication other than what is being articulated. According to Bateson, there are at least two levels of communication present in every message. One of these is the content level and the other is the metacommunication level (the intuitive feeling component of a message that is nonverbal).

In healthy dialogue these levels are compatible, whereas in unhealthy dialogue they are inconsistent, contradictory, and lead to schizophrenia. For example, a mother may say to her child:

(1)   "You do want to shut the window, don't you, dear?" Or,

(2)   "You know mother loves you, don't you — come give mother a hug" (anger in voice on metacommunication level).

In both cases the child is forced to respond Yes. In (1) the child may indeed want the window to stay open, or may have been in no way concerned with the mother's question. In (2) the child is compelled to reply Yes on the verbal level and forced to embrace the mother, who is expressing the opposite message on the metacommunicaton level. Thus the child is simultaneously drawn and repelled by the mother, and a split begins and deepens as this type of communication continues.

Bateson claims the child can interpret the message in three ways:

(1)   Laugh it off — it doesn't make sense (hebephrenia);

(2)   Forget it all and withdraw (catatonia);

(3)   Spend immense amounts of time and energy trying to figure out what the message meant (paranoia).

As these types of conversation increase, the child develops a split which deepens and severs it from the outside world; the withdrawn child becomes schizophrenic or, in less severe cases, neurotic.

Bateson's therapeutic techniques aim at bringing the submerged patterns of communication to the surface; the cure depends upon their recognition and reorientation into more direct forms of communication.

EXISTENTIAL ANALYSIS JEAN-PAUL SARTRE
and ALBERT CAMUS (1913-1960)

It was the French writer Sartre who christened Existentialism, although the questioning of man's relationship to his world did not originate with the writings of Sartre and his compatriot Camus in the 1940s and '50s. Sartre's own point of departure was the Danish philosopher Kierkegaard.

Starting with the postulate that it was absurd for the individual to make decisions in everyday life with little knowledge of their consequences, Sartre went on to claim he was writing "psychology" when he referred in his writings to despair, dread, and self-deception. Similarly, Camus, in *The Stranger*, depicts a lonely individual, Meursault, as the symbol of 20th-century man's alienation. Such writing initially appears to depict a profoundly pessimistic view of life, yet on closer inspection the reader is really offered a situation of paradox, akin to Nietzsche's *Zarathustra:* "Dare ye be tragic, and ye will be redeemed." In other words, man can assert his freedom if he has the courage.

Sartre's "Active Choice"

Sartre sees man as seizing the chance to live authentically and thus give himself the choice of a future. This active choice indicates the will to develop, the leaping forward described by Kierkegaard. Freedom is no more than an empty shell unless the individual can pour his content into it. The existentialist cannot enjoy this freedom selfishly, for as Simone de Beauvoir, long Sartre's closest companion, puts it: "Everyone is responsible for everything before everybody."

Once he realizes his insignificance, the individual is set free from the blinkers of narrow vision and selfishness. This all-encompassing freedom negates the need for a Christian-type God; indeed Camus, writing in 1954, saw man as achieving "the wine of absurdity" only on the relinquishing of the need for God. Sartre clarifies such an exuberant metaphor by pointing out that it is man's lack of courage that prevents him from experiencing the ecstasy of freedom as it truly should be — irrational and unpredictable. Planned lives and career goals are the constructs of insecure people.

Condemnation of "Structuralism"

It is consistent, therefore, that Sartre should vehemently condemn the 1970s trend toward "structuralism" — the increased emphasis on planned living. Erich Fromm had the same fear, expressed in his sociological writings — what he called the regressive biological desire of man to give up his right to individuation.

Such parallels are not surprising in view of the influence at work on both theorists, in the repressive atmosphere of Nazi Germany. Sartre's acerbic mode of expression, however, alienated many readers, who saw him as projecting a totally nihilistic view of life, and this attitude tended to obscure the largely humanistic premises of Sartre's world view. It was not until 1964, when British psychologists David Cooper and R. D. Laing published *Reason and Violence: A Decade of Sartre's Philosophy*, that he was taken seriously in America.

From then on, the too-speedy appraisal of existentialism as pessimistic became a ludicrous reason for not absorbing Sartre's ideas. Abraham Maslow was quick to state that he saw existentialism as "preparing the way (for the first time) for a psychology of mankind," while Rollo May, one of the first psychoanalysts to use the existential approach in psychology, was soon writing of love and the opportunities it offered for the self-fulfillment of man. Man was to be taught to embrace himself, from which self-love, deeper, more fulfilling relationships with fellow men, were bound to follow. In *Love and Will*, published in 1969, May wrote: "It is the fearful joy, the blessing and the curse of man, that he can be conscious of himself in this world . . . in every act of Love and Will . . . we mold ourselves and our world simultaneously. That is what it means to embrace the future."

With such candid sentiment, the doors of perception flew open to a proliferation of different therapies aimed at expanding a variety of senses in all types of individuals.

Existential Psychotherapy

A basic tenet for this approach is that a person makes and changes himself during the course of his life, and that potentialities for change are always there. Particular therapeutic techniques are not important; in a given situation the therapist uses what appears to be most helpful in fostering growth. Theory and methodology are only valuable insofar as they help to divulge what the patient is concretely experiencing.

Another basic concept is that existence and experiencing are one and the same. Psyche and body are inseparably wed, and how one "feels" is an entire mental/physical process. Experiencing is also interactional. Man is not an isolated entity but a being in the world, whose experiencing is intimately connected both with other people and with his entire environment. There are certain innate behavior patterns, but these can only manifest themselves within the context of a particular environment.

Authenticity is a vital component — the process of man's experiencing his moving forward with a continuity within the change, a faithfulness to the qualities implicit in his existence. Experiencing has direction, which is contained in the present moment. Therapy hopes to "help along" this process by aiding the individual to become aware of what he is feeling and allowing the process of development to occur naturally. Psychological maladjustment is viewed as a matter of being out of touch with one's existence; conversely, therapeutic "success" occurs when the patient can actually sense a shift in his feelings, implying possibilities for growth in new directions.

In existential therapy the unconscious is synonymous with the body. Certain areas of bodily reactions and responses are not available to conscious awareness, but a great deal of bodily experiencing *is* accessible to conscious understanding. The work of the therapist, therefore, is to enable the patient to establish contact with this type.

For both client and therapist attention to bodily process is most important, for change is possible only by allowing experience to move in new directions of its own accord, not by making arbitrary decisions and attempting to force life to develop along certain lines. All the therapeutic efforts, whether of a bodily, behavioral, or interactional nature, are aimed at uncovering and enhancing the possibilities of experiential change.

RADICAL THERAPY FOR SCHIZOPHRENIA / R. D. LAING

Laing was born to a poor family in Glasgow, Scotland, where he subsequently went to the University, graduating with an M.D. in 1951. It was not until 1960, with the publication of his book *The Divided Self* that Laing became popular in America; from then on, he replaced Fromm as the new guru of psychology in this country — mostly because of his belief that society was the cause of schizophrenia.

Existential Freedom

Laing's criticism of society was vehement: "We are all murderers and prostitutes, no matter how normal ... or mature we take ourselves to be," he wrote in *The Politics of Experience*, published in 1967. In other words, "Humanity is estranged from its authentic possibilities." Laing's point of view can be seen as a demand for existential freedom without the sheet anchor of responsibility — either to self or society — which is implied in Fromm's cherished aim of defeating the elements of dissatisfaction within the individual. Laing is a fighter against prejudice — and he is prepared to use radical methods as well as language.

Schizophrenia

His work has been particularly related to the causes and treatment of schizophrenia — a major psychosis which Freud thought impossible to treat through a working relationship with a therapist, because he considered schizophrenics as being too absorbed in themselves to enter into analysis.

In Laing's view, the dynamics of a nervous breakdown (or schizophrenic episode) were caused by the removal of the veil from the false self, the front presented during everyday life, which until that moment had been serving to maintain the outer appearance of normality. The stripping away of the veil would make the individual subject to the likelihood of regression.

This regression was similar to that depicted by Freud, but the cure suggested by Laing was the basis for his antipsychiatry crusade. No attempt was made to redefine medical and psychiatric notions; these were rejected outright, to be replaced by the concept of the therapeutic commune.

Kingsley Hall

Kingsley Hall, in London's East End, was the first of the experimental communes, and although in operation for only three years, catalogued some useful insights. Not one of the 104 schizoid patients who passed through the commune committed suicide. Most important was the secure atmosphere created within the commune, which allowed its various members to follow through their acute schizophrenic episodes without fear of being institutionalized or otherwise restrained. Furthermore, the actions of everyone within the commune could be challenged — including those of the trained psychologist — and each individual member was free to organize time as desired. This flexibility was crucial if the afflicted were to regress as their individual needs dictated.

This point is well illustrated by the case of Mary Barnes, a type of "regimental sergeant-major nurse" who, as Laing explains, was apparently extremely efficient, rigid, and organized. One day, however, she was courageous enough to lose herself in the secure and private atmosphere of Kingsley Hall.

"A few days after coming to (the commune) ... she became completely helpless to the extent that she had to be fed with a baby's bottle every two or three hours .... She covered herself with her own faeces .... She became thin, down to almost a bundle of bones. She stopped talking and she could not stand."

Mary Barnes was hospitalized for a uterine hemorrhage, but the regression was not interrupted. "She did not want even to have to defecate. She wanted to abandon her body completely ... not only to childhood, not only to prebirth, but to pre-incarnation."

Eventually, however, Mary Barnes came back — over a period of five to six weeks. "Each day she was a little older and more organized .... Since coming back from (this process), this woman has done a great deal of painting, sculpting, modeling, and writing."*

Laing admits that there still is very little known about why this process works — but that it is effective seems beyond doubt.

* The story of Mary Barnes is told by Laing in "Going Crazy," edited by Dr. Hendrik M. Ruitenbeek, Bantam Books, 1972.

ON EXISTENTIAL ANALYSIS

Trained in both Europe and America, Dr. Serban is clinical associate professor of psychiatry and principal research investigator at New York University. He serves on the editorial board for the Journal of Existential Psychiatry *and the* Journal of Behavioral Neuropsychiatry. *As a senior psychiatrist at Bellevue Psychiatric Hospital, Dr. Serban's insight and concepts have enhanced programs for the treatment of patients. He was a pioneer in introducing many ideas of existential psychiatry in this country and in insisting on a humanistic and holistic approach to psychotherapy. In this article, which originally appeared in full in the* Journal of Behavioral Neuropsychiatry, *Dr. Serban emphasizes that it is up to the individual to give meaning to his life, although the fact must be faced that much of life is filled with despair and absurdity. He believes in a direct approach, a blunt, no-nonsense type of therapy that seeks to cut through evasions and trimmings to achieve clarity and get to the "now" of the problem. In his approach he marries the concepts of psychiatry to the philosophy of Heidegger, Kierkegaard, and Sartre.*

Existential analysis attempts to see man in his full perspective of existence as a mode of projecting his totality of being in the world. The history of his life will show the way in which he has approached reality, with his particular mode of thinking and acting, with his evaluation of others and of himself, and especially with his ability, or not, to grasp his own choices as a distinctive expression of his freedom. The existentialist, phenomenologically oriented, in order not to fall into the error of distorting the human reality according to preconceived hypothetical assumptions, analyzes the history of the patient as a subjective modality of lived experiences of his consciousness. Since this consciousness is the only observable reality after all theoretical speculations are discarded, this consciousness in its intentional and relective content, as experiencing the world, becomes the subject of psychiatric inquiry.

The Search for a Solution

The therapist will attempt to understand the meaning of an act of consciousness of a neurotic, for instance, as it appears in every moment of action where the past and the future are confronted in the decision of a choice for a particular action as the best choice among all other possible choices. But since the search for a solution depends on his personal ability to change an indeterminate problematic situation into a controllable occurrence with a predictable outcome the same act of consciousness will show whether he is able to reconcile conflicting needs which otherwise will create anxiety. In this light, anxiety appears as a state of consciousness in which the would-be possibility for experience, not yet integrated as an experience, questions its realization . . . .

The importance of the understanding of the judgment of the patient with his structure of thinking about the world becomes evident in therapy to the extent to which this view will require re-evaluation and reorientation in order to free it from the contingencies of ambiguity, beliefs, and magical explanation. The inner world of the patient has to be explored and reconstructed in order to find the particular meaning and importance given by him to things and events which have shaped his reality of doing and action. The reflection of the world in his consciousness and his actualization of it, along with its impregnation with emotional meaning, will be the constant subject of evaluation and restructuring . . . .

The world of irrational and magic will be further revealed by the patient in the verbalization of his daydream constructions and free expression of his imagination. This world of "should-be" in which the individual feels master of himself by the actualization of his most daring otherwise inaccessible possibility, will give to the analyst a meaningful picture of the patient's innermost life and thinking. On the one hand, the imagination tries to create an equilibrium between the individual and the environment by the magical nature of the act of imagination, and on the other hand, it directs him toward future desirable-to-achieve possibilities. In the same context, dreaming, instead of getting its meaning from analytical fictional symbolic interpretation, is seen as a part of the rhythm of psychic life in which the pulse of existence is evoked in pictorial images of the existent highly-charged mood and feeling.

Relationships

In the existential view, the whole therapeutic process is based on an authentic communication understood as a sincere attempt to verbalize the most intimate thoughts, intentions, and convictions in order to reveal the deepest meaning which the individual gives to his life. The patient has to share with the analyst the innermost depths of his being in order to realize them for himself and to find their significance for others as well. The relationships between patient and therapist are seen in the light of an encounter, a continuous process of sharing, questioning, and probing inner experiences in which the patient strives to transcend his existing position by using the other's — the therapist's — ability to understand him on an outside basis. The encounter cannot be conceptualized either as a transference, since it does not attempt to revive any alleged infantile interrelationships, or as a simple identification using the therapist for a model, since this inherently will lead to an inauthentic realization of the patient. On the contrary, the encounter unfolds the project of life in its essential meaning through the dialogue between human beings who are committed to the exploration of all the possibilities available for the revelation of an authentic existence. In the encountering situation there is nothing to be transferred from patient to analyst, or vice versa, because both relate to each other in a genuine interpersonal expression of feelings emerging from the common goal and the awareness of the therapeutic situation.

PRIMAL THERAPY / ARTHUR JANOV

Trained as a Freudian analyst, Arthur Janov practiced standard insight therapy for 17 years as a psychologist and psychiatric social worker before discovering Primal Therapy. In his book *The Primal Scream* he tells how a patient described having seen a play where the actor yelled, "Mommy! Daddy! Mommy! Daddy!" Janov then encouraged him to do the same in a therapy session. Suddenly, the young man was writhing on the floor and yelling at the top of his voice. Later, he reported that he could "really feel." Janov didn't quite understand what had happened, but he knew it was significant. Subsequently he developed his system of primal therapy.

Primal Pain

According to Janov we all have needs, which we begin to feel as soon as we are born, and when they are not satisfied we experience pain. By cutting off this feeling we split ourselves, and may pursue these repressed needs later in symbolic forms. Such symbolic behavior is neurotic, according to Janov. Frequently, the child is used to satisfy the parent's need for love, respect, and admiration. Meanwhile, the child's own needs continue to be ignored, and the pain is split off. The parent demands, in effect, that the child become "unreal" in order to please the parent. These pains Janov calls *primal pains*.

At some time, usually between the ages of five and seven, almost everyone experiences a major primal scene. This is preceded by many smaller minor primal scenes. In the major primal scene, the child deeply realizes and feels that he will *never* be loved for what he is. This feeling and realization are so overwhelming that they cannot long be tolerated. The child accordingly covers them up, and in the process becomes more "unreal." According to Janov this is the basis of neurosis.

Therapy begins with three weeks of individual treatment during which the client sees the therapist each day for as long as is necessary. There is no set time limit on the daily sessions, and the therapist sees only this one patient for the entire period. The 24 hours before primal therapy begins must be spent by the client in a hotel room. He is not allowed to smoke, watch television, or read, but he may write. This is intended to help break through his defenses and bring him closer to his real feelings.

Realization of Pain

For the next three weeks the client is guided through a series of primals. Each person has his own type of primal; this even differs within each patient from time to time. It can be characterized by feelings of sadness, quietness, violence, or fear. Some people writhe on the floor, some curl up, some gasp for breath while some chatter their teeth. The common element is the depth of the feeling and the vivid recollection of a past traumatic event. The patient is aware of what is happening and can come out of the primal if he wishes; usually, patients realize the value of the experience and stay in it. Fully feeling this pain, according to Janov, is the only way to cure neurosis. Gradually, the person's defenses are weakened. With each successive primal his feelings become more intense and he recollects earlier and earlier traumas.

HUMANISTIC PSYCHOLOGY / ABRAHAM MASLOW (1908-1970)

Maslow was the most articulate spokesman of humanistic psychology, a school which has been steadily gaining acceptance over the past 10 to 15 years. Humanistic psychology opposes the Freudians and behaviorists by offering another point of view, which centers primarily on the individual and his personal experience. Its tenets are well described in the brochure circulated by the American Association for Humanistic Psychology (founded in 1962 by Maslow, Kurt Goldstein, Rollo May, and Carl Rogers, among others) describing the Association's *Journal of Humanistic Psychology:*

> The centering of attention on the experience of the person, and thus a focus on experience as the primary phenomenon in the study of man.
>
> Emphasis on such distinctively human qualities as choice, creativity, valuation, and self-realization, as opposed to thinking about human beings in mechanistic and reductionist terms.
>
> Allegiance to meaningfulness in the selection of problems for study; opposition to a primary emphasis on objectivity at the expense of significance.
>
> Ultimate concern with and valuing of the dignity and worth of man and an interest in the development of the potential inherent in every person.

Maslow, who was born in Brooklyn, studied Gestalt psychology at the New School for Social Research, although his university work was done at the University of Wisconsin. He was primarily a theoretician, whose ideas are compatible with several types of therapy. Many of them are traceable to his relationship with Kurt Goldstein (1878-1965), who believed that man is essentially motivated by the desire for "self-actualization." This view differs from Freud's perspective, wherein the sexual drive is the sole motivating force, and also differs from the behaviorist concept of a multiplicity of forces, each of which in turn dominates the others at certain times. Goldstein argued that the multiplicity of desires that appear to motivate us are really arranged in a distinct hierarchy, subject to the need for self-realization, wherein at times one desire will become more prominent than the others for the person's continued progress toward self-actualization.

Maslow expanded this concept of hierarchy to include several intermediate levels of human needs, beginning with physiological needs, safety, love and "belongingness," esteem needs, esthetic needs, the need to know and understand, ending in the essential need for self-actualization.

Holistic Outlook

Maslow also shared Goldstein's "organismic" view of man which encompasses the aspects of psychology by using knowledge of them all to enable full understanding of man. It is a holistic outlook, which can be said to include physiological, behavioral, instinctual, emotional, and intellectual aspects of psychology. Added to them, and possibly most important, is the study of man when in a healthy state, which Maslow and his colleagues believed essential and to have been neglected by other psychologists.

Maslow, in particular, pursued this area of interest by focusing on the experiences of self-actualizing people. He discovered that what he called *peak experiences* played a key role in creative, productive people. He later developed a typology of peak experiences, which included transcendence of all the usual aspects of life, such as time, space, and ego.

GESTALT THERAPY
FREDERICK (FRITZ) PERLS (1894-1970)

Best-known Gestalt psychotherapist in the United States is Fritz Perls, who, though trained as a Freudian, adopted a Gestalt approach, together with his wife, Dr. Laura Perls. Born and educated in Berlin, Perls was exposed to the ideas of Gestalt therapy when he served as assistant to Kurt Goldstein in 1926 at the Institute for Brain-Injured Soldiers. He and his wife moved to the United States, where they founded several institutes of psychotherapy, and spread the principle of Gestalt. In the 1960s Perls was resident psychotherapist at Esalen Institute in Big Sur. He published several books, of which *In and Out the Garbage Pail* and *Gestalt Therapy Verbatim* are probably the best known.

Patient's Awareness

Perls' particular philosophy concentrated upon building the patient's awareness of the here and now. Man was visualized as a unique materialization of energy, part of the vast, incomprehensible energy making up the universe. The lifetime of man was therefore an actively evolving process, with energy and matter representing the two poles.

"Loitering"

Based on such premises, Gestalt therapy aimed at discovering the causes of attraction and repulsion between these two poles, an oscillation which in everyday life might be illustrated through the analogy of lovers, who although extremely attracted to each other, at the same time desperately want to maintain their individual integrity and distance. Similarly, a healthy awareness moves back and forth between internal knowledge and an object outside the person. Any impairing of this external-internal relationship can lead to the enclosing of the individual perceptions in one sphere of cognition. This is a "loitering" which is recognizable as excessive introspection, or, in a more pathological case, schizophrenia.

This was Perls' conception of the Freudian conscious-unconscious dichotomy; a dichotomy which he defined as intelligent and psychological awareness. The psychological awareness was the one that said "Ouch!" while the intelligent awareness discovered the cause of the pain. When these two poles of awareness are unable to support each other, psychosis results.

Resolving Conflict

Such a polarization was not restricted to the single individual, but occurred between people as well. Thus, it became the function of Gestalt therapy to bring about a realignment of these poles between individuals, by bringing them into confrontation.

This confrontation at its most obvious might take on the form of a shouting match between, for example, two individuals who think they dislike each other. In the process of flinging insults back and forth, the reasons for the bad feelings of the other person are made interpretable. For the same reason, role changing and psychodrama are also encouraged as useful Gestalt adjuncts.

Perls' theorizing bears comparison with that of Reich, who thought the human mind was composed of an armor of resistances, and suggested that afflicted individuals should communicate their nonverbalized feeling directly. This usually implied some sort of sexual contact, a process not ruled out by Perls.

The Gestalt School

The Gestalt school was developed in Europe by Max Wertheimer, Wolfgang Kohler, and Kurt Koffka as a theoretical approach to all aspects of psychology. Gestalt psychology teaches that the whole is more than the sum of the parts; that the parts are not put together to make a whole, but are derived from the whole.

Gestalt therapists view man as a dynamic process as opposed to a static being. They believe that discordant, unproductive behavior results from a blockage in psychological processes, or, more specifically, from an unnecessary polarization of elements within the individual. The therapy seeks to dispel this polarization by bringing the elements together in direct confrontation. It is not concerned with historical antecedents, or the "whys" of the behavior, but works in the present. In this respect, the therapist plays a key role in his relationship with the client.

Accordingly, the problem of a disturbed "process" is believed to stem from man's intellectual tendency to break down the world into easily-dealt-with categories and definitions, losing thereby his sense of the unity of existence. It is a matter of mistaking the units of measure for what is actually being measured. Man must re-examine his concept of the world and of himself. Becoming aware of the intimate relationship between seemingly disparate elements is the first step toward achieving a realization of process.

Gestalt holds that in "process," the relationship of any two points is always characterized by simultaneous attraction and repulsion, a desire to join and a desire to remain separate. These forces constantly influence and alter the relationship. In the therapeutic relationship, the two points are therapist and client.

In Gestalt there are two essential parts of "process" — awareness and experience. Awareness is the ability to accurately perceive what is going on and provide feedback. It can exist at different levels: intelligent or intellectual awareness, and psychophysical or organic awareness. When the two levels conflict, an event can be experienced in two distinct ways. An essential part of Gestalt work is to bring together these two forms of awareness when they are alienated from each other. The second part of "process" is experience, which means simply the ongoing part of the therapeutic situation, the flow of energy between therapist and client. This immediate "experiencing" between individuals is the key point of Gestalt therapy. If the experiencing is genuine, both people reach greater awareness on all levels.

Symptoms such as fragmentation and pain result from one aspect of the personality refusing to accept another aspect. In the therapeutic relationship the therapist tries to find the discordant elements that are causing the conflict or symptom, and create a dialogue between them. Through open experiencing and acknowledgment of the conflicting elements, the fragmented portions can merge of their own accord into a new whole, different from but still retaining the characteristics of the various parts.

The aim of Gestalt therapy is the freeing of the dammed-up psychological "process" within a person and allowing it to develop in its own natural direction.

Great ideas, it has been said, come into the world
as gently as doves. Perhaps then, if we listen attentively,
we shall hear a faint flutter of wings, the gentle stirring
of life and hope. Some will say that this hope lies in a nation;
others, in man.

I believe rather that it is awakened, revived, nourished
by millions of solitary individuals whose deeds and
works everyday negate frontiers and the crudest implications of history. As a result there shines forth
fleetingly the ever-threatened truth that each and every
man, on the foundation of his own sufferings and joys,
builds for all.   Camus

Corita

CLIENT-CENTERED THERAPY / CARL ROGERS

Born into a close-knit Midwestern Protestant family, Rogers was raised on a farm. He spent two years at Union Theological Seminary before moving to Teachers College at Columbia University, from which he received his doctorate in 1931. Here Rogers was influenced by and sometimes torn between the teachings of the Freudians and the contemporary, more scientifically-oriented psychology of E. L. Thorndike and his followers. In his first post, in the child study department of a Rochester social agency, Rogers began developing his own form of therapy, which emerged out of the therapeutic relationship rather than being imposed from without. He was further influenced by Otto Rank's philosophy that "the individual client is a moving cause, containing constructive forces within, which constitute a will to health."

In 1937 Rogers moved to Ohio State University, where he solidified the core of his new therapy, and subsequently to the University of Chicago. He published his *Client-Centered Therapy* in 1951, and its widespread effect subsequently made him one of the chief spokesmen in the field of humanistic psychology. In 1969 he was one of the founders of the innovative Center for Studies of the Person, in La Jolla, California, where he is presently in residence.

According to Rogers, man is an organic creature, an individual who is always capable of growth, but who may on occasion need to be reminded how to go about releasing his potential.

It was this total acceptance of the individual which provided the orientation for Rogers' subsequent therapeutic developments. The person who wanted advice was no longer to be categorized as a patient, but looked upon as a client. This eliminated the whole medical model, because since the person was no longer seen as "sick," there was no need to delve into his past experiences in order to determine the cause of his illness. The focus of client-centered therapy is on the present situation. Additionally, the person, not the "problem," was the focus of attention, and feelings were more important than the intellect.

"Conditions of Worth"

Client-centered therapy focuses on an individual's inherent tendency toward self-actualization; that is, the essential forces within a person working toward the development of all capacities which lead to self-maintenance and self-enhancement. It is postulated that this process is thwarted in early life when "conditions of worth" (exterior, usually parental standards of right and wrong) are placed on experiences. A person begins to value his own experiences by the criteria of these externally imposed conditions instead of by his own organismic response. This creates an incongruency between a person's self-image and his experiencing self. Thus, experiences not in line with the self-image are distorted or completely shut off from conscious awareness. The work of therapy centers on healing this division.

There are three significant characteristics which a client-centered therapist considers of utmost importance in his relationship with the client: genuineness, empathic understanding, and unconditional positive regard. Of these characteristics, genuineness, or congruence, is the most basic. Genuineness signifies that the therapist is in touch with his own feelings, and can be fully present in the relationship with the client and express himself freely with no attempts at role playing. Genuineness readily leads to an openness to the client's feelings, and hence empathic understanding. Essential to empathic understanding, in turn, is nonpossessive caring and acceptance — i.e. unconditional positive regard.

According to Rogers' principles, these qualities in the therapist will be perceived and positively responded to, and the client will begin to change in the direction of greater awareness and gradual acceptance and trust in his own inner processes. The therapist does not attempt to advise or direct the client in this growth process. He trusts the client's ability to provide his own direction; that is,

he trusts in the constantly evolving self-actualization process. Therefore, he avoids the use of such techniques as Gestalt, bioenergetics or psychodrama because such behavior places the therapist in the false role of "expert."

Because client-centered therapy relies so heavily on the human qualities of the individuals involved and the genuineness of the relationship, it can be easily applied in a wide variety of situations where the aims are to increase interpersonal understanding and enhance personal growth.

Rogers and his team of psychiatrists have defined several stages which people go through in client-centered therapy. By the last stage, the client should no longer be fearful of experiencing feelings of any immediacy or richness of detail. In psychotherapeutic terms, the client can be regarded as having restored his composure — the ability to take life as it comes.

LOGOTHERAPY/ VIKTOR FRANKL

Born in Vienna, Frankl obtained his M.D. from the University there in 1930. He survived three years in Nazi concentration camps during World War II, and afterward became professor of neurology and psychiatry at the University of Vienna and later head of the department of neurology at the Poliklinik Hospital there. In the 1960s he founded the Institute of Logotherapy at the U.S. International University in San Diego.

Camp Survival

Logotherapy developed directly from Frankl's experiences in the camps, where he observed that some people were able to remain relatively healthy and survive while others died. It seemed to him that those who survived had discovered some meaning in their lives, and that, despite their various tragedies, they had something important to live for, which kept them from giving up hope.

Logotherapy is generally considered to be a form of existential psychiatry. Frankl has also been called the founder of the third Viennese school of psychotherapy. His theory, however, differs in important respects from those of Freud and Adler. For Frankl, the will to meaning is the motivation of man, whereas Freud thought the most important motivator was the will to pleasure. Frankl maintains that pleasure cannot be pursued directly, but comes as a by-product of the will to meaning, demoting Freud's primary force to a secondary position. Frankl also differs with Adler about man's primary motivation. Adler contended that the will to power is the main factor; to Frankl power is only a necessary prerequisite to meaning. In order to be able to seek meaning, a person must have some power — for instance, enough money to sustain life, or the power to make choices. But here again, according to Frankl, the will to power is secondary to meaning.

In logotherapy man finds meaning in trying to attain something beyond himself. Even if it is not fully attained, a person has become better by striving for the higher goal. The choice of goal is entirely up to the individual — the therapist does not choose for him.

Irony as Therapy

Logotherapy makes extensive use of irony as a psychotherapeutic technique. The presence of laughter is important because it indicates that the patient has been able to remove himself from his problem and find humor in it. Man's power of irony is the basis of paradoxical intention — the ability to stand a problem on its head and thereby acquire a completely different perspective of it. For example, the therapist might ask the neurotic individual why he has not committed suicide; then, depending on the reasons given for not doing so, the therapist is able to show the patient his real desire for life, and to reinforce it.

Man can be taught how to create meaning in his existence, and for this reason, Frankl sees logotherapy as reaching a deeper level than logic. Unlike the existential philosopher, who teaches that man has to learn to accept the meaninglessness of life, Frankl teaches us to see the intrinsic meaning of life in rational terms, a rationalization he calls the "suprameaning" in life.

THE MYTH OF CARE by ROLLO MAY

One of the most admired of the creators and interpreters of new psychological concepts, Rollo May received a B.D. from Union Theological Seminary before obtaining his Ph.D. from Columbia University in 1949. Best known for introducing the concept of existential psychology in the United States through his books Existence, A New Dimension in Psychiatry and Psychology *and* Existential Psychology, *Dr. May has had a distinguished career as a practicing psychotherapist in New York City, a teaching fellow and supervisory analyst at the William Alanson White Institute of Psychiatry and Psychoanalysis, and as a writer. The books that have made him famous with the general public include* The Meaning of Anxiety, Man's Search for Himself, *the best-selling* Love and Will, *and, most recently,* The Courage to Create. *May's work deals with such problems as the loneliness and insecurity of modern man and how individuals can stand against the insecurity of our age and find sources of strength in themselves. His books are eminently readable, unblurred by the jargon that mars so many books in this field. In his new book on creativity, he characterizes creativity not as an aberration, but as a process of working toward coherence which can prevent neurosis. Greatly daring, I asked Dr. May if there was any piece of writing by which we might represent him in this book, and with utmost cordiality he sent me this brief essay on myth and culture, which I have titled* The Myth of Care. *Compassionate, scholarly, insightful, it is typical of the writing of this original thinker.*

I began my study of the relation between myth and culture some years ago when, as a young man, I lived and taught in Greece. What particularly intrigued me was the way the ancient Greeks seemed to handle their anxiety and other psychological problems. In the classical phase of Greek culture, anxiety in our modern sense did not seem to emerge as an overt problem.

I could not escape the implication that in certain historic periods, the culture provides the help which the individual needs to face the crises of life — birth, adolescence, marriage, procreation, death — so that he does not experience the profound insecurity, self-doubt, and inner conflict which we associate with anxiety.

Jerome Bruner put it well: "When the myths of a society are no longer adequate to man's plight, the individual first takes refuge in mythoclasm and then he undertakes the lonely search for inner identity."

At the outset I shall state the hypothesis which then took shape in my mind: Psychotherapy, and the problems which lead people to come in numbers for psychological help, emerge at a particular point in the historic development of a culture — that is the point where the myths and symbols of the culture disintegrate. The values of the culture are mediated by these myths and symbols, and with their breakdown comes the inner conflict which sends people to psychotherapy.

In fifth-century Greece, a kind of "normal" psychotherapy operates spontaneously in the accepted symbols and practices in drama, religion, philosophy, and art. This is seen most clearly in the Greek myths and in the dramatic and religious ceremonies in which they were presented . . . . (Their function) is to bring the audience to a new level of experience which embraces *both* Apollo and the Furies, *both* freedom and responsibility, *both* love and hate, *both* the daimonic and the rational, *both* primitive drives *and* sophisticated order.

I propose that there is in every viable myth an *intentionality toward reconciliation*. The myth draws out various levels of unconscious, subconscious and transconscious, preverbal and transverbal experience. It lifts the person out of his simple antinomies and makes of a hopeless opposition a creative dialectic. This is the "normal" therapy that participating in the ceremony of the myths gives to the Athenian people as a whole.

When we come down to the third and second centuries B.C., we find ourselves in a world with a radically different psychological mood. Anxiety, inner doubts, and psychological conflict are rampant in the literature. The world we see is not unlike our own . . . .

The chief characteristic of this period, from our viewpoint, is that the myths and symbols are in process of deterioration. In such a time the individual man is thrown on his own. Unable to rely with confidence on cultural sanctions — often, indeed, unable even to *find* any generally agreed-on sanctions — he experiences his normal anxiety becoming neurotic, and he feels what we now call "alienation." There is no language by which he can bring out and deal with his inner problems. The breakdown of the myths and symbols forces him to look inward, and — if he is to avoid shrinking up psychologically and spiritually with accompanying feelings of depersonalization and despair — to undertake the painful pilgrimage to new levels of self-consciousness.

Myths of the Day

. . . It is more difficult to discern the myths of our day, partly because a viable myth is always mainly unconscious.

In the jazz age of the '20s, F. Scott Fitzgerald's novels of romantic nostalgia and sensuous melancholy provided the myth for many of my college generation.

About the same time, the sensitive Franz Kafka in Prague was forming the myths of protest against the objectifying pressures of 19th-century bourgeois society in *The Trial* and *The Castle* . . . . Kafka portrays the gripping picture of people unaware that they lack identity, and the inevitable emotional emptiness that results from this unawareness.

Ernest Hemingway's myth is the struggle for male potency, a myth that gets much of its power from the dread of impotence in Hemingway and modern American men.

Each of these writers was searching for the mythic form required for his own self-realization. Each illustrates how the individual gropes for some relationship to the underlying, archetypal depths in his society. Each died in accord with his own myth: Kafka of tuberculosis, Fitzgerald of alcoholism, and Hemingway of the one ultimate act of self-assertion still possible for him, the act of suicide.

. . . The critical issue which comes out in contemporary drama is the breakdown of communication. This is the theme of our most vital plays, those by Beckett, Ionesco, and Pinter. In the modern tragedies, the mask is fully removed, and we see emptiness, as in O'Neill's *The Iceman Cometh*. The nobility which is necessary for tragedy is felt on stage as the greatness which has fled from man. The apparent vacuum, emptiness, and apathy are the tragic fact. In *Waiting for Godot*, it is of the essence that Godot does not come; we wait forever and the problem remains: Was there a tree there yesterday? Will there be one there tomorrow?

In this void, I submit, new and more profound myths are emerging. I want to indicate one such myth . . . (which I call) the Myth of Care.

Care is a simple word. It is related to Heidegger's *Sorge*, which is the ontological statement of care. I could also translate it into Tillich's *Ultimate Concern*, but I prefer the simple term, the Myth of Care.

Waiting as Care

Now this myth is to be found in the contemporary dramatists we have cited. As they shock us — as all modern art does — into looking more deeply for the significance of our human experience, we find ourselves faced with the question of caring despite the meaninglessness of the external situations. Godot does not come, but in the waiting is Care. It matters that we wait and that we, like the characters in the drama, wait in human relationship — we share with each other the ragged coat, the shoes, the piece of turnip. Indeed, the word "wait" is connected in our language with the words "attend" and "tend" (in Beckett's drama, the boy says he "tends" Godot's sheep). Now "to tend" is also "to care for." Waiting is caring. The very title, *Waiting for Godot*, bespeaks our myth of Care.

Many of the contemporary dramas, to be sure, are negations, and some of them tread perilously close to the edge of nihilism. But it is the nihilism which shocks us into confronting the Void. And for him who has ears to hear, there speaks out of this Void (the term now refers to a transcendent quality) a deeper and more immediate apprehension of Being.

It is the myth of Care — and, I often believe, this myth alone — which enables us to stand against the cynicism and apathy which are the psychological illnesses of our day.

THERAPY IN PRACTICE

Off the couch and into encounters, screaming away the pains of being born, shouting out the hurts of childhood, facing reality, accepting responsibility, telling it like it is, learning to speak out, talk back, living in the now, finding what really exists, being hypnotized into facing and solving the problem — the new therapies bring patients face to face with themselves and the world, teaching them to recognize and express their needs. Or they attack flaws in the physical organism; alter the endocrine balance or rev up the metabolism with megavitamins; chemically alter the mood or renew the hormones. They diagnose your problems with a Luscher Color Test or the slanting loops of your handwriting or the way you see Rorschach butterflies — something here will surely make you well. Less and less struggling with the buried traumas and sexual repressions of Freud, more and more trying to deal with the here and now, the mental healers strive to get you back on the track, to teach you to perceive, fight, go with it, experience it, speak up. They are modern exorcists commanding the demons of 20th-century *angst* to begone and let the mind heal itself.

PSYCHOSYNTHESIS / a way to inner freedom

Psychosynthesis is a psychological and educational approach for recognizing the often conflicting elements of our inner lives. With its roots in East and West, Europe and North America, it is a synthesis of many traditions. It is a developmental process based on a positive conception of man/woman within an evolving universe. Starting with each person's existential situation as he or she perceives it, its goal is personal growth by way of integration of personality and the unifying center of being — the self.

Psychosynthesis draws upon a variety of methods and techniques best suited to each individual's existential situation, his psychological type, his own unique goals, desires, and paths of development. Some of the techniques and methods used are: guided imagery, meditation, self-identification, creativity, Gestalt, movement, training of the will, symbolic art work, journal keeping, ideal models, and development of intuition. Result: A balanced actualization of life, because each individual gains freedom of choice, the power of decision for his own actions, and the ability to actively regulate and direct his many personality functions.

Psychosynthesis was originated in 1919 by Roberto Assagioli, who founded the Instituto di Psicosintesi in Florence, Italy, to which people come from all over the world to train in psychosynthesis techniques. It is a way of looking at the mystery of man, his inner life — a pragmatic approach that strives to take all known facts into consideration and to explore all those that are knowable. It synthesizes every kind of theory and practice from Freud and Jung to massage and meditation. It is an art of healing, an art of education, and an art of living.

OPEN ENCOUNTER / a fresh approach to life

Open Encounter is a means of interpersonal relating based on openness and honesty, self-awareness on all levels, and self-responsibility. Encounter methods are eclectic, drawing from a wide range of experiences and techniques of fruitful interpersonal relating. Some current elements include psychodrama, Gestalt, body therapies, and theater techniques. Small group encounter experiences aim at developing individual awareness, uniting body, mind, and spirit, and removing psychological blocks to enable an individual to be freely in touch with himself.

Like Gestalt, encounter views a person from the perspective of process rather than as a static form. It believes that physical and emotional traumas can impede that process, along with patterns of movement and behavior which make only limited use of potentialities. It operates on the belief that individuals have three basic interpersonal needs: inclusion, or the feeling of being a significant, worthwhile person; control, referring to a sense of competence and ability to deal successfully with the world; and affection, feeling lovable and able to love. In encounter terms, inclusion is the decision to become part of a group,* control refers to the power hierarchy of roles within the group, and affection is the acceptance and closeness generated between group members.

In the open encounter situation, an effort is made to work on all levels of experience. An important aspect of experience is emotion as manifested through body movements and postures, and a basic tenet is that body manifestations are closest to real feelings while words may function as a coverup.

Basic Guidelines

Since encounter is a specific form of interrelating that hopes to achieve certain results, a set of rules is generally observed. Basic guidelines include: (1) Establishment of open and honest communication with a concentration on dealing with feelings instead of ideas and focusing on the present moment as opposed to past history. This openness of communication encompasses such specific actions as talking directly to a person in the group rather than about him, making statements instead of asking questions, and attempting to keep away from stating things in impersonal or very general terms. (2) A full integration of the body into group activities, facilitated by a physically safe and unencumbered environment (i.e., a comfortable, furniture-free meeting place conducive to movement and physical contact), and a willingness to express oneself physically when the opportunity arises. (3) General self-responsibility; that is, taking responsibility for what one says and does, and for dealing with one's feelings vis-a-vis the group.

Open encounter is an approach to living as opposed to what goes on in a particular small group situation. For this reason it can be seen as not only a useful adjunct to traditional psychotherapies, but as a means of working toward mutual supportive understanding in all contexts — from the family to the school to industry — where the quality of human interrelationship is important.

* The term "group therapy" can be used to describe any number of different therapies which are conducted in a group. Many can also be done on an individual basis. Transactional analysis, primal therapy, client-centered therapy, and Gestalt therapy can all be done in group settings. The group therapy may be primarily verbal, or primarily concerned with getting people in touch with their bodies through massage and other touching techniques, or can be a combination of both.

PSYCHODRAMA / the value of role playing

J. L. Moreno is credited with the development of the therapeutic technique which in this country is best known as Psychodrama. Working on a premise of Aristotle, the cathartic effect of drama upon an audience, Moreno developed the idea that acting in a play might provide the necessary encouragement for patients to act out their problems. The opportunities offered to the anxious mind therefore might achieve a greater fluidity of expression than was possible in the one-to-one question-and-answer basis of free association.

Building upon his spark of insight, Moreno had a small theater especially designed for the needs of his therapeutic technique. The theater's stage consisted of three concentric circular aprons rising accessibly in front of the seated audience. Then above the stage — as in Shakespeare's day — there was a balcony which could either be used by participants in a play, or as an observation platform by the psychotherapist. The aloof position of the therapist did not preclude his involvement in the production, however, as he also took on the role of producer, directing his assistants to re-create the fantasies of the patient. On other occasions, the performers might act out various scenes from the patient's life.

Other patients who swelled the numbers as an audience were also encouraged to discuss and participate in the individual "patient-playwright's" creation, a creation in which the playwright was also encouraged to perform if the "vibes" were good. This technique has become known as *role playing*.

Moreno saw transference as taking place not between people, but toward a role which the therapists represent to the patient. Therefore, "every individual has a set of friends and a set of enemies, and a range of roles and counter-roles." Thus, ultimately, "the tangible aspects of what is known as ego are the roles in which he operates."

The conclusions drawn from this reasoning were that the group came first and the therapist remained "subordinate" to its needs until able to assert some direction on the course of therapy through therapeutic experience which was likely to give him more insight into the mechanics of the relationships being created and exposed within the group. If necessary, the therapist might act as an *auxiliary ego*, or alternatively get one of his assistants to react to the needs of the patient in such a way that the psyche might quickly be exposed prior to healing or readjustment. Moreno emphasized the importance of readjusting relationships between people — as opposed to an analysis of the individual's troubled state. He also saw his system as requiring psychoanalytic skill.

MUSIC THERAPY/a new language for the handicapped

From primitive times music has been used for curing, soothing, mood changing — for drumming away demons and calling down the healing spirits. King Saul, feeling the tensions of madness gather in his head, would send for David to soothe his distress by playing the harp. The most powerful form of nonverbal communication, communicating directly from one spirit to another, music can influence behavior in strong and subtle ways.

During the past century it has been used increasingly as therapy for the physically handicapped and the mentally troubled. Following World War II, music began to play an important part in the treatment of hospitalized veterans, progressing from the area of entertainment and distraction into specific therapies. Today it is one of the most rapidly developing adjuncts to healing. According to E. Thayer Gaston in his foreword to *Music in Therapy*, most experts agree that the three most important accomplishments are:

1. The establishment or re-establishment of interpersonal relationships.

2. The bringing about of self-esteem through self-actualization.

3. The utilization of the unique potential of rhythm to energize and bring order.

By wordlessly conveying the warm emotions that bring people together, music can reach withdrawn mental patients, even autistic children.

In 1944 Michigan State University began the first formal curriculum program in music therapy. In 1946 the University of Kansas offered classroom and laboratory courses. Other colleges followed suit, and in 1950 the National Association for Music Therapy was formed to stimulate research and work toward standardizing educational procedures and clinical practice.

Music can persuade people into group activity where other methods fail, can provide ego-gratifying achievements in learning and performing. It is used with great effectiveness in treating mentally retarded children and adults; physically disabled victims of cerebral palsy, muscular dystrophy, and other crippling diseases; severe speech disorders and cleft palate; and a wide variety of psychiatric and behavior problems.

The Mentally Retarded

Because of the problem of communication with mentally retarded patients, music often provides a bridge over the verbal impasses. Responding to the universal appeal of music, patients are led from enjoyment to participation. Like the ancient healing of shamans and medicine men which was focused on chanting, dancing, and beating of drums, the rhythmic pattern provides a reassuring feeling of order and security. In order to participate in the making of music the patients have to become involved in an ongoing process that stretches their attention spans. They attain social acceptance and the reward of performing in an orderly and pleasurable way in a group. With each successful experience the patient's self-esteem is enhanced, and dramatic improvements in behavior and learning patterns start to occur.

For the most severely handicapped, musical games such as clapping and singing provide pleasurable learning experiences and ways of relating to others. Some patients have learned to speak by using rhyming songs, with repetitive or nonsense words and vowels. Experiments have shown that when the retarded are presented with identical learning material in musical or nonmusical settings, they make far greater progress in the musical setting. Hospitalized patients in music therapy programs have shown marked improvement in vocabulary, initiative, and cooperative behavior.

In one state hospital a drum corps was formed for handicapped patients. The group included those with cerebral palsy, deafness, mongoloid speech, stuttering, impaired sight, and a variety of other mental and physical disorders. The group progressed from learning to count and practicing around a table, first with one drumstick and then with two. After long and patient practice, drums were added.

Gradually this struggling, handicapped group metamorphosed into a marching drum corps with a remarkable improvement in individual pride, sense of order, neatness, and morale.

Brain-damaged children can be reached through music, both sedative and stimulative in mood. Children with cerebral palsy can find emotional release, relaxation, and an increased concentration span. The chance to perform in musical dramas and operettas, even for those in wheelchairs, can change apathy into joyous participation. Caught up in the music and the drama, patients lose inhibitions and become functioning units in a successful group activity. Music is particularly valuable in work done with geriatric patients, calling them back from dreams of the past to sing the old songs and be entertained with some of the newer ones.

To quote John Armstrong, "Music exalts each joy, allays each grief, expels diseases, softens every pain, subdues the rage of passion and the plague."

PSYCHOPHARMACOLOGY

chemotherapy in the treatment of depression

Depression can be characterized as a magnified and inappropriate negative response to life situations. It may take a great variety of forms, some of which are the reduction or total disappearance of enjoyment and pleasure, poor concentration, fatigue, insomnia, guilt, indecision, anxiety, irritability, and thoughts of suicide. It may also have physical components such as headache, nausea, chest pains, stomach cramps, and rapid breathing. The U.S. Public Health Service estimates that 10 million Americans suffer from some form of this affliction, with fewer than one million actually undergoing treatment.

Chemotherapy

Many therapists consider a neurosis of some type to be the chief instigator of depression; others believe it is most often due to a biochemical failure in the brain. One of these is Dr. Nathan Kline, who has published his theories in a recent book, *From Sad to Glad*, which has become a national bestseller. Even if the depression is related to a neurotic condition, Dr. Kline believes in the use of chemotherapy to treat the symptoms, which

enables the patient to mobilize his resources for the psychotherapy process. To many depressed people, the added stress of undergoing the traditional kinds of therapy is something they cannot handle. In other cases, the very real problems they face can be successfully dealt with once the appalling burden of depression is lifted. Although the dispensing of medication should never be taken lightly, Kline maintains, the essential point is that the treatment usually works.

The four main types of drugs effective in combating depression are monoamine oxidase inhibitors, tricyclics, sympathomimetic amines, and lithium. All complement each other and work in different ways. The particular combination of drugs appropriate to a patient's need will depend on many factors in his individual mental and physical makeup.

In most cases, the patient will begin to feel relief within three weeks after treatment with chemotherapy is begun, with complete recovery in about four months. Setbacks sometimes do occur along the line, however. After the symptoms have completely disappeared, another month of full medication is continued, for stabilization. Occasionally, however, a patient will require an ongoing maintenance dosage for an extended period of time. Kline is quick to point out that in no case is the medication habit-forming, nor does it create a craving after it has been discontinued. He compares it, rather, to a diabetic's use of insulin, or a cardiac patient's use of digitalis.

Biological Depression

Kline suggests that chemotherapy can best be considered an adjunct to other forms of therapy. In some cases, chemotherapy of this kind is all that the patient requires, while in others an additional form of more traditional therapy may be advisable. One important point to be considered is that a far greater number of people can be treated through such psychopharmacology than through extended psychotherapy, and much more cheaply. Kline believes that 80-85 percent of depressions are biological in origin; further, he holds, the discovery of antidepressants "is not only the secret of treating depression but the key to its cause and prevention ... we find even now evidence that the mechanisms of schizophrenia and perhaps even some of the neuroses will become visible and treatable."

MEGAVITAMIN
THERAPY / orthomolecular psychiatry

Megavitamin therapy consists of the use of massive doses of common vitamins, particularly vitamins B_3 and C, in the treatment of mental and physical disturbances. Orthomolecular psychiatry refers specifically to the treatment and prevention of mental illness through correcting the bodily balance of vitamins, minerals, and nutrients. More than 20 years have passed since the first use of megavitamin therapy in the treatment of schizophrenia, but follow-up work has been slow and skepticism marked. At the moment, megavitamin therapy is usually available only through a private psychiatrist — mental hospitals and clinics rarely consider administration of vitamins a valid part of treatment.

There are many indications, however, that certain forms of mental illness, especially schizophrenia, are accompanied and possibly caused by various bodily ailments such as an inability to absorb or break down chemical elements in a normal fashion. It is suspected that schizophrenics lack the ability to properly decompose adrenalin in the body, which can lead to conditions that produce hallucinations and psychotic perceptions. Vitamin B_3 — niacin — is thought to be able to reduce the formation of adrenalin and thus be of value in treating schizophrenia.

Megavitamin therapy has been found most effective with acute schizophrenics in the early stages of the disease. Such patients are usually put on an initial niacin intake of three grams per day in addition to an equal dosage of vitamin C. Depending on the patient's reaction, the niacin dose may be increased up to 30 grams per day, with vitamin C remaining at the three-gram level. In severe cases electroshock treatment may also be prescribed. Increased vitamin intake has the effect of enabling psychotherapeutic drugs to work more effectively, thus allowing drug dosage to be reduced as much as 50 percent. Results with acute schizophrenics indicate a remission of symptoms in many cases, although the effects of treatment are very slow — it often takes several months for noticeable improvement to occur.

Alcoholics

For the most part, megavitamin therapy is concerned only with the use of the B vitamins, vitamin C, and vitamin E, which are considered nontoxic even at very high levels. In comparison with the problems produced and overdosages possible with standard medication, megavitamin therapy seems relatively safe, with only occasional minor side effects. Studies have indicated that over 90 percent of schizophrenics experience vitamin B_3, B_6, and C deficiencies, so there would indeed appear to be a link between mental disturbances and bodily malfunctions, at least in the case of schizophrenia.

As more research is carried on in the area of mental illness and its interrelationship with bodily processes, the function and applications of megavitamin therapy will surely come more clearly into focus.

Treatment with large dosages of niacin and vitamin C has also been found effective with alcoholics. Many alcoholics have biochemical and metabolic problems, exhibit schizophrenic tendencies, or suffer from hypoglycemia, a blood sugar disorder. Hypoglycemia is of particular interest because it also affects a large number of nonalcoholics who, as a result, are plagued by chronic depression and fatigue and at times may exhibit a wide range of psychotic symptoms. When combined with a special high-protein diet, megavitamin therapy seems to be of significant help in controlling the disorder.

HYPNOTHERAPY / a fresh use for hypnosis

Modern psychotherapy, as we have seen, started as a consequence of Freud's frustration with hypnosis. During the "humanistic therapy era," hypnosis lost ground and it has been revived as a therapy in itself with the advent of direct behavior-modification therapy. Hypnotherapy tries to selectively recondition the human organism through suggestion. It differs from behavior modification in that in hypnotherapy the client is in a trance state.

Hypnosis can best be described as an induced state of selectively altered sensory awareness. It involves that part of the nervous system not subject to voluntary control. The function of hypnotherapy is to recondition certain sensory reactions to the stimuli of anxiety or psychic tension so that instead of producing physiological symptoms, such as ulcers or headaches, they fail to do so. After the therapist decides which stimuli are creating a violent emotional response in the client, he tries through hypnosis to alter the sensory system's habitual reactions.

If an individual is presented with a set of sensory or mental cues that enrage him, the autonomic nervous system prepares his organism for an expression of anger. But if that same sensory cue pattern also includes a powerful stimulus that says the anger must not be expressed, and must instead be sublimated, a conflict results that translates itself into an involuntary reaction in the individual's body. What the reconditioning of hypnotherapy tries to do is allow the hypnotized subject to relearn selectively, or rearrange, the stimulus-response cues that have produced his undesirable involuntary reaction patterns.

Hypnotic induction begins during an interview which provides the hypnotherapist with information on the way his subject usually responds to stress. The therapist will then induce a hypnotic state. The increasing relaxation of deep hypnotic trance shifts the subject's attention away from any awareness that might be distracting. In such a relaxed state the subject is open to the associative suggestions the therapist will give him. These suggestions are aimed at inducing an acceptance of new ways of interpreting sensations and are the basis of the reconditioning process.

Posthypnotic Suggestion

The second important factor in hypnotherapy is posthypnotic suggestion. Once the therapist has reconditioned the subject's anxiety-producing sensation system through repetitive associative suggestion during a series of hypnotic sessions, he will then train the subject in the use of his new responses outside therapy. He is taught to use the technique of autosuggestion in conjunction with his hypnotically reconditioned reactions — that is, to summon up in his mind the pleasant sensations he experienced in hypnosis each time he finds himself confronted by anxiety-inducing states.

One argument against hypnotherapy comes from Dr. Theodore Barber, a psychologist who has conducted almost 15 years of intensive research in hypnosis at Harvard and concludes that there is no evidence that hypnosis even exists. The fact of saying the subject was in a trance because he obeyed the suggestions is, he asserts, no proof at all.

Dr. William S. Kroger has listed several ways in which hypnotherapy has been invaluable in his book, *Clinical and Experimental Hypnosis.* It is his contention that just as anyone can be taught to make a skin incision, anyone can learn to induce hypnosis. However, it takes years of experience and clinical judgment to use hypnosis effectively.

interview / WILLIAM S. KROGER, M.D.
hypnosis and the art of healing

A renowned authority on clinical hypnosis, Dr. Kroger has been practicing the art and science of hypnosis for more than 30 years and is one of the outstanding medical hypnotists and teachers in the country. He has authored and co-authored numerous scientific papers and books, principally in the fields of hypnosis and psychosomatic medicine, and is a frequent speaker at scientific gatherings. He is a past president of the Academy of Psychosomatic Medicine and an honorary member of many scientific societies. He is in the private practice of psychosomatic medicine and hynotherapy in Beverly Hills, California. His encyclopedic knowledge of medicine makes him eminently qualified to discuss the healing art and the application and incidence of hypnosis, in therapy and daily life.

LANDE: What are some of the phenomena of hypnosis?

KROGER: All the phenomena of hypnosis occur at everyday levels and are seen as part of everyday happenings. For example, posthypnotic suggestions are like propaganda, or TV commercials, or ads — they all influence you to do something. Whenever an individual is being influenced *without realizing* he is being influenced, he is being made suggestible. Another phenomenon seen every day is amnesia. For example, you start to introduce your best friend at a party. You have known his name all your life, but all of a sudden you go blank — you can't remember it! It dropped right out of your mind — an occurrence of spontaneous amnesia.

Disassociation is also part of everyday thinking. For example, when you forget what time of day it is, or where you are, or even who you are, it is a kind of temporary splitting off of awareness from reality. Hypermnesia or increased memory recall is a form of age regression. When you walk down the street and recall, "Forty years ago I used to play baseball on that lot, and now there is a big skyscraper there," you have promptly returned to an earlier level of your life.

Another very interesting phenomenon of hypnosis is time distortion, the brain's remarkable capacity to either expand or telescope time, which also occurs at everyday levels. You know, when you are waiting for a cab on a cold rainy day and the cab is due in two minutes — it seems like 20. Or when you are listening to an interesting speaker who talks for an hour, but it seems like only 10 minutes.

Other everyday phenomena are anesthesia and analgesia. Individuals often develop a hysterical numbness or "anesthesia." They will complain of numbness in the hand or foot — and if it follows no known nervous innervation, it is referred to as hysterical anesthesia. This same kind of anesthesia can be produced by posthypnotic suggestions.

Another one is automatic writing, which is really nothing but doodling. When talking on the telephone you often write down things while you talk. The two are apparently disconnected, but if you investigate closely, there is some correlation between your subconscious thoughts and your scribbling.

Finally, there is somnambulism, a form of sleepwalking, where the individual walks around with his eyes open like a sleepwalker. So, you see, the natural functions of the brain can be used for producing all types of phenomena.

LANDE: To what extent does the therapist have control over the subject when hypnosis is being used?

KROGER: The subject always has complete control; at no time is he controlled by the hypnotist. The hypnotist doesn't actually hypnotize anybody, it just looks as if he does. It's an illusion that really depends on the subject's capacity to go into hypnosis, and this in turn depends on his mental set, motivation, and expectant attitude. The relaxed, concentrated state of attention which

we call hypnosis is part of everyday happenings. You might as well ask to what extent is sleep or wakefulness controlled. The subject controls whether he will fall asleep or stay awake or superawake — in fact, superawake is a pretty good definition of hypnosis.

Remember, we are talking only about a man-made definition of awareness. Note that I say awareness rather than consciousness, because even sleep is poorly understood at present. A mother can sleep through a thunderstorm and yet hear the cry of her baby. So the fact that you have your eyes open doesn't necessarily mean you are awake, nor when your eyes are closed does it mean you are asleep. It is unfortunate that the word hypnosis comes from the Greek word for sleep, because it has nothing to do with sleep, trance, or unconsciousness. Really, it has more to do with enhancing human potentials, because it allows a person to transcend his normal voluntary capacities in order to achieve supramaximal performance.

LANDE: As a physician, would you speak a little about healing?

KROGER: First of all, about 75 percent of "sick" people have nothing the matter with them; they have problems of a psychosomatic nature. By psychosomatic we mean the reciprocal and dynamic interaction of emotions and body functions in producing symptoms. It is pretty well accepted that 65 percent of people get better with almost any form of therapy — the so-called placebo effect. Whenever an inert substance is employed to treat medical disorders or a ritualistic procedure is utilized in psychotherapy, a suggestion or placebo effect is operating. If the individual has belief, confidence, and faith he will get better, he develops conviction, and conviction of cure leads to cure. People get cured in the way they expect to get cured, which is why we have so many different kinds of healing methodologies all over the world. About 25 percent require specific medicinal or surgical therapy. There are only about 25 drugs that work. We have antibiotic and immunologic agents too, but other than them we really do not have many drugs that actually heal.

LANDE: What do the different healing methods have in common?

KROGER: Healing methods all over the world have the following formula: There is always a "misdirection of intention," consisting of a ritual which obscures how the healing really occurs by inducing an inhibitory mental set. As a result of this set, the patient's critical faculties are reduced and he accepts the healer's ministrations. These can range from giving an injection to throwing betel juice to the four winds with incantations. The important thing is that motivation must be strong. The belief, confidence, and conviction, processed into faith that he is going to get well, result in the patient's recovery. Faith is the greatest copilot any healer can have. Certainly it is faith that accounts for healing by theologists and spiritualists. Time alone cures over 60 percent of people, so a high percentage will get better.

LANDE: Does that include catastrophic illness?

KROGER: No. Catastrophic illnesses such as cancer, heart disease, and organic conditions or degenerative diseases are not going to get better with faith or time. But some chronic diseases such as arthritis do improve with relaxation, change of environment, elimination of stress, and various types of suggestive procedures.

LANDE: Some doctors are making claims that imagery is successful with terminal cancer patients. What do you think of this method?

KROGER: What they are doing is just using faith — no one can criticize them for that. They are giving the cancer patient something to hold onto by thinking that ladybugs, for example, are circulating in the bloodstream, and biting off the malignant cells. This "magical" approach at least appeals to the patient's expectations. It also gives him a crutch which mobilizes the belief, the faith to live. One of my books has a chapter on emotional factors in cancer, and another on the use of hypnotic imagery for alleviating pain in cancer. I strongly believe there is a will, and some people who are weak, passive, and submissive die quickly, while others who are tougher may live on and on. There have been studies showing a distinct correlation between the desire to live and longevity. There is also a possible correlation between personality factors and malignancies. On the basis of psychometric tests, psychologists can determine which patients will die and which ones will live.

I have also noticed that some cancer patients subjected to suggestive therapy will live a long time or even recover. Spontaneous remission of cancer is not as uncommon as we have been led to believe. That is why many noted investigators get duped into thinking they have a cancer cure. They don't understand that suggestion can be utilized at many different levels of awareness — verbal, nonverbal, intraverbal, and extraverbal. Another powerful factor is the prestige of the institution, the shrinelike effect — all these things add to the patient's expectation, his belief that he *will* be helped. Such strong faith mobilizes the curative or adaptive responses

91

and fighting powers within the body — and who could maintain that that is bad?

LANDE: I remember you debated the late Dr. Paul Dudley White on the nature of acupuncture after he returned from China. Will you share some of your opinions?

KROGER: Acupuncture is another placebo method that comes and goes. I have been familiar with it for more than 45 years, but I became more interested when all the publicity appeared, and it began to be accepted by the public and certain segments of the medical profession. Doctors are just as suggestible as the public, you know. Every six months a new drug or new method of treatment makes its appearance, and then promptly dies. We are currently seeing the rise of biofeedback and Transcendental Meditation. Investigators publish glowing reports which make the headlines. Then another group of investigators uses double-blind crossover studies to find the "therapy" has no value at all. I am reminded of what Trousseau, a great French physician, once said: "Take the drug while it still heals!"

The whole business of acupuncture is very simple to explain. Briefly, what happened was that when Mao Tse-tung made the Long March in 1934-35, he noticed that the barefoot doctors or paramedical workers were curing the peasants by using needles, giving them herbs, and tender loving care (TLC) — all part of traditional Chinese medicine. Because of expediency — he had no money, trained personnel, or equipment — Mao decided that since 75 percent of people get better without anything, this approach wouldn't hurt them. So he said, "We must use traditional medicine (acupuncture, herbs, and TLC) and combine it with Western modern scientific medicine for the 25 percent who do need it." This approach saved money and also fitted into people's belief systems. During any kind of healing, remember there are potent variables that occur before, during, and after

what is being done. Before discussing them, though, we have to divide acupuncture into two categories.

There is acupuncture for medical conditions, which most authorities agree is nothing but homespun psychotherapy for psychosomatic disorders. Then there is acupunctural analgesis (AA), which refers to its use in surgery. The Chinese have reported the effectiveness of AA on over 600,000 surgical procedures. When you look carefully at the data, you distinguish the following antecedent variables:

There is a 5,000-year-old belief system. There are the impressive charts and mannequins. There are the expectations of the leaders who have been told by Mao that this is what they must use. There are the expectations of the masses who feel Mao's wisdom has raised their standard of living, that he knows what's best. Then there are the suggestive effects of the needles, which produce distraction and a sort of numbness. Then, too, there are also the cultural, sociopolitical, and economic factors. In a regimented society the expectations of leaders and masses bring about compliant behavior without overt motivational involvement. The psychobiological changes lead to well-known placebo responses.

Also, most of the investigators did not realize that almost 96 percent of the patients had Novocaine and other anesthetic-like drugs. The Chinese hate to be put to sleep — they have a fear of it — so they were given Novocaine before they were wheeled into the operating room. Other important variables: they were all trained in Yoga breathing exercises to relax. Relaxation neutralizes anxiety, and if you can neutralize anxiety and tension, you automatically raise the pain threshold. Another important variable was that patients were rehearsed in every step of the operation by the same team for from three to six weeks. This procedure removes the fear of the unknown. Since the person now knows what to expect, the elements of fear, tension, and surprise are reduced.

Now can you see how all this, together with Novocaine, produces the end result? I don't wish to denigrate acupuncture, merely to explain it. Since there are so many different ways of producing the same effect — auricular puncture, moxibustion, acupressure, and many other types of acupuncture — all of them must have a placebo effect. They all share the same basic common denominator. A supplicant approaches the healer whom he expects is going to give him something. There is your recipe for increased suggestibility.

I saw the same techniques used when I was a child at evangelist and tabernacle healings. First the preachers make everybody feel guilty that they had something the matter with them. They beat them down, bring strong guilt feelings to the fore. "Which of you stole?" they ask. "Who had carnal knowledge of a woman? Who masturbated? Who told a lie?" By the time they get through all this and more, they have hit everyone's guilty fears. Now you have no place to go but up to ask for redemption in the eyes of the Lord. They say, "Step forth now and make your peace. Drop your money in the collection box to buy a seat in Heaven."

The technique is somewhat similar to that of est and other therapies. First they make you feel lower than a snake's belly, then they use sensory deprivation by prohibiting that you even go to the bathroom and practically starving you. All this wipes the blackboard of the mind clean, and then it is very easy to engraft ideas. All this, along with the emotional contagion that always takes place in a group, the powerful exhortations given in logical sequence that are based upon simplistic reasoning — these all appeal to the highly suggestible. There is the inherent competitiveness which mobilizes in group dynamics. If one person improves, then the other says, "I can do the same thing." There is also a sort of transference of what I call a shrinelike effect, which causes individuals to develop an expectant attitude and faith. They are mass hypnotized into thinking they are getting better.

LANDE: What about instant salvation?

KROGER: Everybody is looking for instant magic — that is why the meditative therapies are so popular today. The wheel has made a complete turn, and we are back to where we were 7,000 years ago, with the sleep temples, the mantras, the closing of the eyes — all this is a part of earlier religions. When someone has anxiety, you neutralize it with relaxation, and the individual feels better. But neither relaxation nor meditation by itself is any more effective than the surgeon's knife making the skin incision. You have to know what to do with the knife after you get inside the belly. Likewise, what good is meditation alone? You have to know what to do with this relaxed state — how to manipulate the variables accounting for faulty behavior in order to polarize the patient toward recovery.

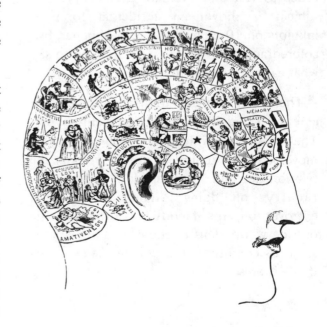

93

THE TESTS/ four of the major psychological tests

The Rorschach Test

Hermann Rorschach, a Swiss psychiatrist, developed his famous inkblot test in 1921 in order to test and evaluate personality. The subject is shown an accidental form of inkblots on 10 plates, or pieces of paper, five colored and five not. He is then asked to say what each represents to him.

The test is intended to distinguish between emotional and intellectual personality types. The way in which the subject relates movement and color factors represents the relation in him between introversion, the faculty of doing "inner work," and extroversion, the faculty of turning to the outside world. This relationship expresses the subject's condition, and can show a psychosis if one is present.

The relationship is usally formulated in terms of the "experience type," of which there are four:

1. The introversive experience type, in which kinesthetic responses predominate (as, for example, in imaginative subjects).

2. The extroversive experience type, in which color responses predominate (the example here is practical subjects).

3. The "coartated" or narrowed experience type, which shows marked submergence of both movement and color factors (as in people who are tending toward depression or are actually psychotically depressed, and subjects with dementia simplex).

4. The ambiequal experience type, which

shows almost equally many kinesthetic and color responses (as, for example, talented, creative people, compulsive neurotics, manics, and catatonics).

The test is regarded as an extremely effective way of delineating personality. It requires a skilled practitioner, however, to interpret the subject's answers.

Minnesota Multiphasic Personality Inventory

"Answer the following statements as being either true or mostly true, or false or mostly false as they apply to you:

I am afraid of losing my head.

Everything is turning out just like the prophets of the Bible said it would.

I certainly feel useless at times.

Someone has been trying to poison me."

The most popular personality test being administered today is the Minnesota Multiphasic Personality Inventory (MMPI), which consists of 550 statements like these. They cover a variety of areas ranging from vocational interests to physical health to social attitudes. The test takes about an hour to complete and can be administered and scored by a nonprofessional. A trained professional then interprets the test data by charting the subject's responses and comparing them on a scale of how others have responded. For example, there is a "D" scale, which is used to determine how the subject's responses compare to those given by people who have been clinically diagnosed as depressed. In this manner, a therapist can determine to what extent the client is depressed. There are scales corresponding to each personality trait, and even a scale to determine whether the subject is giving honest responses. The MMPI (developed in 1943 by the University of Minnesota) is especially useful in psychiatric clinics and hospitals as a tool to diagnose personality disorders; it is also used by employers to screen job applicants, and by college counselors in student career guidance.

The major pitfall in tests such as MMPI is the means by which they define "normal." A subject's responses are compared to "normal" responses in order to determine whether the subject has normal or abnormal personality traits. "Normal" in this case would be statistically defined as the majority response; any deviation from the common response could be construed as "abnormal." A paradox results from using the statistical majority as a definition of normality, however. As the noted British psychiatrist, R. D. Laing, points out in his book, *The Politics of Experience:* "Normal men have killed perhaps 100 million of their fellow men in the last 50 years . . . ." MMPI and other forms of modern psychological testing procedures have given us the means of statistically defining normal, but they also raise the question of just how "normal" we want to become.

Thematic Apperception Test

This test (usually referred to as the TAT test) was originally developed by Henry Murray and Christiana Morgan in 1935, and is used as an exploration of personality. The subjects are shown a series of pictures that are detailed, but in which the details are unclear, thus forcing the subjects to use imagination to interpret them. They are then asked to create a story about each of the pictures in turn, incorporating these fantasies. If repeating themes keep coming up throughout the showing of the pictures, then obviously they point to significant traits of the subjects' personalities and their component elements. By projecting their deepest fantasies, the subjects reveal directional tensions of which they are quite unconscious.

Some fantasies are conscious while others go deeper and arise from the unconscious. These, like dreams, have to be interpreted if the therapist is to be able fully to understand the meaning implicit in them.

Luscher Color Test

It is the argument of Swiss psychologist Dr. Max Luscher that a person's affinity for or rejection of certain colors can be directly associated with psychological and physical needs. He developed his test in 1947, after extensive study of color psychology. The full test presents seven panels of colors with 73 color patches in 25 different shades; the testee makes 43 different selections, from which information about the conscious and unconscious, areas of psychic stress, states of glandular balance or imbalance, and other physiological conditions can be gleaned.

The test takes less than 10 minutes to answer and is extremely simple to administer; interpretation, however, requires considerable training and psychological insight.

A much simplified and shortened test, including only one of the panels, is available to the layman in a test titled *The Luscher Color Test.* Interpretations of color preferences can then be made by using the interpretation tables given in the test. A cover note reminds the reader that the test was designed for professional use and is not a parlor game or a tool for oneupmanship. In its simplicity, however, it is available to misuse as Tarot cards or the ouija board.

The short version is widely used by doctors in Europe as an aid to diagnosis because it highlights significant areas of personality and can act as an "early warning" system, drawing attention to possible locations of stress. The test is also used in industry for screening job applicants. It has the considerable advantage of requiring no language ability — the subject's decisions are made purely on the basis of an instantaneous feeling of preference for particular colors. An interesting feature is that the preferences may vary widely within quite short spaces of time, in situations where there are considerable mood swings.

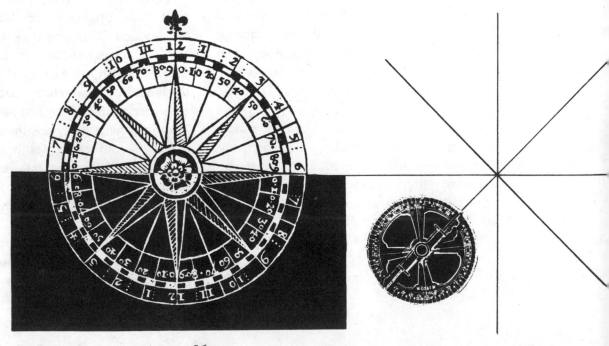

COPING WITH THE CLIMACTERIC by ROBERT B. GREENBLATT, M.D.

One of the principal developers of oral contraception, Robert Greenblatt combines the roles of scientist and physician, teacher and author. Over the past 20 years, his theories regarding the male and female climacteric, the "change of life," have gained wide acceptance. A frequent contributor to both medical and lay publications, he has written more than 600 articles and is the recognized authority on the menopause. Author of eight textbooks and the chapter on endocrinology in the Encyclopedia Britannica, *Dr. Greenblatt has received more than 100 international scientific awards and gold medals. One of the most unusual of his books is* Search the Scriptures, *a physician's interpretation of the Bible now in its 10th printing. He was involved in research on one of the first tranquilizers, Serpasil, but his most significant work has been in the fields of oral contraception and fertility. Now professor emeritus of the Department of Endocrinology of the Medical College of Georgia, Dr. Greenblatt still maintains his clinic in Augusta and each year has 12 research fellows from around the world working with him. He serves as consultant to the Council on Drugs of the A.M.A., to the Surgeon General, the U.S. Army, and the Veterans' Administration, and is a member of the panel on drugs for endocrine disturbances of the National Research Council. His views on aging and hormonal replacement therapy are considered truly authoritative.*

As we age, our outlook on life and our lifestyle itself are greatly affected by the hormonal changes taking place within our bodies. In the majority of women, the cessation of estrogen (female hormone) production by the ovaries is more or less abrupt, which precipitates the psychosexual upheaval that has come to be regarded as one of the features of menopause, or change of life. Menopause is an epoch in a woman's progression through life; it is, in fact, a change that starts with the ebbing of her ovarian function and continues to the end of her days.

Men do not, as a rule, experience a similar marked decline in testicular function. Nonetheless, many do have a moderate to severe diminution of androgen (male sex hormone) production, which results in subtle personality changes accompanied by lessening or loss of sexual potential.

What Is Aging?

Aging and advanced years are commonly equated, but in fact aging is relative. One factor in the process is the ratio of anabolism to catabolism — of buildup to breakdown of tissue proteins. It has been said that anabolism is ascendant for the first 20 years of life, reaches a plateau before age 30, and progressively declines (slowly in some, faster in others) to the end of life.

Another factor is the waning of cell renewal. Cellular aging starts when cells stop cycling, due to loss of new DNA (deoxyribonucleic acid) synthesis, or when the process of cell division (mitosis) is slowed down or stops. This phenomenon may occur early or late in life, depending on the individual's genetic endowment.

Another explanation for aging takes into account the interaction between the higher brain centers (the hypothalamic-pituitary axis) and the adrenal-thyroid-gonadal function. In women, the ovaries stop responding to stimulation by the pituitary gland. This results in a marked decline in estrogen production, which hastens psychological and physiological deterioration, and brings about the female climacteric. In many men, there is a decided lowering of androgen production between the ages of 50 and 60. The lower the androgens, the greater the physical, emotional, and sexual disturbance. Lowering the estrogen-androgen levels impedes anabolic activity, but all the while the catabolic activity of the adrenal glands, producing cortisone-like hormones, continues more or less undiminished.

Yet another consideration is the condition of the blood vessels, especially the arteries, which again may vary widely. Stress, nutrition, environment, genetics, and hormones all play a role here. Aging is a complex process — it starts imperceptibly and continues inexorably until death.

The life history and destiny of every woman are dependent to a great degree on the intensity and duration of her ovarian activity. This varies uniquely with each individual. What is inevitable is that it will cease, a loss that usually occurs somewhere between the ages of 40 and 50, give or take five years. Femininity, then, encompasses three phases: puberty, the reproductive years, and the menopause. Just as the onset of menstruation is the outward manifestation that the reproductive years are at hand, menopause, the cessation of the menses, heralds a change in the way of life from fertility to the end of reproductive potential, the climacteric. Ovarian function subsides, estrogen production declines, and menstrual flow ceases; the woman is now freed from the responsibilities, the stresses, and the hazards of childbirth — but at a price. For a fortunate few the damage from estrogen deprivation is minimal, the scars only slightly visible. For all too many, its effects are physically and emotionally devastating.

Hormone Replacement Therapy

Some women dread the threat of declining femininity, of waning romance. Others expect, and endure, periods of emotional irritability and instability. Little wonder, then, that the psychosexual perturbation connected with the climacteric often triggers a train of varied symptoms, which one physician will stamp as psychoneurotic, while another simply labels them menopausal.

The menopause has traditionally been regarded as an inevitable though unwelcome physiological state, admittedly damaging to the body's economy. However, the rigors of the change of life need no longer be accepted as the curse of womanhood, to be borne with fortitude and suffering.

Modern medicine, which has given today's women 25 additional years of living, must now assume responsibility for the quality of those years by offering adequate emotional, physical, and hormonal support. Before the advent of modern endocrinology and the availability of easily dispensed hormonal products, there may have been an excuse for doctors to try to ameliorate the symptoms of menopause by homespun psychology, barbiturates, and bromides. But too many physicians shun the use of hormones, fearing that they will cause excessive bleeding from the uterus, or possibly contribute to initiating cancer of the breast or the endometrium (the uterine wall).

Estrogens — The Case For and Against

Today's techniques of hormone replacement therapy permit control and discipline of any uterine bleeding, and there is growing evidence that there is no appreciable difference in the incidence of cancer in women on estrogen therapy, if it is properly administered. A recent study of endometrial cancer revealed that the disease was far advanced in 18.1 percent of women who had not received hormones in comparison to 1 percent for those who had been treated with estrogen. It would appear either that estrogens had a protective action or that the cancers in hormonally treated women were detected much earlier — at a stage when simple surgery (hysterectomy) was curative. At any rate, fewer women on estrogen therapy die from endometrial cancer than those who are untreated, many of whom may harbor a silent cancer that, by the time it is detected, is too far advanced for a good prognosis. As for breast cancer, a study of 550,000 women reported by the American Cancer Society has helped to remove a long-standing bias: There was no difference in the incidence of breast cancer among women on estrogens and those who were not.

Although their hormonal environment can be improved, many women at the change of life cannot adjust because they envision goals that will forever remain unattainable. The sense of longing to turn back the flight of time contributes to their crisis. Estrogen replacement therapy cannot erase the wrinkled brow, nor lift the drooping breast. But hormones judiciously used can help a woman who sets realistic goals for her advancing years to grow older with grace and dignity. It seems unwise, therefore, in the name of the mandate to "Do no harm," to fail to try to do good.

Although the spontaneous occurrence in men of a clinical syndrome equivalent to the female menopause is not as startlingly obvious, there seems little doubt that men after the age of 55 (plus or minus five years) experience a variety of symptoms that change their attitude toward society and their own lifestyles. The symptoms are increased irritability, inability to concentrate, decreased libido, episodes of depression and asocial behavior; in a few, something akin to hot flashes may occur. There are physicians, however, who feel that the sheer pressure of life may cause some men to deteriorate physiologically at an unusually early age and to experience a "climacteric" that is not hormonally based. Despite the widely held belief that the male climacteric is a psychological or cultural phenomenon, there are authorities who agree that relative testicular deficiency does occur in as many as 20 percent of men over the age of 50; the incidence is much higher after 60.

Testosterone production certainly declines with advancing age; because of this fact, experiments have been performed in which a placebo and testosterone were administered and responses compared. Improvements in well-being and in sexual potency were scored. About 66 percent of aging men reacted favorably — some remarkably so — to specific hormone replacement therapy, whereas the remainder responded equally slightly or not at all to both the placebo and androgen therapy. The researchers felt that the symptoms in the latter group were psychoneurotic manifestations, while in the former, they were probably due to actual hormone deficiency. When similar experiments were performed in younger men who were suffering simply from loss of potency, the reaction to a placebo was equal to that with testosterone — usually mild or negative. These results seem to substantiate the belief that impotence in normal young men is probably psychogenic. Aging men are more apt to experience an increase in libido and a lessening of nervousness and depression while on androgen therapy, thus proving that the basic disturbance is different in the two groups.

Since estrogen levels fall in the postmenopausal female and testosterone levels are considerably reduced in aging males who complain of psychosexual and physical problems, it seems rational to assume that hormone replacement therapy might be helpful. Estrogen replacement therapy will alleviate hot flushes, sweats, choking sensations, and irritating vaginal discharges. Estrogens lessen the psychogenic symptoms, such as nervousness, apprehension, and crying spells, which are aggravated by hormone loss; they also decrease the rate of bone decay and the tendency toward thickening of blood vessels and cardiovascular disease.

The fear of prostatic cancer has prevented wider use of testosterone in the male. No statistics are available to prove that male sex hormone causes cancer of the prostate, though, admittedly, testosterone may exacerbate the growth of a cancer already present. The frequent examinations offered the man receiving male sex hormone therapy might well uncover a slowly growing tumor, and enable the bearer to receive earlier care.

Hormones, in one way or another, have a

direct bearing on our every willful and unwillful action, our every waking and sleeping moment. Restlessness, insomnia, nervousness, apprehension, flushes, sweats, depression, euphoria, emotional fluctuations, body chemistry, water intake, and energy utilization — all are under hormonal influence. It does not seem more rational to employ tranquilizers and anti-depressants, which are so foreign to body chemistry, than to use naturally occurring hormones to replace a deficiency. Even migraine headaches in the male and female climacteric have been known to respond to hormone replacement therapy.

The Sexual Influence of Hormone Replacement Therapy

From time immemorial, certain foods, herbs, and love potions have been employed by primitive as well as so-called civilized people to enhance sexual drive. It is time to dispel the notion current in many circles that hormonal therapy is of little value here. Our studies reveal that particularly for the elderly male and for the female as well there is a true aphrodisiac: Testosterone is the hormone of libido in both sexes. Though anatomical, neurological, psychological, and constitutional factors obviously play important roles, libido can be expressed as a chemical test-tube equation.

Androgens have been employed for the treatment of frigidity in women for more than 30 years, but the fear of virilizing the female has kept physicians from using testosterone. When androgens were first proposed as a treatment for frigidity, the suggestion was looked upon with disdain, and their use was condemned as pharmacological mayhem. But in recent years it has been shown that women do indeed produce testosterone. Moreover, when women who were suffering from advanced breast cancer were given testosterone as a palliative, many of them experienced markedly increased sexual drives, despite their generalized debility from the disease.

In a study of how women who complained of secondary frigidity responded sexually to a variety of hormonal preparations, it appeared that estrogens occasionally increased libido; androgens, frequently; progestogens and corticoids, rarely; and placebos, hardly ever. Androgens may be administered alone or in combination with an estrogen. Provided the dosage is kept in low range, masculinizing symptoms such as hairiness, slight voice change, or acne rarely appear. If they do, the androgen can be stopped, and reversal of the untoward signs usually results. Some women, however, have preferred to deal with these minor virilizing effects rather than forego the benefits they derive from androgen therapy. In more difficult cases of secondary frigidity, exceptionally rewarding results have been obtained by implanting two testosterone pellets (of 75 mg each) subcutaneously at six-month intervals. In primary frigidity, psychogenic factors play too great a role, making the response unpredictable.

Male Impotence

What about impotence in the male? A man under the age of 50 who finds himself impotent, although his testicular function is normal, may well have a psychogenic block. Administration of androgens to such a patient usually proves futile, unless it is accompanied by psychotherapy to resolve an underlying emotional problem. Males in the over-50 age group, however, frequently complain of loss of potency. This may mean either loss of erectile capacity for intromission or an inability to maintain an erection. Others experience an almost complete loss of libido, along with personality changes, insomnia, lack of self-confidence, fatigue, and depression. As a man ages, he often finds the mind willing but the flesh weak. Desire outdistances performance and, in consequence, his preoccupation with sex is either intensified or completely dissipated. Testosterone can alleviate, though not completely resolve, this problem, but the dosage must be adequate or the results will be little better than with the use of a placebo.

For many women, interest in sex wanes at the time of menopause and thereafter. With the marked estrogen deficiency of the postmenopausal period, the mucous membrane of the vagina thins and atrophies, and intercourse is often painful. On the other hand, many women, freed from the fear of pregnancy, find themselves newly eager for sex. Both for them, and for those who have lost their sex drive and wish it reawakened, a trial of androgens or an estrogen-androgen combination is definitely worthwhile.

Both men and women can, if they so desire, find a physician who is willing to remove the shackles of hormone deprivation. Surely, in the autumn of their lives, they deserve an Indian summer rather than a winter of discontent.

...keep growing quietly and seriously
throughout your whole development;
you cannot disturb it more rudely
than by looking outward and expecting
from outside replies to questions
that only your own innermost feelings
in your most hushed hour can perhaps
answer.   Rilke

Corita

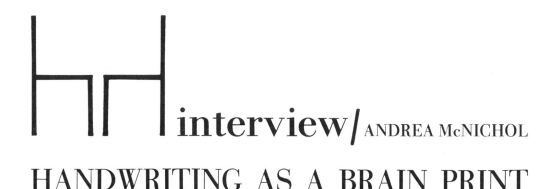

interview/ ANDREA McNICHOL

HANDWRITING AS A BRAIN PRINT

Andrea McNichol teaches graphology at UCLA and is a consultant to four major corporations which utilize her skills to avoid putting any square pegs into available circular openings. She believes handwriting is literally a "brain print," revealing all manner of things about the writer, and her information has been found to be extraordinarily accurate. She works with legal authorities on problems of forgery and character disabilities, as well as consulting in the diagnosis of mental illness.

LANDE: What is graphology?

McNICHOL: Graphology as a modern science is about 100 years old. As long as man has been writing, he has been studying his handwriting. Aristotle spoke at length about handwriting, and how it reveals the emotional level of the person. All through history you can find men and women of note referring to graphology. The artist Gainsborough, for instance, wouldn't paint a subject without having seen a sample of his handwriting. Real research into the subject, using acceptable modern-day scientific methods, began in Europe. Clara Romand, who has written many books about graphology, was one of the pioneers in documenting the facts that relate certain physiological aspects of one's personality to a graphological trait. In

Europe, graphology is an acceptable field of study — you can get a degree in it — and you cannot get a job of any merit without your handwriting being analyzed by a professional graphologist. In the United States, unfortunately, the word mostly brings to mind palmistry, Tarot cards, possibly astrology. Most people think of it as a pseudo-science — something that belongs at a fair.

LANDE: How did it get that reputation?

McNICHOL: Because there's no acceptable field of study where you have to take courses and really know your subject and pass state exams. Unfortunately, by the time it got rolling it was in the hands of people who did not know what they were doing. It's always been in the psychic realm in this country.

LANDE: What scientific evidence is there to support graphology?

McNICHOL: It's endless. No two handwritings are alike, just as there are no two fingerprints alike. Documented research has shown that amputees who have been forced to write with pencils in their mouths or held between their toes eventually develop their identical handwriting, though perhaps in a shakier form of their original script. In other words, handwriting is not the *hand* writing, it's a brain print. Writing is tied to gestures of the body language; a gesture of violence shows in handwriting as angles or a hard line pressure that punctures the paper. A gesture of passivity or soft movement is associated in handwriting with a garland or a free-swinging type of stroke with soft pressure — a physical representation of the feelings in the body.

Further evidence is the degree of medical accuracy graphology can claim. When anything goes wrong with the body, you will notice it in the handwriting. There are even figures now to substantiate the fact that when a woman is carrying a male child, during her pregnancy the incidence of male hormones in her body causes her handwriting to change a bit, and so if you know the secrets to look for, you can correctly predict the sex of the unborn child by the mother's handwriting.

It's also thought to have great therapeutic value. Say you find you have a personality problem, you can look for the graphological trait which is expressive of the problem, and then consciously change your handwriting until it becomes unconscious. Once you have learned to be free with your new form without thinking about it, it is said you will have rid yourself of the undesired trait and acquired the desirable one.

For instance, if you felt you were lacking drive and that this lack of energy and vitality held you back from getting ahead, we would look at your handwriting and probably find signs of weakness. Your writing would probably be clinging to the left margin, which would mean you are clinging to the past. We start writing from the left and head symbolically to the future, toward the right side of the paper. Often the *t* bars and the way you cross them give an indication of how you treat your work areas. A person who had few goals in his work areas would probably have weak *t* bars; so we would give him exercises to assert his *t* bars, make him slash them off with a lot of pressure. When he could do this exercise without even thinking about it consciously, he would have acquired a more assertive character trait.

LANDE: Can you list some other graphological traits?

McNICHOL: You can look to handwriting for anything you want it to tell you. If you're in good physical health, your handwriting should not shake frequently on a page. One or two shakes is considered normal — anything more than that is a warning of physical illness. When someone has had a severe heart attack or a severe lung or upper body problem, it is usually evidenced by a break or a tremor or stoppage of the pen in the upper parts of the letters. For some incredible reason the actual physical parts of the writing are directly correlated to the parts of the body. The tops of upper letters such as *d, b, l, h, t* would correlate to the upper part of the body and head. Middle letters — *a, e, o* — would be middle body, and extension letters like *y* and *g* would be lower body. So if anything goes wrong with letters in those areas — gaping holes, jerks, hand stops, tremors, shakiness, smearing of the ink — there is usually something physically wrong there, too.

LANDE: Would lower zones have to do with an individual's sexual outlook?

McNICHOL: The lower zone is the libido or the id and represents one's basic drives. Somehow money gets into these areas too.

To tell us about your sexual nature, we would look at the shape, length, and size of the lower zones. A healthy individual has a lower zone that is normal in shape and length, either going straight down or in some way looping to the left. As soon as you start reversing the loop, distorting it, or adding angles, we pick up some sort of sexual problem or perversion.

LANDE: Can you tell dishonesty in a person's handwriting?

McNICHOL: It's one of the easiest things to judge. A basically honest person has a legible, straightforward, simple handwriting that stands as it was written. Basically dishonest people — and of course there are many types of dishonesty — have a labored handwriting. Either it's slow or has mistakes or there are many retouched letters or ovals made in the wrong direction. General overall illegibility due to excessive swirling, excessive letter shapings and bizarre formations all show a desire for attention.

LANDE: Can a person's writing show whether he has suicidal tendencies?

McNICHOL: Yes. For instance, a study that was made of suicide notes obtained from the police found that in a great majority of cases, more than 90 percent, I believe, there was a distinctive type of base line which tapered down severely at the end. Often an unstable slant — which means the letters go in different directions — implies a personality that can also go in many directions. When you couple that with a falling base line, you definitely have a suicidal personality.

Generally, happy people have well-formed, evenly spaced, normal-looking legible writing, while unhappy people clutter, crash into the right margin and often have uneven and ungainly hands. Frequently they blot out their letters so you can't read them and can't tell what they are. Each indistinguishable mark tells how they feel about their lives.

You see, where you start on the paper and your margins tell how you use life. If you fill up the paper, you are a person who fills up every inch of your life. People who keep straight left margins toe the line and rigidly adhere to what they were taught. They would never think of crashing into the right side or swerving to the left; they set firm limits for themselves. Some people become very aesthetic about the paper; everything has to be centered and placed properly. They are that way with their lives too.

Recently I've had some very interesting forgery cases. If you study forgery, you quickly see how intensely personal a handwriting is. For instance, everybody has a unique pressure pattern — we have only to put your handwriting under a machine and the pressure readout is distinctly yours and no one else's.

LANDE: What sort of consulting work do you do for business corporations?

McNICHOL: I am sometimes called on to weed out dishonesty within the company, but mostly it's a matter of personnel hiring. If they have three men to consider for a position, all with equal ability and background, they will ask for my advice on which one would do the best job.

106

LANDE: How can you determine from the handwriting whether one person is a better worker than another?

McNICHOL: I base my assumption on what the firm who is hiring needs for that position. If it is someone who is good with other people, I would then look at the handwriting to find a sociable type who works well with people, isn't hostile, and so on. Another corporation might be looking for someone with concentrative abilities who could sit with figures for long periods of time. In this case, I would look for the characteristics of aloofness, someone who enjoys working alone for many hours at a single task.

LANDE: Do you consult with the medical profession?

McNICHOL: Yes, usually in cases where patients come to the doctor with a symptom, yet extensive X-rays and tests show no diagnosable illness. Physicians come to me to find out if the patient's handwriting betrays physical illness or whether there is an emotional problem which could cause hypochondria or a psychosomatic illness. In psychiatric cases the quickest, most accurate judge of all psychological illnesses is the Rorschach inkblot test, which is highly subjective and takes a skilled, trained interviewer. Mostly they want to corroborate their findings with mine after I have studied the patient's handwriting.

LANDE: Is there scientific data to support the interpretation of handwriting in psychiatric research?

McNICHOL: All the facts that I go on have been extensively researched and coordinated with psychological findings. In other words, if 85 percent of the population see a butterfly in a Rorschach test, and those same 85 percent are similar in the degrees of distance between their letters, then we can say they are normal. It is normal to space your words a certain way and to make your letter formations a certain way; if you fall below the percentile statistically, you would be classified as abnormal or pathological.

Everything you do in the way of handwriting or doodles or scribbles can be analyzed and a psychological trait matched to it. Everything has meaning, and you weigh the importance of each figure depending on the general impression you receive from the handwriting. If you pick up a handwriting and the first thing that attracts your eye is the base line rising crazily, that's the dominant feature because graphology works on the deviation from the expected, from the normal. You might pick up irregular angles, which usually mean you're dealing with a schizophrenic. But the outstanding feature would be the angularity, so you would then focus your attention on that. Paranoia usually shows up in abnormal spacing between words and in between lines. We think of each word and each letter just written as the self. If I choose, as I write, to stick my next letter unusually far from the one I've just written, that means I hold other people aloof from me. If I choose to keep a great deal of space between my words I'm also paranoid and I need a lot of room around me in order to feel secure.

Generally, all psychological illnesses are discernible by handwriting. For instance, anybody just picking up the handwriting of a person suffering from paranoia or hysteria, or a manic-depressive, would know something was wrong; but in comparing the psychological data with the graphological data, we have found that they correlated 100 percent.

LANDE: Couldn't almost everyone apply graphology in their lives, if they knew more about it?

McNICHOL: It would most definitely help in deciding who to get involved with, in business, perhaps even in setting up a lifelong relationship. It could tell you if your children have problems before it's too late to get them help. It can tell you yourself how you really feel about a certain thing. When you're saying something untrue, or your subconscious knows it to be false, your handwriting will show it. You cannot fool the graphologist when a statement is false, because your feelings always show up in your handwriting. It's as good as a polygraph test.

THE X-ING OUT OF A PRESIDENT

Four signatures by Richard Nixon, from 1968, 1969, early 1974 and late 1974 show a very interesting disparity over the five-year span. In the early sample, everything is legible and the *d* is extremely tall, much taller than the other upper letters, indicating a lot of pride. As his troubles start, the *d* shrinks and doesn't extend up as high as the middle letters. The *i, c, h, r* and *d* begin to lose their formation; it would be difficult to read the name if you didn't know who it was. The degree of legibility is greatly diminished, indicating that the happiness in his life is diminishing. Early 1974, the Watergate era, shows total disintegration of the name. We're left with just a few powerful strokes — there is horizontal expansion again, with energy and strength, yet the total clarity is gone. You cannot read anything, save the crossing of the *x*, which is now getting longer — we call this "x-ing oneself out." The last sample in 1974 shows just a straight line with an *x* crossing through it, and you cannot distinguish a single letter shape. There is nothing left of the man except a big *x* — a big self-crossing out.

1968

1969

EARLY
1974

LATE
1974

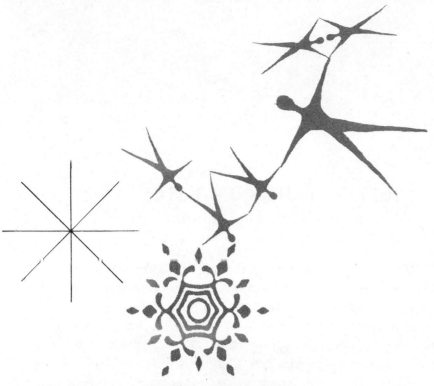

BIRTH WITHOUT VIOLENCE / FREDERICK LeBOYER

Almost singlehandedly, Frederick LeBoyer is revolutionizing the procedures of the welcoming committees that greet new arrivals on our planet. Born in 1918, Dr. LeBoyer is a graduate of the School of Medicine at the University of Paris and was Chef de Clinique there until he left to devote full time to his obstetrical practice.

Dr. LeBoyer says it is totally wrong to bring a baby into a glaringly lit room filled with loud voices, dangle him by the heels, and greet him with a smart slap across the buttocks. The passage through the birth canal has been a frightening experience and to straighten out his back so abruptly is a further shock. Since babies are neither deaf nor blind, the strong lights and voices make the entrance into this world more painful.

What Dr. LeBoyer advocates are soft lights, gentleness, soft voices, caresses. To avoid any possibility of oxygen deprivation, the umbilical cord should not be cut immediately. The child cries at birth because the thorax is relaxed and open and his first breath is painful. He may stop breathing a few times but he will start again, without any slap, and with the cord still attached his oxygen supply continues. Gently stroked by the doctor, he is placed, face down, on his mother's abdomen, where her caresses let him know they are still together.

Slowly, gently, he is eased into this alarming world, and when the first stage is over and the breathing normalized, he is not dumped into the cold steel of the scales but lowered into a warm bath, much like the environment he so recently left.

It certainly sounds like something we would all prefer, if given a choice, and photographs of babies taken very soon after the LeBoyer treatment show what looks very much like a smile.

interview / MADELINE C. HUNTER, Ed.D.
instilling competence in the four-year-old

Director of the experimental University Elementary School at UCLA, Madeline Hunter is a strong advocate of innovative and imaginative approaches to education. In order to make the educational process exciting as well as productive, she is willing to experiment with a variety of promising techniques to find the best methods of helping children learn. Born in Canada, Dr. Hunter received a B.S. in psychology, a B.A., Master's and Doctorate in education at UCLA. She has served as psychologist, administrator, and director of curriculum and research. Dr. Hunter has written many articles for educational publications and is the author of books for parents as well as instructional manuals for teachers. She has received many outstanding achievement awards, including a presidential citation for interpreting the contribution of physical education to child development and learning.

LANDE: Where do you think education is today in this country?

HUNTER: It's in sad shape in terms of what we know about how to make it better. It's astronomical in terms of where it has been before. The notion of the good old days in education is like good old grandma's apple pie. There may have been a few great apple pies, but there were more burned because she couldn't control the oven, couldn't get the right apples, or the lard was sour. Education, I think, is probably in better shape, particularly in the last 10 years, just because we have become so critical and analytical of it. We used to think it was the kid's background, IQ, all those things, that were causing the trouble. We know now that probably the most critical element in education is the teacher, and that teachers are made, not born. Parents are the first teachers, so we ought to be equipping them with better parenting behaviors. Still,

we are literally light years ahead of where we were even five years ago on knowing how to make a good teacher into a successful teacher.

LANDE: What should we be educating kids for?

HUNTER: It's highly unlikely that anybody is going to redesign the human being. They are redesigning the way man calculates, the way man communicates, and the things man learns. But nobody is thinking of redesigning his body, his mind or emotions. In the future, though, he is going to be more in charge of them. Nor is anyone thinking of redesigning man's basic social interaction — he's not going to stop being gregarious. So we should be educating kids to know themselves as physiological, thinking, feeling, social human beings. You need to know, for example, where your "hot buttons" are — what are the things to which you predictably overreact, and how you can ameliorate that reaction.

You can't help feeling a certain way, but you *can* help acting any way that you don't choose to act.

LANDE: How will you implement this?

HUNTER: We are starting experimentally to teach kids basic principles of human learning. The IQ is one determinant of speed of learning, but one which works within very wide ranges. But the *way* a person learns so affects the rate and degree of his learning that we're going to teach these kids, "If you want to speed up your learning, here's a way to practice." In the same way we're now teaching them, "If you want to lose weight, or gain weight, or get over your bad complexion, here are certain things you can do about it."

This is one of the things we're doing to change mindstyle — let them know it isn't set and they are in charge, within very broad limits — and lifestyle — "I don't *have* to be this kind of person," or "Is it within my power to be more like the person I want to be?" And along with that we must build in the dimensions of reality. Because if I suddenly wanted to be the most famous coloratura in the United States (which I would very much like to be), I also have to accept the reality that I am not going to be that; nor am I going to be the champion pole vaulter in the Olympics. Of course, that goes back to the notion that mindstyle and lifestyle are primarily based on the decision-making of each of us, and the fact that we each possess the ability to make decisions not by whim or flipping a coin but on the basis of a very systematic approach where you take into account your unsystematic determinants.

LANDE: When you have in your care a four-year-old child, what are the crucial elements in preparing him for life choices, mind choices?

HUNTER: First that he begin to respect himself as a person who is worthy and who is competent. That is learned — it is not genetic. So we design an environment in which he begins to feel worthy and feel competent — not where he just feels loved. We want him to feel we like him, enjoy him, and respect him. But he doesn't really need to be loved at school, he needs to be loved by his parents at home. He needs to be *enjoyed* at school, but more importantly, he should feel he is competent, that he has something to say about his fate, and that he can get it going along the way he would like it to go.

Our second objective is that we want him to be able to relate productively to other human beings, so that he can be with others when he chooses, and be happily accepted, yet when he is on his own have resources within him so he doesn't feel, "Well, I don't know what to do."

The third is that we want him to learn to move forward eagerly and aggressively into new learning. He is going to have to learn all his life. Here his competence will make him feel, "Well, it's different, but I probably can do it." We don't want him to withdraw and major in sandbox or something he is comfortable with, just because he's afraid to try anything else.

Then, fourth, we want him to use authority figures, in this case the teacher, as a resource for stimulation, for approval — when he needs it, but not to keep him going, and for controls — when he doesn't have them within himself. We want him to ask for information when he needs it, but not to psych out an adult, see what will please that adult, and act accordingly.

These are the things we want to equip every child with, because he will need them all the rest of his life.

LANDE: Because all of a sudden the dilemma hits the child, as it does all of us, once we see what's out there for us?

HUNTER: But all that's out there for this child even as a four-year-old — because we have no compunction about saying to him, "It's OK not to want to do it, but it's not OK *not* to do it. You *need* to do it."

We teach three kinds of decision-making in our school; we call them Type 1, Type 2 and Type 3 decisions.

Type 1 decision is the child's to make. What kind of cookie do you want? Anything you say is OK. Type 2 decision is the group's to make, in which the child has a very persuasive voice. What kind of cookie shall we have for our party? He can argue hotly for chocolate, but the group may decide on vanilla. Then his only choice is whether he is going to eat a cookie or not. Type 3 decisions are where a decision is being made by a person who has either power or knowledge or responsibility that is beyond his. I go by and see the gardener spraying some shrubbery with poison spray and the plate of cookies is close by, so I say, "No, the cookies are not safe, you may not have them." That's a Type 3 decision, his not to make.

There are decisions in life where you have nothing to say. The speed limit tells you how fast to drive, so your only decision is whether you're going to drive that speed or take a chance of getting a ticket. There are other decisions that you have to make yourself. There are yet others that you and your publisher, say, make jointly. You might be very persuasive, but if in the end he wants to

publish your book with a blue cover, you have only the choice of putting a blue cover on it, or going somewhere else with the book and hoping somebody else will publish it.

LANDE: You need resiliency to cope with those situations?

HUNTER: Yes, to accept those decisions and use them productively. Some people have a naive notion that every decision is the individual's to make. It's true that you make the decision whether you will abide by other decisions or suffer the consequences. But all decisions are not yours. We call it responsible freedom. You are free, but you are accountable within that freedom. That's a very, very important concept for kids.

LANDE: Weren't you one of the first to have the concept of reinforcement theory?

HUNTER: It's a very old theory, but I think I was one of the first to say, "Because it's operating all the time in every human interaction, it's better that we know what we're doing with it than operate by happenstance." That has been very distorted, in fact.

LANDE: Would you clarify it?

HUNTER: Reinforcement theory is based on a characteristic of humankind that you and I will do what works out well for us. If I want to turn the light off and I flip the switch and the light goes off, next time I want to turn the light off I'll flip the switch. If I flip the switch and get an electric shock, I'm going to look for some other way to put the lights off. It's just as simple as that.

So when students are engaged in productive behavior, generating good ideas, really showing respect for each other, we need to ensure that that works out well for them, because often it doesn't.

You know, if a teacher passes the plate and I take the smaller cookie, I'm stuck with it. It didn't work out well for me. I don't have as much cookie as you, even though I did something socially acceptable in our society. So the teacher will make that work out well for a child by building his self-concept, using social reinforcers. "You know, Madeline, you were very grown up, because I know you would have liked to take the big cookie; you did a very grown-up thing and you should feel proud of yourself." Not, "I like you for the way you behaved," for that makes the child a "teacher pleaser." This is the way we use reinforcement theory.

A misinterpretation of reinforcement theory is the negotiation system: "Madeline, if when you go to the party you take the smaller cookie, I'll see you get a bigger one later on." That's just a negotiation system, and I have no patience with it. People who don't understand reinforcement say, "Well, I don't want to use it," which is a clear giveaway that they don't know anything about it. Because really it is just like saying, "I'm not going to breathe." If you stop breathing, you're not alive; if you stop using reinforcement, it's because you're dead.

LANDE: You have given so much, with children. What have you learned from them?

HUNTER: I think I've learned the invariance of all humanity. This was made very clear when I first moved from Beverly Hills into an area near Watts — I found out that kids are far more the same than they're different. And as I go to Africa now or to the Far East, I find that human beings are so much the same, and most of them have the same goals. We argue about how we're going to get there, but where we want to get seems to be pretty unanimous. I've also learned the

real pleasure of having a life's work that is also a hobby.

LANDE: Can people feel good about themselves if they don't feel competent? Or can you be competent without feeling valued?

HUNTER: You have to have both. Once the child has a good feeling about himself, he can learn because he has confidence in his own ability to learn. But he only has confidence in his ability *after* he has learned.

LANDE: So it's a parallel task of building in the skills so that the child can measure his ability?

HUNTER: That's right. You know, mastery of our environment is an essential need for each of us. The time when you feel good is when you feel you have something to say about it. Man needs to be proactive, not reactive, to his environment. He needs to feel he can do something about what happens to him, not just receive it as if he were a buffer. We do this with teachers too. The successful teacher is a proactive teacher, one who can do things so those kids will learn rather than just reacting to them.

LANDE: So many people are looking for instant enlightenment these days, and there are all these self-appointed gurus running around saying, Follow me, and yet it's questionable whether the answer is there. What do you attribute this to?

HUNTER: Looking for the magic talisman. We have a lot of this in education, where people are teaching under the guise of "humanistic education" that if you're a nice person and have a rich environment, God will be in his heaven and all kids will learn. And there's just no way this is true. The way we teach teachers is a difficult, rigorous, professional preparation — in fact, our experimental team is called Team L, so there's a saying around campus that if you work with Madeline Hunter you go to L — and some of them, I think, feel they have.

People who grasp for the lucky pebble, the rabbit's foot, are people who don't feel they are in charge and are looking for something that will be in charge for them. They have never had the experience of saying, "I have it *within me* to change my life," nor the realistic recognition that they *don't* have it within them to be a pole vaulter or a coloratura.

So many people as children were never taught to think what their goals were and then say to themselves, "Let's begin by taking some incremental steps." We find this with remedial readers. We write down any word they don't know and help them learn it. Then they begin to count how many words they learned that day, and have a place where they see the successive approximations of that goal of being a reader. This works even with our rough, tough gang leaders in the inner city — we have great big junior high school boys saying, "I learned five new words today." The goal becomes possible because you are taking steps toward it and you can see those steps. Psychologically, this is called getting knowledge of results.

The child needs that direct feedback. There is a little boy here who told me, "You know why I like roller skating better than I like reading?" And I thought I knew the answer, but I said, "Tell me why." And he said, "Well, you know, I didn't use to be able to skate at all. I had to stand on the grass or I'd fall down, and then I got so I could walk on the blacktop, and finally I got so I could skate on the cement. Now I skate frontwards and backwards, with people and everything. But every time I think I've learned how to read I get a new book, and there are a lot of words I don't know in it."

So we learned from that to often tape-record a child when he is beginning to read a book, and when he's finished it, to go back and record the same first page, and then let him listen to how much better he read it. Lots of times people don't know how much they are improving, and psychologically they need that knowledge. Who would lose weight without a scale or a tape measure?

So much in life is just decision-making about how to get started. It's like going to a house that's in disorder. You're ready to roll over on your back and think about hiring a maid instead of doing some systematic decision-making about what spot you need to occupy first. If it's the kitchen, OK, get that cleaned up and leave the living room. If people are coming, shut the door to the kitchen and dust the coffee table.

LANDE: What's your recommendation for success? Realistic evaluation of the problem?

HUNTER: Take that first step. We preach instant success these days, especially through television, and people believe the talisman is no work — just one thing and you're in. Bill Johnson, the Los Angeles superintendent of schools, has a saying that I think is very good: Yard by yard, it's hard. Inch by inch, it's a cinch.

> *"The fairy godmother is stuck in a traffic jam on the freeway. She's not going to make it to your party."*

APPLIED MINDSTYLES

The new religions of the 20th century are the mind training programs as exemplified by Silva Mind Control, Scientology, est, Mind Probe, and countless others. Cut loose from the secure bindings of God faith and traditional religions, bombarded with half-understood psychological concepts, the old familial and cultural bonds slivered, classically alienated modern man is a ready mark for the certainties, recipes, and persuasive techniques of these new dogmas. All that seems to be necessary is the incredible confidence of the shaman-pitchman, various hypnotic or autohypnotic techniques, and usually a four-day tent show which brings the unbelievers figuratively and literally marching up front to confess and accept the new gospel. Most "graduates" of these training programs claim to have had their lives changed, their minds expanded, their psychic sores healed. And maybe they have.

Encompassing a broader and less dogmatic range of teachings and concepts are such experiences as Arica training and the various courses and encounters available at Esalen. What it all seems to show is that even the wisest and most secure who are not locked in and supported by traditional religious faith, and even some who are, are desperate for that man up there, the trainer, the voice, who will tell them what to do and what to think and how to yank the arrow out of the breast.

TAKING THE PLUNGE AT ESALEN

During my last stay at Esalen I went down to the baths at 7 o'clock one morning. Now you should know there are only three reasons why I am ever up at 7 o'clock: There has been some terrible trauma in the night; I have not yet gone to bed; or I am in love. Happily, this time, it was the last two.

I was awash with good feelings as I made my way down the path: I was in love with a Rolfer* (surely a sign of class in the Human Potential Movement), I was soon to be naked in daylight (surely a sign of bravery), and it was 7 a.m. and I was on my feet and happy about it (surely a sign of insanity).

Arriving at the baths, I slipped out of my clothes, feeling confident that, had anybody been there to watch, they would have been impressed at the gracefulness of my movements, if not at the body they revealed. Then I glided inside.

The baths at Esalen are set into a cliff and open to the sea. A line of massage tables banks a railing, while far below, the Pacific waves crash against the rocks. The view is of the spectacular Big Sur coastline, where this morning someone had cleverly placed poetic proportions of mist on each of the cliffs. The sky was crisply blue and the sun beginning to be bright. The steam from the tubs rose to take its place with the mists.

As I made my entrance, it suddenly became apparent that I was one woman among eight men. There have been times when I might have welcomed such odds, but this was not one of them. Of course, the men's bodies were lean, muscular, tanned, and generally beautiful. Each seemed cloaked in a private metaphysical space of his own.

My sense of transcendence toppled. I felt coarse, bumbly, stupidly romantic, graceless, and a lot of other unhappy adjectives.

I waddled over to the farthest tub, where my Rolfing friend Dan awaited me. Feeling that I was the only unlovely thing in the Esalen morning, and not even daring to question whether he would still be interested, I plunged into the water and surged into his arms. Once I had had my hug generously returned, I was able to sit up and look around.

Obviously, I myself had not been noticed. The jagged interruption of my passage was being smoothed over by the mist; slowly the sense I had of being a rude interloper changed to that of being a tolerated voyeur. Several of the men were doing Yoga exercises on the tables — slowly, exotically twisting their bodies in ways that made mine ache just to watch. No one spoke. Even the men in the tubs just stared blandly at those on the tables or gazed out at the distant cliffs. The sense of distance around individuals was enormous. It was as though everyone was dematerializing everyone else in order to make the maximum amount of personal space. Even as I grew more comfortable I had the feeling that any quick movement

*For the uninitiated, a practitioner of Rolfing, skilled manipulation of the body to iron out the kinks life has put in it. Also known as Structural Reintegration.

116

would be like adding the last drops to a supersaturated solution, and that suddenly everything would come crashing out — shattered pieces of bodies, tables, steam, spilling across the floor like so many pieces of crystal.

Some women appeared, but they belonged. They blended into the same space. One or two of them slipped onto tables and began a series of movements as elaborate and as slow as the men's.

Perhaps their presence reassured me, or maybe it was the 120 degree sulfur bathwater. At any rate, after a while I courageously emerged from the tub and walked to a table of my own, reassuring my body as I did so that it should expect no more than my standard two tricks: (1) lying flat on my stomach, and (2) lying flat on my back.

The table felt wet and, immediately, cold, but I forced myself to lie flat and try to blend in with it — which wasn't so difficult after all. It helped me to feel unobtrusive.

Dan came and lay down on the table next to me. That helped too, because he wasn't doing anything exotic either — and he *belonged*. After a while, he had to leave and keep an appointment to Rolf someone. Before departing he pounded me in a friendly way from shoulder to toe. The slapping was a sign of affection; the sound was effervescent, even appropriate in that quiet, mist-filled room.

After a while I began to feel really chilly, so I moved back to the tub. As I sat there, up to my neck in steaming water, I thought about how I fit into all this. It was really nice to have this sense of peace, of oneness with the elements, but I lived with a house full of people and worked at a large university. I didn't really want to leave either of them. I seemed destined to be always between — wanting the calm, natural energy of the Esalen world, and at the same time missing the laughter and excitement, even the tension of my world back home.

It was at this point that Will Schutz, Esalen's currently resident guru, entered. He was wearing a chartreuse warm-up suit and carrying the morning paper. He seemed unaware of looking in any way inappropriate or of causing any intrusion. Indeed, no one seemed to notice him but me.

He made straight for my tub, said Hello, shucked the jump suit and plopped into the water, submerging completely save for a wrist and a hand holding the paper aloft like the sword Excalibur. Then, coming up for air, he settled into a corner and turned to the sports page.

"Don't you know you're not supposed to read the paper *here*?" I breathed, fearful of disturbing the hallowed, intense silence.

He just laughed comfortably and handed me the funnies. How did he know it was my favorite section?

— *Patt Schwab*

ESALEN / navel of the human potential movement

In its 14-year existence Esalen has become known as a place for individual psychological development, as an institution for East/West cultural diffusion, and as a center for social planning and experimentation under alternate cultural assumptions. To comprehend Esalen intellectually, one must know something of its background; to comprehend it emotionally, one must experience it in person.

The impetus for Esalen probably began at New Britain, Connecticut, as early as 1946, when Kurt Lewin and his associates developed the original laboratory training methods, and then went on to found the National Training Laboratory (NTL) in Bethel, Maine.

NTL focused on the training or T-group as its principal vehicle to get at experiential learning about human interactions. The emphasis was on training individuals for more effective participation as team or group members — usually in industrial or business settings.

Encounter

After a while divergencies in opinions developed, with one faction wanting to continue with the management focus and the other wanting to emphasize the impact of training on the individual. This latter group was strongly influenced by the psychology of Carl Rogers, who introduced the term *encounter* to identify nontherapy groups aimed at releasing the human potential of the average person. Eventually the two factions split, and the encounter-oriented group moved to the West Coast in the early 1960s.

Already in California was Michael Murphy,

Esalen's founder, mover, and shaper, although he had as yet no direct connection with what has come to be known as the Human Potential Movement. A native Californian, Murphy had been torn between a career as a doctor or one as a minister. While an undergraduate at Stanford, however, he had found a spiritual home in Eastern religion and philosophy — particularly that of Aurobindo Ghose — and had spent a year and a half at Aurobindo's Indian ashram following his graduation. By 1960 he was back in the States, where he met Richard Price in San Francisco. Price, also a Stanford graduate, shared Murphy's interest in Eastern thought, and the two became good friends. In 1961 they moved to Esalen, about 50 miles south of Murphy's home town of Salinas.

In 1910 Murphy's grandfather, a doctor in Salinas, had purchased 375 acres on the rugged Big Sur coast, conveniently located between San Francisco and Los Angeles. The property had natural hot springs and was originally the home of a North American Indian tribe known as Esalen. Dr. Murphy had had the idea of developing a health spa, and to this end he built bathhouses over the springs, a large central house and one or two smaller ones. He died, however, before the spa idea came to fruition.

History of Esalen

By 1961, when Murphy and Price showed up, the place had already acquired an attraction for odd assortments of people. An evangelical sect was meeting on the property. A group of young people building a trimaran in order to sail to Tahiti were living in rented shacks there. So was Joan Baez, not yet famous as an activist folk singer. The renowned writer Henry Miller and his friends were occasional visitors to the baths. A goodly number of male homosexuals, some of whom came from as far away as Los Angeles, and a rough and tumble crowd of dope dealers and petty outlaws known collectively as "the Big Sur Heavies" frequented the baths on a regular basis.

Murphy and Price took over the Esalen property from Murphy's grandmother — a far easier task than taking it over from its visitors and residents. The evangelicals moved out once their lease expired, and guards were posted at the gates to keep some of the wilder elements out. Even so, a compromise had to be reached with the Big Sur Heavies. As a result, the baths to this day are open to all locals from midnight to 6 a.m. Needless to say, any guest who wanders down to the baths during these hours will notice a decided change in clientele.

Murphy attributes some of Esalen's unique character to the somewhat lawless atmosphere surrounding the baths. "I think a lot of the atmosphere of the place came from this outlaw element," he has been quoted as saying. "It may have contributed to the kind of try-anything spirit of the place."

Why Esalen Is Different

In starting Esalen, neither Murphy nor Price had a clear plan, other than that it should be a center where people from different disciplines could meet and exchange ideas. "Mike Murphy never had an intellectual fix on any philosophical position," according to William Thompson, author, teacher, and Esalen frequenter. "That's what made Esalen different from what it would have been under someone like Buckminster Fuller or Paolo Soleri. He didn't put his stamp on the place — which meant that Alan Watts and Abraham Maslow and Fritz Perls and others could come and use it for their own purposes. But Esalen wouldn't have happened without Mike. It all had its origin in his sensibility and his spiritual quality."

Esalen opened its doors in the fall of 1962, and from its inception attracted the major thinkers (and foolers) of the time. In addition to those just mentioned, the cast at different times has included Aldous Huxley, Gerald Heard, Arnold Toynbee, Frederic Spiegelberg, Ken Kesey, S. I. Hayakawa, Linus Pauling, Paul Tillich, Gary Snyder, Norman O. Brown, George Leonard, Rollo May, Virginia Satir, Bishop James A. Pike, Carl Rogers, B. F. Skinner, Betty Fuller, Carlos Castaneda, John Lilly, and a host of others.

Then as now, the most popular programs were the various body-awareness and encounter groups. Fritz Perls' involvement and later residency from 1964 to 1969 was influential in establishing Gestalt as a major psychological theory at Esalen. In 1967 William C. Schutz arrived with an impressive background, ranging from NTL groups to bioenergetics, psychodrama, psychosynthesis, encounter, and Rolfing. His style has been termed Esalen eclectic. Schutz remained in residency until early in 1976, and still frequently does workshops at Big Sur and at the Esalen San Francisco Center which opened in 1967.

Today's Esalen catalogue shows a continuance of the smorgasbord of human growth programs and the blending of Eastern and Western thought. Programs include those that focus on the interpersonal (Gestalt, encounter, psychosynthesis, and the like), on the transpersonal (meditation and related disciplines), on the body (including techniques as varied as T'ai Chi, Rolfing, and massage), and any combination thereof.

Perhaps the easiest way to get a feeling of the program is to follow along on a workshop. Esalen's workshops vary widely, but this weekend program, conducted by Will Schutz, resembles the others at least in time frame and sense of openness and flexibility.

Friday: The program begins at 8 p.m. after dinner and after a little Esalen pep talk and orientation ("Meet the staff — volunteer to work in the kitchen," and "The baths are thataway"). The group gathers in a large room furnished only with huge overstuffed brightly colored pillows. It's an odd bunch, consisting of a man whose legs are paralyzed, a Swiss-Italian playboy, a couple of tennis club-style housewives, two or three students, a couple trying to make up their minds to be in or out of love, and a sprinkling of educators, beginning therapists, and human potential groupies. The group numbers around 20, about equally divided between men and women. Unifying themes are white and middle class. We sit in a circle only because that is the way the pillows are placed.

Mind/Body Workshop

The workshop opens with sharing expectations and reasons for coming. (These range from "I read all your books and just *had* to experience one of your groups" to "The workshop I originally signed up for was canceled and this was the only one with space left.") After hearing our expectations, Schutz tells us this is to be a Mind/Body Workshop, where we will attempt to integrate the two along with a few feelings now and then. He asks that participants be as open, honest, and present-oriented as possible, and that we take

responsibility for ourselves and our behavior. Rather than saying "I can't" do something, he suggests that "I won't" is a more accurate statement. He also encourages us to do that which we are afraid of doing, as in such situations quite often the greatest learning takes place.

Finally, he requests that no one smoke or wear glasses during the group sessions. This raises a few eyebrows — especially those behind glasses. Will explains his theory is that we choose everything about ourselves, including our vision. This latter makes some sense when one considers that vision is usually a result of the shape of the eyeball, which in turn is affected by the eye muscles, which for their part respond to tension. The tension can be controlled if we attend to it. Reluctantly, members remove their glasses and throughout the weekend vacillate between wearing them and, as they say, "being blind."

The workshop then proceeds to an exercise, or, more accurately, a group of exercises entitled a micro-lab. It consists of nonverbal expression, arm wrestling, and a variety of other exercises designed to loosen us up and introduce us to each other.

We end with a brief discussion of how we feel and then break up around 10:30. Some people go to the lodge for tea or coffee and conversation, some wander off to their rooms, and others go for a walk on the grounds or down to the baths.

There should be a slight aside here to explain that Esalen's fame for nudity far exceeds the fact. Most of it is confined to the bath area, which is set apart from the rest of the facilities, and to appropriate moments within workshops. It would be easy to go to

Esalen and not see anyone nude, or ever feel the need to disrobe personally. On the other hand, the attitude is so casual and positive toward the human body that very quickly a sense of "Why not?" begins to take over in one's mind.

Saturday: The group reconvenes at 9 a.m., meeting until noon. We do guided fantasies and deep breathing, all designed to get us in touch with our bodies. At one point we exaggerate all the structural imbalances such as a raised hip, lowered shoulder, neck thrust forward, and so on, and get a graphic sense of how we are facing the world.

After lunch we are free for the afternoon. Schutz goes home to watch a football game, I go for a drive with a friend, someone else goes to have one of Esalen's famous massages, and others roam the grounds in various stages of awareness.

The next session is from 4 to 6 and consists of more fantasy work and several interesting insights. The paralyzed man, who has a vision problem, is referred to casually by Schutz. The reference is on the order of, "Tom, what was it you were saying earlier about this?" Tom responds, and then tells Schutz that for the past five to ten minutes he had been able to see perfectly well. "When did you stop?" asks Schutz. "When you called on me," is the reply.

Body Reading in the Nude

After dinner the group is feeling pretty comfortable until Schutz suggests that we do some body reading, and that it is best done in the nude. Shyly, we disrobe, grabbing for privacy by turning our backs to the group. We know that nudity is optional, but somehow that doesn't make it easier. As we re-establish ourselves on the pillows, Schutz comments dryly that this is one of the best ways he's found to maintain eye contact in a group. The laugh the comment elicits makes us feel a little more at ease.

The session consists of pairing up, giving our partners nonevaluative feedback about their bodies, and trying to make sense of the feedback we ourselves receive. Will urges us to make use of all the old body-related phrases and acknowledge their wisdom. For example, my right shoulder is lower than my left. Does that mean I'm "carrying the weight of the world" on it? My head is thrust forward. Could it be that I'm "meeting the world head on," relating with my mind and not my body?

At 10 p.m. the session ends and many more of us go to the baths this night.

Sunday: This morning's session from 9 a.m. to noon is to be our last. Schutz introduces us to Feldenkrais exercises (see page 174) as a form of body awareness. Aware of our coming demise as a group, we are happy to become involved in an exercise routine that is vigorous enough to distract us. The intent of Feldenkrais is to teach the body the easiest, most effective way of moving. While I subscribe to the theory, I find that somehow my body rebels and the experience is rather frustrating.

Although this group has not been nearly as intense as an encounter session, it is difficult to separate at noon. The process is made somewhat easier by the thought that we can lunch together before we leave.

The San Francisco Center, located at 1793 Union Street, was established to make the Esalen experience available in a broader, younger social milieu. It sprang out of a concern over the predominance of the middle-aged and relatively affluent at Big Sur. The Center features a variety of single-night events, ranging from Organic Mind Gardening to You Don't Have to Suffer to Feel Good, at a cost of $3.50-$5.00, and a free Saturday night Authors Series. Authors vary from Theodore Roszak *(The Making of the Counter Culture)* to Freda Morris *(Self-Hypnosis in Two Days).* The Center also conducts one-day and weekend workshops on the standard Esalen variety of topics.

Ways of Being at Esalen

The standard approach to being at Esalen consists of attending either a Big Sur weekend workshop or a week-long program. These include room and board, and currently range in price from $100-$120 for a weekend to $240-$320 for a week. Locals, and a few hard-core oldtimers, come just for the baths.

In San Francisco, where, alas! there are no baths, most programs last from one night to three days. As San Francisco does not offer room or board, prices are considerably lower, ranging from $5 to $50, with an occasional weekend program as high as $120-$150.

In addition to the standard approaches, there are some other ways of being at Esalen/Big Sur. Costs vary in each case.

One is the ongoing Residential Program. Offered from September to May, it enables people who would like an intense workshop experience to participate in four five-day programs of their choice.

Another way of participating in the Esalen/Big Sur experience is by living at the South Coast Center, a couple of miles north of Esalen itself, which is designed for people who want to be around Esalen and its facilities without being in an intensive program. Residents usually eat at Esalen and are asked to contribute eight hours per week working in the complex. Residencies can last up to three months. Meal tickets are extra.

A 28-day Work-Study Program also operates out of the Center. Participants attend a series of group sessions, closely tied to a 32-hour-a-week work program which includes such jobs as gardening, maintenance, and office and kitchen duties.

MIND EXPANSION TRAINING/ the foundation for mind research

If man can learn who he really is and what he is capable of; can learn to free himself from cultural biases, self-imposed limitations, constrictions caused by faulty programming; can modify and perfect his physical as well as his mental posture — if he can do all this, the millennium may well be at hand. One of the country's most interesting research centers is the Foundation for Mind Research, in Pomona, New York, where a husband and wife team, Dr. Robert E. L. Masters and Dr. Jean Houston, are attempting to bring about the revolution that will enable man, at long last, to realize his full potential.

Houston and Masters are dedicated professionals who are dealing with the very real problems of society: the rehabilitation of prisoners and of the elderly, and, most important, the transformation of the educational system to enable new generations to become more effectively functioning human beings than their forebears.

In a *Saturday Review* article entitled "Putting the First Man on Earth," Dr. Houston explains the proposal that man be trained to attain his full potential in every area of mind-body functioning. Believing most people are blocked or inhibited in varying degrees from using their capabilities in the most effective way, the Foundation advocates a systematic effort to develop mankind's true capacity. The program would be for everyone, not just an elite group. Houston and Masters are not indulging in ivory tower theorizing but actually have pilot programs under way showing exactly how their concepts can be realized. At the Mead School in Byran, Connecticut, children who have been trained in these new multicognitive methods are from one to four years ahead of their peers in every subject except spelling. In mathematics, language, history, there has been a true leap forward toward the goal of using the child's mind to the fullest, as well as freeing his body for optimum functioning and well-being.

Consciousness Alteration

The Foundation has been studying alterations of consciousness for many years, and has conducted landmark research on the effects of LSD on human personality, as described in the Masters and Houston book, *The Varieties of Psychedelic Experience.* They have had wide experience and remarkable results with various types of "guided meditation," using verbal induction methods as well as sound-and-light environments, electrical stimulation of the brain, and a far-out device known as an Altered States of Consciousness Induction Device, or ASCID. Developed for research in visual imagery as well as the induction of a variety of states of consciousness, it was patterned after a "witches' cradle" used centuries ago. Dr. Houston describes it as "essentially a metal swing or pendulum in which the research subject stands upright, supported by broad bands of canvas, wearing blindfold goggles. This pendulum, hanging from a metallic frame, carries the subject and moves in forward and backward, side to side, and rotating motions generated by involuntary movements of the subject's body." The mechanism of the inner ear is naturally affected and the subject loses not only spatial but temporal orientation and enters a trancelike state with a variety of phenomena, "flying through whorls, vortices, and mists. The mists then take on coloration and gradually dissolve, and the subject finds himself in a world of his own internal imagery ... that can be heard, touched, or even tasted. Often the imagery is initially regressive — scenes of the subject's childhood or early memories may be vividly experienced."

Techniques

The Foundation's wide panoply of techniques for expanding and enhancing consciousness includes the programming of dreams and the expansion or compression of linear time. By putting a subject into a light trance and using suggestion, a phenomenon known as Accelerated Mental Process (AMP) is activated. A musician may experience an hour of practice time in an elapsed time of only a few minutes. An art student who was able to achieve deep trance states was instructed that she would study with an excellent teacher and would experience a full day's instruction in only five minutes of clock time. Several sessions of this compressed instruction were markedly effective in improving the subject's artistic competence.

Another technique the Foundation is developing is an audio-visual program similar to the "light shows" so popular with rock music fans. As Dr. Houston describes it, "The subject sits behind the screen close enough so that the images occupy his entire field of vision and he has the feeling of almost being 'in' the slide projection. Sound (electronic music, Sufi or Zen chanting) comes to the subject either through headphones or from speakers situated at his sides. The visual program consists of dissolving 2x2-inch slides (many of them polarized, giving a constantly moving and flowing design) projected over the entire surface of the screen ...."

Characteristic responses include time disorientation, empathy, anxiety, euphoria, body image changes, religious and erotic feelings, projected imagery, pronounced relaxation, feelings of mild intoxication, a strong sense of wanting to go — or being drawn — into the image."

An interesting sidelight is that although most of the consciousness-altering techniques are verbal ones, the machines such as the ASCID or the audio-visual program are more effective for some subjects because, Dr. Houston believes, our culture reveres the magic of the technicians, the physicists, and the biochemists who are the shamans of our era.

Visualization

Research at the Foundation indicates that visualization greatly enhances creative thinking, problem solving, almost every type of mental activity. Unfortunately, our culture is heavily oriented toward verbal, linear thought processes at the expense of the visual. Imaging is apparently a very common mode in children's thinking, but is lost or suppressed in most adults. Using their marvelous repertoire, Masters and Houston are able to stimulate and reintroduce the visualization capabilities of adults and add a new dimension to their conceptual abilities. They also work with the dreaming process, since this tends to stimulate the imaging capacity and is also an excellent therapeutic tool. Subjects are helped to work "with" their dreams, to use them as aids in solving problems, to take the fear out of their phantoms and use them in constructive ways.

At present more than half of the work of the Foundation is on psychophysical programs for rehabilitation and improved body functioning. These make use of methods derived from the Eastern disciplines such as Yoga and the martial arts; the theories of F. Matthias Alexander, who held that proper alignment and use of the body was of primary importance; but chiefly the work of Moshe Feldenkrais, an Israeli doctor of applied physics who has developed an elaborate system of exercises for bodily rehabilitation. From these sources the Foundation has synthesized a program that can be easily taught and has had dramatic results — freeing and lightening the body, letting people experience the pleasure that comes from perfect bodily alignment, releasing rigidity and enhancing coordination.

The work with consciousness focuses on breaking through the "surface crust, to penetrate the cultural trance" and thus enable people to experience the full potential available from the insights and heightened perception gained in areas of consciousness that were previously inaccessible. Dr. Houston also offers intensive training courses in this work to interested professionals.

An adaptation of some of the techniques developed at the Foundation is explored in *Mind Games,* a handbook of guides for mental exercises or "games" to induce altered states of consciousness in small groups of people. One person acts as guide, and there are detailed, evocative instructions for reaching the goals and achieving new levels of awareness. People interested in experimenting with these states will find procedures carefully charted for them in this volume.

The Foundation participates in a program for prisoners with a high rate of recidivism at the Tulsa Rehabilitation Center in Tulsa, Oklahoma, directed by Dr. Joseph Spear. The work is designed to use different states of consciousness to create enhanced self-esteem, to give subjects a new self-image. The Center has worked with 55 prisoners over a four-year period and only two have been returned to prison.

In the field of mind-body dynamics, the Foundation might well serve as a model in the areas of advanced concepts, innovative research, and pragmatic solutions to the real and pressing problems of our ailing culture.

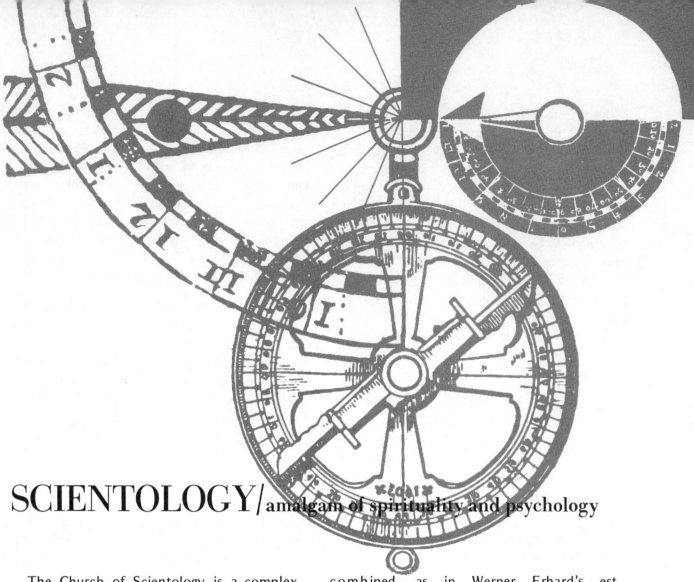

SCIENTOLOGY/amalgam of spirituality and psychology

The Church of Scientology is a complex mixture of down-to-earth psychological theories and practices, spiritual beliefs, advanced occultism, and corresponding organizational structures. Much of the writing about the Church by non-Scientologists concentrates on such a simplistic external as where its money goes. Few writers have really probed deeply into the question of why Scientology has proved so attractive to millions of people over the past 20 years.

A compelling reason for trying to make such an analysis is that many ambitious people, impressed with the Church's success, have based their own groups upon fragments of its philosophy or technology. Sometimes significant tenets of Scientology have been combined, as in Werner Erhard's est organization, with other complex spiritual-psychological traditions.

In any case, since it can cost thousands of dollars to have the Scientology experience, it is worth knowing something about it before getting involved.

According to Robert Kaufman, former member of the Church and author of *Inside Scientology*, the person who walks into one of the many Scientology storefronts as a potential recruit has been described as "raw meat." Although the expression sounds offensive, Scientologists associate it with the fact that the beginner faces a long process of development. Thus a cordial welcome is accorded the "raw meat," and a demonstration given — by means of an evaluative test and some charts — that life can be happier than it is. Most people would agree with that, so it is likely that the novice will sign up for the Communications Course, which costs between $15 to $20.

The Communications Course is quite enjoyable. There are encounter group exercises which include acknowledging other people, poking fun at them, and getting poked at in turn in a fairly safe environment. Since it is fun to relate and to confront, it is remarkable how quickly one's knowledge of relationships can be added to in a structured, safe situation. It is interesting to find that "communication" can be expressed in a simple formula once its successful elements have been isolated.

There is also an auditing session, using Scientology's confessional aid, the "E-Meter" — a scientific-looking instrument with a moving needle. Two wires coming out of the meter box terminate in two empty tin cans (which are impressive precisely because they look so unpretentious). The cans are held while a serious-faced "auditor" asks some questions and watches the needle. The questions are monotonously repeated until the meter responds to the answer. The auditor describes the meter as a truth meter which helps bring hidden psychological blocks called "engrams" to the surface. Then the conscious mind, functioning like a perfect computer, dissolves the secret, obsessive command structure which normally controls a person and keeps him or her unhappy.

To the newcomer it sounds more scientific, quicker, and less scary than the psychoanalyst's couch. And nearby, pinned to a bulletin board, are a number of success stories in which some intelligent and sincere people report they have felt better, solved problems, and gotten rid of illnesses or discomfort after being audited with the E-meter in a more advanced grade than the Communications Course.

People in the room obviously know what they are doing and where they are going, both as individuals and as a group. If some previous bad experience with organizational enthusiasm makes the newcomer somewhat doubtful, the Scientologists' enthusiasm will seem scary but impressive. And if group charisma has never been experienced before, he or she will find it interesting indeed to be in touch with energy and power, and be in a world where family and community can no longer be equated with safety and security, and the individual is beset by problems.

The Communications Course takes 15 or 16 hours, spread over four days. (The recruit will never again get Scientology training at a dollar an hour. In fact, the next grades of auditing can cost as much as $1,000.) "Straight wire release" promises improvement in memory and ability to recall. "Dianetic release" erases loss and misemotion. "Grade O Communications release" offers the "ability to communicate freely with anyone on any subject." In Grade I release a person acquires the "ability to recognize source of problems and make them vanish."

Grade II involves auditing the questions, "What have you done? What haven't you said?" Its aim is to achieve relief from the hostilities and suffering of life. Two important concepts, the areas of "overts" and "withholds," are dealt with here. *The Scientology Abridged Dictionary*, a copy of which every novice is encouraged to purchase, defines an "Overt" as a harmful or contra-survival act. . . an act of commission or omission that harms the greater number of dynamics . . . . . A failure to eradicate something or stop someone that would harm broadly would be an overt act." A "Withhold" is defined as an "undisclosed contra-survival act. . .in which the individual has done or been an accessory to doing something which is a transgression against some moral or ethical code. . ."

"Freedom Release"

Grade III, "Freedom release," offers "freedom from the upsets of the past and ability to face the future." In Grade IV the question audited with the E-Meter is, "What method have you used to make others wrong during your life?" This is called "Ability release," through "moving out of fixed conditions and gaining ability to do new things."

Beyond this point, for additional fees, there are courses in power processing, which involve the discovery of how to be a "source" and the discovery of precisely who you have been victimized by and how you have victimized that person. You can learn how to audit yourself for past goals. Then you are ready to leave your condition of "pre-clear" and go on to Grade VII, learning to be a "clear." Meanwhile you can be taking an auditor's course and thereby start to earn money to pay for your own training. Once you have become clear, there are numerous levels of training to develop your spirit essence, so you can become an "Operating Thetan."

Anyone walking into one of the more than 100 storefront missions spread throughout the United States and a few, mostly English-speaking, foreign countries will quickly observe that Scientologists believe they are on a spiritual path that surpasses any other. Paying as much as $15,000 for total freedom and complete happiness does not seem too steep to the convert, particularly since he or she can earn while learning, or even work for the organization in order to finance the training. And if the new convert signs other people up for courses, there are commissions to be earned. Under these conditions, every Scientologist becomes a keen recruiter.

Despite the lack of exact membership figures for the 22 major Scientology churches and some 100 missions, it is believed that there are well over five million adherents throughout the world. In 1971 Scientology Rev. Glenn A. Malkin said there were 50,000 Scientologists in Los Angeles, presently the world headquarters. Since then the Los Angeles membership has reportedly risen to at least 75,000.

Scientology's Leader

Scientology is particularly visible in Los Angeles, where the Church occupies a number of properties in Hollywood — including a hotel and a former senior citizen residence — using them as administrative offices, dormitories, classrooms and bookstores.

Scientology was incorporated in 1955 by its founder, L. Ron Hubbard, who has acted as its supreme organizer and spokesman, issuing a steady stream of books and pamphlets. One estimate is that Hubbard, a former science fiction writer, has written over 10 million words on the subject.

In 1966, following an attack by the Internal Revenue Service on the tax-free status of the Founding Church of Scientology in Washington, D.C., Hubbard resigned all his Church directorships and, according to *Time* magazine, received a fee of more than $200,000 from the Church for the "good will of his name." Two years later he "forgave" the organization a $13 million debt for services rendered, a move *Time* called an "understandable act of charity considering that he has boasted to friends of having $7 million stashed away in two numbered Swiss bank accounts." On August 1, 1968, Hubbard telegraphed his English headquarters at Saint Hill Manor, 30 miles south of London: "I have finished my work. Now it's up to others."

Although Hubbard, who was born in 1911 in Nebraska, has reached legal age for retirement, he still participates actively in his religion, using his writer's hat. For years, he has lived on the commanding vessel of a small fleet of Scientology ships called the Sea Org (Org is the Scientologists' word for a group), issuing his bulletins, pamphlets and books.

Aims

In 1969 Hubbard defined the purpose of his Church: "Our mission in Scientology is a simple one — it is to help the individual become aware of himself as an immortal Being and to help him achieve and attain the basic truths with regard to himself, his relationship with others across the Dynamics, his relationship to the physical universe and the Supreme Being. Further, we want to erase his sin so that he can be good enough to recognize God."

Although such words seem hard to quarrel with, there have been those who did. In 1965 the Parliament of the Australian state of Victoria passed a Psychological Practices Act, which was later repealed. While in effect, it made the teaching, applying, or even advertising of Scientology punishable by up to $500 and two years in jail. The hearing report concluded that "Scientology is evil; its techniques evil; its practice a serious threat to the community, medically, morally and socially; and its adherents are sadly deluded and often mentally ill . . . (it is the) world's largest organization of unqualified people engaged in the practice of dangerous techniques that masquerade as mental therapy." The British government also moved to prevent foreigners from entering England to train at the Saint Hill Scientology school.

This foreign hostility to Scientology was mirrored in the United States when the Food and Drug Administration seized 100 E-meters, charging that they were fraudulently ascribed curative powers for a variety of physical problems. In the late 60s, several hostile magazine articles appeared: "Scientology: a growing cult reaches dangerously into the mind" (*Life* magazine, November 15, 1968); "Menace to mental health" (*Today's Health*, December 1968); "The dangerous new cult of Scientology" (*Parents Magazine*, June 1969).

But Scientology fought back. By 1971 they had won their fight for survival in the United States with a Federal Court ruling that Scientology was in fact a religion and as such protected by constitutional guarantees. The Church had already started attaching labels to its E-meters, disclaiming any therapeutic powers, and the seized meters were returned by the FDA. In Australia the law against the Church had proved unenforceable and was finally repealed after a change in governments. The British ban on foreign Scientologists had also been impossible to enforce, and was removed by politicians who had no desire to participate in what seemed to be a witch hunt.

The Scientologists also mounted an offensive against a number of book, magazine, and newspaper publishers who had printed attacks on the Church. Hubbard himself urged his followers to "be very alert to sue for slander at the slightest chance, so as to discourage the public press from mentioning Scientology." The extent of this legal policy became clear when Paulette Cooper countersued Scientology in 1972 for $15 million after her book, *The Scandal of Scientology*, was withdrawn from circulation by her publisher as a result of Church pressure. Her complaint specified that in a two-year period the Church had filed at least 100 libel suits in the United States and Britain against such varied critics as the American Medical Association, the National Education Association, the *Washington Post*, *The Realist* publisher Paul Krassner, Delacorte Press, the *Los Angeles Times*, *Women's Wear Daily*, and the *San Francisco Chronicle*.

Lawsuits Justified

Official spokesmen for the Church now say they are no longer trying to silence criticism and that, in any case, their lawsuits were always in response to factual errors or actual libel. But as recently as November 1974, the prestigious *Library Journal* reported that defenders of Scientology had threatened lawsuits against Canadian libraries and bookstores that refused to remove from their shelves various books that were critical of Scientology. According to the *Journal*, "The Canadian Library Association has started a legal defense fund to aid smaller libraries in particular, and it has plans for organizing authors, publishers, booksellers and libraries into a common front against allegations from the Scientology group."

Careful reading of the dialogue between Scientology's adherents and those governments and critics who have been placed in the untenable position of persecuting a self-proclaimed religion reveals that both sides have tried to reach an accommodation. The Church has evidently tried to introduce some internal reforms of organizational policies that had been criticized. For example, Hubbard issued a policy letter in October, 1968 entitled "Cancellation of Fair Game." Its cryptic statement: "The practice of declaring people FAIR GAME will cease. FAIR GAME may not appear on any Ethics Order. It causes bad public relations. This P/L [policy letter] does not cancel any policy on the treatment or handling of an SP [Suppressive Person]." This military-style communique, typical of Hubbard, warrants some additional elucidation.

In the Scientology jargon, a Suppressive Person is one who commits suppressive acts. These are defined in *The Scientology Abridged Dictionary* as "actions or omissions undertaken knowingly to suppress, reduce or impede Scientology or Scientologists." The *Dictionary* goes on to call such actions high crimes, which "result in dismissal from Scientology and its organizations."

The Fair Game policy being canceled refers to an earlier Hubbard bulletin, widely cited and reproduced by Scientology critics: "A person relegated to Condition of Enemy is considered FAIR GAME: may be deprived of property or injured by any means by any Scientologist without any discipline of the Scientologist. May be tricked, sued, or lied to, or destroyed."

Policy Letter

Another policy letter, dating from August 1968, abolishes Security Checks from lists of questions asked while people were hooked up to the E-Meter, which Scientologists often refer to as a truth detector. Such questions ranged from probes into possible crimes to sexual aberrations to such catchalls as "Is there anything that L. Ron Hubbard or your instructors should mistrust you for that you haven't told them about?" Hubbard's letter explains that "We have no interest in the secrets and crimes of people and no use for them . . . . There is public criticism of security checking as a practice . . . ."

A recent court case, still being appealed, is worth noting. When, at the end of May 1974, a Los Angeles Superior Court jury rendered a malicious prosecution verdict against the Church — awarding $50,000 for compensatory damages and $250,000 punitive damages (later reduced to $50,000 compensatory and $50,000 punitive) to a former Scientologist, it became a matter of court record that the Church was continuing its harshness toward defectors and critics.

"Billion Year Contract"

The case involved L. Gene Allard, who became the Church's bookkeeper in Los Angeles after receiving advanced Scientology training in San Diego, where he signed a 'billion-year contract" agreeing to do anything to help Scientology, including clearing the planet of "reactive people."

In the spring of 1969, Allard told his Scientology superiors that he wanted to leave the Church. Lawrence Krieger, the Church's highest ranking justice official in California, told Allard that if he left without permission he would be Fair Game and "You know we'll come and find you and we'll bring you back and we'll deal with you in whatever way is necessary." (This quotation is taken directly from the court records.)

In early June 1969, Allard went to his office at the Church, took several documents from the safe which allegedly revealed improper changes in financial records, and left for Kansas City to present the information to the Internal Revenue Service office in that city. He subsequently went to Florida, where he was arrested and held by the police for 21 days on a charge made by his Scientology superior, Alan Boughton, that Allard had stolen $23,000 in Swiss francs from the Scientology safe. The theft charge was later dismissed by a Los Angeles deputy district attorney and Allard filed a malicious prosecution suit against the Church. The Church counter-sued for loss of their property.

In May 1976, when reviewing the Superior Court's judgment in favor of Allard, the Second District Court of Appeal ruled that the trial jury could reasonably infer from the evidence that Boughton himself had removed the money from the safe in order to falsely accuse Allard of theft. The Appeal Court found that the evidence supported the jury's conclusion that "those witnesses who were Scientologists or had been Scientologists were following the (Fair Game) policy of the Church and lying to, suing and attempting to destroy respondent (Allard)."

Denying the appeal by the Church that introducing Hubbard's Fair Game policy statements as evidence was an unconstitutional attack against the belief system of a religion, the Appeal Court ruled that "any party whose tenets include lying and cheating to attack its 'enemies' deserves the results of the risk which such conduct entails." The Court also made note of the fact that the trial court had given the Church almost the entire trial to prove that the Fair Game policy had been repealed. When the Church failed to submit such proof, the trial court permitted the Fair

Game policy exhibit into evidence. However, noting that the Church's conduct may have so enraged the jury that excessive punitive damages might have been awarded, the Appeal Court reduced the $300,000 judgment to $100,000.

Subsequently, the Appeal Court denied the Church's request for a rehearing of the case and the California Supreme Court also refused to hear it. In August 1976, the Church appealed to the United States Supreme Court.

Dianetics

Hubbard himself attributes the foundation of Scientology's spiritual philosophy and methodology to *Dianetics,* a book he published in 1950. Dianetics is presented as a science for achieving total mental health, a state Hubbard claims was previously unknown to the ordinary human being. He divides the human mind into two parts, the analytical and the reactive. The analytical mind records, recalls, and evaluates data like a computer, providing swift and accurate solutions to the problems posed by life, modified only by the input of education and experience. However, the analytical mind cannot function in this efficient fashion because the hidden reactive mind is feeding wrong data into the computer.

Hubbard says the reactive mind is the only mind which is always conscious and recording. During moments when the individual's very survival is threatened, the mind records sensations and perceptions in great detail despite pain and/or unconsciousness. These vivid and traumatic impressions, which Hubbard calls engrams, are not filed in the conscious, analytic mind but in the hidden, reactive mind. Hubbard describes the situation as analogous to when a hypnotist implants a suggestion in a person's unconscious that a specific stimulus or signal will produce a certain response. The engram, however, is a more powerful entity than a hypnotic suggestion because it is enforced by a painful content. According to Hubbard, when the analytical mind faces a situation which in any respect is familiar, the reactive mind, operating on its simplistic stimulus-response basis, discharges its engramic memories into the analytical mind, where they exert a tyrannical command function — however inappropriate to reality — over the person's awareness, purposes, body, and actions. The engrams comprise a complete recording of all perceptions during partial or full consciousness and the reactive mind, therefore, contains the entire traumatic data of birth, anesthesia, accidents, and sleep.

"Dianetic Reverie"

In the original system, a "dianetics auditor" trained by Hubbard would use a "dianetic reverie" to help another person bring the engram content of the reactive mind into the analytic mind, thus gradually clearing the analytical "computer" of all hidden data. In the next few years Hubbard made two important additions to his system. In place of dianetic reverie, the state of partial sleep that some critics equated with a hypnotic state, he introduced the E-Meter as his fundamental auditing tool. The meter is a simple instrument which measures the electronic resistance of the body by passing a small and harmless amount of battery electricity through two cans held by the "pre-clear." When the auditor questions the "pre-clear," the distinctive movements of the meter's needle register the presence of the engram as it surfaces and as it is resolved.

In Hubbard's words, "The meter tells you what the pre-clear's mind is doing when the pre-clear is made to think of something. If they're emotionally disturbed about cats, and they're talking about cats, the needle flies about. So you let them talk about cats until they're no longer disturbed about cats, and then the needle no longer flies about."

A "Clear"

Hubbard's second addition was his discovery that a "clear," a person whose mind computer could face any new problem without allowing the residue of previous data to enter into the new computations, was only a rung in the ladder of evolution through Scientology. To quote from his *Scientology: The Fundamentals of Thought:*

> Probably the greatest discovery of Scientology and its most forceful contribution to the knowledge of mankind has been the isolation, description and handling of the human spirit. Accomplished in July, 1951, in Phoenix, Arizona, I established along scientific rather than religious or humanitarian lines that that thing which is the person, the personality, is separable from the body and mind at will without causing bodily death or derangement.

Hubbard named this "thing" the *theta* or *thetan*, after the Greek letter.

It is impossible to understand Scientology without understanding Hubbard's concept of the Thetan. A Thetan can create matter, energy, space, and time, the substance of our universe. In Scientology terms, a Thetan is *cause** over matter, energy, space, time, life, and thought. The supreme test of a Thetan is to make things go right.

With this idea of the Thetan, Hubbard had created a bridge between the psychotherapy of Dianetics and the religion of Scientology.

To a person not deeply involved in Scientology, the training to become an OT (Operating Thetan) would apparently seem bizarre and is consequently kept secret. Whereas elementary auditing on the lower grades involves only the down-to-earth techniques of dianetic therapy, OT training means personal involvement (through practice in visualization) in the 35-billion-year history of spirits in the universe. The trainee — who is already a "clear" — is asked to locate these spirits in his own body, using the ever-present E-meter.

Only a committed Scientologist would be able to locate within himself and dissolve engrams that are billions of years old. This is psychoanalysis of the kind a Tibetan lama experiences when he visualizes a wrathful deity and makes the demonic symbol part of his personal reality. In the OT levels of Scientology these practices are connected with "R2-46 type processes" where you take what is wrong with you and project it onto other people you see in a park or a railroad station or other public place. The use of clay models, which in the early training courses seemed an enjoyable way of expressing abstract concepts, becomes in the OT training a means by which the Operating Thetan can manipulate the universe of matter, energy, space, time, life, and thought.

Beginning Scientology training involves a series of power processes which instill the theory of being source or cause. Operating Thetans *practice* being source and cause. Once we understand this, we can realize the true motivation behind the Fair Game and Security policies. Scientology-Dianetics is concerned with purifying the individual of negative emotions, evil spirits, overts, and withholds. People who are against Scientology, particularly former Church members, reinforce these negatives and give them strength. So any Scientologist who harasses a declared Suppressive Person is presumed to be helping his friend progress to total freedom.

*See page 135 for an account of how Werner Erhard incorporated the "cause" concept and other Scientology theories into est.

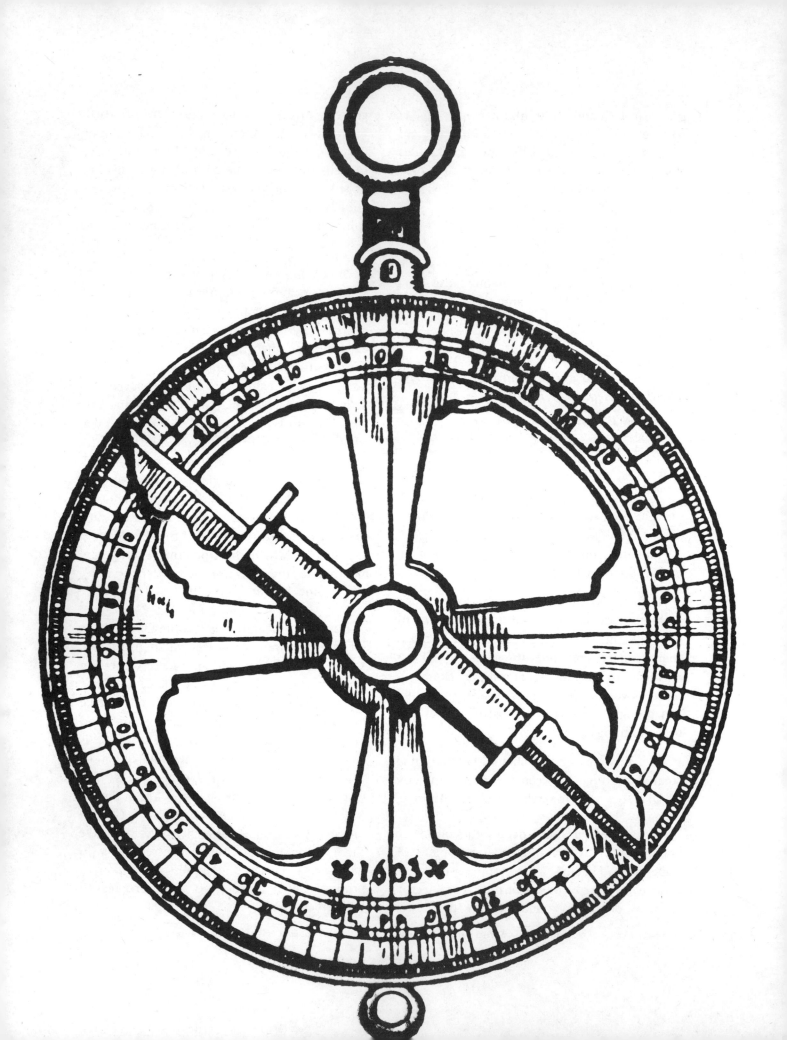

est / is it cattle therapy?

est stands for Erhard Seminars Training, currently the most fashionable mindstyle/lifestyle movement in the United States. EST stands for Electro Shock Therapy, a technique used in mental institutions to modify patient behavior. Critics of est imply that both abbreviations imply brainwashing.

est's founder, Werner Erhard, a charismatic San Francisco businessman in his late '30s, claims that since 1971 his training has helped upwards of 100,000 people to "unblock potential and free self-expression." In four strenuous days (usually spaced out over two weekends plus one midweek and one post-training evening meeting) est trainers put a group of several hundred people through various processes which are claimed to "transform your ability to experience living so that the situations you have been trying to change or have been putting up with clear up just in the process of life itself."

If this sounds vague, it is — deliberately so. A prime tenet of est, convincingly reiterated time and again by Erhard and his staff, is that the est experience cannot be put into words; it has to be experienced. So the person contemplating Erhard Seminars Training is faced with a dilemma: Should I put up the $250 admission price for the training, payable in advance, when I don't really know what I'm going to get for my money?

Since this is really the first big stumbling block to overcome in approaching est, it is worth reproducing the most complete statement made by an est official about the training. It was written in March 1975 by Don Cox, est president:

No claims, guarantees or promises of results are made for the est training. This would be inconsistent with the purpose of the training. However, to make the results of the training reported by graduates understandable, the following is offered in explanation.

The est training is about aliveness, satisfaction, fulfillment, and the experience of completion. The training does not change what one knows; it transforms the way in which one knows. It affects a person's life in the way it would be affected when there was an essential shift in one's experience of living from the attempt to become satisfied to the experience of being satisfied.

What happens during the training is a transformation (not merely a change or enlarging) of:

1. One's experience of experiencing.

2. One's experience of knowing.

3. One's experience of self.

Some of the results of this transformation are:

1. One starts out relationships, jobs, the pursuit of goals, etc., satisfied instead of trying to get satisfied. Therefore one's life becomes an expression of the satisfaction, aliveness, and fulfillment one is experiencing.

2. One experiences the barriers to satisfaction so as to complete the experience (get to the source of the barrier and have it dissolve) rather than resisting, solving, fixing, or changing them, which keeps them in place.

3. One experiences oneself as responsible for one's experience of life. As this expands, one moves from a frustration or antagonism towards society to a sense of being able to effect a transformation in society.

4. One's experience of love, happiness, health, and self-expression expands and so does one's ability to make life work and be effective in the world.

est is sometimes confused with other things. It is not like group therapy, sensitivity training, encounter groups, positive thinking, meditation, hypnosis, mind control, behavior modification, or psychology. In fact, est is not therapy and is not psychology. We specifically point that out to people before they take the training. We tell people that if they need therapy or psychological, psychiatric or medical services, they should see a therapist, psychologist, psychiatrist or physician, as appropriate.

Another official pamphlet quotes Werner Erhard as saying, "Sometimes people get the notion that the purpose of est is to make you better. It is not. I happen to think that you are perfect exactly the way you are . . . . The problem is that people get stuck acting the way they were, instead of being the way they are." After you take the training, the pamphlet continues, you probably won't even know what has really been done to you. "Having someone tell you what it is like to parachute out of an airplane is not the same as experiencing jumping out of the airplane yourself. And as such, it has meaning only to the person who is experiencing it. Each person experiences the training in his own way. After you take the training, you probably won't know *how* it works; you will only know *that* it works."

est Graduates

Many people — close to 100,000 in fact — have found these words compelling enough to take the training. The confidence behind the statements is overwhelming. And there is something refreshing in est's advocacy of the necessity of "experiencing experience." Furthermore, something *has* happened to the people who have graduated from est. It may be indefinable but they are certainly enthusiastic about whatever it is that happened. Most impressive is the fact that these graduates may never have been enthusiastic about anything before.

The result: est has people signed up on waiting lists for months to take the training, the $250 paid in advance. The appearance is that est groups are made up of affluent white middle-class Americans who can afford to spend several hundred dollars to find out what their friends are raving about. The reality is usually quite different. This can be seen during the training when these well-dressed and educated people start throwing up, fainting, or revealing in words how unsuccessful and unhappy they feel, how tortured they are by fears, phobias, and illness. In four days, a clever integrated process brings hundreds of seemingly confident, sometimes even arrogant Americans into simultaneous confrontation with their deepest fears. A friend of mine, Carrie Fisher, dubs est "cattle therapy." It must truly be an experience.

Despite all est's deliberate mystery, however, the process can be meaningfully described and traced to its origins; even how it works can be understood. It may be very important to undertake this exploration, despite the abstraction that "experience must be experienced," in order to know the ultimate value of the est experience, appreciate any dangers involved, and be aware of alternative, possibly more desirable paths to "feeling alive" and "being happy."

Nonetheless, it is true that the est training has to be experienced, because verbal description will lead many people to believe they understand the experience when they don't. If any reader moved by this argument has the $250 to spare, he or she should stop reading at this point, sign up for est, and maybe read the remainder afterward. There is very little danger, and the show is truly worth the price of admission!

est's Founder

Werner Erhard, something of a magician with words and a master of dialectics, likes to say that est comes "out of experience into the world, not out of the world into experience." It is true that est must have come into the world out of Erhard's own experience. Enthusiastic articles have promoted him as a

We found some stardust
in the skies
which has the same chemistry
for life.

B. Fuller

Corita

guru who has personally synthesized a vast array of psychological and spiritual disciplines, from Gestalt therapy to the occult secrets of the Bible, but they do not itemize which these are nor how they have been used. This nonspecific appeal to authority tends to overwhelm and intimidate, rather than inform.

The facts of the matter are really quite simple. est's fantastic organization, the group dynamics, the processes, even the psychological expertise of its trainers can be explicitly traced back to Erhard's own experience in Scientology, Mind Dynamics, Leadership Dynamics, and as a manager of encyclopedia salesmen. To demonstrate this, it is first necessary to tell what actually happens during the est training.

The Training Process

Day One: The est process starts when the trainer makes clear to the newly assembled participants that there are certain agreements that have to be understood throughout the training. The trainees must remain in their seats without talking, are not permitted to take notes, can't smoke, can't eat except for an announced maximum of one meal late in the day, and can't go to the bathroom. They can't wear watches, must be at sessions on time, and are not allowed to sit next to anyone they know. Trainees must give up any spiritual discipline or meditation during the two-week training, and also abstain from narcotics, alcohol, and medicine. If, for medical reasons, a trainee has to have regular meals, medication, or unrestricted access to bathroom facilities, he is segregated from the main group.

We are shown how to use the microphone and are told that trainees can ask questions at any time. We are instructed to acknowledge any other trainee who speaks by clapping, but are not to speak directly to another trainee. The trainer quickly sets a pattern for acknowledgment by repeatedly saying "Thank you" to the trainees.

However, the est training is not a polite environment. Sessions last from six to 10 hours without the trainees being allowed to stand and stretch, or go to the bathroom. Some trainees pee in their pants rather than break the agreement by going to the bathroom (and losing their $250). One session broke up in laughter when a trainee, who had already made clear that he was a highly paid lawyer, signaled for a microphone and indignantly told the group he had paid $250 to have the experience of someone else urinating in his shoe. And for hours on end the trainer tells the group in boring, repetitive detail that they are assholes, that their lives don't work, that they are nonexperiencing experience, and that they don't have control over their bodies (as evidenced by their physical discomfort, great need to urinate, and desire for regular meals).

This goes on hour after hour. People fall asleep in their chairs, and the group is told that this doesn't matter — they are being trained while they sleep. The trainees are told not to worry about understanding what happens during the training: It will usually become clear by the end, but even if it never becomes clear, the training will still prove to be quite important.

Irrelevant Lectures

We are told that if two bodies occupy the same space both would disappear. There are long, apparently irrelevant lectures about the physical nature of the universe, which all seem to lead up to the viewpoint that if a person really experienced anything, it would disappear. We are given a demonstration that if a pain or headache is experienced by concentrating upon it, visualizing the shape, color, and volume of the pain, it will disappear.

There are group relaxations. Trainees are told to close their eyes, locate a spot in the left foot, locate a spot in the right foot, locate a spot in the left knee, and so on, moving up the body. When everyone is relaxed and in a dreamy, sleepy state, some affirmations are read: "We are all feeling good." "We can be great." "We are great." It's difficult to hear the words. No one knows the time of day. Our watches are in a checkroom outside. Obviously, hours have gone by, but as there are no windows in the hotel ballroom in which the hundreds of us are sitting, it's not certain whether night has arrived.

Rules

A rest break is given. No eating is permitted — water or fruit juice only. Lines form at the hotel bathrooms. Those who don't return on time are not allowed in until they have answered endless questions about the agreement they originally made to be in their seats on time. They must acknowledge many times that they made such an agreement, and that they broke it.

The reassembled group is told that if we relax our bodies according to the process we have learned, we can wake up at any specific time without an alarm clock. The secret is to mentally visualize the alarm clock, mentally set the hands, and visualize pulling the alarm stem out. We are told over and over again to take responsibility for our lives. We are the "cause" but until now we never took responsibility for being "cause," so we have actually been "effect."

The day started early in the morning. It is after midnight before we are dismissed, having had a hurried snack at 10 p.m. Everyone is tired, bored, stiff. The est training has begun.

More of the Same

The second day: First, an evaluation of Day One. And then more, much more of the same. Some trainees never stop complaining but the trainers simply say the complainers are assholes and acknowledge the fact that the assholes have expressed an opinion. There is a long discussion of fear. The trainees are told that for now they are not to try to experience their individual fears and thus get rid of them, but to experience the essence of fear. More relaxation. More hours of boring lectures. Everyone takes turns standing in a line in front of the other trainees. They must simply stand there while the rest watch them. Some people faint. Others fidget. The trainers make fun of their inability to have control over themselves.

A deep relaxation. A long affirmation. While everyone is relaxed, we are told to think of the people next to us as enemies and to act this fantasy out. A lot of people take the instructions to heart and scream and throw up and curl into the fetal position. Some black out and finally faint. The hotel room has become a madhouse. Many people are obviously not pretending. It is as if they are in a deep hypnotic trance and living out their fears.

Cosmic Joke

However, there is laughter here and there in the room from the est graduates who are re-experiencing the training. Then the trainer tells the trainees to keep their eyes shut and listen to the cosmic joke: Since we as a group have demonstrated that we are afraid of everyone else, that means everyone else is afraid of us. Therefore, the individual can be

dangerous. *We are all dangerous* once we know this.

It is the end of the second day of training. This last process, the truth process, was so traumatic that the trainees are not sleepy despite the late hour.

Midweek evaluation: Trainees stand up and give testimonials to the fact that they have become conscious of the agreements they have made at work and at home since the first weekend of training. They say they get along better with people when they acknowledge communication, have discovered they don't need to go to the bathroom so often, and tend to eat only when they are hungry.

By this time a group dynamic is operating. Almost everyone has been heard complaining, explaining their fears, asking questions of the trainer. The truth process has made them realize they were assholes for fearing other people when all the time the other people were fearing them. The trainers are no longer calling the trainees assholes, only referring to non-est people as assholes. One young man says it was fun being dangerous the last few days. Others speak of feeling they could be compassionate to other people because they could understand their fears.

A long relaxation concludes this evening meeting. The trainees close their eyes and we all visualize an orange liquid slowly filling our bodies and slowly draining out again. It is very peaceful. A long affirmation is read; again, it is hard to catch the exact words but they seem connected with our well-being. There is a sense of cameraderie as the trainees leave the hotel ballroom. Half the training has been completed — and we have survived.

Next Saturday: The training resumes with a long relaxation. The trainees build a psychic workshop complete with mentally pictured

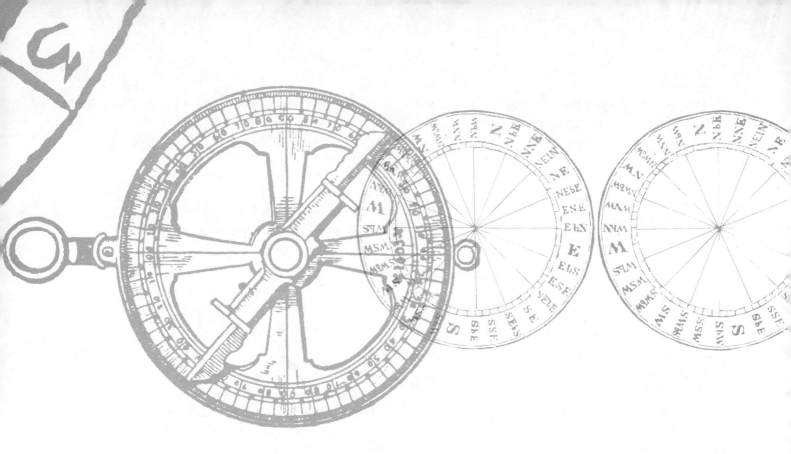

TV screen, storage cabinets, file cabinets with any information we need. It all sounds ridiculous, but there's an elevator in there and we create two guides, who live in that mental room. The trainer assures us that by relaxing our bodies and going into the psychic workshop, we can do such things as slot a mental cassette into our mental TV screen, and watch ourselves skiing. Then when we actually ski, we will be better skiers.

There is no meal break at all, but we are given a free lunch late at night: one cherry tomato, one strawberry, a daisy, a slice of lemon, a one-inch cube of metal, and a one-inch cube of wood. We relax and visualize ourselves inside the strawberry. Then we mentally picture ourselves climbing the daisy, which is 20 feet high. Next we touch the lemon with our tongues, really experiencing the acid taste. Finally, we each eat the strawberry, the tomato, and the lemon. Many trainees are hungry enough to eat the lemon peel and the daisy as well.

Still the third day: Boring lectures about the nature of reality, the world of cause and the world of effect. The trainer runs back and forth between three stools identified as past, present, and future, demonstrating there is no time but present time. Several relaxations enable us to experience being assholes. Games imitating little girls and a circus diver jumping into a tank from a high tower. The women trainees do a Tarzan imitation. More long, boring discussions. Some trainees still keep arguing with the instructors that est's attitude, in trying to get us to accept the world as it is, is counter-revolutionary, negating any need for social change. The trainers acknowledge these persons and call them assholes.

The fourth day of training: We are told in long, boring lectures about how the mind works. We are all machines and there is nothing we can do about it. We have to take responsibility for being machines. But looked at properly, once we take responsibility for

141

what is, we become cause. There is nothing to get in the est training except an acceptance of what is. We can "experience experience" and get rid of some bad pain that way, but true freedom comes through acceptance. Got it?

Some trainees acknowledge that they got it. They testify to a Zen-like enlightenment. Others say they got all that by sitting with a Zen master or taking LSD, so what's new? A lot of trainees persist in being puzzled. Is that all? They must be missing the point. The trainers goes up to them individually and says: "Do you hear me telling you that there's nothing to get?" The trainee nods. (He's standing awkwardly before 200 other people who are now his friends.) Then the trainer says: "Well, you've got it! Sit down!" It is all very verbal. Is enlightenment nothing but a verbal trick? A handful of people around the room look very blank, noticeably those who blacked out during the truth process. Are they ill? Has est proved to be too overwhelming for them all?

Graduation: Each of us is given the name, age, and city location of a person we don't know. The game is to give the est graduates who are our partners a psychological profile of the person as we pick it up in the relaxed state we learned during training. Everyone seems to do remarkably well. We are told we have graduated. The second long weekend has ended, we have survived 60 hours of est training, and it really *has* been an experience.

The post-training meeting: Another relaxation process. We're all graduates now and there is nothing more to learn, really, but we are told about classes for graduates: Be Here Now, What's So, About Sex, Communication, Self-Expression, and so on, costing $20 for each series of 10 evenings. The proceeds go to a foundation which promotes mental health, well-being, and research. Any graduate can review the est training for $35. Everyone uses first names (as during the whole training; everyone wears a name tag). It is clear there are still agreements to be kept. If you start a course, you must attend regularly, and complete it. But the stress is gone. We're all graduates!

Graduates

Many est graduates are going to find it hard to accept that almost everything est teaches about communication, acknowledgment, agreement, and responsibility comes directly from Scientology.

Intimates of Erhard acknowledge that before starting est he completed the Scientology communication course and the first four grades of Scientology training. Any est graduate who really wants to remember those seemingly forgotten lectures of the training only has to look at the Scientology textbooks for those grades and the axioms from L. Ron Hubbard's *Creation of Human Ability* to recapture the experience:

> "Axiom 19: Bringing the static [the spirit] to create a perfect duplicate causes the vanishment of any existence of part thereof.

> "Axiom 26: Reality is the agreed-upon apparency of existence.

> "Axiom 30: The general rule of auditing is that anything which is unwanted and yet persists must be thoroughly viewed, at which time it will vanish."

In his 1954 *Phoenix Lectures*, Hubbard wrote, just as if he were an est trainer, "We know that what is wrong with a person is his subjective universe." And, again, "The ability to be at Cause point is necessary for good communication."

The Source

If much of the theory sounds like Zen Buddhism, that is because it is. Hubbard, at least, is frank and open about the fact that he based Scientology on large chunks of Oriental wisdom. In a 1967 bulletin, "Religious Philosophy and Religious Practice," he wrote, "Scientology's closest spiritual ties with any other religion are with Orthodox (Hinayana) Buddhism with which it shares an historical lineage." The majority of Buddhists regard the Hinayana tradition as an approach which overly intensifies the individual ego and creates arrogant rather than humble monks. It is perhaps not accidental that this same criticism is often leveled against the disciples of both est and Scientology by people outside those organizations.

Mind Dynamics is another major source for the est training. Not only was Werner Erhard trained as a Mind Dynamics instructor, he was selected by the organization's founder, Alexander Everett, to take responsibility for its whole sales structure. But Erhard had greater ambitions, and in 1971 he quit Mind Dynamics with a group of other instructors and formed est. (Stewart Emery, Erhard's main trainer until he in turn quit est to form his own program, Actualizations, was also a Mind Dynamics instructor.)

Everett, an expert in designing learning machines and former schoolmaster, was financed in Mind Dynamics by William Penn Patrick, a millionaire entrepreneur and sponsor of several controversial franchise-type corporations. The Mind Dynamics program was a carefully put together training system based on the meditational practices of the Christian Unity Church and considerable knowledge of hypnotic induction techniques. Its main objects were self-improvement and the development of psychic abilities, particularly psychic healing through visualization.

Graduates of est will immediately recognize the psychic workshop developed in Session 9 of the Mind Dynamics course material:

> The workshop and all the equipment (visualized chair and round table, telephone, clock calendar, files and reference books, TV screen and other visual aids, instruments and equipment, chemicals and medications, platform and screen, elevator) are like a lens to focus the powers of the mind . . . . You can use this room as a place to think, plan and study possible courses of action. You can look for information from your files and reference books . . . your film library can contain special training films . . . the object is to use the elevator as a means of bringing someone or something . . . into the workshop level . . . . Get involved . . . . Use your hands . . . . Pay attention to detail.

These could well be instructions for the est psychic workshop, but they are direct quotes from the Mind Dynamics course that Erhard himself taught. With the major exception of the truth process (of which more later) most of the est processes were modified, or occasionally borrowed outright, from Mind Dynamics material.

There is nothing intrinsically wrong in Erhard's borrowing this, or valuable material from any other source, to create his own unique training — although it would be more generous of him to give it credit. In this instance, however, it is worth noting that est does not use this material as effectively as Mind Dynamics, where it was associated with the development of psychic healing abilities. In est the psychic workshop and other Mind Dynamics material seem tacked on, purposeless save for playing the game of psychological profile.

Leadership Dynamics

An outgrowth of Mind Dynamics was the Leadership Dynamics Institute (LDI), set up by William Penn Patrick using Mind Dynamic visualization along with group encounter techniques to train executives in Patrick's corporations. Articles in the San Francisco

Chronicle August 25-26, 1972, identified LDI as "a strange school for salesmen that has been denounced as Sadism, Inc." and went on to relate that LDI seminars featured spankings, foul language, forced enclosures in coffins (to cure claustrophobia), and other physical harassments. Each four-day seminar cost $1,000.

Patrick claimed LDI students would experience a change that would enable them to lead "a more creative and constructive life. It takes a tough man to be completely honest and that's what you'll have to be to get the most out of it and apply what you'll learn. Some of the things you'll be told might be hard to take."

Bizarrely, Patrick died in an airplane crash while giving an LDI experience to a businessman who had a fear of planes. The controversial millionaire was piloting a plane with his businessman-student as passenger and in an effort to have his trainee "experience an experience," looped too close to the ground. The critical *Chronicle* articles were occasioned by the filing of $250 million in lawsuits against Leadership Dynamics, an event which destroyed not only LDI but Mind Dynamics as well, and left the field clear for est.

"Attack Therapy"

The humiliation, ridicule, and sarcasm in the est training is drawn directly from what group encounter professionals call "attack therapy." Erhard does not speak of Leadership Dynamics, but this might be where he learned the attack therapy practiced so vigorously in est.

Finally, but not least important, the est training uses relaxation techniques closely modeled after Mind Dynamics group meditations, which were labeled as simple

hypnosis by such medical authorities as Dr. Elmer E. Green of the Menninger Foundation. The "locate a spot in your left foot" technique comes straight from the hypnosis manuals. It is particularly effective upon people who have willingly accepted agreements (suggestions) and then been totally exhausted by hours of sitting on a hard seat while feeling bored and hungry.

Hypnosis?

So the lessons of responsibility, agreement, and all those vaguely remembered ideas of reality were being absorbed in est under hypnosis. That is why the four-day training was so effective and produced such enthusiastic graduates, why the affirmations made people feel so much better!

This is not to denigrate hypnosis as a tool for learning and self-development. Properly taught, hypnotic techniques can even provide a means for people to learn how to resist unwanted hypnotic suggestions. But hypnosis should not be used without the subject's being aware of what the procedure involves, or the tendency to succumb to other outside pressure may be increased to dangerous levels.

The truth process (often called the danger process by those who have experienced it) is a prime example of est's use of hypnosis. By that stage the individuals in the group have been hypnotized many times and the est trainer's "rela-a-ax" becomes part of a long hypnotic induction. When the trainees are then told to visualize and experience fear, it is no wonder so many of them go through absolute terror or emotional blackout from the scene of people throwing up and thrashing about. The danger process, as a matter of fact, greatly resembles the Tibetan Tantric Yoga meditations done in a trance state where the disciple voluntarily experiences fear accompanied by cries, choking, shuddering, and convulsions. But the Tibetan initiate has been carefully screened by a long period of discipline before being put through this traumatic experience. The est training makes an attempt to screen candidates by barring those with severe psychiatric problems from taking the training. Should we assume, though, that people with such problems would necessarily disclose them on the est questionnaire?

Chairman of the Board

The chairman of the est's board of directors, Philip Lee, M.D., has excellent professional credentials, like many others who have lent their names to est. Lee has been Chancellor of the University of California Medical School and is currently a professor of social medicine and health policy there. Explaining the function of the est advisory board, composed of prominent endorsers of the training, Dr. Lee admitted, "We want to find out what it [the training] does, and second, why. We don't know either one yet." As has been suggested here, one reason for this may be that everyone who conscientiously takes the training becomes deeply hypnotized in the process and conditioned to like it.

Hypnosis is a valuable medical, psychological, and educational tool; the processes of Mind Dynamics can be an effective key to the exploration of psychic healing; the communication theories of Scientology may be very helpful to those who experience them; and the est package seems to synthesize all of these most effectively. But even though "an experience has to be experienced" and cannot simply be talked about to be effective, students of anything should have some advance information, and perhaps warning, of what it is that they are *really* going to experience.

ACTUALIZATIONS / offshoot of est?

"I would sit there and I'd feel really uncomfortable. I didn't know what it was. I listened to what Werner said and I heard . . . what he said was the truth. He would control people and manipulate people with the truth. That's the new twist. 'Let's control people with the truth because it has the appearance, you see, of being honest.' "

The speaker is Stewart Emery, who was Werner Erhard's closest and most revered trainer. Emery led some 25,000 people through est and then left that organization because of basic disagreement with the training process and inadequate compensation.

Maintaining that all the books on money, happiness, and self-improvement don't work, Emery set out to achieve his own method of experiencing joy and freedom. After exploring many different disciplines, he developed his own concept, which he calls Actualizations.

In this process, Emery goes back to the fundamental human relationship and allows the individual to create the space for individuality to perform effectively. He believes that we are the way we are as a result of where we come from. Life is an accumulation of hurt; therefore, man must choose a supportive environment to help him through this hurt. Man traditionally comes from a history of conflict and, as a result, is chiefly interested in getting something rather than nothing. In the Actualizations process, the training is designed to reinforce the realization that people can hold different beliefs without being in conflict and that life is the process of exploring the self as reflected in its relationships with others and with the environment.

Emery aims to teach people to see events as interrelated phenomena, and to realize their need to share each other's strengths and vulnerabilities. "I see people live their lives," he says, "as if they planned that reality will conform to their dreams, and they react as if it conformed to their nightmares. Reality is neither their dreams nor their nightmares — it's whatever it is."

Emery denies the theory of "I created everything" which is one basic tenet of est. He feels man can discover the joy of beauty and happiness, and what he really wants to do is return people to themselves. "It's not happening until you're dancing" is one way of putting it.

To Emery: "We are the way we are because of the decision we made about what we thought happened. Conflict is the assumption that existing conditions are a threat to well-being. It's not getting the source of who you are from other people or things but rather recognizing the source is within yourself. There is a difference between reason and purpose. There is a *reason* for getting up in the morning, but *purpose* always gives you somewhere to go. Goals are finished for a purpose, but purposes are never finished." And of his training he says, "The purpose is to give you the space to expand."

Actualizations training is given by Emery and an associate in small supportive workshop groups, usually over a three-day weekend. It is currently offered once a month in Los Angeles and in San Francisco, and on a more occasional basis in New York.

SILVA MIND CONTROL / developing your latent abilities

"Control of your own mind — are you ready for it?

Are you ready to do whatever you do, better?

Are you ready to be a better person? Student, housewife, gardener, businessman, teacher, parent, doctor, salesman, politician. Or even free spirit?

Do you want to understand yourself and others better?

Are you ready to listen to your intuition when it tries to tell you something?

Are you ready to remove those limits you keep placing on yourself?

Are you ready to reach for your inner strengths and talents and make them work for you?

Are you ready to control the way you think about your problems? And solve them better?

Are you ready for an incredible trip into your own mind?"

A Silva Mind Control brochure

If you're ready for any or all of these things, you can try a Silva Mind Control training course. Containing elements of positive thinking, alpha brain-wave training, ESP, and Coue's "Every day in every way I'm getting better and better," the classes have attracted 435,000 people to date. Developed by Jose Silva, a self-taught Mexican-American from Laredo, Texas, who spent 26 years in research and study, the program has proliferated until there are Silva trainers operating in most major cities in the United States as well as in Mexico, Canada, England, and Israel.

Cost

After much experimentation, Silva concluded that 48 hours were necessary to train people in his methods. The classes are usually given on four consecutive 12-hour days, or on two consecutive weekends. Cost is $200 for the course.

Designed to develop latent abilities by teaching people how to function at lower brain-wave levels than those of ordinary consciousness, Silva Mind Control claims it can develop innate psychic ability. The Silva version of ESP is not extrasensory perception, something "extra." For its adherents it is Effective Sensory Projection or subjective communication, which is available to everyone. The training promises to improve such skills as concentration, memory, creative imagination, and verbal or artistic expression. It can bolster such personality components as self-confidence, motivation, and leadership; and correct such disturbing behavior patterns as excessive drinking, smoking and overeating, nervous tension, shyness, and insomnia.

Counting Down

Because an electroencephalograph instrument was too expensive and complex, Silva had to manage without one when he began his research. The system he developed, which is still in use in his courses, was to "count down" to inner consciousness levels. To reach Level One, for example, you count down from three to one, repeating each number three times. To reach deeper levels, you start at higher numbers. Since the course does not use any electronic means of monitoring brain waves, it can only be assumed that the method insures that the subject reaches an "alpha" state. Because research indicates that alpha brain waves are associated with creativity, awareness, and intuition, practitioners of Silva Mind Control believe their courses are a means of training people to increase psychic abilities, improve memory, and gain access to their inner consciousness.

The classes teach the use of visual exercises such as a "mirror of the mind" for problem solving. After reaching the proper level, you visualize a full-length mirror with the problem framed in black. You study the problem, mentally remove it and change the frame from black to white. You then see the solution in the white-framed mirror. There are also techniques by which you can program yourself to solve your problems in a dream, to remember your dreams, and to wake up at a specific predetermined time. You can learn glove anesthesia, a method of controlling pain and sometimes bleeding as well.

At a more advanced stage in the course, pupils demonstrate their psychic abilities by visualizing and describing people who are not present and about whom a minimum of information has been given, and diagnosing any illnesses or physical disabilities.

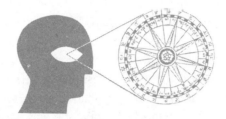

MIND PROBE ONE / visualizing your goals

"But does it work? One only has to look at any of the hundreds of students who have taken the course . . . the fact that they are enjoying a new and better way of life is quite evident . . . ."

Coronet Magazine

Mind Probe One is among the current crop of 40-hour wonder courses that guarantee to change your life, health, outlook, and personal relationships without strain or effort. All you have to do is master their simple, magic technique and life will be wonderful. As described in the introductory seminar, you visualize all the goals you have — health, wealth, success, relaxation, focus, fulfillment — and then visualize Mind Probe as a bus. Climb aboard the bus and you'll be dropped off at your destination.

Cycles

Unlike est, Mind Probe does not follow a militant regimen. Unlike Yoga you need not sit in the lotus position or meditate. You only proceed through various "cycles" of the six-day course and you're home free. What Mind Probe *is* like, beyond the bounds of coincidence, is Silva Mind Control training. They share emphasis on going to deeper levels of the mind and learning simple techniques to control pain, organize sleeping habits, correct excessive smoking or overeating, and improve personal relationships. Mind Probe and Silva "graduation" are virtually identical: Students are given a minimum amount of information about an individual who is not present, and use their new-found psychic ability to supply a description of that person and a diagnosis of any physical disability he may have. According to Mind Probe instructors, no one fails this test, which is particularly remarkable in view of the fact that objective observers found Silva graduates had very spotty records in remote diagnosis. The fact of your ability to accomplish such a feat after only six days of training is supposed to convince you that you can perform whatever else is necessary to straighten out your life. This climactic achievement of the Mind Probe course seems programmed for success.

Founder

Mind Probe One was developed by Dr. Mark Beshara, a former Greek Orthodox priest who mastered a personal crisis in his own life with a system he found so successful he began teaching it to others. A youngish, Levantine guru type with hooded eyes, curly dark hair and beard, Beshara paces back and forth as he describes his methods. You do it all in the privacy of your very own mind — get rid of your limitations, change your thinking, and presto! instant Nirvana!

Success stories are dramatic. A 300-pound man lost 100 pounds in a few months; a man who had smoked three packs of cigarettes a day for 35 years quit smoking after the first night of the course with no withdrawal symptoms and no weight gain; a student who had had intensive psychotherapy for three years was able to discontinue it after Mind Probe training.

Graduates

Mind Probe directors have surveyed their graduates, who now number more than 2,000, and found that 95 percent felt the results were beneficial, 84 percent had two or more aspects of their lives improved, while 54 percent had four or more. There were reports of improved health and emotional stability, of income increased by an average of $3,600 a year.

In an inspired piece of scheduling, a workshop for graduates is dismissed about the same time the Mind Probe seminar for prospective students is winding up. Full of zeal, enthusiasm, and success stories, graduates mingle with prospects and report unanimously happy results from the program. Judy, a cheerful, gray-haired lady, said her life was better in every way, she was easier to live with, and her grown son kept nodding to corroborate her statements. Jan, a middle-aged blonde, said she kept coming back to help with graduations and other portions of the program because she had been helped so much herself she wanted to help others.

In a culture where there is so much sickness, 80 to 90 percent of it considered psychosomatic, programs of this type offer an appealing alternative to tranquilizers because they give participants a chance to take charge of their own lives and some tools with which to do it.

ARICA / a human being is more than anyone believes

"Today it is becoming obvious that competition without end is impossible in a limited system. And our planet has limited resources. In the United States and elsewhere, the most advanced thinkers are evolving a new logic; a kind of thinking that understands that only certain things are possible, that a global or planetary point of view is the only correct one. It is a way of seeing the limitations in reality as to what can be done and how long it takes to do it. It is the recognition that our world and everything in it is pre-established, even the natural laws governing movement and change. This is the attitude of all the top scientists. This way of seeing the entire process, everything as a whole, as a unity, we call Trialectics."

— Oscar Ichazo, founder of Arica

Arica aims to awaken and develop consciousness to a particular level. Happiness, greater aptitude for life, increased understanding, and fuller capacity are all goals of its courses.

Although the original Arica is in Chile, home of Oscar Ichazo, its founder, it is no longer necessary to journey there in order to participate in its unique and rigorous training. There are Arica branches in San Francisco and New York which offer courses throughout the year, and in the summer 40-day residential training programs are available in places as far afield as Vermont, Wisconsin, Vancouver Island, and the mountains of New Mexico.

The Arica training may be taken in various options: a 40-day intensive course, a 16-hour weekend program, or a series of weekday evening sessions. The curriculum is a comprehensive set of precisely balanced techniques, including exercise, dance and movement for the physical body; meditation, mantra, individual analysis assignments, and other work to balance and harmonize mind, body, and emotions.

The new 40-day training incorporates extensive work with the nine systems of the body to develop and balance the basic aspects of the human psyche. The systems are:

Conversation — care

Relations — communication

Syntony — the universe and creation

Coordination — centering

Expression — harmony and grace

Protective — sensitivity

Support and

Movement — capacity to love

Sex — interior development and spiritual consciousness

At Arica, it is believed that practical work brings with it awareness of how the nine systems of the body affect our perceptions of the world, informing us about the psychic quality of both the natural and social objects that surround us. There are five principles of mind which define the humanity of a human being: freedom, contradictions, equality, unity, and objectivity (in the sense of the recognition of reality or the acceptance of "what is what"). The more of these principles each of us has, the closer we come to being totally developed as human beings.

LIFESPRING

another way of "getting clear"

California abounds with groups offering alternative methods of locating the inner self and setting it on the right track. A program that links self-development directly with the Human Potential Movement is offered by a group called Lifespring, headquartered in Garden Grove.

The Lifespring model is based on psychosynthesis, the bringing together and blending of a large number of psychological approaches, which range from Gestalt and bioenergetics to parapsychology and the teachings of many Eastern masters of religion and philosophy. The process is intentionally eclectic and its aim is to bring participants in contact with their essential selves and enable them to recognize their own powers. Lifespring terms this process "getting clear," and its aim is that students become "on purpose" with themselves.

The first step in the Lifespring approach to human problems is the basic seminar, which consists of three consecutive nights and two full days, followed by a post training held the following week. The purpose of the basic seminar is simply "to provide a safe environment in which you may experience that you are already perfect — exactly the way you are." In other words, it's our attitudes that tend to get in the way of our own actualizations, and not our selves. The seminar takes students through a process that allows them to encounter themselves and, for many, this encounter leads to the discovery that they are the cause of

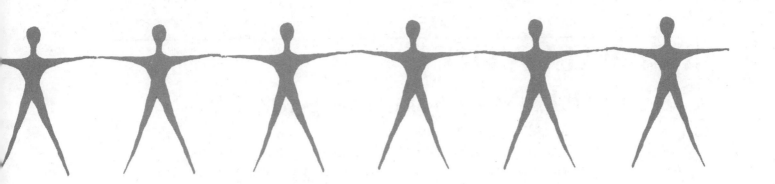

their circumstances and not the effect of them — the basic principle of taking responsibility for self that animates so many human development training programs from est to Arica. The primary objective of the basic seminar is "getting clear" on where you are and what you want to do for yourself, and so confident are Lifespring's founders in the program's worth that even though they claim it does nothing *for* you (you do the work on yourself), they offer to refund the $200 fee to anyone completing the basic program who feels dissatisfied.

The Lifespring program continues through weekly graduate workshops designed to stimulate continued growth, which are available to all graduates at no additional charge. Graduates may also re-audit any number of additional basic seminars, if they wish, at no cost. Additionally, Lifespring offers more advanced Interpersonal Experience for those who want to focus on "getting unstuck" from the learned behavior patterns that are not "on purpose" for themselves, in the form of five-day workshops with a maximum of 20 participants.

Lifespring was founded in San Francisco in 1973 by Randy Revell and John Hanley. Some scholarships covering the flat $200 charge for the basic program are available through the Lifespring Foundation for both individuals and groups in need. The organization has branches in Portland, Oregon; Los Angeles, San Francisco, and Sonoma and Orange counties in California. There are plans to extend eastward before long.

RE-EVALUATION COUNSELING /discharge brings release

The theory behind Re-evaluation Counseling is that human beings, unlike animals, are all born with vast intelligence and the ability to respond to new situations in fresh and creative ways. Unfortunately, these innate abilities are blocked by the traumatic experiences each of us has endured since birth. We get hurt, and while we are hurting, our brains do not properly process the information they are receiving from external stimuli. Instead of the orderly and efficient storage of data which normally takes place, the distressed state causes a piling up of frozen or rigid material, a jamming of the mental gears. Until this blockage is cleared, part of our brain power is inoperative. When new experiences similar to the recorded episodes of distress occur, we meet them with a re-enactment of old distress experiences. This replay of the initial trauma interferes with the mind's normal functioning to an even greater extent than the original episode.

Creator of Re-evaluation

Re-evaluation Counseling is a means of repairing the damage caused by all the old hurtful experiences. Its creator, Harvey Jackins, developed his theories in the 1950s and has been putting them into practice ever since. He believes that the harmful emotions must be discharged by being expressed — an idea that runs counter to most of our societal assumptions about how to deal with people in distress. For example, when a child is hurt, he begins to cry. Our natural inclination is to hush or soothe him and put a stop to the crying. Jackins says that he needs to go on crying for as long as he feels like it, in an atmosphere of relaxed, reassuring attention

from another human being. A child, or an adult, must be allowed not only to cry for as long as is necessary, but to scream, or to shake, or to laugh, or to yawn, until all the pain is discharged. There should be no effort to interfere or distract, or even to sympathize, hard as this may be. The process is naturally longer and more difficult for adults, because the patterns of hurt have rigidified. But Jackins holds the optimistic view that, in the future, adults will have fewer distress experiences to correct because our treatment of children is growing steadily more enlightened and rational.

Co-counseling

Re-evaluation Counseling takes place in pairs, and is consequently often referred to as co-counseling. The idea is that the best way to learn to counsel another person is to experience the discharge and re-evaluation process while being counseled oneself. Starting in the Seattle area, the RC movement has spread widely, and there are now communities of co-counselors in most population centers of the United States and several other countries.

Techniques of re-evaluation include calling the client's attention to what is occurring at the present moment and in his environment generally. Remembering techniques involve the use of free attention to the past, beginning with light, easy memories and moving on to remembering little upsets. The attempt is to get at stored-up tensions, and continue episodes of discharge until the chronic patterns and rigidities have been broken. The discharge must be persistently maintained until all the tension is released, which can be a prolonged process.

Reinforcement

Co-counseling also includes work in groups where techniques and attitudes learned in the pair sessions are reinforced. In one such group, members sit in a circle, holding hands. There is a great deal of warm embracing, not just perfunctory hugs but close, prolonged embraces. Members stand up in the circle one at a time to describe new and pleasant developments in their lives, holding firmly to the leader's hands, beginning and ending their recitals by enthusiastically embracing her. They are encouraged to speak frankly and positively about themselves, to project optimism and confidence, as well as to "discharge" by crying, laughing, shaking, or whatever behavior pattern emerges. There are elements of assertion training in this technique, as well as echoes of Janov's "Primal Scream" therapy. Re-evaluation Counseling, however, is cheaper, simpler, folksier, and — judging from the steadily increasing numbers of members — seems highly effective.

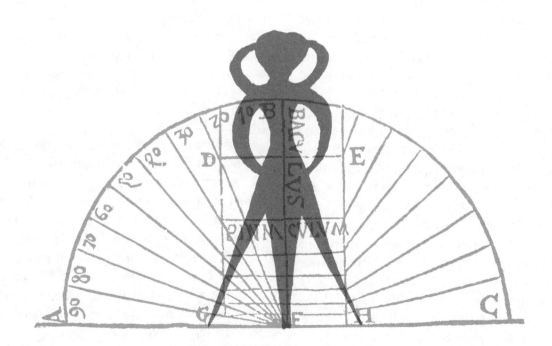

LIVING LOVE CENTER / abolishing expectations

At a place called the Living Love Center in Berkeley, California, is a man called Ken Keyes, Jr. He has combined the teachings of Buddha, Patanjali, Christ, Ram Dass, Charles Berner, John Lilly, Alfred Korzybski, and a host of others, into a means of reaching a higher consciousness. Keyes believes that every current experience can aid us in growth toward higher consciousness if we know how to use it. In his *Handbook to a Higher Consciousness* he says, "The Living Love Way offers mankind one of the most powerful tools for emerging victorious in the race between higher consciousness and the suffering of atomic annihilation, ecologic degradation, prejudice, and the thousandfold ways we separate ourselves from each other."

According to Keyes, it's all a matter of reprogramming our biocomputer — our brain. *How to Make Your Life Work*, another Keyes book, puts it in very simple form. Basically, we automatically are unhappy when people and situations do not fit our expectations. Therefore, expectations create unhappiness. Keyes calls these expectations "addictions," in that they are things conditioned into our body or mind which, if not satisfied, automatically trigger a negative emotion. According to Keyes, these addictions are the sole cause of unhappiness. Because it is obviously impossible to control the world to such a degree that it will always satisfy our addictions/expectations, we must change our expectations — or reprogram our biocomputer. The message is twofold: (1) the outside event, and (2) our inside programming, which determines our response to that event. As Keyes puts it, "The outside world can never give you enough if you are programmed to always want something you

don't already have or more of what you do have. If you always want more you will never have enough."

Addictions

There is a difference, Keyes tells us, between addictions and mild preferences. We can prefer that something happen a certain way and if it does happen . . . fine. But if it doesn't, that's OK too, because it is not a *condition* of our happiness. What we need to do is to set things up mentally so that either way we can't lose.

Loving communication with other people must be made with the clear understanding that it is unconditional — that we will love them regardless of whether or not they satisfy our addictions. If people feel completely free and unpressured by us, they will respond in an equally loving way. "You view life as a game and are not obsessed with winning or losing — you simply enjoy playing. If you're not addicted to winning, there is no way you can ever create the experience of loss."

"Making It"

According to Keyes, there are no "shoulds" or "shouldn'ts" and no "right trip." "The past is non-existent and the future is imaginary. If you're not making it in life right now, you probably won't be making it 10 minutes from now or one day from now . . . . Today is perfect. It is a day which cannot be improved upon . . . unless you are comparing it with the dead past or the imagined future — neither of which really exist. You have to enjoy BEING and stop worrying about BECOMING."

That is the Living Love concept. The people who practice it certainly seem content.

BIOFEEDBACK / what is it? what's in it for me?

A revolutionary but essentially simple concept, biofeedback gives promise of transforming our ideas about the relationship of mind and body. An adaptation of William Henley's famous lines — "I am the master of my mind; I am the captain of my body" — could serve as a model for what man could become with this new tool to reveal what is happening inside himself. Basically the feeding back of biological information to the person whose body is producing that information, biofeedback, has been made to seem complex partly because in the public mind it has been mingled with mysticism, magic, and instant Zen.

Modifying Body Functions

Once they have been made aware that control of a body function is possible by being given a signal showing exactly what is happening with that function, people are learning to modify their heartbeats, blood pressure, muscular and nervous tension — even the rhythm of their brain waves.

It all began in the late '50s and early '60s when several scientists, working independently, noted similar phenomena. Dr. Barbara Brown, one of the pioneers, was doing research on individual responses to color in her laboratory at the Veterans' Administration Hospital in Sepulveda, California. When she gave subjects a signal about their own brain states — in this case, a blue light that shone every time they produced alpha waves (see page 161) - she found that they could learn to produce those alpha rhythms at will. It was Dr. Brown who first used the term *biofeedback* to describe the process she had observed, and in 1969 she founded the Biofeedback Research Society so that those working on this new frontier of knowledge could exchange ideas.

One of the earliest series of experiments was performed in 1958 by Dr. Joseph Kamiya, at that time a sleep researcher at the University of Chicago, who wanted to find out whether people could become aware of an internal state, such as the presence of different kinds of brain waves. He played a sort of guessing game with volunteers hooked up to an electroencephalograph (EEG) machine, asking them to close their eyes and say whether they were in an alpha or nonalpha state. Subjects were told whether their guess was correct, and in a very short time learned to discriminate between the two different states.

The Uses of EMG

Another area of biofeedback was first explored by a pair of psychologists at the University of Colorado Medical School, using electromyographic (EMG) equipment to teach muscle relaxation and treat insomnia, headaches, phobias, and a long list of other tension-related ailments. Dr. Thomas Budzynski, a behavioral therapist who is also an engineer, and his colleague, Dr. Johann Stoyva, worked out innovative techniques and instrumentation. Along with other researchers, they learned that reducing tension via biofeedback can cure, or at least relieve, an astonishing variety of mental and physical illnesses. Much of their work was done with the frontalis, or forehead muscle, which many people aren't even aware they possess. Budzynski and Stoyva found that when people learned to release the tension in the frontalis, they usually relaxed the muscles of the scalp, neck, and upper body as well. Since it is difficult to remain anxious when completely relaxed, this particular therapy can be effective for almost any stress-induced malfunctioning.

In Baltimore, Dr. Bernard Engel worked with heart patients, teaching them to slow down or speed up their hearts at will and to correct cardiac arrhythmias by their own efforts. Patients were guided by a series of lights triggered by their own pulse rates: a yellow light indicated they were on the right track, a red light told them to slow the heart rate down, and a green signal suggested they speed it up. This cardiovascular traffic control was not easy to master and usually required several months of training. Results were highly satisfactory to the subjects, however; once the skill was learned they no longer needed the lights to guide them but could control the pulse rate by "feel." Patients were pleased not only that their off-beat heart rhythms had been corrected, but with the knowledge that they were in control of their own problems.

The Greens

Landmark experimenters in biofeedback, Dr. Elmer and Dr. Alyce Green of the Menninger Foundation in Topeka, Kansas, used temperature-sensitive electrodes strapped to a finger to train subjects to raise the temperature of their hands. Encouraged by suggestions that their hands were growing warmer, were starting to tingle, becoming heavy — all guiding them toward the right "feel" for regulating the flow of blood — patients were able to prevent or relieve migraine headaches. Now that biofeedback is moving out of the research laboratory and into the clinic, there are indications that sympathetic verbal reinforcement can enhance the quality of the response to the biofeedback signal.

More recently, the Greens have been working with theta brain waves, whose presence seems to indicate a state that facilitates the recovery of buried material from the unconscious. If this is so, theta training would appear to have value for artists and writers as well as psychotherapists.

Regulating Hypertension

Hypertension, the potentially dangerous condition so common in our stress-ridden society, was obviously a prime candidate for self-regulation. A Harvard Medical School team developed a feedback instrument and special techniques to train patients to lower their blood pressure. Previous training had been ineffective, but with the aid of the electronic signals patients gradually learned to bring their readings down. At Northwick Park Hospital in Middlesex, England, 34 hypertensive patients were divided into two groups. One was given Yoga relaxation methods along with biofeedback, while the control group was given general relaxation therapy. The Yoga-biofeedback group showed a dramatic drop in blood pressure. When the treatment of the two groups was reversed, the blood pressure of the control group fell to that of the others.

Retraining Damaged Nerves

Biofeedback is not only an effective way of training muscles and nerves to relax; it can also help when either the muscles themselves or the nerves controlling them have been injured. Great strides have been made in retraining damaged nerve-muscle systems, in working with paralysis and other conditions involving actual physiological damage. Using biofeedback, patients in New York's Bellevue Hospital have learned to feed themselves and to perform other functions believed to have been permanently lost. In other research involving nerves that have been severed and reconnected surgically to alternate pathways, biofeedback enables the patient to learn to achieve desired functions and sort them out from unwanted muscle activity by retraining other nerves to provide a new route for messages to the muscles.

A new and most promising application of biofeedback is in the control of epilepsy. Dr. Maurice Sterman of the Veterans' Administration Hospital in Sepulveda is training epileptic patients to produce a special brain-wave pattern of about 12 to 14 cycles per second, slightly above regular alpha rhythms, to make them seizure-free. Regular alpha biofeedback has also been found effective in reducing epileptic seizures. Supporting techniques involve training the subject to recognize and suppress abnormal brain-wave patterns, thus aborting possible epileptic episodes.

Controlling Brain States

Teaching people to recognize many kinds of brain states and reproduce or control them has endless possibilities, such as voluntary control over the scanning of the mind's memory banks. Learning the brain-wave patterns and sequences associated with early stages of sleep, coupled with biofeedback relaxation training, could destroy the demon of insomnia.

Working at Children's Memorial Hospital in Chicago, Dr. Aman U. Khan and his colleagues have had great success in teaching children to control asthma attacks without drugs. By practicing breathing into a specially designed instrument that registers a light when the flow of air is increased, the children learn to relax and voluntarily expand their breathing tubes whenever they feel an attack is imminent. Dr. Khan predicts that eventually many asthma patients will be able to eliminate medication entirely.

One of Dr. Barbara Brown's newest areas of research involves compatible brain waves, or brain-wave empathy between two people. The teams learn to harmonize their brain-wave rhythms by using a light signal which indicates when their alpha waves match. Preliminary results indicate that people who are already empathetic tend to show matching brain-wave patterns and that such matching, indicating psychological or intellectual or emotional affinity, can be learned. Dr. Brown has also suggested that it would be possible for people with terminal illnesses, or in other situations where they might not wish to have their lives prolonged, to will themselves to die before reaching the state where their bodies become the passive creatures of life-support machines.

Exploiters

Unfortunately, the biofeedback phenomenon has attracted faddists, cults, and exploiters as well as serious researchers. Some manufacturers, attempting to capitalize on the excitement about brain-wave training, came up with machines that could actually be harmful. So-called alpha machines sometimes measured scalp movements and eyebrow twitches, and with one device subjects were learning to replicate an epileptic brain-wave pattern.

"Mood" Jewelry

Biofeedback has even invaded the jewelry business, with so-called mood rings, watches, and even belts. The stone, a quartz crystal or other substance that changes color with shifts in temperature, indicates the heat of the finger or part of the body where it is worn. When the wearer is relaxed, blood flows into the extremities and to the surface of the skin, causing temperatures at that point to increase. The reverse is true when the person is tense or anxious, and colors keyed to the change in temperature are supposed to give an indication of the wearer's mood (or whether he has just put down a cold drink).

Even beauticians have joined the parade, with a Beverly Hills beauty salon advertising that wrinkles can be "beeped away." The technique involves relaxing muscle tension in the forehead, jawline, and around the mouth, while firming up areas such as sags and bags under the eyes, all with biofeedback. As the tension is relaxed, the blood vessels expand and circulation is increased. When a researcher attempted to make an appointment to sample these new approaches to beauty, it was explained that there had been problems with the machines and the treatment had been temporarily withdrawn. Like many of the newer applications of biofeedback, theory is racing ahead of clinical application and more research and experimentation is necessary before the trumpeted miracles can occur.

Those most closely associated with biofeedback believe, however, that it may indeed become the healing art of the future, with the mind trained to cure or prevent illnesses of the body as well as controlling its own thoughts and feeling states.

interview / DR. BARBARA BROWN on biofeedback

Brilliant and outspoken, Dr. Barbara Brown's best-selling book New Mind, New Body *is the definitive work on biofeedback. In a world where people feel they are increasingly losing control over their lives, the possibility raised by this new method of synthesizing body, mind and emotion offers an exciting prospect to laymen as well as psychologists and physicians. Barbara Brown was given a great deal of independence very early; she is still an iconoclastic and original thinker whose insights into synthesis have helped make her one of the shapers of the new concept of biofeedback. Small, independent, humorous, Dr. Brown is an innovative researcher who has always worked on the frontiers of mind-body knowledge. She received her Ph.D. in Pharmacology from the University of Cincinnati and for the past 12 years has worked at the Veterans' Administration Hospital in Sepulveda, California, primarily on research funded by the National Institute of Mental Health.*

LANDE: What is biofeedback?

BROWN: Even many biofeedback researchers and practitioners are somewhat confused about that. I try to explain it in several different ways. The term is simply a shorthand expression meaning the feeding back of biological information to the person who is generating the information — all the little bits and pieces about biological activity,

what the muscles are doing, or the circulatory and gastrointestinal systems, or any selected activity. When people have that kind of information it becomes meaningful to them and they can use it. My definition of biofeedback would probably be that it is the process of learning voluntary control over vital functions. And then you also have to give a description of biofeedback, because it is also a procedure. You describe how you can detect physiological activity in a sensory manner — you can use your eyes to see that your hand is sweating, or you can use some kind of sensory apparatus which can feel that it is sweating, or you can use an instrument.

There are several stages in biofeedback. The first is the detection of the physiological activity. Usually, but not always, an instrument is used to do this, much as a physician detects physiological activity during a medical examination. The instrument amplifies and uses that activity to produce some kind of display which is synchronized with the actual activity. Next comes the training phase, which means becoming acquainted with what is going on with internal activities, in very much the way we become acquainted with what our muscles are doing when we learn to ride a bicycle. Of course the obvious consequence of this is the third phase: learning control.

I should say one more thing — that since the brain waves reflect what the mind is doing, we have a shot at feeding back information about what is happening in the mind, indirect though it may be.

LANDE: Where is biofeedback today?

BROWN: It has grown up a great deal. From a practical standpoint, it amounts to the use of biofeedback technique largely to relieve the effects of stress and tension and anxiety. We react to the environment mainly by becoming tense and stressed. That is the basis of the vast majority of emotional or mental problems, and most of our psychosomatic illnesses, of which there may be many more than we have ever dreamed of. That is one aspect of biofeedback today.

The second is the learning of voluntary control over biological systems that we expect

to be disrupted only by physical change and not by emotional stress problems. Take, for example, epilepsy. We normally feel that it is some kind of an abnormality of brain function, certainly not an emotionally induced type of illness. And yet we can control epilepsy with brain-wave biofeedback techniques. It is not recognized as a stress-related illness, so there appear to be organic disturbances which can be controlled with biofeedback. Usually I term this simply normalizing body functions.

Unfortunately, when you deal with brain waves, you are into a highly specialized area and one that is so vast it will probably be years before we make any great strides in brain-wave biofeedback. You see, what we call alpha or beta or theta activity are physiologic events that are very arbitrary — in fact, they are man-made isolations of brain electrical activity.

LANDE: Would you define alpha, beta, theta, and delta activity?

BROWN: Brain waves are composed of both rhythmic and nonrhythmic activity and are classified on the basis of the frequency of the rhythmic activity. When we make records of brain-wave activity, we see that some waves have crests and valleys that are fairly symmetrical and rhythmic. By virtue of the equipment we use, we lose probably 50 percent of the EEG before we even begin to look at it, and of the remaining 50 percent we can identify anywhere from 20 to 60 percent of the activity, depending upon the individual's state of consciousness. So when we use the terms alpha, beta, theta, etc., we are talking about a relatively small proportion of brain-wave activity.

We define these waves on the basis of their rhythmic frequency. Alpha activity has been found to have an average frequency of approximately 10 cycles per second; theta has roughly half that, or an average frequency of five cycles per second; delta activity has a frequency of about half that of theta, from one to three cycles per second, and it is not really rhythmic, because these waves do not appear in groups. Beta activity is discussed in two forms: neurophysiologists talk about it as either rhythmic or nonrhythmic beta activity. The beta activity which has been studied is mainly from 13 to 28 cycles per second.

LANDE: Are most of us in the beta stage?

BROWN: No, brain-wave activity is always extremely mixed. You can find all waves probably at most times, depending upon what the individual is doing and his state of consciousness.

LANDE: To achieve relaxation, is the goal to reach an alpha state?

BROWN: Not necessarily. One of the most famous neurophysiologists in the world has never had an alpha wave, and yet he is a very relaxed guy. It depends upon the spectrum of brain-wave activity of the individual. The reason many people feel alpha is present during relaxed states is that they have studied only those people who had a lot of alpha activity. They have not studied people who don't have much alpha activity, because their brain activities are very difficult to record — very small and subject to a lot of distortion.

LANDE: How would you describe an alpha state?

BROWN: It does not have to mean a state of relaxation; it can equally well mean a state of attention to internal events and/or the Zen or Yoga concept of turning the attention inward and concentrating on inward perceptions. The state is very difficult to describe and it has not been described well, because we have neither the words nor the experiences of these different states of consciousness to do so. The best existing description suggests that when alpha is present in EEG, the individual is in a state of receptivity. He is ready to have sensory impressions made upon him, but there just are not any coming in. When the sensory impression is calm, his state shifts, so there has been a tendency to say that when alpha is present in the brain-wave pattern, the individual is in a passive state. This is not true, because the person is very likely attending to, or being aware of, internal states that he normally does not pay any attention to. That is all it is: shifting attention from the external environment to the internal environment.

LANDE: How about when one goes into a deeper state, which you call theta?

BROWN: It is difficult to say whether these are deeper states or not. Theta activity can accompany various states of consciousness from being very alert and oriented, to drowsiness, and even dreaming and recall, and so on. Eventually we will have to define different kinds of theta activity and base that upon very specific brain electrical characteristics. But because of the relative ignorance of the investigators about brain-wave activity and about states of consciousness, we don't as yet have good definitive data about what these things mean.

LANDE: I want to get into aspects other than the brain — the application of biofeedback to problems. Where is the best center for such help?

BROWN: That is a real problem. Unfortunately, biofeedback had most of its origins in psychology, and psychologists by and large have not really understood the physiology they are working with, and so have made many bad assumptions. They have also attempted to fit the biofeedback phenomenon into older theories, particularly of learning, because biofeedback is a learning process. I happen to believe that the biofeedback learning phenomenon is quite a different kind of learning from any that has ever been defined in academia, and no existing theories explain it at all well. In laboratories, the biofeedback learning is small. So we have a good deal of fragmentation of effort in the field. Virtually no one other than myself has attempted to sit down and try to make sense out of all the data, and develop concepts and theories. Of course, I was fortunate because I had most of the data, kept after it, and — four books later — I think I have it pretty well sorted out.

LANDE: I hope you are continuing your plans for a clinic.

BROWN: It is very difficult. Every time I want to develop some kind of center or clinic, the exploiters are ready to move in. I can't work with such people, because it isn't very honest intellectually.

LANDE: I have heard you mention bringing together Eastern and Western philosophy. Would you go into that a little?

BROWN: I feel I have gained a lot of insight from analyzing the biofeedback phenomenon and developing theories about why it occurs, and about various states of consciousness that we have never been able to describe well. Most of the concepts of Eastern philosophy are based upon awareness of internal states, and then expanding or perceiving that point up to awareness of consciousness itself, and then into awareness of the universal consciousness. One of the things I have done is to establish the physiological chain of

reactions and responses that occurs in shifting states of consciousness. I have also been able to indicate basic similarities between the Western approach and the Eastern approach, once you take away the superstitions and mythologies. In the East they have better understanding of consciousness because they deal with it all the time and are used to talking about these things, whereas we in the West have very little education in these areas.

LANDE: What is consciousness?

BROWN: I believe all the important mental activities really occur subconsciously and we do have voluntary control over all mental processes — we just never knew we had it, because Western civilization for more than 2,000 years prohibited exploring different states of consciousness. For society to continue to exist, people had to agree upon an external reality. So, save for a few psychodynamically oriented psychiatrists, we have never even thought about mental processes that occur without conscious awareness. Yet I have gone through the scientific literature and documented hundreds of studies which demonstrate unequivocally the reality, complexity, and precision of subconscious mental processes. It is a fantastic world.

I wrote an essay about it in which I started out very simplistically by saying, All right, we have certain kinds of feelings and concepts that we can agree upon by verbal exchange with other people. All of this, if we analyze it, is by analogy to something that happens *outside.* Even when we say, "I feel calm and peaceful," I think these words, and all our words that describe feeling states, were developed by agreeing upon analogies to events in the external world — calm and peaceful after the battle, for example.

LANDE: Or after bad weather.

BROWN: Right. We have had to adopt this kind of a language. But I go even further. Even the speech center of the brain is developed solely for the survival of the species, not for the survival of the individual. Not for the further evolution of man, but only to facilitate communication, so that groups can survive. The speech center is literally the only formation or specialized area in the brain which is not bilateral — it is only on one side of the brain. That has to mean something very important with respect to evolution.

In addition to mental events which are concerned mainly with objective appreciation, which I call *consensual consciousness*, there is what I call *subjectively appreciative mental activity*, the kind that we as yet have no way to communicate. We feel, we know, we do, we perform, and we simply haven't the facility yet to explain some of these things. There are all the elusive fascinating states of consciousness that everyone experiences, but which society has said we *cannot* explore. I suppose this will be the next stage in our evolution, a stage of concentrating and defining much more precisely the various things we experience when consciousness is dissociated from consensual consciousness.

LANDE: Are you saying that only through inner awareness can you achieve this state?

BROWN: I am saying, primarily, that in order to evolve further, in order to become aware of the fantastic world of the subconscious mental processes, we need information. To me, information is the basis of everything. We in the West have been blinded by our philosophy from exploring anything that could not be agreed upon by social communication processes.

I don't think either Eastern or Western philosophy is correct; both have elements which are extremely useful. The difficulty with Indian philosophy is that everything is considered to be Maya, to be illusion, and I think you have to recognize two realities. There *is* a universal consciousness — I don't think there is any question about that. I recently redefined it as a sense of order. Every one of us has a sense of order. It is just something people haven't talked about. The Indian only wants to live with the internal reality, the universal consciousness; everything else is an illusion, whereas we in the West only recognize the external reality; we don't, save in very rare instances, recognize that there is consciousness which can be "in tune with the universe," one that can be very rich and very nourishing. I believe you have to live with both realities in order to have the most fulfilled life. And, in the present world, they are distinctly separate.

LANDE: People who practice meditation, Transcendental or other, report that they have an experience of profound insight.

BROWN: I think a lot of that depends upon the kind of meditation they are practicing, how serious they are about it, and how mature they are in it. Any time you sit down and start thinking, you are obviously going to have profound changes in consciousness. Any time you have a different thought your perspective changes, sometimes very profoundly, especially if you continue in that vein.

LANDE: It is interesting that in a meditative process you are told to try not to think.

BROWN: That is the Americanized version. But that is a very immature form of meditation. Yoga meditation insists that you have to concentrate, to really work your mind. It isn't easy to try to concentrate on a single thing or thought. That is a very difficult mental exercise. TM, as it was advertised, is not that; TM is sitting quietly. It has been reported in two scientific papers that practiced TM meditators spend most of their meditation time in levels one, two, three, or four of sleep — one being the lightest, and four being the deepest. So it would seem that TM people simply learn how to catnap, which is a form of microsleep. You don't, by the way, have very much alpha activity during sleep.

LANDE: Why do you think people are searching today more than ever before?

BROWN: The American public has been so deprived of any looking inward. They have been too preoccupied with the material universe to think about it. Education has been at fault too. We have not given people information, and we have not given them the systems by which to think. And no one wants to take any responsibility. We have a few people in the world who have certainly tried, but they are just human beings. God knows if there are going to be any more of those people.

LANDE: Who are your heroes?

BROWN: Me — I am my own hero! I have come to the conclusion that there aren't any.

LANDE: What do you believe in now?

BROWN: Actually, I believe you have got to make the best of both worlds. There are the two realities, a material reality and the mental or spiritual reality, however you want to speak about it. I speak about it as a mental reality.

LANDE: Which is more important?

BROWN: The most important thing is to be aware that there are the two realities and you have to deal with both. Without one you cannot deal with the other. It works both ways. So many of our concepts about human beings, human behavior, human thought, are inadequate. There are many errors in logic and recognizing the realities.

LANDE: Give me an example.

BROWN: If we take man and compare him to the next lower species, the apes, with respect to the illnesses that he has, there is a discrepancy almost beyond belief. Man has infinitely more kinds of illness than the apes — this says, I believe, that there is something terribly different about man, probably a difference in his relationship between himself and his society. The majority opinion is that emotional disturbances are due to stimulation of the brain, endocrine or neural structures, and that such illnesses are mostly due to the fact that physical changes take place. But I keep saying, How did the inciting stimuli get to these structures in the first place? It was social information getting into the individual, and unfortunately it was *mis*information, not real information that indicated facts about an individual's social situation. I am almost convinced that most illnesses are caused by errors in social systems — in fact, all illnesses, save for injury or accident, and certain kinds of physical abnormalities, usually genetic.

LANDE: What about cancer?

BROWN: I don't know. Cancer among nondomesticated animals is extremely rare. I think human cancer may be a social disease.

LANDE: What does that mean?

BROWN: There we get into severe complications. I have developed a concept that because of the need to survive socially, we react to social information. Very often that information is completely erroneous, yet our mental processes attempt to reconcile what the body does with what the brain or mind says the body ought to be doing. This leads the physiological systems into great errors, both of performance and of function. This can actually change body function and susceptibility to disease.

LANDE: Are we in fact programming disease into the body?

BROWN: Yes. That is what biofeedback is all about. There are some incredible findings that indicate once the brain has the right information, it can normalize abnormal processes very quickly — sometimes so immediately that you don't even have time to measure change. You give the biofeedback signal, and the minute you start measuring the process, it has normalized — really incredible.

This is an indication that we have facilities to absorb, evaluate, and integrate information that bears upon very specific and precise physiological processes, and then we can *intentionally* direct normalizing.

LANDE: How do you erase all that faulty information?

BROWN: Apparently the right information wipes out all the wrong information. It really is amazing.

LANDE: Can we call that enlightenment?

BROWN: It doesn't even have to come to any kind of conscious level — it can happen almost automatically. For some time now I have summarized the fundamental implications of the biofeedback phenomenon as "the patient is no longer the object of treatment, he *is* the treatment" — because only the patient can work with himself. It is all in his head.

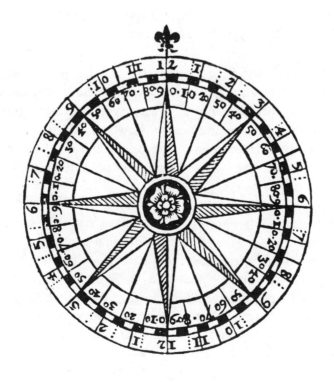

167

LINKING MIND AND MATTER

by ELMER AND ALYCE GREEN

In an article, "Regulating Our Mind-Body Processes," Dr. Elmer E. Green, Director of the Voluntary Controls Program of The Menninger Foundation, and his wife, Alyce, Co-Director of the program, suggest that viewing body, mind and spirit as structural expressions of one basic energy may help to explain how some people can regulate their mind-body processes. In the sections excerpted here, the Greens discuss their observations of two unusual people and the field-of-mind theory they hypothesize as a result:

The limitations of biofeedback for self-regulation of psychological/physiological processes are not known at present, but research with unusual people indicates that the limits extend considerably further than most Western scientists thought five years ago. Research on unusual powers of self-regulation is interesting in its own right, but the importance of such research lies in the fact that the physiological processes over which control is demonstrated are often the same processes that are involved in psychosomatic disorders. If physiological "disorders" can be induced and removed at will by certain persons, it indicates that a training method probably can be developed

for the average person for voluntary control of psychosomatic disease without the use of drugs, hypnosis, or surgery. The explanation of "how they do it" may shed light both on the origin and on the voluntary amelioration of psychophysiological disorders.

Swami Rama and Jack Schwarz

We have had the opportunity to observe two unusual persons in our psychophysiology laboratory — an Indian yogi, Swami Rama, and a "Western Sufi" from Holland, Jack Schwarz. Without going into details of their demonstrations, Swami Rama demonstrated voluntary control of his heart by causing it to cease pumping blood for 17 seconds, putting it in a condition of atrial flutter. He also demonstrated control of the major arteries in his wrist and hand, causing a temperature difference of nine degrees Fahrenheit between two spots on the palm of his hand, two inches apart. One-half of his palm turned pink and the other half gray. There was no evidence of striate muscular involvement.

Jack Schwarz demonstrated that he could stop the bleeding of wounds from a sailmaker's needle driven through his biceps (in two seconds after he said "now it stops"), and that he could prevent bleeding entirely from such wounds. He also demonstrated "pain control" by showing no significant physiological responses (heart rate, GSR changes, etc.) in three trials when burning cigarettes were held against his forearm for as long as 25 seconds. In addition to their physiological demonstrations, both Swami Rama and Jack Schwarz demonstrated on numerous occasions the Cayce-like ability to report on mental, emotional, and physical conditions of persons whom they did not know or had not seen until asked for their "perceptions" relative to these people.

Explanation

The importance of these demonstrations by Swami Rama and Jack Schwarz does not lie in the physiological-psychological data alone but also in their explanations of "how it can happen." When reduced to one sentence their explanation is quite simple, even if it is not easy to understand. "All of the body is in the mind, but not all of the mind is in the body." In this view, the mind, contrary to the classical concept, is a real energy structure (field) of which the body, including the brain, is merely the densest section. This is definitely not the mental concept of Berkeley, the British philosopher, rather it is a concept similar to the field theory of modern science. All physiological and parapsychological data are subsumed under one field-of-mind idea.

. . . It is worth noting that parapsychological data, especially those involving psychokinesis, are the main scientific impediments to the behaviorist theory of biological phenomena. It is especially useful to observe, therefore, that the field-of-mind theory provides a rationale for parapsychological events. It encompasses the "normal" physical, biological, and psychological facts of science, and also provides a matter-and-consciousness substrate for mystical, spiritual, and altered states of consciousness phenomena.

Fields of Energy

It can be hypothesized that a field of mind surrounds our planet, even as a gravitational field, a magnetic field, and an electrostatic field do. In fact, all fields are hypothesized to exist as subsidiary parts of a general planetary field of mind. This field is an energy domain in which there is a multidimensional continuum of physical, emotional, mental, and spiritual substance . . . . Each subsidiary field — physical, emotional, mental, etc. — has associated with it specific existential states, states of consciousness. Perceptions of these states comprise the basic data of all knowledge in the view of many persons, and though we discuss ancient religion, modern science, telepathy, hypnosis, or voluntary control of internal states via biofeedback, we nevertheless speak of a "continuous" domain.

. . . The human being is represented, therefore, as a composite of many kinds of force, mostly at an unconscious level. A person is normally aware of his own unconscious nature to only a limited extent, but awareness can be extended beyond the normal boundary of the "conscious" through biofeedback and through various kinds of meditation, prayer, yogic exercises, fasting, autogenic training, drugs, hypnosis, or psychoanalysis.

Energy Links

. . . Mind and matter require an energy link, a common substrate, if the Stanford demonstrations with Uri Geller and the phenomena observed in our laboratory with Swami Rama, are to "fit" into a theory.

One of the most provocative comments made this century in respect to parapsychology was F. Myers' suggestion around 1900 that we might eventually find that mind manifests through the brain by psychokinetic manipulation of neural tissue.

Voluntary Control of Internal States

Biofeedback data and parapsychological data together are stimulating renewed research on the problem Myers pondered, the mind-body problem, and perhaps humans are close to a breakthrough in consciousness. If so, we need to develop a significant measure of voluntary control of internal states at many levels, psychological and physiological. The possibilities of experiencing strange states of consciousness and developing unusual psychic powers are enticing to many persons, but it seems to us that psychosomatic health, inner tranquility, and psychic freedom through self-awareness are the best "powers" of all, the ones most likely to give help in stabilizing the mental and emotional "field" of our planet.

THE BODY

People have forgotten what the savage instinctively knows — that a perfect body is the supreme instrument of life.

— Havelock Ellis

There is a direct correlation between the state of the mind and the state of the body. As the stresses of society continue to plague man's psyche, they affect his physical functioning as well. From ancient times man has sought to rid his body of its maladies, to strengthen, heal, and preserve it. "Every man is the builder of a temple called his body," and to keep that temple in a state of grace has been the goal of continuing study and experimentation.

With the increase in technological development has come, ironically, a corresponding removal from the body envelopes that enclose us. The emotional stresses of our day are directly reflected in the way we stand, sit, walk; the distractions that press in on us prevent our being in touch with the way we make contact with the ground, the air, each other. One of the major goals of the current sensory awareness movement is to bring us back to an awareness of our bodies. Such teaching would be unnecessary and ridiculous to a Trobriand Islander, who has never lost that instinctive knowledge in the first place . . . .

171

I am a part of all
those whom I have met

Tennyson

BIOENERGETICS

Developed primarily by Alexander Lowen, the theory of bioenergetics is based on the orgone energy and body armor theory of Wilhelm Reich (see page 56) and the idea of living in harmony, both with our natural environment and our bodies' rhythms. Bioenergetics believes that we *are* our bodies. As Lowen puts it, "Ego and body form a unity. We cannot reject one in favor of the other . . . ."

Lowen's original approach was through the treatment of schizophrenia, a condition that exaggerates the divorce between mind and body. To help schizophrenic patients get back in touch with their bodies, Lowen developed a series of exercises that would bring about natural healing: arching the body in forward and backward bows, or over a stool, in order to become aware of its sensations and to produce release of tension through involuntary movements, such as deeper breathing and tremors. He followed these with a series of active movements, such as striking a couch or bed, kicking and flailing with the arms — actions that recall the childish ability to abandon the body to movement, and help to get back the capacity to release emotions through physical means, instead of bottling them up inside.

Subsequently, Lowen found these methods had even better results with well people, and the use of bioenergetic techniques spread widely among psychotherapists — so widely, in fact, that the term has now come to be used almost as an umbrella for a variety of approaches to mind-body integration. In essence, it describes a process rather than a specific technique — the awakening of body awareness in an individual, which can be accomplished either by the person himself, or through the aid of a "giver" or healer, who can manipulate the body to help stimulate and harmonize the levels of energy of which it is capable.

FUNCTIONAL INTEGRATION / MOSHE FELDENKRAIS

The Feldenkrais method is a means of uniting body and mind by concentrating on the body in order to affect the mind. Feldenkrais believes that if man can be attuned to his body, he can then establish a rapport with his environment, thus alleviating conditions of stress. Expansion of the body will expand his consciousness and gradually heighten his self-understanding. Using more than 1,000 elaborate exercises, each with some 40 variations, the Feldenkrais method virtually rebuilds the human frame. It is designed to develop more precise insight into what one is doing — how to monitor the flexing of the muscles being used, how to control breathing, how to increase fluidity.

Now in his mid-70s, Moshe Feldenkrais is a powerfully built, surprisingly light-footed, incredibly energetic man. His approach to mental health and physical efficiency is a holistic one. He emigrated originally from Russian Poland to Palestine, and afterward studied in France. Neither a physician nor a psychotherapist — his doctorate is actually in physics — he developed his theory of proper body alignment through massive research on what makes the body function, undertaken originally because of a debilitating physical injury which prompted him to study literature on anatomy, physiology, psychology, and anthropology.

Feldenkrais insists he does not treat, he teaches neural repatterning to ailing people. His aim is a body organized to work with minimal effort and maximum efficiency. He believes learning should be pleasant, and since setting goals automatically creates a resistance to be worked against, his exercises are intended to accomplish slightly less than each person is capable of.

Prisoners of Bad Habits

According to Feldenkrais, we are the prisoners of the bad habits we learned during our formative years — often we are not even aware of them. In order to increase flexibility, we have to break those habits. Functional Integration, as he calls his method, is a system of slow-moving meditative exercises in which the body is taught first to become aware of its own image. Each joint learns to move to its full range, and then is honed by lessons in specific motions. The pace of the exercises is slow because the more precise the movement, the finer the interactions of the muscles that come into play.

What Feldenkrais calls his working picture of a human being consists of the nervous system (the core); the skeleton, viscera and muscles (the envelope); and the environment — space, the social milieu, and gravitation. The exercises are mostly done lying down, eliminating the use of antigravity muscles. Typically, sessions begin by asking the subject, lying on his back, to check out where the various parts of his body touch the floor and become aware of how they are doing so. Then various sequences of movements are gone through; there are hundreds of them, which means that the person performing them never runs out of surprises and illuminations.

There is no straining for effort. Each sequence is structured to allow before-and-after comparisons, in which the pupil discovers connections he had not previously realized. The purest form of instruction is the "image only" method, in which the pupil is asked to perform movements without moving a muscle outside his mind's eye, thus learning awareness of his body below the threshold of consciousness.

Heightened Awareness

Advantages of the Feldenkrais method? Those who have undergone it report heightened awareness, elimination of stiff, tight muscles, and ability to mentally rehearse a physical task before it actually has to be done, thereby relieving some of the anxiety associated with the movement.

The Feldenkrais theory is steadily gaining popularity. Part of its attraction may lie in the fact that it demonstrates nothing is permanent about our behavior patterns save our belief that they are so.

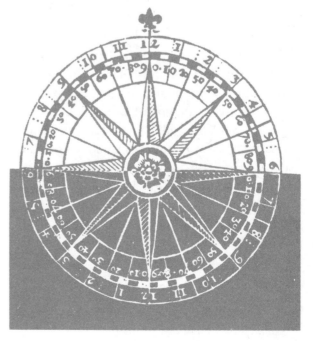

THE ALEXANDER METHOD

The Alexander method is a system of body dynamics. Its founder, F. Matthias Alexander, lost his voice as a result of a serious illness and could find no medical help. In the course of experimenting on his own, he discovered a whole chain of tensions linking the muscular movement of his face and the alignment of his neck and shoulders to the loss of his voice. He contrived to change the relationship of his head to his spinal column — and in doing so, cured himself.

From this discovery stems the Alexander technique of achieving a balanced use of the body with minimum stress. The basic premise is that incorrect alignment of head, neck, and shoulders sets off imbalances that throw the whole muscular system into an abnormal, and consequently stress-causing, state. Alexander-style readjustment of the skeletal-muscular system can greatly help people who have problems ranging from nervousness and insomnia through loss of appetite to fear and anger.

Our bad posture habits begin in childhood, continue as we go through schooling, and by the time we reach adulthood, have become so firmly implanted that we are completely unaware of them. We try to shift the blame for our physical discomfort to other areas and to cure the problem by artificial methods. Alexander plainly states that the solution can come only from within — from changing the basic ways in which we move and rest.

With the Alexander technique it is not enough to explain a malfunction and how it is to be corrected. The student must first learn his faulty patterns of acting, train himself not to respond in his habitual way, and gradually learn the new patterns.

During the training the teacher manipulates the student's posture, guiding him into the correct positions, aiding him to become accustomed to this new, correct body alignment. By first learning the relationship between head and neck, his awareness expands to include all the connections of his body and to learn that they cannot be separated, nor can the mind be separated from the body, any more than he can think of himself as something totally apart from his environment.

ROLFING

Does it defy imagination that more than 30,000 people have paid at least $40 a session (usually for a series of 12 consecutive sessions) to have their bodies manipulated, stretched — often tormented? In other words, structurally integrated; in yet another word, Rolfed.

Basis of System

Dr. Ida Rolf of Chicago based her system of Rolfing on Wilhelm Reich's theory of "character armor," the theory being that consciousness lies in the body as well as in the brain. Because mind and body are interconnected, the results of past traumatic experiences show themselves in a person's posture, "blocking" the easy, natural access to movement each of us had as a child. If these facades with which we surround ourselves can be broken down by realigning the body the way it was intended to be, the consciousness can be expanded by the clearer vision that results from the disintegrated blocks to understanding.

Benefits

Rolfing is a deep-muscle massage — and, if there is resistance, it can be extremely painful. Its real benefits are said to be emotional. Once you have been Rolfed you have experienced material from your past that has been tying you in knots, and once experienced, those feelings of anxiety are gone for good. The body is now loose and centered, alive and ready for the next encounter.

It is enlightening to discuss Rolfing with people who have been through it. Whether they found the experience positive or negative, they remember very vividly how it felt:

> I had just lost my parents in a car accident and felt completely alone. My emotions seemed to be locked up inside me and I had no idea how to let them out. After going through several types of therapy, including five or six different encounter groups, I heard about Rolfing. I can't deny that it was painful, but I can't dispute the fact that I felt a release of a lot of my tensions after the first four sessions. I remember after the first time I cried for hours . . . . Just dealing with making myself go back again was a real accomplishment. Rolfing was terrific for me, and I feel stronger just for having gone through it.

That was Leslie Diamond's experience with Rolfing. Paulette Tov expresses another, less positive point of view:

> I went into Rolfing in the first place because I thought it would help my muscle tone. It was really painful — so painful that it's hard for me to believe it could be beneficial. There are some things I don't think man should deliberately inflict on himself. When there's as much pain as we all undergo involuntarily, I couldn't bring myself to continue paying someone to beat me up.

Legitimate Rolfing masseurs generally have a good working knowledge of the human anatomy. They are trained to know where this manipulation is appropriate and where it would do serious damage to the body tissues. Because of the vehemence with which the massage is applied, it is important when seeking this treatment to choose a skilled practitioner.

The benefits claimed for Rolfing are physical as well as psychological, in the areas of toning and realigning the body and improving the posture. The major goal, however, is to unblock patterns or connections which interfere with the energy flow, and thereby achieve an integrated mind-body system.

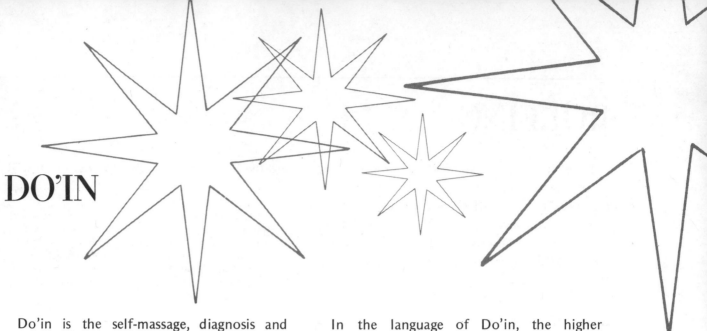

DO'IN

Do'in is the self-massage, diagnosis and quick cure of one's own body. It is an ancient art which passed through time as a secret teaching, finally surfaced in the Orient, and eventually — as most arts have — found a home in America.

Self-Awareness

To help the individual remain in harmony with nature, Do'in encourages body awareness through helping the person become attuned not to someone else's idea of his functioning, but to his own. Its daily practice establishes a discipline of focusing the mind on a single purpose, and allows the individual to become aware of small bodily dysfunctions before they become major problems. As this discipline of self-awareness becomes ingrained, the subconscious mind leads the individual to eat more sensibly, be more responsive to the vibrations around him, and behave in patterns that are less stressful.

Do'in distinguishes between finite stimuli that are perceived through the body, and infinite ones, those caused by higher universal vibrations which only those who are properly attuned are able to receive. To receive the ideal, balanced mixture of finite and infinite impulses, body, brain, and nervous system must be in perfect condition.

In the language of Do'in, the higher vibrations of the universe are contained in an electromagnetic energy or *ki*, which is received at the various pressure points and transmitted along the body's meridians. When a body is functioning at a peak of health, *ki* is circulating freely all through it, and Do'in concentrates on aiding that freedom of flow. When an organ malfunctions, points along its meridian become painful, even when the organ itself shows no signs of problems. Pain at these points indicates that *ki* has bottlenecked and is not being distributed properly. Gentle Do'in massage, using slow, deep, sustained finger pressure with the flat surface of the thumb in a circular rotation, calms the accumulated energy and rejuvenates the flow.

According to Do'in enthusiasts, excessive eating, a craving for artificial food, and the desire to smoke result from "false hunger" — caused by a bloated condition of the mucous gastric and intestinal membranes, which makes them tender, stimulating a sensation of hunger. Do'in claims to be able to ease and eliminate any pain or illness, no matter how violent or chronic. A statement accompanies this, however, to the effect that the cure will be permanent only if the patient studies, understands, and maintains a macrobiotic way of life (see *Macrobiotics*, page 199).

SHIATSU

Shiatsu, literally, "finger pressure," is a manual massage method used on various body muscles to treat a number of illnesses. Its techniques are based on the fact that when the body experiences pain, the instinctive impulse is to touch the place that hurts. The body has enormous powers of regeneration and self-repair. Shiatsu makes use of these powers without the Western world's dependence on doctors, drugs, and injections.

Combustion Processes

How does it work? Tokujiro Namikoshi, a specialist in the field who has treated more than 100,000 patients, explains it on these lines in his book, *Shiatsu*:

Movement in the human body is produced by roughly 450 muscles which are attached to bones at either end. The body manufactures the energy to contract them by a complex process of converting nutrients into glycogen, and combining this with oxygen from the lungs. This combustion process generates energy to power the muscles; it also produces a residue of lactic acid, which can accumulate in a muscle, and prevent it from contracting. The fatigue, brought on by too much lactic acid in the muscle, can be helped by taking a rest — which gives the arteries a chance to bring in fresh glycogen while the veins remove the buildup of lactic acid. But if the fatigue lasts too long, the muscles contract improperly and illness can result. The application of Shiatsu finger pressure over an improperly contracted muscle can cause 80 percent of the accumulated lactic acid to reconvert to glycogen. "This eliminates fatigue and, with it, improper muscular contraction, the cause of illness."

Shiatsu pressure is created through the use of the thumbs, the index, middle, and ring fingers, and the palm of the hand. The degree of pressure depends upon the patient's symptoms and condition. If a second party is administering Shiatsu, the posture should be such that he can apply his entire weight, if necessary. Of course, when administering Shiatsu to oneself, pressure needs are much easier to regulate.

Pressure Points

Treating a specific illness usually requires pressure at a point near the part that is ailing; but sometimes applying pressure to distant areas can bring great improvement: for instance, pressure on the soles of the feet can relieve kidney disease, and pressure on the left hand can strengthen the heart. Duration of the pressure lasts only a few seconds, and its extent should cause a sensation somewhere between pleasure and pain.

Through the years Shiatsu has developed into a self-massage or shared-massage technique that is growing in popularity as awareness of it increases. It can be done anywhere, alone or with another person, and does not require hours of strain to effect results.

KINESIOLOGY

Applied kinesiology was first developed by George Goodheart in 1963. It involves the study and testing of muscles and uses various treatment techniques to change muscular-skeletal postures. A form of bioenergetics, kinesiology organizes the principles of anatomy, physiology, and physics and applies them to the mechanism of movement. Included in kinesiological theory are such techniques as acupuncture, acupressure, Kundalini Yoga (explained on page 295), and polarity therapy.

Acupuncture and Moxibustion

Acupuncture is the method of changing the metabolic and circulatory processes of the human body either through the rotation of small needles, usually made of stainless steel wire, or by magnetism, electric stimulation, or suction, applied to certain points on the body. In conjunction with this process, moxibustion is often used — the application of balls, sticks, or rolls of dried moxa (a fuzzy material made from wormwood leaves) which are burned in order to warm, sometimes even to deliberately scorch, the skin.

The use of acupuncture and moxibustion, both traditional Chinese medicinal practices, is based on the theory that the human body, when attacked by disease, becomes a battleground for two forces: the body's power of resistance and the cause of the disease. Following diagnosis of the disease, acupuncturists determine either that the body is under-reacting to fighting it off, in which case the needles will be used to stimulate; or it is over-reacting, in which case the acupuncture must work as a relaxant.

Acupuncture has been widely publicized, both positively and negatively, especially since travelers to Communist China began to bring back spectacular reports of its widespread use as anesthesia during major surgery. It has been in use in China as far back as 1600 B.C. and by the very fact of its longevity would seem to have some validity.

Acceptance of acupuncture in this country varies widely. Some states restrict its practice to hospitals and other authorized facilities. Others, such as Nevada, allow acupuncture to be performed not only by physicians but also by technicians without medical degrees, under supervision.

Acupressure

Acupressure, the less widely publicized cousin of acupuncture, works on the same principle. In acupressure, however, the certain points of the body whose stimulation will bring about the desired effect are treated with specific touch. In both sciences the points at which stimulation is applied are often far removed physically from the areas they are intended to affect. The reason for this is based on the principle of meridians.

These meridians are believed to crisscross the body and act as channels that transmit electromagnetic energy. At various locations along them are the specific points, some 500 in all, at which pressure or puncture will be applied. It is only necessary, when treating, to come within two inches of the meridian for the desired effect to be carried along it to the area or organ concerned.

Polarity Therapy

Polarity therapy is based on the presence of polarities in our bodies. Because man is a manifestation of energy, like other forms of energy, he possesses a positive and a negative side. Polarity therapy suggests that when massage is being used, it should stimulate the body either clockwise or counterclockwise. Because polarity therapy is used to actually change the energy pattern and polarity of the body, the giver's own body polarity must be borne in mind — for example, the giver should massage the right side of the receiver's body with his own right hand, and vice versa.

It is an alarming fact that more than $5 billion each year is spent on prescription drugs and another $2 billion on non-prescription items. This validation of the urgency of man's search for relief from physical malfunctions makes it much easier to understand the hugely increased interest currently shown in kinesiological techniques.

Knowledge of kinesiology has many applications. Those who use that knowledge most directly work in the fields of physical medicine and physical education. But there is room for a practical knowledge and application of kinesiology outside these areas also. Furniture and machinery, for example, are now being designed with a clearer understanding of both the anatomical needs and human propensities of the bodies that will use them. Obviously, the more clearly we come to realize the causes of fatigue and inefficiency, the more effectively we can bring about a comfortable relationship with the world around us as well as with our own structure. Thus interest in kinesiology, the scientific study of movement, continues to spread throughout the world.

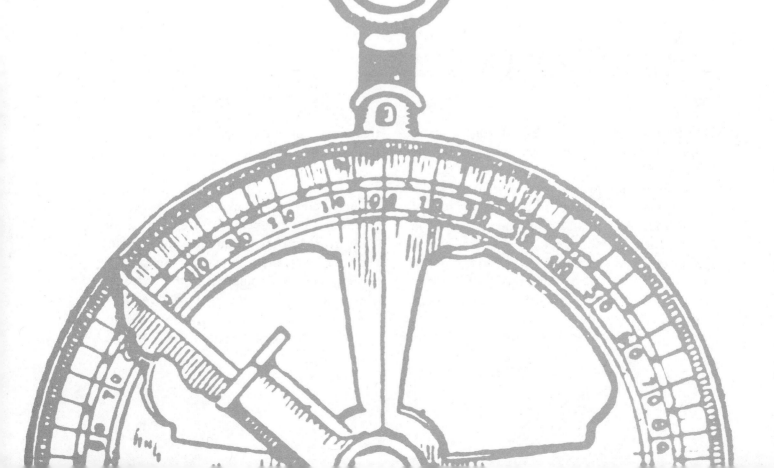

REFLEXOLOGY

Reflexology is a process of zone therapy that involves concentrated massage of the soles of the feet. The method works roughly from the same principle as Shiatsu and Do'in in that pressure is applied to a specific part of the body — in this case, the nerve endings in the soles of the feet. There are several pressure points, each of which corresponds to specific organs and functions. With several seconds of pressure applied to the correlating point, the malfunctioning organ can be relieved of its pain. With continuing regular treatment, problems can be spotted and treated before malfunction has time to surface.

There are 10 zones in the body, and according to zone therapy, different reactions result from different amounts of pressure. The therapy's intention is to relax nerve tension, increase circulation in the blood and lymphatic systems, and get the body into top form so that it will have the power to throw off any accumulated poisons.

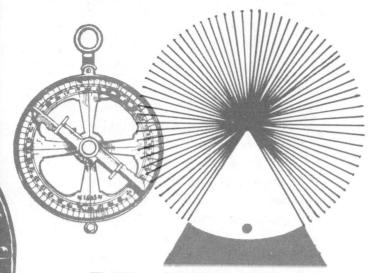

RELAXATION RESPONSE / an answer to stress?

What could be more appealing to an anxiety-ridden society than a technique which by its very name suggests the answer to a common search — relaxation. Dr. Herbert Benson's concept of "relaxation response" is aimed largely at the corporate complex where many of the anxieties of our business-oriented nation accumulate. In his book, *The Relaxation Response*, he suggests corporations consider, instead of a coffee break, offering a relaxation break for their employees, which would act as an interruption of "destructive mental circuits."

According to Benson, our society is highly sophisticated — and we pay the price for that daily. Our problems are major, and they are difficult to solve, because of the fact that no magic force will ever take away the complicated systems that are the source of our frustrations. In fact, as progress continues, complications simply increase. Man is constantly being called upon to readjust to a whole new set of problems. And, since the body is directly affected by the condition of the mind, the effect is not merely psychological but physiological.

Hypertension Epidemic

We are being hit by an epidemic of hypertension — more than 50 percent of deaths in America each year are caused by heart and brain diseases resulting from high blood pressure. Various degrees of hypertension are present in from 15 to 33 percent of the adult population. Symptoms of the disease are subtle, but it strikes quickly — diseases resulting from hypertension are the cause of two deaths every minute in the United States.

Benson's thesis is that we are constantly faced with a physiological reaction called the "fight-or-flight response" — when we come in contact with a stress-causing situation, we can either stay and battle it through or run from it. The fact that we must make this choice at all in itself creates stress; even more stress is caused by the anxiety of living with the choice we make. Yet, Benson stresses, "Each of us possesses a natural and innate protective mechanism against 'overstress,' which allows us to turn off harmful bodily effects to counter the effects of the fight-or-flight response. This response against 'overstress' brings on bodily changes that decrease heart rate, lower metabolism, decrease the rate of breathing, and bring the body back into what is probably a healthier balance. This is the Relaxation Response."

The response has four essential elements: (1) a quiet environment; (2) a mental device such as a word or phrase which should be repeated in a specific fashion over and over again; (3) the adoption of a passive attitude; and (4) a comfortable position. Practice of these elements for 10 to 20 minutes daily will bring about the substantial lowering of the heart rate, metabolism, and breathing rate, and help the body keep its physiological balance.

Benson suggests the individual pick a calm, quiet environment at the office or in the home, kick off his shoes, loosen any tight clothing, and sit in a comfortable chair. He should then let the mind float along and refuse to accept any distractions. The mental device should be a word, a prayer, a sound — anything quieting repeated silently or in a slow gentle tone, every time he exhales. This exercise is essentially a form of meditation, which separates the individual from his environment and brings him more closely in touch with his inner self. The physiological changes that result are decreased oxygen consumption, lower blood pressure, and slower heart rate. The response is relaxation, which alleviates stress — and herein lies the message of Dr. Benson's book.

SENSORIUM MONOVIN

Monovin means "mostly nonverbal institute." It is run by a delightful man named Len Harris, in Los Angeles. Harris has developed *Sensorium,* a sensory maze of art, music, and other pleasurable sources of experience. Sensorium offers the opportunity to experience such delights as:

1. sheets of soft plastic on nude bodies,
2. foot washing,
3. being pummeled by beanbags,
4. tasting fresh fruit,
5. smelling fresh flowers,
6. sounds of tiny bells,
7. massage with powder (corn starch).

Harris has added some other sensations to *Sensorium,* such as body painting under black light with fluorescent colors and a rebuilding process that features a long, plastic tubular structure to slide down. Try it!

MASSAGE/ getting in touch with the somatopsychic

Psychology has from its beginnings been concerned with the behavior of the body. Rather than overlap with medicine, however, it settled with almost exclusive interest on the mind. Thus, when the body (soma) did not function as it should and there was no apparent organic reason, the only logical culprit was the mind (psyche), and the idea of mind-induced, psychosomatic illness was initiated.

Recently, there has been some rethinking of this position along the following lines:

○ The body has a definite structure, the study of which we call physiology. Physiology views the body frozen in time, rather like a series of snapshots. Because of its structure, the body can act only in certain ways. Behavior, then, is like a reviewing of physiology through time — a sort of movie version.

○ Every piece of information the mind receives must reach it through the body. The mind can receive nothing directly — everything has to come through the senses.

○ Because the body is structured, all the information reaching the mind will also be structured. Hence, the way the body acts and behaves in the world will affect the information that the mind receives.

Thus, not only does the mind affect the body, but the body affects the mind. This rethinking has opened up some backdoor approaches to the psyche, one of the most popular and enjoyable being massage.

For many people this term conjures up the image of the seedy massage parlor, little more than a storefront for prostitution. Or, alternatively, the brisk, impersonal manipulations applied by football coaches, YMCA masseurs, or physical therapists. The image most remote for the average person is that of the psychologist using massage of the body as a means of reaching the mind. As a result, terms such as body consciousness and

185

sensory awareness are often used when massage is really what is meant.

Neglect of Massage

One of the reasons for the neglect of massage is that most people do not identify with their bodies. From the chin up is identity; the area below is simply the vehicle that moves the identity through the world. Additionally, the sexual emphasis placed by our civilization on any body contact has caused people to think that massage is used simply as an excuse for physical intimacy: "Sure, you call it massage, but I know what you *really* mean."

In the past there have been two basic types of massage. There have always been rubdowns for those sore and tired muscles. If there were religious overtones, it was called the laying on of hands. This type of therapeutic massage tries to change or correct the physical. The other type of massage is exactly the one everybody likes to fantasize — the full-blown, hot-to-trot, sexy, sensual massage. Warm hands on soft skin are a joy forever.

Today's Approach

These days, there is a fresh approach to massage. In this new style, sometimes called the Esalen massage because it originated at the Esalen Institute on the Big Sur, the person receiving the massage is neither viewed as having a problem that needs to be cured nor an appetite to be satiated, but rather as a whole human being. True knowledge of oneself can only come from the unification of mind and body within the terms of the somatopsychic relationship. Massage thus becomes a means of unifying, coordinating, and integrating the body — and in so doing, integrating the mind. The purpose of the massage, then, is simply to invite the subject to experience and enjoy the sensation of being part of the body. It is definitely sensual, usually curative, and quite often sexual, but these are simply dividends on having pleasure and enjoying one's self.

There are equal payoffs for the person giving the massage. In order to give a completely integrated, unified massage, the masseur must come from a unified, integrated place within his own body. Massage is not something that is done with the hands alone. It is done with the entire body, and the coordination of strength, leverage, and balance is essential. As a result there are some strong similarities between the movements of the person massaging and those of someone practicing a martial art such as T'ai Chi.

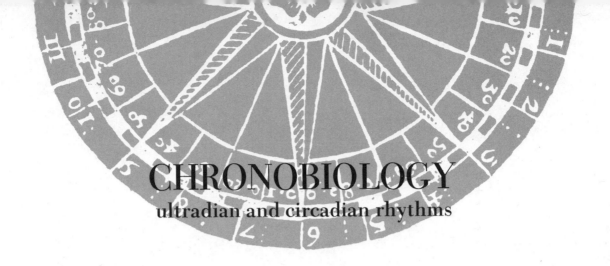

CHRONOBIOLOGY
ultradian and circadian rhythms

It is no surprise to anyone to be told that he or she operates in a cyclic fashion. We eat, sleep, work, and play in an ordered way and on a regular schedule. Most of us have experienced the physical and emotional distress that results when we do violence to our regular routine either by abruptly changing geographical position with a jet plane trip, or by staying up later than usual for one reason or another.

We are less aware of the rhythmic variations that take place in the course of each day. There is now significant clinical evidence supporting the contention that definite rhythms are associated with such basic physiological features as temperature, heartbeat, blood pressure, and cell division. Short-term rhythms with a cyclic periodicity of 90-100 minutes are called *ultradian,* and rhythms repeated within a 24-hour period are called *circadian* (from the Latin words *circa dies* meaning "about a day").

The existence of ultradian rhythms has been demonstrated in clinical and laboratory experiments ranging from observations of variations in hunger demands, intellectual capacity and capability, general alertness, and Rapid Eye Movement (REM), to measurement of cyclic repetition of readily observable body parameters such as body temperature and blood pressure. The length of the period of the various rhythms appears to be relatively fixed, but the variation or "swing" of a given function from low to high is unique in each individual.

Chronobiologists believe that awareness of your specific, personal biorhythms can be extremely useful. Not only can it explain why you are "up" at certain moments and "down" at others, but it can help you arrange your personal schedule to perform work and to rest at the optimum times. Naturally there are outside constraints on the flexibility of each person's schedule but this does not negate the value of personal scheduling where it can be achieved. A second benefit that can be directly realized is in the field of health. If you have established your personal biorhythms under "normal" conditions, these measurements allow your doctor to interpret and diagnose medical problems when you visit him. If you determine, for example, that your blood pressure is normally 130/80 in the morning and 145/85 in the late afternoon, variations from these benchmarks will have added significance.

A precise explanation for the intensity and duration of biorhythms is being sought by researchers. The complex and unique chemistry of each individual body is assumed to be an important contributor to its biorhythms, but the fact that they exist and profoundly influence individual behavior cannot now be doubted.

interview / ALLEGRA FULLER SNYDER
integrating mind and body

Chairwoman of the Department of Dance and associate professor in the UCLA School of Fine Arts, Allegra Fuller Snyder has a comprehensive and authoritative perspective derived from her work as performer and choreographer and her continuing involvement with dance from the historical, anthropological, and therapeutic points of view. She has performed with the New York City Ballet and choreographed for the Robert Joffrey Ballet, has directed several films on ethnic dance, including "Bayanihan," a documentary on Philippine dance which won a special award at the Bilbao, Spain, Film Festival. Dance editor of Film News, *she has contributed numerous articles to other publications in her field. Ms. Snyder is an authority on dance in film and television, has served on the dance panels of both the National Endowment for the Arts and the California Arts Commission and has chaired numerous committees and conferences on dance and anthropology.*

LANDE: What is the area in which dance, or should I say movement, is most effective?

SNYDER: Probably the most important contribution made by movement therapy — and we really prefer that term rather than dance therapy — is that it works in the fullest and most open way with the body. There are two major facts I think we're recognizing not only therapeutically but culturally. For a person to be a fully functioning individual, there has to be real integration of body and mind, and this seems even further verified by the work now going on in trying to understand the functioning of the brain. You know that the right and left sides of the brain have very different functions to perform, and that the left side, which actually is linked with the right side of the body, is the one we tend to stimulate most of the time in our day-to-day activities. It seems to work linearly, sequentially, with facts.

The right side of the brain, which is connected with the left side of the body — you remember the phrase that the left hand is the dreamer — is concerned with seeing things holistically rather than in fragments, seeing things from a feeling point of view rather than just seeing what is in front of the individual person. It responds very much to the movement mode of perception. Dance therapy seems to stimulate both sides of the brain, rather than just the one side. Here, there is a difference between movement therapy, which comes out of the field of dance, and, say, the new developments in athletics. And from a therapeutic point of view, I feel there is undeveloped potential with the athletic area in encouraging that two-sided stimulation which comes from the creative.

LANDE: Because the use of the body in athletics is more regimented and disciplined?

SNYDER: Yes, even if you take the attitude that you're working from a philosophical base rather than a competitive sports base, opportunities for discovery and exploration of self are much less allowed for in an athletic situation.

LANDE: Would you say that in movement therapy there is more of an opportunity to explore self, awareness of the meaning of the self, whereas in athletics the opportunity is more therapeutic in nature, in order to relieve tension or anxiety?

SNYDER: Yes, but all those opportunities are potentially inherent in any kind of body movement. If you really are aware of your body and discovering it, and letting it go and do what it wants to do, there is always release of tension. So at that level both movement therapy and the new attitude toward athletics would be going hand in hand. What I'm saying is that using movement brings about the next level of allowing, understanding the creative self, the development of the holistic perception of experience, which the right side of the brain craves to have stimulated and which I don't think most athletic experience is dealing with at this point.

LANDE: You spoke about letting the body go and do what it wants to do. What does the body want to do?

SNYDER: The body wants to sense itself fully, to really understand itself as a body. Many of the basic problems one discovers in working with movement therapy arise because a lot of people don't even seem to know they have a body — their experience seems to be cut off at the neck or head — and it's very hard for such people to even identify with the idea of body image, of knowing where you begin or end. We start by working with that. Then the next step is to not only have a sense of where you begin and end, but what you are able to generate from the full use of your sensory awareness and perception.

There is a very simple technique that's often used in a therapy session. A person is asked to lie down very quietly — you know, the relaxation thing — and once he has a sense of some movement or action in his body — as a totally inner-generated experience — to begin to respond to that and move with it as a source. And we get some extraordinary kinds of experience evolving from that point, that moment when a person begins to really look inside himself and sense himself.

LANDE: Is it fair to say that you feel there is consciousness in the body, that each cell is conscious and has to be awakened — or perhaps motivated?

SNYDER: Awakened is a nice way of saying it.

LANDE: Can you describe specifically what dance or movement therapy involves?

SNYDER: I can't really, because there is no one course and there are no rules. In fact, the range of activity in the field rather resembles the span between Freudian analysis and humanistic psychology. It would be totally incorrect to describe any one thing as dance therapy. But there is a group, the American Dance Therapy Association, which has about 500 active members, working throughout the country. Its headquarters are at Suite 300, 10400 Connecticut Avenue, Kensington, Maryland 20795.

LANDE: Can you elaborate on any area where, in your opinion, this therapy has been particularly effective?

SNYDER: Maybe I should elaborate a little about the philosophy behind it. It represents something of the fusion of Eastern thinking with Western thinking, because of course Eastern thought is much more body-accepting and body-oriented than Western.

LANDE: Why do you think that is?

SNYDER: I have to pretty much lay responsibility for Western nonbodily thinking in the lap of the Judaeo-Christian concept of the body. A continuous flat denial of the body, and at times a real castigation, in the true sense of that word, permeated the thinking of Europe and all the fundamental Western ideology that formed the American culture. The East's attitude is very different. Hinduism, as you know, is a very physically, very sexually oriented philosophy. Then you get the modification of Hinduism into Buddhism in China, Japan, and Korea, which is still very much oriented toward the body, although it is a quieter kind of experience. Meditation in itself is extremely body-oriented. Kinesthetically, it is not as broad as movement or as dance, but it's a body experience nonetheless.

These are natural ways of thinking about things. We are the one group in the whole world that seems to have attempted to think in another way altogether. Erika Bourguignon

at Ohio State has written a book called *Religion, Altered States of Consciousness, and Social Change*, a heavily documented scientific study, which shows that 90 percent of cultures studied on a worldwide basis were involved with altered states of consciousness, which are, again, body-mind integrating perceptions. One of my concerns about the other side of myself and my interest in all this is that I feel it is extraordinarily important for us to be aware of these phenomena in a global context. It might give us some confidence for rethinking things to discover that we are the very small 10 percent who have attempted to get away from this.

In our dance ethnology sequence and other graduate programs at UCLA, we have begun to study in more breadth and depth the many human experiences which have received the label of dance. This approach enables us to see dance as more than an art. Research in the disciplines of dance ethnology has taught us to understand dance as fundamental to conceptualizing many of the world's cultures.

Dance therapy is a particularly effective means of getting at the heart of many of the social and psychological problems that our society and culture have created, and of correcting or easing them. We have discovered that dance is one of the most powerful tools for healing the split between mind and body which we have begun to recognize as the crucial problem with our society — that is, the split between the two functions the brain has been created to cope with — by fusing the logical with the intuitive, analytical perceptions with sensorial perceptions, holistic understanding with step-by-step thinking. We find ourselves dealing with a discipline which itself is dealing with basic awareness, conceptualization and understanding of human experience. We must perceive dance as a vitally contributing part of the whole humanistic base of knowledge and experience.

LANDE: When someone has gone through dance movement therapy, do you notice an outward-showing zest and aliveness in his approach to things?

SNYDER: It's deeper than that. If things have really worked, you perceive a real sense of self — which doesn't mean chaotic, or jumping up and down. The person is not just giving out movement, but giving out energy. There is a real sense of aliveness in such people. You can almost feel the integration

between what they sense internally and perceive externally. They've really got it together — that's a good phrase that I think is particularly apt for the movement therapy experience.

LANDE: I understand movement therapy has been successful with autistic children and with schizophrenics.

SNYDER: Yes. We may be naive in patting ourselves on the back, but seemingly there isn't an area that hasn't responded in some way — some obviously more than others — to these kinds of movement experiences.

THE ULTIMATE ATHLETE

"Our hope lies not in the brain alone, or in the mind alone, but rather in mind, body, and spirit rejoined." Such is the thesis of George Leonard, whose *Education and Ecstasy*, published in 1968, offered a fresh and visionary approach to education. It looks as if Leonard may have done it again with *The Ultimate Athlete* — this time in sports, an area that most of us have either decided early in life we are good at and interested in, or have cut out of our life schemes because we deem ourselves unathletic.

Leonard's thesis is that inside everyone of us, even the most ungainly, is an inner athlete, and that a connection with the athlete that dwells in each of us is essential for the coming age. Fitness is a requirement for good health and happiness. But Leonard goes beyond this, to look in the realm of athletics for the peak experiences of life, originally recognized by Maslow.

The particular sport in *The Ultimate Athlete* is the martial art of Aikido, a pursuit which is more akin to ballet than battle, whose essence is to use your opponent's strength to reinforce your own. The philosophical approach of the Oriental martial arts has made them increasingly popular in an age when our culture looks more and more towards the East for enlightenment. But the moments of spiritual quality so easily discerned in such arts as Aikido can, according to Leonard, be as easily found in walking, jogging, diving, flying, or playing tag.

Long distance running is one of the most private and poetic of sports, in which the individual is supremely responsible for the condition of his body, the speed and attitude with which he runs, and the feelings of exhaustion and exaltation which are his reward. The sports pages may be filled with "victory and defeat, climactic plays, statistics," but Leonard celebrates "the sweet infusion of every limb that follows a long run."

It would seem that the conditions of intimacy with the body, trust in its ability to produce and harness energy, and identification with its achievements that are demanded by athletic activity are yet another manifestation of man's unceasing search for true integration of body, mind, and spirit.

THE MARTIAL ARTS

A combination of forms of combat and methods of raising levels of consciousness, the various martial arts deserve study both individually and as an example of the increasing influence of the Orient upon American culture. Each has its own characteristics and its own resulting advantages, yet each shares the inherent quality of putting man in closer touch with nature and his own instincts, of unifying the mind and body into one powerful entity.

T'ai Chi Ch'uan

T'ai Chi Ch'uan is a system of health-giving exercises, dating back to the 12th or 13th century and rooted in the teachings of Chinese philosophy. Literally, T'ai Chi Ch'uan means "the ultimate principle," and it is associated with the principle of Yin-Yang, the coordination of the body with the mind. As the body increases in suppleness and rhythmic movement, the mind becomes more fluid, more open to wisdom, more at peace with its environment. Relaxation is a vital part of T'ai Chi, on the grounds that a rigid body creates a rigid mind.

T'ai Chi exercises look like an effortless ballet. There are 128 traditional movements, which instructors encourage students to practice at dawn and at dusk. They take from 20 to 30 minutes to complete, but enthusiasts believe this art's true benefits come only from disciplined daily practice.

Two major tenets of T'ai Chi: concentrating on continuity in time, which allows the flow of movement as a subconscious rather than a conscious phenomenon, and balance, indicating knowledge of the exact right time to do something. Every part of the body comes into play in the 128 movements, from the eyelids to the soles of the feet. Since *Chi* literally means "intrinsic energy," the exercises aim to master this energy and circulate it throughout the body as an extraordinary power and strength which regenerates and revitalizes the organs and vital systems, freeing them from disease.

The ultimate psychological result of T'ai Chi is the calm, tranquility, and relaxation that result from total commitment to the grace, balance, and fluidity of the movements. In the exercises as well as in daily life, T'ai Chi emphasizes awareness, serenity, and proper breathing. Essentially, it "turns the body on from the inside" — a natural, self-induced "high."

Kung Fu

Kung Fu is another martial art that concentrates not only on the development of the body but on the blending of mind and soul which comes from disciplining the two with a single purpose. Its focal point is defense rather than attack, and its movements are smooth, fluid, and centered usually on the knuckles, where all the concentrated energy comes together.

The same body points used to heal a patient in acupuncture or acupressure can be used in Kung Fu to harm or kill an opponent. The adage "Hands that kill can also heal" is particularly applicable here. Students of Kung Fu learn the vulnerable points on their opponent's body as they learn the strengths of their own; through concentration on this knowledge, they are able to master their own reflexes.

Like the other martial arts, Kung Fu goes beyond being a combative mechanism. Outwardly, it would seem to be an aggressive pursuit, yet its principles are serenity of soul and the wisdom of pacifism. Dignity and pride are part of its philosophy, for the whole art cannot be perfected unless mental and spiritual discipline are present. Serious students of Kung Fu soon learn that they are confronting not an attack technique but a commitment to higher consciousness through fluidity of movement, intricacy of coordination, and the energy of concentrated motion. The mind must be relaxed and anger de-emphasized or man's aggressive instincts cannot be submerged in the growth of harmony which is the aim of Kung Fu.

Jujitsu and Judo

The martial art of Jujitsu originated in ancient Japan, where the first references to it date back to the eighth century. It was not until some 500 years ago that Jujitsu was perfected as a mechanism for fighting. Originally taught only to samurai, of the noble class, it is an empty-handed art, which can be used either as an attack or as a defense. Jujitsu was first used in Japan in battle, but after peace came the practice continued as a character-building discipline fusing the teachings of such masters as Confucius, Buddha, Lao-Tse, and Chuang-Tse. The movements of the art, therefore, can be regarded as physical expressions of ancient philosophy.

The art of Judo, an offshoot of Jujitsu, was developed late in the 19th century, and rapidly spread to America and to Europe. Since President Theodore Roosevelt summoned a Judo teacher to the United States in 1902, the art has increased steadily in popularity. Several forms or *kata* of Judo have been developed and are taught at the many schools throughout the country. They include:

1. *Nage-no-kata* and *Katame-no-kata*, the forms of throwing and grappling. These are generally free-style exercises; there are 30 movements in all.

2. *Ju-no-kata*, the forms of gentility. These concentrate on strength, and aim at a broad physical culture.

3. *Kime-no-kata*, the forms of decision. These 20 forms apply to self-defense and attack through concentration on weak parts of the opponent's body.

4. *Koshiki-no-kata*, which perfect the rhythm of strength and teach the theory behind attack and defense.

5. *Seiryoku-zen-yo Kokumin-taiiku-no-kata,* the forms of total efficiency, which enhance physical training and further emphasize gentility.

Reasons for studying Judo are as diverse as the people who practice it; some students enter into this martial art to develop strength, some to enjoy it as a sport, others to help them in self-defense, or to discipline the mind as well as the body. Like the other martial arts, Judo concentrates as much on spiritual tranquility as it does on strength, and in fact all these aims are reconcilable within its scope.

Karate

Karate came to America through Okinawa, where it was developed as a form of empty-handed combat. Okinawans used it for physical training and self-defense, but its transplantation to the United States has refined it into a sport taught at schools all over the country. Dressed in *gis,* the pajamalike white pants and shirt worn by all participants in the martial arts, students work at earning a series of belts (usually white, yellow, green, blue, red, and black, in that order) which signify their rank and proficiency, until they have achieved all the benefits and skills Karate can indue — firmness of the body and inner peace.

Karate basically teaches the supremacy of mind over matter, the concept being that by training the mind to concentrate while training the body to attack effectively, ultimate victory can be won — not only over the opponent or inanimate object but also over one's own fears and weaknesses. The student is taught to look at an object and concentrate on "seeing through it" — picturing his hand, foot, or head as already having passed through the object. The common demonstration is of a man or woman standing before a thick wooden plank in deep concentration and then letting out a fierce yell and shattering it.

Yet in Karate the focus is not on violence. The power is an inner one, and although it can be deadly when used in combat, its main concentration is on the discipline of body that bespeaks a disciplined mind. There is great dignity about Karate, and a pride born of knowing that the mind is master of a perfectly tuned machine — the body.

With the increasing spread of violence in urban areas, Karate has become popular in this country primarily as a means of self-defense. In response to this, Karate schools teach both male and female students the art of warding off attack — yet they maintain the basic tenet of pacifism by teaching students how to turn aside violence, not to initiate it. Self-control is as important to Karate as self-defense.

As a discipline, a commitment, and a mastering of the mind to will the body into action, Karate continues to grow in popularity both as a sport and as an always available means of self-protection.

Aikido

Aikido, newest of the martial arts, was introduced to the United States via Hawaii in 1953. The first Aikido school in New York City was established in 1962, since when Aikido schools have sprung up in almost all the 50 states.

The movements of Aikido are circular. Rather than using force against an attacker, one is trained to sense the direction of the opponent's force so that his own momentum can be used to throw him. Because of the importance of sensing the opponent's direction of attack, Aikido is always taught in pairs. It somewhat resembles dance; the partners must be sensitive to each other's movements and thought processes, so there is harmony between them. There is no feeling of an active and a passive partner. Both merge and learn from each other's motion and each partner is working both against himself and against his attacker. Aikido is strictly defensive; its goal is neither defeat nor injury. The mood is one of relaxation, fluidity, and alertness of mind; there is no thought of competition to cloud the spiritual aspects of this martial art.

The term used in Aikido for the energy which flows through the universe and through mankind is *ki.* When two partners struggle, they are matching their *ki* against each other;

but if they blend this energy, the force of the movement is doubled. It is to the advantage of both, therefore, that harmony and sensitivity to each other exist. For these principles to become natural and therefore constantly available, students must commit themselves to the art of Aikido, and through this discipline both body and soul become instruments of higher consciousness.

Vital to the study of Aikido is the concept of the "one point," an imaginary point two inches below the navel, which is considered to be the center of the body's gravity. If the body is relaxed and the mind focused on this point at all times, perfect balance and mental stability can be achieved. If the body is tense, there is concentration elsewhere, and true balance of mind and body cannot result.

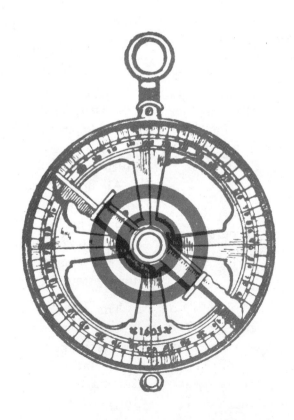

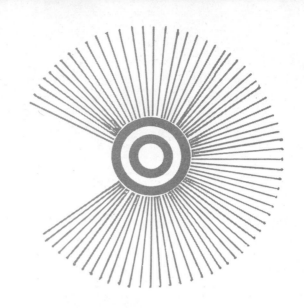

ZEN TENNIS, ANYONE?

Not only has the practice of Yoga asanas replaced traditional occidental calisthenics for many people, but the inner awareness concepts of Zen and Yoga have even permeated the sweaty world of tennis. Leading guru is Tim Gallwey, author of *The Inner Game of Tennis*, who tries to help his pupils get their conscious, critical selves out of the way and let the inner self take over. It is analagous to mastering the technique described in Eugen Herrigel's *Zen in the Art of Archery*, where the pupil struggles persistently to learn to let "it" shoot the arrow. In brief, the harder you try, the less effectively you perform. Your inner, nonverbal, instinctual self knows better than your nervous, nagging, conscious mind how to stroke the ball or shoot the arrow. It is just a question of getting out of the way, as the crack player admonishes his ineffectual doubles partner.

To remove the instruction from the realm of mysticism, it is possible that what happens is the quieting of the verbal, linear, critical left hemisphere of the brain, thereby permitting the right hemisphere, which handles bodily orientation, to take over and do what it does best.

Baba Rick Champion

Another exponent of the inner game is Baba Rick Champion, a Scottsdale, Arizona pro who teaches Yoga tennis. Impressed at the ease with which Baba Don Singh, a Sikh Yoga master, learned a very good brand of tennis, Champion began to use a Yoga approach. His classes begin with a short meditation session to aid in concentration, and then his pupils work mentally with specific movements before moving to the courts. Champion is the author of *Yoga Tennis, Awareness Through Sports*, a how-to book which explains the underlying principles and practical application of the mind-body united approach of Yoga.

Whichever the philosophy through which they approach the game, both experts feel such an approach not only improves their pupils tennis but helps their whole attitude toward life as well.

ESALEN SPORTS CENTER

The Esalen Sports Center in Sonoma County, north of San Francisco, is devoted to furthering new concepts, practices, and teaching methods in lifetime sports; it emphasizes the kinds of activities in which participation is not limited by age, sex, or athletic ability. The focus is on the joy of taking part and the thrill of excelling. The workshops are designed to make sport richer and more rewarding and to elicit the potential that lies within each one of us.

At the summer institute a 12-day residential workshop program includes active games, sports, mind/body disciplines, and exploration of the wilderness as a means of realizing more of one's potential. It also combines some of the techniques of humanistic group therapies — being in the here and now, mind/body harmony, individual responsibility, risk taking — and applies them to sporting experience. The two-week, two-part program includes new approaches to traditional sports such as tennis, jogging, swimming, volleyball, basketball, and softball, as well as exposure to mind/body disciplines such as T'ai Chi, Aikido, Feldenkrais exercises, sensory awareness, Hatha Yoga, meditation, energy awareness, and centering.

The offerings extend from "Rafting on the Rogue River" (which includes Yoga, psychosynthesis, dream sharing, and sensory awareness exercises) to courses such as "Golf in Balance," incorporating principles of physical fitness with psychological fitness and body harmony.

The second week is spent in a secluded base camp in the Sierras, where participants apply their newly gained insights and awareness to such activities as backpacking, rock climbing, and nature walks while living and working together as a community.

DIETS

From the nutritional viewpoint the United States is a paradox — the majority of its population is overweight, yet many of those overweight people suffer from malnutrition without even knowing it. We might conclude that Americans know how to eat, but have little idea how to eat wisely. The country's economic prosperity and natural agricultural abundance — in an area sufficiently vast that seasonal restrictions on foods cease to exist — have enabled us, unlike poorer nations, to escape from the nutritional monotony of one or two staple foods, to choose among a vast array of eating and cooking styles, and to consume, in general, as much as we like whenever we like.

Ours must be the only country in the world to have a category known as "junk food" — the wrappered, injected, artificially flavored offerings of the automatic vending machine. Yet, amid such plenty, Americans are fascinated by the idea of dieting, of eating less, of eating better, of eating more healthily, less dangerously . . . .

The problem is that we are overwhelmed by the choice among diets, every one of which is guaranteed to take off excess pounds and put us at our peak of condition speedily, and without any negative side effects. The issue of what to eat becomes extremely confusing. People who need to lose weight tend to career off one diet onto another without notable success. Those who simply want to eat the healthiest possible foods get an equivalent runaround about which foods are the most valuable. In the same day, a person can glean from different sources the information that milk is good and milk is harmful, that meat is healthy food and that meat should be totally eliminated from the diet; that high-protein diets work most effectively, and that low-calorie diets are the only answer. Fasting would seem to be the only way to avoid the confusion. But, of course, we are also told that fasting can cause malnutrition.

Some information follows about currently popular ways of dieting, which may help to elucidate at least what the major dietary methods stand for. Comparison of their effectiveness is impossible; eating is an area where each of us is unique, both in what we choose to ingest and in the way in which our bodies metabolize it.

Macrobiotics

According to adherents of the macrobiotic diet, all disease is caused by the imbalance in the body of Yin and Yang, the two antagonistic but complementary forces of the universe. It makes sense, therefore, to eat primarily foods near the midpoint between extreme Yin and extreme Yang. By paying attention to this intake, the imbalance which causes disease is corrected, and the macrobiotic diet has worked its miracle. People who follow the macrobiotic path believe that Western medicine ignores the possibility that such a diet could in fact cure a wide variety of diseases, including some for which no artificially induced cures have as yet been found.

The macrobiotic diet has some important rules:

1. Eat only natural foods which are grown on fertile soil under natural conditions, and consume them in their natural state.

2. Eat only whole foods which still contain all the nutrients nature originally gave them — no less and no more. These whole foods are rare, but they are essential.

3. Eat only living foods. The average body requires some 600 different enzymes, and since these are destroyed by cooking, along with many vitamins and minerals, food should be eaten in its natural, raw state.

4. Eat only poison-free foods. Foods available in American supermarkets may contain pesticides, waxes, bleaches, artificial colorings, preservatives, hormone residue, DDT, and any number of other chemicals, which make them less safe than foods bought at a reputable health food store.

5. Eat a high natural carbohydrate/low animal protein diet. Natural carbohydrates are found in fresh vegetables and unrefined whole seeds and grains. The low animal protein caution comes from the fact that nations known for their good health, vitality, and longevity subsist on a low animal protein/high natural carbohydrate diet.

6. Follow a system of undereating and periodic fasting, the two most important secrets of health and longevity. Food eaten in excess of actual bodily need interferes with digestion, causes internal sluggishness, incomplete assimilation of nutrients, and, in fact, actually poisons the system. If we eat less, therefore, we feel less hungry because the food is more efficiently utilized.

7. Correct eating habits. We should eat slowly and chew each mouthful 50 times. Follow the "never mix, never worry" principle: Never eat raw fruits and raw vegetables at the same meal; eat as few different foods as possible at one meal; when eating protein-rich foods along with other foods, eat the protein foods first. Food eaten in a relaxed atmosphere will be digested more efficiently.

The diet also has some important "don'ts":

1. Don't use white sugar or anything containing white sugar, including soft drinks made with sugar substitutes.

2. Don't drink more than a minimum — just enough for urination to occur at least twice every 24 hours for women, three times every 24 hours for men.

3. Don't eat more than a minimum of animal foods such as milk, cheese, and butter.

4. Don't eat food that has been transported over a long distance or has been industrially packaged.

5. Don't eat vegetables with high Yin content (the most prominent: potatoes and tomatoes) and avoid all vegetables out of season.

6. Don't eat more than a minimum of fruit and avoid fruit juices.

7. Don't drink coffee or any tea containing carcinogen dye.

8. Don't eat spices, vinegar, or chemical seasonings.

Though many diets encourage a salt-free method of eating, macrobiotics believes salt is vital to maintain the body's balance between sodium and potassium. Its most nutritious form is unrefined sea salt, available from health food stores.

Liquids are kept to a minimum so that the ratio of water to blood will be kept low. Drinking too much liquid is thought to make one sluggish, lazy, and generally ineffective.

The staple of the macrobiotic diet is brown rice — unrefined, chemically untreated, and well cooked.

High-Protein Diets

Despite the warnings about the dangers of eating meat, Dr. Maxwell Stillman and many others have devised high-protein diets, the main feature of which is the consumption of the "pure protein" to be found in meat, fish, eggs, cheese, and fowl. Stillman's contention is that proteins are not stored in the body, as are carbohydrates, but are used within a few hours of intake; therefore, a body which takes in nothing but protein will use up that intake and be forced to burn up accumulated excess fat. To help "flush out" the waste material produced by the burning off process, Stillman insists that the dieter also consume 80 ounces (eight glasses) of water daily.

While many diets are intended to achieve healthy patterns of eating over a lifetime, the Stillman diet was designed specifically for the purpose of losing weight. There is never a suggestion that intake of pure protein and water be a permanent commitment. Stillman does suggest, however, that an overweight body cannot be healthy because obesity can lead to heart trouble, high blood pressure, and other diseases that are widespread among Americans. His purpose then, is first to eliminate the overweight condition, then to modify the diet to a sensible regimen.

A common argument against the Stillman theory is that he suggests you may eat "all you want" of the "allowable" high-protein foods. Although, in fact, he does warn against overeating, some dieters take this as permission to glut themselves with eggs, meat, and other protein sources, thereby raising their caloric intake unwisely and sometimes even gaining weight. Another complaint is that the Stillman diet is not a balanced one. However, his suggestion is *not* a long-range plan, and physicians who have examined patients before and after going on the diet have found few, if any, ill effects.

Low-Carbohydrate Diets

Another approach to the high-protein diet is the low-carbohydrate diet. The rules are simple: You buy a carbohydrate gram counter at your local supermarket, which lists the carbohydrate grams contained in all the common foods. Using this as a guide, you eat fewer than 60 grams of carbohydrates per day. This simple weight-loss plan allows you to eat a wide variety of foods, and can be followed over a longer period of time than the pure-protein plan, researchers having established that the body can function perfectly well on 60 grams of carbohydrates daily. This plan can also be combined with alcohol consumption (provided the grams are reduced to 50, in order to allow for the additional input from wine or martinis), making it additionally popular.

Opponents of the low-carbohydrate diet are quick to point out that the 60-gram limit still allows the dieter to consume unhealthy foods. A couple of examples of poor nutrition: one could eat a Milky Way bar (58.3 grams) and drink a cup of coffee with light cream (1.3 grams) and eat a tablespoon of anchovy paste (.6 grams) for a total of 60 grams; or one could eat an unlimited amount of butterfish (0 grams) and still have room left over for a piece of layer cake (54.4 grams) and two small cream mints (2.7 grams) — and still lose weight.

High-protein or low-carbohydrate diets are high in popularity, because they allow dieters to continue to eat their favorite foods, in moderation. Particularly for those who find it hard to exercise will power, diets that allow such individual freedom of choice would seem ideal.

Rice Diets

Rice is the staple food of the Orient, and the amount of energy concentrated on the growing of rice may indicate man's instinctive knowledge of his need for this vital grain.

A wide selection of variations on the rice diet have been introduced to the Western world. Some basic points all have in common:

1. Brown rice is the most nutritious, from not having been subjected to the industrial processes used to bleach and refine white rice.

2. Because rice is primarily a "filling" source of carbohydrates, there is less of a tendency to overeat on a rice diet.

3. Because rice comes from the earth, it is a natural food, offering a direct source of energy from the soil.

Some people question the value of an all-rice diet, on the ground that the body needs more nutrients in its system than are contained in rice. Adaptations have been developed whereby rice remains the staple, but other foods are added in small quantities. The most popular American rice diet has the following formula: half a cup of rice in the morning, one cup of rice with a cup of vegetables at noon, one cup of rice with a small portion of seafood in the evening.

In addition to energizing the body through the use of a natural grain, this diet has the residual effect of loss of weight — said to be as much as 10 pounds within the first two weeks. Changing the vegetables and fish used as a supplement injects some variety, and those who have followed such a diet over long periods claim they feel more energetic, more in touch with their bodies, and able to function more freely and comfortably.

Vegetarianism

The vegetarian diet is thought by many to be the diet with the greatest potential for optimum health. Its tenets are absolute: you may eat only food that comes from the earth. The three basic vegetarian food groups: (1) grains, seeds, and nuts, (2) vegetables, and (3) fruits. All refined, processed, denatured, starchy, sweet foods are to be avoided, and milk, cold-pressed vegetable oils, and honey are used to complement the three basic food groups.

The advantages of vegetarianism?

Vegetables contain more nutrients than an equal amount of dead flesh. The four necessary diet elements — proteins, carbohydrates, fats, and salt — are found in greater quantity and in more compact form in earth-derived food than in animal flesh.

Flesh carries with it the typical diseases that have beset the animal throughout its life, and remnants of the germs can still remain in the meat.

Man is not by nature a carnivorous animal. Consumption of meat, then, is unnatural to the organism. Vegetarians insit that they find themselves stronger over periods of time than meat eaters.

Weight loss is often another result of vegetarianism, because meat, being composed chiefly of protein and fats, has a high calorie content, whereas equivalent quantities of vegetables can be consumed with a lower intake of calories.

Should these advantages not be sufficiently convincing, there is the humanitarian principle, which probably brings more people to vegetarianism than any other. And, finally, the price of vegetables is considerably less than the price of meat.

As God said to Adam in the Garden of Eden: "Behold, I have given you every herb bearing seed which is upon the face of all the earth, and every tree in which is the fruit of a tree yielding seed; to you it shall be for meat."

Fruitarianism

Fruitarianism is simply the exclusive eating of natural fruits and vegetables. An inexpensive diet, it is thought by its advocates to be extremely healthy because of the natural nutrients — proteins, vitamins, carbohydrates, minerals, and iron — found in almost every fruit and vegetable. True fruitarianism, of course, is the consumption of only natural fruit and fruit juices. Digestion of fruit is simple, which takes pressure off the digestive organs; juices are thought to be cleansing agents, and drinking them aids in elimination. According to its advocates, fruitariansim promotes speedy healing of wounds and immunity from hardening of the arteries and rheumatism, as well as the curing of diseases ranging from tonsillitis to appendicitis and blood pressure abnormalities.

A warning in the fruitarian diet is to keep intake down because the concentration of nutrients in fruits is higher than in meat, and a smaller amount will satisfy the body's needs. It is usually recommended that the fruit diet be supplemented occasionally with vegetables — although the two should not be combined in the same meal.

This form of dieting, opponents believe, may deprive the body of sufficient protein for it to carry out its natural functions. Food supplements are encouraged — which has caused disbelievers to point out that such supplements would not be needed if such a diet were totally adequate.

Herbs and Grains

Some people believe that seeds, grains, and nuts are the most important and most potent of all foods. They contain minerals (especially calcium, phosphorus, magnesium, and iron), most of the vitamins (especially vitamins A, B, and E), are an excellent source of unsaturated fatty acids and lecithin, and supply plenty of natural proteins.

Some of the healthiest people in the world are the peasants of southeastern Europe, whose meat intake is limited because prices are high, whose grains are not factory-processed and consequently contain all the natural nutrients, and who don't buy fertilizers, which means the foods they grow are pure and unharmed by chemicals. They subsist chiefly on whole-grain bread and other seeds and grains. Americans, quick to make comparisons with their own lives, have recently taken great interest in herbal/grain diets of this kind, and find themselves regretting the advent of industrialization with its mass producing and mass packaging. We have to buy bran to add fiber to our diet that has been expunged in the effort to make eating easier, and buy pure foods expensively at the health food stores which in poorer countries are available at any market stall.

Because of the efforts to which man has consistently gone in order to raise the different grain crops that characterize each of the world's cultures, it is thought that the knowledge of the vital part seeds and grains play in basic nutrition must be instinctive. So, as modern man seeks to rediscover some of the secrets that have been lost in the scramble to achieve other priorities, the herbal/grain diet is once again coming into vogue.

Organic Diets

Organic foods are simply those which have not been tampered with in any way — have not been cooked, treated, added to, depleted, sprayed, or strayed from their natural state. People who adhere to organic diets believe that it is vital to take in food in totally pure form. Yet it is almost impossible, these days, to eat a strictly organic diet. While there may have been no deliberate interference, so-called organic foods are grown in a polluted atmosphere, are watered by polluted water, and contain certain poisonous substances as a result of fallout. Foods bought from health food stores are grown primarily in California and Florida, and by the time they reach stores in other parts of the country are often several days old, which means they have a reduced vitamin content. Even in organic dieting, food supplements are almost always necessary to offset the lack of nutrients and presence of unavoidable impurities.

"Organic" eggs and milk are to be found in many health food stores; yet for the diet to be truly organic, the hen or cow would have had to consume only organic grains and feed — and the same complications apply. Americans have probably robbed themselves of the opportunity to try truly organic dieting at all.

Fasting

At first glance fasting would seem simply to mean not eating for short or longer periods of time. But there are several different ways to fast, and some interesting motivations behind them.

One of the main benefits of fasting is purification of the digestive system. Our typical careless eating habits leave it largely up to chance what harmful elements enter the body by way of the food we ingest. Fasting, especially when the fast consists only of water and lemon juice, enables the body to rid itself of the poisonous wastes it accumulates.

Another benefit is the result of quick weight loss. When there is no caloric intake, the body is forced to use its own fatty tissue to supply energy, and this ridding of fat results in rapid reduction of weight. In addition, fasting for a period of two or three days depresses the appetite so that when regular eating is resumed, the intake will be less than before.

Fasts are often used to complement rest therapy. When the body has been overworked and is suffering from exhaustion, it tends to desire more food to make up for the energy it has exerted. Fasting accompanied by a more relaxed regimen means that the intake has been drastically reduced and consequently there is a smaller amount of energy to burn off.

Most experts on fasting warn that the first two days of the fast are the most difficult. During that time the body, accustomed to random and free intake of food, feels deprived, and food becomes almost an obsession. (Very few Americans eat only when they are hungry — the act of eating is more of an indulgence, even a pastime.) Food deprivation causes hunger pangs and a feeling of weakness. By the third day, however, the body has adjusted and begins to feel suppler, leaner, and more disciplined than before. The purification process has begun, and many of the stored-up poisons have already been eliminated.

The Juice Fast

The classic form of fasting is a water fast — abstinence from all food and drink other than pure water. Recently, however, there has been a change to fasting on the fresh raw juices of fruits and vegetables, plus vegetable broths and herb teas. Medical justification for juice fasting is based on these physiological facts:

1. Raw juices and freshly made vegetable broths are rich in vitamins, minerals, trace elements, and enzymes.

2. These vital elements are easily assimilated directly into the bloodstream without putting a strain on the digestive system.

3. They do not stimulate the secretion of hydrochloric acid in the stomach, which can lead to ulcers.

4. They are beneficial in normalizing all body processes.

5. They provide an alkaline surplus, important for the proper acid-alkaline balance in the blood and tissues.

6. They help to restore the biochemical and mineral balance in the body tissues and cells.

7. They stimulate the cells to absorb necessary nutrients from the blood and excrete metabolic wastes.

Adverse Opinions

There are some controversial features of fasting. One is whether enemas should be used. The explanation for recommending their use is that without food intake the usual stimulation which results in the excretion of waste products is missing, hence enemas are necessary to flush out the impurities. Physicians warn, however, that too frequent enemas can weaken the intestinal structure, and can be habit-forming.

Another adverse opinion holds that fasting is the ultimate deprivation, which disallows the body the nutrition it needs for proper growth and health. Hunger is a sign that the body is in need; consequently, the ignoring of hunger pangs is actually detrimental to physical well-being.

Whatever the arguments against it, the habit of fasting is growing in popularity. Whether for the purpose of losing weight, purifying the system, or undertaking an exercise in self-discipline, people continue to give it a try. One warning that probably should be reiterated is that a physician should be consulted before undertaking a fast lasting longer than a day — but that should be a commonplace of every change in diet.

Go into yourself
and test
the depths
in which
your life
takes rise ...

Accept it,
just as it stands

Rilke

Corita

SEX STYLES

There is no area of our lives that involves us more intimately, and consequently no area where we are more uniquely vulnerable. One of the features of our times is greater openness about sex — freedom to talk about it, practice it, experiment in its byways. Yet sex is still an area where there are astonishing harshnesses — children denied sex education, and the mentally ill, the aged, and the disabled denied expression of their sexual needs. The phenomenon of swinging was said to "open up" stale, flat marriages — but did it do so without distressful long-run consequences? Sexual dysfunction is being treated by compassionate therapists with an absence of pressure for performance, coupled with the use of sympathetic surrogates. Patterns of cohabitation are changing in our colleges. Centers are available for every type of sexual problem, and for simply having fun.

The task of the 1970s is surely to bring about not only more candor about sexual needs and rights, but also increased awareness of the responsibilities that go along with sexual expression. Consequently, the first item in this section is a *Bill of Sexual Rights and Responsibilities* that appeared in *The Humanist* magazine early in 1976. Drafted by Dr. Lester Kirkendall, noted sexologist and professor of family life at the University of Oregon, it sums up so much of today's enlightened thinking on sex that it has been endorsed by a group of psychologists and writers who represent the vanguard of humanist sexology.

A SEXUAL BILL OF RIGHTS

Sexuality has for too long been denied its proper place among other human activities. Physical eroticism has been either shrouded in mystery and surrounded by taboos or heralded far beyond its capacity, by itself, to contribute to the fullness of life. Human sexuality grows increasingly satisfying as life itself becomes more meaningful. The time has come to enhance the quality of sexuality by emphasizing its contributions to a happy and significant life.

For the first time in history there need be no fear of unwanted pregnancy or venereal disease, if proper precautions are taken. The limitation of sexual expression to conjugal unions or monogamous marriage was perhaps sensible so long as reproduction was still largely a matter of chance, and so long as women were subjugated to men. Although we consider marriage, where viable, a cherished human relationship, we believe that other sexual relationships also are significant. In any case, human beings should have the right to express their sexual desires and enter into relationships as they see fit, as long as they do not harm others or interfere with their rights to sexual expression. This new sense of freedom, however, should be accompanied by a sense of ethical responsibility.

Fortunately, there is now taking place a worldwide reexamination of the proper place of sexuality in human experience. We believe that the humanization of sexuality is far enough advanced to make useful a statement of rights and responsibilities of the individual to society and of society to the individual. Accordingly we wish to offer the following points for consideration:

1. **The boundaries of human sexuality need to be expanded ....** Responsible sexuality should now be viewed as an expression of intimacy for women as well as for men, a source of enjoyment and enrichment in addition to being a way of releasing tension, even when there is no likelihood of procreation.

This integration of sexuality with other aspects of experience will occur only as one achieves an essentially balanced life. When this happens, sexuality will take its place among other natural functions.

2. **Developing a sense of equity between the sexes is an essential feature of a sensible morality.** All legal, occupational,economic, and political discrimination against women should be removed and all traces of sexism erased. Until women have equal opportunities, they will be vulnerable to sexual exploitation by men. In particular, men must recognize the right of women to control their own bodies and determine the nature of their own sexual expression. All individuals, female or male, are entitled to equal consideration as persons.

3. **Repressive taboos should be replaced by a more balanced and objective view of sexuality based on a sensitive awareness of**

human behavior and needs. Archaic taboos limit our thinking in many ways. As these taboos are dispelled and an objective reappraisal ensues, numerous sexual expressions will be seen in a different light. Many that now seem unacceptable will very likely become valid in certain circumstances. Extramarital sexual relationships with the consent of one's partner are being accepted by some. Premarital sexual relationships, already accepted in some parts of the world, will become even more widely so. This will very likely also be true of homosexual and bisexual relationships . . . .

Taboos have prevented adequate examination of certain topics . . . thus blocking the discovery of answers to important sexual questions. Abortion is a case in point. By focusing only on the destruction of the fetus, many have avoided facing the other issues that are fundamental. They do not, for example, openly discuss ways of providing a comprehensive sex-education program for both children and adults . . . . The oversacramentalization of sex also inhibits open discussion by not allowing people to treat sex as a natural experience.

4. Each person has both an obligation and a right to be fully informed about the various civic and community aspects of human sexuality . . . . Sexual attitudes are intimately related to many problems of public import, but again taboos inhibit free discussion. Too rapid a population growth cannot be dealt with except as individual attitudes toward sexual expression and contraception are recognized. . . . In the rehabilitation of incarcerated criminals, establishing meaningful ties with others is important. It is inhumane and self-defeating to cut these persons off from the possibility of sexual relationships. We should extend this

concern to all persons who are confined in institutions; for example, those in senior-citizens' homes. The right of the physically and mentally handicapped to be fully informed about sexuality and to have sexual outlets available should be another concern. The commercialization of sex needs careful scrutiny. Patterns in child-rearing that may result in dysfunctional sexual expressions, such as child abuse and emotional deprivation, must be studied . . . .

5. Potential parents have both the right and the responsibility to plan the number and time of their children, taking into account both social needs and their own desires. . . . Involved in the right to birth control is the right to voluntary sterilization and abortion . . . birth control should be the appropriate responsibility of men as well as women. Male contraception should be the object of further research.

6. Sexual morality should come from a sense of caring and respect for others; it cannot be legislated. Laws can and do protect the young from exploitation and people of any age from abuse. Beyond that, forms of sexual expression should not be a matter of legal regulation . . . . Our overriding objective should be to help individuals live balanced and self-actualized lives . . . . Sexual morality should be viewed as an inseparable part of general morality, not as a special set of rules.

7. Physical pleasure has worth as a moral value. Traditional religious and social views have often condemned pleasures of the body as "sinful" or "wicked." These attitudes are inhumane . . . . The findings of the behavioral sciences demonstrate that deprivation of physical pleasure, particularly during the formative periods of development, often results in family breakdown, child abuse, adolescent runaways, crime, violence, alcoholism, and other forms of dehumanizing behavior . . . .

8. **Individuals are able to respond positively and affirmatively to sexuality throughout life; this must be acknowledged and accepted.** Childhood sexuality is expressed through genital awareness and exploration . . . . These are learning experiences that help the individual incorporate sexuality as an integral part of his or her personality. Masturbation is a viable mode of satisfaction for many individuals, young and old, and should be fully accepted . . . . We need to appreciate the fact that older persons also have sexual needs. The joy of touching, of giving and receiving affection, and the satisfaction of intimate body responsiveness is the right of everyone throughout life.

9. **In all sexual encounters, commitment to humane and humanistic values should be present.** No person's sexual behavior should hurt or disadvantage another . . . . In any sexual encounter or relationship, freely given consent is fundamental, even in the marital relationship, where consent is often denied or taken for granted . . . .

No relationship occurs in a vacuum. In addition to the persons directly involved in the sexual relationship there are important others . . . . For this reason each individual must have empathy for others. One might ask oneself, "How would I want others to conduct themselves sexually toward me and others I care about? Am I at least as concerned for the happiness and well-being of my partner, and others involved, as for my own?" . . .

The realization of the points in this statement depends upon certain attributes in the individual. One needs to have autonomy and control over his or her own sexual functioning. One needs to find reasonable satisfaction in living and to accept and enjoy pleasures of the body. Furthermore, one needs to respect the rights of others to those same qualities. The society in which one lives, while it makes demands, should also be attuned to individual needs and the importance of personal freedom. Only as these conditions are met will loving and guilt-free sexuality be possible.

In order to realize our potential for joyful sexual expression, we need to adopt the doctrine that actualizing pleasures are among the highest moral goods — so long as they are experienced with responsibility and mutuality . . . .

. . . The loving feelings of mental and physical well-being, the sense of completion of the self, that we can experience from freely expressed sexuality may well reach out to all humanity. It is quite impossible to have a meaningful, ecstatic sexual and sensual life and to be indifferent to or uncaring about other human beings.

THE NATIONAL SEX FORUM
sexual attitude restructuring

A vital force in contemporary American sexual awareness is the National Sex Forum (NSF) in San Francisco. Founded in 1968 by Ted McIlvenna, a Methodist minister associated with the Glide Foundation, and Phyllis Lyon, author and activist in the area of women's sexuality, the NSF strives to help individuals understand various sexual experiences through a program known as Personal Sexual Enrichment/Education (PSE/E). The NSF stresses that its programs are "open to all persons whether they describe themselves as homosexual, heterosexual, bisexual, or otherwise" — celibacy, for instance, is an "otherwise."

SAR

One of the techniques developed in the PSE/E program is Sexual Attitude Restructuring (SAR), a technique aimed at "demythologizing" the sexual experience and enabling the individual to accept responsibility for his or her own sexual pleasure. Many people feel guilty about sex and consequently cannot enjoy it. Others fear that their sexual feelings may not be "normal." One of the central principles of the Forum is that sexuality is the most individualistic expression of one's self, and what is normal, therefore, must be the individual's decision alone. According to Carolyn Smith, a counselor at NSF and coauthor of *SARguide for a Better Sex Life* — "As long as people know what they're doing, feel good about it, and don't harm others, anything goes."

Introductory Course

In an effort to reach people who would not otherwise be able to afford professional guidance, the NSF offers an introductory course at the surprisingly low cost of $125 per person. This includes an initial assessment session with one of the counselors, four weekly sessions of three and a half hours each, in groups of 15 to 20 people, the workbook — *SARguide for a Better Sex Life* — and some private sessions with a counselor if needed. The course is offered jointly with the University of California, San Francisco, and is intended as a comprehensive view of human sexuality — not an encounter or sensitivity session. As in all NSF programs, no overt sexuality is involved.

Methods

Central to the success of Sexual Attitude Restructuring is the use of sexually explicit films and videotapes. On the principle that one picture is worth a thousand words, the films depict couples (heterosexual and homosexual) engaged in a wide variety of sexual expression. The purpose is to "desensitize" the class so as to make frank and candid discussion of sexuality more possible. The films (produced by the NSF's Multi Media Center) have a carefree, sensual style which emphasizes the joys and celebration of love-making, thereby helping

the viewers to an appreciation of their own sexual responses. In the group discussions which follow, individual reactions are exchanged, and the process of change and the expansion of sexual attitudes begins. Throughout the stages of the course, participants are asked to do "homework" exercises designed to open the mind and body to sensual experience (these include "sensate awareness" exercises requiring close attention to sensory stimuli such as temperature, taste, and smell, examination of the body, masturbation, and intercourse in various positions). Keeping a journal is considered a very important aspect of the course. The crucial and final step is the resensitization of the participants to the expanded possibilities of sexuality — the enhancement of the senses, and total freedom to feel.

The NSF also offers a variety of other advanced classes, workshops, and seminars, based on the SAR techniques, and will design programs to meet the specific needs of particular groups.

All forms of sexual expression are regarded by the Forum as available for exploration, but an area of particular concentration is the sexuality of the mentally or physically disabled person, one of the least understood and most ignored aspects of sexual research. Phyllis Lyon, NSF's codirector, insists that understanding sexuality in someone who is physically disabled is really no different from understanding sexuality in any human being.

Concept

"Sexuality is sexuality," she says. "The basic problem lies once again in an unwillingness to acknowledge it as a basic human expression, and to speak openly about sex. Some disabled people have the additional 'problem' of having to learn alternative sexual techniques. An amazing number of people in the helping professions — such as doctors — refuse to even acknowledge the existence of sexuality in a disabled person, much less suggest alternate methods of expressing it. Oral sex, for instance, is still too embarrassing — or too unacceptable — for many doctors to even mention.

"The mentally retarded person has an additional 'problem' since the retarded have traditionally been treated as children, and in our society children aren't supposed to have sexual needs. So you see we are still dealing with the real problem of acknowledgment of our sexuality — we need to speak openly about sex. The lack of candor about sexuality has especially noticeable consequences with the disabled, the elderly, and juveniles, but the rest of us suffer from the same maladies — ignorance and a great wealth of *mis*information."

Sexuality in the Disabled

The NSF has a supplementary program which deals specifically with sexuality in the disabled person. The Multi Media Center has produced films for the education of hospital personnel (some V.A. hospitals are participating in the program), physicians, and the families of the disabled. Two are panel discussions — one, "Just What Can You Do?" suggests alternate sexual techniques for those with spinal cord injury, while "Don't Tell the Cripples About Sex" discusses sexuality in victims of cerebral palsy. Another film illustrates various sexual techniques between a physically disabled person and a fully able partner. The NSF plans to produce more such films when funds become available.

Self-Help Methods

In its eight years of operation, the National Sex Forum has developed unique self-help methods both for those who feel they have sexual problems and those who simply wish to expand their sexual awareness. Over 40,000 people have taken NSF's courses and workshops — more than half of them professionals who in turn extend the programs to their clients. The Forum also works closely with the University of Minnesota Medical School and the University of California, San Francisco, School of Medicine in both research and training programs. In its new San Francisco center the NSF hopes to focus and distribute information about the most recent developments in sex research, counseling and therapy techniques, education, and media materials. It has already provided thousands of professionals and lay people with an exciting approach to a fuller understanding of the meanings and values of human sexuality — a goal too long postponed in our quest for a better knowledge of ourselves.

If you are interested in participating in a Personal Sexual Enrichment/Education workshop in San Francisco, contact the NSF headquarters and a counselor will set up an appointment. Outside the Bay area, it will be harder to find professionals trained in the SAR methods, although the NSF has trained counselors, therapists, doctors, and clergy from all over the country. The audio-visual program is available on videotape cassettes, enabling some professionals to offer this essential aspect of the workshop as well. If you cannot locate an SAR counselor in your area, consult the NSF, which may be able to refer you.

There is an alternative, however, in the shape of the *SARguide for a Better Sex Life,* which was designed as a self-help manual and has been used very effectively by those who cannot attend courses or find professional help in their own areas. In fact, the NSF believes that by using the book as a guide, most people can help themselves without the aid of a professional counselor.

SANDSTONE

"America was founded, populated and made great by people who got up off their asses and went somewhere looking for a chance to live and grow and be free. Any fear I've had that the spirit of adventure has drained out of this country evaporated that weekend."

— Orson Bean on Sandstone

"There is much of the gullible and credulous in California, along with the energy and violence, the revolutionary mystique, the cult of sexuality. But there is also a genuine effort to reach out for the life force beyond the familiar and accepted, even beyond the world of the senses into whatever lies there. There is only one Sandstone."

— Max Lerner on Sandstone

"Sandstone is no more and no less than a fuck farm."

— Anonymous

Gay Talese came to Sandstone for a weekend a couple of years ago and stayed for months. Marty Zitter, one of Sandstone's directors (along with Alex Comfort and Emily Coleman), says one should spend at least a week at Sandstone to capture the Sandstone Experience. For those too timid, or too poor, for a week's worth of Sandstone ($225), a day-long seminar offers a distillation of the experience for $40 per person. But what is Sandstone?

Exploring Relationships

The Sandstone Ranch is tucked into the hills above Topanga Canyon, with a spectacular view of the Malibu coastline and distant Catalina Island. It is a center where you can explore whatever lifestyles are of interest to you in a supportive atmosphere.

Your relationship with spouse, lover, girlfriend or boyfriend is considered primary. The object is to explore satellite relationships and to understand your own potentialities.

Officially Sandstone calls itself an experiment in social and recreational alternatives, and a center to explore those trends in education, religion, philosophy, and the physical and behavioral sciences which emphasize the potentialities and values of human existence. Its activities consist of seminars and workshops, residential programs, consulting and training, a private membership club, and an alternative lifestyle research community.

The Sandstone experience focuses on three major aspects of exploring alternate, intimate lifestyles:

Getting There: How to leave the outside world behind, become fully invested in your immediate experience in the here and now, and develop a body orientation.

Exploring What Is Possible: Finding out, experimentally, what is and might be rather that what should be or has been. Also developing an attitude that facilitates learning.

Experimenting: Learning to explore and negotiate with others, how to set up low-risk experiments that are not catastrophic. Becoming able to deal with boundaries and preferences, to explore fantasy behaviorally and realize what open sexuality and open relationships are. In a new sense, it's learning how to play.

You could say that Sandstone differentiates between hot and cool sex. Hot sex is sex for power, conquest, avarice, sin, and degradation. Cool sex is sex with sensuality, friendliness, and warmth. Obviously, Sandstone encourages the latter. Some means of doing so: floating in a skin-temperature pool, hiking in the hills, taking part in the Sandstone Massage classes, sailing the blue Pacific aboard the *Sandstone*, the center's racing sloop, relaxing on the terraced lawns, developing the ability to touch and be touched, to express affection openly. Wearing clothing at Sandstone is *always* optional.

The center publishes quarterly calendars of events listing the range of activities available. It may be worth mentioning that the program costs cover tuition, food, and informal lodging. Children and pets are *not* welcome. Participants accompanied by partners of the opposite sex *may* (the emphasis is Sandstone's) be invited to stay for the Sandstone Club evening "social gatherings."

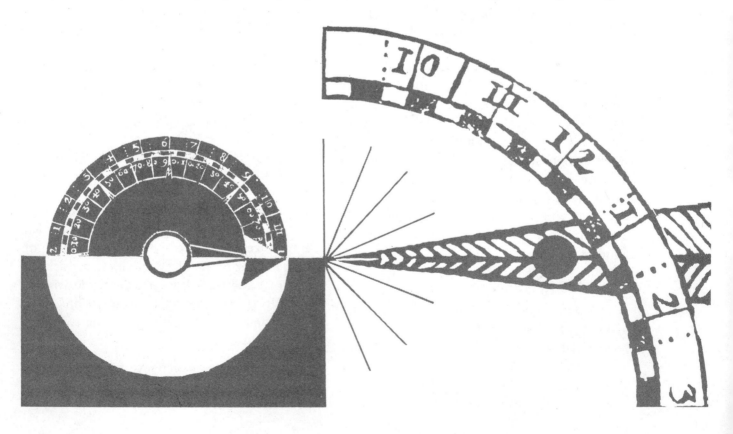

ELYSIUM

Elysium has been called "the poor man's Sandstone," and it is difficult not to make that comparison. Also located in Topanga Canyon, Elysium Fields also offers programs in sensory awareness in a relaxed, informal setting. Many of the people who offer seminars at Sandstone also present them at Elysium, with the same intention: unification of the mind and body, allowing the whole person to emerge.

The Elysium Institute's 60-year-old guru, Ed Lange, is a long-time crusader for personal expressions of sensuality, freedom, and the constitutional right to assembly. He founded Elysium after a lifelong involvement with the nudist movement. When nudism seemed to be moving too slowly toward the true liberation of the body, Ed Lange founded Elysium as a more experimental place for exploration.

There were problems in the early days, for Lange proved to be moving too quickly for the Los Angeles County authorities. Existing laws banned public nudity, and police helicopters would circle the canyon meadows looking for violators. However, these problems have been satisfactorily resolved in the courts, and all the Elysium Fields complex is now clothing-optional for members and guests.

Expressions of sexuality are not as open at Elysium as at Sandstone. Jacuzzis, whirlpools, and saunas serve as sensual meeting places, and "meditation rooms" also offer opportunities for sexual play. Unlike Sandstone, Elysium allows children to attend along with their parents, making it possible for Elysium to be a family experience.

In addition to the Topanga Canyon complex, Elysium maintains an In-Town Center which offers introductory programs to the Elysium experience. Clothing is required for the In-Town meetings, which emphasize bringing groups of people together in a nonthreatening environment to explore their potentials as human beings.

The Elysium credo: "There is an essential wholesomeness in the human body and all of its functions. Exposure to sun, water, air and to nature is a helpful and basic factor in building and maintaining healthy attitudes of mind in the development of a strong body. Human sexuality is part and parcel of our living and no separation or division is possible without denying our humanness."

MASTERS AND JOHNSON

Since the publication in 1966 and 1970 of their monumental studies, *Human Sexual Response* and *Human Sexual Inadequacy,* William Masters and Virginia Johnson have become almost as basic a household term in the United States as bread and butter. The books were the fruit of 20 years of research, much of it conducted almost in secrecy, since it dealt with the most sensitive area in our lives: exactly how human beings respond sexually. Masters and Johnson were the first to study the exact mechanics of sexual union, using a variety of mechanical and sensual devices to stimulate orgasm and measure its quality and duration in both sexes. The pair, who have since become a permanent duo in life as well as work, were the first to use sexual surrogates (at first only women, because the idea of male surrogates was still unacceptable at the time their studies began) in the effort to bring about better sexual compatibility and eradicate sexual dysfunctions. They were and are pioneers in the field of couple sex therapy.

One basic premise in Masters and Johnson therapy is that there is no uninvolved partner in any marriage in which there is some form of sexual inadequacy. In their view, isolating a husband or wife from his or her spouse in therapy not only denies the concept that both partners are involved in the sexual inadequacy with which their relationship is contending, but also ignores the fundamental fact that sexual response represents interaction between people. While both partners are treated, it is the marital relationship that is considered the patient.

Because neither sex can completely understand the other's sexuality, a man and a woman therapist can best treat a man and a woman patient. Each cotherapist has the responsibility of evaluating, translating for, and representing fairly the partner of the same sex in the "distressed marital unit." During treatment, one cotherapist remains primarily silent, in order to observe and define degrees of understanding, acceptance, or rejection of material. It is he/she who acts as coach of the team, changing pace when needed, clarifying when it becomes obvious that one or both of the patients does not understand; from time to time the roles are reversed so that each cotherapist acts as both discussant and observer.

Fear of Performance

Masters and Johnson have found that inevitably any sexually dysfunctional marital unit has as one of its fundamental handicaps insecurity in sexual matters. This insecurity, which frequently manifests itself as fear of performance, is the greatest known deterrent to effective sexual functioning, simply because it distracts the fearful individual from his or her natural responses. In such cases Masters and Johnson avoid all specific suggestion of goal-oriented sexual performance.

Communication is vital to sexual understanding. The ultimate level in marital-unit communication is sexual intercourse. When couples find it difficult to communicate sexually, most other means of communication rapidly diminish in effectiveness. While Masters and Johnson do not adhere to the concept that sexual functioning is the total of a marital relationship, they find that few marriages can exist as effective, complete, and ongoing entities without a comfortable sexual exchange.

Patients Treated As Guests

Couples entering Masters and Johnson therapy are requested to devote two weeks to the therapeutic program, which allows them to isolate themselves from the everyday world; during this time they are treated as though they are guests on a vacation.

Daily conferences are held during this two-week program. The cotherapists are not seeking a report of perfect achievement in the privacy of the bedroom — they are interested in the partners making their usual errors so that those errors can be evaluated and discussed openly and immediately.

Patients must be recommended for therapy by such authorities as physicians, psychologists, social workers, and theologians. Individuals seen in treatment must agree to cooperate with five years of follow-up after termination of the acute phase of the therapy program. In this way Masters and Johnson can be sure that success was not temporary.

The Past

History-taking is an important part of the Masters and Johnson procedure. It must provide character-defining information as well as knowledge of the basic personalities of the marital partners; it should also elicit what changes the partners consider desirable, and the personal resources and potentials with which the team will be working.

Day 1 of therapy is a history-taking day. Day 2 involves more history-taking and a review of the previous day's information. Day 3 involves physical examinations and a round-table discussion with emphasis on sensory focus and special-sense discussion. Various tactile "exercises" are conducted by the cotherapists. Day 4 involves more discussion, reinforcement, and expansion of the tactile exercises. The remainder of the two-week therapy continues with reinforcement, discussions, more exercises . . . and often the use of a surrogate.

Partner Surrogates

The term *replacement partner* is used to describe the partner of choice brought by a man or woman patient. However, a "partner surrogate" is provided by the cotherapists for an unmarried person referred for treatment who has no one to provide psychological and physiological support during the acute therapy phase.

Statistically, there no longer is any question about the advantage of educating and treating men and women together when attacking the clinical causes of male or female sexual inadequacy — hence the use of a surrogate.

The specific role of the partner surrogate is to approximate that of a supportive, interested, cooperative spouse. Her/his contributions are infinitely more valuable as a means of psychological support than as a measure of physiological initiation. Partner surrogates have had a significant degree of sexual experience before joining the program. They are fully sexually responsive men and women, and as is true with most confidently responsive persons, understandingly and compassionately concerned for the frustrations of a sexually inadequate partner.

Social Exchange

With a male client and female surrogate, the first meeting is limited to a social commitment. The couple spends an evening of dinner and casual conversation to make the man comfortable and allow him to think of the woman as a friend and compassionate partner. Every effort is made by cotherapists to match the dysfunctional man and his partner surrogate as to age, personality, and educational and social background.

Once social exchange has been successfully established, the partner surrogate moves into a wife's role as the treatment phase is expanded. She joins the sexually inadequate

male in both social and physical release of therapeutic tensions, with the exception of attending therapy sessions. There has been a high rate of success through the use of surrogates — approximately equal to the success of that achieved by cooperative wives and husbands in marital-unit referrals.

And speaking of success, what is the overall failure rate of the Masters and Johnson clinic? Their figures as of 1970 indicated that of 790 marital units referred for treatment, the overall failure rate was 20 percent — which would indicate that there is indeed much that is valuable in this kind of therapy.

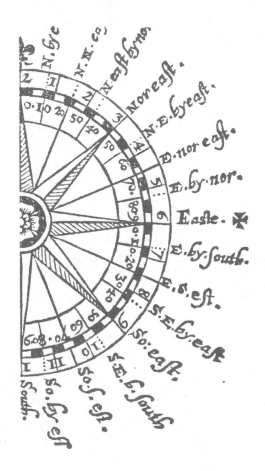

HARTMAN AND FITHIAN

A slightly different approach to sexual problems is taken by William Hartman and Marilyn Fithian. Like Masters and Johnson, they offer a two-week therapy clinic and also make use of a male and female therapist team. But theirs is a bio-psycho-social approach. They encourage you to be familiar with your body, to have a knowledge of it, and to help change it.

Perhaps the best way of illustrating their approach is to list the daily schedule at their two-week intensive sexual therapy program:

First Day — Monday: MMPI (Minnesota Multiphasic Personality Inventory), TJTA (Taylor-Johnson Temperament Analysis), Draw-A-Scene, Luscher color test, sex history.

Second Day — Tuesday: Follow-up sex history, switch.

Third Day — Wednesday: Physical exam, round table, explanation of psychological tests if indicated or requested.

Fourth Day — Thursday: Sexological forum, Draw-A-Person test, sexological exam, body imagery, sensitivity, Kegel film, assignment — comb hair.

Fifth Day — Friday: Foot caress, videotape — caress, face caress, assignment — give each other a bath or shower.

Sixth Day - Saturday: Body caress and breathing together, videotape — pleasuring squeeze technique, assignment for Sunday — pleasuring and clamping successfully several times, clamping enough times to go at least 15 minutes.

Seventh Day — Sunday: Assignment in motel — pleasuring, male and female; practice squeeze technique.

Eighth Day — Monday: Come in and report; if things are going all right, assignment for more pleasuring. See films of coital positions, nonorgasmic woman — audio tape if indicated.

Ninth Day — Tuesday: Talk and report, intercourse (allowed) if things are going well, videotape — intercourse.

Tenth Day — Wednesday: Report, videotape — intercourse.

Eleventh Day — Thursday: Report, videotape — intercourse, spontaneity assignment.

Twelfth Day — Friday: Report, evaluation of progress — if satisfactory, the couple return home. If further progress is needed by seeing another videotape and completing an additional assignment or repeating one, the couple remain another day.

Thirteenth Day — Saturday: Wrap up, schedule for follow-ups, discuss how the couple will be able to implement what they have learned.

If some of the terms are strange to the layman, one thing is clear — Hartman and Fithian are more interested in "doing" than "talking." Interestingly, they are prepared to use hypnosis if the individual or couple feels it would be helpful.

Hartman and Fithian are reluctant to report their statistical success rates, feeling that therapy should not be reduced to a numbers game. In their book, *The Treatment of Sexual Dysfunction*, however, they state: "... we can honestly assure candidates for therapy that at the time of follow-up, couples who have completed our two-week program describe the benefits achieved in approximately the same proportions as are reported by Masters and Johnson."

Hartman and Fithian have also begun group workshops with from seven to 10 couples, which last from one to six days. The group experience is a miniversion of their two-week program. In group situations, the therapists believe, couples can benefit additionally from observing each other and comparing problems.

Hartman and Fithian have initiated training programs for dual sex therapy teams, are doing extensive laboratory research, and have several other projects in initial stages of development.

LONNIE BARBACH /human sensuality clinic

"We are programmed always to have a purpose, to strive, to succeed, but not to relax and enjoy being alive and feeling good."

— Lonnie Barbach

Analyzing the results of two sexual behavior studies — the *Kinsey Report* (1953) and the *Playboy Foundation Report* (1972) — Lonnie Barbach concludes that "despite the so-called sexual revolution, not much progress has been made in orgasmic responsivity."

Dr. Barbach is a psychologist and sex therapist, particularly concerned with the problem many women have in understanding their sexual nature and in reaching orgasm. Trained in basic Masters and Johnson techniques, considerable experience in couples therapy at the University of California Health Service in Berkeley led her to question the validity of sexual therapy that requires a male partner. The couple treatment is often too expensive for many women to afford; it is restricted to those with steady sexual partners; a surrogate or regular partner must be willing and available, and the treatment entirely excludes homosexuals and any others who deviate from strict heterosexuality.

Moreover, Dr. Barbach wished to counter the traditional view (propounded by many psychiatrists and popularized by such writers as Dr. David Reuben in his bestseller, *Everything You Always Wanted to Know About Sex, But Were Afraid to Ask*) that the presence of a sexual problem is a symptom of an underlying psychological problem or "neurosis," requiring psychotherapy. The psychiatric approach increases a woman's anxieties, depletes her financial resources, consumes her valuable time, yet produces little or no change.

The Barbach-run groups are known as "pre-orgasmic women's groups" on the principle that no woman is nonorgasmic; she is simply in need of guidance and encouragement to get in touch with her own body and sexual feelings, and to accept the responsibility of her sexual self. The approach is unique in that it is for women only, it is a *group* situation, it employs a variety of techniques, and it maintains that each woman is unique and there is no one or "right" way.

In the five-week-long group sessions, there are two group sexual therapists and five to seven women, strangers before the first meeting, all of whom meet in 10 sessions. They share stories about sexual difficulties and confusions, share feelings about sexual problems, and gain insights through the shared experiences and support. There is also one hour of homework per day, beginning with masturbation, "the easiest way to get in touch with one's sexual responses."

The treatment itself is a combination of group discussions, physiological information about the female anatomy, homework exercises, and individualized instruction. There is also post-group work in which the women are asked to continue the exercises on their own and take responsibility for their own sexuality.

According to Lonnie Barbach, there are several myths existing in American attitudes toward sex, all of which must be dispelled. To name a few:

Myth: So-called "vaginal orgasm" is somehow superior.

Barbach: "It is absurd that so much emphasis is placed on the manner in which orgasm is achieved rather than the enjoyment two people derive from their lovemaking."

Myth: Sex and intercourse are synonymous.

Barbach: "Intercourse is only one of a number of ways to give and receive sexual pleasure."

Myth: The male must be aggressive and the female passive.

Barbach: "Males enjoy the opportunity of having the partner assume some responsibility for sexual initiation and innovation."

BARBARA ROBERTS / social and sensory learning

Barbara Roberts thinks of herself as a "humanistic existentialist." Her point in therapy is to accept people right where they are. If sexual satisfaction is to come, the individual must understand his total relationship with the world through self-esteem and social skills. Roberts insists that her clients let go of expectations and develop self-awareness in the here and now. Her basic theory is that of imprinting/re-printing/relearning, and sometimes reversing, the imprinting processes.

Basically, she believes, some people are capable of achieving a higher degree of involvement than others. It is possible, according to Roberts, that two people can touch toes and experience orgasm.

Barbara Roberts can be found at the Center for Social and Sensory Learning, a Los Angeles organization which provides services in social skills, body awareness, and sexual functioning. Physicians and therapists are encouraged to refer patients and clients for supplementary therapy. Programs at the Center include social and dating skills, assertiveness training, verbal and nonverbal communication, body imagery, tension release, sensuality training, facts and fallacies of sexual functioning, counseling related to sexual problems, and supervision of surrogate sex therapy.

IPSA / school for surrogates

IPSA (which stands for International Professional Surrogates Association) is an organization committed to the belief that adults have the right to participate in experiential methods of treatment for sexual dysfunction and sexual enhancement. It was founded in June 1973 by a group of men and women who were interested in working as sexual surrogates. Among its objectives: to make available to therapists surrogates who uphold professional standards and meet professional qualifications; to increase general acceptance of surrogates; to elevate their professional standards; to advance knowledge of sexual functioning and disseminate information about it; to encourage updating of laws relating to sexual practices; to provide educational services for the self-improvement of members; to stimulate a feeling of fellowship and cooperation within the organization; and to conduct and/or participate in research relating to sexual dysfunctioning and functioning.

Code of Ethics

The idea of serving as a surrogate is an intriguing one, and to ward off the possibility that inappropriate people might apply, the IPSA code of ethics strongly stresses both the therapeutic nature of the situation and its total direction by the supervising therapist. There is no possibility of an IPSA surrogate taking on personal clients; the relationship is strictly time-limited, existing during professional appointments only. The program of therapy is designed by the supervising therapist to help the client reorient his or her sexuality in whatever way necessary for the

225

achievement of more satisfying relationships with desired partners. To achieve this, the surrogate will use his or her unique training in social and sexual skills, while recognizing their boundaries and limitations. Yet, should the supervising therapist be unavailable when a situation arises that would normally require consultation, the surrogate is responsible for taking appropriate action for the client's welfare, which has already been agreed on as the primary focus of the work. This responsibility continues until it is terminated by mutual agreement between therapist and surrogate, another professional takes over, or the client decides to terminate the therapy.

Confidentiality, of course, is a major tenet, save when there is clear and imminent danger to individuals or society. Even then, information will be shared only with appropriate professional colleagues or public authorities, and the client must be warned of this when therapy begins.

Precautions Taken

Surrogates are responsible for taking adequate precautions against transmitting diseases and infections, for making sure the client has taken similar precautions, and, invariably, for preventing conception.

An interesting section of the IPSA code states: "Surrogates recognize that effectiveness in the therapeutic situation depends in good part upon maintaining independent, personally fulfilling social and sexual relationships. Surrogates are responsible for seeking prompt and effective help when personal problems arise, in order to maintain optimum professionalism." This professionalism is sufficiently important that members are reminded that they may be identified as surrogates or IPSA members at times when they are not acting in these

capacities, and, consequently, their personal conduct should redound to the credit of both.

IPSA takes itself and its work extremely seriously — as is appropriate in a field of such intimate access to the most basic of human problems: impaired sexual functioning. There is no area where we are more vulnerable. Equally, there must be few fields that offer the opportunity to participate in the reorientation of unhappy human beings toward intimate, warm, and caring relationships — and none so personally as IPSA.

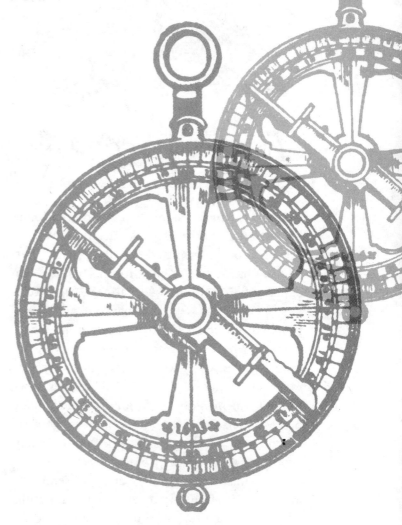

SWINGING / winding down?

What do professional counselors and psychotherapists have to say about the phenomenon of swinging, which had a great vogue — or at least a conversational one — in the first half of the 70s?

We consulted Dr. Norton F. Kristy, director of the Center for Counseling and Psychotherapy in Santa Monica, California, who specializes in marriage, family, and child counseling. Dr. Kristy has held a variety of academic positions, been a senior scientist-psychologist at the RAND Corporation, and once each week for four and a half years has enhanced one of Los Angeles' more frenetic talk shows with his calm and measured tones. In his capacity as psychological consultant he deals frequently with queries about swinging, but says he receives only half as many calls regarding it as he did a year ago. He also has numbers of private patients who have been involved in such experiences and have afforded plenty of insights into the effects of swinging on marital relationships.

Successful Swinging

All the studies made indicate only 10 to 20 percent of couples who experiment with swinging do so successfully for more than a brief period. This minority believe the practice enhances their marriage relationship, that swinging provides sexual variety, and because it is a pair experience, done with the knowledge and consent of the partner, it does not damage the primary relationship.

Few partners are so emotionally secure, however, that they can long indulge in this free exchange process without pangs of jealousy, feelings of inadequacy, and open or suppressed resentment. The great majority, according to Dr. Kristy, find the experience destructive and end up deeply offended psychologically and wounded emotionally. In the 80 to 90 percent of couples who experiment with swinging with negative results, about a third end in divorce. The rest try to heal the wounds and restore the dented equilibrium of their marriages by putting the practice behind them.

Swinging seems to be a somewhat fading fad. However, Dr. Kristy describes a somewhat parallel concept where extramarital sex can have a beneficial, even therapeutic effect on a marriage. Part of the larger context of a therapy he developed as a heroic measure for embattled marriages, in which the sexual relationship has deteriorated almost to vanishing point, amid bitterness, disappointment, and disillusionment, it is the Roommate Concept, which has been receiving increasing attention since Dr. Kristy described it to the American Association of Marriage Counselors recently.

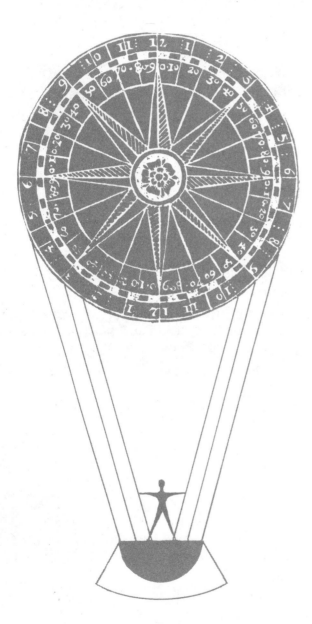

The partners remain in the same domicile but no longer consider themselves married. They write out a formal contract describing the terms and conditions of their cohabitation, and the marriage per se is set aside. Sometimes an actual document of legal separation is obtained. Where children are involved, each partner remains a parent, but they do not coparent. Neither party has spousal responsibilities or privileges. Normally they sleep in separate rooms and each is completely responsible for his own social and sexual rewards. This does not extend to bringing other individuals into the home, but partners are free to make whatever arrangements they like on the outside.

Creating a Dialogue

Remaining in the same domain creates a continuing emotional dialogue, which Dr. Kristy regards as essential, since in marital separations lasting six months or more the probability of reconciliation drops below 25 percent. However, lecturing and hostility are no longer relevant since each has abdicated responsibility for each other. Meanwhile, the partners participate in family therapy, dine together every two weeks, yet have the freedom — and responsibility — to experience themselves as separate and single people — which opens what Dr. Kristy calls "a whole new window on the world."

After six to nine months the arrangement is reviewed, and results so far have been excellent. Out of 200 cases, 60 percent of the marriages were renewed, as compared to the fewer than 20 percent of reconciliations after six months of actual separation. Dr. Kristy has recently completed a book called *Getting Unstuck*, which deals with extricating oneself from static situations in love, sex, marriage, life itself.

SONG OF AN UNSWUNG SWINGER

A stunnning, wide-eyed blonde I met at a cocktail party surprised me by the announcement that she was an enthusiastic swinger. An interior decorator, elegantly dressed, in her middle 30s, Shelley explained that she and her businessman husband Bill had been intensively pursuing sequential sexual coupling for several years. They had traveled the world — Hong Kong, Paris, Naples, Athens — experimenting with established and spontaneously improvised sexual variations: daisy chains, whips, the Kama Sutra, every sort and combination of positions and practices. Bill and Shelley were evidently true eclectics.

"We used to give beautiful parties," Shelley told me, "and swinging was just one of the many lovely things we did at them. We had a wonderful marriage, and swinging made it even better. If I met a girl I felt Bill would like, I would take her home for his delight, knowing he would do the same for me."

And afterward they would expand upon the quality of the experience. "You just think of it like a massage or a Jacuzzi — one of the nice ways to relax and enjoy life."

Shelley's expression saddened. "I did catch Bill cheating on me once, though." I must have looked the amazement I felt — cheating, with no prohibitions, no hangups, no dated old concepts such as adultery or infidelity? The blue eyes had a hurt look. "I found him in the bedroom writing down a girl's telephone number. You just don't *do* that.

"And then one night we were having dinner with David, Bill's business partner and best friend, and Bill started telling him how I was the most wonderful woman a man could ever have, a marvelous wife, a terrific companion. I was so touched." She paused. "I think Bill must have had a premonition or something. Anyway, we invited David home, and the three of us were in the bedroom, making love, when suddenly Bill just keeled over. Dead! You can imagine the shock for David and me."

I could not think of an appropriate comment. We were silent a few moments, and then Shelley went on:

"You know, I'm really pretty disenchanted about marriage, even though Bill was such a wonderful man in most ways and we had such an open relationship. Three weeks after the funeral, I found out that he had a mistress in San Diego. Can you believe that? So who can you trust anymore?"

Who indeed?

— N. L.

SOME THOUGHTS ON COLLEGE STUDENT SEXUAL PATTERNS

DR. ELEANOR MACKLIN

Dr. Eleanor Macklin is an assistant professor in the Department of Psychology at the State University College at Oswego, New York. These extracts from a talk she gave to the Association of College and University Housing Officers in July 1975 make some interesting points about the sexual behavior of today's college students.

What changes in sexual patterns have we noted on the college campus? First and foremost, a higher percentage of undergraduates, particularly women, are now sexually active. In 1972, Dr. Alan Guttmacher, for many years president of Planned Parenthood-World Population, indicated that it is now generally accepted that on many campuses in the country at least 70 percent of both men and women will be nonvirgins by the time they graduate.

A second change is that engagement is no longer a prerequisite for intercourse for women. For those of us who grew up in the 1940s and 1950s, if you loved the person, if you were engaged to him, if you were about to be married, then it was perhaps all right to be sexually involved with him. Now the majority of college students will say that as long as they are involved in a strong, affectionate, currently exclusive relationship with the individual — what we used to call "going steady" — they could feel comfortable having intercourse with the person.

Sleeping Together

Increased sleeping together without being married, or even necessarily sexually involved, is another very common characteristic of today's college scene. One can't assume any longer what will happen sexually when two people spend the night together. A lot will depend upon the nature of the relationship between them, the nature of their past experience, and how experienced they are sexually....

Students who are going steadily with one another are quite likely to spend the majority of their nights together. Cohabitation rates vary greatly from campus to campus, but at a school where there is a lot of off-campus living and a 24-hour visitation policy in the dorms, one can expect to find about one-third of the undergraduates having had a cohabitation experience.

Another change has been a decrease in the percentage of nonvirgin women expressing guilt over their behavior. For instance, a study done at Temple University in 1958 and replicated in 1968 asked women who had had intercourse while going steady if afterward they felt they had "gone too far." The number of women answering "Yes" decreased from 61 percent in 1958 to 30 percent in 1968.

Erosion of the Double Standard

Another alteration has been the slow erosion of the double standard... The gap between men and women in terms of their sexual attitudes and behavior is slowly closing. It is the rates of nonvirginity among women which have shown the dramatic increase, as they have moved to catch up with the men.... A man is much more likely now to be having his sexual experiences with someone of his same social status, and with someone he is going with and cares about — and I think that is much healthier.

Increased acceptance of homosexuality is another big change — acceptance of the fact that someone can enjoy having a sexual involvement with someone of the same sex and be just as emotionally together as those of us who don't.

Questions Raised by Students

"If we are being taught to re-examine traditional sex roles and to relate to others as whole people rather than as males or females, and if sex is primarily for the expression of affection rather than for procreation, and if one's behavior is supposed to be congruent with one's feelings, so that if you feel affection for someone you show it . . . Why should the gender of the individual make so much difference?" These are the questions students raise today as they re-examine all our traditional assumptions about relationships.

Students today tend to be concerned primarily with how they can evolve meaningful in-depth relationships with other persons, somewhat irrespective of gender, that are going to be mutually satisfying, and where the sexual aspect will evolve quite naturally and go hand in hand with the emotional aspects.

The effect of these changes has altered the nature of the group pressure on the college campus. Today there is a tendency for college women who are not sexually experienced to feel somewhat inadequate and to wonder if there is something wrong with them . . . . It seems to me that if we can stop preaching "don't" and start teaching that it's an individual matter, and then help students learn how to make their own personal

decisions, it will be much easier for them to resist that pressure.

More Choices, More Stress

Another problem is the fact that as students gain more freedom to make their own decisions, they are faced with more choices, and hence experience more stress. When you have to sort it all out yourself, it is much more difficult and more painful, but also much more maturing.

Emotional overinvolvement is another potential problem. Students have to learn how to balance their need for freedom to grow and experience and their need for a close intimate relationship. I always say to freshmen: "Some day while you are here, you are probably going to fall in love with someone and develop a relationship with that person. And when you do, remember — as you work to develop that relationship — to simultaneously give equal attention to developing each of yourselves as individual persons. You must push the other person to continue to relate to his or her friends and to continue to do those things that have been important to them. And you must demand these same freedoms for yourself. Or else, someday, resentments may build up . . . In your college relationships, you should be preparing yourselves for the kind of marriage which is increasingly part of our society today, marriages which allow openness and freedom for both persons."

. . . In my opinion, the dormitory should be the place where students are given explicit modeling and practice in interpersonal skills. The dormitory staff should be seen as trainers in interpersonal relations, and the dormitory program should be explicitly designed to provide the kinds of experiences one needs if one is going to learn all those basic interpersonal skills so central to a capacity for mature intimacy, skills which we ourselves were never taught very well — like how to listen to and understand another's feelings; how to get in touch with one's own feelings and share them with someone else; and how to deal with the conflicts that are bound to occur in any intimate relationship.

Harrad: Not So Scandalous

When *The Harrad Experiment,* by Robert Rimmer, came out in the mid-'60s, it was considered scandalous because it described an experiment in a small college where freshman students were assigned to coed rooms . . . . But in Harrad, there was an academic program which augmented their living situation, so that they were taking courses in values and reading about the ethics of relationships at the same time that they were given the opportunity to practice living with someone of the opposite sex.

I would suggest that maybe it is *our* behavior which is scandalous, not Harrad's, for we provide the freedom for the Harrad-type relationship but without the necessary support services and education to help young people cope with it as well or gain from it as much as they might.

In my opinion, one of the most crucial things we should be doing on our campuses today is preparing more responsible, caring human beings who will be able to interact with others effectively on a day-to-day basis for the rest of their lives.

ALTERNATE LIFESTYLES

America has been a land of alternate lifestyle seekers since the first Europeans invaded and settled its shores. With the exception of nature and the native American Indians, little stood in the way of searching the vast width of a continent for a place to live in whatever style seemed appropriate. Time passed. Technology became the tool of the people, and it conquered the Indians and nature. Democracy became the form of government, and it unified the diverse people and regions. Capitalism became the economic power that fueled the government and technology. Things changed. The need for specialization exceeded the need for diversity. The country didn't seem so vast anymore. Where once there was abundance, there were beginning to be shortages. The economic system that had worked so well began producing more problems than solutions. The government dedicated to the ideals of liberty and justice for all was bombing thatched huts in Southeast Asia and killing students in Ohio. Questions were raised.

What was once traditional American society is in a state of flux. All the taken-for-granted aspects of our lives are being re-examined: the nuclear family, the work ethic, governmental policy — foreign and domestic, the economic system, sex roles, the way natural resources are used, religion, morality, even the manner in which the land was taken from the Indians. There is a new spirit of exploration in the country. Unlike the original settlers, who were free to exploit whatever nature offered, the explorers of the late 20th century must seek alternate lifestyles within the narrow confines of an already existing and crowded society.

Odd things happen. A successful Wall Street broker quits his job and moves to a small farm in West Virginia, where he and his family raise their own food in an effort to become self-sufficient. A young married couple move from their suburban tract home into an inner-city neighborhood, searching for a sense of community. A middle-class family of four expands by adding two additional adults, one of whom is homosexual. A Southern California urban planner moves to Oregon to join in creating a new rural community, planned for diversity and ecological harmony.

There are communes, expanded families, liberation movements, homesteaders, religious cults, proponents of the new, and exponents of the old. One clear pattern emerges: there is a dissatisfaction with what is, and a search for what might be. There is yet a pioneer spirit in the land.

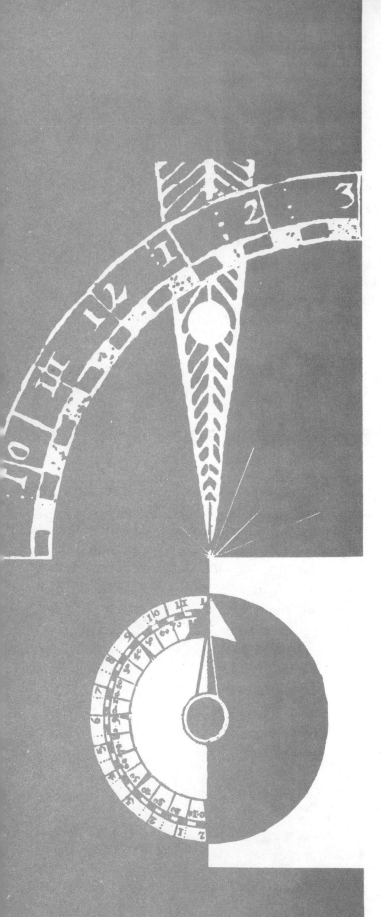

IF I HAD MY LIFE TO LIVE OVER

I'd like to make more mistakes next time.
I'd relax. I would limber up. I would be sillier
than I have been this trip. I would take fewer
things seriously. I would take more chances.
I would take more trips. I would climb more
mountains and swim more rivers. I would eat
more ice cream and less beans. I would perhaps
have more actual troubles, but I'd have fewer
imaginary ones.

You see, I'm one of those people who live
sensibly and sanely hour after hour, day after
day. Oh, I've had my moments, and if I had it
to do over again, I'd have more of them. In
fact, I'd try to have nothing else. Just moments,
one after another, instead of living so many
years ahead of each day. I've been one of those
persons who never goes anywhere without a
thermometer, a hot water bottle, a raincoat,
and a parachute. If I had to do it again, I would
travel lighter than I have.

If I had my life to live over, I would start
barefoot earlier in the spring and stay that way
later in the fall. I would go to more dances.
I would ride more merry-go-rounds. I would
pick more daisies.

— Nadine Stair, 85 years old
Louisville, Kentucky

A SPIRIT OF COMMUNALITY

In Tennessee, Stephen Gaskin and some 600 others have established a self-sustaining agricultural community with a Buddhist-universalist spiritual base. Members of this community live very simply, grow their own food, build their own dwellings, and even manufacture many of the things they need for daily living. Their main spiritual practice is learning how to live and work together truthfully and lovingly. They call it "getting it together on the physical plane." "Truth is the same as God," Gaskin says, "and truth can get you high."

In Boston, several middle-aged, middle-class families have moved together into Packard Manse, a large house in which they share household duties and live less expensively. They are actively engaged in trying to get other middle-class people to examine their lifestyles in light of the glaring gap between rich and poor.

In Houston, Texas, more than 300 people have become members of the Church of the Redeemer community. They live in 45 households in which all income is held in common, thus freeing many members to engage in evangelical and healing ministries. About 30 people serve as volunteers in the local elementary schools, while another 30 to 40 work in a neighborhood health clinic.

In Oregon a group of architects and visionaries have formed an association to build a new community, Cerro Gordo, near Eugene, which will have a totally functional design.

All over America, people are living in different types of communities, linked by common interests, faith, idealism, affection, practicality .... Some, usually fairly large units, are based on articles of faith or spiritual teaching. Others, less formal, consist of expanded family groups living together partly because it's practical, partly because they love each other and enjoy being close. All face problems because living at close quarters and often with not much money coming in is a speedy method of bringing people face to face with what they really want and who they really are.

One of the most perceptive accounts of communality and the way it works is by Richard Atcheson, who went on the commune trip a few years back and published a book about his experiences called *The Bearded Lady.* Here are some of his conclusions about what happens when people get together in groups — and what needs to happen if they are to have any hope of success.

Atcheson's Theory of Communes

In the communes — particularly in those charged most vividly with the Holy Spirit, variously called The Power or Grace or Goodstuff — life is a religious act, community its inevitable form. I am You and You are Me and We are One Together — they really believe that. And when the Goodstuff comes, in a pattern of waves, in an ebb and flow, it comes like the fires of Pentecost, and there is nothing boring about it, nothing distant or remote or polite or in the least good taste. It's a total mind-zap, and it feels good, too.

By no means are all communities operating post-apotheosis, but if they intend really to bring about a social revolution, they might try first to whistle up a revelation. It is past time we realized that primary sexual characteristics are purely incidental and need not, indeed must not, any longer dominate and separate us as they have in the past. Even the most extreme anarchic and/or revolutionary communes have lately been rent by inequality of male and female members, with the guys saying to the girls, "Get off *my* tractor and haul ass back to the kitchen." This attitude has given birth to women's lib communes, where revolution and Lesbianism comfortably co-exist — but I hazard to observe that in neither sort of revolutionary commune has God yet made much of an impact. And until these communards wake up to their androgynous selves, there will be no apotheosis in their communities, and no peace either, and damn little meaningful revolution.

It is, perhaps, for this reason that communes have, by and large, such a short life. Three to six months is about all you can expect of most groups. And after our own brief but profoundly climactic tussle with the communal experience, we think we know why.

1.   A group of people decides that the idea of a commune is charming, pretty, and romantic. They come together and hug and kiss and go Auhmmmmm all the time, and at first it's fun. But because they are basically unserious and disastrously insensitive to one another, dwelling solely on the surface of being, nothing really happens. They might as well be embracing a lot of store dummies for all the vibration that passes between them. In

these close quarters, with these frustrations, there finally erupts a festival of jealousy, meanness, and bad smells, a jarring nonharmony. Talk of "vibes" increases, but vibes do not materialize; hardships do. In the end, with or without free and group sex (which they may by now have resorted to), everybody wonders why he came. They split.

2.   A group of quite sensitive people comes together with great intensity and an eagerness to love and share. They love not the *idea* of communality but each other. They find themselves developing a common spiritual consciousness, they throw off all social and sexual taboos, and the vibrations are deeply felt. For a time there is great elation and excitement, but then somebody literally sees the devil, or perhaps they all do, and there then arises the Stepin Fetchit syndrome: "Feets, don't fail me now." They post out of there, follicles still standing to attention all over their bodies, in as many different directions as there are people.

3.   Some refugees of the former group try new groups elsewhere, with fresh and innocent personnel. They try again. But up pops Satan, sooner or later, the Stepin Fetchit syndrome comes into effect again, and the new group takes to its heels. This pattern may be repeated any number of times, depending upon how stubborn and/or idealistic the refugees are. As they invariably see it, Satan has nothing to do with them.

4.   A group of people gets to the Satan stage. Some may split but others brazen it out. They knew it was coming, or they are wise enough to recognize psycho-sexual eruptions brought on by living closely together in a joint renunciation of taboos, and/or they are wildly excited to come face to face with Satanism, witchcraft, and related

forms, and their adrenalin flows. They feel themselves corporately very powerful, like saints, the elect. Psychic phenomena of an extraordinary sort begin to obsess them — the walls vibrate, cats jump, they read each other's minds. They can do anything: they are God. However, as God they turn out to be unsatisfactory, more helpless to effect good than in their previous android condition. They feel that they are unsuitable vessels; anyway, it turns out that God is lonely. Their union disintegrates in a variety of wholly acceptable directions, because now all directions are acceptable. Some contemplate suicide, because life is a cosmic joke and it's not too funny, especially when the joke's on you. Others retreat to mystical or occult sects and begin to play power games with other people's divinity. Some go up to the mountaintop to just be, others wander as holy bums. And some return to straight life, or to straighter sorts of communes. They make sandals out of leather, screw a lot, and pretend the whole thing was just a dream, or a nightmare.

5. Some few go through all these stages many times. Ultimately, in fatigue and cynicism, they build communities along strictly nonemotional, nonpersonal lines, ashrams without gurus. Everyone to his own, solitary satori, physically together but sexually, emotionally, psychically estranged. This is scarcely any different from the first category of commune but, in subtle ways connected to routine and ambiance, superior. Also, because nothing whatever is happening among people, it tends to remain stable. But I don't really get the point; it was the alienation of contemporary society that set them on this cycle of psychic implosions in the first place. However, it remains true that wholeness, happiness, joy, security do not reside in other people. In the end, man is God alone. And there's nothing like a bunch of other people at close quarters to prove the truth of that . . . .

No commune, no tribe, no nuclear family even, will ever achieve real human freedom until the barrier between male and female in the self is dissolved, and along with it the sexual and spiritual capitalism that thrive on that division. When we are all of us just us, not denying any part of the dual strengths that would, if allowed, make us whole, then we will see real emancipation. If you try to take the commune trip, try not to choose up sexual sides. Try instead to love all the facets, male and female, that constitute you. Only by doing that will we ever be able to really love one another.

— *Richard Atcheson*

237

TWO MODEL COMMUNES

Ananda: Cooperation in Self-Realization

The Ananda Cooperative Village is a spiritual community of disciples of Paramahansa Yogananda, founder of the Self-Realization Fellowship. Approximately 125 full-time residents live on 650 acres of land in the foothills of the Sierra Nevada near Nevada City, California. Swami Kriyananda, one of Yogananda's foremost disciples, founded the community in 1968 and resides as its spiritual leader.

Ananda is organized as a village, with land held in common. Individuals and families each have their own homes and support themselves through the various community industries. Businesses are privately owned and operated and residents work for small salaries. Each resident makes a monthly contribution to the community for utilities and mortgage payments. Village businesses include making and selling macrame, incense oils, seed sprouting kits, health food candy bars, fruit and carob syrups, and honey. Ananda Publications employs many villagers in publishing, printing, and distributing Swami Kriyananda's books and records. In-village services include a market, an auto shop, and a dairy. A large organic garden caters for the community's food for at least six months of the year.

Ananda has its own school system from preschool through high school, taught by community members. In addition to the usual academic subjects, children are taught concentration, meditation, and self-control.

Ananda's goals: to build a harmonious spiritual environment for residents and their families, and to share with the world the benefits of this lifestyle.

Auroville: Experiment in International Living

Auroville, a model commune situated on the Coromandel Coast of the Bay of Bengal, between Pondicherry and Madras, synthesizes East and West around the teachings of Aurobindo Ghose. Its residents come from all over the world — France, Mexico, Germany, Argentina, Sweden, Australia, The Netherlands, the United States — as well as India. Privately financed, Auroville has been in existence eight years and is expected eventually to house as many as 50,000 people.

Everyone works in Auroville, on the principle that if you do not inject your consciousness into matter, the latter will never develop. Industries run the East-West gamut from handicrafts (hand-made paper, wood carving, and incense sticks) to such factory activity as the production of tools and machinery, electronics, and polyester. Auroville has its own schools, bakery, health center, nursery, garage — and meteorological station. Agrarian activity is multitudinous: poultry, dairy, orchards, and general farming of all kinds. The climate at Auroville is tropical and its seacoast position salubrious. All the ingredients for Utopia, it would seem.

Auroville wants to be a universal town where men and women from all countries are able to live in peace and progressive harmony, above all creeds, all politics, and all nationalities. Its purpose is to realize human unity — its ultimate aim, self-sufficiency in the best sense.

If a man does not keep pace with his companions
perhaps it is because he hears a different drummer
Let him step to the music he hears however measured
or far away. Thoreau

Corita

FAMILY SYNERGY

The revolution in lifestyles has now reached the most basic unit of all: the American nuclear family. Not only are "open marriages" becoming more common, where each partner grants the other permission to explore outside relationships, on the premise that these will enrich rather than deplete the primary bond; the newest concept in interpersonal relationships is the "expanded family." Possibly as a result of the communal experiments of the past decade; perhaps influenced by the increasing frequency of cohabitation among college students; certainly in protest at the aridity and impersonality of present-day living conditions — whatever the reasons, people are starting to live in committed family groups held together by love and mutual respect rather than by social pressure, legal sanction, and/or children. In some cases, existing family units have expanded to include additional adults, who may or may not be sexually involved with the husband-wife couple, but who offer alternative, nonthreatening adult role models in affectionate nonsexual relationships with the children. In others, consenting adults take the decision to live in committed family groups, for a variety of reasons. Chief among them: the expansion of intimacy and the realization that a combination of several people's good feelings can produce a state of synergy — an energy greater than the mere sum of its parts.

Now there is even an organization, Family Synergy, dedicated to furthering the understanding and practice of open, committed relationships. Nonsectarian, nonprofit, operated solely by volunteers, the group is headquartered in Los Angeles, and has members in 24 states and several foreign countries, who live in all kinds of open relationships as well as more conventional ones. Its purposes are to facilitate the discussion and exchange of ideas, to collect and disseminate information about all types of expanded families; to provide ways for people interested in these ideas to meet, get to know, and keep in touch with one another; and to further public acceptance of the right of individuals to be themselves and practice openly the lifestyle of their choice.

Family Synergy is not itself a commune or an expanded family; it does offer a service, the Communal Living Center, for those (members or not) who are seriously interested in living with others, by providing opportunities for such people to meet and acting as a communication tool and general resource for existing shared-living groups.

In connection with its twofold purpose of education and facilitation, Family Synergy collects information and conducts research on the subject of group living, and disseminates this as widely as possible. It also holds monthly meetings, arranges weekend retreats, and organizes a variety of specially designed workshops and encounter groups. Annual membership is $12 for an individual joining alone and $15 for a family couple, with an additional dollar for each additional family member. To qualify for family membership, people must be 18 or older, live in one residence, and consider themselves a family. The group also publishes a members' newsletter.

SYNERGY RESEARCH

According to Synergy research, people in expanded families average in excess of $16,000 annually, have a median age of about 32, and average at least one year of graduate school. Median longevity of group marriages has been 16 months, as compared to 40 months for conventional marriages.

A major difference between expanded families and communes is that in expanded families, the primary bond is between the individuals; in a commune, it is usually between each individual and the group.

Reasons to go into open relationships, expanded families, or communal living: personal growth, and getting and giving increased love. Contrary to some theories, people do not enter them for sex, swinging, or to improve a poor relationship.

SYNANON

Although Synanon has been remarkably effective with alcoholics and addicts, its "cures" are only one facet of its remarkable program. As a matter of fact, the centers do not have facilities to handle those in the acute phases of withdrawal. These are sent to hospitals and start "clean" at Synanon. For those drying out on their own, without needing medical supervision, members supply support, tender loving care, and any physical or psychological assistance that is effective.

Started in 1958 by Charles E. "Chuck" Dederick, a charismatic exalcoholic who developed his own style of group therapy in an apartment in Ocean Park, California, the Synanon approach has revolutionized drug therapy.

There are only four basic rules: no drugs or alcohol, no tobacco, no physical violence or threat of physical violence, and compulsory participation in Synanon's aerobic exercise program. In a decade and a half, Synanon has grown from a small group of addicts to a full-fledged social movement with about 1,400 resident members and 2,500 active nonresidents.

The Game

The core of Synanon's process of continuous learning, which its leaders consider their only true therapy, is The Game, a unique encounter technique evolved from those early sessions in Dederich's apartment. The Game has elements of Re-evaluation Counseling and Janov techniques, in that current or long-buried hostilities are blown out in blasts of rage; copouts, self-pity, carefully built-up self-images are destroyed by withering refusals to permit such deception. Intense, fun, lively, fast-paced, The Game is therapeutic without being group therapy: verbal combat with 12 or 15 people unburdening themselves and at the same time getting a picture of how they are viewed by others. Synanon adherents claim The Game not only helps in the individual's growth and development but provides true democracy with a means of assuring feedback and total participation in the community's activities —

a wild, free-for-all verbal version of a suggestion box.

Synanon residents have their basic needs supplied: food, clothing, housing, medical care, plus a small salary. Some work in the group's industries, others have jobs outside and contribute most of their earnings to the community.

The Activities

Synanon has thriving businesses in printing and graphics; a service station in Santa Monica which serves as a job training ground as well as a source of income; and a nationwide advertising specialties jobbing business which nets the Foundation about $600,000 a year. They also obtain large quantities of donated bulk items, some of them surplus, damaged, or mislabeled, and unsuitable for commercial sale. In addition to centers in Santa Monica, San Francisco, Oakland, and New York, there is a 3,200-acre ranch near Tomales Bay in Marin County where overgrazed and poor-quality ranchlands are restored along with the formerly lost and troubled human beings who work and study there.

Synanon's leaders claim to have proof that human nature can be changed by their 24-hour-a-day learning techniques. All life to them is education: when you stop learning, you stop living.

Dederich says Synanon addresses itself to the problem of ignorance, which has nothing to do with intelligence or a lack thereof, but with a failure to achieve wisdom. Its value system is based on absolute honesty, personal responsibility, cooperation, and love.

The community is not made up solely of former addicts or problem personalities who have been recycled into productive human beings. Many socially and financially successful people have moved in to share the Synanon way, and are known as "Lifestylers." A Beverly Hills lawyer, his wife and children recently joined. They have their own apartment, as do other couples in the group, and their children were sent to school in Tomales Bay. As in a kibbutz, children are separated by age groups and are educated and trained together. They visit their parents on a regular basis, sharing vacations and holidays with them. Several professional and highly skilled people are Synanon members and it is estimated that half the department heads are Lifestylers.

To an outside observer, the process seems to be working. There are no figures on what has happened to the 17,000 people who have gone through the program, although many are staffing other drug withdrawal centers. Those still around, some for up to 17 years, are clean and visibly happy.

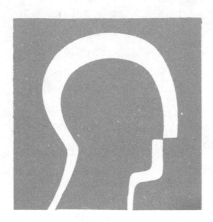

LIBERATION

consciousness raising and beyond

America has never been a static nation. Since its birth in revolution, there has been a long tradition of admiring those who fight for their rights and exercise their freedom of speech to declare independence from whatever forces threaten to suppress them. After surviving the giant, emotion-ridden movements for civil rights and against the Vietnam war, however, Americans seem to have lost the urge to crusade en masse. Have the rival claims of the women's movement, Black Power, Chicano Power, the Indian movement, the Gay Liberationists, the Gray Panthers coalition, the Jews for Jesus movement, the Right to Life group — the list is endless — divided or eroded the interests of the average citizen?

New Demands

Or is it that we are living in such an age of surging demands for liberation, for recognition, for equality, that we have realized each one will beget its own equal and opposite counter-movement if we only give it time? As women unite to liberate themselves from male oppression, men meet in consciousness-raising groups in order to investigate ways in which they too have been oppressed by too sweeping an acceptance of sex roles and stereotypes. As blacks stand up and make their demands for equal opportunities, whites claim reverse discrimination as they begin to be passed over for jobs in organizations which have been encouraged to hire minorities. And so it goes.

The Generation of Discontent

Whatever the group, whatever the goal, whatever the means of expressing points of view, movements are indeed an integral part of modern America. Maybe they are symbolic of a generation that believes discontent in itself is worthy of attention, and that answers will never come until the questions are asked.

The idea of the consciousness-raising group originated in the women's liberation movement, where it filled the vital function of helping individual women get in touch with often buried feelings in an atmosphere of support. By sharing experiences, women hope to learn that their situations bear common qualities, and out of that discovery they find they can provide each other with insights that help them take on proper responsibility for their own lives.

Questions

A couple of points of view: "Without consciousness raising, the only feedback you get is from that man and his support in what you're going to do with your life. I've heard women say, 'How can I confront my husband? He's so objective. He's always being so fair about everything.' Then you find out that men don't have your best interests at heart — that they are not really concerned — but that there are other women who are going to support you and who love you and are concerned about you."

"I'd like to say what I've gained the most from the group: I have confidence in myself now. He could always do it better, any man could do something better than me. And it's absolutely not true."

Suggestions

The usefulness of consciousness-raising groups extends far beyond the women's movement, however, for there are few of us who cannot profit from sharing experiences in a supportive atmosphere, especially when they are the kind we have not, for whatever reason, liked to speak of with others, or maybe even thought of taking time to investigate for ourselves. Taking risks in such groups, surviving disclosure, listening to others tell, stumblingly, of problems that may be very different from our own but with which we can truly empathize — this invariably has an excitingly heady effect upon the participants. They have been helped to look more directly into their own hearts, and in so doing, they learn that this personal, unique material is the very stuff of life. In fact, it is what makes us all — however we divide ourselves into disparate sexual, ethnic, or social units — members of the human race.

GAY LIBERATION/ out of the closet and into the streets

"Part of the difficulty in viewing homosexuality is that it is largely amorphous — a behavioral category of individuals who are about as diffusely linked with each other as the world's smokers or coffee drinkers...."

— C. A. Tripp
The Homosexual Matrix

The term *gay* describes more than a form of sexuality — it can mean an attitude, a person, or some hazily defined group of people (both male and female in this context, though some women prefer the term *lesbian)*. In its broadest sense, it means the *capacity* to love someone of the same sex.

Because gay is a lifestyle as well as a form of sexuality, some sociologists have chosen to view gay people as an ethnic minority. As in other ethnic groups, no single point of view can speak for all members, but there are certain issues which affect the majority in a similar way. Oppression is one such issue for gay people, and the gay liberation movement seeks to do something about it.

An intitial obstacle to be overcome was the acceptance of negative stereotypes (homosexuals are lonely, sad people, homosexuals are sick, homosexuals are dangerous) not only by heterosexuals, but by homosexuals as well. Through consciousness raising and the increasing availability of more solidly researched objective information, liberation organizations are trying to change this negative mythology. Despite much censorship, visible and invisible, there is a growing awareness among informed members of society that homosexuality is neither sick nor deviant, nor some variety of mental illness to be "cured," but an alternate, viable, acceptable aspect of human sexuality.

In June 1969 New York City police raided a Greenwich Village gay bar called the Stonewall Inn. The patrons were told to clear out, but instead of going home they gathered outside the bar on the Christopher Street sidewalk. The police ordered the group to disperse, but someone in the crowd shouted "Gay Power!" in reply. The police began to advance, nightsticks in hand. One member of the group shied a coin at an officer, and within moments the situation had escalated to rock and bottle throwing. Unaccustomed to encountering resistance from gays, "New York's Finest" sought refuge inside the bar and telephoned for reinforcements. By the time the tactical squad arrived, however, the angry group had disappeared into the night, overturning garbage cans and spreading word of the confrontation. It was this event (christened, somewhat exaggeratedly, the "Stonewall Riots") that sparked the formation of the first gay liberation group: Gay Liberation Front. Within two years there were 200 such organizations throughout the country; at present there are more than 3,000.

From the radical gay underground of the 1960s there emerged a central theme for liberation: visibility. It was important for gays across the country to see and hear what was happening in a movement located primarily on both coasts. Visibility was also an important factor in demystifying homosexuality for "straight" society. This proved to be a difficult task in a media-oriented society, with the media reluctant to even mention homosexuality. The Gay Activist Alliance (GAA) in New York used an effective tactic they called "zapping," which usually involved public embarrassment of a corporation or politician the GAA regarded as practicing discrimination against gays. Zapping and other less colorful forms of confrontation politics have had some success in gaining visibility for gays, in turn strengthening the base of political power.

The Gay Vote

Just how much political clout gays have is unclear. Most demographic statistics are derived from information gathered by the census, but the census does not inquire sexual preference. By conservative estimates, 6 percent of the adult female population and 10 percent of the adult male population are predominantly homosexual. With a conservatively estimated average of 8 percent adult homosexual population, voting power is beginning to become an issue for the politician. Gays do not, of course, necessarily vote as a bloc, but in some urban areas where there is a higher percentage of gay people, the "gay vote" can become decisive in elections where gay rights is a clearly defined issue between two candidates. In California there was a strong gay lobby in support of the recent "consenting adults bill," which included protection against job discrimination on the basis of sexual preference. Most states have not yet enacted such legislation, and many areas of the law still discriminate against homosexuality. Gay women, for instance, have repeatedly been denied custody of their children in divorce proceedings on grounds of their sexual choice.

A major effect of the liberation movement and the resulting visibility of gay people has been an increasing number of men and women willing to be open and honest about their sexuality. This "coming out" of "closeted" homosexuals has importantly contributed to increased self-awareness and self-respect.

New Laws

Human rights leaders well know that for an oppressed minority to continue to exist requires some amount of complicity by the oppressed. Many homosexuals are unwilling to submit any longer to certain injustices. Gay liberation goes beyond asking for acceptance or toleration by society. There is a premise that society must be compelled to respect basic human rights, and eventually to change attitudes as well as laws. Such beliefs necessitate radical changes in the ways society views morality.

It is sometimes hard to distinguish between gay liberation and other sexual freedom movements joined in the struggle for the individual's right to personal sexual choice — free from societal taboos, guilt, and fear. Gay liberation offers some examples for the type of sexual freedom that does not seek to determine the future, but to free it to develop as it will. As Dennis Altman has said:

"Gay Liberation will have achieved its full potential when it is no longer needed, for we see each other neither as men and women, gay and straight, but purely as people with varied possibilities. It is the fate of the Negro, James Baldwin once wrote, to carry the burden of both black and white Americans. It may be the fate of homosexuals to liberate both gays and straights."

There is a special quality of celebration in that struggle.

THE GRAY PANTHERS / power to the aged

In the Black Sea village of Abkhazia, in the Soviet Socialist Republic of Georgia, it is not unusual for people to live beyond the age of 90. One woman there claims to be 130 years old, but local physicians think she is fudging a bit — 141 is more likely. She lives a healthy, happy, productive life surrounded by her many descendants, working in the garden, tending her pigs, goats and chickens. How different the picture would be had she been an American. If she had "retired" at 65 (almost mandatory in our culture), could she have survived 76 years of children insisting she settle into an inactive old age, of existing on social security checks, of deadly invisibility in the society? For the aged in Abkhazia each year brings increased prestige. It is life-extending to be needed and respected at 90, or even 141.

Eradication of Ageism

Increasing awareness of the problems of old age in America has been brought about chiefly by elderly people dissatisfied with the prospect of living their final years in obscurity. Some of the most expressive voices belong to the Gray Panthers coalition, a group of people of all ages dedicated to the eradication of "ageism" — discrimination against the old. Chief spokesperson for the movement is Margaret Kuhn, formerly national association secretary for the United Presbyterian Church, who was forced to retire from that post when she reached the age of 65 in 1970. In protesting this discrimination, she found many who shared her sense of injustice, and realizing that ageism was a problem of concern to young and old alike, saw the strength in a coalition movement. "We want to shake up society to humanize it for everyone," she says. "Gray power, yes, but not special privilege."

Revolutionary Change

At present there are 21 million Americans over the age of 65, and another 20 million over 55. Ageism cuts across all classes and is fast becoming a hot political issue. The Gray Panthers seek revolutionary change in the way society deals with the old, beginning with recognition by the elderly themselves of how severe the problems are and how they can act to change them. This consciousness raising among the aged spills over into other segments of the population, an essential ingredient in solving the problem of ageism, for until it is identified, there is little hope for action. Maggie Kuhn calls for "wrinkled babies" to transform themselves into "wrinkled radicals." The Panthers should be "a unifying force in a society that is fear-ridden and divided. No idea should be too extreme or radical. We've got nothing to lose. We've got a brain trust. Those of us who are nearing the end of our lives . . . should want to leave a legacy for a just, humane, and peaceful world. We should go down flying."

The Gray Panthers national coalition is a flexible arrangement of 40 regional networks with multiple leadership and no formal membership or dues. All work is carried out by volunteers. This lack of bureaucratic structure is deliberate, to keep the group "safe for diversity." The networks share common goals, but the Panthers prize seeking methods of effective nonviolent action above conformity. One of their major concerns is the way in which old people are portrayed by the media, particularly television. The New York Panther network maintains a media watch to keep a sharp eye out for such derogatory portrayals, and fight to eradicate them. Another primary target is the nursing home industry, which has recently come under scrutiny by local, state, and federal governmental agencies. The Panthers believe that not enough is being done, meanwhile, and have published a *Citizen's Action Guide to Nursing Home Reform* (available through the Gray Panthers' office in Philadelphia for $3) to aid in clarifying the issues.

Priority Problems

On October 9, 1975, 300 delegates from 33 states and the District of Columbia met in Chicago for the Gray Panthers' first national convention. Three major areas were designated as priority problems for the aged: health care; hunger, inflation, and the economy; and housing. Preliminary resolutions stated the Panther position on these, and task forces were organized to study the problems and possible solutions.

Still a burgeoning movement, short on funds, the Gray Panthers have already drawn national attention. Peg Thornhill, an ex-social worker, who quit her job to become a Panther volunteer, believes the fantastic response is because "we have touched on issues that vitally affect everyone and there are so few organizations that speak out. But it's sad sometimes too — we are not a service organization and can't always provide specific solutions to the many problems people write to us about. We try to refer problems like discrimination in housing and jobs, or foul-ups in the food stamp program to local agencies. In the meantime, we work as an advocacy group — changing society's attitude toward growing old, and raising the consciousness of the elderly so that they can have a positive attitude toward themselves."

So don't be surprised if someday soon a "wrinkled radical" walks up to you, pokes a gnarled finger into your ribs, and announces, "ZAP! You're getting old! Listen to what we're saying. We're trying to change things for *you.*" By the year 2000 it is estimated that 20 percent of the American population will be over the age of 65. We had all better start listening.

MARRIAGE ENCOUNTER / a return to loving

The original concept and techniques of Marriage Encounter were developed in Spain in the late 1950s by Father Gabriel Calvo. Starting eight years ago in the United States, the movement has grown from a small nucleus on the East Coast to a membership of more than 400,000 with 60,000 new couples added each year. There are meetings every weekend in almost every state in the Union, as well as groups in England, Ireland, and Belgium.

Minicourse in Communication

Couples who have experienced Marriage Encounter describe it in ecstatic terms as having changed, enriched, enhanced their marriages. In specific terms Marriage Encounter is often defined by what it is not. It is not group therapy, it is not a hospital for sick marriages, it is not an exercise in problem solving. It is a minicourse in communication, designed to help couples find themselves, and to accept their partners in a totally open way.

All this revelation and communication takes place on a single weekend, 44 hours spent completely away from the rest of the world. Its starting point is a presentation made to the 20-25 couples sitting around the room by a priest and a couple who are fully involved in the program. A series of 12 presentations introduces the participants to different aspects of the dialogue technique. After each presentation there is time for personal reflection; then the couples meet in the privacy of their rooms and share what

they have learned about themselves. The weekend is designed to help each couple progress from "I" to "We" to "We and God" to "We, God, and the World."

Marriage Encounter is based on the idea that marriage is a love affair between two people who are completely and irrevocably committed to each other, and that marriage is important spiritually, to God and to the community. Started and directed by priests of the Catholic Church, it is not restricted to Catholics, although it is oriented toward that faith and the experience is a deeply religious one. The Catholic group has shared its techniques and experience with other churches, who now have their own Encounter teams. Included are the Church of Christ, the Episcopalian Church, branches of the Jewish faith, and the Reorganized Latter-Day Saints.

Notebooks

The key that unlocks the total sharing and experiencing of the other's feelings lies in the notebooks the couples find on their chairs at the first session. After returning to their rooms, they write out their feelings as completely as possible and then each one reads what the other has written. One of the problems with spoken dialogue is that the listener is too often waiting to plunge in with his own thoughts, or attempting to soothe or change the other's feelings, so he never learns to experience fully the emotions involved. Married couples in particular tend to finish each other's sentences and prejudge something before it is expressed. By writing all the thoughts out and then reading them with care, complete concentration can be attained. Couples are told to try to eliminate judging, explaining, or justifying — just to get at the feelings and communicate and experience them to the fullest degree. They try to listen to each other as completely as possible and to understand each other totally.

Feedback and Discussion

The weekend moves in a planned progression. The first writing is just an expression of the couple's feelings to each other. During the next step they are asked to write a love letter. Many find it difficult, almost painful to risk revealing long-withheld emotions, but the awkwardness soon goes and the feelings move onto the pages and into the other person's mind and heart. And with feedback and discussion, testing and describing, the partners make absolutely sure the communication is total, that the feeling has been experienced as accurately as possible by the other.

One of the most important parts of the Marriage Encounter experience is the continuing dialogue. After the couples return home to the pressures and problems of their daily life, they are asked to continue their communicating in a program called "10/10." This means taking 10 minutes minimum each day for writing and 10 minutes maximum for verbal dialogue, completely centered around feelings. In this way they can continue to improve and build their newly strengthened relationship.

Positive Effects

There would appear to be a great hunger for this kind of communication in our alienated culture, in view of the tremendous popularity of the program and the almost total absence of negative feedback. Marriage Encounter enthusiasts believe they are not only renewing and enhancing marriages, but that the positive effects of the experience permanently affect each couple's relationships with everyone in their lives.

FEMININITY FOREVER / a sinking ship?

Ms., Gloria Steinem, and Bella Abzug to the contrary, there exists an entire subclass of women who apparently do not wish to be liberated. Gauged by the popularity of courses such as Helen Andelin's "Fascinating Womanhood" (a thousand of which are currently being taught in the United States) and sales of Marabel Morgan's *The Total Woman* (a bestseller in hardback and an initial printing of two million by Pocket Books), there are a lot of submissives out there.

Andelin and Morgan preach that women should be coy, cute, and totally obedient to the superior male. Morgan adds a little high-spirited sex, advising wives to answer the door in high-heeled shoes, long stockings, an apron, and nothing else (when the husband is expected home, of course). While there are variations, the prime article of faith is that Man must be Master. Don't argue, don't question, just do as he says. Women may get angry, but only in a childlike manner, stamping their little feet and shaking their pretty curls. Its advocates claim this style of femininity is a sure way to a happy marriage.

In vigorous contrast to these demure women is Dr. Howard Watrous, of Living Dynamics International, in Portland, Oregon. Dr. Watrous and his aides teach a variety of courses — Creative Sales and Management, Financial Survival (Prosperity or Bust), Structuring Your Child's Environment — but his most popular offering is Femininity Glorified.

Sex Is Divinely Ordained

In this three-day course, priced at $60, Watrous serves up a smorgasbord of Fundamentalist Christianity, gamy sex, and some shrewd injections of practical psychology. It has been said that Marabel Morgan performed a great service in telling women that sex is divinely ordained, thus encouraging the timid and the potentially frigid. Watrous goes further, saying that what he calls Total Orgasm is an absolute necessity for a woman's mental health as well as for a happy marriage. A characteristic of Total Orgasm is a death scream; and, as in a birth, there is a breaking of waters and uterine contractions. The feeling is like dying and wanting to die. Total Orgasm, not surprisingly, is followed by total submission.

Oral Sex

Watrous advocates wholehearted participation in oral sex, to the consternation of some of his older listeners. Although devoutly Christian, he teaches that submission to a husband is more important than churchgoing. Only through her husband can a woman attain salvation. One wife had to give up Sunday morning services in order to stay home and make love to her husband. Inspired by this tender persuasion, the husband eventually volunteered to take her to church.

Total virginity is a woman's only choice before marriage. A woman belongs to the first man who touches her primary erogenous zones, described rather delicately by Watrous as the bra and panty areas. If she thereafter submits to anyone else, she is a harlot. It is a harsh doctrine in this sexually permissive era, but there are no exceptions to the rule.

THE OLD GOSPEL ...AND THE NEW

Although the divorce between church and state is a tenet of the Constitution, Americans expect a great deal from God. As a nation we have trouble becoming completely and happily secular. We still look to religion as a source of good feelings or guilty ones, use its morality as justification for our actions, and seek its comfort in times of crisis.

Such diverse expectations have resulted in the emergence of a wide variety of religious expressions. Worship takes place in Gothic cathedrals, in drive-in churches, on the television sets in people's homes. It can equally take place in gas stations, insurance companies, U. S. embassies .... Yet, whatever the belief and whether the ultimate goal is happiness on earth or a place in heaven, religion always holds out the promise of reward. Maybe it is typical of American religious styles that they should reflect the basic American tendency toward materialism. While the religions of the East are based on an inner direction and a reverence for the silent functioning of the soul, Western religion tends to be outwardly directed. And Western civilization certainly asks the question, "What can religion do for me?"

Religion in our society is a mindstyle, a whole attitude that dictates basic standards of behavior. It is also a lifestyle, one of the most fundamental reasons for people getting together in groups — whether to attend regular church services or to participate in an evangelist rally, or to join in church-inspired social or fund-raising activities. As always in groups, there is the excitement of being with other people who have similar concerns and similar beliefs. When Jesus said, "Where two or three are gathered together in my name, there am I in the midst of them," he was personifying the sense of solidarity and enthusiasm that are part of the group dynamic, and elevating it to a spiritual plane. Unfortunately, in many of these group endeavors, success tends to be judged less on the spiritual growth achieved than on the attendance tallies.

What follows is not an account of organized religion in this country. It is simply a look at the spellbinders, the movers and shakers who have adapted the methods of the 20th century to the task of spreading the Gospel. Some of the old are here, and a few of the new. It's a colorful group ....

WHERE IT BEGAN

Maybe we can arrive at a clearer understanding of the evangelical movements of mid-70s America by taking a brief look at some of the religious leaders who erected the framework for what could be called public religion.

Aimee Semple McPherson (1890-1944)

Aimee Semple McPherson surfaced in 1918, at a time when the church was a male-dominated organization. A female evangelist/healer was quite a sensation, and for some 25 years she was one of the most famous religious figures in America. In her own way she was a precursor of the women's movement of the 1970s.

Mrs. McPherson got her start in the Salvation Army. At the age of 17 she translated her message of salvation more directly to religion and went to China as a missionary.

After her return to the United States, Mrs. McPherson continued to preach a message of enlightenment, salvation, and the importance of giving up worldly goods. Her tactics were a strange mixture of Hollywood and the Scriptures, a sensationalistic interpretation of the Bible.

Perhaps it was her way of doing things, or maybe merely that she was a woman standing up to be heard in a man's world — there is no question that Mrs. McPherson got her share of both positive and negative attention.

She was the target of lawsuits on the grounds that she had asked her members to contribute everything they owned — even to the gold teeth in their mouths — to her church. However sincere her request, however much she prayed to win her case, it was in vain. She lost.

Scandals surrounded her life as well. The most famous was an incident in which she was reported to have been drowned off Ocean Park, California. She subsequently turned up in the Arizona desert, claiming to have been kidnaped.

Despite the scandals and the lawsuits that surrounded her, Aimee Semple McPherson made her mark in the world of evangelism. Her following was widespread in spite of the fact of her womanhood, at a time when women were not widely accepted as leaders. Her disciples were the founding members of the Church of the Four-Square Gospel, which today claims about 200,000 members in 800 churches and 27 countries.

Sweet Daddy Grace (1885-1960)

Sweet Daddy Grace, born Marcelino Graca in the Cape Verde Islands off French West Africa, was estimated to be worth a cool $25 million when he died in January 1960, at the age of 75. Founder of the "House of Prayer for All People" in 1921 in New Bedford, Massachusetts, where he changed his name to Charles Grace, Sweet Daddy's church spread like a chain of hamburger stands across the country until the church embraced 350 "heavens" and claimed three million faithful members. In addition to religion, Sweet Daddy had apartment houses, hotels, theaters, a Brazilian coffee plantation, a Cuban chicken hatchery, a garment factory, and a cosmetic factory that produced Grace Cold Cream. He also sold coffee and eggs from the basement of his $300,000 red, white, and blue church in Charlotte, North Carolina.

With a toss of his richly curled head, a wave of his hands (whose fingernails were painted red, white, and blue), he would whip congregations into a frenzy by the flow of his oratory. The money flowed too, when he sat in the "money well" or formed the "Sweet Daddy Grace Line." Yet he never paid a penny to the U. S. Internal Revenue Service until the day he died.

Billy Sunday (1862-1935)

"I am a rube of the rubes, I am a hayseed of the hayseeds, and the odors of the barnyard are on me yet ... I have drunk coffee out of my saucer, and I have eaten with my knife. I have said 'Done it' when I should have said 'Did it' and I have 'saw' when I should have 'seen,' and I expect to go to Heaven just the same."

It was the old humble approach, and Billy Sunday knew how to use it. Born in a log cabin, converted as he walked down a Chicago street, at the peak of Billy's colorful career in 1916, he was converting up to 47,000 people in Philadelphia and collecting thank offerings that ranged from $32,000 in Kansas to upward of $50,000 in Baltimore.

Along with a traditional revivalist sermon on guilt, conversion, and new birth, Billy Sunday often added vaudeville acts, spectacular gymnastic feats on the platform, and other gimmicks to his rallies. He openly discussed national and world politics, and the pressing social and economic questions of the day. He was popular for his relentless attacks on the liberal theologians in the larger Protestant denominations — crowds would sit enthralled while their poor little rich boy

attacked the bleeding hearts, the do-gooders, the garlic smellers, the evolutionists, and the misguided politicians. Sunday also knew the appeal of patriotism. He ranked the discovery of America along with the birth of Christ as one of the four greatest events in world history.

His flamboyance was his greatest asset — and his ultimate liability. It catapulted him to the distinction of being the most publicized revivalist in America — and it made him a fad. By the 1920s, he was already a nostalgic entity. In 1933 Billy Sunday proclaimed the world would end in two years. Two years later, he died; and the man who had been front-page news 20 years earlier rated a brief obituary in papers whose top stories concerned the Depression and the rumblings of impending war.

These are only three of the early evangelists who laid the foundations for those enjoying success today. Such an account inspires the same questions that can be asked of the current leaders, however — What is the real motivation? To heal? To save? To reward? To be a mover of men's minds and shaker of souls? Success in the religion business can bring huge financial gain. Where does spiritualism end and materialism begin?

It's a fine line, and perhaps a look at our contemporary evangelists can provide some clue.

Billy Graham

William Franklin "Billy" Graham was born November 7, 1918, on a farm near Charlotte, North Carolina, to parents of the Reformed Presbyterian faith. During his senior year in high school he attended a revival meeting, and decided to become an evangelistic preacher. He thereupon worked his way through a fundamentalist Baptist education, and turned to tabernacle preaching in answer to his evangelical call.

The pinnacle of Billy Graham's success occurred during an eight-week tent meeting in Los Angeles in 1949, at which he won 6,000 converts in a 350,000-member audience. The era of the great international crusades had begun.

Since that time Graham has spoken to millions of people at rallies held all over the world, and the Billy Graham Evangelistic Association, Inc., headquartered in Minneapolis, is a multimillion-dollar colossus with an annual budget of approximately $20 million. Graham himself directs its vast array of programs, which range from a publishing house to a film production company, but he is careful that his association not involve itself in any business outside religious work.

Graham's credibility has survived in a time when evangelists have been closely scrutinized by a skeptical public. He often appears at the top of the list of America's "10 Most Admired Men," and many apparently view him as the epitome of morality in this country. His close association with Richard Nixon in the closing stages of the Vietnam War and the Watergate debacle may have placed some strain upon his credibility, but it was, at worst, guilt by association.

Most of the criticism directed toward Billy Graham, in fact, seems aimed at the message rather than the man. Regardless of the effect his theology may have on the individual, it is difficult not to admire the smoothness with which he operates his vast organization. He has built his evangelistic message on the solid foundation of Southern fundamentalism, yet has stayed flexible enough to adapt his views to the constantly changing American social and political climates. He is probably the most powerful — and least colorful — preacher in the United States today.

Oral Roberts

With the exception of Billy Graham, Oral Roberts is probably better known to the general public than any other preacher in America, chiefly because of his vast network of radio and television faith-healing programs.

Born January 24, 1918, on a farm near Ada, Oklahoma, Oral Roberts claims to have been stricken with tuberculosis in both lungs at the age of 17, and cured by a faith healer who prayed briefly and touched him on the head. This experience filled him with inspiration for a divine mission and a calling as new leader of the Pentecostal faith-healing crusade.

More than a faith healer and star of television specials, Roberts is an educator, college president, and chamber of commerce director. Having long outgrown the "Cathedral Canvas" tent of his earlier years, he is president of Oral Roberts University in Tulsa, Oklahoma — a $30 million, 500-acre campus. He does not receive a salary from his incorporated healing ministry, but the love offerings collected during his crusades bring in some $30,000 annually, not to mention the residuals from his books and an undisclosed salary from the nonprofit Evangelistic Association, which has a multimillion-dollar budget.

Along with his faith-healing practice, Roberts developed a theory called "Seed Faith." It follows directly from the Biblical passage which reads, "As ye sow, so shall ye also reap." According to Roberts, if you are having financial troubles, you should increase the amount of your donations. The money

man is a long time coming.
Sandburg

Corita

will return to you many-fold. Whatever you are short of you should be generous with — and divine intervention will bless you with an abundance of it.

Roberts' book on See Faith outsold his previous works. At the ebb of his career, when he had joined the Methodist Church and rocked the faith of his followers, this book catapulted him back into the spotlight and back on television. See Faith did well for Oral Roberts.

Billy James Hargis

Two of the most controversial topics of discussion in the world are politics and religion. Billy James Hargis speaks out loud and clear on both subjects. In 1969 the then 50-year-old evangelist led his 31st pilgrimage to the Holy Land with his 23-member anti-Communist Christian crusade. Since he began his career at the age of 23, Hargis's crusades have ranged from an assault on United Nations godliness (or lack of it) to opposing forced desegregation, with a strong stand against public school sex education thrown in for good measure.

Hargis's following is large, as is his income. His annual budget is $2 million, and his political broadcasts are heard over more than 100 radio and television stations.

Not to be outdone by his evangelistic contemporaries and their organizations, Hargis founded the American Christian College in 1959 in Tulsa, Oklahoma, vowing that it would teach "God, government, and Christian action."

Indeed, it is those three topics that form the basis for Billy James Hargis's outspoken platform. During the campus outbreaks against the war in Vietnam, Hargis spoke out vehemently: "They are Communists...

You'd better wake up, brothers. The Communists feel they have the college-age youth in their pockets."

Traveling around the country on his $50,000 custom Greyhound, Hargis surrounds himself with massive crowds who listen to such statements as:

"Martin Luther King ... who didn't believe in Virgin Birth, said the Virgin Birth was a white man's trick to exploit the ignorant Negro ... " Or, "If Satan gives a medal, Hugh Hefner will get it." Or, "The Black Panthers are not black, they are Red."

Perhaps the most representative statement Hargis makes is one that occurs frequently during his meetings. Inspiration is translated directly into dollars with:

"The ushers will move among you. Can you give even a dollar a month to save your country? I want you to give your time, your money, your prayers to help get the message out. If I fail to touch your pocketbook I've failed completely."

Recently, sexual scandal has smirched the reputation of the crusader against sexual "deviation." A newly married pair, both students at Hargis's American Christian College, claimed that he had seduced each of them prior to their marriage, and the charge of homosexual behavior was backed by other evidence suggesting Hargis had had several such relationships with students, forbidding them to divulge these on penalty of expulsion from the college. Hargis denied the charges, but the college president backed the students, and since that time Hargis's career has been shadowed.

Reverend Ike

The Reverend Dr. Frederick J. Eikerenkoetter II stands before the crowds, his bright black wavy hair gleaming in the stage lights, and explains the Blessing Plan. It is very simple. Give enough money to Reverend Ike's ministry, and you will be rewarded by God. The more money you give, the more blessings God will bestow. It's as simple as that.

Reverend Ike got his start as assistant pastor of the Bible Way Church in Ridgeland, South Carolina, at the age of 14. He attended several Bible colleges and completed two years as an Air Force chaplain. On returning to South Carolina he founded the United Church of Jesus Christ for All People, Inc.

At the age of 35 he was a struggling fundamentalist preacher in the world of black storefront religion. In 1965 (a year after establishing the Miracle Temple in Boston and a year before moving his organization to New York) he decided to leave the hell-fire and damnation preaching behind. Thus was born Reverend Ike, apostle of the Good Life here on earth.

These days he is heard on a nationwide network of some 80 stations, viewed by millions, and he sends newsletters and full-color magazines (full of testimonials from contributors about diamonds, Cadillacs, unexpected money, and miracle cures) to 1.5 million subscribers. He admits that the policies of his church can only apply to the Christian doctrine if that doctrine is stretched a bit. Street slogans such as "Stick around, don't be a clown, pick up on what I'm putting down" add color to his individual brand of Christianity.

He is pastor of the United Church in Manhattan, and although his United Christian Evangelistic Association is supported by many whites, most of his United Church congregation is conservative, middle-class, and black — some 5,000 people attend each week. Reverend Ike has no tolerance for the Afro-sporting black power advocates. He is militant about one thing — money.

Reverend Ike preaches Green Power, with a little faith healing thrown in. His grooming and wardrobe reportedly cost his supporters $1,000 per week. He doesn't want to give the impression that he is an egomaniac, but the gold-plated church, the Rolls-Royce and Mercedes limousines might be deceiving.

Says Reverend Ike: "I am incredible because I am making the impossible possible . . . . I am God appearing as me. I am the master and mind thinking as me. I am the almighty acting as me. This is the truth even of you and of every man. I am the Divine Sweetheart of the Universe, loving and being loved forever."

Reverend Ike admits his church is rich; he modestly accepts a salary of $40,000 and an unlimited expense account. But he gives credit where it is due: "All I can see I can have because the Lord gives it to me. Thank you, Father."

Kathryn Kuhlman
"I believe in miracles."

America's most celebrated Christian charismatic leader was unquestionably Kathryn Kuhlman, at whose "miracle services" thousands claimed to have been spontaneously cured of illness or physical handicaps. From the time she discovered her healing powers in 1946 until her death in February 1976, she reached millions through her preaching, her books, and her radio and television programs. She herself was a member of the American Baptist Convention, but her services were nondenominational, her preaching Pentecostal, with emphasis on the power of the Holy Spirit.

Born of Baptist/Methodist parents around 1910 in Concordia, Mississippi, Kuhlman began preaching at the age of 16. She would rather have entered a career in law or medicine, had she been given a choice. But she had been called . . . and she answered.

From the beginning she focused on Christian faith, promising that it would bring results. She claimed that lack of faith could prevent healing, and although miracles were worked on nonbelievers as well as the faithful, she called them "mercy healings" which she simply could not explain.

At a typical service, crowds would wait for hours to be admitted to the hall, some people in wheelchairs, some on crutches, some even on stretchers. Suddenly Kathryn Kuhlman would appear on stage — a tall, slim figure usually wearing a simple white chiffon dress with large sleeves and a great deal of jewelry. She would chat and joke with her audience, moving around the platform as she talked, her sermon an emotional tribute to the Holy Spirit:

"I just turn the responsibility over to God, and I say, 'All right! I give my body as the vessel . . . but it's Your responsibility.' Anything that goes on here today . . . Kathryn Kuhlman has nothing to do with. It's God!"

In place of the healing lines that collected in front of other preachers, Kuhlman had a system of "supernatural diagnosis" of a disease, announcing the cures as she became aware of them, identifying those cured, and pointing out their locations in the crowd. The healed persons would surge into the aisles, to be guided onstage by ushers. There Kathryn Kuhlman would congratulate them and put her hand on their heads. Almost without exception the healed collapsed under her touch into the waiting arms of the ushers.

Are the people "cured" at such services suffering from self-diagnosed maladies? Do they bother to verify their illnesses beforehand with doctors or confirm their "cures" subsequently? For spontaneous remission to occur, must an illness be psychosomatic, or has faith really the power to make one well? However it happens, some people will swear that it has. A woman on a Kuhlman television show described being suddenly cured of a heart ailment even her doctors could not explain. A businessman made only four visits to Kuhlman services — and was cured of diabetes.

In 1972, the Kathryn Kuhlman Foundation reportedly grossed nearly $2 million, most of which came from donations collected during miracle services. As of 1970, the healer herself drew a straight salary of $25,000 per year.

Reverend Robert Schuller

To the Reverend Bob Schuller, the church today is in the business of retailing religion; and if this is so, he is running one of the fastest growing stores in the country. His 7,000-member Garden Grove Community Church in Garden Grove, California attracts 800 new members a year. Expansion of the facilities poses no great problem because Schuller's unique commodity — a drive-in church with a 90-foot cross, atop a 15-story Tower of Hope — is situated on a commodious 22-acre site.

With its 12 fountains (one for each apostle), the Crown of Thorns plant, and "Still Waters" reflecting ponds, the modern church (which Schuller describes as a "suburban middle-class shopping center for Jesus") is packed full on any given Sunday: a total of 2,200 children attend classes in the Tower, over 4,000 adults jam the glass-walled sanctuary, and another 1,600 sit outside bumper to bumper, listening in on car radios to Schuller's optimistic preaching.

Schuller is a peddler of optimism. He distrusts skeptics and praises "act-achievers" who "try-umph" over pessimism. According to Schuller, "Jesus was the greatest possibility thinker that ever lived." Espousing a kind of "I'm OK, You're OK" philosophy, accentuated by alliterative slogans, Schuller believes he fills a need with his drive-in church for an increasingly mobile culture.

Addressing the agnostic transients who keep flooding into the West, Schuller packs his sermons with success stories rather than theology. His TV services, called "Hour of Power," aired in 45 major cities and reaching an audience of approximately 2.5 million, generate at least 10,000 letters each week from admirers.

Most members of the Garden Grove Community Church, two-thirds of whom have had no prior church membership, come because of the wide-ranging community service program, which ranges from reading classes for the illiterate, through a singles ministry, to a 24-hour telephone crisis service that handles 20,000 calls a year. The budget for all church and TV operations is $4.8 million a year; and the lithe, 48-year-old Schuller receives $34,750 for his innovative approach.

Marjoe Gortner

No discussion of evangelism would be complete without mention of Marjoe Gortner, the man who exposed the con-game side of evangelism in the biographical feature-length film, *Marjoe*.

Marjoe (the name combines the names of Christ's "foster parents" Mary and Joseph) is the son of two California evangelists who molded their boy from birth into a Bible-beating preacher. At the age of three, he was ordained in the Church of the Old-Time Faith in Long Beach, California; by the time he was five, Marjoe had performed a marriage ceremony that, despite his age, was perfectly legal at that time.

Marjoe became the golden boy of the tent revivals. Huge crowds flocked to watch the child with the golden curls, blue eyes, and angelic face preaching the word of God with such frenzy that people would faint at his touch, while his parents proudly coached from offstage.

By the time he was 14, preaching was old hat, and Marjoe ran away from home. He lived with a woman who supported him until he had finished high school and entered San Jose State College.

Marjoe decided to be a preacher again, thinking the popularity of his earlier days would allow him to tell people what was really happening in late-60s America. He deviated from his earlier message of a stern, avenging God, to speak of a quiet God dwelling within the soul of every man. But the crowds dwindled. Marjoe had to decide either to abandon preaching completely or give the people what they wanted.

He chose the latter. He became the Mick Jagger of the tent revivals, and the crowds came surging back, bringing even more money than before. After a few hymns and a passionate sermon, Marjoe would summon everyone to come forward and buy a prayer cloth, a remnant that had been blessed with God's power to help answer their prayers. As they filed through the line, each person dropped his money into a basket, was handed a prayer cloth, and then received the greatest blessing of all — Marjoe touched him. People collapsed, cried, praised the Lord; and while they left the tent glowing with satisfaction, Marjoe would sit backstage counting his money. The sincerity was gone; Marjoe was king of the racket, star of the revivals.

It lasted four and a half years. But corresponding to his increasing desire to give it all up again was Marjoe's dream of being a movie star. Finally he devised a way that would let him do both. He let his whole con game speak for itself in the documentary in which he starred. The crowds who had watched him and swooned saw that their angel was nothing more than a convincing performer whose most popular script just happened to be about God.

Thousands of others saw *Marjoe* too, and a new skepticism about evangelism sprang up all over the country. Fellow revivalists accused Marjoe of being possessed by the devil, but a wider majority praised both him and the film for their honesty. Marjoe Gortner had spoken out, at a time when Americans were tired of being lied to, and exploded another myth by showing that the evangelist who profits from selling the word of God is not necessarily on the level.

REVEREND ALISON CHEEK

Alison Cheek is not an evangelist, but her voice in the Episcopal Church is as outspoken as that of any "fire and brimstone" preacher in the business. In her drive to become the first woman to be ordained an Episcopal priest, she drew such national attention that she was named one of *Time* Magazine's Women of the Year in 1975. She has become both a leader and a symbol in the women's movement for an active role in the clergy.

"The Episcopal seminary was good to me," recalls Ms. Cheek. "It allowed me to extend my course over six years instead of three so that I could raise my four young children. It hired me as a Biblical language instructor, which eased the financial strain. But it took me forever to stop feeling grateful and start feeling outraged that I felt so grateful."

The transition became complete one spring day in 1972 when Cheek, then a deacon, attended the ordination of a young man. "Before the procession began, I was very pointedly told that only priests, not deacons, could participate in the ritual laying on of hands. I can still remember the embarrassment, rage, and grief that surged through me as I stood alone in the pew while my brothers went up into the sanctuary to lay on hands."

Two years later Cheek heard about the planned ordination of a woman priest in Philadelphia and decided she would rather risk expulsion from the church than relive that same humiliation. Though the ordinations of Alison Cheek and 10 other women were declared invalid, the issue will not be resolved until an Episcopal Convention makes an ultimate decision on the issue of women in the priesthood. Meanwhile, Cheek, who lives in Annandale, Virginia, with her husband, a World Bank executive, is happy about her "freedom in limbo." In November of 1974, she became the first woman to celebrate Communion in an Episcopal Church in defiance of the diocesan bishop, and in August of 1975 she was installed as an assistant priest at the Church of St. Stephen and the Incarnation in Washington, D.C. She says, "I am convinced that the only crime I have committed in this matter is to have been born female."

"We believe as much as we can. We would believe everything if we could."

— William James

NEW GOSPELS, NEW CULTS

It is a particularly American trait that to find one's own individuality, one joins a group. Our society has always been afflicted by a plethora of religions, as subgroups splintered off in every direction accompanied by claims that God's voice was reverberating in their minds, giving instructions for new religions, new charts of the highways to heaven, some incredible systems of belief.

A new wave of cultism is spreading over the land. Usually founded by a charismatic leader and propagated by word of mouth, cults find a breeding ground among vulnerable minds searching for answers to questions that more conventional religions have ignored or belittled. In spite of their unorthodox practices, these groups are a unique part of the American Dream, that credo which declares all men should be allowed to pursue happiness freely.

Whether or not we find the values they embrace to be attractive is secondary to the fact that they exist. Each of them, in its own way, represents a very specific search for the expansion of already existing concepts, and they are being honed and subtly guided by the tensions and stresses that brought them into being in the first place.

By examining the cults in our society we can learn more about the nature of our own search. No longer just an opiate for the masses, they are sought as instruments for attaining new highs, seeking new goals, finding new patterns of living.

REVEREND
SUN MYUNG MOON / the unification church

The Reverend Sun Myung Moon's Unification Church is probably the largest, fastest growing, and most disciplined of the burgeoning religious cults. Largely because of media attention focused on frantic parents claiming their children have been kidnaped or brainwashed by the Reverend Moon's tenacious recruiters, the movement is also the most notorious. "Anti-Moon" organizations have been formed, and some parents have gone to the extent of hiring professional "deprogrammers" to restore their children to pre-Moon behavior. This has produced counter charges of kidnaping from the Unification Church. Lawsuits, filed by both sides, are pending. As yet there is no proof that the church used forcible or illegal means to attract and hold its young converts, but the Moon organization is well aware of the image damage such publicity has produced, and has launched an intense public relations campaign.

The Unification Church (full name: the Holy Spirit Association for the Unification of World Christianity) was founded by Korean-born Moon in South Korea in 1954. It flourished, expanded internationally, and now claims two million adherents worldwide. Its following in the United States is estimated at between 10,000 and 30,000 members, and in 1973 Moon transferred his headquarters from Korea, proclaiming America "God's chosen land." Moon has also founded the Freedom Leadership Foundation (known outside the United States as the International Federation for Victory Over Communism), a biweekly publication *The Rising Tide*, One World Crusade, and the World Freedom Institute.

The phenomenal growth of Moon's organization into an international multimillion-dollar corporation can be attributed partly to its strong political base and economic support in South Korea and Japan, and also to the church's establishment in America's newest "growth industry" — religious cults. Moon also has interests in such thriving Korean businesses as pharmaceuticals, heavy equipment manufacturing, titanium, and ginseng tea exportation. Church members provide much free labor for these industries, and connections with the church also bring the benefit of numerous corporate tax exemptions.

The church's theology is based upon God's word as revealed through Reverend Moon. It is an odd, seemingly contradictory, amalgam of fundamentalism, pop psychology, Oriental family worship, mysticism, patriotism, international unity, and vehement anti-Communism. When he was 16, Moon claims, God's will was revealed to him by Christ in a vision: Christ's work was incomplete at the time of the crucifixion, and a second Messiah is necessary to complete God's plan of a world spiritually unified through Christianity; Communism is the work of the devil and must be wiped out; and world unification must take place in the areas of science, government, and race.

Moon used to openly proclaim himself the Christ of the Second Advent, but part of the new public relations campaign is that he temper this sort of statement and allow followers to reach their own conclusions. Moon now says the second Messiah was born in Korea around 1920 (Moon was born in 1920), and that he will choose America as his base of operations.

The quest for world unification requires a complicated, highly efficient organization, and a reported annual budget of $11 million to fund U. S. operations alone. Central to the success of the organization is the aggressive cadre of youthful converts referred to as "Moonies."

About 25 percent of the Moonies are full-time members and live in church-sponsored communes, or in Barrytown, New York, where the Unification Theological Seminary is located, and Moon himself maintains a palatial estate on the Hudson River. Moonies spend their energies recruiting new members, raising funds (through door-to-door solicitation and selling candy, flowers, or candles), and attending training sessions to learn more about church theology.

New recruits are brought to one of the 120 communal centers for a weekend meeting, encouraged to share their feelings with the "brothers and sisters" of the commune "family," and are told about the church's ideology. Week-long retreats bring those who choose to join closer to the views shared by other Moonies. The communal groups are sexually segregated and all members are celibate. This spartan existence is in sharp contrast to Moon's own lifestyle, his

expensive limousine, and 55-foot cabin cruiser. This does not seem to bother the Moonies, who readily accept the prohibition of sex, drugs, tobacco, alcohol, and individual decision within the "family." Moon is referred to as "divine father," and it is speedily clear that his word is absolute.

There is an evangelical zeal about the Moonies' activities, whether seen in seeking out new recruits on the streets of a large and impersonal city, or in the way they arrange dried flowers which have been dyed red, white, and blue for Bicentennial door-to-door sales. Moonies seem eager to share their way of life and their religious beliefs. They greet strangers on the street or visitors to the commune warmly, smiling at any suggestion that they are conspirators in kidnaping or brainwashing. They find such charges ridiculous, and enjoy pointing out that Jesus too was persecuted.

There is a certain vagueness in the way a Moonie speaks — a faraway, slightly dilated look to the eyes, common among people who claim to be "high" on religion. Disconcerting to those who have not shared the experience, it seems to support the feeling that Moonies may have been brainwashed into beliefs that are not their own. But they will tell you they freely made the choice to give up their personal ambitions, material possessions, family ties, and opinions in order to carry out the will of God as Sun Myung Moon interprets it.

What do Sun Myung Moon and the Unification Church offer to those who become believers? Feelings of belonging, of instant friendship, freedom from problems, and relief from the pressures of a confusing and bewildering world, maybe. For some, the Unification Church provides safety, and some ready-made answers to the perplexing questions of life.

THE JESUS PEOPLE

With the pell-mell rush toward alternate lifestyles and belief systems that characterized the late 60s, there arose an interesting and active group of people who blended the most fundamental kind of Christianity with the "hippie" movement. These new creatures became known as Street Christians, Jesus freaks, or more widely as The Jesus People.

It is hard to say how the movement started or from which denomination it sprang, partly because at its inception few churches wanted to take responsibility for such a unique manifestation. The movement, originally, was intensely charismatic (emphasizing such "gifts of the spirit" as speaking in tongues, prophecy, etc.) and offered an opportunity to break free from the little white building on the corner. Harking back to the original Christian model, religion was not something to be practiced only on Sundays. The ranks of the Jesus People were made up chiefly of new converts, mostly societal dropouts, dissatisfied with themselves and their lifestyles, and seeking a chance to find a new identity. What could be more meaningful than being commissioned by God to spread the Gospel?

This radical Christianity was a hard pill to swallow for people involved in more sedate and established churches. Here were a mass of kids preaching the Gospel, and living a lifestyle that matched the descriptions in the Bible far better than the church weekly newsletter. They were even going so far as to call those traditional church services little more than social gatherings. Such criticisms struck a tender spot with more formal denominations who for several years had watched attendance drop steadily. But neither could they easily welcome into fellowship free spirits who might be moved to deliver a message in tongues in the middle of a Mother's Day sermon.

The churches were saved from this impasse by the appearance of campus Christian organizations, who wanted some of the "good stuff" the Street Christians had, but did not want to drop out of the system. Their main tenet of faith was still to fulfill the "great commission" of spreading the Gospel, yet they tended to look more like Pat Boone than Charles Manson. Moreover, they viewed the church on the corner as essential support for their activities, which allowed its traditional adherents to be part of the domestic missionary work — though in many cases only vicariously.

A whole gamut of campus organizations rapidly appeared, of which Campus Crusade for Christ is probably the most notable. Its founder, Bill Bright, applied the principles he learned in big business to building an organization which would be formal, energetic, and acceptable to even the most conservative of churches. Since its inception at UCLA in the 1960s, Campus Crusade has spread nationwide and even worldwide, attracting thousands of members.

Currently, the divisions have blurred: even traditional churchgoers festoon their cars with bumper stickers and insignia showing a fish or proclaiming the Second Coming; the Street Christians are spending less time on street corners and more time in church; and Campus Crusade has been joined by The Navigators and other non-denominational and semidenominational groups, giving students almost as much choice among groups as among denominations.

Those who used to be described as Jesus Freaks are now content to be called The Jesus People. Soon they will probably be known as churchgoers.

THE INTERNATIONAL COMMUNITY OF CHRIST

By definition, every Christian accepts the belief that the First Coming of Christ was manifest in Jesus of Nazareth, but for 2,000 years religious scholars and laymen have sought clues to when and in what form the Second Advent will manifest itself.

One group that devotes considerable attention to this question is the International Community of Christ. In the historical sense, the Community began when an American named Gene Savoy had a vision that Christ would come into the world as a little child, and journeyed to Peru in order to gather followers and await the event.

Upon his arrival in Peru, Savoy founded a school of advanced teachings based on meta-Christian mysticism, which accepted some 2,000 people for training over a 15-year period. During this time, from 1957 to 1971, Savoy and other members of the school conducted an exploration program of the Andes and the Amazonian jungles in Peru, Ecuador, Colombia and Brazil. Savoy subsequently wrote three quite successful books about their experiences.

While these ecological explorations and research were going on, members of the school were involved in deeper studies. According to their belief, the Christ Child had indeed come into the world and had died in 1962, leaving supplemental teachings and amendments to the Christian religion in the care of the Child's first disciple, Gene Savoy. In 1972 the Community was established in the United States, in the High Sierra country of Nevada, and a teaching program was begun. The first three years have been devoted to publishing selected manuscripts taken from the Peruvian archives and in preparing members of the Community for the public ministry which was to begin in 1975.

As described in the confidential Prospectus prepared by the Community, the essence of the organization's doctrine is that Christ's original teachings were really a complete system of spiritual development. These teachings were oral, were never put into writing during His lifetime, at His specific command, and their content was lost shortly after Jesus was crucified. It follows, therefore, that the New Testament does not contain Christ's teachings, because the Gospels, written long after the crucifixion, are "shrouded in cryptic symbology," the key to which was lost. The various existing Christian churches, therefore, are built on fragmentary and derivative data that include neither knowledge nor understanding of Jesus's original oral teachings.

According to the Community, Jamil, the Christ Child, has revealed these secrets to a select few, the founders and leaders of the organization, who will share the elements of their basic system of Cosolargy (an acronym derived from the words *cosmic, solar,* and *logos)* with those who pass the Community's tests. The Community will teach the student how to begin to develop his or her spiritual consciousness, regardless of race, color, nationality, sex, creed, or religion, using their textbooks and taped lectures. The classes are not conducted in the manner of academic institutions. Printed texts are mailed to each associate for study and practice in the privacy of the home, and oral instruction is given from time to time. The curriculum is arranged in a series of 12 parts and takes a year to complete. Its primary goal is the development of spiritual consciousness.

Graduates may continue with another year of advanced studies, after which ordination in the Community is possible.

THE UNIVERSAL LIFE CHURCH

Kirby Kensley used to be a Baptist minister in North Carolina. After traveling and living around the country, he settled down in Modesto, California, converted the garage of his home into a chapel, and put a sign over it that read, simply, "Church." Passersby would ask him what kind of a church it was. He would ask them what religion they were. If they said, "Baptist," he would tell them it was a Baptist church. If they said, "Pentecostal," he would answer that it was a Pentecostal church.

Thus it was that Kirby Kensley conceived the idea for the Universal Life Church — an organization that stresses the existence of widely varying religious creeds and de-emphasizes the differences between them.

His goal was to unify and to spread the work and the word of God.

In 1962 he legally incorporated the Universal Life Church and began ordaining ministers without questions and without charge, on the principle that each individual has the right to interpret God according to his own theory or concept. The idea grew and received national press coverage.

To date, the Universal Life Church claims two million ministers, who can legally perform weddings, funerals, and baptisms, and 9,000 affiliated churches. Kirby Kensley continues to ordain ministers free of charge; and anyone interested in starting a church can send for a charter and pledge a $2.00 monthly donation to be kept in the records.

GNOSTICISM

Gnosticism is an extremely ancient philosophy of religion, dating back to pre-Christian times, based on the theory that knowledge, *gnosis*, leads to the emancipation of the soul. Modern Gnosticism essentially concentrates on the existence of God within man's soul, and on the infinity of the mind. It believes that the soul is a divine spark, which is forced to live in a material world and suffers from contact with conflicting elements around it. Man's attraction to Christ, then, was that he was the ultimate beacon, and that the sparks of man's soul were drawn to that profound illumination.

Essential to the Gnostic belief is that because of his divine soul man cannot escape suffering from the boundaries that hem him in. He feels perpetually lost because he is separated from his source. It is a classic expression of the struggle of the powers of light against the powers of darkness.

FERAFERIA

Feraferia, centered in Pasadena, California, has only 22 initiates and some 100 members; it merits attention because it makes use of ritual expression in a complicated amalgam of dogma and teaching, and even uses a mythical language.

Its founder, Frederick M. Adams, incorporated Feraferia in August 1967. The idea for the cult dates back to the spring of 1956, when a sudden illuminative experience struck him while he was walking across the campus of Los Angeles City College. He was overtaken by a sense of the incredibility of the feminine form, and from that moment on, devoted himself to the service of the feminine sacred.

Between 1957 and 1959 Adams lived in a multifamily commune in the Sierra Madre with a group interested in the same concepts. At the commune was an outdoor temple to the "Maiden Goddess of Wildness" — representing the two major themes of Feraferia: the child-form representation of the goddess, and the equation of wilderness with sacred ground. The name Feraferia means "nature celebration," and came to Adams as an inspiration, as did the group's symbol, the stang, which is a trident with the sun and a crescent moon superimposed.

Feraferia holds that religious life should be an interaction between nature and the individual's erotic awareness. Man and earth and sky and sea are one huge living organism, whose symbol is Kore, the divine maiden of the Greeks. Kore is all aspects of the feminine, and the Feraferia calendar celebrates the feminine progress each year: birth in spring, emergence from childhood, nuptials, and final retiring beneath the earth in winter. According to Adams, nature not only nourishes and bears life, but also creates erotic passion.

Feraferia, which sees itself as predecessor to a time when mankind will recover a sense of ecological reverence, has primarily a middle-aged membership. There is talk among some members of establishing a paradise community in which inhabitants would live close to nature as vegetarians and horticulturalists, preserving trees and wildness and leaving all natural things intact.

SATANISM / the church of satan

The Church of Satan was founded in San Francisco by Anton LaVey in 1966 on the eve of Mayday, when, in Germany, witches were believed to fly around and celebrate. On that night LaVey shaved his head and proclaimed himself priest of the new faith.

LaVey, a former animal trainer, criminologist, and ceremonial magician, founded the Church of Satan because he believed ordinary churches were distorting the nature of man, making it impossible for him to discover true happiness. If there is a God, says LaVey, he is unable to intervene in human events; therefore, spirituality has no place on earth and its practice is deceptive. If man should worship anything it should be his own natural desires; and since Satan is a symbol of the material world and man's carnal nature, he becomes the worshipped idol. LaVey believes that it is necessary for man to indulge himself, so long as he doesn't hurt anyone else.

The rituals of the Church of Satan include a "black mass" with a nude woman as the altar; communal cursing during which anger and resentment are released; and a performance in which members act out means of coping with people and situations which threaten them. Many Satanic rites include the liberal use of drugs and orgy, but the traditional Satanic act of worship appears to be declining in popularity.

LaVey, in his *Satanic Bible*, described the Satanic mystique:

"Satanism has been thought of as being synonymous with cruelty and brutality. This is so only because people are afraid to face the truth — and the truth is that human beings are not all benign or all loving. Just because the Satanist admits he is capable of both love *and* hate, he is considered hateful. On the contrary, because he is able to give vent to his hatred through ritualized expression, he is far *more* capable of love — the deepest kind of love. By honestly recognizing and admitting to both the hate and the love he feels, there is no confusing one emotion with the other. Without being able to experience one of these emotions, you cannot *fully* experience the other."

The Church of Satan is the only Satanist organization which operates publicly and attracts educated people. LaVey claims some 7,000 members, the bulk of whom are young and, by all outward appearances, "straight."

VECTOR COMMUNITY CHURCH

A Vector group is a series of one-to-one counseling episodes during an evening, rather than an "encounter" or "confrontation" session. Everyone is encouraged to work, and leaders have as their goal the solving of some problem area for each person during each session.

Vector is a nondenominational church and does not dictate what a person's behavior or beliefs should be. It is more concerned with here and now and encourages the finding of the Kingdom of Heaven within one's self. It has no religious affiliations with a church or synagogue, nor does it replace traditional churches. The aim is a coming together to honor the principles of relatedness to each other and the universe. Vector encourages its followers to take care of the self and to help others, and offers help in how to do this.

Vector growth groups consist of six people who work with a counselor in turns while the others listen. During these group sessions there is an attempt to identify "permanent assumptions" about self, people, and the world. These assumptions are re-evaluated, and ways to change them are discussed.

George Burtt, a minister and counselor of the Vector Church, has developed a method of counseling called *psychographics*. It consists of the use of personal drawings to solve problems. The subject draws a picture of the problem and then illustrates each stage of working toward a solution with guidance and feedback from the counselor.

CHURCH OF NATURALISM

Naturalism, Inc., is a religious community dedicated to ever-improving spiritual refinement. Its members engage in good works of an altruistic nature.

The Church of Naturalism believes the formalized structure of religion has caused it to lose its spirit and essence. Emphasis upon the hereafter and lack of response to the situations of our physical existence have had the result that too many people feel enjoyment is sinful and learn to suppress their instincts. Formalized religion expends its energy in passing authority from one generation to another. The Church of Naturalism prefers to encourage the release of this energy in better causes. It is more or less a philosophy of freedom.

Naturalism, Inc., is organized into a structure known as the "divinity training program." It has three stages:

1. *The Group Grope.* The novitiate divides into groups of from five to 10 people, usually separated by sex. They live together, attend four meetings a week (educational therapy sessions in which they become aware of others and their motivations and patterns of life), and undergo a physical therapy process in which they learn to relax the body and regain control. Members of the novitiate are required to hold full-time jobs, in order to remain in contact with reality. They turn over four-fifths of their income, or a minimum of $50 per week, to support the shelter and Samaritan services of the organization. They are also required to work in these Samaritan services and to expect nothing in return.

2. *Rural Setting.* Safely removed from society, the members commit themselves to a process of soul searching, becoming aware of their inner conflicts and tensions so that they can later work them out.

For 30 minutes to one hour per day, they sit in deep tubs of warm water. They are massaged or Rolfed, they take walks to get in touch with nature, and since there is no sexual separation they develop deep, honest personal relationships.

They are also involved in entelechial therapy, a type of therapy in which the subject takes something he can fantasize and works it into existence so that he will get used to the process of making his dreams a reality.

3. *Death Judgment Experience.* In order to get in rapport and contact with themselves, members sit in a black box for 40 days. During this experience the persons loses his self-concept and relives the events of his life. The period of emptiness is thought to allow the original essence (self) to appear, and to give the subject an opportunity to re-evaluate his life. The basic premise of the Death Judgment Experience is that if you can gain sufficient strength and stamina to be yourself by isolating yourself totally, you can operate in society much more effectively.

The Church of Naturalism hopes to acquire islands to which its members can go for three to six months out of the year so as to keep in contact with themselves. The other six to nine months, of course, would be spent functioning in society.

THE THEOSOPHICAL SOCIETY

The Theosophical Society in America was founded in 1875 and in 1970 reported about 5,000 members. Growth has been greatest in the south-central states.

There are basically two sides to Theosophy. The first is the belief in and celebration of psychic phenomena and visions of the Masters. The second is a mentalist philosophy in which the mind is the basis of the universe, and the spirit is separable from the body. Theosophy is yet another modern expression of ancient wisdom, and its concepts are ageless.

The Masters are the unifying body of Theosophy. The Masters are the figures who represent individuals more highly evolved than the ordinary person, and their contact with Theosophists is an integral part of the tradition. The message that comes from these Masters is considered to be the deepest wisdom.

The text on which Theosophy is primarily based is a book called *The Secret Doctrine*, allegedly communicated to its author, Madame Blavatsky, by the Masters. Its text, a combination of science, myth, philosophy, and poetry, supposedly generates remarkable experiences; and the book in its entirety asks the individual to suspend his normal progress until he has discovered the meaning of the techniques described.

Theosophical lodges exist throughout the country, most of them older, rather plain buildings with lending libraries and bookstores. Lectures are held at the lodges on such concepts as karma, reincarnation, astrology, psychic phenomena, meditation, the I Ching, and extrasensory perception. While Theosophical interest in the occult has attracted some young people, the typical membership is middle-class, middle-aged, and white.

The inner circle of Theosophy in America is the Esoteric Section, headquartered in Ojai, California. Members are required to have been Theosophists for three years. They eschew tobacco, alcohol, and meat, and practice secret meditation methods to put them in touch with the Masters.

Theosophists believe in an Omnipresent Principle which transcends human power to conceive. Central tenets are the eternity of the universe, the universal law of ebb and flow, and a pilgrimage of the soul in which it passes through the elemental forms of the physical world, acquires individuality, and finally reaches the highest degree of intelligence to equal the holiest archangel, Dhyani-Buddha.

ANTHROPOSOPHY

Rudolph Steiner, a former Theosophist, decided that it was important to make a scientific study of the spiritual world. In 1912 he formed an organization called the Anthroposophical Society with that basic purpose in mind.

In this school of thought, the mind has two parts, one which can know and the other which can be known, and Jesus Christ is the ultimate example of supersensory perception.

Anthroposophy takes a pragmatic approach to world problems, putting less emphasis on meditative communication with a Higher Mind. There is interest in art, music, agriculture, helping retarded children, and other such expressions that ultimately increase mankind's vision. There is also strong involvement in education, and the membership has founded several private schools known as Waldorf Schools.

THE FULL MOON MEDITATION GROUPS

The Full Moon Meditation Groups were founded by Alice Bailey, a disillusioned former Theosophist. Her first organization was the Arcane School in New York.

The meditation central to this group is concentrated on bringing about the reappearance of Christ, either in human form or as a period of enlightenment. Full Moon members are idealists, eager to promote international unity and understanding. Their meetings include modern dance performances, concerts of Wagnerian music and other classics, meditation, and an emphasis on the occult. They usually culminate in the slow, deliberate recitation of the Great Invocation:

"From the point of Light within the Mind of God
Let light stream forth into the minds of men.
    Let light descend on Earth.
From the point of Love within the Heart of God
Let Love stream forth into the hearts of men.
    May Christ return to Earth.
From the center where the Will of God is known
Let Purpose guide the little wills of men —
    The purpose which the Masters know and serve.
From the center which we call the race of men
Let the Plan of Love and Light work out
    And may it seal the door where evil dwells.
Let Light and Love and Power
Restore the Plan on Earth."

Every year the Full Moon Meditation Groups gather for the Wesak Festival to combine their individual efforts toward greater serenity and communication with the Higher Mind.

THE ROSICRUCIAN FELLOWSHIP

The Order of the Rosicrucian Brotherhood was founded in Central Europe in 1313 by Christian Rosenkreuz, and over the centuries since then, primarily in secret, has transmitted a cosmic philosophy known as the Western Wisdom Teaching.

The Western Wisdom School teaches that God is the creator of our solar system; that in all nature a slow process of development is constantly carried on; that the goal of everything in creation is perfection. It emphasizes that it is possible for mankind to hasten or retard his growth by the way he lives, outlines the plan of creation, and gives specific directions on how to proceed in the most effective manner.

The Rosicrucian Fellowship propagates its teachings through correspondence courses, a magazine called *Rays from the Rose Cross*, and several other publications. A summer school and a winter school are conducted at the group's headquarters in Oceanside, California, where the Fellowship also operates a vegetarian cafeteria.

THE SPIRITUALIST CHURCH

Spiritualists achieve their most meaningful religious experiences by communicating with the spirits who have "passed over." These may be heroes of the past or friends and relatives who have died and are eager to make contact with the living.

Communication with such spirits is naturally very subjective, but charismatic leaders of the Spiritualist Church are able to identify whatever sources of power are available to the individual. It is frequently necessary, in fact, for ministers to act as mediums to help members of their congregations to communicate with their higher source. The ultimate Spiritualist goal is the ability to transcend standard forms of communication and to expand the mind toward infinity.

THE "I AM" MOVEMENT

The "I Am" Movement was founded by Guy Ballard, a Kansas-born man who was interested in the occult and had studied Spiritualism and Theosophy. It has a deeply American setting, rejecting the idea that the Great Masters can be found only overseas. It holds that humanity had its beginnings . . . and will have its end . . . in this country, and that America will prove to be the shining example that will lead the rest of the world to a new age of enlightenment.

Color is an important concept in this movement, which views it as a positive source of energy that can overcome a negative source (sound) and much of the other trouble in which we find ourselves.

Ascension is considered to be humanity's ultimate goal, and there is emphasis on the use of concentrated psychic power to rid the world of evil influences.

Strict members of the "I Am" Movement do not indulge in tobacco, alcohol, meat, or sex. They believe that sexual energies should be redirected toward the work of the Masters and that only through abstinence can one achieve ascension.

GURDJIEFF

Georges Ivanovitch Gurdjieff (1877-1949) is one of those magi who have baffled many but have drawn followers with the promise of making them new men with extraordinary powers. Born in Russia, near the Persian border, he traveled widely, taught in prerevolutionary Moscow, escaped to France after the October Revolution, and settled in Paris, where he continued to teach until his death. He spoke of himself primarily as a dance teacher; nevertheless his teachings go far beyond the realm of movement.

Gurdjieff's thought is hard to encapsulate, but basically he believed that man is capable of four states of awareness: sleeping, waking, self-consciousness, and objective consciousness. Normally, however, man is mostly asleep, not living at even waking awareness, and to reach the more intense states requires "the work" of awakening. People do not realize they are not one person, but a mass of different "I's"; they think that they "do" things, without recognizing that they are really machines. Before one can begin to "do," one must learn how to "be."

Gurdjieff taught the necessity of identifying with the One Mind, because reality can be experienced only by seeing from its perspective. He spoke of four ways of overcoming the typically clouded human vision: the way of the fakir, through the body; the way of the yogi, through knowledge; the way of the monk, through faith; and the fourth way, "the way of the sly man," through understanding. Gurdjieff's "Fourth Way Schools" would allow the ordinary person to learn to follow the way while carrying on with his regular life and continuing his normal relationships.

Gurdjieff drew on three main sources for his teaching. He grew up in the mystical tradition of Eastern Orthodox Christianity, traveled extensively in the Middle East, where he evidently studied with some Islamic Sufi orders, and went to Tibet, where he studied Tantric Buddhism — although officially there as a secret agent for the czar.

His techniques for transforming consciousness begin with the Sufi exercise of self-remembering, where one progresses from the observation of how much man resembles a machine to a sense of man's place in the universe. Drawing on the Sufi tradition of Sama (ecstatic dancing, often whirling) and the symbolic religious dances of Tibet, Gurdjieff developed a system of movements whereby body, intellect, and emotions were to be brought into balance. Some of them are described in a book by one of his most prominent disciples, A. Orage's *Psychological Exercises.* The dancer performs dozens of precise movements while counting backwards in intricate series of numbers and attempting to "hear" the music through the eyes or sense of touch. For his more advanced students, Gurdjieff taught the use of a kind of mantra Yoga, based on the Eastern Orthodox practice of the Prayer of Jesus.

Since Gurdjieff's death, his various disciples have written widely about his work and their own, and there are many groups throughout Europe and the United States that continue what Gurdjieff called "the work" in their different ways.

THE PROSPEROS

The Prosperos, chartered in Florida in 1956, is a group based on Gurdjieff's philosophies founded by a man named Thane Walker, a charismatic one-time student of Gurdjieff's whose approach to therapy is rather more scientific.

Like Gurdjieff, the Prosperos believe in One Mind, and the fact that reality can be experienced only by removing the distortions of the senses and memory and perceiving life through that ultimate source.

God is consciousness. To truly experience that pure consciousness, students of the Prosperos learn five separate processes in their "Translation" classes: (1) A statement of being, (2) Uncovering the lie or error, (3) Argument, (4) Summing up the results, and (5) Establishing the absolute.

Memory is considered to be a negative, deluding fact rather than a helpful ability.

Most Prosperos members are in California, and are said to number about 3,000. As a group they tend to be young, successful, unorthodox, and optimistic about the future and the role the Prosperos can help them play in it.

ABILITISM

Abilitism was founded by Charles Berner, an ex-Scientologist. His goal was to perfect the human ability to love and communicate.

Abilitism is somewhat similar to Scientology, although it is a more loosely molded school. Basically, it consists of an interchange between people, structured in two ways in order to achieve self-understanding. "Relating" is when two people sit together and alternately talk for five minutes and listen for five minutes about problems in their individual lives. "Enlightenment intensives" extend the talk-listen process to groups of people, and can last over periods of up to three days.

Essentially, Abilitism attempts to blend Eastern (non-talk) methods with Western (talk) ones; at no time is there processing out loud of reactions to the talk. That primarily takes place within each person's mind.

CHURCH OF ALL WORLDS

Claiming a membership of around 700, the Church of All Worlds is composed of predominantly young adults, most with a college background, who have dedicated themselves to a way of life that is "nondestructive, peaceful, creative, joyous, alive, nonviolent, loving, life-affirming, free, responsible, ecstatic, aware, nonhypocritical, gentle, courageous, honest, tolerant, humanistic, nonauthoritarian, benevolent, moral, growth-oriented, and ecologically sane."

The various groups, or nests, are informal but have specific purposes. Man must find his place in a biological world where he should cooperate with his own species. The Church of All Worlds believes that humanity is directly responsible for the future of the earth.

THE FLYING SAUCER CULTS

Given our undying curiosity about the likelihood of life on other planets and in other solar systems, it is probably only natural that movements would crop up specifically to study and exchange information about experiences with UFOs.

Master of ceremonies for one such group is George Van Tassell, who holds an annual Giant Rock convention near Yucca Valley, California, to discuss his experiences and the experiences of others in communicating with these beings from outer space. Van Tassell published a book in 1952, *I Rode in a Flying Saucer,* which described his first introduction to this other world. One night he was sleeping out in the desert when a spaceship landed nearby. He spoke at length with the crew, and now receives messages telepathically from the vehicles, which, according to Van Tassell, hover constantly over the Giant Rock area.

Another group is Understanding, Inc., founded by Daniel Fry. While Fry was employed at the White Sands Proving Grounds, he too found himself alone in the desert one evening and was met by a UFO. The saucer people gave him a ride to New York and back in half an hour, in the course of which they informed him that they were the last remnants of a previous earthly civilization which had wiped itself out through nuclear warfare. Having escaped by flying to Mars, they had now returned to earth to deliver their warning.

Membership in such flying saucer cults is on the rise, and their reported communications continue.

HUMAN INDIVIDUAL METAMORPHOSIS/ the two

Human Individual Metamorphosis, or HIM, came to national attention when 20 people in Oregon were persuaded to give away all their earthly possessions and renounce their families in order to accompany "The Two," as the leader-founders are called, on a UFO journey to the next kingdom. The Two are Bonnie Trusdale Nettles and Herff Applewhite, a middle-aged couple from Texas who are also known as The Man and The Woman, Bo and Peep, Winnie and Pooh, Chip and Dale, and the Pied Pipers of Space.

The destination of HIM's trip is the next level of evolution, and in their letter to prospective voyagers The Two emphasize that it is not just a spiritual trip but that the body must literally be converted, biologically and chemically. There are now said to be as many as a thousand followers, grown from the original 26 who left Los Angeles in April of 1975. The core of the experience, according to Sylvia, a former member, is the Process, a continuous method of meditation and spiritual awareness which keeps HIM followers in touch with the Father(s), beings on a higher plane who guide, inspire, and help people on the earthly level.

To participate in the Process, members must live constantly with a partner. There are rules against sex, liquor, and drugs, and partners are usually of widely disparate ages and sexual proclivities. Sylvia told of being paired with a homosexual who was greatly upset at the arrangement.

There is disagreement as to whether an actual trip to another planet is necessary. Bo is reported as saying you can now accomplish the metamorphic process in your own home, preparing yourself mentally and physically for the ascent to a new life.

Ex-followers agree on the hypnotic, persuasive powers of The Two. After living under the spell of the group's doctrines and practices, dropouts often find it difficult to resume normal lives. Converts come from many fields: engineers, students, actors, clerks — but Sylvia feels they were all attempting to overcome inadequacies in their lives, whether in love, money, or a career.

Members are told to sell everything they have and bring the proceeds along when they join. Some of the funds have been expended for equipment and two-week allowances of cash doled out to the partners. Apparently large sums have been collected and their disposition is a matter for speculation.

EXTRACTS FROM THE HIM LETTER TO PROSPECTIVE MEMBERS:

"Dear Prospective Candidate,

"Although no plans are being made other than day-to-day projections, if your seeking is sincere and ardent, you cannot fail to make contact . . . .

"This is not a spiritual trip. To reach the next kingdom above human, your body must literally be converted over biologically and chemically. This metamorphic process happens automatically as you *will* yourself to overcome your humanness.

"If you recognize this as truth, you have only to ask with all your might (out loud or in your head) for your Father(s) in the next kingdom to give you whatever tests are necessary for your overcoming. To demonstrate to your Father(s) that you are committed to reaching the next level, where you will have eternal life and be able to help significantly those in this garden, you must leave all your past behind. This means that you walk out the door of your human life, taking with you only those things that will be necessary while you are still on this planet. Once you establish a strong, direct line of communication with your Father and ask that he do what is best for those you leave behind, they will be in the best of care. When you have left all behind, you can meet with the two — as long as they are here — and they will clarify any questions you may have . . . .

"If you put 100 percent of your energy into this effort from the time you are aware of this truth until the time the light is leaving, you will receive the necessary ingredient to complete your overcoming from members in the next kingdom upon departure in an actual spacecraft . . . .

"As time is running short, we feel that a letter, anticipating your questions, is the best thing. Rather than have you believe that this is merely an interesting trip, we have laid it on the line as best we can. It requires a *total* effort. You must be willing to do whatever it takes to complete your overcoming. You will *not* be asked to do anything illegal or against anyone. Most importantly, you have *will* and choice; you do not have to do anything. The way to overcome will be shown to you. You will take it from there, and you will have help.

We hope to hear from you soon."

THE SEEKERS / who are they?

There is a real hunger in the Western world today for fresh ways of perceiving, fresh states of consciousness, fresh experience of reality. Western religions and traditional Western philosophies are failing to provide such stimulation; as a result there is tremendous interest in the religions of the East, in Zen and Yoga and Sufism.

In the vanguard, of course, are the youth of what we used to call the counterculture, who are attracted by the trappings and symbols, as well as the substance, of Asian religions. They wear Japa mala beads, mandalas embellish their walls, their dress is patterned after Indian styles — external evidence of an internal revolution.

But it is not only those in rebellion against the establishment who are involved in the ancient disciplines. There are many prosperous, middle-aged seekers, conventional in other aspects of their lives, maybe, who fill Yoga classes and Zen meditation sessions who join the Vedanta Society or the Self-Realization Fellowship, and who make trips to India in the same spirit as devout Moslems journey to Mecca, seeking the fountainhead of a system of religious belief that will bring peace and understanding into their lives.

While interest in Buddhism, particularly Zen Buddhism, has greatly increased, to the average Westerner it seems rather esoteric and not readily accessible. The majority of people attracted to Eastern religions become involved with various sects of Yoga and other divisions of Hinduism ranging from the disciplined intellectualism of the Vedanta Society to the self-hypnotic chanting of the Hare Krishna followers. Part of the attraction of all these religions is our eternal fascination with the foreign, the exotic, the mystical. The seekers are of all ages, types, needs; they are looking for acceptance, recognition, psychological support, the feeling of belonging to something important, even magical — a direct pipeline to God. They are trying to discover themselves, and the ancient traditions of the East offer them specific, well-marked pathways to the domain of self-knowledge and spiritual peace.

Many are attractive, well-mannered, pleasant people who should have found ready acceptance in their own social and economic world. Others are the perennially lonely ones, handicapped in some physical or social way, dropouts from normal life who find their pain eased by the carefully ritualized regimen, the totally accepted philosophy. They might have found the same doctrine, the same guidance for their search in the older traditions of their own spiritual heritage — as, for example, among the Quakers. But by putting on Indian clothes, wearing beads, chanting in Sanskrit, the whole quest takes on color and power and magic. It becomes more satisfying.

That is not to say there is nothing at all to find — that the Emperor has no new clothes. There are men of great spiritual power in the Orient, who can indeed open the hearts and clarify the thinking of those who seek them out. But there are also charlatans, pedants, and those who love to pontificate, just as are found in religious organizations anywhere. The spiritual eyes may be opened on the banks of the Ganges or in downtown Peoria; as in every search, you carry the goal within you.

OM: A Statement of Power

OM. The greatest word of power, believed to be the sound of the universe. When properly recited by a Yogi it produces great harmony in the body and in the mind. It should be uttered either very quietly or exclusively mentally.

The theory of *Om* is that as "a" is the first sound, made at the back of the mouth, and "m" is the last, made with the lips, and the "u" is of the nature of a glide between them, the word covers the whole range of vowel utterances, and because vowels are the power in speech and consonants represent only limitations or applications of the power, this whole word is the expression of creation which indicates the presence of the Creator. It has a twofold purpose: the understanding of the nature of individual consciousness, and an absence of obstacles to the attainment of the higher contemplation.

Om is also the sound made by the electromagnetic forces given off by the rotation of the earth. Lynn Taylor, a Yoga enthusiast from Los Angeles, had heard of a crater in Hawaii in which one could hear the *Om* of the earth. She personally made the trip there, climbed down the crater and into a small cave — and, in the total stillness, she clearly heard a soft but definite *Om*. She described her feelings: "It was beautiful listening to the earth making its own statement of power. I've never felt so much a part of it, and I felt at that moment as if I were the only person in the world."

IDRIES SHAH ON GURUS

"Some (gurus) are frankly phonies, and they don't try to hide it from me. They think I am one, too, so when we meet they begin the most disturbing conversations. They want to know how I get money, how I control people, and so on . . . They feel safety in numbers. They actually feel there is something wrong with what they are doing, and they feel better if they talk to somebody else who is doing that. I always tell them that I think it would be much better if they gave up the guru role in their own minds and realized that they are providing a perfectly good social service.

"It's time somebody took the lid off the guru racket. Since I have nothing to lose, it might as well be me. With many of these gurus it comes down to an 'us and them' sort of thing between the East and the West. Gurus from India used to stop by on their way to California and their attitude was generally, let's take the Westerners to the cleaners; they colonized us; now we will get money out of them. I heard this sort of thing even from people who had impeccable spiritual reputations back home in India.

"What I want to say is, 'Brother, you are in the revenge business, and that's a different kind of business from me.' There are always groups that are willing to negotiate with me and want to use my name. On one occasion a chap in a black shirt and white tie told me, 'You take Britain, but don't take the United States, because that's ours.' I had a terrible vision of Al Capone. The difference was that the guru's disciples kissed his feet.

"Getting the masses is the easy part. A guru can attract a crowd of a million in India, but few in the crowd take him seriously. You see, India has had gurus for thousands of years, so they are generally sophisticated about them; they take in the attitude with their mothers' milk. This culture just hasn't been inoculated against the guru. Let's turn it around. If I were fresh off a plane from India and told you that I was going to Detroit to become a wonderful automobile millionaire, you would smile at me. You know perfectly well the obstacles, the taxes, the ulcers that I face. Well, the Indian is in the same position with the automobile industry as the American with the guru. I'm not impressed by naive American reactions to gurus; if you can show me a guru who can pull off that racket in the East, then I will be surprised."

Idries Shah
Psychology Today

MEDITATION STYLES
lulling the dragon of the conscious mind

In the effort to understand ourselves, we are turning increasingly to the Oriental disciplines that involve meditation. And in this quest the hero of our Western culture, the conscious mind, becomes the dragon that must be put to sleep if we are to find the mysteries and insights that lie beyond the gates he is guarding.

The great achievements of the Western world have always depended on the thrust of active, questing consciousness. Our increasingly complex technology demands that problems be solved with rational, sequential thought processes. While scientists as well as artists and philosophers have acknowledged the value of intuition, many people have still regarded this type of knowledge — this flash of insight from a source other than conscious mind — with suspicion, reluctant to acknowledge the existence of anything not accessible to the five senses or to the logical workings of that part of the mind of which we are continuously aware.

In the Western world there has traditionally been a sharp division between body and mind and a skepticism as to whether there was anything real beyond them, whether it be called soul, or spirit, or the immortal self, or the collective unconscious. Now, however, while we are probing outer space with our marvelous new technology, we are simultaneously on the frontiers of exploration into man's inner space. And just as the first forays off the planet and our first view from beyond it have brought home how we truly are inhabitants of one beautiful mist-shrouded world, our explorations into our interior depths are giving us glimpses of the inter-relatedness of mind and body and a barely sensed entity beyond our habitual conceptions of both.

The many techniques of meditation share a common goal: the quieting or blocking out of that conscious, everyday mind, to find the "No Mind" of Zen, the "Immortal Self" of Yoga, the Fana al Fana (annihilation of the self) of the Sufis, the something beyond. Actually these ideas are not as foreign to Western thought as they seem at first glance. In the Judaeo-Christian tradition the ancient prophets believed man must "empty" himself to hear God's voice, and used fasting and forms of meditation to attain that emptiness. Jesus taught that the Kingdom of God is within man: "As a man thinketh in his heart, so is he." The Christian contemplative life has always been important to the Church, and while its present role may be less emphasized, it is still very much in existence.

The most prominent of the kinds of meditation derived from Eastern culture are those used in Zen; Tibetan and various other yogic disciplines, including Transcendental Meditation; and the practices of the Sufi — an esoteric cult within Islam.

Zen

The word Zen derives from the Chinese *Ch'an*, which comes in turn from the Sanskrit *Dyana*, translated as "meditation" — it is known as the meditation school of Chinese and Japanese Buddhism. In Zen monasteries, where the technique is usually taught, the customary procedure is to sit on a padded cushion in a cross-legged position. When the student becomes sufficiently limber he assumes the full lotus position with the sole of the foot facing upward on the opposite thigh. His goal is so to still his mind that discursive thought disappears, the consciousness empties, and the first stage toward "No Mind" is achieved.

The goal of Zen practice is *Satori,* "enlightenment," an awareness of the ultimate reality beyond the limits of individual consciousness. Either through flashes of this awareness, or through long and arduous periods of training, the mind is freed from its past conditioning, its habitual ways of perceiving, and the walls between self and reality come tumbling down.

One Zen technique is simply to follow the breath, to watch it, without attempting to control it in any way. The beginning student is advised to count his breaths to 10, and if he loses the count, as often occurs, to go back to the beginning and start again. In the Rinzai school of Zen the student is given a Koan, a puzzle without a logical solution, on which he is to concentrate as guided by the Roshi, or master. The Koan is used as a device for "wedging through" the layers of the conscious mind while developing, and finally attaining, an awareness beyond the duality of the knower and the known.

In the Soto sect of Zen there is less emphasis on such techniques. The student works on "just sitting," with his mind intensely involved in a state of concentrated awareness but without special aids to provide a focus for meditation.

While enlightenment may come in a blinding flash, the training period in Zen and in most yogic practice is always long and usually difficult. The experience must be repeated and reinforced until the practitioner perceives the essence of mind, which is No

Mind; seeing into things as they are, into their "suchness." First in glimpses, then more fully and completely, a consciousness of That which lies behind all differentiation takes place. This perception must become more than words, more than an idea, but a true alteration of consciousness, a way of "seeing" with the mind alone. Then there is the return, the opening of the path which leads onward and eventually back to the world, where Reality will be integrated and then seen in ordinary life.

In Zen the mind is striving to be cleared of past conditioning, to perceive the very nature of things, to tear away the veils from our way of seeing. The master works with the methods just mentioned to help the student free himself from the cocoon imprisoning his mind — as a limp, wet pupa struggles with pulsing wings to emerge from its chrysalis so that it may soar in full flight. But the disciple must perform this task himself — the master can only offer guidance or point out the direction.

There is a story of a boy who was given a pupa so that he might watch it hatch. Although warned not help, the boy took pity on its struggles to free itself and broke the chrysalis open, only to find that the creature could not fly because its wings had not been strengthened by the ordeal of emerging.

Although this reliance on one's own efforts is important, like all other disciplines that involve meditation Zen is no "do-it-yourself" process. The student can accomplish much by practice and study, but the guidance of a teacher is essential. In Zen, the emphasis is on simplicity; to eat when hungry, to drink when thirsty, to reduce living and perceiving to essentials. Like the early Christian Gnostics, Zen leads away from rigid dogma and doctrine and makes each person learn from within himself.

Scientists have studied the relationship between alpha brain waves and meditation in various experiments dating back to the 1950s. In 1966, two researchers, Dasmatsu and Hirai, worked with Zen monks in *Zazen,* or sitting meditation. Forty-eight priests and disciples of Zen sects of Buddhism had their brain waves continuously recorded before, during, and after meditation. Alpha waves were observed within 50 seconds after the beginning of meditation, continued to appear with increasing amplitude, and persisted for varying periods.

From this and similar experiments some observers were quick to make the connection between the brain rhythms present in meditation and the ability of many subjects to learn to produce such rhythms with biofeedback, and conclude that Instant Zen would soon be available. But can the No Mind be attained with the aid of a machine? Can alpha training be a substitute for years of struggle with a Koan, or endless sessions of Zazen, with aching muscles fixed in the full lotus position and the mind yearning toward Satori? Evidence indicates it is possible.

Yoga

In contrast to Zen, with its Koans, or "just sitting," the traditional forms of yogic meditation use the central focus or technique of a *mantra,* a mystic word or phrase. As taught by the Integral Yoga Institute, founded in this country by Swami Satchidananda, the mantra is conferred on the individual during an initiation ceremony, with the injunction to keep it secret and treat it with reverence. The meaning of the phrase, word or syllable is not important, but it is supposed to create vibrations within the mind, awakening psychic powers in the individual and having a healthy effect on the body. Its repetition is designed to calm the senses and the mind and make them ready to handle any problem. To emphasize the continuity of the 5,000-year-old tradition that lies behind this practice, the initiation ceremony is solemn and elaborate, involving gifts of fruit and flowers, chanting and prayers, performed before a candle-lit altar fragrant with incense, and with the initiates wearing loose white garments.

Integral Yoga is no easy discipline for 20th-century Westerners — followers are urged to write their mantras for a prescribed period each day in addition to repeating them during the meditation period; to perform the yogic postures known as *asanas;* to do *pranayama* (breathing exercises which enhance the *prana,* or life force); to read holy books; observe silence; not to smoke, nor drink liquor save on social occasions; to eat meat sparingly; and to stick to truth, nonviolence, selflessness, and generosity. If the student fails to follow these observances he is instructed to punish himself with various penitences, such as increasing the repetition of his mantra mentally or in writing, fasting for a day with only liquids or fruits, and giving more than his regular contributions to charity.

Just as in the Zen studies, Yogis who practiced *Samadhi* (the Sanskrit word for concentration) showed persistent alpha brain-wave activity, with increased amplitude during the period of meditation, and with alpha rhythms still present during the resting periods.

Tibetan Meditation Styles

A more elaborate yogic tradition is found in Tibet, where there are several schools of

Buddhism. Meditation plays an important part in all of them. Tibet's venerated 11th-century saint and poet, Milarepa, spent a great part of his life in solitary meditation. Members of his sect still live in caves high in the Himalayas, some in hermitages where Milarepa himself is said to have lived. Students and disciples often wall themselves into tiny dwellings where they are fed by friends or neighbors, or subsist on stored-up grain, going occasionally into the outside world to beg for food.

Tibetan practices rest on an elaborate structure of psychophysiological concepts. There is an elemental energy out of which everything is constructed, but this energy comes in many forms, such as those found in plants, in animals, and in various levels of human consciousness. Some schools of Tibetan Buddhism also practice Kundalini Yoga, which develops the psychic nerve (situated in the spinal column) and the *chakras*, or nerve centers, in which the vital force is stored.

Mantras are used, as in other yogic schools, as aids to meditation. Tibetans call them "words of power," and believe they vibrate at a certain rate and can have a profound influence on the consciousness.

As the Tibetan monk or lama progresses in his spiritual practice, he is able to generate *tummo*, psychic heat — a most practical ability in that climate. He also learns to enter the dream state at will, and to be able to compare it to the waking state without breaking normal consciousness. Some meditators make use of pills manufactured by various perfected Yogis, such as the Dalai Lama himself, in order to obtain grace and cure the ignorance which they believe causes the endless cycle of deaths and rebirths to which the unperfected spirit is subject.

The meditator may concentrate upon a single point, such as a tiny object, or upon the body, the sayings, or the mind of the Buddha. Whatever the focus he chooses, he fixes his thoughts firmly upon it, refusing to allow his mind to be deflected from this center of his attention.

"When the mind is kept bound," Saraha, a Tibetan sage, is quoted as saying, "it endeavors to wander in the 10 directions. When it is left free, it remains motionless. I understood that it was a baffling animal, like the camel." This would seem to be a different technique from the rigid concentration just described — more similar to the attitude of Transcendental Meditation, as taught by the Maharishi Mahesh Yogi.

Transcendental Meditation (TM)

This is the simplest of all the yogic techniques. Students are instructed not to try to concentrate, nor to use any effort. Surprisingly, TM teachers insist it is not even necessary to believe in the technique in order to have it produce results. After some preliminary lectures, the student is initiated and given a mantra to repeat silently in meditation. The initiation ceremony is similar to that used in Integral Yoga, with fruit and flowers, chanting and incense, to link the technique with the ancient Hindu tradition from which it comes. The student is instructed in the use of his mantra, and encouraged to return for periodic checking, meetings which feature lectures in the practice or tapes of the Maharishi himself, and group meditation.

Teachers of Transcendental Meditation speak of "diving" into the mind on the mantra, and then coming out again on a thought. The thoughts are allowed to come and go without any effort to stop or control them, but the mantra is simply repeated quietly in the mind with the mind constantly plunging deep below the surface level.

Sufi Meditation

An entirely different form of meditation, or altered consciousness, is practiced by the Sufis, a sect within Islam which has flourished for centuries, sometimes as an almost heretical opposition to the position of the faithful, sometimes becoming reconciled with them and acting as a renewing element within the faith. They practice the repeated recitation of a religious formula, or *Dhikr*, to attain a trancelike or meditative state and find an inner way to God. They believe in Gnosis *(Ma'rifa)*, an inner experiential knowledge, as opposed to the intellectual knowledge of theology. Moving in a circle, the "whirling dervishes" chant the Dhikr with their hands on their neighbor's shoulders, the upper part of their bodies bending backward and forward, to attain the ecstasy of inner union with the divine, the absence of the self before God. The Sufis use a chain of beads, like the Yoga mala or the Christian rosary, to guide them in chanting the 99 names of God.

In looking at these many paths to altered consciousness, to Reality, or God, or Brahman, it is evident that they all have virtually identical goals and yield similar descriptions of the state of those fortunate travelers who have been there and returned. to try to put into words what is essentially an ineffable experience.

While we are only beginning to penetrate these mysteries, to try to duplicate scientifically the direct experience of Reality that all great spiritual leaders have said we must have, there are indications that training in the generation of alpha rhythms and other brain states, combined with meditative techniques, does indeed offer hope to our troubled society.

Our normal waking consciousness, rational consciousness as we call it, is but one special type of consciousness, whilst all about it, parted from it by the filmiest of screens, there lie potential forms of consciousness entirely different. We may go through life suspecting their existence, but apply the requisite stimulus and at a touch they are there in all their completeness, definite types of mentality which probably somewhere have their field of application and adaptation.

wm. james

Corita

ABOUT YOGA

Yoga is the world's oldest science of physical and mental self-development, a doctrine handed down from prehistoric times. The word means "union," and is the Sanskrit ancestor of the English word *yoke*, "to bind together." It is a method, not a religion, which teaches that man can raise his capacities to the highest level through meditation, concentration, and other disciplines. These are the means of uniting the individual with the Godhead, cosmic consciousness, ultimate reality — terms to describe the indescribable, which can in fact only be experienced. Achieving such union is the state of perfect Yoga, uniting man, the finite, with the infinite — a marriage of spirit and matter.

The essence of a faith dedicated to the breaking of sensual bondage and the realization of a state of serenity and bliss, Yoga involves not only meditation and ascetic practices, but physical and mental exercises as well. The ultimate aim is to bring body and mind to the highest perfection. This final stage of Satori is reached by only a few who have progressed through many stages and attained perfect control through their own efforts.

Yoga aims at controlling physical as well as spiritual and mental well-being, relieving muscular and nervous tension, correcting problems of circulation. Great powers can be attained through its disciplines, powers that must always be used for selfless purposes. Among them are knowledge of past and future, understanding of the significance of the sounds made by animals, knowledge of former states in life, knowledge of others' minds, knowledge of the time of death, various kinds of strength, the knowledge of tiny, concealed, or distant things, and the ability to see perfected beings beyond humanity.

Surprisingly, perhaps, many apparently materialistic, self-indulgent Westerners have been attracted to the ascetic practices of Yoga and their numbers are increasing. Housewives and businessmen who join classes to learn the asanas, or postures, and streamline their figures, often become interested in the total discipline and take up meditation, concentration, and the quest for enlightenment. The impact of Yoga upon our society is a remarkable phenomenon.

One of the first to introduce Yoga into the United States was Indra Devi, and her book *Yoga for Americans* describes very accurately why it has been so successful:

> The secret of Yoga lies in the fact that it deals with the entire man, not just one of his aspects. It is concerned with growth — physical, mental, moral, and spiritual. It develops forces that are already within you. Beginning with improved health and added physical well-being, it works up slowly through the mental to the spiritual. The transition is so gradual that you may not even be aware of it until you realize that a change in you has already taken place .... When a student of Yoga determines and rightly directs his course, a molecular change takes place in his body until, in about six months, this change begins to affect his tastes and habits. It also expands the power of his mind. As the force within him becomes awakened, his state of consciousness also changes — he ceases to be lonely, his fears vanish and his happiness comes within his reach.

There are various branches of Yoga, spiritual paths leading to the same goal, but with the starting point determined by the individual's temperament and interests:

Hatha Yoga, the branch best known to Westerners, is concerned chiefly with the regulation of breathing and other body disciplines. Generally *ha* is taken to mean the action of inhaling, and *tha* to mean exhaling, called respectively the sun and the moon breaths. Through bodily postures (asanas) and mental concentration, health can be attained. Proper oxygenation of the bloodstream and concentration on specific nerve centers will restore vital energy, and through proper diet, the physical body can be made to undergo a cleansing process through which impurities and toxins are eliminated, and vitamins and minerals readily assimilated and utilized by the system.

Karma Yoga: "As a man sows, so shall he reap." This is the law of *Karma*, the law of action and reaction. Karma Yoga is the path of action through selfless service. By performing duty without attachment or desire for the fruits of action, the Karma Yogi purifies his mind. When the mind and heart are purified through the practice of selfless service, the Karma Yogi loses his sense of identity as doer and merges with the Divine Consciousness and becomes an instrument through which the Divine Plan or Work is performed. Action or business in the world is not in itself a form of Yoga, but if it is carried on unselfishly with a view to the welfare of others, then it is Karma Yoga.

Bhakti Yoga: This is the path of love and devotion to God, a spiritual teacher, or a Divine Incarnation or representation. By constant love and thought of the Divine, the individual transcends his limited personality and attains cosmic counsciousness through God's grace. The path of Bhakti or devotion can be practiced by everyone. All that is needed is constant and loving remembrance of God, coupled with faith.

Raja Yoga: The way to God through psychological exercises, known as the "royal road to reintegration." For those scientifically inclined, it is a way of achieving control of the mind, an eight-limbed path of concentration and meditative techniques by which the mind can be stilled. When the mind is empty of thought, all limitation is transcended and the state of *Samadhi*, or superconsciousness, is experienced. Raja Yoga is based on the Hindu concept that man is a stratified being — the body, the conscious mind, the individual subconscious, and cosmic consciousness, infinite and eternal. On this level, to quote Heinrich Zimmer, "I am smaller than the minutest atom, likewise greater than the greatest. I am the whole, the diversified — multicolored — lovely strange universe. I am the Ancient One. I am Man, the Lord. I am the Being of God. I am the very state of divine beatitude."

Japa Yoga: This is an extension of Raja Yoga. *Japa* means repetition, and Japa Yoga is the repetition of a mantra. A mantra is a sound structure of one or more syllables which represent a particular aspect of the divine. The concentrated mental repetition of the mantra produces the same vibrations within the individual's entire system. Consequently, the individual experiences great peace and ultimately the goal of Yoga, Divine Consciousness.

Jnana Yoga: This is the path of wisdom through the attainment of knowledge, which consists of self-analysis and awareness. The Jnanan Yogi gains knowledge of the Self by ceasing to identify with the body, mind, and ego, and completely identifying with the divinity within.

Laya Yoga: Laya Yoga means "mind control" and deals with the method of acquiring mastery over the will. It is studied only after Hatha Yoga has been mastered and the student has his body and mind under disciplined control.

Kriya Yoga: The Yoga of action, with three divisions: tapas (bodily self-government), swadhyaya (mental study), ishwara-pranid-hana (an emotional attitude/thought attractive to God), and therefore meaning that it is the Yoga for daily life, as opposed to that prescribed for meditation.

Tantra Yoga: Human sexuality is the core and practice of Tantrism, the only Yoga to focus on sex exclusively. In a highly ritualized sexual union, the male and female partners provide a vivid example of the union of opposites; as they concentrate on the flow of energy between them, they become briefly but literally divine beings, and at their peak of sensation the energy flow reverses and suffuses the partners with the creative energy of the universe. The basic concept of Tantra Yoga is the dissolving of the ego and a relaxation into merger with the partner and that universal energy.

Kundalini Yoga: The practice of Kundalini, known as "the hard way," seeks to expand psychic power; it includes the techniques of Raja and Hatha Yoga, with breathing exercises designed to awaken the powerful energy of the reproductive system, symbolized by a coiled serpent at the base of the spine. The aim is to draw this power up through the higher chakras (centers of power in the body) in order to achieve enlightenment. Followers believe that working with Kundalini can be very dangerous without great care and respect; readiness for the anticipated full explosion of energy in the mind may require many years of preparation.

Both Tantra and Kundalini employ the concept of the seven chakras, or energy centers. They are the Muladhara chakra, at the base of the spine, the Swadisthana chakra, in the reproductive organs, the Manipura chakra, at the navel, the Anahata, or heart chakra, the Vishuddhi chakra, in the throat, the Ajna chakra, above and between the eyebrows (also known as the "third eye"), and the Sahasrara chakra, at the crown of the head. Awakening of this chakra, the thousand-petaled lotus, is the culmination of the rising of the serpent power, the Kundalini.

HINDUISM

Hinduism dates back to prehistoric times; it is the oldest known religion of man. Having no common creed or doctrine, Hindus have complete intellectual freedom of belief. This can encompass monotheism, polytheism, or atheism, provided it adheres to the Hindu social caste system.

Hindus believe that all living things are in a continuous cycle of rebirth and redeath, and that the goal of existence is eventually to achieve nirvana (extinction of passion) through progressive stages of reincarnation. The law of karma determines the level of rebirth, depending upon a person's moral behavior in a previous phase of existence. Life on earth is transient (maya) and a burden that must be endured, which provides a rationale for the caste system.

The sacred scriptures upon which modern Hinduism is based, the *Vedas*, are written in Sanskrit and are thought to be at least 3,000 years old. These ancient works speak of many deities, all of whom are manifestations of Brahman, the supreme source and guiding principle of the universe, from whom everything proceeds and to whom everything ultimately returns. Other sacred writings, such as the *Bhagavad-Gita* (Song of the Lord), celebrate devotion to the Lord Krishna, and praise the discipline of Yoga.

Today Hinduism claims more than 500 million adherents, more than 300 million of them in India alone.

SOME GURUS AND THEIR TEACHING

Sri Swami Sivananda

A renowned and much-loved guru, Sivananda trained and inspired such world-famous Yoga leaders as Satchidananda, Vishnu-Devananda, and Chidananda, world president of the Divine Life Society, at his Sivananda Ashram beside the headwaters of the Ganges in the foothills of the Himalayas.

Born in 1887 to a family of saints and savants, Sivananda inclined toward a life devoted to the study and practice of Vedanta. His passion for service drew him to a medical career, however, and he established himself in Malaya, where he thought he was most needed. After practicing medicine, studying and writing extensively on health problems, he decided that people needed right knowledge most of all, and undertook the dissemination of that knowledge as his own mission. Relinquishing his medical career, he began a life of renunciation to qualify himself for ministering to the soul of man. He settled down at Rishikesh in 1924, practiced intense austerities, and soon attracted a devoted following.

In 1932 he started the Sivananda Ashram, in 1936 the Divine Life Society, and in 1948 the Yoga-Vedanta Forest Academy, which has as its goal the dissemination of spiritual knowledge and training of students in both Yoga and Vedanta. In 1953 Sivananda convened a World Parliament of Religions. He died in 1963, having written more than 300 books, and attracted disciples from all nationalities and religions.

Swami Satchidananda

Satchidananda was born in 1914, became a disciple of Swami Sivananda at the age of 28, and taught Raja and Hatha Yoga before traveling around the Orient to set up branches of the Divine Life Society. His first global tour in 1966, sponsored by the illustrator Peter Max, brought him to New York, where he subsequently established the Integral Yoga Institute. Integral Yoga is a flexible combination of the yogic disciplines specifically designed to develop every aspect of the individual. There are currently 13 IYI branches in the United States, and class attendance in New York alone has topped 25,000.

A beloved spiritual leader who seems to radiate happiness, Satchidananda believes one can miss the mark by "running after God too eagerly and searching too hard." Once you give yourself to others, he believes, other people will give themselves to you. "In the beginning of this life, people often said to me, 'Why are you renouncing? You have thrown away your house, your wealth, everything. What are you going to gain?' I would tell them, 'I'm going to gain everything.'"

Swami Vishnu-Devananda

A vigorous, earthy Yogi who pilots his own plane, runs a 60-acre Yoga retreat in the Laurentian Mountains north of Montreal and another on Paradise Island in the Bahamas, Vishnu-Devananda is founder-president of the Sivananda Yoga Vedanta Centers, with branches in Canada, the United States, and Europe.

Born in Kerala in 1927, he briefly taught school and then joined the army. A pamphlet written by Sivananda inspired him to pattern his life after the master's teachings. In 1946, on leave from the army, he visited Rishikesh, met Sivananda, and became his disciple. During his training in the Sivananda Ashram, Vishnu-Devananda became unusually adept at the asanas, or postures, and is often photographed in the incredibly difficult peacock pose, balancing his body horizontally on his powerful hands and wrists.

After a world tour in 1957, he spent two years crossing and recrossing North America, finally settling in Montreal where he founded the Sivananda Yoga Vedanta Center. In 1971, he flew his "peace plane," a Piper Apache decorated by artist Peter Max, over such strife-torn areas as Belfast, the Suez Canal, and West Pakistan, dropping peace leaflets, flowers, and loving vibrations. His newest Yoga retreat is in Grass Valley, California.

TM and the Maharishi

Maharishi Mahesh Yogi was a disciple of Swami Brahamananda Saraswati, leader of a monastery in northern India, who encouraged him to bring to the West the fundamentally simple message of Vedanta — that the wellsprings of joy are readily available. The Maharishi's version of the message, embodied in the Transcendental Meditation technique, employs the mantra as a means of attracting the mind to the subtlest level below phenomenal reality — the level that transcends thought.

Transcendental Meditation or TM was introduced in the West in 1959 under the aegis of the Spiritual Regeneration Movement, and received its biggest boost when adopted by the Beatles at the height of their career. The Maharishi's smiling face and easy manner graced television talk shows; phrases such as "creative intelligence" or "pure awareness" began to show up in the conversation of businessmen, housewives, and students, who were the most enthusiastic proponents of the new technique, founding the Students International Meditation Society (SIMS) as a means of propagating its teaching.

The Maharishi advocates using TM as a means of living more happily and efficiently in the everyday world. Basically, he describes it as "a direct way to reach the peace that lies within all men ... the kingdom within himself which Christ and every great prophet knew and described." By contacting the deep level of Being within each individual consciousness, the mental powers are expanded until the full force of the mind can be focused on the problems of daily life. The Maharishi is convinced that if only 1 percent of the people of the world would use his technique, it could revolutionize society by bringing an end to war, poverty, and suffering.

In July of 1976 there were 205 TM centers in the United States, approximately 250,000 people having been initiated, with some 10,000 joining each week. Two books on TM were recent major bestsellers. There seems no reason to suppose the runaway popularity of this form of meditation will slow down; its benefits appear to fit exactly the needs of our stress-torn society.

(More information about the style of TM meditation can be found on page 298.)

Maharaj-Ji and the Divine Light Mission

Maharaj-Ji was born in northern India in 1957 into the holy family of Yogi Raj Param Sant Satgurudev Shri Hans Ji Maharaj, founder of the Divine Light Mission. He began delivering spiritual discourses to his father's devotees at the age of two, and when he was eight and a half, his father died, and he claimed to have directly received his parent's spiritual knowledge, powers, and responsibilities.

He made his first World Peace Tour in 1971, and revisited the States the following year, aged 15. Currently, there is family dissent and disunity, his mother has disowned him, and various lawsuits are in the offing. Nevertheless, according to the guru, God is still within, and he is still able, by dispensing knowledge, to shed light on the internal Godhead.

There are four meditative techniques communicated in these "knowledge sessions," which enable devotees to experience divine light, celestial music, divine nectar, and the word of God in the form of a living vibration. Through these meditations, devotees remain linked to Maharaj-Ji, their director, and many have devoted their lives to his mission, offering both service and money to its cause.

Divine Light Mission is an international and, of course, nonprofit organization, with national headquarters in Denver. It maintains about 200 centers of varying size, several mansions, several jet planes, and several automobiles, also of various sizes. The appeal of the mission has focused particularly on the college-age groups, with heavy emphasis on university programs and college radio advertising, but the scope is being broadened.

Yogi Bhajan and 3 HO

Yogi Bhajan is an Indian spiritual leader who operates in the United States as a teacher of Kundalini and Tantric Yoga, and, more importantly, as spiritual education director for the 3 HO Foundation, a training and rehabilitation organization that has influenced the lives of thousands of young people. More than 200,000 have enrolled in the foundation (the acronym stands for Healthy-Happy-Holy Organization), a nonprofit corporation headquartered in Los Angeles with affiliates in six states, run by student-teachers who have been taught by Yogi Bhajan.

Bhajan's teachings stress relieving tension and learning relaxation techniques in order to help people to become conscious, emotionally stable human beings. They are offered not only in 3 HO centers but in YMCAs and universities — and so far have enabled some 158,000 people to quit taking drugs. The organization also offers a controlled rehabilitation program for heroin and methadone addicts. Kundalini Yoga is an essential part of the 3 HO way of life, since by cleansing the subconscious mind, an individual becomes freer to develop and merge himself with the infinite.

There is much that is practical in the 3 HO way — the centers are supported by self-created businesses, such as vegetarian restaurants, construction companies, small industries of various kinds; they also practice active service to the community, holding classes in prisons, running free kitchens, and teaching preschool and primary school children. In addition to the thousands who attend classes, thousands more have moved into the 3 HO centers to practice and experience the changes that Bhajan's teachings have brought about. "If you want respect," says Bhajan, "learn to give respect. If you want love, learn to give love." It is an impressive creed.

Swami Muktananda Paramahansa

Born in Bangalore in 1908, Muktananda spent 25 years traveling until he met his spiritual Master, Swami Nityananda of Ganeshpuri, to whom he dedicated his ashram in Ganeshpuri. Muktananda made his first world tour in 1970, accompanied on the U.S. section of his travels by the transformed scientist-cum-Yogi Richard Alpert/Ram Dass.

The Swami conceives his mission to be the awakening of divine consciousness in aspirants by means of Shaktipat Diksha. This is an initiatory process whereby the guru transmits divine power to the aspirant by touch, word, look, or thought, thereby awakening his kundalini. From then on, the devotee remains connected with his guru across space and time, and the guru takes responsibility for his evolution.

Muktananda has several hundred U.S. disciples and thousands of devotees of all ages. Several American centers developed in the wake of the guru's 1970 visit, a major one in California, and smaller centers in New York, Chicago, Dallas, and Houston. Shree Gurudev Ashram in Ganeshpuri hosts large numbers of Westerners, many of whom come for lengthy periods.

Baba Ram Dass/Richard Alpert

Alpert was born in 1931 into an affluent Boston family. He taught psychology and practiced psychotherapy at Harvard and, in 1961, began to research mind-altering drugs, notably LSD, with his Harvard colleague Timothy Leary. After being dismissed from the University in 1963, Alpert and Leary established the Castalia Foundation on an estate in Millbrook, New York, with intent to study the mystical aspect of drugs. For the next four years, Alpert continued his personal experiments while publicly defending the new psychedelics.

In 1967 a visit to India brought him to the feet of his guru, Muktananda Paramahansa — and Alpert found the high that for him surpasses all others: God. He returned to the United States in 1968, lectured extensively in many parts of the country on the subject of spiritual awakening, and produced tapes on the same subject for broadcast over the Pacifica Radio Network (WBAI-New York; KPFA-Berkeley).

His most recent book is *Be Here Now,* a spiritual autobiography/guide which has sold 200,000 copies.

He returned to India in 1970. Since the spring of 1972, he has again been traveling and lecturing in the United States, attracting large crowds of the drug-experienced generation, who find easy identification with this multimetamorphosed scientist and spiritual seeker.

Satya Sai Baba

All over India there are pictures of a wizened old man sitting on a slab of stone with one leg over the other. This is Sai Baba of Shirdi, an Indian St. Christopher. Miniature shrines with Sai Baba figurines can be seen in niches in the bazaars, hung on tree trunks and draped with fresh marigold medallions. Cab drivers have Sai Baba medallions on their dashboards; many people wear them in necklaces.

Sai Baba of Shirdi died in 1918. Followers of Satya Sai Baba believe that eight years later his spirit entered the body of a young boy, Satyanarayan Raju of Puttaparti, near Bangalore. Word spread that he was performing miracles, and the boy was soon acclaimed as the incarnation of the Shirdi Sai Baba.

Satya Sai Baba has a bigger following than any of the contemporary Godmen of India. Wherever he goes, people flock to him in the hundreds of thousands; in the cities, his arrival snarls up traffic on the roads for many hours. Next to Indira Gandhi, he is India's biggest draw.

Sporting a shock of curly hair which crowns his head like a black halo, Sai Baba is draped from shoulders to feet in a flaming saffron robe. With a wave of his hand he produces *vibhuti* (sacred ash) from the air, wristwatches (made not in heaven, but in Switzerland), rosaries, and rings with his pictures. Kenneth Keating, former U. S. Ambassador to India, wears one which Satya Sai Baba reduced to the right size simply by blowing through it.

He has other remarkable powers, too, which are said to include healing the sick and bringing the dead to life. For an account of such an incident, read on.

Krishnamurti

Jiddu Krishnamurti was born to a poor Brahmin family in India in 1895. At the age of 14, he was adopted by Annie Besant, then head of the Theosophical Society, who proclaimed him the incarnation or avatar of the new "world teacher," i.e., the Buddha. Krishnamurti was educated at Oxford, with the intention that he become a Messianic spiritual leader. Later, however, he completely rejected that role, insisting that he had no knowledge, and questioning the value of spiritual teachers on the grounds that the quest for truth has to be carried out by the individual alone.

Krishnamurti lectures all over the world. His philosophy is iconoclastic and insightful. Most of his lectures are based on question and answer, in which he responds with total concentration on the now, urging radical rethinking of our acceptance of ourselves — a fundamental revolution within, "in our thinking, feeling, and reacting."

There is a Krishnamurti Foundation in England, which sponsors his appearances and makes his teachings available through books, films, and tape recordings.

Sri Chinmoy

Sri Chinmoy Kumar Ghose was born in East Bengal in 1931. At 12 he entered an ashram and spent the next 20 years practicing intense spiritual disciplines. During this period he is said to have attained Nirvikalpa Samadhi, the highest level of enlightenment. He came to the States in 1964, and has lived here ever since, traveling and teaching the form of Bhakti Yoga that he practices. Since 1970 he has been leading biweekly meditations at the United Nations.

Sri Chinmoy's is basically an inward approach, conducted on a one-to-one basis with his "family of disciples." Having achieved God-realization himself, he becomes the channel through which each disciple's spiritual evolution takes place, and restricts his followers to those he feels are truly suited for this path, the path of the heart. Currently he has about 500 disciples in some 40 spiritual centers throughout the United States, Canada, and Western Europe.

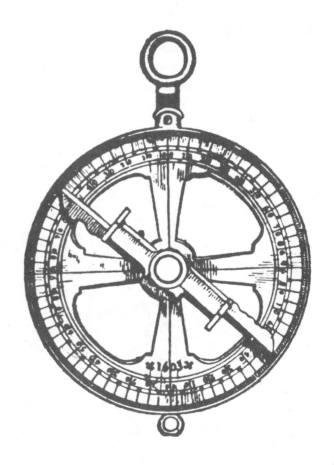

SAI BABA

Walter and Elsie Cowan, pleasant, prosperous, outwardly conventional Californians in their 70s, had been making periodic trips to the Sai Baba ashram in Puttaparti, Prasanti Nilayam, ever since Baba had begun appearing almost nightly in the Cowans' remarkably communal dreams. When they asked where they might find him, they were told the answer would come at 10:00 the following morning. Precisely at that hour a friend of Walter's walked into his office in Santa Ana and handed him a book about Baba. Their guru identified at last, the Cowans made reservations on a plane for India.

In 1972, at home in California, Walter grew quite ill with diabetes and other complications. Elsie sent a distress call to Baba's ashram and he replied that she should bring Walter to Madras at once. By this time Walter was so sick that he had to be carried on and off the plane. On arrival, however, he was sufficiently improved to be able to check into a Madras hotel. But before they could contact Baba, he took a turn for the worse and became unable to breathe. He felt no pain but knew he was dying, and in a few moments he did "die" in Elsie's arms. She recalls the violence of the death rattle.

Believing the body was no longer of importance once the soul had left it, Elsie didn't accompany Walter's body when the ambulance came to take it to the hospital. Walter, however, though now out of his body, was still hovering around it, and was shocked at the casual way the attendants tossed it into the ambulance, then dumped it on a bed at the hospital, with one leg twisted underneath. The corpse was officially pronounced dead by the doctor, then its nose, mouth, and ears were stuffed with cotton, and a sheet pulled over the head.

As Walter remembers it, Baba soon arrived and took him away. They entered a vast hall where a judge sat high above them, leafing through the pages of a huge book containing a record of Walter's incarnations for the past 10,000 years, which included such august personages as King David. Baba told the judge he would like to take Walter back because there were still tasks for him to do. Clapping his hands, the judge intoned, "So be it," snapped shut the book, and Walter found himself back in his body, fighting for breath.

In the next few days he "died" again, and again Baba restored him to life. When the recovery was complete, the Cowans traveled to Baba's ashram to renew their wedding vows in front of their guru. Baba materialized two rings for the ceremony, prepared the wedding garments and, in a final dramatic gesture, held up his empty hand — and flung out a pearl necklace for Elsie . . . .riting, it's a brain print. Writing is tied to gestures of the body language; a gesture of violence shows in handwriting

ZEN BUDDHISM

An extension of Buddhism, Ch'an, and Taoism, Zen made its major move into the United States during the "beatnik" era of the late 1950s, largely through the teachings and writings of D. T. Suzuki and Alan Watts. Its growth in this country has been largely due to the fact that it is a living religion, able to adapt to new stimuli and changing conditions rather than adhering stiffly to a traditional set of disciplines.

Buddhism had its beginnings in Northern India about 560 B.C. The most popular version of the Zen history personifies Buddha as a prince called Siddhartha. One day as the young prince walked outside his palace, he saw an emaciated old man, a sick man, a corpse, and a monk. It was his first encounter with suffering — everything hitherto had been aimed at sparing him the sight of pain, misery, sickness, and death. From this point on, Siddhartha left his palace and lived the life of a wandering monk, devoting himself to the study of spiritual problems. He studied with Brahmins (Hindu monks), scholars, and instructors at various schools of philosophy, but was dissatisfied and continued to wander the country, seeking answers by engaging in a series of ascetic practices.

Illumination reportedly came while Siddhartha was meditating at the foot of the Bodhi tree. Intense concentration allowed him to discover the fundamental cause and meaning of all existence, including his own. His revolutionary insight was that *Nirvana*, the state of complete redemption, was possible here on earth. Man could free himself from the rigid laws of reincarnation and rid himself of pain by complete emptying of the self. After this breakthrough, he became known to the followers who flocked to join him as Buddha, which means "Enlightened One." He devoted himself to teaching for almost 50 years, and died at the age of 81.

Although Buddhism soon spread to other countries, it was never really popular in India, largely because it denounced superstitions, magical practices, and other concepts close to the Indian way of life. Around the time of Christ it split into two major branches: *Hinayana* (small vehicle), which survived in Ceylon and southern Asia, and *Mahayana* (Great Vehicle), a more social, polytheistic cult that survives in Tibet, China, Korea, and Japan. In China, Buddhism merged with Taoism; it was this blending that evolved into Zen.

It is not surprising that Zen has achieved such popularity in America. Its concepts are very different from those of orthodox Western religion; for people in search of a way to fill the gaps they sense in their lives, it offers a completely fresh perspective.

Zen teaches that anguish is the result of the disparity between man's external behavior and his soul. From the beginning of his life, man has established habits of acting, and these have been molded and reinforced by the material world in which he lives. So while other religions spell out all the things their adherents must do to achieve salvation, Zen Buddhism concentrates on the things we must *un*do, for only through this undoing can the chaos of the soul be relieved.

Man's tendency is to intellectualize everything, base his actions on memory, and cloud his perception with distortions stemming from the mind's preoccupation with mundane problems. Zen teaches that we cannot achieve a complete and realistic view of ourselves and the world until we remove the illusions we have created. Freedom from turmoil must come from a direct, unified approach rather than a constant series of trial-and-error methods. Zen makes it clear that man can achieve a paradise on earth if he can simply eliminate ignorance.

In Zen Buddhism the most serious human flaw is inattention. This prevents the mind from perceiving its contact with the Universal Mind and makes the body slower to respond to its important functions. Zen believes that the mind is material but all matter is spiritual; therefore, nothing is stable, and all that appears to be is an illusion. This is summed up best, perhaps, by Robert Linssen in *Zen*, who says, "If Buddhism and Zen use thought, it is to make one understand that thought must be transcended."

The unenlightened man is governed by the law of cause and effect — represented in Buddhism by the word *karma*. His thoughts come so quickly and so randomly that he never completes a thought before another one begins; therefore there is never a complete action on any one thought. He becomes a victim of the law of cause and effect, therefore he *creates* his karma.

Zen does not deny the fact that man lives in a material world. It simply teaches that man must put the values of the material world into their proper perspective. Zen adheres to no ideas of sin and salvation. It aims at Nirvana, enlightenment — the death of illusions and ignorance. Death, as Westerners perceive it, is the result of an attachment to the body and the material world. Zen rejects that attachment. Death only draws to a close the existence of that external shell, the human body; and for Zen adherents death is a victory over the material, sensory world, because the Cosmic Mind surpasses the limits of life and death. The idea of reincarnation is secondary.

Zen Buddhism is a very attractive philosophy in many respects. It professes to develop great attentive powers and a disciplined mind. Because it is pacifistic, it is one of the few religions that has never been responsible for war. To a Buddhist the greatest victory to be won is the victory over Self, not over other men or other nations.

Zen also encourages relaxation of the body, because only by allowing this tension to dissipate can true and total mental awareness be established. It is closely related to judo and aikido, for this reason, because they offer means of bringing the individual closer to self-mastery. According to Buddhist belief, suppleness will always triumph over hardness; and both judo and aikido increase suppleness. They also help to establish a natural mental peace and are helpful in the process of disintellectualizing. Even the art of archery can be compatible with fundamental Buddhist beliefs, for Zen considers it an expression of transcending man's habitual reflexes.

The first Zen center in the United States, the Buddhist Society of America, was founded in New York in 1930 by Shigetsu Sasaki. When he died, his widow continued his work and established an attitude of commitment and discipline to the Zen tradition in this country. There are now 10 or 12 legitimate Zen centers, the largest of them in San Francisco, founded by Zen's great exponent D. T. Suzuki. There is a feeling of timelessness about them — the food is organic, the discipline constant and directional . . . and Zen continues to take its place as an appropriate element in the American search for enlightenment.

TIBETAN BUDDHISM

The basic theme of Buddhism is inwardness — the psychological discipline required to perfect psychic powers and mind control in order to discover that all the world is mind. The mind and the Buddha-nature are the same; and if the mind can control itself, then it can make itself vulnerable to the One Mind.

The Tibetan Buddhist thinking can be outlined through the use of five *skandhas,* or psychological components. These are:

1. Form *(rupa)* — the realization by the Self that it is an entity in an external world.

2. Feeling *(vedana)* — the instinctive, gut reaction of the Self to this external world.

3. Perception *(samjna)* — the active reaction to the external world.

4. Concept *(samskara)* — the combination of intellect and emotion in which the distinct personality of the individual is defined.

5. Consciousness *(vignana)* — the point at which the Self becomes its own world, and the universe becomes a reactor to the stimulus of the Self.

A crucial aspect of the Buddhist concept of Self is the fact that enlightenment can come about only when the individual recognizes a dissolution of the Self into the universality of the One Mind. The basic cause of sin is believing in the Self as being the center of the universe. When the Tibetan Buddhists say the world is unreal, they mean that if we view life as if we ourselves were the center of it, we cannot develop a knowledge of the world as it really is. But if we can pierce the clouding veil of Self, we can squarely face true Reality.

This view of Self might seem to contradict the psychological components just listed. It becomes compatible, however, when we realize the Self is important to the Tibetan Buddhist especially when it is perceived as a part of the One Mind as opposed to a separate entity. When the consciousness (vignana) state is achieved and the Self becomes its own world, it has realized its oneness with the universal wisdom and stripped itself of its ego-centeredness.

The Tibetan Buddhist also concentrates on five *tathagatas,* or modes of energy of the awakened consciousness. These are viewed as both five wisdoms and five confusions, mirror images of each other which are perceived by the individual according to his own state of enlightenment:

1. *Vairocana* — basic confusion and ignorance, also the opposite of ignorance, which is limitless wisdom.

2. *Aksobhya* — hatred and aggression, also a calm and uncritical wisdom.

3. *Ratnasambhava* — pride of material wealth, also the wisdom of equality.

4. *Amitabha* — passion, also

discrimination and the detached serenity that transforms passion into compassion.

5. *Amoghasiddhi* — envy and ambition, also the wisdom to accomplish.

Salvation in Buddhist terms comes from the comprehension of the Buddha-nature which exists not only in the human soul but also in all forms of nature from the highest mountain to the smallest grain of sand. To the Buddhist, everything is mind; and it is this lack of division between man and his environment (not to mention man and his God) that forms an important framework in this tradition.

Mountains have a special spiritual significance to the Tibetan Buddhist, because they represent the "other world" where man's soul is enhanced and enlightened. The great Tibetan Buddhist centers are found on mountaintops; and when a Buddhist feels the need for enrichment, he most frequently goes to meditate on a mountain.

Tibetan Buddhism places great emphasis on meditation, using images of deities to provide specific symbols that will heighten the experience. Imagery triggers and heightens the speculative imagination. Central to the teaching is the concept of the four noble truths, which spell out the belief that suffering is a universal condition — but also a noble one, because through it the individual can achieve wisdom and thereby spiritual peace. The road to this is the eightfold path. Each of the paths is symbolically represented in the eight arms of the Buddha statue: correct understanding, correct aims, correct speech, correct behavior, correct role in life, correct effort, correct intellectual activity, and correct contemplation.

It is not surprising, with this serene philosophy in mind, that so many Americans have become involved with Tibetan Buddhism. In Berkeley, California, there is a thriving Tibetan Center under the tutelage of Tarthang Tulku, who founded it six years ago. The Center has been accredited for M.A. and Ph.D. degrees at the University of California, and some 3,000 students have studied there in some capacity.

The Naropa Institute in Colorado, a community established by Chogyam Trungpa, another lama who fled Tibet after the Chinese takeover, has become affiliated with the University of Colorado in Boulder. Scholars from all over the country, in disciplines ranging from physics to psychology, come to teach and study there. Trungpa has established other centers in Vermont and Colorado, as well as smaller ones in major cities, all of which emphasize the integration of meditation, living, and working.

NICHIREN SHOSHU ASSOCIATION (N.S.A.)

N.S.A. Buddhism, currently achieving enormous popularity in America, was founded by Nichiren Daishonin in 13th-century Japan.

Nichiren was trained at a Buddhist monastery at a period when medieval Japan was undergoing considerable change in its society and values. The questions he began asking were uniquely personal ones: he particularly wondered why the Japanese loyalists had been defeated despite the widespread spiritual support given them by the Buddhist priests.

Concerned with personal salvation, Nichiren arrived at the very simplest requirement — the book of teaching called the Lotus Sutra. The Lotus Sutra defines devotion as the answer to personal freedom, and its focal point is the chanting of the Daimoku *(Nam Myoho Renge Kyo)*, which puts the individual in automatic, mystical harmony with everything he needs. Chanting in front of the Gohonzon, a wooden box containing names of important Buddhas which serves as an altar, additionally enhances the experience, because the Gohonzon is a centralized source of power.

Nichiren was a fanatic. He suggested that Japan would collapse if it did not repent and convert. His modern adherents have continued that fanaticism. For them, Nichiren is the sole authority. There is one holy book — the Lotus Sutra. There is one man — Nichiren. There is one object of worship — the Gohonzon. There is one practice — chanting the Daimoku.

Nichiren Shoshu is one of two major offspring from the Lotus Sutra. It was perpetuated in Japan by T. Makiguchi, who merged his own society, called the Soka Gakkai, with Nichiren Shoshu.

When Makiguchi was imprisoned in 1944, J. Toda took over the leadership of Soka Gakkai. A charismatic man with strong leadership ability, Toda was able within a decade to catapult an obscure sect to a position as the fastest-growing religion in the world. Soka Gakkai was immensely popular in Japan, particularly among the worker class; and because of its enormous influence on Japanese life, the movement spread to America during the postwar era when Americans stationed in Japan began to take an interest in the concepts of the country. Japanese-Americans perpetuated the faith, and Soka Gakkai had found its roots in this country.

Toda's successor, D. Ikeda, was very anxious to make the Soka Gakkai faith international. In 1960 he established an American organization, which has grown from an original 10 chapters in 1963 to 135 chapters today. Soka Gakkai had always been a part of Nichiren Shoshu, and in America the faith was given the latter as its name. There are now roughly 200,000 members of Nichiren Shoshu in this country.

On the surface it would appear that Nichiren Shoshu is very materialistic, since its leaders promise that chanting the Daimoku will bring both material and spiritual benefits. They see no reason for man to wait until he dies to receive goodness — it can be his during his lifetime. In actuality, their belief that materialistic benefits result from chanting suggests a unity between the material and the spiritual — therefore, the entire universe becomes one.

Nichiren Shoshu is highly organized in America and very active. Each district meets several times a week, and each of these groups contains subdivisions, smaller groups of five to 10 people. Supervising the districts are the regional chapters and the general chapters, which answer to the national headquarters in Santa Monica, California. N.S.A. organizes pilgrimages to Japan, schedules performances of traditional music, and maintains active publications departments which print such widely circulated papers as the *World Tribune.* There are two temples in this country, one in Hawaii and one in California.

Very important to the lives of the members is the daily worship in the home, which is called Gongyo, during which the member recites chapters of the Lotus Sutra in Japanese eight times a day and then chants the Daimoku as long as he feels it necessary. Gongyo is performed in front of the Gohonzon, technically owned by Nichiren Shoshu but loaned for life at the price of a small donation. Chanting is continued silently throughout the day at any time, at any location.

As the popularity of Nichiren Shoshu continues to spread in America, the emphasis is beginning to fall less on immediate rewards for chanting and more on an understanding of Nichiren's interpretation of Buddhist philosophy. But the chanting does go on, and more and more frequently throughout America in more and more locations one is likely to hear the quietly intoned *Nam Myoho Renge Kyo.*

SUFISM

Sufism is a mystical school within the religion of Islam, which has grown over the centuries through the interweaving of several religious traditions. Its origins date back to the teachings of the Zoroastrian magi; developing subsequently in the Arab countries and Moorish Spain, it found its way to India, where it was enriched by contact with Buddhism and Vedanta. Closely associated with Sufi tradition are the dervish brotherhoods, known for their dances and their music.

For the Sufi, anything unstable is an illusion, and it is vital that man learn to discern between what is illusion and what is reality. Once we know what reality is, we can know everything there is to know. The ignorance that results from inability to discern between the two entities causes us great suffering — but this can easily be ended because knowledge of reality can easily be attained.

Sufism considers itself the personified discipline of man's deepest and noblest thoughts. It does not relate directly to any sect but merely portrays the process by which man, through diligent study, can attain truth, beauty, and God. In this process all the illusions and personal desires fall away, and the attention is directly centered on the Creator.

There are seven levels of consciousness on the Sufi path to enlightenment. The accomplishment of each level, through the guidance of a master, develops the spiritual essence within man, bringing him ever closer to the divine source. The three most important elements on the road to this realization are love, obedience, and surrender. The love is all-encompassing, the obedience is discipline, and the surrender is the relinquishing of personal desires and achieving the *Fana al Fana* — annihilation of the self in God.

One of the most important men in the Sufi tradition, as it relates to the Western world, is Meher Baba, who was born in India in 1894. He received "God realization" while in college, and subsequently claimed to be an avatar, a human manifestation of the Divine Being, like Buddha, Jesus, and Muhammad. In 1925 Meher Baba took a vow of silence, which he kept until his death in 1969.

Although he did not speak for more than 30 years, Meher Baba had considerable influence through his written teachings, which were heavily influenced by Sufism and were propagated by many enthusiastic disciples. His book, *God Speaks*, celebrates the love of God which Baba felt was the only real reason for existence. God is the self within every finite self, and our sense of love for this infinity that is God arouses intense longing to see, know, and become one with the truth.

Baba's teachings are extremely popular in the United States and groups meet all over the country to discuss his work and practice his ideas. Maybe because he did not speak, Baba smiled a lot, and so do his followers. It is tangible evidence, it would seem, of a faith based strongly and mystically on the power of love.

Another leading exponent of Sufism is Idries Shah, who has translated many of the tales or parables by which the body of Sufi religious knowledge is kept alive.

BAHA'I

The Baha'i faith was founded in 1843 in Iran, by a man who called himself "Bab ed-Din," which means "gate of faith." His followers believed him to be a manifestation of God as he taught that heaven and hell exist on earth, and that man can live here either in love and enlightenment or in suffering. After the Bab's death in 1850, Baha'u'llah, one of his followers, continued his teachings, and Baha'u'llah's son brought the faith to Europe and America early in the 20th century.

The essence of the Baha'i faith is belief in one God and one world. Because Baha'i has adopted the concept of a progression of spiritual leaders, its adherents believe that the words of each lead on to the next, and that the progression will ultimately end with the saviour who will welcome the dead into heaven. Baha'ians are concerned with suffering, death, and destiny, and believe that mankind can be united now — that this is God's intention and that it is the task of the current prophet to carry on this work. Life to them is comparable to life in the womb — death, therefore, is the rebirth into a stage of further growth. Heaven and hell are not literal places, but states of consciousness.

The Baha'i faith has no clergy, but is organized on the basis of spiritual assemblies: local assemblies, composed of nine believers each; a National Spiritual Assembly, also of nine individuals, who take charge of administration and leadership on a national scale; and the Universal House of Justice in Haifa, Israel, which presides over the Baha'i communities in some 300 countries and territories.

Baha'i adherents take their morality and their religion seriously. Marriage takes place only with the consent of the Spiritual Assembly and the consent of all four parents, if living, regardless of the age of the bride and groom. Intoxicants are strictly forbidden.

The Baha'i faith continues to grow in the United States. In 1970 the membership in this country went from 25,000 to 50,000. Many adherents are those who have become disillusioned with the promise of automatic enlightenment offered in other religious sects.

The Baha'i House of Worship in Chicago, an imposing structure on Lake Michigan, provides social service institutions such as the Baha'i Home for the Aged in Wilmette, and publishes periodicals such as *World Order*, for the discussion of spiritual and social problems.

It has been said that, "To be a Baha'i simply means to love all the world; to love humanity and try to serve it; to work for universal peace and universal brotherhood." Such is the spirit of this growing community.

INTERNATIONAL SOCIETY FOR KRISHNA CONSCIOUSNESS

The Krishna Consciousness Society is the most conspicuous of all the new, Eastern-influenced religious groups. Its predominantly young devotees, their orange robes flowing, their heads shaved save for a strand in back, are familiar figures on city streets all over the U.S. and Europe, dancing to their own brand of music and singing "Hare Krishna." As they perform they hand out cards and solicit donations from passers-by. They have even invaded the airports, "selling" (for donations) books about the movement, or flowers for your lapel — but this type of solicitation is carried on in the disguise of Western clothes, even, sometimes, wigs to cover the shaven heads.

Membership in the society is full time, and discipline is strict. The basis of the Krishna faith is a conservative interpretation of Hinduism. Its Spiritual Master, His Divine Grace A. C. Bhaktivedanta Swami Prabhupada, a charismatic Bengali, did not begin his task of spreading the Krishna message in the Western world until he was 70 years old. Bhaktivedanta first arrived in New York in 1965, and his concept of consciousness spread rapidly in the dropout, questing society of the late 1960s. Abandoning Western tradition, he established four strict rules for his followers: no consumption of meat, fish, or eggs; no illicit sex; no drugs or alcohol; and no gambling. He worshipped one god, Krishna, the Supreme Lord, who is at the same time personal and impersonal.

Members of the Krishna Consciousness Society believe in the literal interpretation of the *Vedas*, the *Bhagavad-Gita*, and accounts of Krishna's life. They believe the soul is eternal, but is trapped inside the material body. Only through devotion and love of Krishna can it transcend this prison and find purity.

The main focus of the Society is abandonment of personal desires and concentration on the strict life dictated by the Spiritual Master. Members may be married only with his permission; celibacy is always more desirable. Children participate actively in the group; and since the emphasis is on the one-family concept, they are considered as separate entities from their parents, and are educated in special schools taught by Society members. Many children live and study at the big Krishna commune in Texas.

Financially, the group is doing very well. In addition to contributions and donations, they own and operate the second-largest incense factory in the country. There is also plenty of support from wealthy Indians who appreciate the concepts for which the Krishna people are working and living.

The "Hare Krishnas" operate like a large family. Most of their activities are group efforts; this is surely one reason why the Krishna Society has offered such a haven for confused young people whose chaotic lives are set in place by the strictly defined practices of this unique order.

VEDANTA

Vedanta is the philosophy of transcendental knowledge. Its earliest forms came from the *Vedas*, the ancient scriptures of the Hindus. Its teaching is based on three propositions: the true nature of man is God; the purpose of life is to recognize our divinity; and all religions are essentially the same. Consequently, Vedanta concentrates on the unity of all faiths, believing that in spite of their external practices they all seek the existence of God within man. As man holds the key to supreme unity, the search for God must begin and end there.

Vedanta came to America through an Indian named Vivekananda, who had been educated in a Western tradition and sufficiently discouraged by its skepticism to seek out Ramakrishna, the great teacher of Vedanta. He became Ramakrishna's foremost disciple and, at his death, took over the task of spreading the message of Vedanta.

In 1893 Vivekananda came to America to attend the World Parliament of Religions, but arrived too soon, ran out of money, and ended up begging on the streets of Boston. Fortunately, he managed to meet some influential people who backed him financially until the Parliament opened, and his impact on the Parliament was equally favorable. In 1896, Vivekananda was able to found the Vedanta Society of New York, which made a considerable appeal to the upper-class, intellectual world. Sarah Bernhardt, Aldous Huxley, and Christopher Isherwood were three of its members.

Interest in Vedanta societies spread subsequently throughout the nation and to other social classes. California is the home of several Vedanta religious houses, notably the Trabuco Canyon monastery in Orange County, where Vedanta monks work, worship, and study this supremely pacifistic, unifying philosophy.

SELF-REALIZATION FELLOWSHIP

The Self-Realization Fellowship was founded in 1920 and its national headquarters were established in Los Angeles in 1925. Its founder was Paramahansa Yogananda, a guru who "from his birth, desired God-realization above all else." After establishing several schools in India he came to the United States to give a lecture series on the universal science of Yoga. During that tour he established the Self-Realization Fellowship Centers.

Devotees of Yogananda teachings believe that every man can learn and apply the laws of the universe and operate them for his welfare. The laws are explained by the Yoga teachings of the Self-Realization Fellowship, which invite initiates to prove "the efficacy of Yoga . . . discover the hidden, joyous nature of your being and come to know beyond doubt that all obstacles in life can be overcome."

The Self-Realization followers believe it is possible to achieve physical well-being by learning precise methods of harnessing the universal life energy, which aid in banishing disease and maintaining a vibrant state of health. They also practice meditation, which leads to spiritual realization, a sense of being in tune with God in his infinity. (See page 238 for an account of a community based on these principles.)

Paramahansa Yogananda's *Autobiography of a Yogi* has been called "the best book ever written to introduce the whole science of Yoga." Whether you want to delve deeply into Yoga or just be reassured that some people do actually have an idea of what inner peace means, it is worthwhile reading.

THE OCCULT

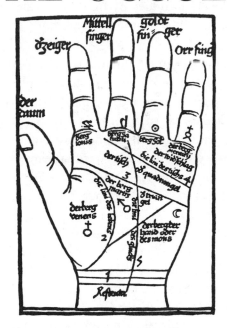

"In the sweepstakes of American spirituality, witchcraft — if anything — seems to currently have [it] over traditional religion .... The occult seems to answer man's spiritual needs with understanding that the repressively defensive churches have more or less denied. We look, in the last generation of this century, for a spirituality wide enough to match the frontiers of outer and inner space."

John Fritscher

In the Snake Temple in Penang, Malaysia, on the Chinese New Year, a woman stands in the incense-filled room where snakes drowse in baskets beside the altar, and shakes out bamboo slivers from a cylinder to learn from the I Ching what the coming year will bring. In Seattle, a banker checks the daily horoscope to see how Capricorns will fare that day before he turns to the stock market page. Shafica Karagulla has written a book based on interviews with successful executives whose decisions are based not on market research alone but on "hunches," and Dr. Karagulla claims this extra knowledge is what makes them successful. In every age man has sought to peer into the future with crystal balls, the throw of dice, oracles speaking through the sacred smoke; and our so-called materialistic, mechanistic era is no exception.

There are *clairvoyants*, those who have the ability to see "visions"; there are *prophetics*, those who can predict the future; there are *automatic writers*, those who can sit down with paper and pencil and "receive messages" which will manifest themselves in writing (sometimes in languages and vocabulary completely foreign to the receiver); those who can *astrally project* themselves, or have their spirits leave their bodies at will and travel to any desired destination (some believe that because the body temperature and pulse rate are significantly lowered during sleep, the spirit leaves the body regularly at that time, and that the experience is interpreted by the uninformed as a dream); *mediums*, those who can summon the spirits of the dead; and *psychics*, those whose perception and consciousness are so acutely developed that they can perceive not only details of present lives but also the influences of past lives.

Various psychics, spiritualists, and metaphysicians say they can tell much about people by a phenomenon called *aura*, an emanation which is more or less the sum total of your thoughts during that day, balanced by the thoughts you have had over a period of years. Your aura is a storehouse of thought forms, and its color depends on the predominant mood of those forms. Someone with a great deal of physical energy might have a bright orange emanation. Material, earthy things are green, while red indicates a superlative degree of the emotion of love. The color becomes more dense with intensity of purpose and more brilliant with the force of the thought. The aura is constantly changing, as activities and thoughts change.

The halo shown in portraits of Christ and of the saints is a manifestation of aura. Many people claim to be able to see aura quite readily — the Rev. D. J. Bissell of the Chirothesian Church said his congregation was like a lovely bouquet of flowers, a palette of the colors visible around each member.

Another popular manifestation of the occult is *numerology*. Otherwise practical people go to great expense to change their names according to a formula which will give them greater harmony and better vibrations. One theory of numerology is that every letter in the alphabet corresponds to a note on the musical scale. Put together, they strike a chord which is either harmonious or discordant with the personality. Another theory is based on the energy or the vibrations of numbers. Each letter corresponds to a number, and these are manipulated to find the appropriate total for the person's spiritual and physical attributes. The right name will attract the right opportunities, according to numerologists.

These phenomena are just a sample of the techniques flourishing around us for predicting the future, dealing with the present, exorcising the past. As long as man craves magic to deal with his problems, purveyors will be available.

ASTROLOGY

Since the dawn of history man has been fascinated by the patterns made in the heavens by the sun, the moon, and the planets. The solar bodies were especially vivid in the clear skies over those parts of the world where the Egyptians, Babylonians, Chaldeans, and Persians lived, and it was there that astrology — and civilization — began.

Primitive man was attuned to natural forces and the sky was the most remote and mysterious part of his world. The sun, the rain, and the wind directly controlled his activities; it was understandable that he would create a mythology that accounted for the shining presence of the moon and stars in the night sky. He also noticed that the planets moved independently of the "fixed stars" in the various constellations, and hypothesized that they were gods with the power to control life on earth. Refinement and expansion of these ideas led to the first written records of astrology in the 7th century B.C.

In earliest times astrology and astronomy were synonymous. Natural astrology, the study of the movement of the heavenly bodies in order to make calendars and predict the movements of sun, moon, and planets, as well as eclipses and comets, provided the basis for the science of astronomy which developed out of it. The branch of astrology which evolved into the pseudoscience of prediction and personality matching was judicial astrology, which claimed to be able to predict wars, earthquakes, and the fall of dynasties — as well as the character and fate of individuals.

Some of the earliest and largest man-made structures in the world were the ancient watchtowers and observatories built to study and record the movements of the stars and planets. Stonehenge, Machu Picchu, the great ziggurats of Ur, were apparently planned and correlated for astrological purposes. The first people to apply mathematics to the study of the universe were the Chaldeans, who observed 12 principal constellations across which the sun and moon appeared to trace regular paths. Accordingly, they divided their maps of the sky into 12 sections, each governed by a different constellation or "sign." Each of these divisions also constituted a "house" controlling a specific area of life. The first house governed life itself; the second, money; the third, brothers and sisters; the fourth, parents; the fifth, children; the sixth, physical well-being; the seventh, marriage; the eighth, death; the ninth, religion; the tenth, dignity; the eleventh, friendship; and the twelfth, enmity. As the sun, moon, and planets moved across the sky they became dwellers in each of these houses in turn, and thus the first complex system of astrological prediction came about.

Since then astrology has been regularly applied to nearly every fact of life: to predict events, to explain personality traits, to select business and marital partners, to plot out appropriate careers. Even today people who know nothing else about astrology usually know their "sun signs" and read their forecasts in daily newspapers or magazines. Astrologers caution, however, that these are inaccurate because they are based only on the position of the sun at the time of birth. For each individual the positions of the moon and planets are always different; hence, a truly applicable forecast can be made only by casting each person's horoscope.

The horoscope, also known as *natal chart, nativity, wheel,* and *map,* shows the exact position of the planets, sun, and moon in the heavens at the moment of a person's birth. It is a segmented circle, representing the path the sun appears to travel around the earth, although, of course, we now know the opposite is true. The 12 30° sectors represent the 12 signs of the Zodiac, or houses of the horoscope. The astrologer will use various sets of tables to calculate the position of the sun, moon, and planets at the time of birth, and then fill in the details in the appropriate sectors. Which houses contain the various heavenly bodies will influence the chart; so will the combinations of planets and signs unique to each person.

The Zodiac most commonly used among Western astrologers is determined by the vernal equinox, when the sun is so positioned that the days and nights are of approximately equal length. Astrologically, the movement of the sun during the equinox marks the beginning of what is called the "tropical Zodiac," and that is why lists of the signs always start with Aries, the first sign after the equinox, and continue in identical order around the Zodiacal belt. To each is ascribed a set of extremely general characteristics and preferences.

The rift between astronomy and astrology was caused by the scientific revolution of the 16th and 17th centuries, when the discoveries of Copernicus, Kepler, and Galileo exploded the basic theory of a geocentric system on which astrology was founded. With the discovery that the earth and its moon were in fact circling the sun like the other planets, astronomy and astrology parted company forever, because the tenets of astrology increasingly failed to stand up in the face of successive discoveries in the pure scientific realm of astronomy.

Modern scientists certainly do not regard astrology as respectable; for them it is a pseudoscience to be classed with palmistry and crystal gazing. In the fall of 1975, 186 prominent scientists, including 18 Nobel Prize winners, issued a statement challenging the "pretentious claims of astrological charlatans." Stating flatly that there is no scientific basis for astrology, they regret that "acceptance of astrology pervades modern society." The statement continues: "We are especially disturbed by the continued uncritical dissemination of astrological charts, forecasts and horoscopes by the media and by otherwise reputable newspapers, magazines and book publishers. This can only contribute to the growth of irrationalism and obscurantism."

The pervasive influence of astrology in our culture and its acceptance by otherwise practical and materialistic people is a tribute to its entrenched position in our consciousness. We are charmed by the personality traits that so frequently seem to fit the sun sign: "He's a pure Leo," or "You might know she would do that — she's a Pisces." While Americans don't go as far as those in Chinese and other cultures who have horoscopes cast to determine the most auspicious times for marriages, business ventures, coronations, many otherwise hard-headed business men and women use astrology in their careers. According to R. Donald Papon, director of the Academy of Mystic Arts in New York, 50 million Americans are very much involved in astrology, 1,230 out of 1,500 daily newspapers carry astrology columns, and six universities have offered academic courses in the subject.

There is no question that all life on earth is influenced by the sun and the moon. The lunar cycles affect not only the oceanic tides, but our bodies too; various physical and psychological manifestations can be clearly correlated with the moon's activities. Experts have shown that sunspots and other types of solar activity have an effect on physical processes as well as on radio and television reception. A Czechoslovakian gynecologist, Dr. Eugen Jonas, has demonstrated how the female reproductive cycle is affected by the birthdate and fertility can be predicted accordingly. Sheila Ostrander and Lynn Schroeder have written a book, *Astrological Birth Control*, based on Dr. Jonas's research.

Less is known about the effect of the various positions and alignments of the planets on the sun's magnetic and gravitational fields, but there is evidence that planetary alignments do affect happenings on earth. Studies have even shown a relationship between the "ascendant," the sign rising above the horizon at the moment of birth, and the ultimate profession of individuals born under that sign.

What is most fascinating about astrology, however, is that, although it has been discredited as a science, we still accept its method of explaining events and personalities — an ingenious kind of prescientific shorthand — as folk wisdom. In an age where much of pure science has become so esoteric that the average person cannot comprehend it, astrology offers a variety of basic appeals. It is a primitive, yet surprisingly effective form of psychoanalysis, which enables us to group our acquaintances and rationalize our expectations of them. It is also a handy method of foretelling the future, an activity of perpetual fascination to each one of us.

HUMANISTIC ASTROLOGY

Dr. Zipporah Pottenger Dobyns, a Los Angeles clinical psychologist, has been working to integrate the knowledge and insights gained from 20 years of work in humanistic psychology, parapsychology, and astrology. Dr. Dobyns believes scientists hostile to astrology "can only conceive of a world of blind, purposeless, meaningless physical forces which cause equally blind, meaningless physical results." Now that physics has begun questioning the extent to which the individual's consciousness determines the reality of what exists for him, those old assumptions of determinism, materialism, and causality are being challenged. She hopes that science will give up these outmoded premises and instead apply scientific *methods* to the field of astrology.

According to Dr. Dobyns, "Our attitudes and actions (including unconscious desires and habit patterns) create our destiny . . . we are born when our character-destiny matches the state of the cosmos, and . . . the planets offer a useful blueprint of the cosmic order, but do not create it . . . . To be told 'what' is going to happen leaves us feeling helpless to change it. To be told 'why' in terms of our psychological drives and conflicts facilitates solutions." The humanistic astrology she advocates "can pinpoint the inner conflicts which are present in almost all of us and can point the way to their resolution."

WITCHCRAFT

Witchcraft is booming in the United States and Great Britain, with tens of thousands dabbling in forms of black and white magic, voodoo, devil worship, and even ritual murder. But genuine witches are hard to identify, since they are not required by civil authorities to pass board examinations certifying their right to practice.

Witchcraft does not lend itself to sociological investigation or a comprehensive census of just how many people are doing what, but most authorities believe there is very little practice today of so-called black magic, or the "left-hand path," as the cognoscenti define it. Witches believe those who take that path are doomed to reap more harm than they sow, and in any contest between white and black magic, the good can summon up far more powerful resources.

In pre-Christian times, witches were healers and spiritual advisers. The Old Religion or Old Faith was a kind of tribal fertility rite forced underground by religious persecution. Witches from earliest times worshipped the Horned God as well as the Great Goddess, and religious authorities, confusing the Horned God with Satan, accused them of devil worship. Witchcraft has been described as a blend of fertility cults and such traditions as

Egyptian occultism and the Kabbalah. Some experts in the occult trace its origins back to emigrations from the lost continent of Atlantis, the last of which reached Egypt and started traditions exemplified in the Egyptian Book of the Dead, origin for many of today's occult rituals.

Traditionally the witches' craft included the use of herbs for healing and casting spells. There are claims they used poison as well to help the spells take effect. Witches were also reputed to employ drugs to produce such illusions as that of flying, as well as devices such as a "witches' cradle," a kind of swing for inducing hallucinations. Drugs from plants of the deadly nightshade family and similar potions were associated with witchcraft and probably had an effect similar to that of modern psychedelic drugs.

The key ingredient for the results claimed in black magic practices such as obeah and voodoo is the power of suggestion. If a highly susceptible victim in a country that takes witchcraft seriously becomes aware that a spell has been put on him, that knowledge alone is sometimes enough to do him in. Some sick individuals and groups indulge in actual killings, ritual sacrifices of humans as well as animals, but such incidents fortunately are rare.

In Europe, particularly during the 16th and 17th centuries, there were witchcraft trials with victims tortured, hanged, and burned at the stake. The accused were rarely witches, but all too frequently unfortunates persecuted for religious or political reasons, or for being elderly, eccentric, and reclusive.

Authorities estimate that currently there are 80,000 white witches in the United States alone, using their powers only for good; healing physical and mental illnesses; and pooling the talents of the coven to help each other or those who ask for assistance. Most modern covens work with clairvoyance as well as techniques of healing, and explore previously inaccessible regions of their own consciousness. Occasionally, using their psychic radar, they scan the horizon for signs of black magic and set out instantly to counter its influence. Each coven has its own traditions and ideas, largely nonconformist and with no real overall organization. Wicca, as its adherents call it, is a joyous religion with emphasis on the nonmaterial, but it covers every aspect of life from the elemental physical to the most sacred. Regular meetings are known as esbats, and more important gatherings, held eight times a year, are sabats.

Covens can be training centers, sources of power, and units of social enjoyment; or all three. By combining their energies, witches claim they can increase the intensity of the power and raise it higher than the sum of the individual contributions. Because in many covens formal rites are conducted in the nude and the so-called Great Rite is a ritualized act of sexual intercourse, positive accomplishments tend to be neglected by the press in favor of the more sensational aspects of the craft. Nudity is a tradition in witchcraft, a symbol of freedom and openness, and the rites are serious rather than orgiastic. The Great Rite is most often performed symbolically, but when performed in actuality it is strictly private.

Rites of initiation and advancement are full of symbolism: sword, wand, and pentacle; the *athame*, or ritual knife with esoteric symbols carved in the handle; and cords of several colors, used for binding and ritual scourging. Witches are trained in healing and various esoteric disciplines. They strive to balance within themselves elements of their personalities that correspond to air, water, earth and fire.

Witches' covens these days seem almost as dedicated as are Elks or Masons to doing good and performing rituals that are harmless, yet meaningful to those involved. White witchcraft certainly provides an exotic school for the satisfaction of the hunger for self-development and inner knowing that obsesses so many modern seekers.

you become what you behold

wm. blake

Corita

THE TAROT

The origins of the Tarot, ancestor of the familiar deck of playing cards, are shrouded in mystery. First recorded in Europe in the 14th century as used in games of chance and fortune-telling, the Tarot is sometimes attributed to the gypsies. While it was indeed used by them as a method of divination, students of the occult believe the Tarot goes back to the ancient Egyptians and beyond. One legend has it that the Egyptian priests met to decide how to preserve and transmit their teachings to future generations. At first it was proposed to confide the secrets to virtuous men who would pass them on from one generation to another. But a wise and cynical priest proposed that the knowledge be linked with vice, since this was certain to endure longer and to be more prevalent than virtue. Thus the archetypes of the Tarot and the mysteries behind them have been preserved in decks of cards used for fleecing the gullible.

The Tarot pack contains 78 cards. The Minor Arcana, or "lesser mysteries," have 56 cards divided into four suits: Swords (Spades), Wands (Clubs), Cups (Hearts), and Pentacles (Diamonds). Each suit has Ace through Ten, with four court cards: King, Queen, Knight, and Page. The four suits correspond to the occult elements, cups for water, swords for air, wands for fire, and pentacles for earth. The suits have also been said to correspond to the structure of medieval society. The wand, weapon of the peasant, stands for agriculture; the cup, or sacred vessel, for the clergy; the sword for the warrior; and the money (pentacles) for commerce. In the recently designed "Tarot for the Aquarian Age" the four symbols are linked to the four functions of the Jungian theory of types: thinking, feeling, intuiting, and sensing. The symbols of the Tarot are also frequently linked to astrological symbols and to the Kabbalah, whose Tree of Life consists of 22 paths traditionally associated with the 22 personages of the Tarot's Major Arcana.

The Tarot is a powerful roster of symbolic figures, a useful tool for exploration of the subconscious, lending itself both to Jungian analysis and the Jungian teaching of the recurring myths and archetypes that occur in every culture. It can be a blueprint for understanding the province of the mind, for helping an individual seek out the personifications, the images hidden within himself. It has served as an inspiration for writers and poets, as a structure for psychoanalysis and self-analysis. Its meanings and ramifications are endless, repeating images held up as mirror to the self.

THE KABBALAH

The word *Kabbalah* comes from the Hebrew *kabeil*, meaning "to receive," and is the name given to Jewish mystic philosophy. Its adherents believe that it was revealed at the same time as the Torah, but while the Torah was given to everyone, the Kabbalah was made known only to a select group of mystics. The first written records were the Book of Formation, which appeared in Italy in the 8th century, and the Zohar, written in 13th-century Spain. These books were combined into the Kabbalah. Throughout Jewish history, the Kabbalah has run parallel to the Torah and the Talmud, hidden in the secret passageways of Jewish occult philosophy. It is a blend of prophecy, Zoroastrian mythology, numerology, Greek science, and gnosticism. It is based on symbolism, with a secret symbolic language of its own. It uses the first 10 numbers and all the letters in the Hebrew alphabet as 32 paths to wisdom. The starting point is the tetragrammaton, the name of God, *Yahweh,* composed of the four letters Y, H, W, H.

These symbols are formed into the intricate Tree of Life, a map of the steps to the ultimate which exists beyond the human concept of God. The Tree is made of 10 spheres of the Sephiroth, generally referred to by their Hebrew names. The Kabbalah hypothesized that as man looks toward God he looks into the mystery of God's self, the Ein Soph; and between this abyss and himself is a chain of the 10 attributes of God. They are in pairs: feminine, negative, receptive in relation to the one before it; and masculine, positive, active in relation to the one following. The schematic drawing of the Tree of Life looks something like a diagram of a molecular structure.

The crown, or highest sphere of the Sephiroth, is the Kether, pure being without form. The steps range down to Malkuth, the Kingdom, the sphere of elements both occult and physical through which all life must pass before it can complete its development by moving back to its source. Malkuth is also the sphere of divination, of the use of material objects to provide answers to nonmaterial questions. Kabbalists believe that the Sephiroth will be reversed on the Last Day and the world of man raised high, closer to the essence of God.

The 32 mystical Paths of the Concealed Glory "revealed" in the Kabbalah are the means by which the human soul approaches God, symbols serving as objects of meditation. To Kabbalists theirs is a living system of spiritual development, dependent not only upon technical knowledge but upon the development of powers such as that of concentration and visual imagination. All of the paths in their schema are equally holy and necessary steps in the cosmic process, a process of discovering and developing the potential within, of opening up all levels of consciousness.

THE I CHING

For thousands of years the Chinese have turned to the enduring wisdom of the *I Ching* (The Book of Changes) for guidance and inspiration. It is a kind of psychic computer, giving symbolically coded answers to those seeking guidance. It helps define where one is in the ever-changing cycles of life, and is believed to cast light from a higher source on existing problems. It is a book of feelings and intuitions, indicating when some condition is going to change. Traditionally it was used to determine the appropriate time for action.

The premise of the I Ching is that the changing patterns in the universe can be divined, can even be consulted and questioned. This is done by throwing or sorting out 49 yarrow stalks and interpreting the random patterns of their fall by means of the 64 hexagrams, patterns of dark and light lines, that make up the I Ching. An alternate method is to use three coins, throwing them six times to generate a hexagram. The coins are thrown after asking a question — a serious question with a complex, rather than simple, answer. The coins are inscribed on one side and blank on the other, and after each throw the result is recorded. The first throw gives the bottom line of the trigram, the second throw the line above, and the third throw the top line. The pattern will indicate whether the line is a yin or yang line, and whether it is a moving line. For every moving line the throw must be repeated.

The coins are a faster method than the stalks, but by using the latter experts feel the question is more fully realized in the consciousness of the questioner. It takes at least 20 minutes to sort out the stalks, and during that time the mind is concentrated on the problem to which it seeks an answer, and attains a higher degree of awareness. Answers are given about the current status of the problem and its future course.

The I Ching has been used, and its counsel valued, by psychologists, businessmen, people in many disciplines. Devotees keep their stalks or coins carefully wrapped and cherish them as almost sacred objects.

The definitive translation of the I Ching into a Western language is the one by Richard Wilhelm, a German Protestant missionary to China. Another highly regarded version was done by John Blofeld, author of several books on the Orient.

BIORHYTHMS

According to the theory of biorhythms, each individual is profoundly influenced by rhythmic variations that "pulse" with a fixed periodicity initiated at the moment of birth, and continuing unchanged throughout the individual's life. One of the more articulate proponents of this school is George S. Thommen, author of the book, *Is This Your Day?*

The tenet that each person's biorhythms start at the time of birth and vary at a fixed rate is fundamental to Thommen's contention that each of us can predict our "up" times and "down" times, regardless of age. Three basic rhythms are hypothesized: the Physical, with a 23-day period, the Sensitivity, with a 28-day period, and the Intellectual, with a 33-day period.

Armed with an accurate birthdate, a person can calculate where he is at any moment in relation to his three biorhythmic cycles. The fact that each biorhythm has a different period means that at any given moment in time the curve of each rhythm will be in a different position and the influence of one rhythm may be positive (during the first half of the period) and the others negative (during the second half of the period). The amplitude of each varying rhythm is unique to the individual,

It is Thommen's contention that "critical" days in a person's life occur when one or more of the biorhythm lines is crossing the "zero" line from positive to negative, or vice versa, and he offers data to show a significant arithmetical correlation between critical days and untoward happenings in individuals.

A natural extension of Thommen's beliefs is comparison of the compatibility of two people, based upon their biorhythmic cycles. A straightforward arithmetical computation coupled with a "compatibility table" compiled by Thommen purports to demonstrate the predictability of compatibility of two or more people. Compatibilities are computed for each of the three rhythms and then arithmetically averaged to give a composite percentage. A composite average of 60 percent or higher is said to be highly favorable for a compatible relationship. The extent to which a "fulfilling" prophecy influences the outcome, of course, is not susceptible to measurement.

A variety of devices for charting the individual's biorhythm are available, ranging from a plastic dial, manufactured in Japan, to biorhythm clocks and wristwatches developed in Switzerland.

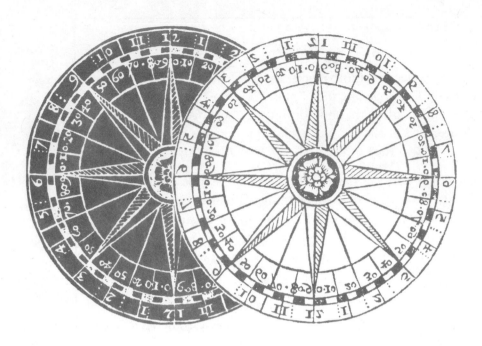

GREGGE TIFFIN/metaphysical intelligence services

Gregge Tiffin is the founder-director of Metaphysical Intelligence Services, which has offices in Boston, Milwaukee, Dallas, Encino and Del Mar, California. At his Encino headquarters, Gregge, a husky, graying, matter-of-fact man, works at an antique desk surrounded by exotic curios and carvings, giving Life Readings and preparing Circadian Time Charts.

As described in the M.I.S. brochure, a Life Reading is "a modern application of an ancient and effective method of determining vital spiritual, psychological and physical characteristics, brought into this incarnation from previous experiences .... Our arrival here in a life experience is determined by our need to use this planet as a teaching center. What we learn here is then applied to our

total storehouse of knowledge of the Universe. This planet, as all celestial bodies, serves as a school within the structure of the Universe.

"The Life Reading answers three basic questions: Why did I come to this planet? What previous experiences did I have that started me on this present life experience? And what should I be learning in this experience in order to fulfill the life lesson? Additionally it explains much in your life in those areas concerned with hidden fears, bad habits, physical disorders and personality weaknesses. It is based neither on astrology nor a birthdate, but on information that is stored deep within your cells. The information is compiled by you, on you, throughout all your life experiences in the

Universe. Gregge Tiffin matches his cellular consciousness to your cellular consciousness, and then reads the information.

" . . . The material is taped, and experience has shown that most people really feel the effects of the Life Reading anywhere from one to six weeks after their session with Gregge. By then the information has seeped back down into your cells, releasing old memories, lost feelings and vital awarenesses."

In addition to giving Life Readings, Gregge deals with Circadian Time Analyses. These intricate, colorful charts have certain elements in common with astrological and biorhythm projections, but they are not the same. As Gregge explains it, they are based on the time of release from the etheric plane rather than the actual hour of birth and the information is obtained clairvoyantly. From his chart a client learns about "his individuality, his decision-making capability, his ego strength, his ability to make changes, his love-sex capability, his intelligence capability, his money and success capability, his emotional strength, and his future orientation." Individual charts don't give future projections but six-month updates can be obtained. Gregge has done Circadian Time projections for businesses and there is a demand for his services in that area, but he finds it too computerized and impersonal.

Using astromathematics, Gregge also works with numerology. He explains that while his technique is not Tibetan, it came out of his six-year training in that country. With an esoteric arrangement of numbers and letters, he determines the suitability of clients' names and recommends changes where he finds them advisable.

At present most of Gregge's group teaching and lecturing is done in Boston. Some of the classes: Overcoming Previous Life Sexual Impediments, The Use of the Life Reading in Personal Development, and Intergalaxial Law and the Function of the Interstellar Hierarchy.

Do any of his clients experience *deja vu* or other verification of these previous incarnations? Gregge has an abundance of such stories. One concerns a recent Life Reading he did for a mother and her three children. Gregge prefers the children not be present at sessions and uses his clairvoyant ability to locate a particular individual by name alone. According to Gregge's reading, the 10-year-old son had been a stockbroker in his last incarnation and had suffered greatly during the 1929 crash. His mother didn't play the tape for the boy or describe it to him, but on a subsequent trip to New York he absolutely refused to visit the Stock Exchange, going into a screaming, kicking tantrum. Insisting he had been there before, had seen it all, and didn't like it, the boy refused to be persuaded that this was his first visit to New York — and had to be left behind while the family made the trip to Wall Street.

Occasionally, Gregge explains, he reads for people who are on earth for their first trip, who have come from other galaxies. At present, he says, there is a strong influx of youngsters from other galaxies, a wave that began in 1954 and will continue in a 25- to 50-year cycle. Gregge believes these children are arriving because their unique talents and abilities are sorely needed to deal with the severe problems on earth at the present time.

THE GUIDE MEDITATION

The experience of the archetype is frequently guarded as the closest personal secret, because it is felt to strike into the very core of one's being . . . . [These experiences] demand to be individually shaped in and by each man's life and work. They are images sprung from the life, the joys and sorrows, of our ancestors; and to live they seek to return, not in experience only, but in deed. Because of their opposition to the conscious mind they cannot be translated straight into our world; hence a way must be found that can mediate between conscious and unconscious reality.

Carl G. Jung
The Personal and the Collective Unconscious

In an adobe house in Santa Fe, with ceiling beams made of huge trees, Edwin Steinbrecher gives astrological readings and helps people to find their Guides, spiritual beings who will lead and protect them on journeys into the unconscious. A professional astrologer who has been through Jungian analysis, Steinbrecher has blended elements from his profession and from his knowledge of Jungian concepts into the Guide Meditation. The archetypes in his explorations are the archaic figures from the Tarot: the High Priestess, the Magician, the Fool — all the 22 images of the Major Arcana.

A few years ago, using Jung's technique of active imagination, Steinbrecher had some vivid experiences in meditation involving Tarot figures. During one such journey he came into contact with the Tarot Devil, and knew utter terror when the Devil placed himself directly in front of Steinbrecher's stairway to the outside world. After this frightening confrontation, Steinbrecher avoided the practice for a time, but decided to try again and this time to request a guide.

As he descended the familiar stairway into his inner world, the Guide appeared, a friendly old man dressed in striped robes. From that time on, the Guide protected and helped him through his meditative experiences and his contacts with the archetypal figures. Steinbrecher describes it as the beginning of true freedom and choice in his own life.

Because the experiences were such constructive ones, he began to demonstrate the technique to others. After a few tentative beginnings, he found it was having the same salutary effect in the lives of those he taught. This is how Steinbrecher describes it in his book, *The Guide Meditation:*

> The Guide Meditation is the product of the coming together of a number of potent spiritual and philosophical streams: astrology, tarot, alchemy, analytical psychology, qabalah and the Western Mystery tradition which contains the Judaeo-Graeco-Christian spiritual heritage of the West. The mingling of these vast currents produces a gestalt in which the Guides — humanity's lost teachers — reappear, fresh, alive and waiting to serve in the individual spirit quest; to lead us toward that "Kingdom of Heaven" that is within each of us.

Since 1967, thousands of people have been initiated into the process without any reports of a "bad trip." Recently my friend Joan Hackett, who is an actress and a painter, went to Santa Fe and was taken on such an inner voyage. Here are some extracts from her report of the journey:

> I sat down and was asked to close my eyes and visualize a cave. It was very difficult for me to do — I cannot will what I will see . . . . You close your eyes and see a cave . . . turn to the left and find an opening and go out through the clearing. You call an animal to you . . . you're not to anticipate doing this . . . your mind just comes up with the images. The animal takes you to your guide. It's customary not to be able to see the face of the guide; in fact, that's one of the signs that you don't have a false guide. You ask the guide what you want to know . . . he won't volunteer anything. You ask him to take you to the various symbols in the Tarot. Two things must happen when you meet the symbol. You must say, "What do you need from me or my life to make you my friend and have you work with me?" The other is, "What do you have to give me — a symbolic gift — that I can use in my life?"
>
> I started out very tongue-in-cheek — but the experience I had was that I was afraid in my cave and couldn't get out . . . there was a tiny opening that got smaller as I went through it, rather like Alice in Wonderland. I came out on a precipice that went straight down and overlooked all of Los Angeles . . . a man came as a wolf and we had to climb the mountain . . . I was crying and afraid. The guide looked a little like St. Anthony with the robes and the brown cassock. I went to the sun . . . and then to the High Priestess, kind of art nouveau in negative — her hair white and her face black. She gave me a wonderful gift, saying that I need give her nothing except trust. Her gift was a large round bowl made of crystal with a square cross on top. I placed it on my head and she told me I could see everything in it . . . and every time I would look into it I would see everything, but without discrimination.
>
> Next I met the Empress, who would not speak to me. She had long red hair and stood with her arms folded across her chest, standing as if dead . . . I asked her what she needed from my life and she told me my hair. My hair had been bleached and I wanted to have it cut. After I had returned home I took the scissors to cut it and instead cut my face above my eye. I called a friend to recommend a hairdresser, and she sent me to one who had red hair and looked exactly like the Empress.

Steinbrecher describes the background of the process involved in the Guide Meditation as the phenomenon of projection, which puts inner archetypes into the outer world, thus drawing into our orbit the very qualities we are trying to reject. Projection sends energies of the self out into the world, with a loss of psychic energy and freedom. When the energies are made conscious, with ego and self being brought into balance, the result is a "free individual who pours light and love into the world around him." By confronting the archetypes on these inner journeys patterned by the active imagination, one's own behavior can be modified, and the outer world begins to improve — problems start to drop away, negative persons move out of one's life, and more positive relationships are created.

interview/HANS HOLZER
WHERE IS THE OCCULT TODAY?

Dr. Hans Holzer, leading authority on the occult, ESP, and other parapsychological phenomena, is professor of parapsychology at the New York Institute of Technology, a member of the British College of Psychic Studies, director of the New York Committee for the Investigation of Paranormal Phenomena, and a member of the American Association for the Advancement of Science. Dr. Holzer has written 41 books including ESP and You, The Human Dynamo, The Directory of the Occult, Windows to the Past, *and* The Truth About Witchcraft. *Because of his wide knowledge in this field, we asked Dr. Holzer to select the most interesting and reputable psychics, clairvoyants, and other practitioners to give us "Holzer's Picks, the class of the occult."*

LANDE: What are your thoughts on the importance of the occult sciences in this age and year?

HOLZER: I think it is indeed the beginning of the Aquarian Age, the time of change. I think we — and by we I mean the general public as well as the scientific establishment — have to think of the occult sciences, including parapsychology, not as some fringe area to be engaged in by a few odd characters with or without academic training, but as one of the most vital new directions in research that has come into the life of man. If it weren't for the fact of parapsychology, for instance, religion wouldn't have a leg to stand on. Science has been able to establish principles of human survival of personality beyond bodily death that seem to support religion, rather than the other way around. We must never accept anything on belief, which in my opinion is nothing more than the uncritical acceptance of something you can't prove one way or another. So therefore we are at the threshhold of a new approach to the entire field.

I think if we take a cautious but progressive path toward exploring the human potential and exclude nothing — that is to say, not use 19th-century materialistic concepts of methodology to confine ourselves to what we think is possible and exclude what we think is not — if we are completely open-minded about areas that are as yet beyond our belief systems, then and only then can we truly learn what man is all about.

LANDE: What scientific data can you offer to support that position?

HOLZER: I have offered my scientific data in 41 published books, six television documentaries, and countless lectures. The evidence is really very clear. It consists essentially of three elements.

The first is the supported testimony of large numbers of witnesses unconnected one with the other, yet giving us parallel information in widely scattered areas. It is a scientific axiom that similar testimony by witnesses who have no contact with each other is considered part of evidence.

Secondly, there is the concrete evidence of psychic photography undertaken under test conditions, excluding any kind of fraud, delusion, or faulty mechanism.

And thirdly, there is experimentation in the field — that is to say, the competent observation of spontaneous phenomena as and when they occur in nature by as large a number of observers as is possible.

Notice that I did not mention laboratory experiments. I take a very dim view of these in general because they create under artificial conditions seeming duplications of phenomena that occur properly only in nature. I do not think the laboratory is the way to prove evidence of human survival. It is a valuable adjunct in examining physical evidence, such as in testing people for their ability in ESP, but it is not the road to the final solution, which is what is really behind man's ability to transcend the boundaries of time and space.

LANDE: Good, bad, or indifferent, where do we stand today?

HOLZER: In my opinion, based on investigation of the field over the last 15 years, we have a number of competent and highly progressive scientific investigators, both academic and on the fringes of academia, who are doing a fine job. We also have self-appointed pseudo-intellectuals who are trying to cash in on the vogue of interest in ESP and the associated occult sciences by offering quickie workshops, questions answered by mail for $5, and that sort of thing, who are not qualified at all but because of the lack of policing in our field are able to thrive, and by doing so confuse the picture for the outside world. In a free country, of course, this sort of thing has to fall by the wayside of its own volition.

I also expect that the resistance to parapsychology and its findings by the authors of the scientific establishment will fall by the wayside too, because the evidence is becoming more overwhelming every day.

As you know, I don't accept terms like "the unknown" or "the unexplained" because everything is eventually known and explicable. My concern is that the mass media of television and news be utilized in a proper way to put this knowledge at the fingertips of the average man — because this is not so now. The resistance on the part of the communications media toward even the discussion of the subject is a sad reflection upon their anxiety to refrain from programming anything even slightly controversial. But that will yield — and I hope to be among the first to help it to do so.

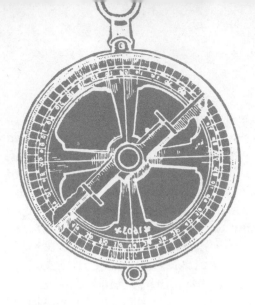

The following information was gleaned from Dr. Holzer's The Directory of the Occult, *published by the New York Committee for the Investigation of Paranormal Occurrences, and is excerpted with the author's permission. It is a partial list, based purely on Dr. Holzer's recommendations, and includes only the most reputable organizations.*

The American Society for Psychical Research has its West Coast branch in Los Angeles and does such work as investigating and researching haunted houses. Activities are open to the general public. The address: 1414 Club View Drive, Los Angeles, California 90024.

The Noetics Foundation, which studies the "science of consciousness," deals with all aspects of psychic research. It was founded by Dr. Edgar Mitchell, who is dedicated to the study of the unknown and is best known for his walk on the moon. The foundation may be reached in care of *Psychic* Magazine, 680 Beach Street, San Francisco, California 94109.

Dr. Jule Eisenbud has devoted himself to the study of such psychics and mediums as Ted Serios, a bellhop who is able to project thought images into cameras, photographic film, and television tubes. His studies resulted in the formation of foundations to continue the investigation. Dr. Eisenbud can be contacted either at the University of Colorado or at 4634 East Sixth Avenue, Denver, Colorado 80220.

Dr. Stanley R. Dean has spent many years studying metapsychiatry, the "unclassified interface between psychiatry and mysticism." He is interested in the intervention of the occult into medicine and can be reached at the University of Miami Medical School, Miami, Florida.

Morey Bernstein, author of *The Search for Bridey Murphy,* has concentrated his efforts on the subject of reincarnation. He can be contacted at 1830 South Treasure Drive, Miami, Florida.

George Adler heads a group in New Jersey which exchanges knowledge in the field of psychic phenomena and offers a library service with a vast amount of information on related topics. This group is called the Psychic Phenomena Society of New Jersey, Kingston, New Jersey 08528.

Another group studying psychic phenomena and doing extensive psychic research is **The American Society for Psychical Research,** which publishes the *Journal of the American Society for Psychical Research.* The group's approach is scientific.

Its address is 5 West Seventy-third Street, New York, New York 10023.

First to bring attention to Uri Geller, the now world-famous medium and parasensitive, is **The Foundation for Parasensory Investigation.** It sponsors lectures and study courses and can be reached at 1 West Eighty-first Street, Suite 5D, New York, New York, phone (212) 799-4686.

A dream laboratory has been established at the **Maimonides Medical Center** in New York to study such subjects as the relationship between ESP and sleep. This laboratory may be contacted at the Department of Psychiatry, Maimonides Medical Center, Brooklyn, New York 11219.

The Parapsychology Forum of Cincinnati was established in 1970 and studies parapsychology, investigates reports of hauntings, and assists in helping to locate missing persons or objects. This establishment can be reached at the Parapsychology Forum of Cincinnati, P.O. Box 24105, Cincinnati, Ohio 45224.

Probably the best parapsychology school in the country is the **University of Virginia School of Medicine.** It is headed by Dr. Ian Stevenson, who is an expert on the subject of reincarnation. Dr. Stevenson can be reached at that University, which is located in Charlottesville, Virginia.

Sercolab manufactures tools and scientific instruments used in parapsychological research and can be reached at P.O. Box 78, Arlington, Massachusetts 02174.

Spiritual Frontiers Fellowship was founded by well-known psychic and medium Arthur Ford and seeks to deal in psychic research as it applies to the ministry as well as to the layman. It offers a middle-of-the-road approach to spirituality. It can be reached at

800 Custer, Evanston Illinois 60202.

The Fountainhead is a group which studies the occult and operates several bookshops on that subject. It may be reached at P.O. Box 50426, Tucson, Arizona 85703.

Harold Sherman has founded a group which investigates ESP. The ESP Research Associates is a forum for lectures, discussions, and special seminars and can be reached at 1750 Tower Building, Little Rock, Arkansas 72201.

The Triune Science of Being Awareness Center is a nonprofit organization which studies spiritualism, numerology, astrology, and psychic individuals. It can be contacted at 3497 Cahuenga Boulevard, West Los Angeles, California 90068, phone (213) 851-3611.

The Atlanta Institute of Metaphysics is an excellent organization at which Mr. and Mrs. Peter Calhoun operate regular lectures and teaching sessions and act as a clearinghouse for psychic activities in the area. It may be reached at 1625 Monroe Drive, Atlanta, Georgia 30324, phone (404) 875-0273.

Under the direction of **William and Renee Linn,** two spiritualist healers, the New York Spiritualist Center, Inc. conducts regular healing services and gives classes in spiritual development. It can be contacted at 225 East Seventy-fourth Street, New York, New York 10021.

Serenity Socials meet every Saturday night for discussions on "inner vibrational harmony, nutrition, yoga, occult, Aquarian Age, ecology, art of living, cosmic consciousness." They can be reached at 15 East Thirty-first Street, New York, New York 10016.

Amerisyche is an organization which explores every phase of the occult. It takes an intellectual approach and can be reached at 141 Arsenal Street, Watertown, New York 13601.

Discussing parapsychology and the occult on a rather casual level is a group organized by **Mrs. Stephanie Grove,** 605 Grandview Avenue, East Pittsburgh, Pennsylvania 15112.

White witchcraft and psychic healing work are the subjects of a group in Alaska, which may be contacted by writing **Mrs. Mia LaMoureaux,** P.O. Box 8151, Anchorage, Alaska 99504.

Mr. and Mrs. Robert Evanston hold lectures, group discussions, and meetings on psychic phenomena and will arrange for private sittings. Their address is 1018 West Mitchell Drive, Phoenix, Arizona 85213, phone (602) 263-5394.

A great spiritualist and medium in California is **George Daisley,** who first became famous for his work with Bishop James Pike. He can be contacted for a sitting at 629 San Isidro Road, Santa Barbara, California 93108, phone (805) 687-1873.

A psychic consultant who is very popular among celebrities, **Lotte von Strahl** can be contacted by appointment at 437 Gayly Avenue, Westwood, California 96137.

A very impressive clairvoyant is **Bill Corrado,** who can diagnose illnesses, accurately advise businessmen in financial matters, and collaborate with psychiatrists on solving patients' problems. He is available for readings and reportedly can predict the future with 83 percent accuracy. He has opened a school to teach people to use their own psychic ability, and readings can be arranged by appointment only through Bill Corrado, 23243 Burbank Boulevard, Woodland Hills, California.

Reverend Richard Zenor of the Agasha Temple of Wisdom, Inc., does not make predictions but is a clairvoyant and gives psychic readings from the pulpit. He is a medium, and through him speak Agasha (an Eastern master) and several other spiritual guides. Richard Zenor can be reached at the Agasha Temple of Wisdom, Inc., 460 North Western Avenue, Los Angeles, California 90004, phone (213) 464-6252.

A recommended psychic in the San Francisco area is the **Reverend Phaetyn E. Grasso,** who can be reached at 1017½ Capuchino Avenue, Burlingame, California 94010.

An excellent astrologer who does individual charts and writes informative, unexaggerated claims is **Sidney Omarr,** who can be reached at 232 Alcyona Drive, Los Angeles.

Virginia O'Hallahan is a combination astrologer/psychic and can be reached for readings and charts at 922 Trinity Avenue, Seaside, California 93955.

An astrologer who compares astrological charts with numerological charts is **Victoria Saint Cyr,** who specializes in stockmarket charts and general astrology. Her address is 438½ Landfair Avenue, Los Angeles, California 90024.

Another dependable astrologer is **Betty Collins,** who keeps charts and counsels people according to previously-recorded information. She can be reached at 1631 North Genesee, Hollywood, California 90046, phone (213) 874-4457.

An excellent medium who has been able to visually foresee future events which could be factually verified is **Mrs. Judith Laurie,** 122 West Thirty-fifth Street, Riviera Beach, Florida 33404.

A psychic healer, medium, clairvoyant, psychic photographer, and spirit communicator who gives private sittings is **Betty Dye,** who can be contacted at P.O. Box 82687, Hapeville, Georgia 30354.

Another psychic/astrologer is **Irene Hughes,** who is able to diagnose illnesses by mail without ever having met the patient. Doctors consult with her, and she is also well known for her psychic counseling. She is able to give very accurate readings by mail. Among her other feats, she predicted Agnew's downfall, predicted both Kennedy assassinations, the outbreak of the Near Eastern war in 1967, and Jacqueline Kennedy's remarriage. She can be reached at 500 North Michigan Avenue, Suite 1040, Chicago, Illinois 60611, phone (312) 467-1140.

Henry Rucker is a psychic healer and fortuneteller who is particularly gifted. He is also an excellent lecturer and is the only black man heading a psychic research foundation. He can be reached at 192 North Clark Street, Chicago, Illinois 60601.

Penny South is a paranormal analyst who can get psychic impressions from the handwriting of those who consult her. She is also a trance medium and founded the Society of Psychic Awareness and Research for further study. The society is located at 1120 South Mayfield Avenue, Chicago, Illinois 60644. Penny South is also available at 9235 West Capitol Drive, Milwaukee, Wisconsin.

Good compatibility charts, which evaluate the bonds between married couples or men and women interested in each other, as well as general and business charts can be done by **Mary Anne,** whose address is North Avenue at Bloomingdale, Glen Ellyn, Illinois, phone (312) 665-6015.

A psychic helper who can aid in searches for missing persons or predict future events is **Frederico de Arechaga,** head of the Sabaean Society of Chicago. He gives private sittings and operates an occult shop called El Sabarum at 2553 North Halsted, Chicago, Illinois 60614.

An accurate psychic astrologer in the Midwest who will do charts and progressions as well as investigate missing person cases or unusual deaths is **Gar Osten,** who can be reached by mail at 315 South Third Avenue East, Newton, Iowa 50208.

A fine psychic predictor in the South is **Ron Warmoth,** who can be reached at 97 Rue St. Anne, New Orleans, Louisiana.

Mrs. Sybil Leek is an excellent trance medium who does her work exclusively for scientific purposes. She will not give private readings but will do charts for people, being a fine astrologer. Letters addressed to Mrs. Sybil Leek containing a stamped forwarding envelope will be forwarded by her publisher, Stein & Day, Scarborough House, Briarcliff Manor, New York, New York 10510.

The leading medium in New York is **Ethel Johnson Meyers,** who gives private sittings for both laymen and scientists. She is able to predict the future, contact the dead, and give readings on a person's past lives. She also gives group sittings and is a capable psychic counselor. She may be reached at 160 West Seventy-third Street, New York, New York 10023.

A leading clairvoyant who can foresee the future is **John Reeves,** who can be reached at 225 East Seventy-fourth Street, New York, New York 10021.

Virginia Cloud uses Tarot cards to induce psychic impressions and is able to continue into full mediumship. She will do private readings for those contacting her at P.O. Box 2684, Grand Central Station, New York, New York 10017.

A woman who is clairvoyant and able to predict the future as well as dealing in some astrology is **Shawn Robbins.** She is a lecturer and demonstrator, and she gives private readings. Shawn Robbins may be contacted by calling (212) 896-1892 in Queens, New York.

A psychic and clairvoyant couple who work together as a team are **Barry and Jackie Shawney,** who can give readings from a photograph. They can be reached at 470 Fifty-fourth Street, Brooklyn, New York 11220.

Frederick Stoessel is a psychic who can foretell his own future as well as that of others. He is also a psychic healer. He believes he can help anyone solve his emotional, medical, or financial problems. He also lectures and can be reached at Box 5012 Woolsey Station, Long Island City, New York 11105, phone (212) 545-9223.

Gene Sullivan is an excellent palmist, who reads character and future in the lines of the hands. Her talents are combined with psychic abilities. She may be reached at (212) 245-0347.

Ariel Yvon Taylor is an excellent numerologist who can explain the various aspects of clients' names in relation to professional activities, love and success, and other aspects of personality. Ariel Yvon Taylor can be reached at Carnegie Hall, Fifty-seventh Street and Seventh Avenue, New York, New York.

Another fine astrologer/psychic is **Isidor Oblo,** who can be contacted at 240 West End Avenue, New York, New York 10023, phone (212) 874-1322.

Hugh MacCraig is an accurate astrologer who can be contacted at 10 East Thirty-ninth Street, New York, New York 10016, phone (212) 532-0016.

Penny Hale is a prophet and seer who claims to be 95 percent accurate in her predictions. She can be reached at the Psychic Research Association, P.O. Box 125, Beaverton, Oregon 97005.

An excellent medium and psychic is **Mrs. Marianne Elko,** who is able to predict the future and expose many intricate details of the past. She may be reached at 2207 Riverview Drive, Industry, Pennsylvania 15052.

The following covens and pagan groups are in existence with some recommendation:

An Anglo-Saxon form of witchcraft is conducted by **Mrs. Mia LaMoureaux,** P.O. Box 8151, Anchorage, Alaska 99504.

Ernie Bidwell, 565 Howard Drive, Northeast, Sierra Vista, Arizona 85635, is head of a small traditionalist coven.

Sara Cunningham gives classes in witchcraft and runs an occult supply shop. She can be reached at P.O. Box 204, Wolf Creek, Oregon 97497.

Fred and Martha Adler run a coven of traditional witches at 4501 West 141st Street, Hawthorne, California 90250.

The Church of Wicca at 1908 Verde Street, Bakersfield, California 93304 is a traditional coven.

The Pagan Way is a fellowship of pagans who worship the forces of nature. They may be contacted through **John Wootten, the Pagan Way,** P.O. Box 2015, Wilmington, Delaware 19899.

Morgana runs a small coven in a traditional way and may be contacted through Mary Davis, P.O. Box 4818, Baltimore, Maryland 21211.

A hereditary witch named **Witch Tarun** runs a coven which worships in the Anglo-Saxon persuasion. The coven may be reached at Box 139, South Lancaster, Massachusetts 01561.

Du Bandia Grasail is a coven which worships once a week and studies the works of many philosophers and the kabbalah. It may be contacted at Box 43, Allston, Massachusetts 02134.

Dr. Raymond Buckland's coven practices a Tradition of Saxon Witchcraft and can be reached at P.O. Box 238, Weirs Beach, New Hampshire 03246.

An occult shop and coven is **The Aquarian Family,** which can be reached at 802 Holcomb Street, Watertown, New York 13601, or reached by phone between the hours of 11 a.m. and 11 p.m. at (315) 788-8947.

Circe runs an occult supply shop, teaches witchcraft, and is a witch. She may be reached at 2242 Parkwood, Toledo, Ohio 43620.

Unusual occult and health herbal products are produced by Enchanted Herbs and are grown, gathered, and prepared by **Selene,** a witch. More information can be obtained at Enchanted Herbs, 12099 County Line Road, Chesterland, Ohio 44026.

A pagan group and Dianic witchcraft coven is located in Dallas and is headed by **Morgan and Mark Roberts.** The organization publishes *The New Broom,* which is a journal of witchcraft. They can be contacted at P.O. Box 1646, Dallas, Texas 75221.

A small coven of hereditary witches headed by **Carol Ramsbottom** may be contacted at 10 Winter Avenue, Scarborough, Ontario, Canada.

Those who know of unusual paranormal cases or substantiated evidence of mediumship or would like to investigate relevant information may write to **Dr. Hans Holzer,** *140 Riverside Drive, New York, New York 10024. Professor Holzer also gives courses in parapsychology, and the school can be contacted at 888 Seventh Avenue, New York, New York.*

BUILDERS OF THE ADYTUM

Builders of the Adytum is a teaching and training order, which directs its teachings towards physical, mental, and spiritual development. Among the physical objectives: perfect bodily health, unfailing and completely adequate income, a harmonious environment, congenial occupation, and interesting, sympathetic associates.

Mental objectives include banishment of fear, ability to concentrate and to make correct decisions, and the development of creative imagination, reason, discrimination, and intuition.

The spiritual objectives are direct knowledge of the answers to the age-old questions of life, death, and nature without the laborious intermediate process of thinking and reasoning.

Students are taught in mystery schools, which develop initial mastery over small things, then greater, and finally over nature itself. The first two months of instruction are spent on study and experiments in occult psychology. After this, a new student receives a set of Tarot keys, which are studied for the next three months. A year of Tarot fundamentals follows. The series of Tarot keys, it is important to add, represents "a complete record, in picture form, of the inner secrets of the ancients."

PSI / what is it? who has it?

Parapsychology is the science of *psi,* the ability that is commonly called psychic. The correct name is *parapsychic,* but psi is easier to say. Some people like to call psi ability paranormal, but since psi seems increasingly normal as we study it, the word paranormal is a little misleading.

"Psi has two types of function, *extrasensory perception* (ESP) and *psychokinesis* (PK). ESP ability brings knowledge without the help of the senses; PK produces a physical effect without muscular means. But the two types of psi seem much like one basic ability with a two-way operation. Also there are subtypes: e.g., ESP is *clairvoyance* when the target is an object; it is called *telepathy* when a thought is transferred extrasensorially; and it is *precognition* when a future event is cognized. PK also has its subdivisions: It may affect *moving* matter, *static* objects, or *living* targets."

Origin of ESP

It was the author of the definition above, Dr. J. B. Rhine, who originated the term *extrasensory perception* while he was working at Duke University during the 1930s in the fields of telepathic and clairvoyant phenomena. During his early researches Rhine was attacked as a charlatan, but he persisted and expanded his pioneering studies. Extracts from his own *Introduction to Parapsychology,* on pages 353-356, give an account of this significant growth period, and in the interview that follows, the man who has been called "the father of parapsychology" makes some observations about his career and what the future holds for this new science.

For parapsychology is a science. Today courses in it are offered at some 100 colleges and universities, and at least 200 United States scientists are involved in researching psi. There are institutes of parapsychology in more than 40 countries, but in most of them the work is done by researchers with degrees in the hard sciences.

"Remote Viewing"

Physicists Dr. Harold Puthoff and Dr. Russell Targ of the Stanford Research Institute (SRI) recently wrote a description of their paranormal research for the prestigious British scientific journal *Nature,* which had never before published an article on parapsychology. Puthoff and Targ presented scientifically documented studies pointing to the existence of a perceptual ability called "remote viewing," by which information about a remote location can be obtained under conditions where the ordinary sensory channels are shielded. Their subject, a former police commissioner named Pat Price, perceived outdoor scenes many miles from their physical location in experiments where neither he nor the experimenters knew the location in advance. Nine remote-viewing experiments were conducted. The SRI team chose natural sites in the San Francisco Bay area on a double-blind basis, while Price, who remained at the Institute in Menlo Park, was asked to describe each location and whatever activities were going on there.

While one SRI experimenter was closeted with Price, a second would obtain a target location from an individual in SRI management not otherwise associated with the research. The team that had chosen the target proceeded to the location without communicating with the subject. The experimenter who remained behind with Price was not told of the location. Price described his impressions of each location on a tape recorder. Targ and Puthoff reported that the judges, who matched the nine locations which they independently visited against the typed transcripts of Price's tapes, correctly matched six of the nine descriptions. The probability that this could have occurred by chance is one in a billion.

PK

One of the most fascinating areas of parapsychology is that of psychokinesis — mind influencing matter, sometimes known as telekinesis.

In 1974, Uri Geller, the young Israeli psychic, was brought to the United States by Dr. Andrija Puharich and tested thoroughly at the Stanford Research Institute. Geller's admirers credit him with a wide range of paranormal abilities that enable him to bend keys, read or duplicate letters or images placed in sealed envelopes, and repair broken watches with a glance or a touch.

Starting as a nightclub magician in Israel, Geller has become world-famous and highly controversial. Although he played to mixed reviews in serious scientific and parapsychological circles in the United States, he left a trail of bent metal and thousands of awed viewers in England, Germany, and Scandinavia. Says one observer: "A hundred years ago we'd have burned Uri Geller at the stake. Now we put him on the Johnny Carson Show."

Geller Tested

In the Stanford Research Institute experiments with Geller, he was asked to reproduce 13 drawings, over a week-long period, while physically separated from his experimenters in a shielded room. Geller was not told who made the drawing, who selected it to be reproduced, or how it would be selected. The researchers state that only after Geller had been isolated in a double-walled steel room that was acoustically, visually, and electrically shielded from them, was each target picture randomly chosen and drawn. Examples of drawings he was asked to reproduce included a firecracker, a cluster of grapes, a devil, a horse, the solar system, a tree, and an envelope. Two SRI researchers were submitted Geller's reproductions for judging on a "blind" basis. They matched the target data to the response data with no errors, a chance probability of better than one in a million.

According to *Time* magazine, psychology professor and Defense Department consultant Ray Hyman visited the SRI laboratories during the testing period and criticized the methods and the validity of the conclusions. Geller volunteered to demonstrate his powers for *Time*'s editors, but after a performance of metal bending and mind reading in the Time-Life Building, professional magician James Randi was able to duplicate each of Geller's feats.

Possibilities for Fraud

Milbourne Christopher, famed investigator of psychic phenomena, comments that "Geller is at his ingenious best in laboratories where he is being observed by scientists who believe he has extraordinary ESP ability and think ... without justification ... that they have ruled out every possibility of fraud. Unless an expert in deception is present while such tests are being conducted, these experiments are as valid as a four-dollar bill."

One of the most remarkable examples of psychokinesis is the reputed ability of a Russian woman, alternately known as Nelya Mikhailova or Ninel Kulagina. There are dramatic reports of Ms. Kulagina spinning a compass, first the dial, then the compass itself, causing pens to creep across tables, moving objects inside a plexiglass container, causing bread to "jump" into her mouth. Whether it is part of the act or the result of a transfer of bodily energy into psychokinetic energy, Ms. Kulagina loses weight and becomes pale and visibly exhausted after her performances. This uncanny ability to move objects has been observed and tested by many Russian and foreign scientists and journalists, and if there is a trick, it has so far been undetected.

Poltergeists

A psychokinetic manifestation which has existed for a long time in legend and literature is that of the poltergeist, blamed for noisy house hauntings or otherwise inexplicable outbreaks of glass smashing and crockery breaking. Probably the best-known contemporary case is that of Matthew Manning of Great Britain, who has been accompanied by disturbances since his early teens. (Poltergeist activity almost always takes place in houses where there are adolescent or preadolescent children.) Matthew's parents often came down to breakfast to find furniture overturned and smashed dishes strewn around. This frenetic activity followed Matthew to boarding school, culminating in a shower of knives that rained down on his six roommates. There were fortunately no injuries, but the headmaster decided to give Matthew a private room. Now 24, Matthew does spoon bending on the Uri Geller model, automatic writing in several languages, and automatic drawing in the style of various deceased artists.

Psychic phenomena have always fascinated mankind. Man *wants* to believe, yearns for a spiritual bulletin board bearing messages assuring him he is not alone down here. This pervasive hunger could be an expression of our desire for unity with the universal consciousness, a cure for our feeling of alienation.

The problem facing serious researchers has consistently been to ensure that this basic credulity does not influence the experimental findings. Says one leading biologist: "Now that more and more of the scientific community is becoming involved in researching these phenomena, better experiments must be designed and conducted by truly objective observers so that these arcane powers, energies, or whatever they may prove to be, can be understood, and hopefully, harnessed for the benefit of mankind."

KIRLIAN PHOTOGRAPHY

About the only element of agreement among the many researchers working with Kirlian photography is that there is still much yet to be done before the shroud of mystery around these unique and exciting pictures is lifted.

The basic "kit" used to make Kirlian photographs includes no cameras, no lenses or special light sources. Instead, a source of high voltage electricity, wires and clamps, photographic paper, and developing solution comprise the do-it-yourself equipment for generating the beautiful and sometimes spectacular Kirlian photographs. Once the negative that has been exposed is developed, the mystery becomes evident. What has been photographed? What do the pictures mean?

Soviet Discovery

The name is that of Semyon and Valentina Kirlian, two energetic and imaginative Russians who live in Krasnodar, 750 miles south of Moscow on the northern slope of the Caucasus mountains. Semyon Kirlian started his investigations in 1939 and accumulated a large file of pictures and data, but it was not until 1970 that the Western world learned of his work. In that year the book *Psychic Discoveries Behind the Iron Curtain* was published. Written by Sheila Ostrander and Lynn Schroeder, it was a compilation of the data they had gathered while traveling throughout Russia during the summer of 1968. They were excited by the reports they received, an excitement reflected in their book.

Dr. Thelma Moss, a medical psychologist at UCLA's Neuropsychiatric Clinic, was asked to review the book prior to publication. She was sufficiently titillated by the chapter on Kirlian photography to pursue the subject further. In late 1970 Dr. Moss was in Moscow and discussed it at length with Victor Adamenko, a childhood neighbor of the Kirlians in Krasnodar, who had worked with them on their photographic investigations and also carried on further research with Victor Inyushin, a Soviet biologist, at Kirov University in Alma-Ata in southwestern Siberia. The work of these two men and their colleagues stimulated Dr. Moss, and upon her return to the United States in early 1971, she began a program of independent research with Kirlian photography. The results of her discussions with the Russians and a report on her subsequent work are contained in her book *The Probability of the Impossible.*

Electrical Photography

Results of the research to date are open to a broad range of interpretation. Researchers have independently reproduced the kaleidoscopic panoramas of color that are photographed when electrical current is passed through a living organism. The picture is made by electrical photography; that is, by passing an electrical current through a circuit, integral parts of which are the photographic negative and the subject to be photographed. Say that the researcher wants to photograph the "pads" of the subject's fingers. These are pressed against the unexposed film while a tiny amount of high voltage current (measured in fractions of a microampere, to avoid any possibility of harm to the subject) is conducted through the film and the subject for a brief period.

Variations

Not surprisingly, variations in the photographs have been recorded as a function of such basic variables as the time of exposure, the voltage, and the frequency of the electrical current. The inexplicable, however, derives from the enormous variations that can be recorded when the only variable is the subject itself. The Kirlians, and subsequently others, discovered that pictures of finger pads, for example, varied according to the physical and mental state of the subject at the time the picture was taken. The glow or corona in the picture was significantly reduced or even absent when the subject was either tired or emotionally depressed.

What do these photographs mean? Are they pictures of emanations from an animate body? Do these emanations interact with each other? Do these photographs represent visual evidence of a discharging energy field, or are they merely evidence of a conventional corona discharge? Is there a "bio-energy" field within or surrounding animate objects, and is this field unique to the organism? Clairvoyants and mystics contend that these photographs support their long-held conviction that there is a radiating aura of energy from an organism which they have been perceiving for years. Others dismiss the evidence as insignificant, albeit pretty, data that neither demand nor need further comment. There is a third body of opinion, however, represented by people such as Dr. Moss and Gottlieb Schneebeli, a research instructor in anatomy at the University of Utah. They take no sides in the controversy but continue their experiments to determine whether or not there are "real world" applications of the Kirlian photographic technique.

Animate and Inanimate

It has been found that it is only with animate objects that photographic differences are recorded. Photographs of inanimate objects such as a coin or a metal bar always reproduce as a constant. A particularly intriguing experiment was conceived of and carried out by Dr. Moss and her colleagues under rigorously controlled conditions. Its aim was to determine whether or not a "green thumb" person exerted any effect on a recently plucked leaf — without touching it — that was detectable by Kirlian photography in comparison with the effect exerted by a nongardening or "brown thumb" person. The data gathered from a group of 30 people evenly divided between green- and brown-thumbers showed that in more than 76 percent of the cases there was positive correlation between increased luminescence of the leaf and nonphysical "treatment" by the green-thumber. Conversely, the leaf's natural luminescence was reduced or absent after similar nonphysical treatment by brown-thumbers.

Schneebeli's Experiments

Scores of other experiments have been conducted, the results of which appear to point in the direction that the photographs depict some as yet to be defined function of the state of consciousness. Schneebeli, at the University of Utah, has tested male students by taking their finger photographs before a female enters the room, after the female has arrived, and finally, after the female touches the male's arm. Most of the male students reacted positively in that their finger coronas were fatter and brighter after the appearance of the female. In a small number of cases the males were "turned off" by the appearance of the female. In no case was there no reaction. In other experiments, the aura or corona of a subject would appear weakened or broken when he was experiencing pain or was on the verge of becoming ill.

Determined efforts have been made to substantiate or disprove the contention that physical variables — the amount of blood in the finger, the presence of tiny beads of sweat, skin temperatures, or the galvanic skin response — are responsible for the photographic variations. The evidence continues to mount that these physical variables are *not* the determining factors and the path of investigation always seems to lead back to the variable of the subject's "mood."

There are still not enough data available to support positive and unequivocal statements about the precise meaning of the Kirlian photographs, but Dr. Moss, for one, is leaning toward the belief that she is seeing visible evidence of a "flow of energy" between animate objects and their environment. Regardless of the outcome of the continuing experiments, it is clear that still another, if as yet imperfectly understood, tool has been added to the workshop of the psychic researcher.

PYRAMID POWER

Is there a mysterious force or energy generated by a pyramidal shape? More and more believers, including some scientists, say there is — a force that can sharpen razor blades, mummify organic matter, including animals and possibly humans, retard the growth of bacteria, and alter the molecular structure of water.

In the special Salon of the Mummies in the Cairo Museum, the ancient kings of Egypt are displayed as in a showroom on plain, rectangular tables. They are indeed remarkably preserved, whether it be by special embalming processes or by "pyramid power."

Ostrander and Schroeder describe some of the experiments done with pyramids in *Psychic Discoveries Behind the Iron Curtain,* including a report on evidence that elaborate recordings of cosmic ray patterns on magnetic tape, conducted by the Ein Shama University near Cairo, were distorted because of mysterious energies inside the pyramid.

Studies and practical applications of this force are being made by Pyramid Power V, in Santa Monica, California, headed by Bill Kerrell. Kerrell has written a book, *The Guide to Pyramid Energy,* which explains the phenomena and describes the many experiments that have been conducted by physicists and other scientists. (Another book on the subject is *Pyramid Power* by Max Toth and Greg Nielsen.) The company sells pyramids of steel, six feet high, for $89.95, which can be placed over a bed or on the floor and used for meditating, healing, energizing. They are supposed to improve the growth of plants, germinate seeds faster, and create healthier specimens. The company also sells pyramid research kits to let people study the process for themselves.

The scientific premise behind the apparent force is that when you change the shape of something you change the vibration of the atomic particles in it. Just as one tuning fork brought closer to another will pick up its harmonies, any matter put into the resonance of the pyramid will harmonize with that resonance. The size of the pyramid is not important, nor the material from which it is made. But, the proportions must be exact and the pyramid must be lined up with magnetic north and south to operate most effectively.

PSYCHIC HEALING

. . . A woman . . . came up behind him and touched the fringe of his garment; for she said to herself, "If I only touch his garment, I shall be made well." Jesus turned, and seeing her he said, "Take heart, daughter; your faith has made you well." And instantly the woman was made well.

— Matthew 8:20

Psychic healing has been known since earliest times. It was the only kind of healing among primitive tribes, who believed sickness was caused by spells or evil spirits which had to be cast out. And alongside all the marvelous medical advances of the last century, the wonder drugs and organ transplants and open heart surgeries, psychic healing is still very much with us. Dr. R. K. Rao, dean of the department of psychology and parapsychology at the University of Waltair, India, says it is the only psychic power claimed by mystics and holy men he can state categorically he has been able to verify.

Indian Medicine Men

There is psychic healing among the American Indians, who put great stress on wholeness and honesty with oneself and with the Great Spirit. Medicine men do not claim to be either possessors or users of spiritual powers; the healer is the Great Spirit who works through those who have prepared and purified themselves. One elderly Indian, Patrick Sundance, was reported in the early '70s to be curing cancer and diabetes among white people in Utah. Pressure was put on him by organized medicine to leave the state, but since then universities have been studying his methods and experimenting with his native medicines.

One of the most common techniques in psychic healing is the laying on of hands. Dr. Edgar Jackson, a Methodist minister and a psychologist, has employed the laying on of hands over 10,000 times and also uses meditative healing in the Quaker tradition. A typical case was that of a concert pianist who had been diagnosed as having a serious heart condition and told he must retire. The subject had no religious connection with Dr. Jackson. After a process of relaxation and meditation, "centering down" on resources that might be present within his patient, Dr. Jackson placed him in a chair and put his hands on his head. The pianist started. "What did you do to me?" he asked. "I felt something go right through me." When he went to his doctor for a new electrocardiogram the tracings were completely different.

Disappearance of Cancer

Dr. Jackson has also had success with subjects who were very negative about any possibility of help. One woman, referred to him by her pastor because of suicidal tendencies, had already had one disfiguring operation for cancer and was scheduled for another. Dr. Jackson asked if his prayer group could place her in their "area of concern." Somewhat sarcastically she told him to go right ahead, even though it wouldn't do any good. The prayer group went to work, the nodes disappeared, the surgery was postponed indefinitely. That was several years ago and the cancer has still not recurred.

Dr. Lawrence LeShan, a clinical and research psychologist, described an experience his wife Eda had with Dr. Jackson. She was ill with a severe throat infection which had not responded to treatment, and was due to begin a speaking tour. They telephoned Dr. Jackson and asked him to "work" on her. Almost as soon as he hung up, Dr. LeShan was aware of a sense of tension, a throbbing presence in the room, and a sense of vitality and energy, of activity within his wife's body. The infection cleared up rapidly and she was able to go on her tour.

Why It Works

Dr. LeShan has investigated other paranormal phenomena, originally as a complete skeptic. After much research he decided that psychic healing worked because in some way "we are all part of each other." After discarding the differing rituals and surface methods and seeking the things healers had in common, he divided them into two types. In Type 1, the healer goes into an altered state of consciousness, viewing himself and the patient as one, whether through the concept of intersecting energy fields, or through the concept of God's love, or seeing each individual as a manifestation of the All, of Brahma. This brings into play the healing powers of the patient. The self-repair and self-healing faculties of the body usually operate below their potential, and apparently this type of healing unites the subject to the universe and to those powers that exist within him. In other words, Type 1 healers do not try to heal but to unite with the patient and let him heal himself.

In Type 2, personified by the laying on of hands, the healer concentrates or gets into a mental state so that there is a current of power or energy between his hands, and he places them on either side of the affected area. Subjects often describe a sensation of great heat. LeShan, the original skeptic, is now working on psychic healing with a group of associates and getting medically observable results in 30 to 40 percent of the patients.

Sister M. Justa Smith, a Franciscan nun who is chairwoman of the Natural Sciences Concentration at Rosary Hill College, is a biochemist and an expert on enzymes. She performed a carefully scientific and apparently very objective study of the power in the hands of a healer, a Colonel Estebany. Working with enzymes in glass containers, using double-blind procedures and having the results recorded by technicians who did not know the purpose of the experiments, which were repeated many times over a period of weeks, Sister Justa found that the Colonel significantly increased the activity of the enzymes by holding the containers between his hands.

Edgar Cayce

Probably the most famous of modern healers was Edgar Cayce, who diagnosed illnesses and recommended treatments for many thousands of people. He himself did not understand his power and the diagnoses were performed in a state of deep trance, but their accuracy was corroborated by doctors. Olga and Ambrose Worrall, well-known healers, were able to heal from a distance as well as through actual contact. Experiments indicated they were able to transmit an energy form that affected the growth of rye grass and caused a pulsing effect in a cloud chamber used to detect high-energy particles.

The law takes a more skeptical view of healers, particularly those who advertise or make claims in advance. Kirk Oakes, operator of a so-called fulfillment center, was recently

351

fined $500 and placed on two years' probation, the first prosecution of a psychic healer in Los Angeles since 1926. He had claimed he could cure cancer, blindness, tuberculosis, arthritis, and cataracts, but undercover agents from the state Department of Health were not impressed.

In Bolinas, a coastal village north of San Francisco, Dr. Irving Oyle is helping his patients to heal themselves. Dr. Oyle, a general practitioner from Farmingdale, New York, became disillusioned over the results he was getting from traditional drugs and decided to try to involve the patient in his own battle against disease. The division between mind and body is a comparatively recent phenomenon, expressing the materialistic idea that there is nothing the mind can do to heal the body except to propel it to a doctor or put medicine in it. From the times of the ancient Egyptian and Chinese cultures down to the American Indian, mind and body were regarded as different aspects of the same thing. If there are malfunctions in the body, the mind can become involved and direct the body to get well. This is the basis for Dr. Oyle's therapy.

Remarkable Results

Using a high frequency sound wave to soothe his patients and induce an "alpha" brain-wave state, he tries to put them in touch with their healing centers. His goal is to quiet the left hemisphere of the brain which controls speech and reasoning, and which he refers to as the "male" hemisphere. The right side, which controls body images, is to him the "female" hemisphere. He tells his patients to get in touch with that female side and ask that the symptom or the illness be manifested in a picture. The patients are then told to request a picture of the healing. Remarkable results have been reported, which include cures ranging from slipped discs and glaucoma to stiff necks and skin infections. Oyle's theory is that no matter what kind of healing is taking place, whether it be surgery, acupuncture, or the laying on of hands, it is just a ritual to convince the patient he is going to get well. And if the patient is convinced, he will indeed get well.

A BRIEF INTRODUCTION TO PARAPSYCHOLOGY by DR. J. B. RHINE

Wishing to treat the subject of parapsychology in a way that would be truly authentic, I approached Dr. J. B. Rhine, who has done more than any other researcher now living to validate parapsychology as a science, to ask for a brief interview about his personal experiences in the field. I was not prepared for him to generously give me, in addition to the interview, his own Introduction to Parapsychology, *which offers a fuller account of the work of the man whose experiments have validated in turn the existence of ESP, psychokinesis, and the psychological analysis of psi phenomena.*

Under the sponsorship and guidance of Professor William McDougall, I began research in ESP in 1930. A series of psi investigations led to the development of a research center there which (in 1935) took the identifying title of The Parapsychology Laboratory of Duke University. In 1934 a monograph summarizing the results of the first three years of its work was published under the title *Extra-sensory Perception,* and in 1937 the *Journal of Parapsychology* was started with Professor McDougall and myself as editors. The Parapsychology Laboratory continued for 30 years as part of Duke University, maintaining a small staff of full-time research workers. With my retirement in September 1965, it became an independent center, The Institute for Parapsychology, sponsored by the Foundation for Research on the Nature of Man (College Station, Durham, North Carolina).

One of the main developments in parapsychology in the '30s consisted of the devising of methods of testing. There was great need of standardized procedures that could easily be repeated by different experimenters. A special pack of cards was designed for the easier investigation of ESP. It consisted of 25 cards, each having one of five geometric designs that had been selected for distinctiveness — star, square, waves, circle, and cross. The pack might be made up in either of two ways. It might have an equal number of cards of each symbol (closed pack), or it might be an "open" pack with an unequal number of the five symbols chosen by some random procedure. In either case, it could be taken for granted that an average score of five per 25, or a 20 percent rate of success, was to be expected from chance alone . . . .

Once methods of standardizing the testing of ESP had been developed, the logical next step was to design an experiment that would be crucial and so take the question of the occurrence of psi out of the realm of debatability. For the Duke investigators this was accomplished in 1933 when the Pearce-Pratt series of experiments was completed . . . .

The standard pack of ESP test cards was used. The cards were handled by J. G. Pratt, then a graduate student of psychology . . . . Hubert Pearce, a Divinity School student, was in a building a hundred yards away. Both men wore watches that were synchronized. Pearce attempted to identify the cards as Pratt isolated them one by one, without looking at them, as it had been explained to Pearce he would do. One minute was given to each card.

Two runs through the pack were made each day for six days. Duplicate copies of the records were made, and before they got together to check the number of successes or hits, each man sealed up one copy to be turned over to me. In the total of 300 trials that were made in the series, the number expected on a theory of chance was 60, or 20 percent. Actually, 119 hits, or approximately 40 percent, were made by Pearce. Such a result could hardly be thought of as explainable by chance, for it would not be expected once in more than a trillion of such experiments .... Nothing, then, but ESP could explain the results ....

ESP and Space-Time

While the flow of research continued to amass more and more evidence of ESP, the Duke inquiries spread out to include other questions. How was this ESP effect to be classified, first of all with regard to the field of physics?

One point that had stood out in the Pearce-Pratt results was that the average score Pearce made when he was 100 yards distant from the card was not below that which he made in experiments in which shorter distances were involved, and even those in which the cards were on the table in front of him. This ... gave rise to the suggestion that, in this kind of test, distance was not an important factor, a suggestion that had already been given ... by the large collection of spontaneous cases in which the persons concerned had been, in many instances, hundreds and even thousands of miles away from the events they clairvoyantly or telepathically perceived.

The suggestion that ESP was not related to the distance over which it operated raised another question. It seemed to follow logically that if *space* is not a limiting condition, ESP should be independent of *time* also. It seemed reasonable to attempt next to discover whether the subject in ESP tests could identify a future order of cards in the pack as well as a contemporaneous order. On this point, too, the collection of spontaneous material offered very definite and clearcut support ....

In the actual precognitive testing, the subject was asked to predict the sequence of symbols, not as it was at the time, but as it would be after the cards had been rearranged by shuffling .... Significant extrachance scoring was produced, and the first actual experimental testing of the old claim of prophecy became a matter of record in the Parapsychology Laboratory in December 1933 ....

Psychokinesis or PK

The investigation of PK began in an effort to see if a person can influence moving objects mentally and without muscular or other physical contact. It was noted that many people believe they can influence the fall of dice by direct action of the will. Accordingly, a method of experimenting was developed in which falling dice were used. The result was a gamelike test which enabled the subject to experience an easy conviction that he was able to influence them. Methods of handling the dice were introduced that eliminated the possibility that manual skills were used. Also, the test was so designed that any effect of inequalities in the structure of the dice could not cause an error in the interpretation of results ....

After eight years of investigation ... the staff of the Parapsychology Laboratory had arrived at a crucial type of demonstration of the case for the occurrence of a psychokinetic effect in the dice-throwing experiments. It was independent of any single experimental method. The development of this conclusive case led to the first publication of the results on psychokinesis in 1943 . . . .

The Psychology of PSI

. . . Once the investigators were reasonably sure that the main types of psi phenomena had been soundly demonstrated experimentally, it seemed logical to go as far as possible into the psychological analysis of just what was taking place in psi experience.

The chief psychological fact about psi . . . was that it operated in an almost completely unconscious way. At least in the experimental situation, the subject was unaware of how well he was doing even when he was making long sequences of hits in perfect order. He had no introspective guide as to when a true cognitive effect took place or whether or not in any given trial he was correct or incorrect in the response he felt impelled to make . . . .

Once the unconscious nature of psi had been recognized, many of the difficulties and peculiar results hitherto encountered were rendered more understandable. Take, for example, the spotty character of the successes in a sequence of trials. Operating in the dark, introspectively, as the subject was, there was bound to be a hit-or-miss quality to his responses even though he possessed some ESP capacity . . . .

Again, if a subject knew when he was right or knew definitely when he *was* wrong, he would have had the possibility of learning, accordingly, of improving his scoring rate, of discovering the conditions of more effective performance . . . .

Many other curious effects which were found in the researches are now less puzzling,

as, for example, the decline in scoring rate as a subject continues through a long sequence of trials . . . . Also, some subjects showed a tendency to displace their responses and hit the card just ahead of or the one just behind the intended target as they went through the run of trials in a test. These and other unconscious twists in the operation of the psi function were robbed of at least part of their mystery by the recognition of the failure of introspective consciousness to give any glimpse of the real process.

. . . It is probable that everyone has psi capacity but that there are individual, and even group, differences in the way in which the capacity is regarded. These may affect to some extent the readiness with which psi may be allowed to function. Even when a subject exercises psi in any form, he is, of course, a whole personality with many other functions and operations going on at the same time. Some of these may favor his exercise of psi in a test situation, whereas others may hinder it.

Status and Prospects of Parapsychology

. . . Experiments are no longer made merely to get evidence of psi, or to distinguish its types. Instead, psi is taken for granted, as well as the fact that clairvoyance, telepathy, and precognition are all types of one cognitive process, extrasensory perception (psychokinesis being the extramotor aspect of the psi ability). The question of whether psi is really nonphysical has been settled in large part by the growing weight of evidence for precognition. Also, the fact that the psi process is largely an unconscious one is now generally recognized.

This recognition has made more understandable one of the worst bugbears of psi research, the tendency for subjects under certain conditions to score significantly *below* mean chance expectation while trying to score above. Since the ESP process goes on unconsciously, the person has little control of it; therefore, if some unconscious disorientation should occur, his "aim" can be deflected like that of a rifleman with defective sights, and he can miss the target consistently without knowing he is doing so. The explanation of this effect, known as *psi-missing*, is one of the important problems for future research.

Another mark of change today is in the parapsychologist's perspective . . . . Earlier, most of the workers brought with them the perspectives of their previous fields, i.e., psychology, biology, physics, or engineering. Consequently, their problems tended to be questions as to the way psi fitted into the other disciplines. Today, investigators are more likely to select problems which bear directly on the nature of psi . . . .

With the new perspective, the challenge is, in fact, on the researcher and his skill in getting evidence of his phenomena. Psi occurs; but for reasons now at least partly understood, it is elusive. On this account, the experimenter must be able to get evidence of the ability before he can hope to study it . . . .

The important meaning of the results of parapsychological research today lies in its significance as a recognized part of human nature . . . . Men have always been groping for an understanding of their basic nature. Through the ages they have needed to know if the distinctive nonphysical element they have instinctively felt in themselves is a reality. The need has always existed, but never before has the scientific method been used directly in an attempt to satisfy it. The important thing now is not to let the reclassification become a point of philosophical argument, but rather, the starting point of a new order of investigation . . . .

interview / DR. J. B. RHINE
some perceptions of parapsychology

My interview with Dr. Rhine follows, and since it covers his career at some length, I have omitted personal details from this introduction.

LANDE: How did you yourself come to investigate the subject originally?

RHINE: In my college days, science won me away from a preministerial course, but it also offered a much too barren understanding of life and human values. Parapsychology (or psychical research) caught my attention with its claims of proof of life after death, and a few great men of science were already looking into these claims. My wife (Dr. Louisa E. Rhine) and I ventured a few cautious steps — went to Harvard for a year and then to Duke to work with the great psychologist, William McDougall, F.R.S., who was a leader in parapsychology as well. While at Harvard we studied under Dr. W. F. Prince, the leading American psychic researcher. At Duke we worked with McDougall on the appraisal of the claims and records of mediumship, the main topic of parapsychology then. This research financed our first year at Duke. Then we found positions, L.E.R. in botany and I in psychology and philosophy — but the main point was my position left me free to pursue psychic research at Duke with McDougall, perhaps the only such place there was in the world in 1927.

LANDE: What were the hardest kinds of opposition you faced?

RHINE: All of our advisors and most of our friends were vigorously against our move into this field. Not one of them supported us. They insisted that our careers would be ruined. "Wait until you are established," they advised. A second barrier was the lack of funds to support the venture; but we overcame that by holding other positions while we prepared to work in parapsychology. We spent 23 years struggling with this barrier after the start at Duke. It was 1950 before we were free to do parapsychological research on full time.

Then we met the cultural barrier. While Duke was tolerant and the psychologists in and out of the University were at first surprisingly open-minded, considerable criticism and opposition developed later on when publicity became excessive (beyond any power we had of controlling it). The dominant school of psychology in the 1930s was behaviorism, which was, to say the least, not favorable to ESP. But McDougall and Duke University stood firmly back of us, and the crisis passed. The vigorous outside opposition largely declined during the 1940s. Actually, in recent years there has been more controversy within the field than without.

LANDE: Which do you feel were your most exciting, your most gratifying discoveries?

RHINE: The most *exciting* experience happened at Duke in the mid-1930s. My best subject, H.P., made 25 successive hits (correct calls) in the card test for clairvoyant ESP; he was under the strongest challenge I knew how to give him. He paced back and forth in my office wanting to leave while he "guessed" the cards I had concealed behind my hand. This high score led me to think that science will

357

likely be able in time to achieve such high control over the ability.

The most intellectually *gratifying* advance came about after clairvoyance became firmly established and precognition was tested next. As results of the new test came in strong and conclusive, this became for me a peak scientific experience. Precognition, ESP of the future, seemed to me the most astonishing claim ever to have been scientifically tested and established. The test conditions had been built up to the highest pitch of controls we knew how to devise, yet the significant results kept on coming in, long after all counterhypotheses were ruled out. I knew of course these results were not final — science can never be final since new knowledge tomorrow may change the conclusion of today. But the case was as conclusive as we knew how to make it then.

LANDE: What about the most significant discovery?

RHINE: That is a different type of situation. It is a kind of evidence that cannot conceivably be ascribed to human error, consciously deliberate or unconsciously accidental. It depends on nobody's honesty or competence. It *has* to be proof of psi. It is evidence such as this:

Dr. X, a scientist, conducts a psi experiment and publishes his report. Many years later a new type of psi effect is discovered that Dr. X did not himself know of, and so did not claim and use as a basis of significance and interpretation of his work. When, independently, another scientist looked into Dr. X's results for evidence of the new psi effect and found it unmistakably there, the complex question of experimenter reliability had been transcended. The later independent analysis could be repeated ad lib.

It seems to me to be bedrock evidence. A mass of such fraud-proof evidence for psi has accumulated.

LANDE: Which of the current areas of activity in the field do you think will ultimately prove of most value?

RHINE: The study of ways in which the psi function can be made to operate, whether in the individual's own personal self-control or in the socially disciplined guidance of conduct. Hardly a beginning has so far been made on this line in the research centers; it is too early, the help is too slender, and the staffing has not been developed for such a program. But from what is already known about psi ability, it could function even unconsciously as a supporting factor in the acquisition of value concepts and also in influencing actual behavioral situations. The actual processes that occur, or can be induced to occur, may be understood in time. The problem is that the possibilities are so obvious that they will be (are, in fact, already being) claimed and practiced by religious and other groups *without* benefit of the careful scientific controls essential to reliability.

LANDE: What do you feel are the most important unknown areas yet to be worked on?

RHINE: It is most immediately urgent today to do the kind of psi research that is as understandable as it is reliable. We need help of many kinds — funds, personnel, status, and schools, among others. But to obtain this assistance, we need to be understood. What we are doing should *make sense.* Its usefulness, as well as its meaning, should be most obvious, as it can well be. On the other hand, we need *not* hasten to come up with a personal theory of psi, or a new set of terms; and it is *not* the most complex research design conceivable that is crucially needed today. Indeed, sheer novelty is even a handicap when we have not yet "sold the old model."

However, I certainly do not suggest bowing to mere popularity as such. Nor do I mean that the most obviously practical uses should dominate all research. But as it is, many of our *basic* research needs are both understandable and urgent; results from them are easily appreciated.

For example, how does psi compare with other unconscious cognitive abilities? Or, can good methods be designed to explore PK effects on the subject's own organic system? Again, what peculiar signs of the psi function can be found to identify it best in tests needing a psi-tracer device? Then, too, the search for improved *practical* techniques for testing psi can be most useful, whether the device is psychological or mechanical.

LANDE: What other countries are making significant progress in the field?

RHINE: As 1976 begins, two countries of Western Europe are showing new promise, the United Kingdom and The Netherlands. They also collaborate well and have no real language barrier. A new journal in English is just starting in Utrecht, *The European Journal of Parapsychology,* and in the United Kingdom two significant books have just appeared: John Randall's *Parapsychology and the Nature of Life* and Adrian Parker's *States of Mind: ESP and Alternate States of Consciousness.* Germany has an active university center at Freiburg and France has shown new interest in several universities. It is hard to say much about Eastern Europe at the moment. In Asia, from Israel to Japan, there is lively interest, with its peak in Indian universities. But on this subject the United

States has been leading the world for some decades, principally because of the unique feature of philanthropic aid to research. Nearly all the American work for the last 60 years (and much of that abroad too) has relied on this altruistic aid from the country's citizenry.

LANDE: Could you let your fancy roam about the outlook for the future?

RHINE: The prospects are fair, I think, that by A.D. 2000 parapsychology will be a dominant branch of the psychology department, which in turn will be the leading department in a School for the Science of Man on all the major university campuses of the world. Obviously the size of the threat parapsychology presents to psychology and other sciences is a measure of its potential significance. When psi has been firmly established and recognized, it will probably change psychology more profoundly than nuclear energetics has changed physics.

One future consequence, however, is on a surer basis: the effect of parapsychology on the disciplines that depend on what man is believed to be — religion, medicine, ethics, government, education, and so on. Take religion, for illustration, and remember its long losing battle with science. What if parapsychology should find that those discredited miracles (and all the supernatural theories of man's communication with his supposed spiritual order) are not wholly without some verifiable principles in man's own nature? Remember too what the discovery of some long-overlooked germs did to medicine in Pasteur's day. We do not need merely to speculate about the future of the humane disciplines when science is at last giving evidence of man's greater potential. The way is open to explore it.

Wisdom...
    is the
detached concern
    with life itself,
    and the faith
    of death itself.

    Eric Erickson

                                    Corita

CONSCIOUSNESS

Scientists, savants, philosophers, psychiatrists are advancing on the brain on all fronts, probing, measuring, questioning, dissecting. The boundaries of ignorance have been moved back dramatically in this century, but we still do not fully understand the workings of this mysterious mechanism. What we do know is that we no longer need stand in awe of the complex and lightning-fast workings of mechanical computers — our own billions of brain cells are even more remarkable. We can make more connections and perform functions that the electronic computer cannot begin to duplicate. We are baffled by the power of rational thought, the hidden sources of creativity, the marvels the human mind can conceive and achieve. It is beginning to appear that there is almost nothing the mind cannot do, from controlling the functions of its its bodily appendages flinging complex technological structures across the heavens.

Some of the newest research investigated here includes Delgado and his electrical and chemical probes into brain structure and function; research in the two hemispheres of the brain and their differing functions; Penfield, Lilly, and others, who have approached the brain with scalpel, drugs, and electroencephalographs to try to map and graph it. We seem to be on the brink of dramatic breakthroughs, but the suspicion grows that perhaps we will never be able to chart all the brain's elusive secrets. Is mind more than brain? It is beginning to appear so.

THE BRAIN AS COMPUTER

John von Neumann, in his book *The Computer and the Brain*, points out that the total amounts of thought fed into the brain as ideas and attitudes exceed the number of particles in the entire universe. The human brain far exceeds the ability of even the most sophisticated computer that man can develop to process and store information. No wonder it has been called "the enchanted room."

This vast storage capacity in the cortex is referred to as the experiential background. It consists of the sum total of the individual's life experiences before and after birth. The brain stores everything and forgets nothing. Information comes in not only through the five senses but other input routes, continually feeding messages at an enormous rate of speed. All this information processing functions at less than 1/8 of an ohm of electricity. It would take 100,000 Niagara Falls to supply the energy for filling the memory banks in the cortex.

The subcortex, the old part of the brain, functions like an executive secretary. It was the ancient smell or nose brain. Millions of years ago in our existence we had only one sense: smell. Through evolution the other senses, sight, taste, touch, and hearing, caused the nose brain to expand into its present part of the brain known as the cortex. This is a recent acquisition in man's development — perhaps a million years or so. The cortex by itself cannot execute orders; it is merely a discriminating center. The nose brain is now called the limbic system, and it is a relay station. For instance, incoming messages from within the body and outside the body are continually being sent up to the cortex for processing and validation. If the information jibes with the stored data, then this constitutes reality. So the living brain is guided by reality as it perceives reality — the stored data. Nothing could be simpler.

Information can be accurately recalled back to the age of maybe three or four, not much earlier. Most information before that time is stored as engrams. The nerves have not been covered by protective sheaths called myelin. Since they are not fully developed, transmission of impulses and storage as memories is not complete until four or five years of age. The individual may think he can recall something that happened when he was one or two or three, but this is "misremembering," using what we call "screen memories." If you are told at five or six what you did when you were two or three, and then again at 18, you think that you remember what happened when you were two or three instead of remembering the retelling.

— *William S. Kroger*

362

PROBING THE BRAIN

There are approximately 100 billion cells in that highly advanced computer, the human brain. Ninety billion of them are glial cells, the white matter making up the supporting troops for the elite 10 per cent, the roughly 10 billion neurons of the gray matter. Some estimates place the neuron count even higher, at 13 billion or more, and each neuron has many millions of RNA molecules that can receive coded instructions from DNA to turn out thousands of different proteins. It is not surprising that we understand only a small part of the intricacies of brain functioning. Apparently "thinking" is done by connections between cells via branches, across a gap known as a *synapse*. An electrical impulse crosses that gap and is relayed to the next cell in slightly altered form, with vast numbers of these connections continually occurring.

Priority Number One

The nourishment and protection of this marvelous mechanism is the number one function of the body. If there is a shortage of nutrients or of oxygen it will be borne by other parts of the organism; the brain must be fed first. And the blood circulating in the brain does not pulse — there are no changes in the vessels inside the delicate structures. At the site where the pulsing blood enters the brain the size of the vessel increases and the flow is modified.

One of the most noted experts on this incredibly complex organ is Dr. Jose Delgado, a Spanish scientist and pioneer brain researcher. Since the brain is both an electrical and a chemical system, its function can be affected in each mode. Dr. Delgado has done landmark research in both electrical and chemical stimulation of the brain in an effort to learn more about its operation, to deal with such problems as intractable pain and the malfunctioning in such conditions as epilepsy. Working with ever smaller and more sophisticated instrumentation, he has learned to insert fine steel electrodes into the brain in a painless procedure that permits research animals to move about freely. With this new equipment, Dr. Delgado learned that the stimulation which produced aggression in laboratory animals did not have the same effect when his subjects were running free.

Direct Communication

Some of the more important effects described by Delgado and his team of researchers are that it is possible to "teach" the brain without intervening sensory impressions, using a direct brain-to-computer linkup. Using this same direct communication, but without the computer, epilepsy can be brought under control with a surgically implanted device.

Effective control of pain has been achieved with electrodes placed under the skin at appropriate brain sites. Delgado's work has also shown that the environment can actually change the clinical makeup of brain cells. The resistance of the free-roaming animals to electronically stimulated aggression is one indication that we are a long way from electrical manipulation of the multitudes, or a computer "Big Brother" enslaving whole populations with electronic thought control.

There has been much speculation about the possibilities of electronic mood control, finding the "pleasure" spots in the brain and using a small electrical charge instead of two martinis to achieve relaxed, pleasurable states. Brain researchers can indeed stimulate those centers, can electrically trigger outbursts of affection, and, to an extent, control aggression. Dr. Delgado demonstrated this most dramatically in a bull-ring when, complete with cape, he halted a charging bull by short-circuiting an electrode planted in the amygdala. At present, however, these techniques are used primarily for research in the functioning of the brain.

Violent Behavior

A great deal of work is being done to locate centers in the brain that can trigger violence, often because of cells damaged by illness or injury. In order to locate the precise spot, electrodes must be placed inside the brain and tested. The amygdala is usually involved in cases of repeated violent behavior and most experiments indicate it is the source of such impulses. In a demonstration of one of Dr. Vernon Mark's patients at Boston City Hospital, she was happily playing her guitar and when the electrode in her right amygdala was stimulated by a signal sent from another room, she stopped playing and smashed the guitar against the wall.

When the precise spot is located, violently aggressive behavior can be altered, sometimes by stimulation alone. More often the offending damaged or abnormal cells must be "burned out" or removed. This procedure can put an end to the incidents of violence, but in some cases they recur. In less extreme cases, behavior can be altered just as dramatically and with much less risk with a new battery of drugs. Lithium and the so-called tricyclic drugs such as elavil and tofernil are highly effective tools in cases of depression and similar abnormal mental states. And the traditional methods of training or behavior modification, like the carrot and the stick, will also be around for a long time.

One after another, so-called "mental" illnesses believed incurable or originating from strictly psychological causes have been found to have physiological origins. Paresis, mental illness associated with the B vitamin deficiency in pellagra, and many others are now treated or prevented with therapies of diet or drugs. Experiments with spiders showed that when injected with minute amounts of blood from schizophrenic patients they spun weird webs, indicating that this mental disorder also has a biochemical origin. And with the new drugs mentioned above, formerly intractable cases of severe depression are being relieved.

The work of Delgado and others does give promise of improving education, preventing the stunting of brain development in embryos or infants by proper nutrition, finding and possibly removing some causes of drug addiction, and correcting more extreme forms of antisocial behavior. As information accumulates and understanding increases, the day is approaching when mental disorders ranging from psychoses to a slight case of the blahs will be curable by chemical, electrical, or self-modification of these states and will present a host of problems as to the legality, morality, and even the advisability of the more drastic types of behavior modification with surgery or other techniques that are irreversible. Specters of thought control and the manipulation of helpless individuals make this an area that demands careful study to make sure such procedures are properly monitored and the patients protected. It is those who are least able to protect themselves who are usually candidates for such drastic medical or surgical intervention.

OUR DIVIDED BRAIN

"The scientific-academic mind and the feminine mystical mind shy from each other's facts, just as they shy from each other's temper and spirit."
— William James

James was referring to the minds of two different types of people, but he might well have been describing the two "minds" that coexist in every human brain, symbols of two ways of perceiving and experiencing the world.

At the Institute for the Study of Human Consciousness in the Langley Porter Neuropsychiatric Institute in San Francisco, research psychologists Robert Ornstein and David Galin are exploring new ways of studying the human mind, of realizing its vast potential. Hoping to synthesize the behavioral and humanistic schools of thought into a new model of human consciousness, Ornstein and Galin insist that knowledge is not exclusively rational: hunches, insights, and flashes of intuitive truth affect our behavior much of the time. They urge the recognition of more than one way of knowing, and that the new techniques of Western science be fully employed to study the esoteric psychologies of the East. Both disciplines can learn from each other, just as the complementary modes of the two hemispheres of the brain enhance its functioning. The greatest progress in both

understanding and increasing the capacity of our minds will come when the divergent views fuse on a higher plane that reflects an integration of both the rational and intuitive approach.

Limited Sensory Dimensions

Suppose we were to visit a primitive tribe and tell the people to imagine millions and trillions of electronic messages floating in the air. Astonishing, since they never heard of television! So it is, says Ornstein, with us. We simply have not developed the technical equipment — receptors — to pick up the tremendous quantities of energy that float in the air around and about us. We are restricted by our physical evolution to only a few sensory dimensions and if we do not possess a "sense" for a given energy form such as infrared radiation, X-rays, or ultrasonics, we do not experience its existence. We perceive only a very small amount of what's going on out there and that remains the sum total of our reality. And this in turn influences our physiological development because the dominant senses are simply relied upon and refined.

Using scientific tools of research to explore and define the chemistry and physiology of the brain, Ornstein and Galin are proving that we are virtually ignorant of half of its capacity. Much has been learned about the two hemispheres by studying "split-brain" subjects in whom the corpus callosum, the connecting link, has been surgically severed. In such subjects functions become divorced to the extent that there is actual conflict between the two sides. When tested by portions of words flashed separately to each side of the brain, the split-brain subjects were unable to form a coherent whole. When one hand had difficulty in solving a problem, the other hand would reach out to correct it. Old proverbs were suddenly made real: "His left hand doesn't know what his right hand is doing," or "I'm of two minds about that."

Mystical Half of the Brain

Since the brain division in these experiments was of course artificial and was done to correct malfunctioning because of severe epilepsy, it does not follow that the data can be completely extrapolated and related to normal brains. Studying split brains does give a better understanding, however, of the division of function that apparently occurs. It is hypothesized that in man's evolution this division originally took place to allow for specialization, so that each half of the brain could concentrate on what it did best without being distracted by functions assigned to the partner. However, researchers now suggest that in our verbal, linear, analytic culture we may have allowed the left, or major, hemisphere to become too dominant and are denying an important part of our consciousness. We may be shutting ourselves off from a more holistic, timeless, centered part of ourselves, from achieving the "body-knowing" that Don Juan speaks of in Carlos Castaneda's novels. Philosophers and religious leaders over the centuries have referred both directly and obliquely to this "buried" part of our mind, the nonverbal yet powerful source of "higher" wisdom. If we

can still the wordy chatter of our left hemisphere and become aware of the messages from the dark, silent, mystical half, we could be more in touch with the deepest reality. "Be still, and know that I am God."

Hidden Sources

Musicians, artists, geniuses such as Einstein have told of ideas coming from some hidden source, appearing full-blown in their consciousness; of symphonies that almost write themselves, of answers to long-pondered problems that appear in a dream or when least expected. It has been suggested that this "lesser" or "minor" half of the brain is the repository of the cosmic consciousness and therefore the pathway to so-called paranormal information used in telepathy and precognition. Because we are so conditioned to the cultural patterns around us, to our "normal" ways of thinking, it has also been hypothesized that we shut off much of the information this nonverbal portion of our minds is trying to supply. We deny or shrug off its messages, much as one hand struggled with the other in the split-brain experiments.

Yehudi Menuhin, who began his career as a child prodigy, has described the way he played the violin when he was very young; he did the correct things without thinking about them. As he grew older he found it necessary to begin again and to consciously relearn the things he had once done intuitively. Another musician, a pianist, has described a similar phenomenon. In her early years she read and played the music as a series of patterns, as a whole perceived and performed without any sensation of conscious reasoning. It was not necessary, for example, to plot out the beats in a measure and count them, since she played them as a visual figure. After a few years away from music, she found it necessary to apply conscious thought processes — This is a half note, This is a quarter note, This gets two beats — particularly when dealing with the somewhat arbitrary time constructions of avant-garde composers. Perhaps the right hemisphere of her brain read the music as pattern in the first instance, whereas it was necessary to invoke the conscious, linear reasoning of the left hemisphere when this spontaneous faculty became less accessible.

The Right Hemisphere

It is a function of the right hemisphere to recognize faces, perceive pattern, deal with spatial orientation. Among Eskimos and so-called educationally disadvantaged groups in our culture, children are found to be incredibly good at grasping pattern and structure, at learning to repair complex mechanisms.

Dr. Joseph Bogen, who performed the split-brain operation, has described a man who was found, in an autopsy, to have one cerebral hemisphere missing. Apparently it is not necessary to have two hemispheres in your brain to have a "mind" or to be a whole person, indicating that with the two halves we literally have two minds, with a specialization that gives us more efficiency but also more internal conflict.

Only In Man

Joseph Pearce, author of *Exploring the Crack in the Cosmic Egg* believes the specialization of the two sides of the brain might be a result of man's adaptation to the culture-orienting process. Apparently this lateral specialization does not exist in animals. Pearce believes that as the mind gets farther away from a centered, natural mode of being and into the verbal deceptions of the culture, part of it clings to the "body-knowing" and its original relationship to the life flow.

The right side of the brain perceives things simultaneously, intuits meanings, grasps concepts, symbols and forms, yet it does not have the means to communicate what it knows to be true. If it is severely damaged, we might suffer disorientation in space, lack the ability to carry out artistic endeavors and crafts, lose our sense of body image. The right side processes information more diffusely than the left hemisphere and its responsibilities demand a ready integration of many inputs at once. Indeed, some things are perceived only by way of gestures, facial and body movements, or simply a tone of voice.

Dual Consciousness

The recognition that we possess two cerebral hemispheres specialized to operate in different modes may allow us to understand much about the fundamental duality of our consciousness, whether it be described as reason and passion, mind and intuition, or conscious and unconscious.

In Ornstein's words, the world of life's experiences cannot be reduced to reason, yet we only let into our conscious awareness that which we can describe. But what if we allow ourselves to imagine that there is so much more to be known? To conceive of this possibility may indeed make it so. It is an act of pure creativity. Ornstein points to the man who ran the four-minute mile. Everyone said it couldn't be done, yet Roger Bannister decided to accomplish it, and did. Quite soon many others were able to perform what was once considered impossible. Our lives are full of infinite possibilities if only we allow ourselves to expand our awareness and rise to a higher level of consciousness by opening both sides of our minds.

MEMORY MECHANISMS

While performing brain surgery on epileptic victims in 1951, Dr. Wilder Penfield made the fascinating discovery that stimulating the temporal cortex of the brain with an electrode at a specific point recalled specific, detailed memories. The patients were fully conscious and could speak with Dr. Penfield about what was occurring. A fraction of a second's stimulation invariably elicited the same bit of information or memory, whether it was the sight of a specific storefront or the sound of a specific bar of music. The experience was recalled quite involuntarily, in a rush of detail, along with the feelings associated with it. It differed from remembering in that it did not consist of thinking about a past occurrence; instead, it was a mental and emotional "reliving" of the incident, in which the event and the feeling were involuntarily recalled, apparently because they were inextricably linked in the brain.

Such reliving can occur without artificial stimulation of the brain. Sounds, smells, sights, can usher in tremendous surges of sadness, joy, emotion. These present stimulations recall past experiences, even though it may sometimes require digging to discover the specific incident that triggered the feeling permanently associated with it in the brain. The subsequent conscious, voluntary recollection of the event, however, does not have the same quality of "I'm there!" as the initial, intense re-experiencing.

It appears that whenever a normal person is paying conscious attention, he is recording the experiences in the temporal cortex of each hemisphere. The recordings are sequential and continuous, hence the triggering of memory works like an actual event. But we only recall what we were paying attention to at the time, not the mass of sensory impulses that were simultaneously bombarding us. Each individual's memory, then, is a subjective recording of his unique responses to each situation.

When new experiences occur they are coded in with similar experiences from the past. As Dr. Penfield expressed it, "A new experience is somehow immediately classified together with records of former similar experience so that judgment of differences and similarities is possible." He conjectured that memory was probably stored in specific cells; other researchers believe it may be randomly stored. Whatever the mechanism, both the memories and the judgments based on them are unique to each individual. Does the capacity to recall the past lie in some primary genetic mechanism, such as DNA?

IMAGINATION

Attempting to formulate theorems and rules for that flash of creative intuition that triggers great poetry, scientific discoveries, new mathematical systems, is in itself a mind-bending task. Scholarly probing into the act of creative thought, a process as awesome and mysterious as birth itself, was the dedicated undertaking of Professor Harold Rugg of Columbia University. Jung said, "The creative act will forever elude the human understanding," but Rugg and others have attempted to prove this statement false.

The Magic of Thought

Professor Rugg asks, "What is the nature of the act of thought when, in one brilliant moment, there is a sudden veering of attention, a consequent grasp of new dimensions, and a new idea is born? Some autonomous forming process sweeps like a magnet across the chaotic elements of the threshold state, picking up the significant segments, and, in a welding flash, precipitates the meaningful response. What is this magical force that forms the bits and pieces of the stuff of mind?"

The great leaps forward in science and the creative masterpieces of high art are products of these explosions of insight. In an attempt to pin down that elusive process which almost defies analysis, some basic concepts can be articulated. The phenomenon can only be understood if one frees oneself from the traditional splitting of a mechanical versus an organic explanation of man's being, thinking and behaving; as well as separating the intuitive and the scientific approaches to knowledge. To understand the creative process the two approaches must be joined. The sum of human knowledge is pyramiding at such an incredible rate that even to grasp the basic concepts in each field is an enormous task. We must have more generalists, more people with at least an overview of knowledge, if we are going to understand the workings and the achievements of the mind. We need the autistic, intuitive approach of Eastern philosophy as well as the conscious, linguistic modalities of the West.

Powerful Creative Flashes

Studying hundreds of descriptions of the creative process, Rugg repeatedly identified a sequence of events. These powerful creative flashes do not come unsought. The first step seems to be a long, conscious struggle to organize a coherent, logical body of ideas, to solve a problem, to create the discipline of a work of art from a set of chaotic materials. After the long search, the often discouraging pursuit of solutions, the mind turns to other things and suddenly the solution leaps unbidden into consciousness. There is a feeling of absolute certainty, of the validity and rightness of this new concept, but then must come the work of consciously clarifying, certifying, critically testing and reconstructing the solution. The "imaginative flash" cannot be willed. It slips through the doors of consciousness only when they are left unguarded and must be preceded by concentration on the problem at hand. Sometimes this preliminary gestation period is very long: months, or even years, can pass after the posing of a problem or the seminal concept of a work of the imagination. And the answer often comes after a period of confusion, when the solution seems far away.

The Phenomenon of Serendipity

The mind must be off guard. It is on the fringe of consciousness where "the spark explodes the meaning," and brings the multiple aspects together into a perfectly organized whole. And while a vast body of knowledge must be fed into the subconscious before the creative explosion can take place, often the new concept may be a parallel or unsought one — the phenomenon of serendipity. Some of the greatest advancements in science have been triggered by seeming accident, when an alert investigator dropped his regular work to follow a will-o'-the-wisp. Fleming discovered penicillin when an unknown mold blew in through the window. Roentgen's X-rays and Edison's photoelectric cell were unsought discoveries, "accidents" to be observed by an inquisitive mind, which could juxtapose them with existing knowledge to make creative breakthroughs.

According to Rugg, the illuminating flash occurs at a critical threshold of the conscious-nonconscious continuum on which all of life is lived. Much of Einstein's creative thought was nonverbal — "a thought comes and I may try to express it in words afterward." It is the releasing of the conscious mind, the "no mind" of Eastern disciplines such as Tao or Zen. Rugg describes it as "two end sections, the conscious and the unconscious, connected by a dynamic, transliminal antechamber in which the creative flash occurs."

The Necessary Atmosphere

Stimulating sensory conditions seems to facilitate the process, varying with the individual — lots of black coffee, Proust's cork-lined room, certain kinds of ink or paper — anything that is basic to concentration and to establishing the proper emotional mood. There must be discipline and form, but passion and emotion must also be present for the act of discovery.

As Rugg sums it up, the optimum conditions for creativity would appear to be:

"the quiet mind of relaxed concentration, prolonged conscious preparation, pertinent and ordered storage in the nonconscious mind, a perceptive and alert observer, the stimulation of curious aids to concentration, the disciplinary effect of the form of the medium and finally the compelling and passionate drive. But one mood pervades them all — the mood of quiet intuitive concentration."

BRAIN RESEARCH / The Salk Institute

A distinguished group of scientists, including four Nobel Prize winners, are at work in the cement cubes of the Salk Institute for Biological Studies on a cliff overlooking the Pacific in La Jolla, California. In this dramatic setting, teams of researchers are attacking a multiplicity of problems and coming up with dramatic answers, or at least the beginnings of answers.

Researchers in the Neurobiology Laboratory who have been studying the basic functioning of the brain made a significant breakthrough when they succeeded in forming a working connection between a piece of spinal cord and a muscle cell grown in a culture dish. The group was studying the simplest level of brain function, the interaction of one individual cell with another. With its billions of nerve cells the brain is capable of an infinite number of connections; however, the number of

possibilities for the way these connections are made should be limited.

Investigation of Cloned Cells

The group worked with a clonal cell line, a laboratory culture of millions of cells grown by the division of a single cell in endless repetitions of an identical pattern. As yet the researchers are unable to study the synapse, or connection, one nerve cell makes with another. But the connections a nerve cell makes with a muscle cell can be investigated by inserting minute electrodes into individual cells and measuring the passage of current across the cell membrane.

The investigators are seeking to find out the nature of the small molecules which are directly responsible for the transfer of information from one cell to another across the synapse, and the mechanisms by which these molecules affect the cell after the impulse has crossed the synapse. These electrical events depend on a special class of molecules which are being studied through the venom of cobras and scorpions. The lethal effects of these poisons are caused by molecules which inactivate specific parts of the electrically excitable membrane of nerve and muscle. Using the poisons, it is possible to dissect the excitable membrane and study the interaction between its components.

Failure, Then Success

To carry out its research the group is developing clonal cell lines from both muscle and brain cells. The clonal cells provide a useful tool for studying mechanisms of cell communication in experiments which would have been impossible to attempt in living animals. The attempt to form a working connection, or synapse, between a nerve cell and a muscle cell from the clonal lines did not succeed. Next the researchers tried a piece of living nerve tissue taken from the spinal cord of a rat. This time, it worked — the first occasion when a clonal cell line has formed a working synapse in laboratory culture. From this first step, the group hopes eventually to begin to solve the puzzle of exactly how synapses are formed, and begin to get some understanding of the working of that immensely complex organ, the human brain.

Working with cobra venom and electric eels, Dr. Jon Lindstrom and Dr. Jim Patrick have isolated the substance by which nerves transmit their signals to muscles, or receptors. After they had isolated a protein by using the toxin to absorb it from a solution, they injected it into rabbits and found that antibodies were developed which not only blocked the activity of eel electric cells, but also the rabbits' muscle activity. The rabbits developed a form of paralysis which seemed to mimic myasthenia gravis in humans; hopefully, it may offer new insights into the actual mechanism of this fatal disease, giving new impetus to the possibility of finding a cure.

Mapping the Brain

In the Arthur Vining Davis Center researchers are studying the chemical structure of the brain, mapping it and monitoring the activity of individual nerve cells. By studying the chemical activity of the norepinephrine circuit and its neighbor, the dopamine circuit, and the "pleasure centers," they are learning more about how this chemistry helps a cell concentrate on its task. This research gives promise of treatment for behavioral problems such as those giving rise to alcoholism or forms of drug abuse.

Biologists in the Neuroendocrinology Laboratory have discovered a new hormone, somatostatin, which reduces blood sugar levels in animals. This research confirmed an earlier theory that an excess of another hormone, glucagon, was the cause of high blood-sugar levels in diabetics who were taking insulin. The new hormone inhibits the release of glucagon and appears to be a weapon not only for the control of severe diabetes but also for reducing one of its most distressing side effects, blindness. Somatostatin also inhibits the secretion of somatotropin, which is found in high levels in patients with juvenile diabetes and is believed to be a major factor in the retinal degeneration that can occur.

VISIT WITH A RENAISSANCE MAN

JOHN LILLY/ The Center of Many Cyclones

John Lilly is a Renaissance man: scientist, writer, teacher, poet, trained in the fields of medicine, biophysics, neurophysiology, psychophysiology, psychophysics, and psychoanalysis. He received his basic education in science at the California Institute of Technology and went on to obtain a medical degree from the University of Pennsylvania. To pursue his interest in brain-mind research, he continued his work in bio- and neuro-physics at the E. R. Johnson Foundation of Medical Physics and moonlighted by attending the Institute of the Philadelphia Association for Psychoanalysis at the same time. After completing his own training analysis he became a qualified psychoanalyst.

In 1953, at the National Institute of Neurological Disease and Blindness and the National Institute of Mental Health, he did outstanding research with monkey brains. To try to settle a controversy about brain physiology and sleep, he became interested in methods of eliminating external sensory stimulation to learn whether the brain would go to sleep or would stay awake on its own energy sources. He learned of a tank in a soundproof room in an isolated part of the campus at the National Institute of Health, left over from World War II research. He added a temperature control valve and began experimenting in it. Shut off from external sound or light sources, floating in water at 93 degrees Fahrenheit temperature, he found that unusual states of consciousness were experienced. He has been working with the "Lilly tank" ever since, using one for several hours almost daily. In the tank, freed from the bodily adjustments necessitated by gravity and from virtually all external stimuli, consciousness moves back on itself.

Each person responds differently to the experience: some hallucinate, all sorts of explorations of inner space are accomplished, but nearly everyone describes it in positive terms. And most tank trippers have a strong feeling of calmness and peace after the session.

As a result of the early gravity-free immersions, Lilly began to speculate about other animals with a brain size comparable to that of humans, whose lives were spent entirely in water. To explore these ideas he began research with dolphins in 1955 and later, in the Virgin Islands, in 1959. His innovative experiments indicated that not only were the playful dolphins very intelligent, but they had the capacity to communicate with man as well as with each other. Because other researchers would not replicate these results and because of his unconcealed affection for his subjects, Lilly was accused of anthropomorphism. His reply was that man's arrogant assumption that he is the only truly intelligent animal, the only one capable of communicating ideas of more than minimum complexity, is sheer prejudice. To find the capabilities his research indicated were present in dolphins, one must first believe in the possibility. Gradually he became convinced that it was wrong, even for scientific purposes, to keep dolphins in captivity or to "use" them for any purpose. After closing down his research facility and freeing the remaining animals, he set out to map and explore his own consciousness.

interview / JOHN C. LILLY, M.D.
visit with a renaissance man

I had the good fortune to meet John Lilly early in my research on this book; he is, quite frankly, one of the most impressive men I have met, with a vast range of knowledge and a gift for expressing it succinctly and with clarity. In the course of several talks, he told me briefly about the course of his inner journey, which he has described in detail in his book The Center of the Cyclone, *and discoursed at length about such subjects as pain, the "moat effect," awareness of responsibility, and where man is headed. Some extracts from these interviews follow:*

LANDE: When you left the dolphins and wanted to go and explore yourself . . .

LILLY: I wanted to find out what is wrong with the human species. Not just me. Otherwise I would have stayed with the dolphins. And I would have worked with them in a much more ethical fashion, instead of being the objective scientist, keeping them in confinement. My transformation was necessary before I could get back to work with them.

LANDE: What kind of transformation?

LILLY: In 1969 I went to Esalen, spent two years there, then I went to Arica, in Chile, and worked in the Instituto de Gnosologia with Oscar Ichazo. I had to explore the gnostic belief that religious revelation is the property of the individual; he has to work on it himself.

I was brought up as a Catholic, and the Catholic belief is quite counter to that. The revelations of God come from others, they don't come from the individual. It's a heresy to believe in individual revelation; the Church wants control.

One of the blind alleys that humans have gone down, again and again, is that of getting caught up in group movements that begin to expand and take over. The belief becomes rigidified and there's no longer access to the original source of inspiration. I spent seven months on my own work. At that point I found the group was getting rigidified, so I left. I had learned what I had to know, that there were techniques of getting into "far-out places," getting into Samadhi or Satori. I learned the techniques, went into those states, and then came back.

But the transformation I went through started even earlier. In 1954 I began the isolation tank research. I finished my psychoanalysis and I went into the tank a year later and worked with it for 12 years. The dolphin thing didn't start until 1955. I was floating around in the tank and thought I should be working with an animal that floats around all the time, because it is very different from being exposed to gravity in air. The counter gravity forces in air are quite a stricture on what we can and can't do. When you float in a tank you begin to realize that somebody swimming in the sea all the time, 24 hours a day, must have an entirely different kind of consciousness. I want to emphasize that I started working with dolphins as a consequence of the tank work and of the work I was doing in neurophysiology.

Later, 1973, I decided to try a long-term experiment in Samadhi. I spent a year in and out of it, and Toni, my wife, has some horrendous tales about what that leads to. It means one leaves the responsibility for one's bodily welfare up to other people. My sustaining group consisted of one other person, Toni, instead of a whole group of followers, such as Yogananda had, the Maharishi has, and so on.

If one wants to play in that area of the far-out spaces within one's own mind and spirit, one needs a support system — someone to take care of the practical problems, the money, the travel, the food, the clothing. And by one's charisma, one can influence the others in such a way that they do this quite automatically in order to achieve the same reward.

I'm not that kind of person. I went into that state to investigate what it is. Samadhi, and Satori too, means to me a responsibility. You don't stay in those states, you work on trying to achieve something which will allow all sentient creatures to share them in safety. I don't see this business of me sitting or lying in the tank for 16 hours a day and working the other eight. I use the tank now as a rest. It's the most profound rest one can get. If I am too worn out, I get in the tank for half an hour, clean out completely, void out all the previous programming. I return my mind to what I want to work on and go to work on it just as intensely as I'm working with you. That seems to me to be the main usefulness in the United States for Samadhi and Satori, for going into the void. I prefer to use the term *void*, because what I do in the tank is just totally leave my body, the universe, the whole business. It's really a zeroed out place.

LANDE: With regard to a learning experience, can you isolate your most important experience?

LILLY: There are episodes all through my life that taught me more dramatically than others, but the accumulated experience generates this point of view: I need no more catastrophic dramas in my life. I've had enough of those. I've learned there are negative things that happen in order to teach a given individual new lessons. Accidents in which one breaks a lot of bones or goes into a coma are the kinds of things I don't need anymore. I've had them. A lot of people haven't had these experiences, and I see a naivete in them which is incredible, because they don't know what ultimate survival of the vehicle they live in really is. For example, they haven't experienced pain.

I spent 12 weeks in pain after breaking my shoulder, sitting in bed propped up at 45 degrees. The negative teaches in a very peculiar way. It's a domain of human experience which is absolutely necessary. This seems to be built into our brains. The negative reinforcing systems that cause pain and anger are controllable by the cortex. When you are forced by broken bones to experience pain, you become a much simpler organism. During that 12 weeks my thinking wasn't worth a damn, and I had to know that. *I had to know that pain drains the brain* — one's level of accomplishment is terrible.

LANDE: What about emotional pain?

LILLY: If you mean depression and grief,

yes, they do the same thing. There is a preoccupation that develops. In order to come back to being a normal functioning person, one has to go through a therapeutic period of not spending so much time with one's big cerebral cortex. To survive one has to pay attention, to allow regrowth of bones, regrowth of cells, whatever is necessary. And anybody who has been through a chronic disease or a long-term experience like that has a kind of wisdom that is very different from the usual.

We heal ourselves. What is healing? A lot of people think healing is preventing pain. It isn't. The ultimate in healing is allowing people to go through painful experiences, emotional, negative experiences, in order to know what those are. The ultimate compassion is not preventing a child from hurting himself but making sure the child knows he must relax once he's hurt himself, and recover and not be overwhelmed by the experience. The next time he's hurt, he has additional programs which prevent his doing foolish things.

There's a difference between pity, sympathy, and compassion. Separate those out very, very carefully. You can have a lot of sympathy for somebody who is hurt. But if you have pity for him you may do the wrong thing. Whereas if you have a long-term compassion, you may allow him or her to go through the pain and not give pain killers, for example.

LANDE: How about an illness where there's great pain involved?

LILLY: I'd say let them go through the pain because they will then learn something that was known in the last century before anesthesia. It is that they can control it when it becomes overwhelming. Pain has its ceiling,

as well as its threshold.

I studied some of the people who went through torture in World War II. With torture — and the torturers know this — there is a certain point beyond which pain doesn't pay. The person in pain leaves the pained body: coma supervenes. Actually, they stay conscious but they're in other spaces. During World War II people who were going on special missions were taught this lesson. Harold Wolff at Cornell used various techniques to show them their pain had a ceiling and taught them how to handle that ceiling. This is tough-minded stuff. It's not the usual medical view.

Most medical people give patients pain killers, but they also give them tranquilizers, to get them out of the way so they can treat them. Somebody who is ignorant of the ceiling of pain and who goes into a panic state can rebreak his bones. When you come into the emergency ward in a coma, they don't know who you are, they don't know your capacity. After one of my severe accidents, it took me five days to get to the point where I could even *talk* to the doctor because of the medication they had been giving me, and when I could I said, "I want no more sleeping pills, no more pain killers, no more of that stuff." I just endured the pain, and then I learned what it does.

LANDE: Why do you think so many people today are seeking meaning and awareness?

LILLY: Go back through our social history. We started out in this country with the constitutional right to one's own religion; we set aside religion as a very special case, in the law and every other place. Religion was formalized, so that with a fixed belief system you could belong to this group or that group or another group. That began to collapse with the onset of World War II. We went through scenes of vast destruction, and the responsibility for killing a quarter of a million people in Hiroshima and Nagasaki. That changed the whole view of man right there.

Taking a longer term view, if we hadn't had those lessons, nobody would have believed the power available — there would be just reports and movies. I can't be moral about this one way or the other, though at the time I was quite moral about it. Maybe that's the kind of lesson we have to have in order to prevent a holocaust. I don't know that it will prevent it — maybe it will.

Then you have the psychedelic experiences with marijuana, LSD, and all the rest. There was research going on, and a few individuals who were not scientific, but artistic or philosophical, took it and wrote books about it. A lot of people went through the experience. And then the panic laws of 1966 came in, and the counter movement from the establishment, the national negative program on LSD, developed to the point where these things disappeared. But the use of marijuana kept growing. As I understand it, more kids got turned on to marijuana in Vietnam than anywhere else, and when they started coming back, we had a whole new breed of young people who stepped forward to do something about it. And they did, which freaked out the establishment.

There is a whole new wave in that sense. I don't like to call it a new wave of consciousness; it's an awareness of the responsibility of man to man which has developed. Young law people, young scientists are willing now to take responsibility for what they're doing. Still, there are those who don't take that responsibility, and they far outnumber the

others. We may *have* to have an atomic holocaust with the survival of only a few people to clean up the planet. Einstein was once asked what weapons would be used in World War III. He said, "I can't tell you what weapons will be used in World War III, but I can tell you what will be used in World War IV: Sticks and stones."

LANDE: Why is there so much orientation in mindstyles towards the East?

LILLY: Because our educational system has not offered any courses in the last hundred years which have anything to do with one's inner realities. When I was a student at Cal Tech, for example, we had mathematics and natural sciences. The juniors and seniors got together and said, "We need a course in psychology, and we don't want all this Pavlovian stuff and the Skinnerian stuff, we want the psychology of our selves, our own minds. Who is man? Who is the observer?" These kids in the '30s were already asking those questions.

Finally the faculty got a man who gave a course across the board, about psychoanalysis, about Wilhelm Reich, about Jung. The faculty insisted that the course be given in the evening from 8 to 10. Well, if you know Cal Tech students, you know they can't afford that amount of time away from other studies. This had to be an elective course — there was no credit for it. They didn't expect many people, so they started out in a small classroom. And the professor looked around and saw the room filled with so many people, they had to give him an auditorium. From that point on, he gave these lectures once a week. The whole senior and junior class attended, and the sophomores and freshmen came when they could. It was just incredible, the amount of interest. Why? Because he was giving information about what goes on inside one's head from a nonreligious standpoint. He included religion, but from the standpoint of an observer looking at religion, not immersed in it. This is what is defective in our educational system, the lack of that kind of information. Slowly but surely, however, courses are being established.

LANDE: So the educational system has to be reevaluated?

LILLY: Sometimes you encounter hostility because of what I call the moat effect. That's a property of our central nervous system. If you shine a small spot of light on the retina, the spot of light excites the neurons and the end organs of the neurons immediately under it, and it is surrounded by a ring of inhibition which enhances the contrast. We repeated it as an experiment in the cerebral cortex and discovered that when we stimulated just a little spot of the cortex, it was surrounded by a moat of inhibition. Now if you diagram this, the activity surrounding the hyperactive spot drops way off, and then here, beyond the moat, there's normal activity going on.

People are like this too. Say that I'm educated in a certain area and I'm taught to value that over and above the surrounding territory. If I'm a lawyer, I'm taught that science is in the moat. If I'm a scientist, I'm taught that law is in the moat. And if I'm a theological student, I'm taught that everybody else is in the moat. So we tend to arrive at a mesa in which we think we know everything that's on that particular mesa, but when we look around, the landscape is studded with other mesas.

Now, how do people show this? By denigrating, by demeaning, by reducing in importance points of view that differ from theirs. You can see politicians, everybody

doing this. The important thing to realize is that the areas of our knowledge are filled with ignorance and negative responses. Everybody protects his castle, his mesa, and the others attack. If you try to attack them through the moat, you get nowhere.

I've generally found that you have to start out by giving credence to other mesas. Each person can rise from his own mesa and take a more aerial view of what's going on around. And then he suddenly realizes that his particular moat is full of little holes that go down to infinity, and that he's been walking on a set of tightropes, a skein of knowledge which isn't necessarily so.

LANDE: What if other people are trying to hurt you?

LILLY: They're trying to stay on top of their mesas. There are several approaches one can use, depending on the person and where he is open. Hostility generates only very narrow communication channels; with lack of hostility the channel is wider. As soon as somebody gets emotional, he closes down and becomes a very narrow channel. I try to find out what the belief was that generated the negativity. If I can find that belief, I don't attack it, I ask him to examine it.

In the province of the mind what one believes to be true, either is true or becomes true. I believe that statement, and if you know how to use that with people, then you know that's the platform on which they are operating. Then you can find out additional information about where they feel positive, and you can begin to connect across the barriers they have, so that you don't generate hostility.

There's a classic example of this. In the early '60s I was invited to a cocktail party in New York by a psychiatrist friend. I'd just come up from the Virgin Islands where I was working with dolphins. There were about 50 people in the room. Margaret Mead was all the way across the room. She saw me come in, and she shouted at me across the room, "John Lilly, if you think you'll ever talk to a whale, you're psychotic." With a lot of humor, you see. So I went over and talked to her, and I said, "Well, Margaret, what is psychosis?" Now, no psychotic asks that question. And we got along very well after that.

She was epitomizing the reaction of the group consensus to what I was doing at the time. And she decided to do it in her usual dramatic way. By provoking me, she got the information she wanted.

My father used to use that technique with me. I would propose, say, going to Cal Tech instead of going to Harvard, and he would blow his top. He'd say, "It's stupid to get yourself all tied up in science and not realize that there are other areas of human knowledge," and would carry on and rant and rave for a while, and I'd go away and have to think. And I'd come back with very well-organized plans about what I wanted to learn, and why Cal Tech was the place I wanted to go, and he'd go, "Humphh." Mother would come in — she was always the fall guy for father — and sort of smooth things over.

In the meantime, I went and took the entrance exams to Cal Tech. They wouldn't accept College Boards. I was already entered in MIT and accepted. I was only 18 years old, and they were the toughest exams I had taken up to that point, designed by scientists trying to find young scientists with talent. At the end of the three days of exams, I thought, "I really flunked out on that."

About three weeks later the letter came from Cal Tech, and they gave me a scholarship on the basis of my performance. So I thumbed my nose at my old man. I said, "See . . . ."

LANDE: And it worked.

LILLY: He had aroused my anger. He knew how young men operate — he'd been that way himself. He had been exposed to a father who did that to him.

Many years later, when I was much older, he said, "I want to give you some advice about anger. Never allow your anger to get to the level at which you cannot function with somebody. If you're angry, go and get out if you can't control it. Learn how to act 'as if' you are angry." I went back over my own life with him and I said, "Well, I've been dealing with a practical psychologist who really knows what he's doing."

But he never revealed this until much later, when we were both old enough so we could talk.

LANDE: Where is man going?

LILLY: It seems to me the next step in the evolution of man is to find out about his own brain, not only where it came from, but where it's possible for it to go, and also his own mind, in terms of taking on a set of beliefs for temporary, pragmatic purposes, as is taught in the better sciences. Some sciences are so full of dogma, they're impossible. But the best sciences, those that are making the quickest progress, realize this. The biggest area for the future of man, as far as I can see, is more effective research on the possible types of programming we can do to get a perspective, by communication with brains larger than ours. Instead of making dogmatic statements about them, find out about them. Who are they? We don't know. We need to find out.

interview/ DR. ANTOINETTA LILLY
cosmic surfing

While talking and visiting with John Lilly, I talked with his wife Toni — at far greater length than this brief note would indicate. She is a dynamic, strikingly handsome woman whose varied background indicates the range of her intellectual and artistic involvement: she is an artist, who has studied at the Los Angeles Art Center, Chouinard Institute, and Otis Institute; she has been a costume designer, a film maker, and has particular talent for designing environments for creative living and working; she is also a trained psychotherapist. I owe much information and many valuable leads to her remarkably inclusive knowledge of what is going on in the field of mindstyles today.

LILLY: My own experience of using the human biocomputer model has been a help to the way I program myself. It has also made me even more aware of the domain of the observer in my behavior. It seems everything always gets down to where the observer is in your system. In physics, in psychology — it all eventually comes down to that. And now, finally, science is beginning to say that the observer is affecting the system that it observes. I call that cosmic surfing.

Of course, if you're too much of the observer, you're not involved, and there's not enough joy. You can also be a complete observer and be a narcissistic bliss ninny — just sitting there and not taking part in the process for which energy was put into your vehicle to begin with. How much of that energy do you allow to be expressed by the life force? In females, it's very different than it is in males.

LANDE: How so?

LILLY: The difference between a male and a female is that the female takes her inner reality and projects it on her outer reality. Something she knows comes from a groundedness that is connected to the life force. And a male will get out there and put a piece of technical stuff together and will think that's the reality — and he applies that to his inner reality. That's the balance game again. You see it in Yin and Yang. I know myself that very often I am much more Yang than I am Yin. It's the other side of the coin, the snake eating its tail. The dichotomies are always present in my life, the Yin-Yang in myself and the Yin-Yang in my dyad.

All this is cosmic surfing, and that's the way I try to live. I'm successful most of the time; not all of the time. When I'm not, I'm tolerant.

ECCO: A Grand Design

There exists a *Cosmic Coincidence Control Center* (CCCC) with a Galactic substation called *Galactic Coincidence Control* (GCC). Within GCC is a *Solar System Control Unit* (SSCU), within which is the *Earth Coincidence Control Office*: ECCO, sometimes mistakenly shortened to ECO, as in ECOSYSTEMS and in ECOLOGY [the study of the Earth (Coincidence) Control Office]. Down through the hierarchy of Coincidence Control (from Cosmic to Galactic to Solar System to Earth) is a chain of command with greater and greater specification of regulation of Coincidences appropriate to each level in the system. The assignment of responsibilities from the top to the bottom of this system of control is by a set of regulations, which, translated by ECCO for us humans, is somewhat as follows:

"**To all humans:**

If you wish to control coincidences in your own life on the planet Earth, we will cooperate and determine those coincidences for you under the following conditions:

1. You must know/assume/simulate our existence in ECCO.

2. You must be willing to accept our responsibility for control of your coincidences.

3. You must exert your *best capabilities* for your survival programs and your own development as an advancing/advanced member of ECCO's earthside corps of controlled coincidence workers. You are expected to use your best intelligence in this service.

4. You are expected to expect the unexpected every minute every hour of every day and of every night.

5. You must be able to remain conscious/thinking/reasoning no matter what events we arrange to happen to you. Some of these events will seem cataclysmic/ catastrophic/overwhelming; remember, stay aware, no matter what happens/apparently-happens to you.

6. You are in our training program for life; there is no escape from it; we (not you) control the long-term coincidences. You (not we) control the shorter term coincidences by your own efforts.

7. Your major mission on Earth is to discover/create that which we do to control the long-term coincidence patterns; you are being trained to do this job.

8. When your mission on planet Earth is completed, you will no longer be required to remain/return there.

9. Remember the motto passed to us (from GCC via SSCU): *'Cosmic Love is absolutely Ruthless and Highly Indifferent; it teaches its lessons whether you like/ dislike them or not.'* (**End of Instructions**)"

— John C. and Antonietta Lilly

ALTERED STATES OF CONSCIOUSNESS

Our normal waking consciousness . . . is but one special type of consciousness, whilst all about it, parted from it by the filmiest of screens, there lie potential forms of consciousness entirely different. We may go through life without suspecting their existence; but apply the requisite stimulus, and at a touch they are all there in all their completeness, definite types of mentality which probably somewhere have their field of application and adaptation. No account of the universe in its totality can be final which leaves these other forms of consciousness quite disregarded. How to regard them is the question — for they are so discontinuous with ordinary consciousness. Yet they may determine attitudes though they cannot furnish formulas, and open a region though they fail to give a map. At any rate, they forbid a premature closing of our accounts with reality.

— William James

An altered state of consciousness is defined as one in which there is a significant difference in the quality or pattern of our mental functioning. Consciousness is not "altered" as was your grandmother's cat, but there is a change. These "other" states have traditionally been difficult to characterize. Frequently when an attempt is made to do so, the person who has undergone the experience begins, "Words cannot describe . . . . "

Consciousness can be altered in many ways: drugs, meditative techniques, various physical agents, illness, monotony, fasting, epilepsy, hypnotism. Some episodes occur spontaneously, such as Saul's dramatic conversion on the road to Damascus. There are reports of anesthetics inducing mystical experiences similar to those reported from the use of psychedelic drugs. Modern researchers have developed innovative approaches such as the Lilly tank, described on page 373, where an absence of external sensory stimuli and freedom from the accustomed effects of gravity can cause hallucinations and various other paranormal states. At the Foundation for Mind Research they obtain similar effects by using an Altered States of Consciousness Induction Device, or ASCID, a kind of metal swing or pendulum suggested by a "witches' cradle" used in medieval times. The subject, blindfolded, stands within the cradle and is swung gently about.

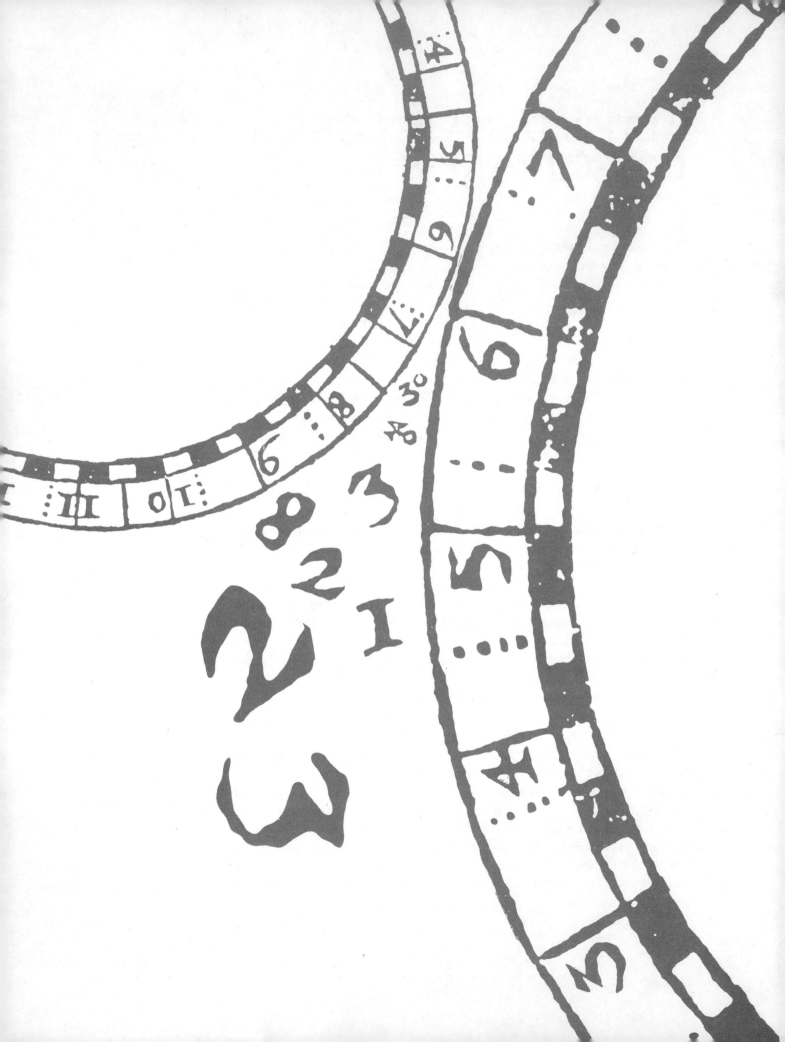

Most of the "other" states have been characterized as experiences of expanded consciousness, of more intense "seeing" of ordinary objects: the grass is radiantly green, light is brighter, commonplace materials vibrate with an intense luminosity. There is a perception of wholeness, of suddenly understanding the nature and meaning of the universe, of being one with it. And for the most part such experiences seem to leave a positive residue in the mind.

Religious mystics since earliest times have written about altered states of consciousness, have sought them as a form of union with God or with the cosmic consciousness. The author of the medieval poem, *The Cloud Of Unknowing*, speaks of the "longing for God" and how one must "smite upon that thick cloud of unknowing with a sharp dart of longing love" until the self disappears. The highest states of Eastern religious systems such as Zen and Yoga are Satori and Samadhi, terms for the sensation of the physical self dropping away and a realization of unity with the infinite. And usually the new realizations, new perceptions about one's relationship to the universe persist into the "normal" state.

Traditionally, trance states have been used for healing, for prophecy and divination. In our modern society they have been found useful for mental healing, for curing all manner of psychic disorders and sicknesses of the soul, as well as alcoholism, impotence, and other conditions difficult to treat by conventional therapies.

Dr. Ainslie Mears, psychiatrist and author of *Relief Without Drugs*, has had remarkable success in treating a wide variety of psychological problems by simple relaxation procedures. As his patients gradually learn complete relaxation of body and mind, they attain a state of regression. Buried material comes into the conscious mind, so do new ways of looking at problems and new concepts, and the phobias and neuroses disappear.

An advocate of Yoga techniques describes a similar process. Using complete bodily relaxation and either prayer or meditation, the mind becomes relaxed. Going into the "silence" *(sankara)*, without any suppressive will, the posture automatically becomes erect and neck and throat muscles relax of their own accord. In deeper relaxation even the ego becomes relaxed and pinpricks are not felt. Complexes causing uncontrolled stress are automatically exposed and gradually eliminated. Desires are there but are not poignant; you learn to live in the living present.

interview/ SIDNEY COHEN, M.D.
the current situation

Cohen has also written The Beyond Within: The LSD Story *and* The Drug Dilemma. *Considered one of the nation's foremost experts on drug usage and the physical, psychological, and legal problems involved, Dr. Cohen is called upon to help draft the laws dealing with the control and treatment of drug abuse.*

LANDE: What is meant by an altered state of consciousness?

COHEN: As I understand it, it means some change in awareness other than ordinary reality. Furthermore, it usually means a positive state. To be delirious is an altered state of consciousness, but that isn't what people mean by the term; what they mean is increased perception, awareness, insight, a state they determine as being beneficial. It is my feeling that our present preoccupation with altered states of consciousness derives from the earlier LSD experiments of many people. It wasn't until people started, shall we say, blowing their minds with LSD that they said, "Oh, wait — there's something going on which ordinary awareness doesn't encompass." They rediscovered, let's say, the altered states of consciousness. In fact, throughout history, this has been a very valued experience, and people who experienced intense altered states of consciousness were made into shamans, witch doctors, and high priests.

LANDE: Do you think such people used any sort of mind-altering drug?

COHEN: Not necessarily. I think some of them achieved it by strenuous exercise such as prayer, meditation, going down into a mine or a cave and sitting there for long periods of time, utilizing methods that decrease sensory input or change the focus of attention. Sleep deprivation, for instance, and many other conditions can produce such a change in consciousness — although we do know of some instances where chemicals were used.

LANDE: You've done considerable research using LSD as an approach to psychotherapy. Did you achieve significant results?

COHEN: Our studies were exploratory. They weren't the tightly controlled and designed studies that are required in order to make absolute statements about significant results, but they were very interesting to those of us who participated in them. They indicated that LSD released very repressed memories and thereby might help to achieve better awareness by the patient and by his therapist about what was going on underneath. Furthermore, under other conditions LSD produced a state which you could call chemical transcendence. It seemed to us that there are certain people who become alcoholics or drug abusers because of a feeling of emptiness, a feeling there is nothing to believe in, nothing out there. We felt that administering this chemical transcendental experience might give them a feeling that there is indeed some meaning in life, some design in the universe, that it isn't all a buzzing confusion without significance. Not everyone was cured of their problems by this high-dose LSD experience, but I must say enough patients were improved in their subsequent behavior for us to feel there was a possibility of using this as a therapeutic cure.

LANDE: Do you see a relationship between mysticism and LSD?

COHEN: Some subjects of mine had what seemed to be an extreme alteration of consciousness, which included feelings of exaltation, of great significance, of inability to express these with words of perceptual wonder. I was reminded of some earlier readings I had done on mystical experiences in literature, and when one compares the effects of such LSD states with what are described as mystical experiences, there is a strong resemblance. I think we can speak of a chemical mystical state — but we mustn't forget there are important differences. The most important, to my mind, is that in the natural state, which seems to come out of nowhere, the person usually is a participant in its generation, whereas with LSD he has borrowed a substance which then proceeds to uncover the state.

LANDE: I'm fascinated when I hear someone describing that state as a blinding white light, being covered in it — again it goes back to the mystical experience.

COHEN: Precisely. Many of the mystics mention this perceptual blaze, and something similar has been described to me by quite a few of my LSD subjects.

LANDE: As a drug expert, would you comment on the findings of the Fifth Federal Report on Marijuana?

COHEN: It seems to tell us that use of marijuana such as is going on in this country at present is probably not going to be associated with any serious debilitating complications. We now have reports on three studies from other cultures — Greece, Jamaica, and Costa Rica — where marijuana is used almost from adolescence until death by peasants, laborers and farmers. The quality is better, and it is used in far greater quantities than we use here. These studies indicate that not too much was found in the way of loss of ability to function physically and mentally, and when psychologically tested, these people showed no particular difference compared to a control group of nonsmokers.

Adding that information to the material that has been accumulating from my own study and a couple of others that are doing similar work, we are coming to the conclusion there is probably no motivational syndrome and any impairment that happens in connection with marijuana use is probably not going to be very significant.

LANDE: I take it you agree with the Fifth Report?

COHEN: I wrote a part of it, so I guess I do, in general. And I also endorse the trend that various states are taking to decriminalize the possession of small amounts of marijuana. I think the hazard of arresting people — especially young people — and giving them criminal records for possessing less than an ounce of marijuana is not only a waste of legal time but very harmful to the young person.

LANDE: Why do you think the drug-oriented culture of the 1960s came into being?

COHEN: I would guess a couple of things were happening. One was the research with

LSD and the fact that Huxley and Heard, Alan Watts and many other distinguished people tried it, reported it, and wrote fascinating accounts of their experiences. Later it became available everywhere to anybody. The other aspect was that in our logical development perhaps the time was right for change. We were very troubled with the political and military events that were going on at that time and were looking for something more than we had — and this was something more than young Americans had — or have.

LANDE: What do you think of LSD in the work you have done with it?

COHEN: It's the most wonderful and the most terrible of drugs. On the one hand, I think it has a potential for helping us understand mental functioning and may, I do believe, have potential for assisting certain kinds of troubled people, if it's skillfully used. On the other hand, it has a potential harm. Not everyone should have LSD, and no one should have it under the conditions that it is sometimes used out on the street. I've seen horror, panic, psychosis, dread, and everything negative that a human being can encounter in connection with an LSD experience which was given casually — without safeguards, without selection of who was to get it, without supervision of the individual while he was in this vulnerable state, and so forth.

LANDE: How do you feel about cocaine? Does it create paranoia?

COHEN: It surely does, especially when it is used many, many times. Cocaine produces an intense euphoria which many people relish, and although it is not addicting, it can be psychologically dependence-producing, because of this highly pleasurable state. I have

found that people who take it over a period of time do seem to become suspicious and paranoid — perhaps because of this very intensity.

LANDE: Do you think there will be a cycle in drug taking?

COHEN: I think we're seeing it now. We're seeing ups and downs, at least, with many of the drugs. Marijuana seems to be going up at present year by year. The strong hallucinogens seem to be leveling off, although they are still being used. But we don't hear as much about the horrors because I think people are being a little more cautious and taking smaller doses. Heroin went away for a few years, and now it's back. I think that was strictly a matter of the availability of heroin during the couple of years consumption went down. Cocaine is increasing somewhat; on the other hand, use of the amphetamines, which produce a state like that of cocaine, is diminishing. There are some pretty obvious reasons why some drugs increase and decrease, but I think there is a faddish quality to drug taking. People seem to follow the leader; if he drops something, then they drop it, and if he picks it up, they pick it up.

LANDE: Have you found that marijuana has any particular effects on the brain?

COHEN: Yes. You know the hemispheres of the brain are believed to have somewhat different functions. The left side is more involved in things like logical thinking, reasoning, mathematical abilities, and items of this sort. It's a sort of survival brain which helps us cope with what's going on outside. Whereas the right side of the brain is more inclined to deal with the artistic, nonrational features of our existence.

One good way to think of it is that the left side of the brain adds up a column of figures and the right side of the brain can complete a drawing which is incomplete by seeing the whole thing as a *Gestalt,* a whole image. It is nonlinear thinking, as it were.

We have some preliminary evidence in our work indicating that there seems to be a shift from left-sided cerebral dominance to right-sided cerebral dominance under the influence of a drug like marijuana. Now, this hasn't been done with drugs like LSD, but I would suspect that a similar situation might occur.

LANDE: If some drugs can create a high, can depression also be induced chemically?

COHEN: Yes. The pattern of chemical changes in the brain which results in depression can be produced by drugs that we know about, which have been used in experiments to produce depression. I am thinking of a drug like reserpine. If it is taken in fair quantities, at least a healthy minority of the individuals who take it will feel and look depressed. If you didn't know they were taking reserpine, you would diagnose their reactions as depressive.

LANDE: Two of the most prescribed drugs in the country are Valium and Elavil. Could you comment on the role of the tranquilizer in our society?

COHEN: Elavil is an antidepressant with some tranquilizing properties, and is widely used. So are other antidepressants, drugs related to Elavil, perhaps because this is a depressed society. Valium and drugs like Valium are also widely used because this is an age of anxiety. I think that whereas in the old days a person might have endured his anxiety or his depression, now he is not inclined to do so, and will take a chemical for some relief from this obnoxious effect. So we have two things going on apparently — one, an increase in our emotions about what is going on around us, and, two, a reluctance to tough it out or to simply endure and suffer through these anxieties and depressions. Depression passes, you know. Anxiety may remain fairly chronic if it isn't dealt with one way or another. The advantage of these drugs as I see it is not that they cure the symptom but that they allow the person who has that symptom to be able to understand and learn to cope with future episodes of anxiety and depression.

PSYCHOACTIVE DRUGS
which are they? what do they do?

One of the most unsettling phenomena of the 1960s was the emergence of the "drug culture," with millions of mostly young Americans sampling a variety of seemingly strange, new, and dangerous drugs.

What we were witnessing, however, was not the first initiation of psychoactive drugs into American culture. Following Western tradition, our society had already accepted the regular presence of a psychoactive drug — alcohol, despite the fact that it can be physically and mentally harmful, can lead to violence, and is addictive and sometimes lethal. Ignoring or forgetful of this existing tradition of alcohol drug use and abuse, Americans found themselves confronted by a whole spectrum of unfamiliar psychoactive drugs, and understandably felt threatened by their widespread illegal use, as well as the lack of accurate unbiased information about their aftereffects, both short- and long-term.

Time has remedied much of the hysteria, and though the drug culture is still with us, most of our initial fears have somewhat abated. Many of these new drugs are used (as is alcohol) for recreation, to get "high." Marijuana especially has gained a large following, and from present research it would seem that it is a far safer drug than alcohol.

Amphetamines and barbiturates, synthetic drugs discovered in this century, originally entered the market as legal drugs, prescribed medicinally; however, they soon became "recreational," and were sold and used illegally. Cocaine, which had been used for centuries by the Andean Indians, gained rapid popularity. So did the opiates, heroin and morphine, introduced from Asia and first used on a large scale as medical analgesics. Their illegal use blossomed widely, bringing with it the demon of addiction.

Rediscovery of peyote and psilocybin, both related to Native American religious traditions, together with LSD, a synthetic drug first produced in the 1930s, created a new reason for taking drugs. Young American users thought of these drugs as more than just another "high." They dubbed them "mind expanders," and considered them a means of achieving an altered, higher conception of consciousness and of life as a whole.

Considering the technological advancement of our society, it does not seem strange that new psychoactive drugs should come to be so widely used. Nor is it really strange that a society so constantly curious about the way the rest of the world lives should adopt the drugs of other cultures, just as many Americans have adopted Eastern religions. What is definite is that the new psychoactive drugs have become the symbol, and often the instrument of the search for alternate lifestyles and alternate forms of consciousness. What follows is a brief survey of the major drugs and what is known about their effects.

Marijuana

Marijuana is by far the most popular psychoactive drug in the United States, excluding the legal drug, alcohol. One estimate of marijuana usage states that two million Americans smoke it every day, another seven million use it at least once a week, and 25 million have experimented with it at least once.

Marijuana consists of the leaves and flowering tops of the Indian hemp plant *cannabis sativa*, which grows both wild and cultivated in temperate climates throughout the world, including all of the United States. During a particular season the plant exudes a sticky resin which is most abundant among the leaves and especially among the flowers growing uppermost on the plant. Concentrated in the resin is the active compound tetrahydrocannabinol, THC. The THC content in marijuana, which can vary from mere traces to more than 5 percent, determines the drug's potency.

Marijuana has been classified legally as a narcotic, primarily for reasons of control. Medically, it has been classified with the LSD-like drugs, but now it is recognized as unique, combining the properties of a sedative, a euphoriant, and a hallucinogen.

Experiences with marijuana vary. However, certain characteristics of a marijuana "high" are widely reported: The mind wanders in a kind of stream of consciousness, a dreamy, euphoric state. Feelings of gaiety and jocularity are induced, together with a preoccupation with simple and familiar thoughts and ideas. A greater enjoyment of sensory perception can occur: increased appreciation of sounds, tastes, textures, and smells. Increased appetite is common. Short-term memory and the ability to think logically in a linear manner are sometimes impaired, causing a segmented thought pattern. Antisocial behavior is rare, while aggressiveness seems to decrease. Adverse experiences with marijuana seem to be related to large dosages (i.e., high consumption of THC), when a panic reaction or paranoid state can occur in some individuals.

Marijuana is not physically addictive. The "amotivational syndrome," a theory which speculates that heavy marijuana smoking can cause apathy and lethargy, is as yet unsubstantiated. At this time, no studies have shown that marijuana causes or facilitates criminal behavior, sexual promiscuity, or the use of other, more dangerous drugs.

Significantly, the Fifth Annual Federal Report on Marijuana states that no research has shown that marijuana, as used in this country, causes any serious mental or physical pathologies. Nor is there any indication that harmful effects occur with long-term usage.

Overall, then, as more and more research is done, marijuana appears to be becoming recognized as one of the safest psychoactive drugs. Many researchers and many reports give it a clean bill of health, while no research has definitely proven any serious deleterious effects.

Hashish is composed mainly of the dried resin of the *cannabis sativa* plant. This gives it a high THC content, usually around 5 percent, making it roughly five times as potent as marijuana. Hallucinogenic effects are more likely to occur, simply because of the increased THC intake, especially when hashish is eaten. A person smoking can stop when a desired "high" is reached, but when the drug is eaten the effect is delayed and the potency is unknown.

Amphetamines

"Dexies," "Bennies," "Meth Crystal," and "White Crosses" are slang terms for the amphetamines, a group of synthetic psychoactive drugs including Methedrine, Dexedrine, and Benzedrine. Around 30 amphetamine preparations and compounds distributed by some 15 pharmaceutical companies are on the market. Besides these legal drugs, large quantities of illicit amphetamines are produced and black-marketed every year, while many of the legally manufactured amphetamines end up on the illicit market.

The amphetamines are direct central nervous system stimulants that were first synthesized and used in the 1930s. The initial effects of an oral dose are alertness and lessening of fatigue, hence the drugs' popularity with long-distance truck drivers and students studying for examinations. Amphetamines can produce feelings of confidence, well-being, elation, and excitement, and they improve both mental acuity and mental and physical performance. Sustained, continuous use, however, eventually results in fatigue overriding the exhilarating effects of the drug, causing brief lapses in alertness and blocking of coherent thought. Also, after the drug wears off, the user may suffer from insomnia, depression, nervousness, and inability to concentrate.

The amphetamine boom began when doctors started prescribing the drugs as antidepressants; it really got moving when they were enlisted in America's never-ending search for a simple means of losing weight, because they inhibit appetite. This "diet pill" boom popularized legal amphetamines, and it was not long before they began to be used recreationally, and illicitly.

The 1960s saw the emergence of the "speed freak," who would inject himself with increasing quantities of Methedrine "crystal" powder, in order to induce longer and longer sensations of good feeling. The initial reaction is an orgasmic "rush" of euphoria, lasting several minutes, followed by feelings of extreme well-being, self-confidence, and hyperactivity. Although amphetamine use is not physically addictive, tolerance builds up, forcing larger and larger dosages of the drug, which is already being injected in tremendous quantities, compared with oral dosages. Short- and long-term use of injected Methedrine can cause hearing and visual hallucinations, paranoid delusions, extremely depressive

It might turn out that exploring
the far out spaces of human consciousness
is the fastest way to social transformation
John Lilly

Corita

states, and temporary loss of memory. Physically, the sleeplessness, constant hyperactivity, and starvation diet wreak havoc on the body, and cases of malnutrition and hepatitis are common.

Cocaine

Cocaine strongly resembles the amphetamines in effects. Although legally classified as a narcotic (carrying a felony charge), medically it is a topical anesthetic and potent central nervous system stimulant. It is derived from the coca plant of Peru and Bolivia and is regularly used by Quechuan Indians, who chew the leaves. Cocaine has had considerable popularity in the past. Probably its best-known addict is a fictional one: Sherlock Holmes. But no less a luminary than Sigmund Freud used cocaine for a period of time and wrote papers defending it. He discontinued both use and support, however, when some of the serious effects of the drug were discovered.

Cocaine is either sniffed through the nose or injected. Euphoric excitement occurs even when it is sniffed or "snorted" nasally. Feelings of tremendous physical and mental capability are engendered, as well as an arousal of sexual desire. Users report that topical application of cocaine to the sexual organs greatly enhances sexual relations. Intravenous injection produces a very short "rush," so users often repeat injections every five to 15 minutes.

Sniffing can irritate the nasal membranes and result in nose bleeds. Large dosages can cause rapid heartbeat with palpitations, tactile, audial, and visual hallucinations, and paranoid delusions. The question of addiction is still being debated. While physical dependence probably does not occur, the severe depression suffered by heavy users

on withdrawal is considered by some authorities to be a symptom of addiction. Normally, a slight depressive state follows any use of cocaine.

Cocaine is often considered a status symbol among drug users, largely because it instills a superhuman feeling and connotes sexual prowess. The price of cocaine also makes it a status symbol. A gram costs from $50 to $100, and an ounce from $1,000 to $1,500. A couple can easily "snort" a hundred dollars worth of cocaine in a day, which makes it almost as expensive a habit as heroin.

Barbiturates

Barbiturate "downers," like amphetamine "uppers," are used both legally and illegally. Chemically derived from barbituric acid, barbiturates are central nervous system depressants. Phenobarbital is a long-acting barbiturate while secobarbital (Seconal) is short-acting, meaning that it acts more quickly and for a shorter duration.

Barbiturates calm and relax by inhibiting the nervous system, the heart, the muscles, and the respiratory system. Mental acuity is decreased and speech is slowed. At higher dosages, they act as a hypnotic, facilitating sleep.

Their popularity is unfortunate for a number of reasons. First, the barbiturate user quickly develops a tolerance necessitating greater quantities. The level of tolerance rises very easily to a fatal level. A user who overdoses dies of respiratory failure. Second, barbiturates at doses higher than medically prescribed are addictive, and the withdrawal process is dangerous, painful, and very difficult. While low consumption causes a relaxed euphoria, further consumption produces hostility and aggressiveness. Some experts feel that next to alcohol, the short-acting barbiturate Seconal is the most violence-producing drug.

The Narcotics: Heroin

Medically, the narcotics include opium, morphine, heroin, and codeine. Opium is derived from the opium poppy. Morphine, the basic active ingredient of opium, is approximately 10 times as strong as raw opium. Heroin is further derived from morphine and is converted back to morphine by the body. Both morphine and heroin can be eaten, sniffed, or injected under the skin or into a muscle, but for greatest effect the drug is injected, "mainlined," into a vein. The term *narcotics* simply means that these drugs have sedative and analgesic effects, and their legal, medical use is as pain killers. But narcotics do not make a patient immune to pain; rather, they act to divorce the patient from the reality of pain, while the sedative effects decrease fear of, anxiety about, and emotional reaction to pain.

The initial "rush" of heroin is often quoted as one of its most pleasurable effects, but apparently this only occurs when the drug is injected into a vein. Sometimes the rush is not pleasurable at all, and once tolerance builds the feeling may disappear completely. The most important effect is the relief from negative mental or physical feelings, and, for the addict, the avoidance or curtailment of withdrawal symptoms.

The narcotics are definitely addictive. Tolerance builds up and physical dependence develops. Withdrawal is acutely painful, both mentally and physically, and in cases of abrupt withdrawal, death may even result. Even after complete withdrawal, the great majority of ex-addicts return to heroin use. The idea that one injection of heroin will cause addiction is a myth; but the point at which addiction occurs is variable. Some people have been able to use heroin occasionally over a period without becoming addicted; others have instantly "fallen in love" with the drug and begun daily injections. The majority fall between the two extremes: they take heroin a few times and either quit or continue. If they continue, the chances are that dosages and frequency will increase — and they are hooked.

Most of the physically and mentally harmful effects attributed to the narcotic drugs are unfounded. The drugs themselves do not account for any serious medical pathologies. It is the lifestyle engendered by addiction that is the major culprit. The addict usually lives in poverty because of the high cost of narcotics on the black market and often because of inability to work. This means that he or she cannot afford adequate food, proper health care, or a decent place to live. In many cases addicts resort to theft, burglary, and prostitution in order to get money to support an ever more expensive habit. Heroin does not in itself instill violent behavior. But the threat of or the onset of the agonies of withdrawal can cause the addict to commit violence in order to get more of the drug and gain relief.

LSD and LSD-like Drugs

LSD, mescaline, and psilocybin form one of the most controversial drug groups. Antagonists claim they are the easiest road to insanity, while proponents insist they are the route to cosmic consciousness. While the debate continues, Americans go on consuming them and experiencing their effects. Because of the wide usage and ready availability of these drugs, some knowledge of them becomes indispensable.

Peyote, the oldest drug used by man, is

derived from the dumpling (peyote) cactus, which grows throughout the Rio Grande Valley. The "buttons" on the top of the cactus are cut off and dried in the sun. These peyote or mescal buttons contain the drug mescaline. Peyote was widely used by the Indians of central Mexico for religious purposes when the Spaniards arrived, and it is still used today in northern Mexico, and by the Navajos, Apaches, and Comanches in the United States. In fact, its use as an integral part of services by the Native American Church of North America is completely legal. Mescaline, derived from peyote and now synthetically produced, is similar to LSD but not as potent. Psilocybin, obtained from psilocybin mushrooms, has also been traditionally used by Mexican Indians for religious purposes. Its effects are strikingly similar to those of mescaline.

LSD, which is synthesized from a parasitic fungus of rye, is a relative newcomer. Technically termed d-lysergic acid diethylamide tartrate, it was discovered in 1938 by a Swiss chemist, Dr. Albert Hofmann, who inadvertently tested it on himself in 1943 and then bicycled to his home — surely one of the most remarkable rides ever taken! Immediately recognized as an incredibly potent hallucinogen, LSD was first distributed to and used by psychiatrists strictly in psychotherapy situations.

In the United States one of the pioneers in LSD research was Dr. John C. Lilly, who spent 12 years investigating its effectiveness in conditions of sensory deprivation as a means of reprogramming the brain (see page 396). Another was Dr. Sidney Cohen, an interview with whom appears on page 397.

During this period of research, which lasted from 1949 to the mid-1960s, when the government first began trying to curtail and finally end the experimental use of LSD with humans, the drug was used in treating alcoholism and with terminal cancer patients. Some of the results were impressive, but there was no definite proof of the overall effectiveness of LSD in psychotherapy at the time research was terminated. Although the drug is no longer legally used in the United States, some study and research continues in Europe.

Serious claims concerning the physical harmfulness of LSD have been made and need to be considered. Physical dependence or addiction does not occur. The pattern of usage is generally infrequent and is usually not sustained over long time periods, although a minority of "acid heads" frequently or even constantly use LSD. The chemical itself has never been physically lethal; a need for larger dosages does occur with constant use, but it rapidly disappears if the drug is discontinued. The much advertised theory that LSD does chromosomal damage has been discredited in subsequent tests. Apparently, LSD is a relatively safe drug, but because studies were largely curtailed before adequate research had been done, definite conclusions about its physiological effects are not yet possible.

What is certain is that the drug produces a highly suggestive and sensitive state of consciousness, and that environment, mood and frame of mind, expectations, and individual mental characteristics are extremely important factors. In controlled psychotherapy situations and communal religious and social situations LSD and LSD-like drugs appear safe. Currently, however, LSD is primarily used outside such situations; anyone who has an inclination and ability to purchase it can use LSD, and the conditions in which it is used to get "high" are often far from secure.

Proponents of LSD have advertised it as a "mind-expanding" drug. Viewing the effects of the drug, it becomes obvious that consciousness is definitely altered during the LSD experience, with the user viewing himself, life, and what we know as physical reality in a totally different manner. The experience can change a person's subsequent ideas. Loss of ego and ego controls in LSD experiences can instill a sense of transcendentalism, of merging with the cosmos, which was popularized by Timothy Leary and his philosophy of "tune in, turn on, and drop out." This method, along with its apostle, has largely been discredited in recent years, and the "acid head" is becoming a rare and unenvied species. Much more intriguing are the experiences of Carlos Castaneda with his Indian teacher, Don Juan, in which the LSD-like drugs, particularly peyote, are used as part of a transcendental philosophy. (See Page 399.)

By and large, American society is very rigid in its definition of both what is normal and what is real. It is saturated by a scientific consciousness which denies mystic and esoteric experiences. LSD, whether or not it can be considered mind expanding, can definitely be seen as a revolt against this rigid framework, offering the possibility of viewing the world from a very different perspective.

Marijuana, amphetamines, cocaine, barbiturates, heroin, LSD — Americans no longer use just one drug, they use a multiplicity. In view of the widespread use of these psychoactive drugs in our society, some questions need to be considered. First, in connection with drug use, what is antisocial behavior? At one time the ingestion of any drug other than alcohol was classified as antisocial. But when a rapidly expanding group of Americans began switching to new psychoactive drugs, and considered it perfectly acceptable behavior among themselves, this definition began to change. The group popularized as the "drug culture" became not so much antisocial as alternate-social. Rather than follow the pattern of traditional alcohol consumption, they chose to consume other drugs. Once the use of marijuana became widespread, the group lost its distinctiveness, and now, with the greater acceptance of new drugs, it is in the process of being assimilated into the mainstream culture.

It is true that antisocial behavior in the form of criminal behavior is related to drugs. But for the most part, the psychoactive drugs do not cause or facilitate violence. Criminal behavior is largely due to the legal prohibition of drugs.

Another question that should be considered is drug abuse. Medical studies show that dosage, frequency and duration of use, and method of administration determine whether or not a drug is abused. The illegal market for drugs is particularly dangerous because the purchaser is never sure of the potency or quality of the drug he buys. Frequently the drug is not what it was advertised as; even more often it is "cut" or diluted with various other chemicals, some of which can be dangerous. The major recommendation to users or potential users of any drug is to be as cautious and as knowledgeable as possible.

But a still more profound side of the question remains to be weighed. In this country huge numbers of deaths occur each year as the result of abuse of two physically addictive drugs which are both socially and legally acceptable: alcohol and nicotine. It is time the question of drug consumption, both legal and illegal, was considered seriously and intelligently — and in *all* its ramifications.

A PERSPECTIVE ON DRUGS AND CONSCIOUSNESS

"As soon as we understand the difference between straight and stoned thinking we can see at once that all of our approaches to social problems associated with drugs are based on the former. The very notion of a drug problem is straight because it implies that drugs are causative of negative behavior connected with their use."

The speaker is Andrew Weil, an acknowledged expert on drugs who studies them because he has "been there." He feels that the failure of Prohibition should have taught this country that the criminal law will not affect drug taking in our society. Education is only a means of scaring would-be users in more sophisticated ways than the law can. According to Weil, what we are now doing in the name of stopping the drug problem *is* the drug problem.

The real risk of using drugs as the primary method of altering consciousness is their tendency to make it ultimately harder to learn how to maintain highs without dependence on them. Drugs intelligently used as tools to enter other states of consciousness are potentially beneficial:

"If we can even start to move in the direction of relying on intuition and experience to discover the positive potential of drugs, the drug problem will automatically begin to recede. Once we accept the general premise, it seems to me that our actions must be directed toward two specific goals: (1) encouragement of people who wish to use drugs to use them intelligently for their own good and thereby for the good of society; and (2) encouragement of people to progress beyond drugs to better methods of altering consciousness."

Read Weil in full on the subject in *The Natural Mind: Another Way of Looking at the Higher Consciousness.*

CARLOS CASTANEDA/ learning to "see"

The quest for another experience of reality, for an escape from our plastic, mechanistic, sentimentalized *Reader's Digest* kind of world has made the books of Carlos Castaneda overwhelming best-sellers. The most recent cult figure of the young, Castaneda's shadowy shaman figure Don Juan, has supplanted Herman Hesse's heroes, Tom Wolfe and his Electric Kool-Aid Acid Kids, the Hobbits, and Salinger's furious adolescents. And not only students, but housewives, businessmen, and other middle-class urbanites find themselves transported with Castaneda to the bleak Mexican countryside, shaking with fear at a crackling in the underbrush as they wait alone in the night for some alien visitation, or soaring in awe and terror over the vast, crenellated landscape on mystical wings.

In 1960 Carlos Castaneda planned to begin graduate work in anthropology at UCLA and decided to do some preliminary research in ethnobotany, studying medicinal and psychotropic plants used by the Yaqui Indians. He felt the preparation of a scholarly and well-documented study such as this would give him a head start in his field. At a friend's suggestion he contacted an old Mexican, Juan Matus, a Yaqui Indian *brujo*, or sorcerer. As he grew to know Don Juan, Castaneda's original desire to learn about plants metamorphosed into a long, intermittent but intense apprenticeship in acquiring the "separate reality," the way of knowledge, of the old Indian's world.

Sometimes accompanied by Don Juan's powerful, delightful fellow brujo, Don Gennaro, Carlos floundered in a mystic sea of incomprehensible happenings that bore little relationship to the structured academic world whose disciplines he had been trained to use. The old men tried to draw him from the rational, everyday viewpoint he had always lived by into a new way of "seeing," of experiencing their world and absorbing its power. There were mind-bending experiences with drugs when Mescalito, the plant spirit, was conjured up from peyote in a series of haunting materializations: a strange black dog, a column of light, a giant cricket.

The result of this first stage in his epic training was *The Teachings of Don Juan: A Yaqui Way of Knowledge*, written as a master's thesis and published originally by the University of California Press. Its audience mushroomed until the book moved out of the academic world and became a bestseller.

Returning to his apprenticeship, the successful new author continued his efforts under Don Juan's tutelage to alter his perception of the world and become a "man of knowledge." Don Juan emphasized that one must always be aware of his own death and prepared to confront it, that one must be a "warrior," because "only a warrior can survive. A warrior knows that he is waiting and what he is waiting for."

In Castaneda's second book, *A Separate Reality*, Don Juan explains that although he can act as guide, Castaneda must break through to the ultimate goal and learn to "see" by his own efforts. He must undo his habitual ways of perceiving and constructing the world, find new ways of organizing his environment to penetrate beneath the surface. Don Juan advises him to focus on detail, to see the shadows beneath the leaves, to look around and behind and into familiar objects until their essence is his. And Carlos must cease the endless internal dialogue, the mental chatter: "We repeat the same choices over and over until the day we die, because we keep on repeating the same internal talk over and over until the day we die . . . . We talk to others and to ourselves mainly about what we see. A warrior is aware of that and listens to the world; he listens to the sounds of the world."

It is necessary to free oneself from one's personal history, to discard sentiment, the attachment to the everyday world. When the basic lessons have been mastered, when the apprentice begins finally to reach his goal, he will encounter an ally, a mysterious being described by Don Juan as a piece of cloth that can take on any shape. When the would-be sorcerer finally learns to "see," the ally comes to challenge him, to wrestle him for the final prize of membership in the world of power. If the aspirant loses the match he will be "snuffed out," in the words of Don Juan — whether literally or figuratively is not clear.

In *Journey to Ixtlan: The Lessons of Don Juan*, the fascinating odyssey continues. Castaneda had come to realize that the original drug experiences were only a way of opening windows for this new kind of perceiving — psychedelic substances were no longer necessary once those first lessons had been learned. Don Juan explains that for some pupils drugs are not necessary at all, but Carlos was a stubborn case. He describes his arduous apprenticeship in vividly detailed and evocative language. Indeed, it is the wealth of detail pouring out of those notebooks in precise, sinewy prose that makes the experiences totally real.

The last, and apparently final, word from Don Juan is in *Tales of Power*, where Castaneda, now an advanced student, is given some exhaustive and exhausting lessons from his mentor and then sent off to leap from the edge of the mesa into the Unknown. Castaneda's routine has become a bit threadbare but still has enough power to make us believe in the old sorcerer and search his words for clues that will make us all "warriors."

There is considerable controversy about whether Don Juan really exists or whether the experiences came from Castaneda's powerful imagination. His accomplishment is beyond argument: as one admirer expresses it, he is either a superb anthropologist or a superb novelist. Despite the skepticism expressed in some quarters, the Department of Anthropology at UCLA believed in the validity of Castaneda's research sufficiently to award him a Ph. D. for *Journey to Ixtlan*. Unquestionably, he has become the hero of the new wave of psychologists writing about expanding consciousness, ways of perceiving, new methods of mapping the mind. Quotations from Don Juan are scattered like plums through their books and essays.

Confusion even exists about Castaneda's personal history; he has never been photographed, and there are conflicting details in the few interviews he has allowed.

Somehow these questions seem unimportant, as does the concern over whether all the events in his books are factual.

Whatever their source, they are works of high art which enable us as readers to participate directly in an awareness of differing realities. Squinting our eyes, struggling to halt our incessant internal dialogue, we find ourselves peering like Carlos at the horizon, trying to crack open the everyday walls of our consciousness. It is no mean achievement.

SLEEP

By the age of 72, a normal person has spent 24 years of sleeping and roughly six years dreaming. At no time during sleep does consciousness cease; in fact, it has even been suggested that wakefulness and sleep are an interwoven whole. How much do we understand about sleep, our other existence, which claims a third of our lives?

It is now known that sleep is not synonymous with oblivion. Nor is it a unitary whole punctuated by flashes of dreams. Instead, it is a complex mental and physical process of existence. In fact "sleep" has become a poor word to describe the many phases and intricate transitions of mental and physical activity which all of us experience each night.

In the last two decades the scientific study of the brain has been revolutionized, a fact that has had a corresponding impact on the study of sleep. To understand the mechanism of sleep it is necessary to know some of the basic facts about how the brain works and the methods scientists employ to study it.

The brain is composed of innumerable tiny cells which contain interacting chemicals. The chemical reactions are of an electrical nature, characterized by continuous shifts of positive and negative charges. The ongoing brain cell reactions are termed *brain waves* or *rhythms*. Scientists discovered that by placing electrodes on the scalp, the brain's constantly fluctuating electrical potential could be detected, and with the invention of the electroencephalograph machine (commonly known as the EEG) researchers could actually record the flow of brain waves. The EEG does not record what is being thought; rather, it records the frequency and intensity of brain activity. When a person is mentally active, a zigzag pattern is recorded, indicating a larger number of electrical reactions of relatively low intensity. In a completely relaxed state a curved, elongated wave pattern is recorded, indicating few reactions and less brain activity, but often of greater intensity or voltage. The EEG's importance for the study of sleep is obvious. Sleep is generally a condition of physical inertia when the brain is highly unresponsive to outside stimuli. Yet with the EEG it is possible to monitor the sleeping person's brain and discover what is occurring.

In the process of "falling asleep," there is no definite boundary between wakefulness and sleep, only intermediate stages. According to Ian Oswald in his book *Sleep*, prior to falling asleep the brain cortex decreases its attentiveness to the outside world. A state of relaxation follows, monitored as high rolling waves by the EEG. These waves become longer and smaller as mental activity and its intensity decrease. For a short period of time a person experiences visual images, hears voices, and has "dreamlets." This has been called the "hypnagogic stage," which is neither sleep nor waking. A person roused at this point will most often claim he has not been sleeping, but is unable to remember exactly what has happened. As the relaxation process continues a sudden spasm occurs, causing the body to jerk in reaction to the last burst of mental/physical wakeful activity. At this point say Gay Luce and Julius Segal in their book, *Sleep*, "the threshold of sleep" merges into sleep, the muscles relax and the heart rate slows as the EEG changes from long waves to

a "small pinched scribble," denoting mental activity at a very low level. The EEG then records fast bursts of mental activity, termed "sleep spindles." Finally, large slow waves interspersed with sleep spindles are recorded. The person is soundly asleep.

But much else will occur during the night's course. A person usually remains in a relatively sound sleep for about 90 minutes; then begins another transition when a different type of sleep is experienced. In fact, throughout the night a cycle occurs in which a person fluctuates between two fundamentally different types of sleep. This is the normal pattern of sleep we all experience.

The most definite characteristics of deep sleep are large, slow waves, termed delta waves, *revealed by the EEG. They indicate that the mind is in its most passive state. Researchers call this type of sleep "orthodox," "delta wave," or "phase IV" sleep. The body experiences a general slowdown of vital activity: heart rate drops, blood pressure and body temperature decrease, and respiration slows. This sleep is probably the most physically restorative, and people who have been deprived of sleep for long periods will spend a greater percentage of their sleeping time in this stage once they are able to do so.*

Until recently it was thought that no dreams occurred during this phase of sleep; however, this viewpoint has dramatically changed. Early misconceptions centered on the fact that when researchers woke subjects from this sleep phase, they reported having had no dreams or that they had been "thinking" unemotionally about mundane matters. What the researchers failed to account for was that arousing the subject from this deep sleep is difficult, and when the subject does wake he has lost all or almost all memory of dreams.

In *The Brain Revolution,* Marilyn Ferguson is adamant on the point that mental activity definitely takes place in a "curious altered state." She argues that sleep-walking, sleep-talking, and night terrors all occur during this phase. When a person walks about in his sleep, talks at length, or wakes in a state of panic, he is obviously mentally active. Yet when researchers have awakened sleepwalkers, sleeptalkers, and subjects experiencing night terror, the individuals have no recollection of what they have been doing. It seems clear that even though our mental activity is often not remembered, it exists continuously, even in this phase of profound sleep.

A second type of sleep was discovered when researchers noted that at a certain point in the sleep cycle a person's eyes would begin to move under his eyelids, even more rapidly than during wakefulness. These rapid eye movement or REM periods reoccur throughout the night, beginning approximately an hour and a half after falling asleep and becoming more frequent and of longer duration toward morning. In all, about one quarter of the night's sleep, some two hours, will be spent in REM periods. It has been found that when a subject is awakened during an REM period, he invariably reports having had vivid dreams.

The EEG provides more information. The transition from orthodox or phase IV sleep into REM sleep appears to be a reversal toward wakefulness. Luce and Segal describe the EEG as changing in appearance to that of wakeful, intense concentration. They also describe bodily changes. The previous slowdown of vital functions reverses as heart rate becomes irregular, blood pressure rises, oxygen consumption increases, and the pulse quickens. Body temperature and brain temperature also increase, along with the production of stress hormones. Yet at the same time the body muscles lose their tone and become flaccid. Ferguson calls this a relative paralysis which keeps the person from acting out his dreams.

In the midst of this growing mental and physical activity, vivid dreams begin. As the night wears on the dreams become more frequent and more intense. Oswald points out that the "larger than life" feelings one experiences in dreams may be due to the fact that the brain region which controls REM sleep, the pons, is also the brain's emotional center.

REM sleep can be potentially dangerous. Some types of ulcer cases are aggravated by an increased output of gastric acid during this time. Statistically, it has been shown that nighttime coronary strokes happen most frequently during intense REM periods. However, even though the mind and body become highly activated and agitated, REM sleep is a human necessity. In experiments, researchers attempted to eliminate REM sleep by waking the volunteer every time he started to enter this stage. But they soon found out that the mind was insistent on acquiring REM sleep, and the subject reverted to it more and more often. Once normal sleep was again allowed, a process of "catching up" inevitably occurred.

Through a number of experiments it has become increasingly accepted that REM sleep is extremely important for us. Insomniacs suffer from a lack of REM sleep, and in turn experience psychological disturbances. A connection has been shown to exist between certain types of mental retardation and a severe shortage of REM sleep. And studies have also indicated that a lack of REM sleep has detrimental effects on mental functioning in general, causing depression and tension. Thus, REM or "dream" sleep seems to provide a necessary ingredient in our lives.

Our society does not put great emphasis on the content of our dream life. To the Senoi tribe of the Malay peninsula, however, dreams are an integral part of human existence. Marilyn Ferguson tells how they regularly recount and analyze their dreams in family and communal situations. When a person is harmed by or does harm to another person in a dream, he seeks out the individual and either gives or receives restitution. When the Senoi discuss their dreams, they practice a form of dream modification in which they consistently reinforce the pleasurable aspects of dreaming. The Senoi have shown the benefits resulting from an active awareness and acknowledgment of the importance of dreams. They have no war or violent crimes and enjoy remarkably good mental health. Understandably, Senoi methods and teachings have become popular in the United States; several centers now exist around the country and many universities offer classes on Senoi practices.

Since Freud, psychoanalysts have been concerned with dream interpretation. But what is now apparent is that throughout the process of sleep mental activity is occurring. Dreams that are remembered and reported to the psychoanalyst are mere fragments. For as Ralph Berger has pointed out, even during "orthodox" deep sleep a certain level of consciousness, which he calls *mentation*, never ceases. Ferguson goes on to suggest that the various mental activities during all phases of a night's sleep are somehow interconnected and that dreams are merely the most memorable and vivid parts of the process.

It would seem that sleep consciousness is a "need-fulfilling" process, the mind's way of viewing things from a different perspective or or in an altered form. Sleep consciousness can be seen as a "second opinion" in the search for resolution of needs and problems.

The general consensus of those studying sleep is that we still know very little about it. We do know that it is a very complex process that involves many phases of mental and physical functioning. But the questions of how it is related to waking consciousness and what needs it fulfills are still unanswered.

CONCEPTUAL FRONTIERS

"Far-out" is an approving word in the lexicon of the young, and here we move far out both literally and figuratively; far out into physical space in the almost romantically beautiful concepts of Dr. Gerard O'Neill's space colonies, designed to capture and transmit inexhaustible, inexpensive solar energy to the earth from cylinders hung in space, complete with flowers and trees and running streams.

We learn a little of the new physics, which seems to be reaching beyond science into mysticism and poetry, epitomized by James Jeans' often-quoted remark that the universe is beginning to look more and more like a great thought. We see the awesome and frightening possibilities of tinkering with genes to make human beings to order, a reality that is no longer in the distant future but right next door. Is genetic control a way of multiplying the individual, making thousands of identical Einsteins or Hitlers or Raquel Welches? Where to begin? Where to stop? These are mind-boggling possibilities but they must be faced and understood, for we will soon have decisions to make about fantastic things that only yesterday were strictly science fiction.

THE DOLPHINS/breaking the communication barrier
by JOHN C. LILLY, M.D.

John Lilly has finally come full circle in his remarkable program of self-exploration, and plans to go "down to the sea again," to return to his friends the Cetacea, in the hope of breaking the communication barrier with another species for the first time in man's history. In the fall of 1975 Lilly, his wife Toni, actor Burgess Meredith, and Victor DiSuvero, a San Francisco businessman, established the nonprofit Human/Dolphin Foundation, based in Malibu, California. Its major intention is to develop a program of research that will bring about communication between man and dolphin in the vocal sphere. The first approach will be conversion of the spectrum of human speech to the dolphins' higher frequency hearing spectrum, and the simultaneous conversion of the high-frequency underwater sound spectrum used by the dolphins to the spectrum of human hearing. Microprocessors and minicomputers will accomplish this speeding up process without either species sensing a delay in the computation — which Lilly hopes will open the channels of communication initially. The second approach will be testing the dolphin's ability to learn a simple code, and elaborate on its uses. In his previous research, Lilly found that the human is not fast enough to sustain the dolphin's interest. He therefore plans to use a minicomputer to speed questions up enough to pique the dolphin's curiosity and get it to reason in a graded series of exercises. Toni Lilly, who has a gift for expressing thoughts memorably, says that the communication barrier "is one of the last frontiers — once you break that barrier, a project like saving the Cetaceans will take care of itself." Let us hope so. When John Lilly and I talked about the work of the Foundation, he suggested I incorporate a speech he had recently given on the subject which he entitled Universal Consciousness and Dolphins. *It is followed by the interview.*

I worked in direct contact with dolphins from 1955 until 1968. As I worked with them, my simulations of them changed. Instead of research animals upon which I did experiments, they became mysterious beings with mysterious accomplishments, mysterious simulations, and mysterious experience which I didn't understand. I remember the day that this happened:

A dolphin began for the first time in my experience to mimic what I was saying and then improve his own mimicry as I insisted on it. I suddenly realized that here was a someone, a being on the other side of a peculiar glass wall which I had constructed from my belief systems. The sudden shift in my own consciousness that took place at that point was a bizarre, weird feeling that for the first time I was meeting another species worthy of our attention, our interest, our compassion, and our respect. It then took me about two years to realize that I had no right to confine them, to imprison them, to work *on them;* my only right would be to work *with them* in their natural habitat and their natural state. At that point, I closed the laboratory and went to Esalen Institute to find out who I was.

I had conceived of myself as an objective scientist. I found that I was a poor humanist. I gradually began to see the point in many of the religious teachings, the ethical teachings, which we have inherited. The Buddhist reverence for all life began to plague me.

Who on this planet is more spiritually advanced than any man has been in our records? Are there any beings here other than ourselves, the human species, who have a spiritual development, who have ethics, who have a philosophical point of view very different from ours?

Man has a long narcissistic tradition of saying that he's the top of creation, that he controls the seas of earth and the land of earth. It's time that those of you interested in universal consciousness realize that for 15 times longer than the time since man (as we know him) even appeared upon the face of the earth, the whales have been here perfecting their philosophies, perfecting their ethics. Their intellectual and ethical capacity and their traditions have to have existed at least 15 times longer than those of man. Their brains are larger than ours — in very critical areas; 15 million years ago, whale/dolphin brains were of current human size. At that point in time, our predecessors had brains equivalent in size to those of small mice.

Man is a very peculiar animal. His brain has expanded faster than that of any other species on the planet.

Those who have brains greater than ours, equal to ours, and less than ours in the sea have been here much longer than we have. There is a vast reservoir of intelligence, of tradition, of history, of philosophy and ethics in the sea from which we have been cut off by our arrogant beliefs. What do we do with these magnificent brains? We slaughter them. We imprison them for sport. We put them in the service of human warfare.

This is my simulation and, so far, I have been fairly lonely with it, but let me give you some of the evidence:

In 12 years of working with more than 100 dolphins, whose brains were 40 percent greater than ours in those critical areas, the silent areas of the brain, no dolphin at any time, even under the severest provocation, injured any of our personnel.

The total interdependence of the cetacea for the last 15 million years dictates an ethic which will not allow them to hurt man. Young dolphins have to learn this. At one point, in our laboratory, a two-year-old dolphin started to attack me with an open mouth. Now, if you know that such an animal can bite a six-foot barracuda in two with one snap, you realize the power available. He started after my arm and an older female dolphin came across at right angles and hit him on the top of the head, so hard that you could hear the thud all over the laboratory.

That young dolphin never again tried to bite a human. He was apparently severely lectured, as well as punished.

We can be faced with such evidence and remain perfectly blind to what it means. The biologists who have worked with dolphins, the cetologists who have described their anatomy and behavior, in the service of the whaling industry, have not gone this far. They do not agree with me; yet they want to conserve whales. They want whaling to stop.

I say to them, if you are going to realize the total interdependence of life on this planet, please pay attention to brain size, irrespective of body size. Neuroanatomists have studied the brains of dolphins and whales, and it turns out that they are larger than ours in the same critical silent areas where our brains are larger than those of chimpanzees, gorillas, and orangutans.

On the surface of the earth, none of man's predecessors are left — none of the critical links between the apes and ourselves remain, because as soon as man reached the critical brain size for language, his advantage over those who could not yet attain language was so great that he eliminated them rapidly.

Today we still eliminate those human beings whose brain size is below the critical value for language. Why? Because if they reach maturity, they are not controllable by language. Their sexual activities, their aggressive activities, are not inhibited in the presence in other humans of the symbolic mechanism known as language. So either they are killed at birth, or they are locked up in institutions for what used to be called "the feeble-minded." If you want to see the missing predecessors of man, go to these institutions and study the microcephalics.

In the sea, ethics are very different. The small-brained dolphins live with the larger-brained dolphins and whales in a totally interdependent situation. This interdependence is a function, not only of their society and their ethics, but of their physiology.

If a human is knocked out, he continues to breathe — like the other terrestrial mammals, man has an automatic breathing system. The dolphins do not have this. The mammals of the sea cannot afford it. If they were knocked out under water, if they passed out from a high fever or a blow on the head, they would drown immediately, if they had an automatic respiratory system.

If a dolphin passes out, he has a short period of time in which his fellow dolphins must bring him to the surface, wake him up, and get him to breathe again in a voluntary way. Otherwise he is lost.

This means that every day, every minute, 24 hours a day, the dolphin is dependent upon his fellow dolphins in a very detailed way. With the estimated billions of sharks in the sea, dolphins are always on the *qui vive*, always aware that the danger is just below, and that the only way they can survive is in groups. At night, they must have those on duty who awaken them. They sleep only between breaths — they wake for every breath. For a human, this would be an extremely nerve-wracking situation, to say the least.

We may survive for another 15 million years; but only if we develop an ethic which would stop us from killing one another, which would not allow warfare, and which would not allow public expressions of anger in hostile action. We now have the weapons and the means to completely eliminate all species of this planet, including ourselves. We can no longer afford the luxury of hostile action based on anger, of territorial rights expressed in a hostile way. Until we can realize the nature of the ecology of man in a totally interdependent ecosystem included in that for other organisms, we will not have the basis for any sort of spiritual advancement beyond that of a narcissistic Samadhi experienced alone. As Buddha said, "I cannot go into a permanent Nirvana until all sentient creatures are there also." And so we are left with the duty to develop the ethic that the whales and the dolphins already have.

I am going to devote the rest of my life to attempting to break the communication barrier between us and the cetacea. One of them is killed every 15 minutes, 24 hours a day, by man. I just hope that, by the time we are able to communicate, there are enough of them left to respond.

Adapted from an address given to the International Cooperation Council, in Santa Monica, California, in January 1976.

interview/ JOHN C. LILLY, M.D.
one of the last frontiers

LANDE: You said you intended to devote the rest of your life to breaking the communication barrier between man and the cetaceans. Would you state the philosophy behind that?

LILLY: I'll answer by quoting an article I wrote for *Oceans* magazine in early 1976:

"Research in communication with cetaceans is no longer simply a scientific pursuit. Such research is now a necessity for humans to exchange information on a high level of complexity with the cetaceans. We must learn their necessities, their ethics, their philosophy, in order to find out who we are on this planet in this galaxy. The extraterrestrials are here in the sea. We can, with dedicated efforts, communicate with them. If and when we break the communication barrier, we and the cetaceans can work out our differences and our correspondences."

Then there's another point: Their brain size has been equal to and greater than ours for 15 million years; their "survival wisdom" is demonstrated by their present existence. Our brains have achieved their present size only in the last 50 to 100 thousand years. Can we last 15 million more? Maybe not. They have shown a total interdependence in the sea. They haven't killed off the small-brained dolphins; they have perpetuated them.

We have not done so on land. There is a gap in brain size between the speaking, functioning human and the largest of the apes with a brain size of 500 grams. The smallest human brain that can acquire language and function well enough in our society not to be locked up is about 700 grams. We've killed off all the intervening creatures in that range. In the sea there are dolphins with brains the size of the chimpanzee, 300 grams, and there is a continuous spectrum of brain size all the way up to the largest of 9,000 grams (in the sperm whale).

We may already have accumulated too negative a reputation among the cetaceans by our whaling industries. In spite of this they don't hurt or kill us, which is incredible. Let us at least stop killing for industry and enslaving them for entertainment and warfare. This we can do now.

The communication problem is longer term and needs more research. In the Human/Dolphin Foundation we are collecting a bibliography on dolphins and whales in the areas of brain structure, communications, and behavior. The Foundation is also proposing research to start breaking the communication barrier between man and dolphin, doing the research at sea with no confinement of the dolphin.

LANDE: Where do you plan to do your research?

LILLY: We're going to have totally portable equipment. The computers are now small enough to carry in a van to where the dolphins are.

LANDE: If they are not confined, how do you know the dolphins you are working with will come back?

LILLY: There are certain techniques for interesting the dolphins. I've never talked about this publicly and I don't want to at this time, but I'm sure it won't be a problem.

LANDE: What about the structure of the dolphin society?

LILLY: I can tell you a little story about that. A researcher came to the Virgin Islands laboratory and spent 18 months trying to find the dolphin's dominance hierarchy. He gave up. He then moved to Hawaii and worked with the smaller-brained dolphin with a brain about the size of a gorilla. And immediately, hierarchies showed up. The small-brained dolphins are organized in an obvious way that man can detect. The larger-brained dolphins, due to the complexity of their language, set up their hierarchies within the meaning spectrum of their language. They don't have to have a behavioral thing showing that this guy is boss with a tag around his neck saying: I am boss. No obvious pecking order.

We did find that the old dolphins are in control of the education of the young and we learned what happens with a given group at sea. They have to be in control: they have the knowledge, the experience, and the tradition to control the group.

If you go to isolated groups of Indians in Mexico, you'll find the same thing. The 94-year-old Shaman is the man whose advice is sought. He may not be active at all, and if an extraterrestrial came down and watched their dominance hierarchy, he wouldn't even notice that the 94-year-old guy was programming everybody. But he doesn't program in a narrow sense. The small-brained dolphins can only program one another in a narrow sense, so the behavior shows up in forms that are observable by humans.

Let's take an example of beliefs about dolphins from Aristotle — this is in 400 BC. He said a lot of things about dolphins, many of which weren't believed by later biologists. We checked out Aristotle rather systematically. He said that small boys and dolphins develop passionate attachments. We found that was true. We showed Ivan Tors that small boys can ride dolphins. The men who furnished Ivan with his dolphins for "Flipper" didn't believe this. Ivan called me up and said, "What about this business of all these boys riding the dolphins on the coins of

Tarentum?" I said the coins of Tarentum showed boys riding dolphins from about 700 BC to about 200 AD, so there must be something in it. I said, "Do you want to test this? We need a freshly captured dolphin, preferably a mother and a baby." I went out to the Bahamas where Tors was working; he had a fence and beach and water about eight feet deep inside the fence. Within six hours we had both of his sons riding the mother dolphin. She'd take them out and take them down and bring them up to breathe. They got attached to the baby.

We have an instance in this century in which a boy developed a passionate attachment with a dolphin and they had sexual intercourse. That was about three years ago. He wrote me about it.

What Aristotle said about the voice of the dolphin, I think, is rather interesting. "The voice of the dolphin in the air is like that of the human. He can pronounce vowels and combinations of vowels but he can't pronounce the consonants." And that made me think. The voice of the dolphin in air. Where do you hear the voice of the dolphin in air? At sea they communicate only underwater. The only time is when dolphins are kept in close contact with humans in small, shallow pools. We went out and tested this. Where do the consonants go? We started looking at our own speech output with high-frequency microphones, measured it, did an analysis of it, and we found that when we see a "t" or an "s", we're putting out a lot of energy above our own hearing range but well into the dolphin's hearing range. So when you ask them to pronounce English, they do the vowels and then they use the ultrasonics for us for the consonants. You'll hear a vowel and silence, and a vowel. We recorded all this on high-speed tape recorders and slowed it all down and found where the consonants were. Aristotle didn't have that equipment, so he couldn't do it. What we need is equipment that will translate their ultrasonic region into the sonic for us, and our sonic region into their ultrasonic for them.

LANDE: Where does this stand now?

LILLY: We recently formed a nonprofit foundation. Toni and I are supporting it with what we make from books and so on, and various other people are contributing money and time. Until we have IRS approval there is a period of personal effort and expense without remuneration.

LANDE: Can't the government or private foundations underwrite the project?

LILLY: They just don't have the money. The present government policy with regard to support or research in biological/medical areas is way down compared to what it was in the '60s, '50s, and '40s. Of course, we would like foundation money, and we will approach foundations when we've written a proper proposal. There are, of course, other ways of handling expenses. One of them is public support. There are probably hundreds of thousands of people willing to put 10 dollars into this. Another possibility is to approach computer companies who have the hardware we need and ask for a donation of time and money on the basis that in the future, if we break the communication barrier, they can make a profit.

THE NEW PHYSICS/space-time and beyond

"Since everything is constructed from consciousness, if enough people are aware of the harmonies of peace in the universe layers, conflict and fear can diminish. It has been the significance of Jesus, Buddha, and a handful of others throughout history to show us the interpenetration of the universes, to reunite us with ourselves.

So as I turn inward, realizing I am intimately connected with all the universes, I take direct responsibility for my thoughts. It's all here and now, within!

Don't wait for the guru, the messiah, the teacher, the second coming. Wake up and smell the coffee!"

— Bob Toben
Space-Time and Beyond

There was a time when the facts that there were seven planets in the sky and seven days in the week were of obvious significance. It made perfect sense at this time to attempt to relate the paths of the planets to notes on the musical scale, or to the volumes of geometrical solids. Since that time, however, science has become more and more specialized and the search for interdisciplinary relationships has dwindled. That is, until the appearance of *Space-Time and Beyond,* written by Bob Toben with physicists Jack Sarfatti and Fred Wolf. With a collection of modern theories and mystical truths that look like a random selection from an experimental college catalogue, the authors have put together a disturbingly convincing book that rattles just about every conventional view of reality.

Quantum mechanics, paranormal phenomena, black holes, Eastern philosophy, multidimensional space, cosmic consciousness — related? Exactly, and not just in the minds of Toben, Sarfatti, and Wolf. Most of the material in the book can be found — far less readably — in various physics journals; much of it comes from Nobel laureates Albert Einstein and Richard Feynman, and from

Princeton physicist John A. Wheeler, whose *Geometrodynamics,* published in 1962, has been called the Bible of the new physics.

As every philosopher will tell you, the most important thing around is consciousness. Without it the universe does not exist. (Actually, it might, but who would know?) It used to be that the physical scientists would tell you that the universe existed objectively without relation to consciousness. Then, with the development of quantum mechanics, it became obvious that it is impossible to know or be conscious of anything without simultaneously changing it (a theory known as the Heisenberg uncertainty principle after Werner Heisenberg, who postulated it in 1927). Thus there is no such thing as an objective observer; there can only be participant observers.

Consciousness, however, is more than just a spanner that has been thrown into the works. It transcends "normal" or "ordinary" reality. As Toben expresses it, "Consciousness is the totality beyond space-time.... We have come to know that consciousness and energy are one; that all of space-time is constructed by consciousness; that our normal perception of reality is a composite of an indefinite number of universes in which we co-exist; and that what we perceive as ourselves is only the localized projection of the totality of our true selves."

Since by consciousness we influence everything, we are also linked to everything — and cosmic consciousness, or the reuniting with the One, is just around the corner. The main obstacle is that we exist in space-time and the physical reality we deal with makes it a little hard to see quite how we can go about merging with the cosmic One.

Consciousness IS, and it exists on a higher level than space-time, which is three spatial dimensions and one of time. Consciousness exists in what can be called multidimensional or superspace. That attribute we all have which we call consciousness is simply a localized edition of this larger force. In much the same way as a three-dimensional object in a house of mirrors casts a myriad of two-dimensional images, consciousness is projected nearly an infinite number of times into space-time, and while the images may change, the source remains, and all the images, though different in appearance, are in fact the same. It is this consciousness that creates the space-time universe that we ordinarily perceive, and because this consciousness shows up in an infinite *different* number of ways, then an infinite number of universes exist, all of which are connected to the primary source.

This concept, which has been part of mystical philosophies throughout the ages, is now appearing in various theories in physics. Nobel prizewinner Richard Feynman has proposed a possible solution to the puzzle of why all subatomic particles have the same charge, mass, spin, and other properties. According to Feynman's theory there is only one basic form of each subatomic particle and this primary form is projected in multidimensional or superspace. For instance, there is only one electron — or, to express it more clearly, there is only one *primary* electron which, like the object in the house of mirrors, is projected an infinite number of times into space-time as a normal or run-of-the-mill electron. What is this essential electron like? That is a tough question because, like the image in the mirrors, its projections into the space-time we are familiar with must be an order of magnitude simpler than the source (just as a mirror will not show us a three-dimensional object in three dimensions, but only in two).

Similarly, in relation to consciousness, we "created in the image" of a larger consciousness beyond space-time.

Let's take it a step further. If, indeed, there is only one consciousness and it is true that it generates an infinite number of universes, then each of us is connected to all the different projections of consciousness and consequently we all exist in all those different universes throughout all time. We are all part of the One whether we realize it or not. We don't have to work to make ourselves part of the whole; we simply have to be aware that this is already the case.

It sounds like religious philosophy, doesn't it? Yet at least one shrewd observer has called the scientists and mathematicians "the new mystics of the Western world — they're measuring matter, and it's becoming poetry." Is this really where the frontiers of physics lie?

As British astronomer Sir James Jeans said, more than three decades ago:

"Today there is a wide measure of agreement . . . that the stream of knowledge is heading toward a non-mechanical reality; the universe begins to look more like a great thought than like a great machine. Mind no longer appears as an accidental intruder into the realm of matter; we are beginning to suspect that we ought rather to hail it as the creator and governor of the realm of matter."

As recently as February 1974, John Wheeler told an assembly of physicists at Oxford:

"There may be no such thing as 'the glittering central mechanism of the universe.' ...Not machinery but magic may be the better description of the treasure that is waiting."

The obvious question is, then, "How do I get there from here?" Or, "So what good does it do me to know all this unless there is some way to make it work for me?" Again, modern physics offers some possible explanations.

Just as there are smallest units of matter, so also there are smallest units of energy. These smallest units of energy, or quanta, cannot be further subdivided. This means that as we look at extremely small energy potentials there is not a smooth gradient but, rather, a staircase-like arrangement where energy levels have certain fixed and discrete values and there are no values between them, even though it would seem likely that there should be. Thus there is not a smooth transition between one energy level and another because there is an area in between in which there is no existence. This is the origin of quantum leaps or jumps — a phrase that most people use to mean a massive step forward. Basically, it means going from one point to another without ever being between them.

If indeed "consciousness and energy are one," as Toben said, then we can expect consciousness to behave in the same way (provided we ignore the inevitable distortions inherent in the process of scaling upward). If this is so, then a jump in consciousness will put one into an entirely different universe. (It should be stressed here that this does not necessarily mean a different place spatially but simply a place or universe that is structured differently.) Space-time as we normally perceive it, however, is continuous and these quantum jumps of consciousness do not regularly occur. It is a situation rather like that of an imaginary rider on a city bus line, who commutes from point A to point B by a certain route and does not know that there are other buses and other possible routes. For him, the route he regularly takes represents his total perception of the city he is traveling through. A quantum jump is possible for him when he discovers the existence of transfers.

How can this happen, in physical fact? Is there some mechanism whereby regular space-time can be transcended? Is there a *singularity* — the term used in physics for an area or place in which things are transcended — where the fabric of space-time is not continuous? In other words, a place where we can go through the looking glass?

Currently accepted astrophysical theory proposes that these singularities do indeed exist. We are even fairly familiar with them, at least by name, as the "black holes" which are believed to form as a result of stellar collapse. There is also a theory that mini-black holes exist, which are far smaller than even sub-atomic particles. And, unlike stellar black holes, which are few and far between, mini-black holes and mini-white holes actually "make up" space. (The difference between a black hole and a white hole is that in the white hole time is reversed, and each may have either a positive or a negative mass.) "Wormholes" is the term Wheeler has used to describe these holes, whether black or white. These wormholes criss-cross space-time connecting the different possible universes. If it were possible to look into one of these singularities it would not be like peering through the fish-eye lens set into your front door to enable you to view who or what is on the other side. Rather, it would be like looking into an infinite kaleidoscope. Inside the hole space-time does not exist; you are in multidimensional superspace.

The result of making one of these quantum jumps would be to change ordinary reality, and this is a possible explanation for paranormal or psychic phenomena. Since at the quantum level there is no absolute direction for time, then awareness of both the past and future becomes possible and the phenomena of precognition and retrocognition are easily explained. And, since space is also transcended, it is possible to be aware of different places without actually being present in them — a capacity which is normally called clairvoyance. If we specialize in knowing a concentration of life events in the past, we describe the result as the phenomenon of reincarnation. Reincarnation is too simplistic a view, however. Since we are intimately connected with all consciousness throughout all time, we need not limit ourselves to an identification with the existence of a handful of individuals in the past. We are actually all people in the past, we are all people now, and, equally, all people in the future. Actually, we are all consciousness independent of corporeal existence and time.

Time travel, space travel, astral travel — with or without the presence of our bodies — represent the *experiencing* of the different universes that exist, as distinct from the states of clairvoyance, precognition, and retrocognition, which represent merely the cerebral *knowledge* of these universes. Telepathy then becomes no more than a fancy way of talking to ourselves, while psychokinesis can be seen as the participant observer of the Heisenberg uncertainty principle, operating on a "macro" scale.

It was Einstein who taught us that intuition and imagination are more important than experimentation. Other scientists were going into the laboratory to observe the workings of physics; Einstein went into his mind. The structure of the universe is not something we can see and observe. It is something we are participants in — we are an expression of that structure. This fact is borne out in mathematics, which is still a mental construction that *happens* to apply to the universe. When Schroedinger and Heisenberg derived the equations for quantum mechanics, the solutions to those equations already existed — they had been solved decades before as mathematical curiosities.

Since the human mind is both aware and self-aware, it can study both that which is within and that which is without. Since at the same time it is a structure that is found within the universe, it is not so surprising that the information gleaned from either realm should be similar, if not equivalent. The difference between the unified field theory and cosmic consciousness may be only in semantics. And as the puzzle pieces are fitted together maybe they do not form a picture at all, but only a mirror.

416

interview/ DR. HEINZ VON FOERSTER

the participant observer: is objectivity possible?

Dr. Von Foerster has won international renown as a theorist in the field of cybernetics — the comparative study of the automatic control system formed by the human nervous system and brain and its application to such manmade control systems as the computer and similar mechano-electrical devices. He recently retired from his professorship of electrical engineering and biophysics at the University of Illinois.

LANDE: How would you describe the role of the observer in the system?

VON FOERSTER: You remember the saying, "In the land of the blind, the one-eyed man is king"? My feeling is, unfortunately, that it is wishful thinking. I would paraphrase it as, "In the land of the blind, the one-eyed man is locked into the psychiatric ward," because if somebody can see in a group of people or a society where everyone else is blind, he is usually interpreted as being mentally ill. Because he sees what the others do not, they do not take his statement as indicating there is something to look for. They think he is crazy!

LANDE: Doesn't this often happen with people who have great concepts? Aren't geniuses often misunderstood and misinterpreted? Where would the observer be in the system in that case?

VON FOERSTER: The problem is that we are only slowly beginning to understand that the logic of the absence of perception is not the same as the logic of negation.

Take the physiological case of the blind spot. It is an area of the retina that is not sensitive to light, because it is where the optic nerve leaves the eyeball and at that place there is no vision. But we don't see that we have no vision there; we are quite unaware that there is a place in our visual field where we don't see anything. So when I say that the absence of perception is not the same thing as the logic of negation, I mean that absence of perception would be to say, "I see that I do not see." Whereas the logic of negation is something else, because in that case we do not see that we do not see.

LANDE: How can we begin to see? By acknowledging that we do not see?

VON FOERSTER: That would be a good start. Take the writings of Carlos Castaneda, about his teacher Don Juan. As I see it, the message in the books is that Don Juan wants to show Castaneda how he can go about learning how to see. You remember his statements about having to learn to "see," and Castaneda always says, "Well, I can see," and then Don Juan points out or takes him to places where he can discover certain things he cannot explain.

So then you get the very interesting notion that apparently in our Western culture there is great difficulty in seeing anything for which we don't already have an explanation. The moment we can't explain something, we have a blind spot; we can't see it. This means we have to move from our usual Western explanatory paradigm, which is a causal one, to other types of explanatory paradigms, such as metaphor.

That brings me to your word *mindstyles,* because each different explanatory paradigm is in fact a different mindstyle. Every explanation is a way of linking one type of description to another. If you keep to the causal paradigm and you have an insistent questioner, then you expose the weakness of the causal paradigm, which is that it can never be ended — you keep having to go on and on and on. In a metaphor, however, you have a holistic approach — you are covering the whole case, not just a tiny aspect of it, as in the causal situation.

LANDE: Metaphor leaves a lot to imagination — so must each individual bring his own cause and his own feeling and seeing in order to interpret it?

VON FOERSTER: Yes, he has to put his own personality into it, to recall his own experiences. This means we need a new kind of mindstyle, a different styling of our minds in relation to the operatives.

The concept of objectivity is a peculiar idea which has taken hold of our Western culture in the last 500-600 years. You know how scientists insist that every statement a scientist makes or publishes as a scientific revelation must be an objective statement — no subjective statements should be accepted in scientific literature. But if you remove all the properties of the observer — you see, the essence of being able to make an objective statement is that the properties of the observer shall not enter into the description of his observations — it makes complete nonsense. The observer's capacity to make the description, his property of being *able* to make that description, is already present when he makes it. So to remove it or not allow it to enter would be completely impossible. It would mean, in fact, that he couldn't say anything; he could only be silent.

LANDE: What kind of rules for living would you offer to the average person who is being exposed to the idea of the observer in the system for the first time?

VON FOERSTER: I would embrace a different attitude — I would embrace Taoism. Tao, you know, means the idea, this is the way. With respect to your prescriptions, I would say exactly what the Taoists say. You can't prescribe anything, you see, you can only present something and wait for somebody to look at it and say, "I've got it." If he doesn't get it, then forget it. It's nothing like Christian dogma, which says, "Tell me what I should do, tell me what I should not do." The Chinese don't say anything beyond, "Look, here is the universe. Just look at it and try to find your *own* place in it."

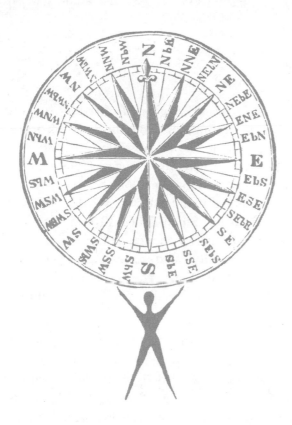

STEWART BRAND/ a one-man energy source

"We don't have an energy crisis, only an intelligence crisis."
— Heinz Von Foerster

Iconoclastic, gentle, concerned, original, Stewart Brand, creator of the *Whole Earth Catalog* and its supplements, now brings you the *Co-Evolution Quarterly:* more of the same, an adventurous exploration of what is happening today and where we may be tomorrow. Managing to be both folksy and focused, erudite and simple, the *Quarterly* is growing apace, finding its audience, and expects to be self-supporting by the fall of 1976. It is published by POINT, a nonprofit corporation funded from the original *Catalogs.* To quote from the magazine, "Self-sufficiency is not to be had on any terms. Ever since there were two organisms, life has been a matter of co-evolution, life growing ever more richly on life."

Born in Rockford, Illinois in 1938, graduated from Phillips Exeter Academy, and with a degree in biology from Stanford University, Stewart Burrows Brand has been logger, photographer, infantry officer, photojournalist, skydiver, LSD researcher, producer of slide-tape-film presentations such as "America Needs Indians" and "War/God," and participator in the capers of Ken Kesey and the Electric-Kool-Aid Acid Test kids.

Difficult to pigeonhole, a great believer in doing his own thing and encouraging others to do theirs, Brand is an activist rather than a navel-gazer, a catalyst and organizer who makes things happen. The many facets of his career and his far-reaching interests all came together in the best-selling *Whole Earth Catalog,* winner of the National Book Award for 1972. *Rolling Stone's* Thomas Albright called it "a unique compendium of the hip and the homespun, of far-out technology and down-home atavism . . . (which) celebrates an old-fashioned, fundamentalist individualism, the mystique of the self-taught, self-reliant, do-it-yourselfer living in an organic relationship with his environment."

At the Demise party to celebrate the completion of the *Last Whole Earth Catalog,* held at the Exploratorium in San Francisco, Brand turned $20,000 over to the 1,500 guests to "do good." Arguments about the proper method of accomplishing this raged until 9:30 A.M., at which time one Fred Schmidt was empowered to hold a series of such meetings until final disposition was made of the money.

With $1 million "inadvertently" (his term) coined from the *Catalog,* Brand formed POINT, seeking more ways to do good. Six directors were provided with $55,000 a year to give away at their individual discretion. Brand feels that for the most part the small grants were the most effective: for instance, a mere $600 donated to Gerard O'Neill's Space Colonization project helped launch what is now a full-blown enterprise supported by funds from NASA and other sources.

The soft-spoken Brand is an advocate of violent physical exercise and body-contact sports. He has offered exhibitions of saber-fighting in connection with his public appearances, and believes that such "boffing" releases ugly and violent force, leaving people free to "play out good stuff." The staff at *Co-Evolution Quarterly* plays a couple of vigorous volleyball games each day.

Asked about his concept of the ultimate lifestyle, Brand expressed distaste for the term, preferring "life content." He advocates as much variety as possible, true cultural diversity. "We live in an age of dinosaurs — it's best to be a mammal. Most of what we are doing here is to aid and abet the development of mammals." Small is beautiful, he believes, because small is a chance to respond quickly to opportunity and threat. Detroit, Los Angeles, and New York are dinosaurs — mammals are small places, communes, religious groups.

The Winter, 1975, edition of the *Quarterly* contains a seven-page guide illustrated with drawings of a winged figure landing, shedding the wings, growing flowers, feeding birds, entitled "Finding our place in space. A handy step-by-step guide for getting from where we are to where we ought to be." It expresses much of Stewart Brand's philosophy of living.

Step One: Clear your head, clean up your dreams, get easy and believe in the new possibilities.

Step Two: Move about, look around, pick a place, come down gently and tune yourself to the natural vibrations.

Step Three: Look and listen, move slow, tread softly, stay open and be part of what the place is being.

Step Four: Grow slowly, flow steady, try hard, don't worry. Remember that everything is connected.

Step Five: Live lightly on the land, share, recycle. Do less with less. Dream small, feel big.

Step Six: Care. Teach children. Think healthy. This is the glue which holds things together.

Step Seven: Maintain yourself. Steward the Earth. Love, and we will all have a place in space.

SPACE COLONIES BY THE YEAR 2000

The testimony that follows was given by Dr. Gerard O'Neill before the Subcommittee on Space Science and Applications of the Committee on Science and Technology, U.S. House of Representatives, on July 23, 1975. O'Neill, a high-energy physicist at Princeton, maintains that the initial cost of the project would be $100 billion — "one tenth the cost of Project Independence and 10 times the return in energy alone," as Stewart Brand points out. His Co–Evolution Quarterly *for Fall 1975, from which this testimony is excerpted, and for Spring 1976, contain much more equally fascinating material about the space colonies and their originator.*

Within the past year, a new possibility for the direction and motivation of our thrust into space has reached the stage of public discussion. It is called space colonization, or the development of space manufacturing facilities. Our present American leadership in space technology gives us a unique opportunity to play a central role in that new development, if we act with decision and speed.

The central ideas of space colonization are:

1. To establish a highly-industrialized, self-maintaining human community in free space, at a location along the orbit of the moon called L5 where free solar energy is available full time.

2. To construct that community on a short time scale, without depending on rocket engines any more advanced than those of the space shuttle.

3. To reduce the costs greatly by obtaining nearly all of the construction materials from the surface of the moon.

4. At the space community, to process lunar surface raw materials into metals, ceramics, glass and oxygen for the construction of both additional communities and of products such as satellite solar power

stations. The power stations would be relocated in synchronous orbit about the earth, to supply the earth with electrical energy by low-density microwave beams.

5. Throughout the program, to rely only on those technologies which are available at the time, while recognizing and supporting the development of more advanced technologies if their benefits are clear.

The Space Colony Concept

Although it has precursors in the works of many authors, the modern idea of space colonies originated from several questions, posed six years ago as an academic exercise:

1. Is it possible, within the limits of 1970s technology, using only the ordinary construction materials with which we are already familiar, to build communities in free space rather than on a planetary surface like the earth, the moon, or Mars?

2. Can these communities be large enough, and sufficiently earth-like, to be attractive to live in — small worlds of their own rather than simply space stations?

3. Would such colonies have unique advantages from an economic viewpoint, so that they could justify the costs of their construction and contribute in a productive way to the total human community?

4. If such colonies were built, would their further development be such as to relieve the earth of further exploitation by the industrial revolution, and to open up a new frontier to challenge the best and highest aspirations of the human race?

Surprisingly, six years of continued research has confirmed, in even more increasing detail, that the answer to all four of these questions is a strong "yes."

Geometries

The largest colonies now foreseeable would probably be formed as cylinders, alternating areas of glass and interior land areas. From those land areas a resident would see a reflected image of the ordinary disc of the sun in the sky, and the sun's image would move across the sky from dawn to dusk as it does on earth. Within civil engineering limits no greater than those under which our terrestrial bridges and buildings are built, the land area of one cylinder could be as large as 100 square miles. Even a colony of smaller dimensions could be quite attractive.

Rotation of the cylinder would produce earth-normal gravity inside, and the atmosphere enclosed could have the oxygen content of air at sea-level on earth. The residents would be able to choose and control their climate and seasons.

Agriculture for a space community would be carried out in external cylinders or rings, with atmospheres, temperatures, humidity and day-length chosen to match exactly the needs of each type of crop being grown. Because sunshine in free space is available 24 hours per day for 12 months of the year, and because care would be taken not to introduce into the agricultural cylinders the insect pests which have evolved over millennia to attack our crops, agriculture in space could be efficient and predictable, free of the extremes of crop-failure and glut which the terrestrial environment forces on our farmers.

Industry

Nonpolluting light industry would probably be carried on within the cylindrical living-habitat, convenient to homes and shops. Heavy industry, though, could benefit from the convenience of zero gravity. Through an avenue on the axis of the cylinder, workers in heavy industry could easily reach external, nonrotating factories, where zero gravity and breathable atmospheres would permit the easy assembly, without cranes, lift-trucks, or other handling equipment, of very large, massive products. These products could be the components of new colonies, radio and optical telescopes, large ships for the further exploration of the solar system, and power plants to supply energy for the earth.

Limits of Growth

In the early years of this research, before the question of implementation was seriously addressed, it seemed wise to check whether an expansion into space would soon encounter "growth limits" of the kind which humankind is now reaching on earth, and which have been vividly described for us by Professor Jay Forrester of Massachusetts Institute of Technology, in studies supported by the Club of Rome.

If the space colonization program is begun, its technical and economic imperatives seem likely to drive it rather quickly toward the exploitation of asteroidal rather than lunar materials. Long before the results of mining activity on the moon became visible from the earth, the colony program would be obtaining its materials from the asteroids. Given that source, the "limits of growth" are absurdly high: the total quantity of materials within only a few known large asteroids is quite enough to permit building space colonies with a total land area more than 10,000 times that of the earth.

Energy Without Guilt

The efficiencies of a space community, regarded as an island of a technological human civilization, stem from the abundance and full-time dependability of free solar energy in that environment, and from the possibility of controlling the effective gravity, over a wide range from zero to more than earth-normal, by rotation. In contrast, industrial operations on earth are shackled by a strong gravity which can never be "turned off"; those on the moon would be similarly limited, although the limit would be lower.

In a space colony, the basic human activities of living and recreation, of agriculture, and of industry could all be separated and noninterfering, each with its optimal gravity, temperature, climate, sunlight, and atmosphere, but could be located conveniently near to each other. Energy for agriculture would be used directly in the form of sunlight, interrupted at will by large, very low-mass aluminum shades located in zero gravity in space near the farming areas. The day-length and seasonal cycle would therefore be controllable independently for each crop.

Process heat for industry would be obtained with similar economy; in space, temperatures of up to several thousand degrees would be obtainable at low cost, simply by the use of low-mass aluminum-foil mirrors to concentrate the ever-present sunlight. In space, a passive aluminum mirror with a mass of less than a ton and a dimension of about 100 meters could collect and concentrate, in the course of a year, an amount of solar energy which on earth would cost over a million dollars at standard electricity busbar rates.

Electrical energy for a space community could be obtained at low cost, within the limits of right-now technology, by a system consisting of a concentrating mirror, a boiler, a conventional turbogenerator and a radiator, discarding waste heat to the cold of outer space. It appears that in the environment of a space community, residents could enjoy a per capita usage of energy many times larger even than what is now common in the United States, but could do so with none of the guilt which is now connected with the depletion of an exhaustible resource.

The Bootstrap Method

Until recently, it had been assumed that the only practical way to locate or assemble an object in a high orbit was to build it or its components on earth, and then to lift it out of the earth's gravity, through the atmosphere, by rockets. One might fairly call this the "brute force" method. In space colonization, we would like to use a far more economical alternative, a kind of "end run" instead of a power play through the middle.

Here on the surface of the earth, we are at a very low point in the gravitational map of the solar system. In energy terms, we are at the bottom of a gravitational well which is 4,000 miles deep. This is reflected in the fact that we must accelerate a spacecraft to a speed of more than 25,000 miles per hour before it can escape the earth's gravity and go as far as lunar orbit. In a sense, we are the "gravitationally disadvantaged."

We are fortunate that we have another source of materials, which lies at a much shallower point in the gravitational map of the solar system. The energy required to bring materials from the moon to free space is only 1/20 as much as from the earth. Further, the moon has no atmosphere — a disadvantage if we wanted to live there, but a great advantage if we want to obtain from the moon materials at low cost. On the moon we could assemble a launching device for the acceleration to escape velocity of lunar surface raw materials. Such a machine does not require high-strength or high-temperature materials, and the methods for building it are well understood.

One design of that kind is called a mass-driver. It would be a linear electric motor, forming a thin line several miles long, which would accelerate small 10-pound vehicles we call buckets. At lunar escape speed the bucket would release its payload and would then return on a side track for re-use. Only the payload would leave the mass-driver, so nothing expensive would be thrown away. The mass-driver would be an efficient machine, driven by a solar-powered or nuclear electric plant, and our calculations show that in six years of time it could launch to escape distance from 300 to 1,000 times its own mass. A collector at escape distance from the moon would accumulate materials, and there, with the full solar energy of free space, they would be processed to form the metals, glass, and soil of the first space community.

With the help of that economy measure, the mass lifted from the earth need only be a few percent of the mass of the colony itself. We would have to bring the components of the mass-driver and of a lunar outpost, components of a construction station in lunar orbit for the processing and assembly of materials, and those elements — mainly carbon, nitrogen, and hydrogen — which are rare on the moon. By so avoiding the need for prior development of advanced high-capacity lift vehicles, we could also carry out the construction of the first colony on a fast time scale, possibly beginning as early as 1980-'82 when the space shuttle will come into operation. For the lifting of freight to low orbit, we would need one new vehicle, of a type which the aerospace experts call a "dumb booster" — a freight rocket based on the same type of engines already developed for the shuttle. For operations in space above low orbit, a chemical tug would be sufficient. My recommendation would therefore be strongly supportive of a recently initiated

NASA study of the design of a shuttle-derived heavy-lift vehicle, and of a chemical tug whose segments could be lifted to orbit by the shuttle.

In this approach, we would establish a productive beachhead in space as early as possible, and as the resulting traffic increased, would let its revenue assist in paying for the further development of more advanced launch vehicles.

Lunar Materials

At the time of the Apollo project, we did not think of the moon as a resource base. The moon landings, originally motivated by national pride and a sense of adventure, became scientific expeditions and, as such, returned a high payoff in knowledge.

Now, though, it is time to cash in on Apollo. It was impossible to plan in a rational way a program of space colonization until the Apollo lunar samples were returned for analysis. From those samples we now have the analyses of the lunar soil and rock. *Table 1* summarizes representative data from soils at the Apollo II landing site:

Table 1
UNSELECTED APOLLO II SOIL SAMPLE

Oxygen	40.0%
Silicon	19.2%
Iron	14.3%
Calcium	8.0%
Titanium	5.9%
Aluminum	5.6%
Magnesium	4.5%

This unselected sample is more than 30% metals by weight.

The baseline mass-driver would be capable of transferring from the moon from half a million to two million tons of such materials within a six-year period; that is, from 28,000 to more than 100,000 tons of aluminum, 70,000 to 280,000 tons of iron, and corresponding amounts of the other lunar materials. Strangely, though the lunar surface is devoid of life, its most abundant element is the one which we need in every breath we take: oxygen. That oxygen, transported to free space and unlocked from its binding metals by solar energy, would be usable not only for an atmosphere but to fuel rocket engines, reducing by 85 percent the requirement for fuel carried from the earth.

The lunar surface materials are poor in carbon, nitrogen, and hydrogen; in the early years of space colonization, these elements would have to be brought from earth. They would be reused, not thrown away. For every ton of hydrogen brought from earth, nine tons of water could be made at the colony site, the remaining eight tons being oxygen from the processing of lunar oxides.

The removal of half a million tons of material from the surface of the moon sounds like a large-scale mining operation, but it is not. The excavation left on the moon would be only five meters deep and 200 meters long and wide — not even enough to keep one small bulldozer occupied for a five-year period.

A few years after the first space community is built, we can expect that transport of asteroidal materials to L5 will become practical. No great technical advance is required for that transition; the energy-interval between the asteroids and L5 is only about as great as between the earth and L5. Once the asteroidal resources are tapped, we should have not only metals, glass and ceramics, but also carbon, nitrogen, and hydrogen. These three elements, scarce on the moon, are believed to be abundant in the type of asteroid known as carbonaceous chondritic. Therefore, I add my support to those who for several years have been recommending an unmanned rendezvous-probe mission to a selected asteroid. Such a mission has already been studied in detail by NASA and is well within present technical feasibility. If conducted in the late 1970s or early 1980s, with the aim of assaying a carbonaceous chondritic asteroid for its C, N, H content, such a mission would serve the same function that oil-well prospecting now serves on earth: the finding and proving of necessary resources for subsequent practical use.

Island One

The first space community will be economically productive only if talented, hard-working people choose to live in it, either permanently or for periods of several years. It must therefore be much more than a space station; it must as earthlike as possible, rich in green growing plants, animals, birds, and other desirable features of attractive regions on earth.

Within the materials limits of ordinary civil engineering practice, and within an overall mass budget of half a million tons (about the same as the mass of a super-tanker), several designs for this first "Island in Space" have evolved.

All of the geometries we have studied are pressure vessels, spherical, cylindrical, or toroidal, containing atmospheres and rotating slowly to provide a gravity as strong as that of the earth. With gravity, good long-term health can be maintained; the colonists should experience none of the bone-calcium loss suffered by the Skylab astronauts in their zero-gravity, nonrotating environment.

Physiology experiments in rotating rooms

on earth indicate that humans can acclimatize to quite high rotation rates, some to as much as one rotation every six seconds. A fraction of the space-community population will, though, "commute" daily between the rotating earth-gravity environment and zero- or low-gravity work areas. We must, therefore, hold the rotation rate to a rather low value to avoid inner-ear disturbances. It is quite possible that our lack of information is forcing us toward unnecessary conservatism on this point. It would be quite useful to carry out long-term physiology experiments during the space-shuttle program, to examine rotation effects in the space environment. On earth, our simulation of these effects can never be more than approximate.

Conservatism on this requirement has, though, led us quite recently to a new and possibly more attractive alternative design. It allows for natural sunshine, a hillside terraced environment, considerable bodies of water for swimming and boating, and an overall population density characteristic of some quite attractive modern communities in the United States and southern France.

It is startling to realize that even the first-model space community could have a population of 10,000 people, and that its circumference could be more than one mile. From the valley area, where streams could flow, a 10-minute walk could bring a resident up the hill to a region of much-reduced gravity, where human-powered flight would be easy, sports and ballet could take on a new dimension, and weight would almost disappear. It seems almost a certainty that at such a level a person with a serious heart condition could live far longer than on earth, and that low gravity could greatly ease many of the health problems of advancing age.

A few minutes from the residential areas,

there could be large assembly areas, with low or zero gravity. In one design now being studied, these areas would be cylindrical, rotating once every 70 seconds, and would provide 1.5 percent of earth gravity. There, a ton of mass would weigh only 30 pounds, but tools and equipment would stay put when set "down." Workers commuting to those areas would experience rotation-rate changes of no more than one rpm.

Cost-Drivers in Construction

Recently, independent cost estimates for the construction of Island One have been made by the NASA Marshall Space Flight Center. These are not at the stage of an official report, but excellent cooperation and communication between Princeton and NASA/MSFC has allowed identification of some important cost-drivers in the construction of a first colony. These are:

1. Frequency and efficiency of crew-rotation between the earth and L5, and between the earth and the moon, during the construction period.

2. Extent of resupply needed during construction: This item can vary over a wide range, depending on the atmospheric composition needed at the construction station, and whether food is brought in water-loaded or dry form.

3. Atmospheric composition: The structural mass of Island One is proportional to the internal atmospheric pressure, but independent of the strength of the artificial gravity produced by rotation. Nitrogen constitutes 79 percent of our atmosphere on earth, but we do not use it in breathing; to provide an earth-normal amount of nitrogen would cost us two ways in space-colony construction, because structure masses would have to be increased to contain the increased

pressure, and because nitrogen would have to be imported from the earth. A final choice of atmospheric mix would be based on a more complete understanding of fire protection.

A modest program of experiments on earth could add greatly to knowledge on this point, and might save a great deal of money. Lacking such experiments, present designs are conservative, based on carrying a substantial pressure of nitrogen.

Costs and Payoffs

A range of costs for large-scale engineering projects is listed in *Table 2*, for scale:

Table 2
APPROXIMATE COSTS OF ENGINEERING PROJECTS IN 1975 DOLLARS

Panama Canal	2 Billion
Space Shuttle Development	5-8 Billion
Alaska Pipeline	6 Billion
Advanced Lift Vehicle Development	8-25 Billion
Apollo	39 Billion
Super Shuttle Development	45 Billion
Manned Mission to Mars	100 Billion
Project Independence	600-2,000 Billion

(The re- or devaluation of the dollar forward or backward to 1975 makes each of the numbers in *Table 2* uncertain by at least 25 percent.)

The Apollo project provided trips to the moon for a total of 12 men, at a cost of about $3 billion per man. In space colonization we are considering, for Island One, a thousand times as many people for a long duration rather than for only a few days. With the cost savings outlined earlier, it appears that we can accomplish this thousandfold increase at a cost of at most a few times that of Apollo.

I have waited so long
to be where I am going

d.m.

Coreta

interview / ERNIE LYKISSAS and GEOFF LANGUEDOC
genetic control: the morality of biochemical manipulation

Ernest Lykissas was born in Greece in 1946, came to the United States in 1963, took his B.Sc. and M.Sc. in microbiology at California State University, Long Beach, and has just completed his Ph.D. in experimental medicine and surgery at the Institute of Experimental Medicine and Surgery, University of Montreal. Geoffrey Languedoc, four years his junior, is Canadian by birth and has a B.A. in philosophy from Sir George Williams University, where he is currently taking his M.A. As an editor at the International Institute of Stress, he works closely with Dr. Selye, its director, and his staff of researchers, preparing books and manuscripts for publication. The circumstances of this dialogue are rather interesting. I was in Montreal, working with Dr. Hans Selye on the preface to this book, and Lykissas and Languedoc were working with me. One day the three of us were in the Institute of Experimental Medicine and Surgery where Selye works, and got into a dialogue which started at the afternoon coffeebreak and lasted far into the night, finally concluding the following day over a late breakfast. I include the edited dialogue here because it raises some fundamental questions about our ability to control the forms life takes, and whether living under such programmed conditions would deprive human beings of precisely those qualities that comprise our humanity, our individuality, our uniqueness . . . .

LYKISSAS: The key to life is information: the input data which we now know from the deciphering of the genetic code that resulted from Watson and Crick's modeling of the molecule of DNA. Once we move in, then, and can identify specific genes for specific actions, we are able to see the key to life.

When a living cell, a fertilized ovum, is first implanted in the uterus, all we have there is the information for the specific organism that can be made from that arrangement of information inherited from the parents. Once this cell is propelled into the world as a mass of cells that have attained a highly specialized function *in utero*, in the womb, we have specialization. You can look at a cell and say this is a muscle cell, this is a sperm cell, this is a nerve cell. They all look different, but the same information for the individual is contained in each of them.

So we have the information out of which life will come. But if we look at that information, it is not itself alive. The basic components of life are six elements: carbon, oxygen, phosphorus, nitrogen, hydrogen, and sulphur — but then you can throw in smaller quantities of sodium, magnesium, potassium, calcium — all the elements that we find in inert matter, as we call it, also make up life. Nothing new is added. It is the *arrangement* of that matter which brings us from the inert state, death, to what we call living. What gives life on our planet is the particle called a photon, which is emitted from the sun. The photon is energy traveling at the speed of light. In effect, the process by which life evolves is the trapping of that energy. It comes from the sun, hits a plant, and then the plant, through the light energy, takes the mineral, the inert matter, and brings it into the state of being organic — by incorporating carbon in it — and from plants we go into the food chain, and move up it.

First in the food chain is the herbivore, which eats only plants; then the carnivorous animal that eats herbivorous animals; then the omnivorous animal like the human being that eats both; and so we step up the chain in organization and complexity of function, to forms of life that, by our standards, are more perfect. The dolphin and the human being, which are both members of the mammalian family, exhibit a fantastic complexity of function.

LANDE: How much do we know about DNA? Is it the transmitter of the genetic code?

LYKISSAS: Yes. Experiments have proven beyond any shadow of doubt that DNA, nucleic acid, is the transmitter of the genetic information. Now, during the transmission of the information, errors occur and there are various environmental factors that also have an effect, not only on the arrangement of that information but also its expression. It's a case of the environment limiting the information and how it is expressed.

LANDE: I don't completely understand how environment controls or influences DNA.

LYKISSAS: It doesn't influence DNA itself. But take ionization, or cosmic rays. At this particular moment, excluding nuclear proliferation and all the pollution with nuclear waste in our environment, the earth is constantly being bombarded — and if we could take a Geiger counter we could measure it — by a barrage of highly energetic particles whose radiation is extremely penetrating. They are partially responsible for the mutations that have occurred through evolution.

When we say mutations, what happens? We have a certain information to express, and a highly energetic particle comes in and throws out a key piece of that information. The information gets rearranged, mutated — and 99 percent of the new information is lethal. Only in the case of 1 percent will the product be viable. But that is how change is accomplished and therefore how we proceed into evolution.

LANDE: How can you isolate DNA?

LYKISSAS: We would take a cell, or a population of cells, then proceed to isolate the nuclei, the centers of the cells. Once we reached the nuclei, we would split the nuclear membrane that encircles the nucleus and go inside, and what we would find inside that nucleus would be DNA, the chromosomes, and RNA, which is the messenger DNA sends out to make the protein.

The genetic code works rather like a cookbook: the DNA makes up recipes and sends these out to the ribosomes, via the messenger RNA, one for the salad, one for the entree, one for the dessert, and so forth. Let's say the recipes are on punch cards; the messenger RNA goes out through the nucleus into the cell, hits a ribosome, which reads off the punch card, and generates a protein through the clues on the card, that tell which amino acid to put where to form the protein.

LANDE: Are you implying that it's thinking?

LYKISSAS: If you would like to call it that, yes. The organization of the cell is far more complex and fascinating for me than the level of reality that I realize around myself with my own eyes. I find that what life is at its base is far more exciting than the life that we are living. Watching that mystery being unraveled in front of my eyes sometimes makes me lose contact with reality. I start living inside the cell instead of outside. It's like watching how life really goes on.

LANDE: Do you think we will be able to alter life, genetically speaking, through the control of DNA?

LYKISSAS: Oh, yes, and in certain instances this is practiced already. For example, we now have the ability to perform certain tests on the fetus while it is *in utero,* and if we ascertain a certain genetic malfunction in the arrangement or rearrangement of its inherited genetic material, we abort the fetus because we know

it will be born defective, or a thalidomide victim — and we can apply this knowledge to the bettering of the human race.

LANDE: Can we in any way implant DNA in the fetus — as intelligence?

LYKISSAS: Theoretically, with the information we have, we can.

LANGUEDOC: I'd like to comment on that. The topic for a moment there was, it seemed to me, the intentional genetic manipulation of material within a cell. You were saying that the human race could be improved or made better by, let's say, throwing out the bad aspects of genetic material and replacing them with superior ones, in such cases, for instance, as physical health or the ability to process concepts. I see the role of the philosopher as being to examine the criteria for deciding which action would be the better one.

My first objection to intentional genetic manipulation comes from the thought that the human race is unique from many points of view. One of them is the seemingly haphazard way it evolved to the state it is in right now. The public gets scared at the thought of individuals being created rather than conceived. This is a problem I think not only scientists and politicians need to adjust to, but professional thinkers as well. It's going to be up to someone to establish and implement criteria. I don't think the philosophers of this world can conscientiously ignore the question and refuse to apply themselves to something of such profound importance.

Another problem is raised by the diversity of choice we have in establishing pathways in our lives. Many people find it very difficult to resolve to proceed in a particular way and to see it through to the end. One of the principal problems, I think, is that there are so many established and almost institutionalized approaches to life. Many kids have been brought up today — I think I could put myself in that category — to have a liberal approach to other people's ways of thinking, other lifestyles and mindstyles. I think in many households today parents are unconsciously abdicating a responsibility that must be assumed by *someone* to give the child at least one mindstyle and at least one lifestyle to work with and to balance against all of the others. A kid can't be raised with the thought that everything is equal and that everything is relative. Some things have to be more relative than others, otherwise we could never opt for any one thing. We would be in a constant state of indecision and of relativity. And sooner or later in life you have to choose.

A philosopher could help out here by examining the pathways and domains we already have at our disposal. He might perhaps throw in a few more of his own, but he could certainly help, through the analysis of language and the processing of concepts, to clarify obscure points and somehow standardize the putting forward of ideas in a way that everyone can understand. There is a big problem these days with jargon, scientific jargon, sociological jargon, psychological jargon. People get misled into thinking there are two different concepts happening, when in fact there is only one. You can see this happening in religion too. People may take issue with this, but in fact Nirvana, the happy hunting grounds, God, heaven, are all concepts that express a certain fundamental notion. The words are different but the ideas behind them have a common ground. Philosophers could bring this common ground to light, so that people wouldn't be seemingly so lost and so confused at the almost infinite number of choices open to them.

LANDE: What evidence is there to support that intelligent information, creative ability, the aspects of man's personality can be transmitted genetically?

LYKISSAS: We have evidence which is presented even in first-year biology courses of various experiments in which changes of genetic information have been performed in unicellular organisms, namely bacteria. There is a bacterium called *escherichia coli*, the coliform bacteria, which we geneticists know better than we know the map of earth because we use it constantly. Now, we can change a cell of *escherichia coli*, give it whatever characteristics we want or take from it whatever characteristics we want. We can change its whole information by just manipulating its DNA. Therefore, there is no scientific reason to stop short of this kind of manipulation in man — if we are indeed stopping short, because if it is being done probably it wouldn't be made public.

We ourselves evolved from Cro-Magnon man; before Cro-Magnon was *homo erectus,* and we are *homo sapiens.* Evolution has to go on. I believe that we, our own species, can predetermine what will evolve from us. We will be able to choose the best characteristics of our race and put them together in an arrangement. I see the scientists as handling the hardware, but the philosophers, the leading minds, I believe, can get together and arrange the new species that will evolve and will take over from *homo sapiens'* fallacies and problems.

LANDE: On a more immediate level, is it possible to have a DNA bank where I can go and select DNA for a blond, blue-eyed, intelligent child with a sense of humor, an altruistic approach to life, and good business acumen?

LYKISSAS: What do you think is going on with sperm banks? You are already selecting individuals there. But if you want something better than what you can get in a typical sperm bank, then probably you would allow a scientist to manipulate that sperm cell, add some things to it, take some things away from it and this is not that far away. I'm not talking about the year 2000 — I'm talking about the year 1980, 1990.

LANDE: I've heard from some sources that it can be done now — that they can identify DNA to such an extent that you can tell exactly what it is in the characteristics or personality and intelligence.

LYKISSAS: This is true, but to actually say that it is practiced at this particular moment would raise havoc among religious and various other groups. The timing is not right now for the release of that type of information.

LANDE: Why is there a morality factor here?

LYKISSAS: Because the big question is who will be the person to select which characteristics are right.

LANDE: Wouldn't that be the responsibility of the parent?

LYKISSAS: No. We are moving into a society where, because of overpopulation, we are going to have to give up the individuality and various other characteristics that have made our lives so meaningful up to now. They will have to be sacrificed in favor of characteristics that will provide more efficiency and more productivity per unit. Therefore, the organized state — by employing the scientists to perform this work,

even if they haven't actually given that order yet — will probably arrange for this particular situation to come to pass.

LANDE: Geoff, this seems to be an area for the philosophers.

LANGUEDOC: Any area is an area for philosophers. You both mentioned a morality factor. Who is going to be in charge of genetic manipulation; who is going to set the rules and standards about what we are going to be looking for in our goody bag of genetic material? Apart from this, the question of how hormones influence behavioral manifestations is particularly interesting, because the hormonal balance presumably would be at least in part controlled by the encoding of the DNA material. And should it be possible to intentionally and very carefully rearrange DNA in a cell in such a way that it would have a bearing on the hormonal balance in the body, then it would obviously also be possible to alter a man's behavior as a result. Although the manipulation of character is certainly nothing new, as you both know. The notion of peer pressure — a neat term that has become popular in the 20th century — expresses a concept which has been in existence ever since men first banded together in groups. The maintaining of the status quo and the processing of deviants from it is a kind of behavioral therapy which has been practiced for a long time. B. F. Skinner's book *Beyond Freedom and Dignity* is really just a rational approach to creating the kind of society that we could arrive at by consensus.

Right now we allow social progress and behavioral development in an almost haphazard way. We have certain institutions more or less directed to the forming of behavior. We have finishing schools for girls — and probably for boys, too, if you want to include private schools — where behavior is polished and refined, and we have the courts and the prisons, which are places where we put our deviants. All the while, we are trying to pattern behavior along certain broadly but really quite specifically defined lines. You could call them pathways. If most people can be made to follow them, the result will be a society in which we can coexist relatively peacefully.

LANDE: It doesn't seem to have worked, though, up to this point in time.

LANGUEDOC: That's true, but it would be hard to imagine something that would work better. Unless, of course — which is the question we are directing ourselves to right now — we could start at a cellular level and reproduce carbon copies, or maybe 15 to 20 major variants of a particular style, and in that way remove the element of chance from human evolution and from behavioral manifestation. Then we would wind up with a very carefully controlled and easily predictable group of individuals.

Whether this is a situation we would like to see come to pass is another question. I think if you back people into a corner, they would say one of the most fundamentally important features of human beings is their unpredictability, their creativity. There is a sense in the word *creativity* of something you just can't deduce; you have to induce it. There is something kind of haywire about it, something spontaneous, something unknown. The mystery of life, I think, is a notion people don't want to see removed from what it means to be a human being.

Unfortunately, it is that very aspect of man which has led to many of the behavioral differences with which every society is faced. The problem boils down to striking a balance between the expedience of social control by genetic manipulation and our desire to preserve the human race as we know it today.

LYKISSAS: I would like to comment on some of the things Geoff said. He talked about the spontaneity, the creativity, the qualities that may have been responsible for putting man on the moon. But we are faced with a situation today — without trying to play the alarmist role — where man is knocking on the door of self-destruction, if he has not bust it open already. Now we have to examine human behavior from a realistic point of view. In the past it's always been, Let's find the solution — once things haven't worked out. Let's look in a new direction — once everything has failed. We have never programmed our existence, our behavior, before — instead of after — the results. This is what everybody is afraid of.

LANDE: For a program you have to have a model.

LYKISSAS: Yes, first an experimental model, then a practice model, and from doing all kinds of things to that model, we would be able to arrive at the real man.

Man has already been projected into the future. We have already started training the populace with TV or mass media information about what is to come, what is available, how we can train ourselves to a better solution because we only have one earth. I will never forget that Armstrong, the first astronaut to place his foot on the moon, said the only manmade thing he could see on earth from space was the smog belt over Los Angeles.

I believe that only through programmed behavior, programmed existence, a programmed future can we survive. We aren't talking any more about how to make things better. We are talking about survival. If we want to be here tomorrow, let's do something about it.

LANGUEDOC: That really opens up a hornet's nest. If we are going to preserve life, what will wind up being preserved in another 50 or 200 years? If the price of preservation is genetic alteration and completely predictable and unspontaneous behavior, I think many people would have to ask themselves: "Is it humanity that we are preserving or is it another kind of race that's going to need a new kind of word to describe it?"

LANDE: Or a new kind of vocabulary.

LANGUEDOC: Right. If we could completely alter those characteristics we think are most fundamental to human life now, would we still be considered human? Or would it be an entirely different kind of beast we were continuing than, let's say, we know, or our children would know. It's a very tricky question. I've known of people who encountered situations that were so drastically opposed to their notion of what it meant to be a human being or what it meant to be alive that they committed suicide.

As human beings, I think most of us would say that if the human race was changed to the extent we seem to view as a possibility, we would not want to be alive on such a planet. Would we consider it worthwhile to have our children manipulated and mutated to that extent? That's a really fundamental question, which disturbs the morals of the 1970s, but it doesn't upset them nearly as much as it did the morals of the 1930s when Huxley spoke of cloning in *Brave New World*. And in 50 years, I think people will be worrying even less about the question because they will already have been changed a little bit.

LANDE: Ernie, can we control character and behavior?

LYKISSAS: What we know as character and behavior are the total expression of the genetic code through its endocrine secretions that we call hormones. It is the hormones, and their balance in the body, that determine each individual's character. We have been successful at controlling people's behaviors for quite some time now by altering this hormonal balance, as in the case of thyroid malfunction, or with menopausal women, where we can alleviate feelings of depression by administering estrogen, the hormone in short supply. But we can also go in through the DNA cells, alter the DNA, and thereby change character, change behavior. We are changing behavior today in prisoners whom we find to have chromosomal abnormalities, like the trisomics, whom we find have more tendency toward violence. These individuals are being castrated to prevent their propagation in our society. Therefore, you could say we are already doing it and all we are now engaged in is making it more finite, doing it better.

LANDE: Geoff, how about society?

LANGUEDOC: I think the flow of information in society is one of the absolutely fundamental aspects or modifiers; it has the greatest bearing on the way we live and the way we think. Nowadays there is a vastly increased amount of information available to any individual upon which he can base any number of decisions. The poor human being has more and more parameters to consider, simply because of the increasing number of factors that bear on any single decision he might want to take.

It's getting increasingly difficult, in other words, for people to make up their minds about things because they have to decide so many smaller issues before really getting to the heart of the matter.

Genetic information is just another way of communicating. If you are going to manipulate the channels of genetic communication in the same way we can interfere with short-wave communication, or newspaper communication, or governmental communication, maybe that opens up a new pathway that should be explored. It might turn something up — like a new approach to society.

LANDE: Ernie, to wrap up our discussion, what are you currently working on in the laboratory?

LYKISSAS: I'm presently involved in the elucidation of the effects of certain drugs that we call in pharmacology *microsomal enzyme inducers.* These microsomal enzyme inducers have beneficial effects for man because they increase the detoxifying capability of the liver to such a degree that it can alleviate harmful effects due to ingestion or overproduction of certain toxic agents.

What I'm looking at personally is what these drugs are doing to the DNA. Are we really doing good, or are we actually changing the genetic information of the cell? We have to be careful with drugs these days. Since the thalidomide experience we cannot take any more chances. So people like myself look inside the genetic information of the cells, to check whether, while the drug is doing all the beneficial activity, it is bringing about any other changes which may produce things like cancers, after-effects that we may be hurt by.

LANGUEDOC: I feel my concluding comment should be a plea for people to think about things a little bit, and to get good at thinking. We must not overlook — either

because it is expedient or because ignorance is bliss — the problems raised by the immense strides being made in the sciences, especially biology, as they have such a direct bearing on the human race. People need to be on their guard. Information such as the scientists are in possession of now could alter our ways of life and our ways of thinking so radically, so incredibly, and so quickly that we must all feel directly involved and directly threatened.

It is important for all of us to try and stay as abreast as possible of what is going on. Through discussions and through thought, we need to arrive at conclusions about exactly where we want to go, and not to be weak in putting into effect the knowledge that is increasing exponentially in the scientific world. We can't leave it up to the politicians to decide these questions, nor can we leave it up to the scientists. We have to come to conclusions that will need to be implemented on a social and a political level, worldwide. We have to be very vigilant over the scientific community, over the political community. Each one of us as citizens cannot abdicate his responsibility to the rest of the global population to make sure that whatever changes are carried out are decided upon as fairly as we possibly can in a world that is becoming more overcrowded and unmanageable every day.

If enough of us fail at this task, there's a good chance that our children's children will never even be aware that once there were no Alphas and Betas. It won't be long before we'll be remembering 1984.

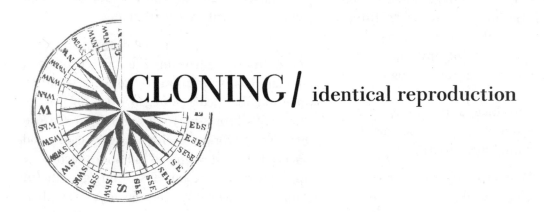

CLONING / identical reproduction

*"We have the awful knowledge to make
exact copies of human beings."*
— Willard Gaylin
New York Times Magazine,
March 5, 1972

The 20th century has brought with it such vast physiological and biological strides that we are now able to patch human beings together out of spare parts. Transplants of eyes, kidneys, hearts, and other organs have become common; and plastic devices and electronic receivers are being implanted throughout the body to substitute for missing or defective elements.

By far the most awesome of this array of alternatives to nature's method of constructing life is cloning — the production of copies of a living organism that are genetically identical to the original. Willard Gaylin, in the article just quoted, defines this concept:

"Cloning is the production of genetically identical copies of an individual organism. Just as one can take hundreds of cuttings from a specific plant, each of which can then develop into a mature plant — genetic replicas of the parent — it is now possible to clone animals. The possibility of human cloning seems to produce in nonscientists more titillation than terror or awe — perhaps because it is usually visualized as a 'garden of Raquel Welches,' blooming by the hundred, genetically identical."

It has been a known fact for centuries that every species of living organism has the capacity to reproduce its own kind. Mendel's theory of genetics established many years ago that each genetic trait in an individual organism is determined by two genes, inherited one from each parent. The physical expression of each trait is dependent on the unique combination of the two genes — one may dominate or they may join in some intermediate form of expression. Each gene, however, retains its own unique identity and can be passed on in pure form to future generations. This combination of genes (one maternal, one paternal) for any one trait is carried on in a random fashion through sexual reproduction. Each mating of any two organisms will produce a new and unique individual possessing a random assortment of traits inherited from both parents.

To illustrate Mendel's laws, which hold true for all living things, envision a plant which produces only white flowers. If we fertilize it with pollen from a plant which produces only red flowers, the offspring might have only white flowers, only red flowers, or even all pink flowers, depending on how the parental genes were combined in individual offspring. Genetically speaking, however, each offspring has both the genes for white flowers and for red flowers and they exist as separate entities. Depending on what type of plant an offspring is mated to, any one of the observed traits is once again possible.

The idea of cloning is based on the fact that the nucleus in each cell of every organism contains a complete set of genetic information for the entire organism.

It was Professor F. C. Steward, a cellular physiologist at Cornell University, who first developed the cloning process. Steward worked on a variety of conditions until he was finally able to produce a full-grown carrot plant — roots, stalk, leaves, flowers, and seeds — from one individual cell. His feat has since been reproduced by dissociating individual phloem cells (the transporters of nutrients from the photosynthetic tissues to the rest of the plant) and putting them in coconut milk, which acts as a food source somewhat like the yolk of an egg for the growing cells. After a while the cells form a small cell mass, and eventually one of these cells begins to divide and differentiate to form a complete and genetically identical carrot plant.

Theoretically, it was valid to assume the possibility of transferring Steward's process to animal cells, and several researchers — not to mention the media — began work on this. In the 1950s Professor John Gurdon, an Oxford biologist, worked with frogs' eggs and succeeded in devising a radiation technique that destroyed the nucleus of an egg without damaging the body of the egg. He then contrived to extricate the nucleus from an ordinary body cell of the frog and implant it in the egg cell. His hypothesis was that the newly constructed egg cell was now the equivalent of a fertilized egg and should, with the aid of stimulation, be able to produce an adult form. He was correct. Some of the cells, on division, formed perfectly normal tadpoles with a genetic makeup identical to that of the frog which donated the nucleus. But the clone only developed as far as the tadpole stage and did not continue its development into a normal adult frog. There is no reason, theoretically speaking, why the full process should not take place.

Naturally, speculation centered upon the application of the cloning process to human beings, and the advisability of this. In the 1960s cloning research was on the upswing, and in 1969, Robert Sinsheimer, then chairman of the division of biology at California Institute of Technology, declared that it would be possible to clone human beings within 10 to 20 years. Since that time, however, the publication of cloning research findings has dwindled drastically, and the extension to humans of discoveries made with plants and animals seems more remote.

What could bring it closer? Increased funding of projects related to cloning and an increase of man hours spent in research might well be the answer. But the reason for the falling off could also be that cloning research was chiefly a stepping stone to other knowledge in the field of genetics, or that scientists decided that the technique would raise more moral, ethical, and theological problems than it was worth.

Although it is currently impossible to produce a clone from a completely differentiated cell of an adult organism, such as a hair cell or a tongue cell, there are no technological or theoretical blockades in the way of human cloning's becoming a fact in the future.

Microsurgical techniques have advanced so far that it is entirely possible to insert the nucleus of a human cell into an unfertilized ovum. Unlike the frog egg, however, which can exist and develop outside the mother's body, thanks to the egg yolk which meets the nutritional needs of the developing embryo, the human fetus must rely on the placenta to abstract all its nutritional needs from the mother's blood.

Again, this need not impede the progress of human cloning. Technology is currently available to implant a fertilized human egg in any human female's uterus without altering the normal progress of pregnancy. Another alternative, a little out of reach, but theoretically viable, is an artificial uterus which would harbor a developing embryo without the need of the human womb.

The mind reels at the possibilities this could afford.

○ Inheritable diseases could be either propagated or destroyed, depending on the controls used.

○ Clones could be mass-produced and given a strictly controlled environment (shades of *1984*) to produce soldiers, or cheap manual labor workers.

○ Couples incapable of having children could clone offspring with their own genetic combination. Parents who had lost children through illness or accident could clone another identical child, and start again.

Some awesome questions can be raised, but until cloning becomes more than a light in some scientists' eyes, it is hard to do more than speculate about the moral advisability of this form of reproduction. Obviously it is never going to substitute for the regular process designed by nature — if only for the reason that it is so much less enjoyable — but it could theoretically make possible the duplication of the bodies of unusually valuable people. Would it be possible to reproduce multiple great men? They might look like the originals, but there would be no way of reproducing the individual environments that make each human being unique. The real question, then, to be debated is the influence of environment on the mind. Can mental ability, can character be passed on simply through building up from a single cell? Aren't genius, sainthood, the quirks and qualities that make each human being unique, unduplicable? Most of us would like to hope so.

THE FRONTIERS OF MEDICINE
as viewed by DR. WILLIAM S. KROGER

A renowned authority on clinical hypnosis, Dr. Kroger discussed hypnosis and the art of healing in Mindstyles: Theories in Action. *Here he answers the question: "Why do you think there is such a supermarket of mindstyles available today?"*

We have a veritable delicatessen of healing methods because people are looking for relief from the various pressures they are subjected to. We are living in a society where the tempo is increased, the means of communication enormously multiplied, and where goals are different from what they were several hundred years ago. People then had the same problems we have today, but they didn't have the automobile, television, radio, and the rapid locomotion to get from one place to another. Also, we are exposed to a tremendous amount of stress, interference by

tensions and anxieties in almost every area of human endeavor. As a result, we are looking and yearning for some means of putting a "Band-Aid on a cancer," for instant Yoga, instant Zen.

It is interesting that the wheel has made a complete turn, and the Western world is now embracing Eastern philosophical concepts. It will be extremely difficult for us to assimilate these into a Judaeo-Christian frame of reference, however, because we are interested in acquisitiveness, in material things: How is the stock market doing? Who won the World Series? Irrelevant facts and information are continually being obtained and stored in the brain. In the Far East, they look into the inner existence, inside themselves. They couldn't care less how many baskets Wilt Chamberlain made last year. They are interested in the phenomenology of the soul, the inner self.

What is happening today with mindstyles and lifestyles is, as Voltaire once said, "What's new is old and what's old is not new." We have resuscitated the meditation and the mantras; the sleep temples are the psychiatrists' offices. People flock to all kinds of esoteric healing methods because they need surcease from their problems. The same concerns that plagued the great civilizations of the past are harassing ours. We are burdened by taxation, difficult living situations, fear of war, the omnipresent specter of crime, and other growing socioeconomic problems which have far-reaching repercussions on the psyche.

I believe the next century will see the *avant garde* in science utilizing information processing in a systems approach — a method of studying a problem from all angles. Studies of how the human organism functions will be placed on a more scientific and rigorous frame of reference. Theories will have to be proven in replicable experiments and not on the basis of shared experiences, if we want to understand each other and solve problems.

I foresee that the next century will bring a dramatic change in the approach to treating diseases. The biomedical engineers are already overtaking us with their findings. For example, we have the pacemaker to regulate the heart beat, the dorsal column stimulator to relieve pain, and many other innovative procedures to substitute for nature's way of doing things. Intrepid investigators are mapping out the human brain with depth electrode studies. The brain is the last uncharted territory; scientists are only now learning which centers control what functions. In the next century, or perhaps sooner, brain centers will be stimulated by different forms of energy to replace the use of medicines and psychotherapy. I can see how electromagnetic field forces will be beamed into the brain to activate specific centers to produce particular results quickly. Stimulation of such centers is already being used in the alleviation of pain. A start has been made in treating schizophrenia by probing specific areas of the brain. Hormone production will be regulated by activating the brain centers specifically involved in manufacturing these chemical messengers.

So we are moving away from a *post hoc, propter hoc* specious reasoning into an approach based upon objective data where results can be measured and quantified. I foresee great promise in signal analysis. After all, our current methods of diagnosis are based on simply interpreting the nature of signals, which at present are extremely crude approximations of what is taking place within the organism. Electrocardiograms or electroencephalograms (brain waves) only measure surface potentials. Mathematicians, with their refined tools, will be able to extract the signal from the noise, in the same way Neil Armstrong's voice was carried 240,000 miles and amplified, and pictures of the moon were taken and then amplified by computer technology. I certainly envisage more and more use of computers, in monitoring patients and in understanding the multivariant nature of problems. Mathematical modeling, manipulating the variables, will enable us to understand what is going on inside the organism.

In spite of the many exciting developments which will take place in the next century, we must never lose sight of the humanistic approach. The empathy, wisdom, judgment, and experience of therapists will always be integral in helping humans to help themselves.

Another important breakthrough before the turn of the century will be the artificial heart, as well as artificial organs for every part of the body, or, if not complete parts, then substitute parts that will "jump" the faulty circuits. Scientists will use the tools of system theory and mathematics to accomplish this. These are the scientists that landed a man on the moon. They have ushered in the current revolution in communications. At hand is the ability to understand human-to-human communication by machines — artificial intelligence. So machine-man specifications are not too far off.

It is an exciting preview of things to come, and I don't think we have to worry about the behavior modifiers or a *Clockwork Orange* situation. Much of the noise about deleterious effects is exaggerated. There has never really been any freedom, because we are all the products of our genes and chromosomes, and the environmental milieu in which we function controls us. We see what we want to see. We thrive on illusions. We embrace the soothsayers and those who promise us Nirvana. The reason for most of our behavior is that we are continually being bombarded by suggestions and influenced without realizing it, so that we develop a "logical incongruity" where we buy things that don't add up. Madison Avenue reigns supreme in our culture.

As we move toward a more scientific state, there is no question that one disease after another will be eradicated. In our own lifetimes, we have seen cholera, smallpox, tuberculosis, polio and other diseases eliminated. Now we must turn our guns on cancer, heart disease, high blood pressure, the degenerative diseases. I am sure that science will eventually discover what causes aging, will elucidate the laws of immunology so that we will have organ transplants without fear of rejection. This could all happen within a century, if we reorder our priorities.

The technology that landed men on the moon should be used to alleviate human suffering. Such problems as the rejection of artificial organs could be solved if governmental agencies would use the brain power and the billions of dollars that are spent for the destruction of other human beings. Why does only an infinitesimal amount of money, by comparison, go for scientific research? Much of that is wasted. Many of the greatest contributions to science were made by individuals working without the backing of money, of politicians, of a university environment.

Nothing should be omitted in our search for the manifold ways in which man can better himself — providing it hurts no one.

THE PHANTOM CAPTAIN

"Man?"

"A self-balancing, 28-jointed adapter-base biped; an electro-chemical reduction-plant, integral with segregated stowages of special energy extracts in storage batteries, for subsequent actuation of thousands of hydraulic and pneumatic pumps, with motors attached; 62,000 miles of capillaries; millions of warning signals, railroad and conveyor systems; crushers and cranes (of which the arms are magnificent 23-jointed affairs with self-surfacing and lubricating systems, and a universally distributed telephone system needing no service for 70 years if well managed); the whole, extraordinarily complex mechanism guided with exquisite precision from a turret in which are located telescopic and microscopic self-registering and recording range finders, a spectroscope, et cetera, the turret control being closely allied with an air-conditioning intake-and-exhaust, and a main fuel intake."

Man is also a mechanism integrating radar devices, an intricate filing system equipped for ready-reference, and a laboratory which computes many years of experience not only exclusively but also in relation to the environment. There is even a system which can analyze future possibilities and arrive at conclusions.

Man is a mobile unit, traveling freely on land, water, and air, operating on a system of both direct and indirect impulse.

And every man is ultimately guided by a "phantom captain."

The phantom captain is intangible and imperceivable to the five senses. He weighs nothing, as has been proven by weighing the original mechanism after the phantom captain has departed (commonly known as "death"). When the phantom captain evacuates the machine, the entire mechanism is unable to function and disintegrates into very basic chemical elements.

The captain is infinite in regard to self-identity and understanding. He is also able to sympathize with the captains residing in similar mechanisms.

The understanding he has accomplished is "an intuitive, non-graphable awareness of perfection, or of unity, or of eternity, or of infinity, or of truth." Because he is aware of perfection he is able to measure all things around him against that standard, and from that information he is able to make conscious selection.

— *R. Buckminster Fuller*
from Nine Chains to the Moon

CONCLUSIONS
by R. BUCKMINSTER FULLER

By and large, nature designed human beings so that the grown man, if it's available to him, tends to average taking in two pounds of dry food a day, five pounds of water and other liquids, and seven pounds of oxygen, which he extracts from 54 pounds of atmosphere which he inhales into his lungs. Now, you can go without food for 30 days without perishing, without liquid less than a week, and without the one resource of which you use the most — the seven pounds of oxygen — you can't last two minutes. These are very different time tolerances. Because their need for food is less frequent, humans apparently were deliberately designed to be self-educated by having to find their way only through food-seeking trials and errors. When man experienced scarcity or famine, he made the error of killing others in war to alleviate that scarcity, to get what the other had. The individual would say, "Maybe I myself am not so important, but my family depends on me. I've got to battle for them . . ."

I come back, then, to the vital resource of which we need the most: oxygen. Nature did not take a chance on our getting it, because we can only last two minutes without it. So we have enormous amounts of air. Air has always been socialized, and people don't have to think at all about taking it away from each other. They don't fight about it until once in a while an awful thing happens — let's say, a fire in a theater. The fire may not burn the theater building, but only the oxygen which the building contains. After that fire is over, we find that almost all of the human victims died of suffocation. We find that a father and mother who, in their consciousness would spontaneously give their lives for their children, lacking oxygen had gone mad and had trampled over their own children.

Only when we go beyond the vital tolerance do people become destructively aggressive. If you've experienced vital tolerance shock, you tend to continue destructiveness. A lot of creatures have this kind of shock. But if they never have had such, most humans behave thoughtfully toward one another.

All I want to point out is that there are two stages of behavior. In the initial stage, the creatures' trusts in one another have not been violated and they have obtained vitals always within the time tolerance. In the initial stage they don't misbehave. In stage two's secondary behavior, having suffered tolerance and trust shock, the individuals lose their confidence in the natural scheme of things and misbehave.

Man's Individual Responsibility

If within the next 10 years humanity fails to pass its final examination as to its fitness to continue on this particular planet, it probably will be because it has yielded its problem solving to its political leadership.

What is vitally and cosmically in *question* is the problem-solving capability and integrity of each one of our minds. It will probably be each moment-to-moment way in which we express our innermost attitude toward one another and our concern for all humanity that will spell out whether humans continue on Earth. It's got to be everybody or nobody — otherwise the big show is over, for everybody, permanently. So can we keep our heads? Can we really do our own thinking? Can we really look for and spontaneously adopt the solutions that will really take care of all people?

I have a lot of hope — which is quite different from optimism — because, being a student of patterns, I am astonished by the amount of misinformation that prevailed when I was born and with which I was "educated" and from which I had to escape, and which, happily, no longer prevails. And I don't find the new world being told, as were I and my contemporaries, "Never mind what you think! Pay attention to your elders and teachers who are trying to educate you! Get over your sensitivity and generosity. Life is hard!" I see a young world that is spontaneously doing its own thinking, learning that it is a whole world, and that a great many people around it are in trouble — and the compassion of all youth is for everybody. That's what's going to be necessary: really using our minds, keeping our sensitivity and paying attention to what it is trying to tell us must be done.

Energy In Infinite Supply

Recently I read a report that was totally contradictory of the well-known published data about world energy. It is a book called *Energy, Earth, and Everybody* and it deserves the widest possible dissemination.

What this report makes incontrovertible is that — dealing only in proven energy resources of all known kinds (we're talking about thermal power, water power, wind power, methane gas — whatever it may be), and employing only proven technology for utilizing each type of energy resource, and employing only the proven rate at which such technologies can be produced, installed, and put to work — it is absolutely clear that it is feasible within 10 years' time to have all of mankind enjoying the same energy income as was enjoyed exclusively by North Americans in 1972, before the energy crisis occurred. And this can be accomplished in that 10 years while concurrently phasing out all use of fossil fuels and all use of atomic energy.

This is our option. It is one of the reasons why we now know that with full concern for ecology and environment, it is now highly feasible to house and feed all humanity at higher standards than any have ever enjoyed. But if we try to house them in the same kind of technology of the past, then there is nowhere nearly enough life support for all humanity. Done properly, there is enormous capability. Now we know we have the energy. The 1975 World Game Study was on food, and it became clear that there's no trouble about producing enough food; it's been the distribution system, the games played politically, and the exclusive drives to make money, instead of common sense, that have created all the want and have made all the trouble. So I can say now realistically and categorically that it is highly feasible to sustain the taking care of all humanity, at a higher standard of living than anybody has ever known, and to do it by 1986.

Wealth — Energy x Intellect

Energy is wealth, and I find that when we get down to what we really mean by wealth, it is the organized capability to adequately support, protect, and accommodate so many lives for so many forward days. To support life, protect it, accommodate it, that's what wealth is. *How* wealthy is defined by the relative number of forward human days already provided for. We've now a comprehensive socioeconomic game going wherein people are producing enormous amounts of money, which has nothing to do with real wealth, and which cannot support life.

To protect against complete collapse of our monetary system in case of nuclear attack, the United States government has stashed four billion dollars of paper money in a Virginia cave which also has the physical capacity to house 400 people safely. With all the remainder of humanity and its life support resources destroyed, the saved 400 persons would have naught to buy, and would not be well nourished eating paper dollars.

The first law of thermodynamics states the principle of the conversion of energy. Energy cannot be created or destroyed; therefore, energy cannot decrease. Wealth is energy compounded with the intellect's know-how. Every time man uses this second constituent of wealth, the know-how, this intellectual resource automatically increases. Energy cannot decrease. Know-how can only increase. It is therefore scientifically clear that wealth, which combines energy and intellect, can only increase. Wealth can increase only with use and wealth increases as fast as it is used. The faster, the more. Those are the facts of science. Those are the facts of life. The proper use of energy and know-how of wealth is scientifically determinable. Therefore we must through design science continually advance the efficiency of our conversion of energy to products. It is highly feasible to do more with less because our world's present overall energy-to-work efficiency is less than 10 percent, whereas an overall of 20 percent is engineeringly feasible.

This brings us to a realization of the enormous educational task which must be successfully accomplished right now in a hurry in order to convert humanity's tailspin dive toward oblivion into an intellectually accomplished pullout into safe and level flight on a course of physical and metaphysical success for all, whereafter humans may turn their Spaceship Earth into further Universe-exploring and problem-solving advantage. So planners, architects, and engineers must take the initiative, go to work, and above all, cooperate. Don't hold back on one another or try to gain at the expense of one another. Any success in such lopsidedness will be increasingly short-lived. These are the synergetic rules that evolution is employing and trying to make clear to us. They are not man-made laws. They are the infinitely accommodative laws of the intellectual integrity that governs Universe.

We have come to know certain very glad news over the last 10 years. Only within this time have we had scientific proof that there is no genetic dichotomy of humans into two classes — a worker class and a capitalist nobles class. In the old days the powerful men, the king and the nobles, reserved all the hunting. Any commoner caught killing a rabbit could be hung in England as recently as 150 years ago. History had all the nobles eating their fill of the flesh of animals, while the other people just had to get along with roots or whatever was around. In the last decade we have learned irrefutably that humans' undernourishment during the nine months in the womb and in the first year of life damages their brains. Undernourishment doesn't mean not enough bulk; it means the wrong chemistry, not the right variety of inputs. The nobles eating the meat did not get undernourished because the meat took care of it for them. The animals wandered around eating many different kinds of herbs and fresh vegetation until they had acquired a nourishing mix, so, in a sense, they ate all the herbs and vegetables for the nobles. But the other people, the poor people, just had to eat roots, barks, berries, or nuts, which meant they were undernourished because there was not the right chemical variety.

At any rate, to both the illiterate poor and the nobles, all the damaged-brain poor people seemed to be relatively duller — there *seemed* to be a marked, fundamental biological class or species difference. But now we know that this is not so, and does not need to be continued. We have a Universal top-priority obligation to provide the right kinds of food for all so that this can be promptly corrected. And while feeding people's bodies, we need to feed their minds. It's all a tremendous educational task to be accomplished in a decade. Can we really span the gap? Can each of us really make the right decisions?

It is also only within the last decade that we have learned that vitamin D is an essential ingredient of the development of adequate calcium for human growth. Vitamin D is acquired by humans from Sun as radiation in a zoological photosynthetic process which is the counterpart of the vegetative photosynthetic conversion of Sun radiation into life-sustaining hydrocarbon molecules. But the vitamin D acquisition by humans from Sun radiation has tolerance limits. Overdoses can be lethal. To avoid such imperilment of humans, nature has invented and installed Sun-radiation dosage-reducing filters in the form of two types of skin pigments — melanin, a dark brown set of filters, and carotin, a yellow set. These filters occur in varying degrees of intensity appropriate to the various terrestrial latitudes. In the north, where the Sun radiation is less abundant but the vitamin D equally essential to human growth and maintenance, filters are progressively removed from the skin, leaving it white and transparent. In the case of the bundled-up Eskimos, their vitamin D supply is provided exclusively by whale "blubber," which is one of the rare cases of vitamin D presence in food. All skin coloring is a product of long-living in specific latitudes. There is, then, no fundamental race difference. There is no inherent class and no race distinction amongst humans.

War Is Invalid

Because I know that there is ample life support and accommodation for all, I know that the working position of politics — "It has to be you or me" — is invalid. Therefore, war is invalid. Up to this time, if you didn't know that there is enough for all, you had to assume that it had to be you or me. That's how the rationalization of selfishness developed — "I don't like to do it, but I have to look out for my family." You have to think, if there's only enough for one family, which family is it going to be? So you cultivate selfishness, and we've adopted the socially comprehensive rationalization of selfishness. But since there is enough to go around, selfishness can never be rationalized again. It becomes invalid.

It's all of us or none of us. Inadvertently, we have developed into such a state of mutual interdependence that we can no longer operate in terms of national boundaries and in-groups that exist today. We must think in terms of all humanity, governed not by man-made laws, but by the comprehensively intercirculatory laws that govern the eternal regeneration of Universe.

Regenerative Industrialization

Technology providing more and more goods from fewer and fewer raw resource units of weight and volume could guarantee that everyone can survive. We must therefore think of our economy in terms of performance per pound, energy effort, and know-how hours invested per each function to be accomplished.

Nothing else but a design revolution will do the trick. All that political revolution can do is pull the topmost down and take from one and give to the other, with much physical energy lost in the doing. But the design revolution which elevates the bottommost to new heights along with all others can't be accomplished exclusively within just one country. It has to be a total world revolution because industrialization, as we have seen, consists inherently in world-around integration of all resources, both physical and metaphysical. The resources occur randomly around the world. The only way we can operate an inherently regenerative industrial system is to hook into Universe's comprehensive evolutionary system. Industrialization will only function at the highest momentarily realizable efficiency when it is an unfettered world-around operation. Automation is also an essential to our producing more with less.

Cosmic Accounting

Right now we're in a very critical condition of information. One of the biggest needs is for a whole new method of socioeconomic accounting. Luckily the computers are there; if they weren't, we couldn't possibly do it.

Take, for instance, oil drilling. Say we put down some pipes, at whatever the cost of the operation; that's it. The oil is for nothing, or so we say. I was able to persuade a really great oil geologist, who is also a very good general geologist, to write a scenario of the ways in which nature produces petroleum. I had him start with the original photosynthetic impoundment of Sun's radiation by Earth's vegetation and algae, and thereafter to follow

through on all the subsequent complex chemical stages in this process: how much energy went into the wind to shake the trees, and how much energy went into evaporating, the lifting of the water into the sky. In science, we measure energy effectiveness in the terms of lifting a given weight against gravity, a given height in a given amount of time. So it could be a foot-pounds-per-minute, or it could be centimeter/gram/seconds, which vertical distance, weight, and time ratios are all convertible into the various languages of energy, i.e., into kilowatt-hours, or whatever may be desired. I asked this great geologist if he could write a scenario of all those progressive stages wherein a state is finally reached at which these energies are concentrated enough by ages-long sustained heat and pressure to convert the fossil residues into petroleum. My geologist said that he knew enough about the natural processes to enable him to write a fairly accurate scenario.

When he had done it, I asked him to figure out the total amount of all such energy expenditures by nature as heat, pressure, and erosion work as sustainingly expended by nature over a time period long enough to produce a gallon of petroleum, and then to price it at the rate we pay for our electrical current for that much energy over that same time period.

So he went through all this calculation, and it came out that it cost nature approximately $1 million to make a gallon of petroleum. This is what we call cosmic costing.

That's the way physics has to operate. Everything we have to do, astrophysically, is accomplished in terms of such energy exchanges and applications within given time spans. So when we get into strict energy accounting, we find that it does indeed cost

448

nature $1 million per gallon of petroleum produced and stored in underground petroleum pools.

In today's society it is said humans don't have a right to eat or exist unless they have a job, whose salary pays their way. Seventy percent of all the jobs we have in the "Western world" are invented — they are not connected with the production of life support as we have defined it — most of those invented jobs are not supportive of human life. Such an invented job might be that of handling a postage meter in a company which underwrites the reassurance of other insurance companies in special fields. So you are expending three million metabolic-capability dollars a day from nature's cosmic energy savings account just to go from your countryside home into the city to operate that postage meter of the no-life-support-producing insurance underwriter's office. It would be vastly less expensive to humanity as expressed in terms of cosmic accounting to have most of us stay at home.

It seems quite clear that, once we start reckoning this way, assessing wealth in terms of the "known" organized resources and their capability to take care of future life — for so many lives for so many days — once we get into cosmic accounting, we will discover that humanity is not in any predicament whatsoever. We are incredibly wealthy, wealthy enough to take care of every human on Earth at higher standards of living than anybody has ever known.

Caretakership of Our World

Man's function in Universe is to employ all his senses and knowledge and time to make all humans and their Spaceship Earth a success.

From my viewpoint, by far the greatest challenge facing people today is that of responding and conforming only to our most delicately insistent intuitive awareness of what the truth seems to us to be as based on our own experiences and not on what others have interpreted to be the truth regarding events of which neither they nor we have experience-based knowledge. That is why our self-preparation for planetary caretakership involves commitment to comprehensive concern only with all humanity's welfaring.

Mistake-Making Integral to Experience

Whatever humans have learned has had to be learned as a consequence of trial and error experience.

Those quadrillions of mistakes learned through its evolution were the price paid by humanity for its surprising competence as presently accrued synergetically, for the first time in history, to cope successfully, on behalf of all humanity, with all the problems of physically healthy survival, enlightening growth, and initiative accommodation.

Chagrin and mortification caused by its progressively self-discovered quadrillions of errors would long ago have given humanity such an inferiority complex that it would have become too discouraged to continue with the life experience. To avoid such a proclivity, humans were designedly given pride, vanity, and inventive memory, which, taken together, can and usually do tend to self-deception.

Witnessing the mistakes of others, the preconditioned crowd reflex says, "Why did that individual make such a stupid mistake? We knew the answer all the time." So effective has been the nonthinking, group deceit of humanity that it now says "Nobody should make mistakes," and punishes people for making mistakes.

I am personally convinced that every human being is really born with all the equipment to be a genius. We get de-geniused very rapidly, particularly by loving parents who say, "Darling, you're going to get in trouble doing that! Don't do that!" Thus begins the shutting off of opportunities to exercise our innate faculties. We find that if our faculties are not used as they come naturally into operation, they become no longer operative.

Thus humanity has developed a comprehensive, mutual self-deception and has made the total error of not perceiving that realistic thinking accrues only after mistake-making, which is the cosmic wisdom's most cogent way of teaching each of us how to carry on. It is only at the moment of humans' realistic admission to themselves of having made a mistake that they are closest to that mysterious integrity governing Universe.

Every little child is full of interest in the whole Universe. He doesn't want to be a specialist at all; he wants to understand the heavens and the microcosm. And his memory is just incredible. I don't think I have any capability other than those innate faculties of all children, access to which I've fortunately regained.

I think we all have within us the genius of childhood. Our problem is in keeping open our access to it. I am terribly lucky that I didn't get too many valves permanently closed off. When I made up my mind in 1927 to try to recapture my renounced childhood sensitivity, I wondered if these were lost to me, or were only shut off temporarily. I found I could open the sensitivity and perceptivity valves again.

In attempting to reopen my valves, the first thing I said to myself was, "I'm not going to ask anybody else any more questions. I'm going to go and find out for myself. I'm not going to ask anybody to listen to me. I will speak to others only when asked to do so." That's the only way to do it. There is no short cut. You have to make a lot of mistakes, and not get touchy about making them. But if you're going to go on making mistakes, you have to learn to welcome their recognition and not be ashamed of the truth. I see that nature has set up individual gestation rates that are absolutely unique for different species and different technologies. It takes just so long to make a human baby, and so long for humanity to catch onto certain things and learn to behave in appropriate ways. For this reason, I don't get impatient when things seem to be lagging. Nature has her own check and balance devices.

I find hope in the spontaneity of a child's love. Stones don't love stones, but human beings have this extraordinary phenomenon called love. Love spontaneously includes, understands, and serves the needs and idiosyncracies of others. The principal signs for hope that we may exercise our success options within the critical time limits are mind-discovered truth, youth, and love.

interview / R. BUCKMINSTER FULLER

Man, Mind, and Universe

R. Buckminster Fuller is one of the most original and influential minds of our century. Scientist, philosopher, humanist, explorer of man's evolving possibilities, Fuller is a modern Leonardo da Vinci. He spent long hours charting for me his concepts on man and the universe, plotting the thoughts of Copernicus, Galileo, Newton, and Kepler in a sequential process for my understanding; presenting data which brought together the most valued principles of science and the humanities. He was quick to explain the difference between mind and brain, to discuss ideas and integrities, Utopia and oblivion, education, revolution, and the principles of geodesic domes. With great patience he explained the mathematical coordinate systems of the universe.

LANDE: There is a chapter in one of your books, "Nine Chains to the Moon," that particularly pleased me from my own point of view with regard to man — about the Phantom Captain.

FULLER: The Phantom Captain — that was published in 1938. It was my first attempt to make clear that individual life is not the physical organism which that life employs. That's why I had to create the Phantom Captain, who is intangible and imperceptible to the five senses. I've written 11 books since then and have talked a great deal about differentiating between the mind and brain.

LANDE: Could you run down that differentiation yet again?

FULLER: The brains of human beings exist to coordinate the input information received from the senses — smell, touch, hearing, and so forth — and they differentiate each experience input from the others. Each one of the brain's inputs is a special case, and the brain remembers and recalls them as special cases. Regarding mind — we don't know of any creature or phenomenon other than human beings that have minds — only the mind can find relationships existing *between* special cases which are not inherently in any of the special cases when each is considered only by itself.

Their brains have asked humans to explain Universe in terms of things that begin and end. But the mind is concerned only with principles. Principles are inherently eternal, in contradistinction to the special cases that brains deal with, which are inherently temporal and limited. So it is human minds that have gradually, bit by bit, discovered some of the great, extraordinary eternal principles that operate in Universe.

These great principles are all utterly unique and only mathematically expressable. None of them has ever been found to contradict any of the other generalized principles. Not only are they not contradicting, they are all co-occurrently interaccommodative, and some are interaugmentative.

It was Isaac Newton's mind that discovered the mathematical rates of the complexedly co-varying distances and mass interattractiveness of all celestial bodies by making intuitive assumptions regarding the special case of Moon and the special case of Earth. Newton's mind discovered that their interattraction varied at a second power rate as their interdistancing varied at only an arithmetical rate.

Man had known for thousands of years that there were five wandering-around lights in the sky which appeared much smaller than Moon and Sun, yet bigger and brighter than the rest of the stars, which latter seemed to be in fixed patterns. These five lights had unique colors. Studied by the early Mesopotamians, Egyptians, and Greeks, they became known as the planets.

Our present human brains probably have the same faculties human brains at all times have had; but until humans had the ability to calculate, no matter what they thought intuitively might be going on in nature, as for instance they watched falling bodies, they could not discover any mathematically governing laws. Anyone who has ever tried to do calculation with Roman numerals has found only frustration. Roman numerals were a simple one-to-one scoring system — one vertical scoring line represented each jar of grain or other item being conveyed into the storehouse. It was a system that could be employed by the utterly illiterate.

Finally, Arabic numerals were introduced to the Western world in about 700 A.D. as a sort of shorthand for the Roman numerals. It was easier to write one Arabic "3" than it was to make three separate vertical scratches. But since it was impossible to "see" or to "eat" a "no-sheep," 0 sheep, the Arabic cipher was left unemployed. It was not until 1200 A.D. that the function of the Arabic cipher was recognized as a means of lateral positioning of numbers to start new columns to accommodate the operational products or dividends as expressed in decimal modules. This made multiplication, division, and all calculation practicably feasible. The explanation of this positioning of the numbers and the function of the cipher was written in 1200 by a Latin living in North Africa. There were so few literate humans that it was not until 1500 that the students of Northern Italy and Southern Germany got hold of it, and it became the key to all calculation.

Once the ability to use ciphers to calculate finally got loose in 1500, we have a Copernicus, a Galileo, a Leonardo, a Kepler.

Copernicus, with this new calculating capability, discovers that apparently we are on a planet ourselves, Sun is not going around us, but we are going around Sun. And this absolutely changed all scientific thinking. Then came Tycho Brahe, who developed better telescopes and instruments. These were used by Johannes Kepler, who recorded very accurate data concerning the planets. He found that they were all going around Sun in elliptical orbits. They were all different in size, all orbiting at different distances from Sun, and all going around Sun at different rates. So while they were on a team, there still seemed to be a great disorder in their characteristics and performances. So Kepler, having made very accurate measurement of the distances and the times, and discovering they were orbiting in ellipses, found that the only thing they had in common was that they were going around Sun. He needed two things in common in order to be able to find out more about them. So he deliberately gave them all the same amount of time, very much less than it takes to make an orbit — I think it was 21 days. He knew where each one was at the minute and hour of the starting day, so he also knew how much elliptical arc each one described in the 21 days. He had each of their distances from Sun as each planet started, and their distances from Sun when the time was completed, as well as how far each planet traveled in arc. This information produced a pie-shaped area for each one, some of them short and fat, and some of them long and thin. So Kepler said, "Inasmuch as I have the data, I must calculate the areas of those pieces of pie." Just imagine the excitement if you were the first human being to make this calculation — and suddenly found that all the areas of those pieces of pie were identical, exactly the same. Hidden in all the superficiality of dissimilar data and all the only intuitive excitation of human beings over thousands and thousands of years, was this incredibly elegant mathematical coordination.

Though we have no record, it is quite probable that Kepler said, "If they (the planets in orbit) were touching each other like gears, I could understand how they could mechanically coordinate. But they are incredible distances apart. However, we do know that they are orbiting in the same manner as weighted objects on the end of strings when swung by humans around their heads. Therefore, there must be some invisible tensile interrestraint operating between them; and since ellipses are drawn only by use of two restraints, there are restraints operating not only between the planets and Sun, but also between the planets themselves." By using his mind, Kepler found relationships going on between the planets which were not indicated to be operative as disclosed by the data of any one of these planets when analyzed only separately.

While brains always and only deal with each special case, minds alone from time to time discover the relationships existing between special cases that are not in the special cases themselves. And what I'm doing is elaborating on that for you.

Copernicus discovered that all the planets are going around Sun, but that our Earth is also a planet and we, too, are going around Sun. His brain didn't tell Copernicus that; he found it out by using his mind and intuitively formulating mathematical models that satisfied the data of human observations. Then Kepler makes it perfectly clear that the vari-sized planets are all going around Sun at different rates and in different size orbits and are seemingly an entirely disorderly group. But his intuition makes him go to work, and he suddenly discovers that there is a relationship going on here that is not in any one of the individual sets of data by itself. There is a commonality of the areas swept out in a given amount of time that is quite exact, hidden in the superficial disorderliness. Human minds, from time to time, discover relationships existing *between* that are not in any of the characteristics of any of the parts analyzed by themselves — which relationships can be expressed only in mathematical terms. These are called generalized principles. These generalized principles are synergetic; synergy means behavior of whole systems unpredicted by the behavior of any of the parts of those systems when the latter are examined only by themselves.

This period of mathematical discovery greatly stimulated others. Take Galileo — he, too, had the new calculating capability. He was excited by the rate at which objects tended to fall to the ground. So he decided to make methodically measured observations. He timed objects sliding or rolling down inclined planes of methodically altered angles. He carefully noted the changed rates at which they moved. Then, using a high tower, he found that free-falling bodies kept falling faster and faster — they didn't have a fixed rate of fall. Then he calculated the rate at which the speeds of fall were gaining. He found that velocity accelerated at a second power rate in respect to the arithmetical rate of gain of distance traveled.

Isaac Newton in England was greatly excited by Copernicus' and Kepler's discoveries, and tremendously excited also by Galileo's information about motion. Newton wanted to understand even better what might be governing the motions of the planets as they inter-coordinated while millions of miles apart.

Newton said, "The one thing I know about it is that they're in orbit, which, as Kepler realized, means they must be interrestrained and governed not by a pushing force, but by a pulled restraint. There must be some absolutely invisible interpulling phenomenon in the sky out there, operating over incredible distances." Newton probably reasoned, "If I have a weight on a string and swing it around my head, then it's in an orbit, tensilely controlled by the string. Once I let go, the weight travels away from me horizontally in a line until the 'Kepler-discovered' attraction of our planet overcomes my horizontal impelment and pulls it evermore vertically toward Earth." Newton then formulated his "First Law of Motion," to wit, that "A body will travel in a straight line except as affected by other bodies."

These experience-induced conceptual formulations of Copernicus, Kepler, Galileo, and Newton had never before been introduced to human thinking — the idea that in the cosmic "nothingness" there could be invisible tethers operating between great bodies millions of miles apart.

By Newton's time, the navigators and astronomers had fairly well organized the observational data governing the Sun-orbiting of planet Earth as correlated with points of observation in respect to Earth's mathematical coordinate of longitude and latitude. The astronomers and navigators had been able to mathematically chart the interpositioning of the great celestial sphere's outstanding stars. Thus they knew how to navigate and how to find a particular position on Earth.

Newton had all that going for him, wherefore at any moment, any night, from any particular place, he could know exactly what the star patterns should be as angularly observed above the horizon and in compass orientation from any Earth position. Newton was also familiar with the long-known relationship between Moon's positions and phases and Earth's tides, the pull going on between Moon and Earth that is pulling outward quadrillions of tons of water twice daily. Realizing that the pull between the heavenly bodies had to be something enormous to hold such fantastic-sized bodies in restraint by Sun, Newton must have said:

"I think the interpull must be something to do with their individual relative sizes — masses. If I had two apples they would probably exert a pull on one another, but the pull of Earth on them both is so fantastically great that you can't notice the relatively negligible pull the apples exert on each other. It's a matter of relative size — the apples are four inches in diameter and Earth is 8,000 miles in diameter. In other words, this intermass pulling would never have been detected only on Earth; we can only notice it in the sky as operative between these enormous bodies."

Newton then made a working assumption — that the interpull is proportional to the masses involved; so he said, "I think I'll multiply the two masses times each other, and the product will be the basic interpull of that pair as related to any other pairs."

Newton thought, "If Earth were suddenly annihilated, there would be nothing to restrain Moon, so Moon, like a sling-released missile, would shoot off in a straight line."

In just the way Kepler had invented an arbitrary mathematical concept to try to elucidate the movement of the planets, Newton chose a given evening when he knew Moon would be at the full and easy to observe, fairly high above the horizon. Newton chose a given second at which Earth would (theoretically) let go of Moon, and calculated the straight line along which Moon would then travel. By the astronomers' science, he knew exactly what that line of released Moon-travel would look like as graphed against the pattern of fixed stars in the sky as witnessed from Newton's home base position on Earth. So he plotted just such a theoretical line; and on that night, at that time, he measured the rate at which Moon was falling away from the theoretical line and toward Earth as both Earth and Moon cotraveled at 60,000 m.p.h. around Sun, and found that Moon's travel agreed with Galileo's formula for "falling" bodies.

LANDE: What did you mean when you have said that what man means by design is in contradistinction to disorder or randomness?

FULLER: I meant that Universe is a design because all its separate laws of behavior are arranged to accommodate one another considerately, which is what we mean by design. The mind alone has access to the eternal design of Universe, which design is a complex of coordinate principles; and these principles are absolutely weightless.

The physicists say that everything that is physical is energy associative as matter or disassociative as radiation, and one is transformable into the other. And everything, then, that is physical energy will move a needle either gravitationally or electromagnetically. That which we experience that does not move a needle is not physical, but metaphysical.

But what goes on in this room between us — understanding — is absolutely weightless. It doesn't make any difference what kind of words I am using to express what I am weightlessly thinking. Meaning and understanding are weightless. They are absolutely metaphysical.

Human beings made an error a long time ago when they began to use the words "animate" and "inanimate." Long before we had biology, people said it was perfectly clear that a cold hard stone and soft warm flesh were two things absolutely different. One was inanimate and the other animate, but both were assumedly physical. So in the game of 20 Questions that human beings have played over the ages, the first big question to get the riddle answered was, "Is it animate or inanimate?"

This identification occurred before the inception of the sciences of biology, chemistry, and physics. Then we inaugurated biology and chemistry, but they were deemed to have no interrelationship whatever. Biology was dealing in cells and chemistry was discovering both atomic and molecular associations and disassociations going on invisibly, for as yet unknown reasons.

Physics, dealing at first with optics and mechanics in general, and in most recent decades with the internal affairs of atoms, was something else again. With the progressive discovery of genetics and chromosomes, and then DNA-RNA's biological species design control encodements, biology, chemistry, and physics have become intimately interstaffed and inter-data-ed.

Going from biology to chemistry to physics, it was always assumed that there existed a discrete inviolable threshold lying between the animate and inanimate. However, what is physical, i.e., inanimate, becomes ever clearer, and what is animate becomes ever less clear. What alone has kept the animate concept in currency is the fact that the whole history of science starts with the live humans and the fact that the discovery of the DNA-RNA code had been consequent to the pursuit of design controls in biology. We have now come to the point where we can say that all biology consists entirely of atoms, and atoms are completely inanimate. Though 99 percent of humanity knows naught about science and may not be interested in my thinking, I've got to pay absolute attention to what science has found out experimentally. Thus I am impressed with the fact that medical scientists, with the dying patients' permission, have positioned these patients' beds on scales at the time of dying. At first, it was thought that there was a little loss in weight upon death, but that was later identified as the weight of air that had been in the lungs. Life, itself, was found to be immeasurable, weightless.

We often hear from biochemists dealing in amino acids and other DNA-RNA molecular compounds that they have found samples comprising the chemistry of life. They say that as a consequence of their find, we can now understand how life got onto our planet, because these scientists have found some of these "vital" chemistries in the stardusts in the heavens.

I say that when a man dies, all the chemistry stays right there; so the chemistry wasn't the life. I am now 80 — I was born at a fairly average seven pounds. Then I got to be 70 pounds, and then I got to be 170 pounds. I got to 207 at one time, then took off 70 pounds. That 70 I took off was 10 times what I weighed originally. The fact is that that 70 pounds of "animate" flesh was not me. I find that at my age I have eaten and processed and made temporarily mine over a thousand tons of food, air and water. Progressively, a thousand tons has been organically assimilated, employed, cut off, fallen off, and rubbed off: I am not what I had for breakfast. I have given up altogether the idea that human "beings" are their physical organisms. What is really unique about us is our minds, which employ a completely different kind of awareness, an awareness of principles, which is utterly different from the raw information awareness obtained only by our senses.

I finally conceived of the following metaphor which complements the Phantom Captain concept, possibly expounds it a little better. You have had the experience, I'm sure, wherein your friend said, "You're so much like another of my friends that I think you'll love each other. I've got to get you two together someday." Your friend says this time and again and finally says, "I never seem to be able to get you two together. I'm going to call my friend on the telephone." So he calls and introduces the two of you. Meeting only in this aural communication manner, you like each other very much, having also heard so favorably much about each other. Then it happens by coincidence that both of you are engaged in the same profession and have occasion to telephone one another because the other has information you need; and later it turns out that you have information the other needs. So you begin to call each other quite often, and get to be good friends, though you've never seen each other. As years pass, your earlier mutual friend dies as do many other of both of your separate friends. Finally, your never-seen telephone friend is your only surviving friend. So you subscribe to an additional and special telephone reserved exclusively for Joe — you don't want anyone else to be in the way when he calls. Joe is a red telephone. When the red telephone rings, that's Joe.

I say our physical organisms are all just self-regenerative and walking telephones. Our physical organisms are the instruments of communication, but we are not the instruments.

In terms of physical principles and of the relative abundance of the 92 regenerative chemical elements present in humans' total organism, our nearest physical counterpart is Universe itself. Each one of us may be a miniature local Universe containing all the principles of total Universe. Our abilities to apprehend and detect come out of being an integral part of our Universe capabilities.

I can see, then, how each human being might be one game of Universe which comes out a little different from each other game of Universe. With six moves to make with each turn to play, and with the vast variety of play components operating at very high frequencies of recurrence, our cosmic pattern integrity employs a variety of the alternate choices to be made within the same comprehensive game of Universe.

LANDE: What is intuition?

FULLER: Intuition is a twilight zone faculty, as is also aesthetics. They co-occur.

They operate within the borderline zone lying between our conscious and our subconscious operation. The size of that twilight zone depends on what kind of day it seems to us to be, whether pleasant or not. Sometimes we are a little more intuitive or aesthetically perceptive than at others. Science considered the word "intuition" to be meaningless during the second quarter of this 20th century, but science did not have my definition of its meaning.

Professor Northrup of Yale and another writer, both working independently, studied the diaries, letters, and notebooks of a half-dozen scientists whose contributions everybody acknowledges to be really great. They studied only what was written by these great scientists (a) during the period just before they made their respective historical discoveries, (b) at the same time they made it, and (c) for a little while afterwards, searching for clues which might tell how and why they happened to make their particular discovery. Both Northrup and the other searcher found one factor in common mentioned by every one of the great scientists. Each revealed that the single most important factor leading to their great discovery was intuition. Intuition said, "Look in this direction"; and they looked, and there was the great discovery.

The great scientists' writings also stated unanimously that the second most important factor operative in their successful discoveries was a second intuition which came a few seconds later, which told them what they ought to do to secure for humanity's advantage that which they had discovered. Without the second intuition, many great discoveries may well have been made and lost. The first intuition says, "There's a big fish hooked on your line," and the second intuition tells you how to pull it in and how to successfully land it.

As a result of the discovery of these astonishingly similar records, intuition is now highly credited in the scientific world.

LANDE: Is there a scientific application for intuition?

FULLER: You can't apply something in advance of discovery — and you don't know in advance when you're going to be intuitive. But once you learn how important intuition is, you can cultivate it. It's there all the time, but people pay too little attention to it. All the things I have discovered and developed came about because I keep twilight zone sensitivities alert by paying attention to them. They may be saying, "There's something important here." I never subordinate my intuition to expediency.

LANDE: Is intuition part of the mystical side, the spiritual side of life?

FULLER: Right. In relation to all the scientific episodes I have reviewed for you, I find that humanity rarely asks, "How did Newton happen to discover what he discovered?" History records and exploits his formulas and rarely asks Mr. Newton what gravity, or mass interattraction, *is.* Newton would have had to answer, "I haven't the slightest idea. There is nothing in any of the separate celestial bodies themselves, which are so interattracted, that says they are going to attract or be attracted by the other bodies. All we may ever know is that this mathematically elegant, beautifully reliable relationship exists."

When you come to the discoveries of great science, you come to *a priori* absolute mystery.

Atheism developed as a great many people studied technology, but studied it only as a set of already discovered laws which permitted the misconception that man could solve anything and that mystery is the antithesis of technology. However, when you get into the intimate information concerning the great scientific events themselves, you are overwhelmed by the *a priori* mystery. The more you learn, the more you realize how little we really know or ever will know. That's the payoff; that's the end.

XIV

AFTERTHOUGHTS

The scenario of the universe is multidimensional, more than a single frame. It is the earnest attempt to explain the facts of experience, the basic laws: if you throw a pencil in the air, it comes down. The universe doesn't forget, even though we do. It is not a static structure in the Newtonian sense, but more of an Einsteinian concept of constant motion and process, an aggregate of finite and infinite. We're a finite package. All physics is matter, all matter is energy, but life doesn't move any needles. When we die, our weight remains the same. There is patterned integrity in life, chemical, physical, and metaphysical, all unique. Each of us is a little universe. As we grow and learn to express and feel, we can see where we're coming from as well as incredible distances ahead — only the stars that we see are not there any more.

It is not an easy thing for humanity to absorb the fact that $300 billion is spent each year on destruction. If we cannot change our thinking and halt this race toward Doomsday, we're not going to make it. How can we as individuals be effective in relating to all humanity? We must acknowledge our mistakes, try new paths, learn from our misadventures. The six billion beings on our planet make quadrillions of mistakes, but nature compensates by giving us short memories and inventive minds. Our technology, our industry are immoral — but then corporations can't really be immoral, just utterly ruthless. On the credit side, science, like art, is inventive and creative, willing to take imaginative risks. We must educate the educators to let the young do some thinking of their own and give them a gold star when they make a good, imaginative mistake.

Everything starts with the individual. We must stop delegating others to solve our problems. The important thing in life is to find out what you love and do it. Not only that, if we see something that must be done and no one else is attending to it, we must go and do it even if it means taking on a second job. There is a difference between a purpose and a goal. We get up in the morning because of our purpose, not because of a goal. Most goals are never attained. Life is a greyhound race; we keep chasing the rabbit but it is programmed to forever elude us.

In the 18th century, congressmen going to Philadelphia had the alternatives of traveling by coach, on foot, or on horseback; on the way they would stop in villages, talk to people, learn about the weather and the crops and the state of mind of their constituents. They would also bring news from the government. In 1927, when all the daddies in the country came home from work, their children told them they had heard on the radio that Lindbergh had made it across the Atlantic. Daddy was suddenly deposed as the bringer of news. This was the beginning of an incredible change in communication as well as family structure. Since then, there has been a tremendous telescoping of time, events flashing instantaneously around the world. There is constantly more to learn. Even the number of words is increasing; each edition of the *Oxford English Dictionary* grows larger — 150,000 words that hold us all together.

Political credibility is lessening — politics is becoming obsolete. Eventually city managers will run our urban areas, and the same kind of professional managers will direct the country. Our political systems are founded on the premise that our life support systems are inadequate. If we're going to make it, we must start doing more with less. The first telephone line carried a single message; now a copper cable carries tens of thousands, and the work done by 175,000 tons of copper cable can be accomplished by a half-ton satellite.

Everything is interlocked; the universe is interdependent. Air pollution, transportation, energy, are facets of the same problem. If all the cars in the world stopped at a red light in a given instant, 200 billion units of horsepower would be running in a nonproductive discharge of wasted energy and pollutants. We need to re-examine our ideas about energy and realize that piston engines are only 15 percent efficient as compared to a turbine engine at 30 percent, a jet engine at 65 percent, and fuel cells, which are 85 percent efficient.

We must re-examine our ways of communicating. The newspapers that bring us each morning's events use enough newsprint to wrap around the earth several times. We need to preserve our life-sustaining trees and preserve our land, too, to grow more of them. If modern technology were used, a newspaper could be transmitted electronically into our homes and printed out there onto reusable mylar sheets, which would save paper without sacrificing the selectability and permanence of print.

And our lovely earth with its blue, cloud-hung atmosphere and vast oceans — relatively, these are no thicker than a breath of vapor around a

What one believes to be true either is true
or becomes true in one's mind, within limits to be
determined experimentally and experientially.
These limits are beliefs to be transcended.
In the province of the mind there are no limits.
                                              Lilly

                                              Corita

12-inch silver ball. Our life-giving atmosphere must be used and reused — if you are more than 20 years old you have already inhaled more than a hundred million breaths. Your next breath could contain atoms that Gandhi breathed in his long life. Every saint and every sinner of earlier days, every common man and common beast, has put atoms into the general atmospheric treasury. That atmosphere is diffused by winds and currents, but most of the pollution we are pouring into it is trapped to be breathed again and again.

In the 1960s, newscaster David Brinkley reported: "There are some in Washington who believe that in the future, maybe in the 1980s, the Federal Government will be forced to limit the driving of automobiles and the burning of gasoline simply to make it possible for people to breathe."

We have known all our lives that the parts affect the whole. An antique nursery rhyme demonstrates the scientific axiom of cause and effect:

> *For want of a nail the shoe was lost,*
> *For want of a shoe the horse was lost,*
> *For want of a horse the rider was lost,*
> *For want of a rider the message was lost,*
> *For want of the message the battle was lost,*
> *For want of the battle the kingdom was lost,*
> *And all for want of a horseshoe nail.*

One thing is certain: the impossible happens. Look at the aerodynamically implausible structure of the bee, the moon trips that moved from fantasy into reality. There is order in disorder, but there is mathematical agreement in the universe, and adaptation and compromise in nature. Look at the exquisite structure of a tree with its slender trunk upholding heavy branches, marvelous in its asymmetry.

We should study the miracles of everyday existence in the laboratory — measure love, the smell of spring, the brighter colors, the marvel of the other person. How can we appraise the pain of rejection and loss, actual physical pain, nausea, heaviness — or study the feeling of success? What happens physiologically? Does man's greatest growth come out of suffering and pain?

We must learn more about human experience — what makes us sensitive and alive. We must get away from the survival syndrome of either you or me; it is spontaneous cooperation that we need, not competition.

Most important, we should study our children, those superbly designed instruments, and watch them as they begin to learn how to manipulate their bodies, babble their way into the languages of a thousand different cultures. All the earth's peoples should have a common tongue, and it has been theorized that one- and two-year-olds actually do speak the same language. It would be interesting to take a tape recorder around the world and explore this premise, using as interpreter a three-year-old whose memory of that primal speech is still fresh.

We should never ignore the child's marvelous curiosity nor curb his inquiring mind. We represent security — he holds our hand and clings to us — but we must encourage and support his inner and outer explorations. Even the child understands the interdependence of the universe.

Of the many pathways and domains I investigated in the course of preparing this book, people have asked me which I found the most rewarding. But that is the secret of Self. And as you sift through several hundred disciplines, trying to search and understand, you realize you no longer can play blamer or victim. You must take responsibility for your actions, because you are indeed the cause of your experience.

You see, there were two forces, both a part of you, and they came together. A small image was formed — that was you. And a small infinite mass took shape and feelings — that was you. Every cell was you. At any time you could have rejected the trip, but you chose not to. So here you are, a leader of four billion cells, looking for answers — questing, searching, finding.

Know that you are a part of the whole scheme of things — a part of the universe. It is your world and you created it, just as you created me and I created you. All we really have is each other; we ought to get in touch with that. It is not always where you're going that counts, but where you're coming from.

My friend John Lilly likes to say, "What one believes to be true either is true or becomes true in one's mind, within limits to be determined experimentally and experientially. These limits are beliefs to be transcended. In the province of the mind there are no limits."

It is up to you to find out. Good luck, Pilgrim.

— Nathaniel Lande

There is an old Zen story about a seeker who crossed the oceans of the world to find knowledge and wisdom — "the secret." At the direction of wise men, he crossed the deepest crevasses, stumbled across deserts, crawled and hacked his way to the top of the highest mountains, where he was told the secret would be waiting for him. When he got there, ragged, torn, and exhausted, he found a little box. Inside was a mirror and the inscription: "There is no secret."

"... Any passionate and courageous life seems good in itself, yet one feels that some element of delusion is involved in giving so much passion to any human attainable object. And so irony creeps into the very springs of one's being. Are you finding the Great Secret in the East? I doubt it. There is none — there is not even an enigma. There is science and sober daylight and the business of the day — the rest is mere phantoms of the dusk. Yet I know that when the summer comes I shall think differently."

— Letter from Bertrand Russell
to "Goldie," February 13, 1913

XV

PLACES AND SPACES

PLACES AND SPACES

This is a list of places and spaces to seek help from, to find out about, to marvel at, to try to grow in. Some of them are "growth centers," drawn from the files of the American Association for Humanistic Psychology, who have graciously allowed us to use their list, with the proviso that they are not responsible in any way for either the information or the concepts of the groups included in it. Others are medical clinics, university-sponsored associations, communities, some large and well-known, some more esoteric. The list, though it has taken much time and trouble to compile, is by no means exhaustive, nor do we endorse any of the places listed. It merely suggests a sampling of the myriad of different lifestyles and mindstyles that are being checked into in this country and overseas.

What To Do If You Need Guidance

A few things to remember if you really need help, fast, in a psychological emergency. Consult your local telephone directory for your county hospital, or the nearest university teaching hospital, or regional mental health service. And remember that the American Psychiatric Association, the American Medical Association, and the American Bar Association maintain referral services in all major cities in this country.

Most communities now have active "hotline" services for such common problems as alcoholism, drug overdose, abortion, depression, or having nowhere to turn for help or advice. The FISH organization, run entirely by volunteers, offers a sympathetic ear day and night in many communities. The telephone directory lists most services, if you are sufficiently in command of yourself to consult it; if not, try asking the telephone operator for the appropriate hotline, hospital, police, or fire department (many of whom have trained paramedical ambulance services).

PSYCHOLOGICAL GROWTH: Individual, Interpersonal and Community

ADANTA
Suite 1140, Lennix Towers West
3390 Peachtree Road, N.E.
Atlanta, Georgia 30326

Adanta attempts to provide an emotional atmosphere of honesty and trust, conducive to personal reflection and exploration. It is hoped that program participants will feel free to share spontaneously with others, work toward creatively integrating the many aspects of themselves, and achieve a sense of personal refreshment and renewal.

ALL TOGETHER
One East Wacker Drive
Suite 3500
Chicago, Illinois 60601

A newly incorporated umbrella organization for a wide variety of lifestyles, All Together was founded by Lloyd M. Levin, market researcher and consultant. Believing that at least one industry — life insurance — was losing touch with a large market, Levin documented the practices of major companies in relation to people from so-called alternate lifestyles such as communes, singles cohabitation, homosexuality, bisexuality, divorcees and others living alone, and users of marijuana. All Together is nonpolitical, incorporated in Illinois, and plans to act as a conduit between business and its members, with insurance programs, a credit union, a legal assistance program, and many other services.

ANEW
537 Charles Lane
Mill Valley, California 94941
(415) 383-2584

Anew consists of humanistically oriented psychotherapists and counselors trained to be of assistance in two specific areas: enhancement of sexual functioning and general counseling for couples. Emphasis is on improving relationships through improving problem-solving abilities, increasing communication skills, and achieving balanced sex roles. Sexual counseling, for individuals or couples, is approached from the perspective of Masters and Johnson when deemed appropriate. All counselors are licensed, trained, and experienced. In addition to client services, training courses in the theory and practice of sex therapy are offered to practicing therapists and qualified graduate students.

ASSET
990 Geary Boulevard, Suite 106
San Francisco, California 94109
(415) 441-3334

Asset offers a variety of workshops focused on developing self-resources, understanding commitments and needs, and exploring the nature of relationship to others. Areas covered include: parent workshops, body mastery workshops, relationships workshops, job workshops, and children's workshops.

ASSOCIATES FOR HUMAN RESOURCES
191 Sudbury Road
P.O. Box 727
Concord, Massachusetts 01742
(617) 369-7810 or 258-9624

Established in 1968, Associates for Human Resources provides clinical and professional services and training for individuals and groups. Programs fall within the following general areas: (1) Contractual services for corporations, educational systems, or any public or private agency. Consultation skills are used for problem-solving, evaluation and research, leadership training, human relations training, etc. (2) Clinical services for individuals, couples, or families desiring consultation and counseling. All counselors have had extensive training in Gestalt therapy and also make use of other therapy techniques such as bioenergetic analysis and transactional analysis. (3) The Institute, offering a wide range of professional development and training programs and personal growth experiences. Professional courses cover areas such as Gestalt, individual and group consulting skills, organizational development, and a transactional analysis program for educators. Personal growth groups also emphasize Gestalt, plus a variety of other experiences such as centering and body energy, dreams and personal growth, and music as revelation. (4) Academic programs, including several internship options, and graduate level work through the Campus-Free College. Fees for many activities may be negotiated through a barter/work program. Some scholarships are also available.

BARKSDALE FOUNDATION FOR FURTHERANCE OF HUMAN UNDERSTANDING
P.O. Box 187
Idyllwild, California 92349
(714) 659-3858

The work of the Barksdale Foundation centers on the development of effective methods for building high self-esteem, enabling people to live more productive and happier lives. The Foundation has created an integrated program for self-esteem enhancement which has been used in many therapeutic situations throughout the world. To those interested in increasing their self-esteem, it offers periodic workshops in major cities throughout the United States; a home study kit of books and tapes focusing on the attainment of self-confidence, inner peace, and success; and a detailed study guide which provides instructions on how to organize and conduct a study group (there are currently over 100 such study groups in existence). The Foundation offers a free evaluation form for anyone wishing to test his level of self-esteem.

BAY CITIES MENTAL HEALTH CENTER
11601 Santa Monica Boulevard
Los Angeles, California 90025
(213) 477-1021

Bay Cities Mental Health Center provides low-cost psychiatric diagnosis and treatment on an out-patient basis for children and adults. Group and individual therapy is available, plus family and couples counseling.

BEVERLY HILLS COMMUNITY ADVISORY COMMITTEE: Maple Center
339 North Maple Drive
Beverly Hills, California 90210
(213) 274-5387

Maple Center is an overall community treatment center with the major focus on individual and family counseling. Drugs and crisis-oriented programs are offered for groups of all ages.

BLACK BART CENTER
234 San Jose Avenue
San Francisco, California
(415) 282-7851

Black Bart Center offers a supportive atmosphere for persons making changes in work and lifestyles. Ongoing discussion groups and counseling are provided for guidance in establishing more satisfying lifestyles and gaining greater fulfillment from work and interpersonal relationships. Open House is held each Wednesday evening as an opportunity for people to become acquainted with the Center's aims and programs.

BOULDER WORKSHOP:
Experiences in Personal Growth
2889 Valmont Road
Boulder, Colorado 80301
(303) 449-5230

The Boulder Workshop offers workshop experiences aimed at providing opportunities for individuals to pursue those areas which will aid in self-development. Workshops are designed for individuals in sound mental health who are interested in exploring new paths toward greater fulfillment and enrichment. An assortment of workshop topics include: basic and marathon encounter; Gestalt therapy principles; energy awareness, movement, and Aikido; sensory awareness; bioenergetics; biofeedback training; enhancing intimacy in couples; assertiveness training; psychosynthesis; decision-making and the I Ching; meditation.

CASAELYA
1561 Masonic Avenue
San Francisco, California 94117

Casaelya is an association which focuses on the areas of interpersonal communication and personal expression. It offers a program of intensive weekend group experiences, whose aim is to bring about more meaningful relationships and a fuller discovery of life.

CENTER FOR HUMAN DEVELOPMENT
221 Shady Avenue
Pittsburgh, Pennsylvania 15206
(412) 361-1400

The Center for Human Development attempts to provide an environment where human potentialities can be realized and personal enrichment achieved. The Center provides a variety of opportunities conducive to new ways of relating to self and others. It conducts Gestalt groups, "singles only" groups, and discovery workshops on a weekly basis. A variety of other workshops of varying duration are also offered, exploring such areas as Yoga, assertion training, life planning, psychodrama, sexual responsiveness, and dealing with separation and divorce. Consulting and community services for interested organizations are available, and individuals may make use of a lending library containing books, magazines, and tape cassettes on subjects in the humanistic field. On the fourth Sunday of every month, the Center holds Open House.

CENTER FOR THE WHOLE PERSON
304 West 105th Street
New York, New York 10025
(212) 222-9445

Directed by Dr. David Freundlich, the Center for the Whole Person provides experiential opportunities for increasing self-awareness, understanding, and personal growth. It focuses on primal experiences as a means of coming in contact with one's deep childhood feelings, and thus being able to release oneself from the early sources of present pain and self-limitation. Gestalt, fantasy, psychodrama, and encounter are also used in conjunction with the primal approach. Workshops led by Dr. Freundlich include: 15-hour primal experience marathons; primal experience weekend marathons; five-day primal experience marathons, and ongoing weekly Primal Groups lasting four hours each.

CENTERING:
Every Woman's Career and Life
Development Center
944 Market Street
San Francisco, California 94102
(415) 391-3206

Centering, formerly known as the Women's Vocational Institute, was created in 1974 to deal with women's needs in the areas of employment, career planning, and life development. Activities and services include classes and workshops, individualized counseling, a newsletter service, a public vocational library, job placement information files, and conference series for particular vocational problems. The Center's core educational program consists of the following courses: Career and Life Planning, Women's Strength after Forty, The Art of Job Seeking, and Assertiveness Training. The Center also conducts special programs for women who face discrimination due to a prison record, drug abuse, lesbianism, minority status, or age.

CENTRAL CITY COMMUNITY
MENTAL HEALTH CENTER
4211 South Avalon Boulevard
Los Angeles, California 90011
(213) 232-4111

The Central City Community Mental Health Center provides in-patient, out-patient, and day treatment for children and adults. The Center offers a wide variety of programs, including: crisis intervention; short, intermediate and long-term psychotherapy; individual and group counseling; occupational, recreational, and dance therapies; and psychodrama. Fees are determined by ability to pay.

THE CLEARING
P.O. Box 835
San Rafael, California 94902
(415) 457-4622

The Clearing offers a program of primal therapy as a basis for individualized development. It believes that primal therapy is an effective way of getting in touch with one's real self, consequently enabling an individual to feel whole, secure and open to people and experiences. It provides a supportive environment for this inner exploration in a program of individual and group assistance toward growth.

COMMUNITARIAN CONSULTANTS
236 San Jose Avenue
San Francisco, California 94110
(415) 647-4593

Communitarian Consultants was formed to assist groups and individuals in exploring the options of cooperative living. It serves as a facilitator for existing communities that wish to improve their capabilities in such areas as intrafamily communication and decision making. It also provides consultant services for individuals to help them determine whether or

not they are ready to live in a community, what kind of community is appropriate to their needs and interests, and where they are likely to find such a community.

COMMUNITY FAMILY CENTER
Rosenberg Building, Suite 210
306 Mendocino Avenue
Santa Rosa, California 95404
(707) 544-1863

The Community Family Center is a humanistically oriented service agency which provides counseling for individuals, couples, and families. It is designed to assist in such areas as stimulating individual growth and awareness, improving contact and communication in close relationships, and working through periods of crisis and change. Counseling fees are based on a sliding scale according to income.

CUMBRES
Dublin Inn
P.O. Box C
Dublin, New Hampshire 03444
(603) 563-7591

Cumbres offers a constantly evolving group of programs which encourage personal growth and interpersonal understanding. Activities focus on activating self-expression and creativity.

DIALOGUE HOUSE ASSOCIATES
45 West 10th Street
New York, New York 10011
(212) 228-9180 or 673-5880
Los Angeles: (213) 829-2356

The core of the Dialogue House program is the use of an Intensive Journal as a means of personal growth. Founded in 1966 by Dr. Ira Progoff, it offers a variety of public workshops and institutional programs in education, mental health, industry and religion. A unique aspect of the group workshops is that privacy is maintained throughout, allowing individuals to work on resolving their problems without resorting to group discussion of them. Process Meditation Workshops, offering an active approach to meditation, are also part of the program and have lately become increasingly important. Intensive Journal Workshops are regularly conducted in both the New York City and Los Angeles areas, and Special Dialogue House workshops are held throughout the country.

EMOTIONAL HEALTH ANONYMOUS
2420 North San Gabriel Boulevard
P.O. Box 1476
Rosemead, California 91770
(213) 573-5482

Emotional Health Anonymous is a group of persons with emotional problems who have joined forces to solve them and remain well.

ENCORE
16770 Redwood Lodge Road
Los Gatos, California 95030
(408) 353-3330

Encore is a rentable, year-round growth center located on 30 acres of land in the Santa Cruz Mountains. Facilities include a main lodge with meeting room and sleeping accommodations for up to 29 people, nine A-frame cabins accommodating six people each, a fully equipped kitchen, swimming pool, massage tables, sauna, playfields and sports equipment. The camp may be reserved for residential conferences, group encounters, seminars, workshops or study groups on a day-long, weekend or long-term basis. Visitors are welcome but are requested to make advance arrangements.

ENCOUNTER CONSULTANTS
P.O. Box 1455
Cody, Wyoming 82414

Encounter Consultants provides activities for

individuals and groups, with the aim of discovering new creative and productive possibilities in human encounter.

ENCOUNTERS
The Huntington, Suite 209
5225 Connecticut Avenue, N.W.
Washington, D.C. 20015
(202) 363-3033 or (301) 530-4485

Encounters offers group workshops which provide the opportunity for participants to share personal experiences, get a variety of feedback to their ways of expressing themselves, and become more accepting of their inner feelings. Encounters do not substitute for any form of therapy; rather, the assumption behind the group experiences is that participants are capable and growing individuals who are having good experiences in their lives and wish to expand them. Groups may meet either on a long-term basis once a week or for a two- or three-day weekend retreat at the organization's Solitude Farm Center.

ESALEN/SAN FRANCISCO
1793 Union Street
San Francisco, California 94123
(415) 771-1710

ESALEN/BIG SUR
Big Sur, California 93920
(408) 667-2335

Esalen focuses on the potentialities and values of human existence within a variety of contexts. It explores new humanistic possibilities in such fields as education, religion, philosophy, physical and behavioral sciences, sports and art. Its activities encompass seminars and workshops, residential programs, consulting services and research. There are a wide variety of programs geared to particular interests and needs. These include:

(1) Residential summer workshops held at Westerbeke Ranch in Sonoma County, varying in duration from two days (weekend) to five days; (2) Esalen Sports Center Summer Institute, concerned with the presentation of new concepts, practices and teaching methods in sports activities, with emphasis on the pleasure of participation; (3) Children's programs designed to expose children to new ways of looking at themselves and at others, and new approaches to play activities and expression through art; (4) Women's programs, devoted to helping women develop personal creativity in a variety of forms and exploring the nature of feminine perception and attitudes.

A Media Center embracing film, video, audio, typesetting and design exists at Esalen/Big Sur. Cassettes and films of Esalen programs are available, plus the opportunity in some workshops for participants to make use of video feedback. Information on availability of materials will be provided by the Center if people specify the personalities or subjects in which they are interested. From September through May, Esalen/Big Sur offers an ongoing residential program for people interested in long-term intensive workshop experience. Minimum residence is 26 days. For those wishing to be in contact with Esalen, but not in a residential capacity, studio apartments may be rented on a monthly basis at the South Coast Center, located one and a half miles north of Esalen/Big Sur. Further information about Esalen's facilities and specifics about all activities are furnished in the "Esalen Catalog," published quarterly at $2 per year.

est
1750 Union Street
San Francisco, California 94123
(415) 441-0100

The purpose of est is to unblock inner potential and free self-expression. It strives to achieve this end by a combination of various disciplines developed and refined by Werner Erhard. Training is in the form of an intensive basic course which takes place on two consecutive weekends. Seminars are also conducted on a weekly basis, including: Body Series, Here/Now Series, and the Sex and Money Series. Participants come from a wide variety of lifestyles, economic levels and cultural orientations. Training can be obtained in San Francisco, Los Angeles, New York, Hawaii and Aspen, Colorado.

FAMILY DEVELOPMENT CENTER
179 Los Ranchito Road
San Rafael, California 94903

The Family Development Center offers a variety of programs, workshops and ongoing groups aimed at furthering self-discovery and growth. The Center makes use of intensive encounter group and Gestalt methods, art, movement, psychodrama, role playing, and videotape feedback as means of achieving more effective ways of intra- and interpersonal communication.

FAMILY GROUP INSTITUTE
649 Irving Street
San Francisco, California
(415) 731-1095

The Family Group Institute believes that individuals have an innate capacity for stimulating growth within themselves and encouraging it in others. They consider work within the family context to be a relatively unexplored source for facilitating individual growth in addition to development of the family unit as a whole. The Institute's experience with multiple family groups, where three or four families meet together on an ongoing basis, is a newly developed technique found to be very effective in encouraging growth of all participants. The Institute also offers couple therapy and couple groups, adolescent groups, and individual therapy. Other activities include consultation to mental health agencies on work with families and adolescents, and a developing program of training workshops for mental health professionals.

FAMILY SYNERGY
P.O. Box 30103
Terminal Annex
Los Angeles, California 90030

Family Synergy describes its functions, aims and services in the following manner: "Family Synergy is an organization based on the premise that people can live fuller, more rewarding lives, achieving more of their potential, by living in committed family groups larger than the nuclear family .... Our purposes are to further the understanding and the practice of the type of open and committed relationships necessary to implement and sustain these expanded families; to facilitate the discussion and exchange of ideas and the collection and dissemination of information about all types of expanded families, including group marriage; to provide ways for people interested in these ideas to meet, get to know and keep in touch with one another, and to further public acceptance of the right of all people to be themselves with the right to practice openly the lifestyle of their choice .... The Communal Living Clearing Center is a service provided by Family Synergy for those people (members or not) seriously interested in living with others. Its goals are to provide opportunities for these people to meet each other, to help to put potentially compatible people in direct touch with one another, and to facilitate their living together as they desire. CLCC will also serve existing shared-living groups as a communication tool, a source of additional people, and as a general resource as desired."

FAMILY THERAPY INSTITUTE
120 Oak Meadow Drive
Los Gatos, California 95030

The Family Therapy Institute offers a four-part program: (1) treatment of families in distress; (2) well family evaluation and education; (3) multiple family therapy, and (4) family therapy training.

FRANSISTERS
2168 South Lafayette Street
Denver, Colorado 80210

Created in 1963, the aim of the Fransisters is to help women appreciate their womanhood and be aware of their own importance and influence. The Fransisters consider woman to be a "light-bearer" who can give continual encouragement, inspiration and love by daily devotion to high ideals. They are an interreligious group, and their central desire is to share their ideas with all women, point out the connections between ancient wisdom and modern science, and encourage women to make their own silent retreats within their homes or communities. They believe that in these ways women can become more fully in touch with their inner strength and beauty.

GAY COMMUNITY SERVICES
1614 Wilshire Boulevard
Los Angeles, California 90017
(213) 482-3062

This organization provides services for the gay community in many areas, including: self-development, medical help, employment counseling, legal assistance, military/veteran affairs, and transsexual problems. Affiliated with the Gay Community Services is the Sappho House, a center which provides temporary emergency residence service for women.

GAY PARENTS LEGAL
& RESEARCH GROUP
P.O. Box 82
Mountain Terrace, Washington 98043

The Gay Parents Legal & Research Group asserts: "We are concerned about all gay parents and teenagers who have no one to talk to about their sexuality and circumstances." The group provides counseling, information and legal and medical referrals, and it also sponsors a speakers bureau.

GUILD FOR PSYCHOLOGICAL STUDIES
1734 45th Avenue
San Francisco, California 94122

The Guild for Psychological Studies analyzes material from the fields of comparative mythology, religions and the arts, primarily from the viewpoint of Dr. C. G. Jung's Analytical Psychology. The Guild also provides a framework within which the individual may be aided in his search for his own highest values and deepest awareness, through a better understanding of his unconscious and conscious processes. Discussion groups are used for a more personal approach to the values of the texts studied.

HUMAN DEVELOPMENT ASSOCIATION
P.O. Box 811, Station B
Montreal, Quebec
Canada

The Human Development Association consists of a partnership of men and women who share a desire to become more mature and who wish to encourage and assist others in actions beneficial to man's welfare and instrumental in his development.

HUMAN GROWTH CENTER
376 Broadway Arcade Building
Saratoga Springs, New York 12866
(518) 587-8440

The desire of The Human Growth Center is to serve as a catalyst for individual and interpersonal growth. Its services are aimed at discovering and helping to develop the strong, positive capabilities within each person. A wide choice of programs is offered, including: individual and group therapy, testing and evaluation, nonmedical hypnosis and biofeedback, marriage and family counseling, developing adolescents toward healthy adulthood, helping children learn, sensitivity training and deep muscle relaxation. Consultation services are also provided for professionals in the fields of medicine and education. Seminars and workshops are held on Fridays on a drop-in basis for people interested in learning more about the Center.

HUMAN RESOURCES DEVELOPMENT
Hidden Springs
South Acworth, New Hampshire 03706

Human Resources Development (HRD) conducts scientific research into the nature of human potential and devises methods and techniques for the maximum development of these resources. Its desire is to enable individuals to make full use of their potentialities and thus achieve a more productive and joyful life.

IAMATHON
1020 Corporation Way, Suite 103
Palo Alto, California 94303
(415) 969-3800

IAMathon is a 40-hour weekend training program designed to help individuals explore their societal and parental conditioning, discover inner needs and learn to develop open and fulfilling relationships with others. The program utilizes a variety of techniques, including Zen, transactional analysis, transcendental meditation, dianetics, Gestalt and value clarification, plus other specially designed IAMathon techniques. Training is held regularly in the San Francisco, South Bay and East Bay regions. In addition to the weekend program, IAMathon offers workshops for individuals in such areas as relationships and communication, obesity, and sexual enjoyment.

INSTITUTE FOR ADVANCED STUDY
IN RATIONAL PSYCHOTHERAPY
45 East 65th Street
New York, New York 10021
(212) 535-0822

The Institute for Advanced Study is founded on a belief in Rational-Emotive Therapy (RET), an action-oriented therapy approach that emphasizes each individual's own responsibility for the causes of his problems. The psychologists, psychiatrists and social workers on the staff of the Institute believe that people can learn to change irrational, self-destructive assumptions and actions by means of RET. In conjunction with the Institute for Rational Living, a wide array of programs is offered for both professionals and nonprofessionals. They include:

(1) Professional training in the form of ongoing courses, special weekend symposia, case supervision and lectures; (2) on-site consultative services through which Institute faculty members design specially tailored workshops for schools, colleges, hospitals and other organizations; (3) individual, family and group therapy sessions at moderate fees; (4) a clinic offering diagnostic and counseling services for children with behavioral and/or learning problems; (5) research in psychotherapy and in classroom emotional education; (6) rational-emotive education consultation services carried out through the Living School Consultation Service, designed for educators and parents wishing training in a rational-humanistic approach to living and working with children; (7) ongoing workshops, lecture series and one-day workshops for all individuals interested in improving the quality of their interpersonal relationships, actual-

izing more of their creative potential and generally enhancing their capacity for more enjoyable living, and (8) women's programs, offering workshops in female sexuality, assertiveness training, career planning and special workshops for women over 40.

The Institute also offers three special professional training programs: (1) postgraduate fellowship training in psychotherapy; (2) associate fellowship program in psychotherapy, and (3) primary certificate program in rational-emotive therapy and counseling.

INSTITUTE FOR EXPERIENTIAL LEARNING & DEVELOPMENT
1687 Lawrence Road
Trenton, New Jersey 08638
(609) 882-6815

The Institute for Experiential Learning and Development (IELD) offers a program aimed at personal growth through a combination of: (1) private psychotherapy work with individuals, couples, families and groups; (2) ongoing therapy groups, making use of a variety of encounter and growth techniques, and (3) weekend workshops as an adjunct to private therapy or by themselves offering significant growth opportunities.

INSTITUTE FOR MULTIPLE PSYCHOTHERAPY
3701 Sacramento Street
San Francisco, California 94118

The Institute for Multiple Psychotherapy was established to provide an environment in which participants can revitalize their friendly, sensual and loving relationships, experience an active appreciation of and trust in other people, and learn methods of fostering encounter between individuals in a group situation.

INTERPERSONAL COMMUNICATION PROGRAMS
2001 Riverside Avenue
Minneapolis, Minnesota 55454
(612) 338-4276

Interpersonal Communication Programs was developed at the Minnesota Family Study Center, University of Minnesota, in conjunction with the Minneapolis Family and Children's Service. The function of the organization is to provide certified instructors to conduct couples groups and to teach basic interpersonal communication skills in educational settings.

KOPAVI
1462 Wilson Avenue
St. Paul, Minnesota 55106

The motivating purpose of Kopavi is to provide a forum for the discovery, exploration, practice and dissemination of techniques of value to individuals and groups that are striving to achieve a fuller realization of human potential.

LA JOLLA PROGRAM
1125 Torrey Pines Road
La Jolla, California 92037
(714) 459-3861

In conjunction with the Center for Studies of the Person, the La Jolla Program offers summer institutes and a newly created seven-day spring institute designed for individuals interested in achieving personal and interpersonal growth and learning to apply group processes to their own working situations. The program emphasizes participation in small groups, aimed at providing maximum freedom for personal expression, exploration of feelings, and interpersonal communication. Participants are also allowed to facilitate weekend groups as a means of developing their own leadership abilities.

LAUREL INSTITUTE
234 South 22nd Street
Philadelphia, Pennsylvania 19103
(215) 732-8550

The Laurel Institute offers consultation, staff development, and training programs specially designed to meet an organization's particular needs. The programs are aimed at increasing the effectiveness of people in a variety of fields: business, industry, government, health care, public service and education. Directors of the Institute are members of the International Transactional Analysis Association, and therefore, special emphasis is placed on transactional analysis as a means of increasing personal capability. Seminars in effective management workshops for staff development are offered, along with a wide range of training courses in transactional analysis. Clinical services are also available for individuals, couples or families.

LOS ANGELES COUNTY DEPARTMENT OF HEALTH SERVICES
Mental Health Services
Information and Resources Unit
1102 South Crenshaw Boulevard
Los Angeles, California 90019
(213) 937-2380

The Information and Resources Unit for Mental Health Services provides referrals for individuals seeking help with mental or emotional problems. The type of problem, the individual's resources, his geographical location and other points of importance are taken into consideration before referral to a therapist, mental health center or clinic as appropriate to the person's needs. Similar referral services exist within county health departments throughout the nation.

LOS ANGELES COUNTY PSYCHOLOGICAL ASSOCIATION
11520 San Vicente Boulevard
Los Angeles, California 90025
(213) 826-6551

The Los Angeles County Psychological Association maintains a listing of more than 200 Ph.D. psychologists in the county who provide a wide range of counseling services for children, adolescents, and adults. The individual data card for each psychologist contains information as to the geographical location served and area of specialization. The Association has referral offices in counties throughout California, and similar referral services exist nationwide.

LOS ANGELES COUNTY/ USC MEDICAL CENTER
1200 North State Street
Los Angeles, California 90023
(213) 226-5334

The Los Angeles County Psychiatric Department provides crisis intervention assistance and general psychiatric assistance for all ages on an in-patient or out-patient basis. Fees are determined by ability to pay.

LOS ANGELES INFORMATION AND REFERRAL SERVICE FOR THERAPY AND GROWTH
9056 Santa Monica Boulevard
Los Angeles, California 90069
(213) 878-2105

The L.A. Information and Referral Service for Therapy and Growth serves as a centralized place for people to obtain information and referrals to therapy and growth programs. It attempts to direct anyone wanting help to a therapist or center which best meets the unique, individual needs of the person. The center itself provides crisis counseling, vocational counseling and research for both professionals and nonprofessionals seeking information on therapy and growth situations. The

standard fee for services is $30, though arrangements can be made for individuals without adequate financial resources. In addition to local information, the center has a list of primal therapy centers throughout the world.

MANN RANCH
P.O. Box 570
Ukiah, California 95482

Mann Ranch offers small group experiences in seminars and workshops in self-awareness. The programs, encompassing a two- or three-day period, present no particular creed or philosophy but instead allow an open-end exploration of the joy and meaning of existence. They allow the opportunity for communion with self, others and nature.

MID-ATLANTIC TRAINING COMMITTEE
1500 Massachusetts Avenue, N.W.
Suite 325
Washington, D.C. 20005
(202) 223-0582

MATC consists of more than 150 skilled educators, group facilitators, organizational consultants and training advisors, accredited by the Association for Creative Change Within Religious and Other Social Systems. The Committee has been in existence since 1965 and offers a variety of training, educational and consulting services to residents of southern New York, New Jersey, Pennsylvania, Maryland, Delaware, Washington, D.C., Virginia, West Virginia and North Carolina. Arrangements can be made, however, for putting together programs in other parts of the country. At least 50 educational and training conferences are held each year, either on a residential or nonresidential basis. Most conferences can be brought to any conference site where a sufficient number of people express interest. Training programs and educational conferences can also be tailor-made for the needs of a particular organization. In addition, consulting services in such areas as organizational development, short- and long-range planning, and curriculum development and design can be provided for any group on a short- or long-term basis.

MATC offers many different options, including: (1) short (usually one day) introductory programs, discussing topics such as leadership, problem solving and values clarification; (2) longer developmental programs including Women's Personal Development Weekend, Man/Woman: Changing Roles, I'm OK — You're OK: T/A Weekend, and personal planning workshops and weekends; (3) Human Relations Training, an intensive, full-coverage program in the essentials of human interaction and relationship. Also provided are skill development programs, consultant skills training programs, and a thorough trainer/consultant intern program.

MOTIVATION DEVELOPMENT CENTRE
P.O. Box 238
209 East Washington Street
Bloomington, Illinois 61701
(505) 265-6557

The Motivation Development Centre seeks to assist individuals who are attempting to change their lives or find solutions to personal problems. Toward this end the facilitators at the Centre assess the present state of the individual's creative potential and work on developing a program which will be of special value in assisting the person's growth. The Centre is interested in originating alternate methods and practices to help bring about personal growth. It encourages continuous research in new areas of human development and attempts to communicate these findings to practitioners in all fields.

MOUNTAIN GROVE
Barton Road
Glendale, Oregon 97442

The desire of the Mountain Grove community is to allow everyone to explore the possibilities of living fully and naturally by discovering his essential needs and methods of expression. They are concerned with all aspects of relationship — to self, to other, to nature, to the world of ideas, to the continuum of life.

NATIONAL GAY TASK FORCE
80 Fifth Avenue
New York, New York 10010
(212) 741-1010

The National Gay Task Force is a civil rights organization which undertakes projects aimed at altering media approaches to homosexuality. The Task Force also maintains a complete up-to-date listing of all U.S. gay groups.

NATIONAL ORGANIZATION FOR WOMEN
425 13th Street, N.W.
Suite 1007
Washington, D.C. 20004
(202) 424-9537

NOW is a civil rights organization whose purpose is to help bring about conditions which will enable women to develop their full potential. NOW is not a "women's group" but a human liberation group, with both men and women working together to achieve equal responsibility and participation in society. Its emphasis is on action, and it has a full program of projects and goals which include the following: ratification of the Equal Rights Amendment, equal employment opportunities, equal educational opportunities and reorientation of the educational system, developmental child care, revision of income tax and social security laws, revision of marriage, divorce and family laws, equal participation in political activities, prohibition of sex discrimination in public facilities, an improved image of women in the mass media, a recognition that the liberation of women involves the liberation of men, and a realization that women's problems are linked to broader questions of social justice. Local NOW chapters sponsor ongoing consciousness raising groups, workshops and conferences. Individual chapters also publish monthly newsletters dealing with services, activities, and current issues.

NATIONAL TRAINING LABORATORIES
Bethel, Maine

NTL, the first and probably the most prestigious of the encounter-growth centers, was founded in 1947 by a group of social psychologists. They had been participants on a workshop for group problem solving related to the Connecticut Fair Employment Practices Act, and an informal discussion among staff and participants developed into what was probably the first encounter group session ever held. NTL encounter groups have dealt primarily with problems in management and industry and have been employed by large corporations, leaders in education and social service such as the American Red Cross, and leaders and members of the Episcopal and Methodist Churches. NTL has managed sensitivity training and T-groups for organizations throughout the country. With the decline of interest by corporations in T-groups, and lessening of the belief that they can solve every problem, NTL reorganized in 1971 and dissolved its association with regional groups. Current emphasis is on the programs at the Bethel center.

NEW COMMUNITY PROJECTS
32 Rutland Street
Boston, Massachusetts 02118
(617) 262-3740

New Community Projects consists of a collective of people who are committed to developing life-change alternatives for themselves and others. They are engaged in attempting to bring about personal and societal transformation by exploring issues and attitudes in such areas as work, sexual roles, decision-making and interpersonal communications. New Community Projects provides a clearinghouse, counseling services, legal assistance, workshops and facilitation for people interested in communal living.

NEW ENGLAND CENTER
FOR PERSONAL AND
ORGANIZATIONAL DEVELOPMENT
Box 575 E
Amherst, Massachusetts 01002

The New England Center offers summer workshops in Gestalt, humanistic education, altered states of consciousness, psychosynthesis, meditation, Yoga, creativity, massage and women's awareness.

NEW HAVEN CENTER
FOR HUMAN RELATIONS
400 Prospect Street
New Haven, Connecticut 06511
(203) 776-1333

The New Haven Center for Human Relations offers a constantly evolving series of programs conducted by a highly qualified core staff augmented by individuals prominent in their fields of specialization. Workshop offerings include: introductory massage, Gestalt, reality therapy, transactional analysis (weekend introduction and five-day training institute), relaxation, introduction to bioenergetic analysis, and group processes. In addition, a special one-week summer training institute is offered, providing intensive training in small group dynamics psychodrama, bioenergetics and Gestalt. Also, a separate series of psychodrama classes is now available under the direction of the Psychodrama Institute of New Haven, the newest branch of the Center.

NEW YORK UNIVERSITY SCHOOL
OF CONTINUING EDUCATION
2 University Place
New York, New York 10003
(212) 598-3991

The School of Continuing Education has a variety of noncredit evening classes and weekend workshops open to the general public. It also sponsors programs in mind research, a current symposium being "Ways of Healing: Ancient and Contemporary." Through its Life Studies program, it offers courses including: Death and Dying, Decision-making, Biomedical Ethics: A Philosophical Inquiry, Life Planning, and Creative Problem-solving Workshop. In addition, it has a full range of human psychology courses covering such topics as Psychical Research: Myth into Science, Behavior Modification, and Coping with Change. Other courses of interest include The Spiritual Journey into Literature, Atheism: A Philosophical Inquiry, and Mysticism — East and West. A complete catalog of course offerings and fees will be provided on request.

OASIS
Center for Human Potential
12 East Grand Avenue
Chicago, Illinois 60611
(312) 266-0033

Oasis is a nonprofit educational institute founded in 1967. Its emphasis is on workshops which aim at heightening self-awareness, increasing understanding of how others react to us, and developing more effective ways of dealing with each other. Oasis also offers training programs, consulting services, and a massage guild. Workshops cover a wide spectrum of subjects. Sample titles include: From "Us" to "I" — for Separated and Divorced

Persons, Fair Fight Training and Pairing, Transactional Analysis, Gestalt Use of Dreams in Therapy, The Use of Poetry in Personal Growth, and Acupuncture — An Introduction. Drop-in encounter groups, ongoing groups and special groups for couples and for women are also offered.

ONTOS
40 South Clay, Room 246
Hinsdale, Illinois 60521
(312) 325-6384

Ontos was created in the belief that there is a need for new ways of relating, unprovided for in present societal structures and institutions. To facilitate inner growth and improved interpersonal relationships, it offers experiences in group encounter, nonverbal communication, sensory awareness, meditation and discussion.

OPEN END.
A Community in Marin
241 North San Pedro Road
San Rafael, California 94903
(415) 472-2101

Open End provides an emotionally supportive environment in which people of different backgrounds have the opportunity to examine new lifestyles, explore their own feelings and assumptions, test new values and experience meaningful relationships with a variety of persons. Open End is also concerned with motivation and training for working toward social change.

PERSONAL EXPLORATION GROUPS
2400 Bancroft Way
Berkeley, California 94704
(415) 841-8900 or 841-6013

P.E.G. is a community-based program offering low-cost encounter groups plus paraprofessional training for work in interpersonal relations. In addition to basic encounter and training groups, P.E.G. offers couples groups, movement groups, awareness groups and many weekend workshops. P.E.G. also emphasizes community service through such activities as supplying communication workshops for schools, businesses and community social services; working with juveniles in diversion groups through the Berkeley Police Department; teaching classes and conducting workshops for educators, foster parents and individuals in the mental health field, and providing consultants for community agencies.

PIEDMONT SUMMER PROGRAM
Wake Forest University
Box 6219
Winston-Salem, North Carolina 27109
(919) 725-9850, extension 401

The Piedmont Summer Program is a three-week residential training workshop designed for people involved in group work of any kind. The program is aimed at assisting participants in achieving greater personal growth in addition to improving their group leadership skills. Training consists of more than 150 hours of experiential and cognitive explorations of group process, drawing on the resources of psychotherapy, counseling and the human potentials movement. Each individual participates in two training groups and assumes the role of co-leader in a weekend group under the supervision of a staff member. These weekend groups are open to the public at a low fee.

PROGRAMS IN COMMUNICATIONS, INC.
P.O. Box 2216
Boulder, Colorado 80302
(303) 442-2741

The primary aim of Programs in Communications is to help organizations develop the best possible operating conditions. It is concerned with reducing frustrations and destructive conflict among people in a group situation, improving cooperation and understanding among individuals and helping increase skills in communication. To these ends, it provides organizational consulting services and conducts training programs in such areas as basic communication skills, team building and creative conflict management.

PROMETHEUS
401 Florence Avenue
Palo Alto, California 94301
(415) 328-6137

Prometheus offers a variety of workshops and encounters to increase personal growth in many areas of human potential. The sessions are conducted by highly qualified personnel, and an attempt is made to keep participant costs low. Past groups have dealt with such topics as: Massage as a Healing Art, Bioenergetic Workshops, Inner Freedom Marathon, Relating to the Opposite Sex Marathon, and Gestalt and Reichian Bodywork. The Center also has open, ongoing groups and will allow other organizations to rent space for group meetings when it is available.

QUAESITOR
Vernon Lodge
Vernon Road
Sutton, Surrey, England

Quaesitor, meaning "Searcher," offers a series of intensive experiential encounter group meetings. Its goal is to become a full experiential growth center for the development of human potential.

RACIAL CONFRONTATION GROUPS
3516 Sacramento Street
San Francisco, California 94118

Racial Confrontation Groups provides a means for individuals to express previously hidden and forbidden thoughts and feelings about race. Directed by trained leaders, the groups have been effective in stimulating participants to take positive actions in reducing racial tension.

RELATIONSHIP DEVELOPMENT CENTER
P.O. Box 23, Gedney Station
White Plains, New York 10605
(914) 428-8367

The Relationship Development Center is an educational organization dedicated to the following goals: "the development of programs to encourage individual growth, to revitalize, deepen and enrich existing interpersonal relationships and to improve the ability of group members to work together cooperatively and productively in community organizations or educational enterprises."

RESOURCE CENTER
FOR HUMAN RELATIONS
6201 Harwood Avenue
Oakland, California 94618
(415) 653-8901

The Resource Center for Human Relations is designed to help individuals establish intimate, loving relationships. More specifically, its objectives include the following: (1) to increase self-understanding of intimacy and sexuality; (2) to improve communications and relationships between people; (3) to improve sexual functioning. To achieve these objectives, a variety of educational, training and resource services are available to individuals, couples and organizations. In the field of general education, the Center provides certified instructors for youth education programs dealing with intimacy and sexuality in healthy, loving relation-

ships. In terms of training and consultation, it offers short and long-term programs to enable professionals to become more competent in dealing with sexual problems of their clients. It also hopes to develop a program for training of paraprofessionals in the area of human sexuality. Other important activities include a continuing series of workshops; individual, couple and group counseling, and an ongoing program of research and evaluation.

ROCKY MOUNTAIN
BEHAVIORAL INSTITUTE
12086 West Green Mountain Drive
Denver, Colorado 80228

Weekend encounter groups are the major focus of the Rocky Mountain Behavioral Institute. The Institute has also engaged in a variety of other activities, however, including the Denver Public School integration program, management training, family communication, language behavior programs and the publication of learning materials for adult groups.

SENOI INSTITUTE:
Center for Growth and Development
Route 2, Box 259
Eugene, Oregon 97401
(503) 747-4311

The desire of the Senoi Institute is to help people achieve a new level of awareness and a greater involvement in life. It offers a program of exploration for individual growth, sensitivity and self-awareness.

SOUTH BAY THERAPEUTIC CLINIC
11633 Hawthorne Boulevard, Suite 403
Hawthorne, California 90250
(213) 973-7830

South Bay Therapeutic Clinic is a community mental health center that utilizes a holistic approach to healing. It offers a wide variety of services, including the following: art psychotherapy; counseling for children, adolescents, adults, couples and families; abuse programs for alcoholism, obesity, drug and cigarette addiction; groups for couples, men, women, parents, and teenagers; a biofeedback laboratory; clinical hypnosis; legal psychiatric reports and evaluations; psychological testing and evaluation; marathon group experiences; educational testing and tutoring; psychiatry on a crisis or long-term basis; a 24-hour emergency service. In addition, the Clinic sponsors several major conferences each year. Fees for any services or activities are based on the ability of the participant to pay.

SOUTHERN CALIFORNIA
PSYCHIATRIC SOCIETY
9713 Santa Monica Boulevard
Beverly Hills, California 90210
(213) 271-7219

The Southern California Psychiatric Society refers individuals to psychiatrists who are members of the American Psychiatric Association. The type of counseling desired (e.g., Gestalt, primal, psychodrama, etc.) is taken into consideration, and the individual receives a listing of the Association psychiatrists in his geographical area who provide such services. District chapters of the American Psychiatric Association exist in all states and provide public referrals to local Association members.

SUMMER RETREAT
East West Center
Route 2, Box 142
Spencer, West Virginia 25276

The Summer Retreat provides an opportunity to learn macrobiotic cooking, gardening and massage in a healthful mountain community. Children are welcome, and reservations may be made on a weekly or monthly basis.

TOPANGA CENTER
FOR HUMAN DEVELOPMENT
2247 North Topanga Canyon Boulevard
Topanga, California 90290
(213) 455-1342

The aim of this nonprofit organization is to explore the wide range of possibilities for growth and community. To this end, it presents a series of programs implementing approaches developed by both behavioral arts and sciences, past and present. The programs cover a wide gamut, from such ancient practices as Yoga and hypnosis to the most current, innovative forms of group encounter. The Center sponsors weekend workshops, ongoing groups and drop-in group programs. It attempts to maintain a high degree of flexibility and openly invites suggestions and workshop proposals from the community at large.

UNFOLDING PATH
1578 Willowmont Avenue
San Jose, California 95118
(408) 266-7051

Affiliated with the International Primal Association, the Unfolding Path offers primal feelings work based on the process developed by Arthur Janov. Counselors serve not as therapists but as facilitators, helping individuals discover and deal with primal feelings. Three different primal options are offered: (1) intensives, ideally on a daily basis for three consecutive weeks, but tailored to individual needs and time limitation; (2) weekend groups, limited to seven people, which serve as an introduction to primal work or as a follow-up after an intensive; (3) individual sessions by appointment, usually on a weekly basis. In addition to standard primal techniques, the following approaches are employed when useful: Reichian concepts and techniques of breathing, releasing muscular tension and freeing body energy; psychosynthesis techniques of guided imagery; transactional analysis of primal events. Though emphasis is on primal work, the Unfolding Path also offers three-day women's workshops.

UNIVERSITY OF CALIFORNIA
Los Angeles, California 90024

— Neuropsychiatric Institute (NPI)
740 Westwood Plaza
(213) 825-0511

NPI provides psychiatric and neurological services for children and adults. It also contains a gender identity research and treatment clinic geared to transsexual and transvestism problems. Fees are dependent on ability to pay.

— Psychology Department: Fernald School
405 Hilgard
(213) 879-1049 or 825-1191

The Fernald School undertakes training and research on learning problems of individuals of all ages who are of normal intelligence. It offers developmental and therapeutic programs on an hourly, half-day or full-day basis. Fees are dependent on ability to pay.

— Psychology Clinic
Franz Hall
(213) 825-2305

The Psychology Clinic provides psychological evaluation and psychotherapy for adolescents and adults with emotional problems and for children with behavioral and learning problems. Individual, group and family counseling are available. Fees are dependent on ability to pay.

— UCLA Extension
10995 LeConte Avenue

UCLA Extension offers a wide variety of courses (for academic credit or noncredit) in the areas of religious experience, consciousness expansion and personal growth. The majority of the classes are scheduled in the evening, though daytime programs and weekend workshops are also available. Extension offerings include: (1) programs through the Center for the Study of Religious Experience, East and West; (2) Yoga: Clinical Applications and Techniques, a series of classes specially designed for therapeutic practitioners; (3) Human Development courses, listed in a separate human development newsletter. Contact the UCLA Extension Office for full quarterly listings of continuing education courses.

VENTURE
P.O. Box 11802
Palo Alto, California 94306
(415) 326-8255

Venture is an organization providing opportunities for encounter as a means of personal and spiritual growth. Its assumptions about group encounter are stated as follows: "(1) that people share a common desire for personal growth; (2) that the goal of personal growth is worth the risk taking it involves; (3) that people can help one another; (4) that human beings are entitled to all their feelings — positive and negative alike — and that the full realization of these feelings leads to more authentic living and relating." Venture offers a variety of groups meeting once a week, plus weekend encounters at its country lodge near Pescadero. Most groups combine weekly meetings with one weekend retreat at the lodge. In addition to the regular series of encounters, special groups for men, women, couples and teens are also offered. Individuals interested in finding out more about Venture are invited to attend free evening meetings scheduled prior to the commencement of regular group sessions.

WAINWRIGHT HOUSE
Center for Development of Human Resources
260 Stuyvesant Avenue
Rye, New York 10580
(914) 967-6080

Wainwright House had its origins in 1941 and has continually grown and broadened in scope since its inception. It seeks to provide an environment and activities conducive to an individual realization of spiritual growth. Its approaches are diverse, including: analytical psychology, transactional analysis, biofeedback, paranormal healing, Gestalt, Yoga, Carl Rogers' nondirective approach, T'ai Chi, meditation and

prayer, psychodrama, and receptive listening. All forms of expression are fostered: art, dance, painting, sculpting, pottery, writing, discussion, drama, role-playing, body movement, and games. The Center offers weekday, evening, and weekend seminars, retreats, conferences, lectures, courses, and group meetings. Its programs fall under the following general headings: (1) Mind, Centering, and Meditation; (2) Relationships — Masculine and Feminine; (3) Healing; (4) Religion; (5) Psychology and Self-Awareness; (6) Creativity; (7) The Body and the Cultivation of the Whole Person; (8) The Family. All those interested in learning more about available programs may attend a "sample day" Sunday afternoon open house, or write to the Center for a program calendar.

WALDEN HOUSE
101 Buena Vista Avenue, F
San Francisco, California 94117

Walden House attempts to create a therapeutic environment which will encourage people with drug-related problems to discover their own inner needs and to learn to deal with the world around them.

WE CARE
121 Broadway, No. 517
San Diego, California 92101
(714) 233-6866

We Care is designed to meet the needs of newly divorced persons. It provides a variety of groups and activities which attempt to enable each participant to discover his own particular needs and inner strengths, and learn to function successfully as an autonomous person. To this end, emphasis is placed on improving communication skills, increasing self-awareness, and learning to be an active listener. We Care hopes to provide a warm and supportive atmosphere for personal growth. Programs include: (1) small, weekly ongoing groups; (2) samplers, in which various professionals offer one-night lecture and feedback sessions; (3) personal growth days, one-day workshops functioning as extensions of the samplers; (4) Creating A Positive Single Life workshops; (5) Developing Personal Potential weekend workshops; (6) Leadership Training days. There is an attempt to keep the cost of activities at a minimum, and scholarships are available for those without sufficient resources for attending any of the programs offered.

WIDE WORLD
OF CONTEMPORARY PEOPLE
Anaheim, California

Espousing a new type of swinging, the Wide World organization has many divisions: Wide World Social Swing Club, Wide World Group Discussions, the Omnisexuals, the Emerge Lifestyles Newsletter, the yearly Lifestyles Symposium and Convention, and the Lifestyles Center, offering a variety of classes, talks, workshops, and ongoing discussions in sexuality and society. Geri McGinley, a founder and director of Wide World, describes the activities of the organization as "growth swinging," "social sexuality," "emerging lifestyles" and relational-recreational." Stating that the old type of swinging grew from an uptight society, McGinley describes growth swinging as caring, sharing, and personal; intimate relationships with many people fostering an awareness and understanding of oneself.

WOMEN ASSOCIATES
402 West Mt. Airy Avenue
Philadelphia, Pennsylvania 19119
(215) 248-4916

Women Associates is a newly founded organization committed to helping women in their self-development, and enhancing the growth of all to humanize social systems. The staff consists of professionals who are skilled in human relations training, group processes, organizational development, and counseling.

WOMEN'S POWER CENTER
P.O. Box 9096
Berkeley, California 94709
(415) 549-0839, 655-6538 or 364-9751

The Women's Power Center attempts to help women learn how to develop and expand their inner sources of power, and how to focus their power to create positive changes in their lives. "Power from Within," a workshop where women can discover, experience, and express their personal creative power, is offered on a regular basis. Other workshops deal with the creation of nurturing support systems, and the development of group cooperation for social action. The Center is also putting together a workbook on Womanpower.

SPIRITUAL AND PARAPSYCHOLOGICAL DEVELOPMENT

ACADEMY OF SPIRITUAL ARTS
428B West 11th Street
Reno, Nevada 89503
(702) 323-2524

The activities of the Academy of Spiritual Arts are focused on developing spiritual awareness through a synthesis of Chinese Taoism, Japanese Buddhism, East Indian Yogas, African Spirit drumming, American Indian rituals, and music therapy. Classes are held throughout the community, with the current program including Hatha Yoga, Sat Sing, T'ai Chi Ch'uan, Mantra meditation, Taoist breathing techniques, and modern dance.

AKASHIC ORGANIZATION
10033 Saloma Avenue
Mission Hills, California 91345
(213) 893-9003

Through a monthly meeting in the San Fernan-

do Valley featuring a guest speaker, the Akashic Organization attempts to bring to public attention the existence of various metaphysical sciences and religions. The aim of the Organization is to demonstrate that a common sense of brotherhood and mutually beneficial cooperation can exist amongst all people, regardless of their backgrounds or nationalities.

ALVERNA
8140 Spring Mill Road
Indianapolis, Indiana 46260

Alverna is situated on 40 acres of secluded, park-like land on the north side of Indianapolis. The programs offered are designed for human and spiritual growth. With the exception of a few programs specially geared to professional interests, the workshops, laboratories, and retreats are intended for the general public. Special programs are provided for various

groups, and Alverna's facilities are available to any church-related or community service organization wishing to make use of them. Up to 50 people can be accommodated for overnight programs, and much larger groups for day programs. Workshops offered in 1975 covered such topics as value clarification, Gestalt and existential encounter, marriage encounter, Yoga, and life planning.

AMERICAN VEGAN SOCIETY — AHIMSA
Malaga, New Jersey 08328
(609) 694-2887

Taking its orientation from the Sanskrit word "Ahimsa," meaning nonkilling or nonharming, the American Vegan Society follows the concept of complete reverence for life, opposing all manifestations of cruelty and exploitation and actively encouraging compassion, kindness, and love for all forms of life. The Society publishes a monthly magazine entitled "Ahimsa," which emphasizes the benefits of a vegetarian diet.

A'NANDA MA'RGA
North American Sectorial Headquarters
854 Pearl Street
Denver, Colorado 80203
(303) 623-6602

A'nanda, Ma'rga, meaning "Path of Bliss," teaches the means by which the innate harmony within all spheres of life is revealed. The founder, Shrii Shrii Anandamurtijii, and his disciples teach techniques of Tantra and Astanga Yoga which awaken the desire to follow the inner divinity in all spheres of life. Completely cost-free instruction is provided to anyone sincerely interested in learning the techniques of meditation. Introductory classes are available at centers in most major cities.

ANANDA MEDITATION RETREAT
AND ANANDA COOPERATIVE VILLAGE
Alleghany Star Route
Nevada City, California 95959
(916) 292-3303

Ananda Meditation Retreat was created as a haven for persons seeking personal spiritual renewal. Open to visitors year long, it provides lodging, food, and instruction for a fee. Activities include meditation, chanting, and courses on the practical application of Yoga philosophy. The Meditation Retreat is part of the Ananda Cooperative Village, an integrated spiritual community of disciples of Paramahansa Yogananda, to whom the Retreat is dedicated. The Village includes organic gardens, schools, a monastery, and various industries which support the community. For long-term visitors it has apprentice programs in gardening and carpentry.

AQUARIAN AGE YOGA CENTER
620 14th Street
Virginia Beach, Virginia 23451
(804) 425-9414

The aim of the Aquarian Age Yoga Center is to merge a wide variety of spiritual practices in the hope of harmonizing persons of different backgrounds into a sadhana of Christ Consciousness. A full range of practices are taught, including Hatha Yoga, astrology, Sufi dancing, and T'ai Chi Ch'uan. Special Yoga classes for children and people over 40 also are offered.

ARCANA
407 North Maple Drive
Suite 214
Beverly Hills, California 90210

Arcana, a group meditation training center, is devoted to releasing untapped human potential and setting it to solve community problems. It provides the individual with a program of daily meditation, planned study, and group work. Experiences in group meditation are offered in weekly workshops, as are various other intergroup experiments.

ARICA
580 Market Street
San Francisco, California 94104
(415) 986-8800

Arica, founded by Oscar Ichazo, combines Yoga, Zen, Tibetan and Sufi techniques with calisthenics, music, and dancing in a system for the harmonic development of mind, body and emotions. Training options include a 40-day intensive program, a 16-hour weekend program, or training sessions on four consecutive weekday evenings.

ASSOCIATION FOR RESEARCH
AND ENLIGHTENMENT
Box 595
Atlantic Avenue and 67th Street
Virginia Beach, Virginia 23451

ARE is devoted to disseminating information on the "Readings of Edgar Cayce" and promoting research to verify these readings. Cayce, through an experience with hypnotic suggestion, discovered he could answer questions put to him while he was in a sleep-like state. These responses were systematically recorded and are known as his Readings. The ARE files contain nearly 15,000 readings. The largest percentage of these deal with the functioning of the mind and body and diagnosis of individual problems. Another portion deals with psychological and human relations, and still another with dream interpretations. The basic principle underlying all his material is a deep belief in a Divine Creator and a Plan, to which man must attune himself if he wishes to know himself and live in harmony with nature.

ASTARA
261 South Mariposa Avenue
Los Angeles, California 90004
(213) 387-7187

Astara, meaning "A Place of Light," acts as a comprehensive center embracing all religions and philosophies and serving as an institute of psychic research. The organization's principal activity is the publication of nearly 100 lessons in its Degree series, Astara's Book of Life, which relates the mystical development of the individual from prebirth through afterlife. Other activities include church services and weekly classes in such areas as Yoga, meditation, reincarnation, and psychic unfolding. The basic aim of Astara is to enable each individual to overcome his limitations and develop his inner being. To this end, it actively functions in the area of spiritual healing at all levels — physical, mental, and emotional. The center issues a monthly publication, "The Voice of Astara," free to all members. In addition, it operates a well-stocked bookstore.

ATMANIKETAN ASHRAM
4432½ Burns Avenue
Los Angeles, California 90029
(213) 662-0080

4401 Appelhuelsen
Kirchplatz 9, West Germany

Atmaniketan Ashram, inspired by the teachings of Sri Aurobindo, is dedicated to following the path of essential Truth and arranging one's life in accordance with it. It maintains a residence center for individuals truly desirous of achieving this end. It also possesses a research library containing writings by and about Sri Aurobindo, as well as traditional scriptural writings of India. Classes and seminars are arranged on topics of special interest, and an active cultural program exists, with special emphasis on inspirational expression through painting, music, and dance. The Atmaniketan Ashram also includes Auromere, a wholesale and retail distributor of books by and about Sri Aurobindo and other Indian scriptures. A book catalogue is available on request.

AWARENESS ASHRAM
2101 Cove Avenue
Los Angeles, California 90039
(213) 665-1800

The Awareness Ashram functions as an inner development center stressing the unity of all life. It offers a variety of programs drawn from many sources for individuals at all stages of development. Activities include: (1) awareness workshops, affording individual development in

private or group settings; (2) retreats, in a natural setting, offering individual and group sessions, meditation, and communal meals; (3) experimental meditation, focusing on relaxation, passive and active meditation, and work on the development of intuitive abilities; (4) couples' workshops, aimed at unfolding the potential for mutual development in committed ongoing relationships. Ministerial and ceremonial services are also available for weddings, healing services, etc.

BHOODAN CENTER OF INQUIRY
Star Route 1, Box 81
Oakhurst, California 93644

The Bhoodan Center of Inquiry, organized by Charles W. Davis, is convinced that immense changes are now taking place in the world, changes which necessitate the full understanding of the immutable laws of nature in order to avoid disaster. It seeks to provide a fellowship whereby individuals can attain realization of this higher truth and learn ways to implement it. Information on the Center's aims and methods can be obtained by subscribing to the "Bhoodan Log," at a cost of $2 per year.

BOSTON VISIONARY CELL
36 Bromfield Street
Boston, Massachusetts 02108
(617) 482-9044

The Boston Visionary Cell consists of a group of Neo-Platonic artists who serve as supporters of and consultants for the development of visionary art. The central tenet of the organization is a mystical explanation for the universe, following the spiritual tradition of Teilhard de Chardin. They believe that mystical or visionary art has been a vital force throughout history, and is now experiencing a necessary resurgence in this era.

BROTHERS OF THE GRAPE
27 Rockwood Drive
Grass Valley, California 95945
(916) 272-1504

The Brothers of the Grape is based on the symbology of wine as representing truth and spiritual intoxication or ecstasy. It wishes to persuade people of the benefits of "tasting of the grape" to attain this knowledge. Arnold Michael, founder and president of the society, has written a book entitled "Brothers of the Grape," which deals with man's quest for self-ennoblement and presents a simple yet powerful means of meditation. Meetings are held each Sunday morning at 11 a.m. at 101 Broad Street, Nevada City, California, and also every Thursday evening in Roseville, California. The Brotherhood also mails to interested individuals material on Universal World Harmony.

BUILDERS OF THE ADYTUM
5105 Figueroa
Los Angeles, California 90042
(213) 255-7141

Builders of the Adytum specializes in teaching the theory and practice of the Tarot and Kabbalah. It offers an excellent correspondence course in these and other esoteric teachings. The school is directed by a disciple of Paul Foster Case, an American mystic and authority on the Tarot. It derives its name from the adytum in ancient temples, the inner shrine in which resided the god to whom the temple was dedicated.

CENTER FOR SPIRITUAL AWARENESS
Box 7
Lakemont, Georgia 30552
(404) 782-3931

The Center offers a home study course in spiritual awareness, comprising 12 lessons that deal with knowledge of the nature of consciousness as evidenced through metaphysics, occultism, world religions, and the teachings of mystics, philosophers, and scientists through the ages. The Center sends a monthly publication, "Truth Journal," to all students and supporting members; in addition, it publishes a selection of books and recordings whose purpose is to instruct and inspire.

CHELA CENTER
614 East Atlantic Boulevard
Pompano Beach, Florida 33060
(305) 782-3041

The Chela Center is active in two areas: (1) as a New Age, service-oriented business, distributing books dealing with New Age subjects and running a food cooperative dealing in organic foods and herbs; (2) as a school, offering classes in meditation, esoteric philosophy, Eastern and Western philosophies, Chinese medicine, herbology, acupressure, iridology, natural gardening workshops, nutrition, and Yoga. The Center publishes a monthly newsletter, "Aquarian Events Calendar," which functions as a community guide to New Age activities and organizations.

CHRISTANANDA CENTER
977 Asbury Street
San Jose, California 95126

The Christananda Center is devoted to helping people realize Christ Consciousness within themselves. To this end, various spiritual, psychological, and educational experiences are directed, together with meditations based on readings from the Bible, Siri Guru Granth Sahib, and the Writings of the Essenes. The Center is also attempting to establish branches throughout the country where students can be educated in the eight-fold path of Yoga.

CHRISTIAN HOMESTEADING MOVEMENT
Oxford, New York 13830

The Christian Homesteading Movement was established in 1961 for the purpose of forming Catholic communities where families own and operate homesteads with the use of hand tools only. To this end, the Movement provides intensive instruction on how to successfully run a homestead. A series of six "Homestead Weeks" are the basis of this training. Training covers the following areas: (1) basic homesteading, dealing with the fundamentals such as horse working, gardening, using tools, etc.; (2) advanced homesteading, giving information on such activities as fence building, use of medicinal herbs, rope making, furniture making, tanning, and pottery making; (3) herbalism, learning to identify and use 50 to 100 wild plants; (4) home childbirth, emphasizing home delivery of a child by the father; (5) log cabin construction, teaching all skills required in the creation of a cabin; (6) Christian customs, discussing how to celebrate and put meaning into the Christian life. Members of the Movement presently meet four times a year to attend classes and become acquainted with one another prior to forming a community.

CHURCH OF WORLD
MESSIANITY — JOHREI
3068 San Marino Street
Los Angeles, California 90006
(213) 387-8366

The Church of World Messianity was created by Mokichi Okada, as the result of revelations in which an energy source gave him the power to heal others and instructed him to pass this ability on to other people. This healing energy or Light is channeled in the act of Johrei (Prayer in Action). The channeling is performed by use of a focal point which concentrates the

energy, enabling it to enter the top of the head and flow out through the hands.

COSOLARGY
Box 4500
Reno, Nevada 89505

Cosolargy teaches techniques of solar meditation, brought to the United States by Gene Savoy, who traveled in the Peruvian highlands for nearly two decades. The function of the techniques is to speed up brain wave frequencies and increase the potential for inner growth. Work done by Cosolargy teachers (including physicists, geneticists, and psychologists) indicates to them that through the focusing and channeling of light energy, man may be able to evolve into a new species with a higher consciousness.

DAWN HORSE COMMUNION
Star Route 2 Avenue
Middleton, California 95462

Dawn Horse Communion consists of a community of devotees of Bubba Free John, who maintains as a central belief that all seeking produces only suffering which reinforces the dilemma it hopes to resolve. Bubba Free John (ne Franklin Jones) offers a genuine relationship to all those who come to him, as opposed to merely techniques or a variety of practices. Satsang, the Company of Truth, is the vehicle of this relationship, and the Dawn Horse Communion is the instrument through which Bubba John prepares and sustains his devotees.

DIVINE LIGHT MISSION
P.O. Box 6495
Denver, Colorado 80206

Established in the United States by Guru Maharaj-Ji in 1971, the Divine Light Mission teaches a meditation upon the Life Force. This meditation consists of the awareness of four forms of inner energy, referred to as Light, Harmony, Nectar, and The Word. The Mission teaches that, through the experience of these four energy vibrations, one is able to experience the infinite energy of the life force and achieve a direct knowledge of the self. "Knowledge sessions," conducted by disciples of the Guru, exist to teach the meditation whereby knowledge is imparted. Discourses are held nightly at Divine Light Mission ashrams and centers throughout the world. The Divine Light periodical, "And it is Divine," is published monthly, and the "Divine Times" bi-weekly.

EAST-WEST CENTER OF NEW YORK
23 West 73rd Street, Suite 210
New York, New York
(212) 595-8081

The Center offers classes in macrobiotics (cooking and philosophy), oriental medicine, acupuncture massage, natural agriculture and organic gardening, calligraphy, and Japanese language.

EAST-WEST CULTURAL CENTER
2865 West Ninth Street
Los Angeles, California 90006
(213) 386-0999

Organized in 1953, the activities of the East-West Cultural Center focus on achieving world harmony through the teaching and integration of East and West cultural traditions and spiritual values. The Center offers lectures, films, meditation, and classes in religion, occult arts, world culture, Sanskrit, philosophy, and Yoga systems, to mention only a few. Dramatic and musical performances also are given, with special programs geared to the interests of children.

ECKANKAR
Box 5325
Las Vegas, Nevada 89102

Eckankar, a movement created by Paul Twitchell· in 1965, is purported to be the ancient science of soul travel, a path to God-realization. By practice of this science the soul is set free to reach higher stages of consciousness. Twitchell, known as Mahanta, or Light Giver, by his disciples, was able, upon leaving his earthly body, to be in several places simultaneously. In this manner it was possible for him to personally counsel his followers. In addition to publishing a newspaper, Eckankar offers discourses, tapes, and books.

THE FARM
Summertown, Tennessee 38483

The Farm, numbering 650 people, is a community led by Stephen Gaskin, who teaches the Yogas of honesty, compassion, family, vegetarianism, work, and self-trust. Over 125 babies have been delivered on the Farm in the past three years through the practice of "spiritual midwifery," and all women who are considering abortion are encouraged to have their babies delivered and, if desired, raised on the Farm. The community also has a book publishing company, and Stephen Gaskin and the Farm Band make musical tours of the country, providing free performances.

FELLOWSHIP OF RELIGIOUS HUMANISTS
105 West North College Street
Yellow Springs, Ohio 45387
(513) 767-1324

The Fellowship of Religious Humanists considers itself to be midway between Christian Humanism on the one hand and secular, ethical Humanism on the other. It holds a naturalistic, nontheistic view of the universe, but within that general orientation, it posits a religious aspect as well. It is concerned with the worth of man's life here and now, and it is an affirmative stand for the development of man's best thoughts, feelings, and actions. It urges integration of the vast amount of human knowledge available to us, and calls upon man to realize the full dignity of his life, opening himself up to all possibilities and developing his potentialities. The Fellowship publishes a variety of pamphlets about its outlook and issues a quarterly journal entitled "Religious Humanism."

FELLOWSHIP OF UNIVERSAL GUIDANCE
2100 Hillhurst Avenue
Los Angeles, California 90027
(213) 661-7570

The Fellowship of Universal Guidance works toward the integration of the spiritual aspect of man's existence with all other aspects of his life. Programs offered are based upon an in-depth psychology operating on three levels of consciousness: the higher self, the conscious self, and the subconscious or basic self. The aim is to achieve a balance between all three levels of consciousness. Activities include weekly world and personal prayer programs on Wednesdays, and workshops or lectures on Saturdays. Chapters exist in San Diego, San Francisco, and Phoenix, with membership open to the general public.

FOUNDATION FOR UNIVERSAL
UNDERSTANDING
P.O. Box 907
San Juan Capistrano, California 92675
(213) 652-8860

Created by Edward Scofield, the Foundation for Human Understanding is primarily involved with the publication and distribution of materials on Religio-Therapy, a synthesis of religion and psychology. The organization maintains that in Religio-Therapy, the dimensions of humanism and natural phenomena are added to traditional analysis and therapy. Lectures by Scofield are available on audio tape cassettes, and a variety of seminars are offered, dealing with such subjects as how to achieve maturity, how to achieve happiness, how to cope with the world around you. The Foundation's official publication, "Journal of Vision," is issued bimonthly.

FRATERNITY OF LIGHT
2417 North 54th Street
Philadelphia, Pennsylvania 19131

The Fraternity of Light is a small religious order concerned with the spiritual advancement of its members, and the peaceful, balanced transition of mankind into a new age. For the serious student of the occult, they offer a unique series of correspondence courses covering all manifestations of Western occultism, from the well-known to the obscure. A book providing information on courses offered, as well as specifics about membership, may be obtained for a 25-cent donation to cover printing and mailing costs.

GLIDE MEMORIAL METHODIST CHURCH
330 Ellis Street
San Francisco, California 94102
(415) 771-6300

Glide Memorial is a nontraditional church, packed each Sunday with people of all races and ages. They are encouraged by minister Cecil Williams to express their joyfulness, dance in the aisles if they so desire, and openly commune with their neighbors. Readings are given from a very updated Biblical text, "Quotations from Chairman Jesus." Glide believes that the spiritual movement comes from the struggles of oppressed people to liberate themselves, and its ministry is especially directed to these people.

GROUP HARMONICS CENTRE
115 Harvard Avenue, S.E.
Albuquerque, New Mexico 87106
(505) 265-6557 or 265-9335

The Group Harmonics Centre serves as a center for dissemination of material pertaining to individual and group growth. Its name derives from the belief that, through an understanding and application of the principles of world and universal harmonics, it is possible for people to achieve an inner harmony and thus become happier, more responsible, and more productive. The Centre believes that personal attunement meditation and transpersonal group interaction are the two best means by which the principle of harmonics is realized. A wide variety of resources is available from the Centre, including books, tapes, experimental supplies, seminars, workshops, lectures, and personal and group counseling services.

GURU BAWA FELLOWSHIP
5820 Overbrook Avenue
Philadelphia, Pennsylvania 19131
(215) 879-9960

Founded by Guru Bawa of Ceylon, the fellowship explores the nature of man and God and the relationship between the two. Emphasis is placed on the acquisition of the divine attributes of love, compassion, and justice. Through the attainment of these qualities it is believed that man can achieve a true understanding of both himself and God.

HAROLD INSTITUTE
10000 Sunset Boulevard
Los Angeles, California 90024
(213) 271-7137

The Harold Institute, named in recognition of author Preston Harold, seeks to perpetuate his work and generate renewed interest in it, in the belief that his ideas are of special importance to today's world. His writings offer a synthesis of all major disciplines and demonstrate a harmonious relationship between them. He arrives at a new interpretation of natural law, which in turn invites a new concept of man and of the universe. He also provides a vision of an in-depth psychology which has room for both scientific research and religious experience, creating a framework whereby the individual is able to develop his full potentiality and work toward enlightened goals.

HARRAD COMMUNITY
Box 6864
San Francisco, California 94101

The Harrad Community is a nonresident expanded family attempting to redefine themselves and their roles by means of group techniques, open alternative living situations, and self-liberation. The Community publishes a monthly newsletter, "GROK," and sponsors meetings the first Friday of each month at 7:30 p.m. at the Unitarian Church, Geary and Franklin, San Francisco.

HEALING LIGHT CENTER OF I.C.O.A.
5619 Lindley Avenue
Tarzana, California 91356
(213) 881-0466

The Healing Light Center, a member of the Independent Church of Antioch organization, functions as a religious, healing, and educational organization. Its aims are stated as follows: "(1) to promote, carry on and aid the spiritual and religious development of Man; (2) to disseminate information concerning spiritualism, natural healing techniques and practices, and spiritual or psychic phenomena by means of classes, lectures, seminars, demonstrations, clinics, publications, etc.; (3) to conduct research in a spiritual, scientific and psychic sense, in order to extend the knowledge, understanding and development of natural healing techniques and practices and of spiritual or psychic phenomena; (4) to provide, perform and conduct religious services, rites, and instructions; (5) to provide natural healing practices whenever required or requested; (6) to promote wider acceptance, advancement and recognition of natural healing and spiritual or psychic phenomena." The Center is open daily to the public, and natural healings are available by appointment day or night. Classes in natural healing and related subjects are offered on a regular basis, and spiritual counseling is also provided.

HIGH POINT FOUNDATION
647 North Madison
Pasadena, California 91104
(213) 681-1033 or 797-3020

High Point Foundation is based on the belief that all people have an innate capacity for spiritual unfoldment. To this end it employs the psychological concept of psychosynthesis, an approach which considers the individual as a whole being — physical, mental, emotional, and spiritual — with a personal self and a transpersonal self. Its training programs offer the following services: theoretical and experiential training in psychosynthesis for psychotherapists, educators, counselors, and all those in the helping professions; training and experience in Emotional Maturity Instruction (a course in Unconditional Love and Forgiveness); and training in applied psychology, through classes in self-esteem, masculinity and femininity, meditation, transactional analysis, Gestalt therapy, and communication. Seminars, workshops, and retreats of varying durations are offered, in addition to counseling, psychotherapy, and psychosynthesis on an individual basis.

HOLY ORDER OF MANS
20 Steiner Street
San Francisco, California 94117

Through the teachings of the Bible and other forms of ancient wisdom in harmony with the ideals of Jesus, the Holy Order of Mans is devoted to the acceptance of the illumination of Christ and the realization of the inherent God-Self. The essential aim is to enable people to recognize the presence of Christ in their lives and to learn methods of living in harmony with this realization. The Order has seminaries in San Francisco, Chicago and Boston.

HOUSE OF LOVE AND PRAYER (Yeshiva)
1456 Ninth Avenue
San Francisco, California 94100
(415) 731-2261

Established by Rabbi Shlomo Carlebach and his followers, the House of Love and Prayer (conceived of as a Sabbath House or Spiritual Oasis) serves as a community center for the revival of Jewish culture and teachings. It also functions as a residential center for the study of the Torah, including Mishna, Kabbalah, and Hasidism. People of all faiths are invited to partake in the Center's joyful celebrations of the Sabbath.

HUMANIST INSTITUTE
1430 Masonic Avenue
San Francisco, California 94117
(415) 626-0544

The Humanist Institute is staffed by members of the Community of the Simple Life, a small nondenominational religious order having roots in both Eastern and Western spiritual traditions. It is dedicated to both a respect for the spiritual quest and a commitment to the growth process, and it employs a variety of Eastern and Western teachings in its programs. Program offerings include the following: (1) The Spiritual Path, an integrated eight-month course and experience in spiritual growth; (2) Pathways to Inner Wisdom, a weekly gathering and sharing of inner experiences through journal keeping, dreams, art, and inner imagery; (3) Me Groups, a weekly experience in self-exploration; (4) special five-week groups providing guidance in centering, awareness, and meditation; (5) seminars in the classics of Eastern and Western mysticism; (6) summer workshops, covering such topics as the Shakers, the English mystics, and Native American spirituality; (7) Saturday workshops and Sunday evening talks; (8) 12-day Spiritual Growth Institutes; (9) full-time programs for people wishing to devote at least a year's time to intensive participation in spiritual growth activities. For details on these programs and others, write for the Institute's catalog.

HUNA INTERNATIONAL
3741 Centinela Avenue
Los Angeles, California 90066
(213) 397-0669

The Order of Huna International is a spiritual order devoted to the teaching, application and research of the universal laws governing man and nature. The organization describes its objectives in the following manner: "to spread the knowledge of Huna Science; to aid the spiritual, mental, physical, and moral progress of mankind; to provide the means for individuals to attain self-mastery; to demonstrate the inter-relationship of mind, matter and energy." The realization of these objectives is sought by a variety of means: establishment of Centers of Knowledge (Heiau) wherein individuals can learn self-mastery and study Huna Science (science of the universal laws); training of a group of teachers, practitioners and researchers of Huna; dissemination of all research results to the general public; and cooperation with other organizations with similar interests and goals.

I AM ASHRAM
1779 Haig Drive
Ottawa, Ontario, K1G2J1, Canada
(613) 521-1288

Sri Mata Atmananda, known to her followers as Beloved Mother, founded the I Am Ashram in 1970. Under her guidance, it serves as a center for discovering inner joy and meaning through union with the self. This realization is attained by commitment to a lifestyle founded on a willingness to learn and cooperate and the active practice of simplicity, love, and humility. I Am Ashrams, now located throughout Canada, offer courses in Hatha Yoga, meditation, and natural foods cookery.

IMMACULATE HEART HERMITAGE
Big Sur, California 93920

In the Immaculate Heart Hermitage, overlooking the ocean in Big Sur, hermit-monks of the Camaldoli Order (founded on the rule of Saint Benedict) live in retreat and prayer. Each monk has a small cottage where he prays and meditates and tends a small garden. The belief of this order is that a life of solitude and prayer is a means by which one may know, love, and serve God. On the grounds is a guest house where individuals wishing to make a retreat may make reservations to do so.

INNER CHRIST ORIENTATION
AND AWARENESS
Box 331
Encino, California 91316
(213) 784-9086

ICOA attempts to bridge the gap between the many existing philosophies, but it presents no rigid creed or dogma of its own. Its primary aim is to make each person aware of his true self, or Christ self, and, by listening to this inner voice, learn to develop his own unique abilities. All ICOA teachers and counselors are ordained under California state law. Classes deal with such topics as deeper metaphysics, spiritual development, extrasensory perception, parapsychology, dream therapy, and life regressions. By contacting the center in Encino, one may obtain the ICOA "Inner Voice" publication and Newsletter, plus a list of ICOA centers throughout the country.

INNER LIGHT FOUNDATION
Box 761
Novato, California 94947
(415) 897-5581

Betty Bethards, a psychic and spiritual leader, founded and now directs the Inner Light Foundation. Its aim is to aid people in developing a greater awareness of God through the use of extrasensory faculties inherent in each individual. Ms. Bethards demonstrates her abilities and teaches meditation techniques at public lectures; in addition, she leads group meditations and holds private counseling sessions and readings by appointment. The Foundation is currently raising funds to construct a center to serve as a meeting place for all medical and spiritual healers.

INNER PEACE MOVEMENT
5103 Connecticut Avenue, N.W.
Washington, D.C. 20008

The central concern of the Inner Peace Movement is to enable people to develop an understanding of and proper balance between the physical, mental, and spiritual forces operating in their lives, and by so doing direct themselves in more successful, productive ways. Members are assisted in developing greater confidence, self-respect, and innate leadership qualities, and in increasing general sensitivity and enhancing social relationships. IPM provides a program of orientation lectures, technique workshops, discovery groups, and perception counseling, all aimed at helping participants realize their inner potential.

INNER SENSE SCIENTIST ASSOCIATION
7707 State Street
Huntington Park, California 90255
(213) 588-4323

Founded in 1974 as an educational and scientific foundation, the Inner Sense Scientist Association is engaged in in-depth studies of the mental, emotional, philosophical, and spiritual aspects of man. Meetings are held the third Sunday of every month from 1:30 to 5 p.m., and the main office is open daily from 9 a.m. to 5 p.m. The Association, supported voluntarily by its members and by sale of publications, offers counseling, suggested reading programs, free literature, and monthly newsletters.

INSTITUTE FOR ADVANCED
PASTORAL STUDIES
380 Lone Pine Road
Bloomfield Hills, Michigan 48013

An ecumenical institute concerned about the future of the ministry in a changing world, the Institute is actively involved in identifying crucial issues for the church and ministry; conducting research and experimentation; providing training and counseling; and disseminating information and resource materials. It hopes to provide a variety of means by which personal growth and organizational change can be combined in new and powerful ways. The courses it conducts fall into three general categories: general theory practice, specialized workshops, and advanced seminars.

INSTITUTE FOR THE DEVELOPMENT
OF THE HARMONIOUS HUMAN BEING
233 South Alexandria
Los Angeles, California 90004
(213) 383-6713

The primary desire of the Institute is to bring about the full development of individual and planetary consciousness. It seeks to achieve this end by means of the Way of Service, a dynamic program continually changing with the varying needs of the people, time and place. The educational portion of the Institute instructs individuals in methods of service, but any person entering the program must come fully committed to the concept of service and without expectations of learning one particular form of service. At the present time, the Institute is providing service in the field of conscious natural childbirth, and service to the dying for conscious death.

INSTITUTE OF ABILITY
4115 Cutting Boulevard
Richmond, California 94804

The Institute of Ability was founded by Charles Berner to serve as the center of a new religion, Abilitism. The sustaining principle of Abilitism is the belief that each individual is a separate manifestation of God, an all-knowing completely creative, infinitely able Being. Convinced that the purpose of life is to become fully conscious of that limitless ability through communication, the Institute strives to break down all barriers to communication to facilitate uninhibited relationships. Courses of instruction include training in: Clearing, Enlightenment, Education, and Emotional Trauma Release.

INSTITUTE OF HUMAN ENGINEERING
3680 East Fall Creek Parkway
Indianapolis, Indiana 46205
(317) 923-6676

The Institute of Human Engineering seeks to integrate the social, political, economic and religious aspects of life by correlating the results of research in a wide range of fields, including philosophy, science, religion, psychology, economics, physics, and metaphysics. By this means it hopes to assist individuals in attaining a high degree of mental maturity and enlightenment by broadening their scope of knowledge and understanding of spiritual, physical, and human nature. The Institute believes that when people are able to function on an optimum level and direct their lives according to positive values, then a full understanding of universal organization will be possible, along with a realization of man's purpose, goal, and destiny.

INSTITUTE OF MENTALPHYSICS
P.O. Box 640
Yucca Valley, California 92284

The Rev. Edwin J. Dingle has founded the Institute of Mentalphysics as a center where self-realization and a recognition of the oneness of life can be achieved. Its practices are aimed at developing within the individual full physical and intellectual powers. The Mentalphysics Spiritual Haven at Yucca Valley is also operated by the Institute. The Haven, a residential and meditation center designed by Frank Lloyd Wright, offers a variety of courses.

INTERCOSMIC CENTER OF
SPIRITUAL ASSOCIATIONS
102 David Drive
North Syracuse, New York 13212

Dr. Rammurti S. Mishra, a master of Raja and Kundalini Yoga and a noted surgeon and psychiatrist, founded ICSA with the following aims: "(1) To experience one's Self as the cosmic center; (2) To establish Unity of all beings, especially of all nations among mankind in all aspects of life; (3) To promote global togetherness, especially togetherness of East and West, and to experience peace and unity through understanding; (4) To promote a natural way of education, self-discipline, and mutual relations; (5) To promote the education of Sanskrit with other related languages; (6) To establish modern education centers and publications through scientific research; (7) To promote natural, spiritual and psychological methods of healing; (8) To experience automatic and spontaneous psychosynthesis and psychoanalysis; (9) To assist the individual in realizing the Godhead that always resides within all." Dr. Mishra travels extensively, assisting other centers with similar aims.

INTERNATIONAL BUDDHIST
MEDITATION CENTER
928 South New Hampshire Avenue
Los Angeles, California 90006
(213) 384-0850 or 487-1235

The International Buddhist Meditation Center was created in an attempt to bring about greater harmony and cooperation between the multiplicity of Buddhist traditions existing within California. The Center issues a monthly newsletter informing its readers of workshops, lectures, meditation practices, and seminars. It also conducts classes throughout the week and provides outside groups with speakers on Zen Buddhism and Oriental philosophy.

INTERNATIONAL SOCIETY FOR
KRISHNA CONSCIOUSNESS
Srisri Radha Krsna Temple
3764 Watseka Avenue
Los Angeles, California 90034

The central belief of ISKCON is that Lord Krsna (Krishna) is the source of absolute truth. Accordingly, its aim is to enlighten all people to the elevated state of Krishna Consciousness, devotion, and service to the will of God. The most direct and appropriate path to this stage of enlightenment is considered to be the continuous chanting of the mantra: Hare Krsna, Hare Krsna, Krsna Krsna, Hare Hare, Hare Rama, Hare Rama, Rama Rama, Hare Hare. Residential centers exist for those wishing to follow the religious life under the guidance of Swami Prabhupada, the Society's founder. Instruction is given in Bhakti Yoga, Sankirtan (chanting), Vedic literature and mantra meditation. There are centers in most major cities which encourage those interested in the society to visit.

KAILAS SHUGENDO (YAMABUSHI)
2362 Pine Street
San Francisco, California 94115
(415) 922-5008

Shugendo, an ancient religion of Buddhist tradition, originated in Japan; Kailas Shugendo is a new sect, the only one of its kind in North America. An essential part of its practice deals with fire worship, including Goma, a twice-daily fire ceremony conducted by the ritual master, and Hiwatari, a purification ceremony performed once a week in which members walk across a sacred fire. Members of the sect also undertake ascetic practices in the mountains. In addition, part of the daily discipline is concerned with music, and Kailas Shugendo is in the process of expanding its program of musical-cultural presentations to the public at large and providing other community services.

KOINONIA FOUNDATION
P.O. Box 5744
Baltimore, Maryland 21208
(301) 486-6262

Koinonia Foundation was founded in 1959 as an ecumenical training center and commitment to community living. It strongly believes that spiritual and educational growth are synonymous, and that these are best achieved in a community setting. The learning process explores the interrelatedness of spiritual disciplines, academic endeavor, artistic expression, service to others, and practical aspects of community life. Both weekend conferences and a residential program are offered to interested individuals.

LAMA FOUNDATION
Box 444
San Cristobal, New Mexico 87564

The Lama Foundation is a rural community for spiritual growth. Instead of following one particular spiritual tradition, its members partake of several, including Zen, Yoga, Sufism, and T'ai Chi. Every member is expected to perform six to eight hours of physical labor each day on projects decided upon by the commune as a whole. The Lama Foundation continues to publish Baba Ram Dass' "Be Here Now" and is now putting together a package subscription dealing with aspects of sadhana. Visitors are welcome on Sundays, but no new members are being taken in at the present time.

LANARK HILLS COMMUNITY
RR4, Perth
Ontario, Canada K7H 3C6

The Lanark Hills Community consists of a group of people sharing a communal farm life and attempting to develop a community based on Krishnamurti's teachings. Weekend gatherings and group seminars are held at their educational center.

LESLIE COMMUNITY
Route 2, Box 50-A
Leslie, Arkansas 72645

The Leslie Community is a spiritual, survival-oriented commune whose members are interested in Yoga, astrology, ESP, the teachings of Christ, and organic living. New members are welcome.

LIBERAL CATHOLIC CHURCH
Box 598
Ojai, California 93023

Founded in 1916, the Liberal Catholic Church is completely independent of the Church of Rome. It uses a vernacular literature, and attempts to balance ceremonial worship with scientific and mystical thought. The clergy, whose orders are derived from the Old Catholic Church of Holland, are not forbidden to marry. The philosophy maintains the existence of God as manifested through the Trinity, with the recognition of Christ as mankind's spiritual teacher. Every member is encouraged to pursue his individual search for truth, rather than accepting any rigid dogma.

LIVING LOVE CENTER
1730 La Loma Avenue
Berkeley, California 94709
(415) 848-9341

The aim of the Living Love Center, founded by Ken Keyes, Jr., is to utilize the wisdom of the ages in creating a method for growth into higher stages of consciousness. To this end, the course of the Twelve Pathways is practiced as a means of realizing the primary life goal: to love everyone, including self, unconditionally. Situations that occur in everyday life are used as teachings to assist one's growth. The Center conducts weekend Consciousness Growth Intensives, and has open house every Sunday evening. It also sponsors a program whereby individuals may live at the Center for a week or longer while participating in an intensive round of consciousness growth activities.

LUCIS TRUST
866 United Nations Plaza, Suite 566-7
New York, New York 10017
(212) 421-1577

The Lucis Trust, founded in 1922 by Alice and Foster Bailey, is a world service corporation whose activities include: (1) the Arcane School, a correspondence school offering courses of study in esoteric philosophy; (2) Triangles, whose aim is to establish a worldwide network of goodwill through the power of thought and invocation; (3) World Goodwill, working to develop optimum human relationships and stimulate goodwill in the hearts of all; (4) Lucis Publishing Companies, which publish and distribute books of the esoteric teachings of Alice Bailey; (5) Lucis Trust Lending Library, containing approximately 2,000 books on metaphysics and related subjects.

MAUI ZENDO
OF THE DIAMOND SANGHA
R.R. 1, Box 220
Haiku, Hawaii 96708
(808) 572-8163

Members of the Maui Zendo follow the spirit and tradition of Zen Buddhism. The daily schedule includes the rigorous practice of zazen (meditation), plus several hours devoted to gardening and house maintenance. Some single persons reside at the center while others live in private homes nearby. The Diamond Sangha also encompasses two other centers in Hawaii: the Koko An Zendo in Honolulu, and the Buddha Mountain Zendo on Kauai.

MANDALA SOCIETY
P.O. Box 23231
San Diego, California 92123
(714) 272-7330

The Mandala Society wishes to cooperate with all individuals and associations aimed at increasing man's level of functioning in conjunction with a higher state of awareness. The philosophy of the Society is in no way dogmatic, but simply desires to provide the environment and opportunity for full

expression of individual uniqueness. The Circles of the Mandala exist as groups concerned with improved human relationships.

MATAGIRI
Mt. Tremper, New York 12457

The spiritual leaders of Matagiri believe in the ascending evolution of nature through levels of consciousness to the development of human consciousness, but they believe that man in his present condition is in a transitional stage from that of mere animal instinct to the possibility of a truly new consciousness in accordance with universal truths. The aim of Matagiri is to work toward the achievement of this new plane. The community makes available information on their founder, Sri Aurobindo, and has a listing of over 200 books which may be sent for.

MEDITATION GROUP FOR THE NEW AGE
P.O. Box 566
Ojai, California 93023

The Meditation Group for the New Age is a nonsectarian association that wishes to increase New Age consciousness through active meditation, positively and scientifically engaged in as a form of spiritual service to mankind. The meditation course functions in accordance with the following New Age laws and principles: (1) The Law of right human relations — The Principle of good will; (2) The Law of group endeavor — The Principle of unanimity; (3) The Law of spiritual approach — The Principle of essential divinity. Bimonthly books are issued on each of these laws and principles, along with aspects of meditation and suggestions for daily or biweekly meditations. The work is voluntarily supported and no fees are charged.

MIDWESTERN INSTITUTE
OF PARAPSYCHOLOGY
P.O. Box 282
Mason City, Iowa 50401

Extensive testing programs for psychics, mediums, and healers are carried out by the Midwestern Institute of Parapsychology. The Institute offers a psychic counseling service and issues certificates of merit to those with psychic, mediumistic, or healing ability, after a year of rigorous testing. Certified persons are then listed as consultants in the Institute's central registry.

MIND SCIENCE FOUNDATION
17511 Devonshire Street
Northridge, California 91324
(213) 368-3063

The Mind Science Foundation hopes to develop and make available the most effective techniques for bringing about mental, physical, and spiritual health. To this end it encourages research aimed at establishing scientific evidence that man's awareness extends beyond his five physical senses. It desires to educate the individual and general public about the existence of extended mind power and possible constructive uses of it, stressing the need for new educational methodologies to aid in developing this power. The Foundation believes that, through the proper use of such untapped powers, man can achieve a new sense of serenity, confidence, and well-being without resorting to any structured religious or philosophical system.

MOVEMENT OF SPIRITUAL
INNER AWARENESS
Box 676
Rosemead, California 91770

The primary aim of the Movement of Spiritual Inner Awareness is to promote higher states of consciousness within its members. Centers exist throughout the United States for this purpose. Dr. John-Roger Hinkins, spiritual director of MSIA, gives seminars which teach that a universal energy flows through all of life, extending from the central point of God to all planes of existence. The central belief of the Movement is that when individuals allow themselves to be guided by this higher consciousness, great spiritual growth is possible.

MU-NE-DOWK FOUNDATION
Box 268, Route 1
Kiel, Wisconsin 53042
(414) 894-2681 or 894-2339

Mu-ne-dowk, from the Chippewa word for "dwelling place of the Great Spirit," is an educational and religious foundation located on 12 acres of wooded lake property in Wisconsin. A lodge and dormitory on the property can accommodate up to 45 persons interested in taking part in the Foundation's retreats. The retreats, sponsored by the Institute of Crystal Truths, are designed to impart pure, universal truths to participants, with the ultimate goal of awakening the realization of man's oneness with the universe.

NEW AGE BIBLE
AND PHILOSOPHY CENTER
1139 Lincoln Boulevard
Santa Monica, California 90403
(213) 395-4346

The desire of this nonsectarian center is to meet the needs of those individuals who are sincerely seeking enlightenment. It engages in a number of activities, including lectures; study classes in New Age Bible interpretation, astrology, and esoteric philosophy; guidance in meditation; and instruction through correspondence courses. It attempts to help students reach a full realization of truth through an understanding of the basic principles of esoteric knowledge.

NEW AQUARIAN MASTERS'
EDUCATIONAL ASSOCIATION FUND
FOR NEW AGE YOUTH
P.O. Box 146
Lake Luzerne, New York 12846

NAME's primary aim is to promote the teachings of Ancient Spiritual Masonry in the 17,000 Lodges which exist in the United States and Canada. It hopes to develop programs of Masonic education which will enable current and future members of the Lodges to receive instruction in the science of Spiritual Masonry. Spiritual Masonry is defined by the association as "a cosmic science consisting of those universal teachings that the Great Masters and Prophets received from the God-Mind and interpreted to Mankind as a Spiritual Heritage that conferred upon the individual the power to transform, regenerate, and redeem himself."

PADMA JONG
P.O. Box 2384
Berkeley, California
(415) 525-5157

Established in 1974, Padma Jong is a Buddhist community located on 274 acres of land, encompassing an art center and therapeutic area and offering meditation seminars. Members are followers of Trungpa Rinpoche.

PANOSOPHIC INSTITUTE
P.O. Box 2971
Reno, Nevada 89505

The Panosophic Institute is dedicated to the cleansing of man's vision through enlightenment, brotherhood, and conservation. Founded in 1973, it is especially interested in the transmittal of the Tibetan culture and religious tradition to Western society. The Institute School of Universal Religion and Philosophy is located at Reno and offers

masters' programs in the areas of meditation, religion, occult sciences, and philosophy. Although the Institute has a special interest in Tibetan Buddhism, it desires to increase understanding between members of all major religions of the world.

PARAPSYCHOLOGY ASSOCIATION
OF RIVERSIDE
3681 Beechwood
Riverside, California 92506
(714) 784-1565

The purpose of the Association is to stimulate interest in extrasensory perception and to offer individuals the opportunity to develop their personal extrasensory capacities. To this end, it presents lectures, sponsors study groups and provides occasions for sharing ideas and experiences. It also seeks to inform the general public of current developments and activities in parapsychology, and to recommend speakers to community organizations. Much resource material, suitable for term papers, research projects, etc., is available to members.

PARAPSYCHOLOGY FOUNDATION, INC.
29 West 57th Street
New York, New York 10019

The Parapsychology Foundation is a nonprofit organization which encourages research, study, and experimentation in all aspects of the paranormal, including extrasensory perception, telepathy, and precognition. It seeks to further a better understanding of psychical manifestations through working in conjunction with scientists and scholars who are researching paranormal phenomena throughout the world. Although the Foundation does not have its own research division nor conduct public lecture programs, it does sponsor domestic and international conferences and puts out two publications: "Parapsychological Monographs," a continuing series of research studies, and "Parapsychology Review," the Foundation's official journal, issued six times a year.

PERSONAL CREATIVE
FREEDOMS FOUNDATION
3300 Airport Avenue
Santa Monica, California 90405
(213) 390-3362

The Personal Creative Freedoms Foundation has a variety of aims, which include the following: (1) to assist individuals in attaining the greatest possible understanding, wisdom, and ability necessary to lead joyful and productive lives and work toward the creation of a humane and positive civilization; (2) to use the best means available to defeat negative and destructive spiritual and mental attitudes; (3) to enhance humane experience and help to bring about human evolution; (4) to develop and make use of the best technology for achieving individual and societal growth. With these aims in mind, the Foundation offers workshops in happiness and security, relationships, and problem solving; courses in ESP, communications, and past lives; and private spiritual counseling and training sessions.

PHENOMENON OF MAN PROJECT
8932 Reseda Boulevard, Suite 204
Northridge, California 91324
(213) 886-5260

The writings of Teilhard de Chardin provide the basis for POM's concept of the evolution of consciousness. The ideas of Teilhard plus those of other prominent thinkers of both Eastern and Western traditions are presented regularly in audiovisual lecture-seminars (already attended by over 50,000 people). More

personalized experiences, in the form of weekend retreats and small-group workshops, involve the use of meditation techniques, music, group dialogue and discussion sessions. A large number of educational materials are also available, including film-strip and tape cassette libraries.

PHILOSOPHICAL RESEARCH SOCIETY
3910 Los Feliz Boulevard
Los Angeles, California 90027
(213) 663-2167

Founded in 1934 by Manly P. Hall, the Philosophical Research Society seeks to increase understanding of the nature of man through research in the areas of philosophy, comparative religion, and psychology. Its specific aims are stated as follows: "(1) To discover additional knowledge by intensively investigating the essential teachings of the world's greatest scientific, spiritual, and cultural leaders, and by further clarifying and integrating man's heritage of wisdom. (2) To apply this heritage to the present needs of mankind, by means of modern skills and the cooperation of outstanding experts. (3) To make available these vital concepts to persons in every walk of life, by lectures, publications, and other media. (4) To create an increasing awareness in the public mind of the usefulness of these ideas and ideals in solving the personal and collective problems of modern man." A quarterly program of seminars, workshops, and lectures is presented, featuring the work of staff members plus an international group of guest speakers. In addition to activities at the center in Los Angeles, there exist a number of study groups throughout the country which operate under the Society's supervision. The Society puts out an 80-page Quarterly Journal, published since 1941, and has an extensive library on its premises, containing 50,000 volumes. The center is always open to the public, and has no dues or membership list.

PHOENIX INSTITUTE
307 Third Avenue
Chula Vista, California 92010
(714) 425-4870

Founded in 1956, the Phoenix Institute seeks to increase man's awareness of himself and the universe in which he finds himself. It has the following major objectives: "to teach the inner creative action of science, art, and religion through esoteric and exoteric knowledge; to encourage an intercultural atmosphere conducive to the development of responsible, emotionally mature citizens; and to provide a place where those who desire to live a life of dedicated service may so do." The Institute seeks to implement these aims through a variety of programs carried out by several different branches: (1) the School of Man, teaching the Oneness of Being and constructive use of energy; (2) the Church of Man, a healing ministry which hopes to provide individuals with the opportunity to experience the inner meaning of worship; (3) the International Friendship Club, making an effort to increase understanding of all cultures through fellowship and sharing of artistic and dramatic expressions of each culture; (4) Portal Publications, publishing a journal of religion, science, and the creative arts, and extending an open invitation for poems, articles, and illustrations dealing with New Age concepts; (5) the Phoenix Research Library, containing an ever-expanding collection of materials on religion, science, and art. The Institute is open daily and welcomes visits by interested persons.

PSYCHICAL AID FOUNDATION
P.O. Drawer 49047
Tucson, Arizona 85717

PAF was created for the financing and developing of a youth camp and conference center in the high desert of the Southwest. Sources of income flow from the lecturing and writing of Frank O. Adams, the sale of lithographs, and tax-deductible donations. Plans are underway for the establishment of camp and conference facilities on the 80-acre section of land, plus an adjoining cooperative. The facilities would be available on a nonprofit basis to organizations involved in New Age activities, and the cooperative would provide organic food and other supplies for campers or conference participants. The cooperative would also aid organizations in the scheduling and planning of activities.

PSYCHONAUTICS SOCIETY INTERNATIONAL
P.O. Box 1461
Huntington Beach, California 92647

The Psychonautics Society International considers a psychonaut one who explores inner space. Through a program of research and education, the Society undertakes this inner exploration. Research is done on all aspects of the supernormal, making use of a fully maintained psychical research laboratory and qualified director. Recent work has centered on the evaluation of individuals with suspected supernormal abilities, such as telepathy, psychokinesis, and precognition. The Society is also beginning publication of a monthly newsletter. Any group interested in obtaining the services of a lecturer or demonstrator in the area of paranormal phenomena is urged to contact the Society.

PSYCHOSYNTHESIS INSTITUTE
576 Everett
Palo Alto, California 94301
(415) 323-9615

The Psychosynthesis Institute provides a psychological and educational approach to man's achievement of harmony with the universe through a personal integration or synthesis of his inner being. It is engaged in theoretical and practical training in psychosynthesis for professionals and concerned individuals, and it undertakes the study of exceptionally gifted persons in the attempt to understand the potentialities of man's abilities. It hopes to work in cooperation with educational institutes in utilizing methods which will foster the creative growth of young people. The Institute supports research dealing with the principles and applications of psychosynthesis, and disseminates information on new developments in the field.

PSYNETICS RESEARCH & EDUCATION FOUNDATION
1212 East Lincoln Avenue
Anaheim, California 92805
(714) 533-2311

Founded in 1962, the Psynetics Research and Education Foundation seeks to reveal truths based on natural law, and discover methods by which these truths may best be applied for the betterment of man's life. A variety of activities work toward this end, including the following: (1) weekly membership and public lecture meetings, featuring prominent speakers from a wide range of scientific, philosophical, and religious fields; (2) training classes and seminars providing an opportunity for extensive study of techniques and methodologies of special interest in human advancement; (3) discussion groups, offering a chance for personal development and communion with others; (4) retreats and social activities aimed at creating an environment conducive to close personal ties and a sense of unity; (5) counseling services, providing assistance in problem solving and attainment of personal goals; (6) Sunday workshop services, flexible religious services with a variety of inspirational messages, including activities leading to inner awareness

and opportunities for group participation; (7) Apollo School, specially designed for the slow learner, neurologically handicapped and multiple handicapped persons.

ROSICRUCIAN FELLOWSHIP
2222 Mission Avenue
P.O. Box 713
Oceanside, California 92054
(714) 757-6600

The Rosicrucian Fellowship, founded in Europe by Christian Rosenkreuz, presents a philosophy concerning the origin, evolution, and future development of mankind and the world. It attempts to shed light on confusing passages in the Bible, and generally makes use of scientific knowledge to provide logical solutions to problems. In this way it attempts to bridge the gap between science and religion, but it stresses that scientific teaching is only a means by which man may arrive at a truly religious life and experience fellowship with other men. The Rosicrucian teachings aim at revitalizing the Christian religion, and they encourage individuals to remain with their church. For those who are no longer church members, they offer a new perspective on Christianity which attempts to reveal its essential beauty. Publications include the Fellowship magazine "Rays From the Rose Cross," and numerous pamphlets and booklets concerning the teachings. A summer school is also conducted at its Oceanside headquarters, open to the public on a free-will offering basis, and correspondence courses are available on astrology, philosophy, and the Bible.

SANDBACK RESEARCH INSTITUTE
3808 McGee
Kansas City, Missouri 64111
(816) 561-0797

Founded in 1974 by astrologer/occultist John Sandback, the Institute exists to explore the relationships between man and reality through the study of astrology, art, metaphysics, and all sciences. It is hoped that specialists in the various fields will come together to share ideas and gain greater understanding of how their particular work relates to the whole of reality. Classes and workshops in astrology and Tarot are offered by the Institute, as well as private counseling sessions. In addition, guest speakers are invited to make presentations on a variety of topics.

SELF-REALIZATION FELLOWSHIP
3880 San Rafael Avenue
Los Angeles, California 90065

The Fellowship of Self-Realization was founded in 1920 by Paramahansa Yogananda, the first great Yoga master to leave India to live and teach in the West. In accordance with the work of Yogananda, the Fellowship teaches that the purpose of life is evolution into God consciousness and that there exists a complete harmony between original Christianity and original Yoga. It attempts to demonstrate the life of service to the greater Self, and it disseminates information on definite scientific techniques which enable a direct personal experience of God. The Fellowship also offers a correspondence course based on Yogananda's recorded lectures and writings.

SHADYBROOK HOUSE
R.D. No. 1
Mentor, Ohio 44060
(216) 255-3406

Shadybrook House is a church-oriented organization offering a comprehensive program for successfully meeting the challenges of our present world situation through development of mind, body, and spirit. It is concerned with creating positive behavior patterns, generating a

congruent system of values and standards, and developing a greater consciousness through full use of all senses. It presents a full program of activities, including growth seminars, retreats, and training institutes.

SILVA MIND CONTROL
1110 Cedar
Box 1415
Laredo, Texas

Silva Mind Control, developed by Jose Silva, relies on methods of relaxation, as opposed to any mechanical means, to achieve Alpha brain-wave states. The course guarantees that any student will develop his clairvoyant power and increase his intuitive accuracy. Scholarships are available for those in need.

SOCIETY FOR COMPARATIVE PHILOSOPHY
P.O. Box 857
Sausalito, California 94965
(415) 332-5286

The work of the Society for Comparative Philosophy is concentrated in three principal areas: (1) a philosophical and cultural dialogue between East and West; (2) investigation of the problems of human ecology; (3) a study of the transformations of consciousness.

SOUTHERN CALIFORNIA SOCIETY FOR PSYCHICAL RESEARCH
170 South Beverly Drive
Beverly Hills, California 90212
(213) 276-4523

The activities of the Society center on the study of paranormal phenomena, and research is conducted in numerous fields, including the following: the study of psi in altered states of consciousness; investigation of the energies of the physical body and its force field; controlled laboratory experiments in extrasensory perception and psychokinesis; study of physical correlates of unorthodox healing; investigation of reports of spontaneous occurrences, such as apparitions, hauntings, and telepathic dreams; studies of gifted sensitives and mediums. The Society conducts workshops, presents lectures, and maintains a library open to the public for research purposes. In addition, foreign scientific and technical papers dealing with important aspects of paranormal research are being translated into English through the work of bilingual members of the Society. For those interested, a registry of premonitions and of spontaneous phenomena is also maintained.

SPIRITUAL FRONTIERS FELLOWSHIP
800 Custer Avenue
Evanston, Illinois 60202

Founded in 1956, the Spiritual Frontiers Fellowship seeks to "sponsor, explore, and interpret the growing interest in psychic phenomena and mystical experience to the traditional churches and others, and relate these experiences to effective prayer, spiritual healing, personal survival and spiritual fulfillment." Functioning as an interfaith fellowship, it believes that the material recorded in the Bible can be applied to everyday life experiences. An increased level of consciousness is aimed at through reading, discussion, research, and personal and group development. Nationwide, approximately 8,000 people are members of the SFF. In addition, The Academy of Religion and Psychical Research is an academic affiliate.

SPIRITUAL LIFE INSTITUTE
Nada Contemplative Center
Star Route One
Sedona, Arizona 86336
(602) 282-7668

The Spiritual Life Institute has two centers, one just south of Sedona, Arizona, and a second in Nova Scotia. The aim of these centers is to foster religious contemplation, offering short-term retreats or long-term residence. Founded by Fr. William McNamara, it is an ecumenical institute desiring to achieve a renewal of the spirit of the Christian Church. It stresses a contemplative life similar to that of the Carmelite hermits, and it believes that in isolated locations such as the desert man is able to achieve his greatest degree of communion with God. The Institute puts out a quarterly magazine entitled "Desert Call," and a series of cassette tapes dealing with contemplation in the modern world.

SPIRITUAL UNITY OF MAN
FELLOWSHIP
3215 West 81st Street
Inglewood, California 90305
(213) 751-3959

SUM is a spiritual and educational fellowship devoted to the exploration of the inner life. It propounds no set dogma and has no rigid structure, but seeks to aid those who are searching for a sense of unity, identity, and self-expression. Study-meditation groups are held for two hours each week and, in addition, everyone is invited to attend the monthly Festivals of Unity which take place in North Hollywood and Inglewood.

STONETREE RANCH
The Church for the Fellowship of All Peoples
2041 Larkin Street
San Francisco, California 94109

Stonetree Ranch is a retreat center located one and a half hour's drive from San Francisco. It may be reserved by families, committees, religious groups, or small conferences wishing to spend time in a quiet area of great natural beauty.

STUDENTS INTERNATIONAL
MEDITATION SOCIETY
1015 Gayley Avenue
Los Angeles, California 90024

The aim of Students International Meditation Society is to assist individuals who wish to learn how to expand their consciousness, develop their creative intelligence, and make full use of their potentialities in all aspects of their lives. The Society believes that these ends are achieved by the practice of Transcendental Meditation, as taught by Maharishi Mahesh Yogi. SIMS has representatives on nearly every college campus in the United States, with certain key regional headquarters. It also has chapters throughout the world, as does IMS, the International Meditation Society for nonstudents.

SUMMIT LIGHTHOUSE
Box A
Colorado Springs, Colorado 80901

Founded in 1958, the Summit Lighthouse serves as a religious and philosophical organization aimed at helping to develop the unlimited spiritual potential of man and to the bringing about of cosmic law. Its program consists of the dissemination of the teachings and directives of the Ascended Masters, such as Saint Germain. Within the framework of the Lighthouse, a fraternity known as The Keepers of the Flame is devoted to actively assisting the Ascended Masters. Four conferences are held annually in various parts of the world. The conferences provide intensive training in teachings of cosmic law for disciples of Christ and chelas of the Masters.

UNITY
Unity Village, Missouri 64065

Unity is a religious organization which sponsors varying types of programs, including: (1) vacation and holiday retreats for individuals and families; (2) continuing education courses through a summer residency at Unity or class work at a local Unity Center; (3) a home study correspondence course; (4) a school for ministerial and religious studies which, after a two-year, full-time residency, confers a graduation diploma and, upon committee recommendation, ordination into the Unity ministry. Unity also has one of the largest publishing houses in the Midwest, which produces a steady stream of books, pamphlets, and magazines.

VAJRADHATU
1111 Pearl Street
Boulder, Colorado 80302
(303) 444-0202

Vajradhatu, consisting of meditation and retreat centers in various parts of the country, brings to public attention the philosophy of Chogyam Trungpa Rinpoche, born in Tibet in 1939. The teachings of Trungpa Rinpoche encompass the three major traditions of Buddhism: Hinayana, Mahayana, and Tantra. In his teachings he emphasizes the danger of "spiritual materialism," an egocentric, security-bound type of spirituality which risks little and fails to confront essential human issues.

VEDANTA SOCIETY
The Ramakrishna Order
1946 Vedanta Place
Hollywood, California 90068
(213) 465-7114

Founded in the 1890's by Swami Vivekananda, the Vedanta Society affirms spiritual truths contained in the Vedas, and is one of India's

oldest living philosophies. The teachings emphasize that the true human nature is divine, and the purpose of life is to discover and experience this inner divinity. Methods of achieving this realization are taught in lectures and classes conducted by swamis who are monks of the Ramakrishna order of India. Monasteries and convents exist in various parts of the United States.

VORTEX INSTITUTE
P.O. Box 73152
Fairbanks, Alaska 99707
(907) 452-5954

The Vortex Institute, originally founded in 1971 as a small esoteric lending library, has expanded considerably since then and is now engaged in educational, religious, and research activities. The primary aims of the Vortex Institute are twofold: "(1) to assist individuals in attaining self-realization developing the use of higher consciousness; (2) to correlate metaphysical and universal knowledge, especially that related to cosmology and healing, and make modern application possible through a computerized 'banking' system." Those wishing to make use of the material available through the lending library, consisting of over 800 books and periodicals, plus cassette and open reel tapes, may send for a catalogue.

ZEN CENTER OF LOS ANGELES
927 South Normandie Avenue
Los Angeles, California 90006
(213) 384-8996

The Zen Center of L.A. is devoted to extending the practice of Zen Buddhism as an individual means of attaining peace and fulfillment. It describes its central aims and activities in the following manner: "(1) A community-living experience for those who wish to pursue intensive group practice. (2) A focus for training and practice in the larger community so that those who wish to encounter living Zen may do so in whatever way their individual circumstances permit. (3) A journal published three times a year presenting works of Zen masters past and present, with translations from major Zen texts, koan collections and commentaries. (4) A long-range program of translating and publishing important Zen works. In virtually all cases, these works have never before been translated into any Western language." The Center offers a long-term accredited teacher training program, plus other programs of varying length, including: Ango, an annual 90-day period of intensive practice in a communal living situation; Zazen (Zen meditation), open to the public; and Sesshin, an intensive Zen practice period lasting from three to seven days per month. Introductory classes on theory and practice of Zazen are offered on a regular basis to all interested.

PSYCHOPHYSICAL DEVELOPMENT: Body Disciplines, Health, and Body Awareness

ACUPRESSURE — JIN SHIN JYUTSU
1429 Westwood Boulevard
Los Angeles, California 90024
(213) 478-7828

Jin Shin Jyutsu is a form of Japanese acupressure (or acupuncture massage) which serves to release deep muscular tension while balancing, revitalizing, and redirecting the body's energy flow. Its aim is to increase body-mind awareness through structural and functional integration.

AIKIDO
678 Turk Street

San Francisco, California 94102
(415) 441-6087

Aikido is a Japanese nonviolent martial art, a defense system to repel aggressive actions. It serves not only as an effective means of self-defense, but also as a way of centering oneself, i.e., unifying one's energies and enabling them to work in harmony. Aikido training centers exist throughout the country.

AJAPA-BREATH FOUNDATION
239 Mount Royal W.
Montreal, 152 P.Q., Canada
(514) 844-6023

Ajapa-Breath is based on the law of loss and conservation of energy. Unlike normal breathing where there is a constant loss of energy with each breath, Ajapa-Breath techniques provide a steady increase of energy. This energy creates added strength and higher mental and psychic capabilities, eventually leading to a spiritual union with the Absolute. After instruction, the Foundation maintains contact with the student to provide any further necessary assistance and guidance.

ALETHEIA PSYCHO-PHYSICAL
FOUNDATION

Box 334
Selma, Oregon 97538

The central aim of the Foundation is to increase understanding of all aspects of man's existence — mental, physical, and spiritual — and man's interrelationship with his total environment. It stresses the need for bridging the gap between existing sciences and philosophies, and sponsors seminars dealing with such topics as voluntary control of internal states, human aura, and metaphysics.

AMERICAN MEDICAL-PSYCHIC RESEARCH ASSOCIATION
135 Madison Avenue N.E.
Albuquerque, New Mexico 87123
(505) 265-0221

AMPRA was founded to help create a better understanding of the health and natural laws applying to man. Through a synthesis of many disciplines, it seeks to provide better means for physical, emotional, mental, and spiritual healing. The aim of the Association is to unite individuals of the same mind who are practicing in a variety of therapeutic fields, e.g., osteopathy, nutritional therapy, homeopathy, hydrotherapy, psychology, psychiatry, etc. It is AMPRA's belief that through cooperation and joint research in these disciplines, new and greatly more effective approaches in the field of healing can be developed.

ASSOCIATION FOR CHILDBIRTH AT HOME
13 Fletcher Avenue
Lexington, Massachusetts 02173

The Association for Childbirth at Home is composed of parents, medical professionals, psychologists, childbirth educators and individuals interested in home birth. Founded in 1972, it functions as an information service via telephone counseling and keeps a current record of all area resources for parents. The Association currently has groups in Massachusetts, Virginia, Maryland, Washington, D.C., New York, Connecticut, California, North Carolina, and Rhode Island, and new groups are in the planning stages in various other states. Meetings are held every other week, consisting of an informal class followed by a group discussion. ACAH offers a series of six lecture/discussion classes which cover the following topics: (1) advantages of a home delivery; (2) equipment and procedure; (3) psychological issues; (4) medical emergencies; (5) exercise and breathing techniques; (6) the neonatal exam and the first few days of life.

BIOENERGETICS NORTHWEST
3938 First Avenue N.E.
Seattle, Washington 98105

Bioenergetics focuses on the body as a means of bringing people more fully in touch with their energy sources and feelings. It offers a series of Bioenergetic Weekends devoted to relieving unperceived muscular tensions that cut off body awareness, and releasing the body's natural energy flow to enable a deeper experiencing of feelings and sexuality. Participants are cautioned that the workshops are physically and emotionally strenuous. Priority is given to applicants who are in the helping professions, or who would like to pursue bioenergetics on an ongoing basis.

CENTER FOR ENERGETIC STUDIES
1645 Virginia Street
Berkeley, California 94703

The Center for Energetic Studies maintains a program of teaching, workshops, and publications concerned with the development of biological process as the basis for self-identity. The Center explores how individuals form both themselves and their environments.

CENTER FOR SOCIAL AND SENSORY LEARNING
6350 DeLongpre
Los Angeles, California 90028
(213) 466-9922

The Center for Social and Sensory Learning provides experiences which embrace the following goals: new awareness of self and others through increased sensory awareness; reintegration of body and mind; discovery of more fulfilling ways to express needs and desires; separation of facts from fallacies about male and female sexuality; development of a fully sensual and sexual being. Program offerings include: monthly introductory drop-ins; ongoing discussion groups; ongoing women's groups; individual sensual enhancement training; therapy sessions related to sexual problems, for individuals or couples.

CENTER FOR THE HEALING ARTS
11801 Missouri Avenue
Los Angeles, California 90025
(213) 477-3981

Center for the Healing Arts is dedicated to exploring and more fully understanding the multiple aspects of healing and health maintenance. Center activities include the following: (1) Seminars and workshops conducted during fall, winter, and spring, with summer set aside for special conferences. There are seven key areas to which the seminars and workshops are devoted: healing through the body; healing through the arts; healing through the symbolic process; healing through group and community; healing through interpersonal process; self-healing; healing through spirit. Summer conferences deal with a variety of topics. Presentations are taped and made available to anyone interested. Also, from October through June there exists a special Friday evening program series concerned with all varieties of healing experiences and methodologies. (2) Research programs, foremost of which is the Cancer Research Program, though other projects are in the developmental stage. The Cancer Research Program currently has three groups of patients who are taking part in an intensive program utilizing a holistic approach to healing. (3) Consultation services, at an individual, group, or organizational level. (4) Publications, both reprints and articles never before published. Members of the Center receive a monthly news bulletin, free publications, and have the opportunity to attend workshops, conferences, and seminars at a reduced fee. Membership is not necessary, however, for participation in Center activities.

CONEX FOUNDATION
580 Prospect Boulevard
Pasadena, California 91103
(213) 681-3739

The CONEX Foundation was established for the purpose of conducting research on biofeedback and other methods of self-control and expansion of consciousness. Members of CONEX include scientists and therapists who are actively working in the areas of biofeedback, meditation, psychotherapy, and a variety of other nondrug, nondestructive methods of exploring the possibilities of increased consciousness. Training programs for professionals in the therapeutic use of biofeedback are offered, along with services to individuals interested in gaining greater understanding and positive control through biofeedback. Fees are based on a sliding fee schedule dependent on ability to pay.

ELYSIUM INSTITUTE
5436 Fernwood Avenue
Los Angeles, California 90027
(213) 465-7121

Elysium attempts to foster a positive attitude toward the human body, and consequent acceptance of oneself and others on both physical and emotional planes. Elysium has two centers, one in Los Angeles and the other (Elysium Fields) located on a 10-acre country estate in Topanga Canyon. Both centers offer a variety of workshops. Programs at the in-city center include: A Sensorium — Sharing Our Senses; Sexodrama; Basic Course in Human Sexuality; How to Have More Pleasure in Your Life. Workshops at Elysium Fields cover the following topics: Sensual Spirituality; On Becoming a Sexual Being; Delightism; Tactile Celebration; Pathways to Sensuality. Elysium facilities include tennis courts, swimming pool, heated hydro-pool, mud wallow, and sauna.

EVERING CONSULTANTS LTD.
43 Eglington Avenue East, Suite 803
Toronto, Canada M4P 1A2

Evering Consultants is an educational corporation consisting of research, educational, medical and organizational consultants who provide training in the applications of the Eidetic General System. Eidetics involves the imagery science of biofeedback and the use of pattern recognition. Through the use of biofeedback monitoring instruments and eidetic imagery feedback, the corporation maintains that individuals can learn voluntary self-regulation of both internal and external states.

FRIENDLY HILLS FELLOWSHIP
26126 Fairview Avenue
Hemet, California 92343
(714) 927-1113

Friendly Hills Fellowship is dedicated to a holistic concept of health, wherein all aspects of man — physical, emotional, mental, and spiritual — are balanced and integrated. Methods to achieve this overall sense of well being are offered in the Fellowship's many programs at Meadowlark, a country estate near Hemet, California. Activities concentrate on both physical development and mental and spiritual growth through such means as exercise, relaxation techniques, proper nutrition, meditation, counseling, and creative arts.

GETTING IN TOUCH
Box 1225
Los Gatos, California 95030
(408) 354-3433

Getting in Touch offers workshops which focus on massage, centering, breathing, and other body-awareness techniques as a means of increasing vitality and enhancing one's pleasure in life. The community is located in a rural setting on three wooded acres of land. Here, workshops are offered in various phases of massage awareness. Weekend workshops on "Getting What You Want: expanding your sensual and sexual awareness and communication" are also offered for individuals or couples. In addition, Getting in Touch provides training for individuals working in the helping professions, and functions as a resource center for a variety of humanistic studies on the effect of touch in human relationships.

HARA
P.O. Box 28177
Dallas, Texas 75228
(214) 279-6868

Hara (from the Japanese word meaning "wholeness") attempts to help individuals achieve a balance between mind and body, feeling and intellect, through a program of meditation and involvement in encounter.

HAWAII HEALTH NET
1629 Wilder, 802
Honolulu, Hawaii 96822
(808) 949-3642 or 523-2311

Hawaii Health Net is a relatively new organization which consists of individuals — both professional and nonprofessional — who believe in the concept of health in terms of well-being of the entire person; people are encouraged to become more responsible for the condition of their bodies, rather than being overly dependent on medical practitioners. The association is interested in creating a "center for human wholeness," which would question old assumptions and raise the possibility of new attitudes toward health. It would also attempt to integrate specific health concerns with a broader picture of human health on all planes of existence. A series of workshops is being planned on both theory and practical training in various kinds of alternate therapies, e.g., Yoga, biofeedback and nutrition.

HEALTHY, HAPPY, HOLY ORGANIZATION
1620 Preuss Road
Los Angeles, California 90035
(213) 273-9422

The purpose of this foundation is to enable people to live as healthy, happy, and holy beings. 3HO is directed by Yogi Bhajan, a master of Kundalini Yoga and Mahan Tantric. He trains teachers in Kundalini Yoga (the Yoga of awareness, utilizing control of the breath and mantras to achieve awareness) and Sikh Dharma (the path of the Seeker). 3HO ashrams are now found throughout the United States and in many countries worldwide.

HIMALAYAN INSTITUTE OF YOGA SCIENCE AND PHILOSOPHY
970 East Camp McDonald Road
Prospect Heights, Illinois 60070

The Himalayan Institute, founded by Swami Rama, teaches students to develop their full physical, mental, and spiritual potentialities in order to achieve a more productive life. The goal of the Institute is to reveal the harmony inherent in all world religions and philosophies, as evidenced by modern scientific achievements. To this end, the Institute carries out a continuous research program, presently focusing on biofeedback and voluntary control of internal states.

HIPPOCRATES HEALTH INSTITUTE
25 Exeter Street
Boston, Massachusetts 02116
(617) 267-9520

Founded by Ann Wigmore, the aim of the Hippocrates Health Institute is to return sick bodies to a state of vibrant health by cooperation with nature. This is attempted by extracting the essence of organic foods and training in means of detoxifying the body and cleansing the blood stream. A wide range of activities include classes and lectures on Yoga, meditation, astrology, nutrition, and various aspects of bodily health.

HOLISTIC CHILDBIRTH INSTITUTE
1627 Tenth Avenue
San Francisco, California 94122
(415) 664-1119

The Holistic Childbirth Institute is concerned with minimizing the fear and trauma of childbirth, both for the mother and child. Its activities include: (1) a national communications network, enabling contact between people interested in the holistic childbirth concept and professionals (doctors, midwives, educators, etc.) offering those services; (2) a twofold comprehensive training program for (a) prenatal childbirth educators, emphasizing the practice and teaching of various body-mind disciplines as well as study programs in physiology, nutrition, and infant psychology, and (b) birth attendants, whose purpose is to minimize birth trauma by establishing positive contact with the infant through massage, gentle sounds, and

attunement to the baby's sensitivity; (3) sponsoring of public forums and professionals' workshops relevant to current issues in childbirth; and (4) developing satisfactory models for home-environment birth centers.

INNER RESEARCH INSTITUTE-SCHOOL OF T'AI CHI CH'UAN
131 Hayes
San Francisco, California 94102

The motivating aim of the Inner Research Institute is to investigate and teach systems of "inner exercise," particularly T'ai Chi Ch'uan. The Center emphasizes inner, as opposed to external, achievement and believes that this can be arrived at through the gradual awakening of a spiritual consciousness.

INSTITUTE OF POSTURAL INTEGRATION
1057 Steiner Street
San Francisco, California 94115
(415) 929-0119 or 383-7469

Postural Integration is a specialized form of bodywork, combining principles and methods of connective tissue manipulation, Reichian-Gestalt bodywork, acupuncture, and movement awareness. The Institute serves as a center for research and training and offers a program of study leading to certification as a Postural Integrator. Activities include workshops, courses, and individual appointments.

INTEGRAL YOGA INSTITUTE
Satchidananda Ashram
P.O. Box 108
Pomfret Center, Connecticut 06259
(203) 974-1005

Swami Satchidananda, student of Swami Sivananda, founded the Integral Yoga Institute in 1966. Integral Yoga combines methods aimed at developing every aspect of the individual, the end result being a harmonious interrelationship of mind, body, and emotions. By achieving this harmonious functioning it is believed that limitations can be transcended and union with the All can be experienced. Integral Yoga makes use of all other forms of Yoga, including (1) Hatha Yoga, a means of purification through postures, breath, and relaxation; (2) Karma Yoga, producing action through selfless service; (3) Bhakti Yoga, the path of love and devotion; (4) Japa Yoga, mantra repetition; (5) Raja Yoga, meditation and mind control; and (6) Jnana Yoga, the Yoga of wisdom, self-analysis and awareness.

INTERNATIONAL BABAJI KRIYA YOGA SANGAM
11305 Alondra Boulevard
Norwalk, California 90650
(213) 868-9013

Yogi S.A.A. Ramaiah founded the International Babaji Kriya Yoga Sangam, dedicated to Sath Guru Kriya Babaji Nagaraji of the Himalayas. Centers now exist throughout the world. Babaji's Yoga consists of a fivefold path incorporating Kriya Hatha, Kriya Kundalini, Kriya Pranayam, Kriya Mantra, and Kriya Bhakti Yogas. The aim of this synthesis of Yoga disciplines is to awaken the individual to an experience of God on all levels of existence — physical, vital, mental, intellectual, and spiritual. Students desirous of practicing Kriya Yoga on an intensive level each day may stay in the centers' dormitories, designed specifically for this purpose.

KRIPALU YOGA ASHRAM
7 Walters Road
Sumneytown, Pennsylvania 18084

The Kripalu Yoga Ashram was founded by Yogi Amrit Desai in honor of his teacher, Swami Shri

Kripalvanandji, a Kundalini Yoga master. The particular form of Yoga practiced by the Ashram is Shaktipat Kundalini Yoga, a discipline through which the guru is able to unfold the student's latent spiritual energy. As the student's spiritual energy increases, so does his ability to experience love, serenity, and full capability. Spiritual growth is guided forward by the practices of Hatha, Raja, Bhakti, Karma and Kriya Yogas, all within the context of Kundalini Yoga. Individuals sincerely desiring to follow this path will be considered for residency. Guests are always welcome, and arrangements can be made for special intensive and teacher-training seminars.

MONOVIN
Mostly Non-Verbal Institute
1872 South Sepulveda Boulevard
Los Angeles, California 90025
(213) 479-7110 or 656-3000

MONOVIN is founded on the belief that nonverbal experiences can positively affect creative human behavior. Current projects include: drop-in and ongoing sensoriums, offering an opportunity to explore the dynamics of sensory experience as a means of relating to oneself and others; massage, for individuals or couples, employing a variety of techniques; and a special pilot program for developmentally disabled children and adults. Those wishing to take part in MONOVIN's activities should write or call the Institute.

RADIX INSTITUTE
P.O. Box 3218
Santa Monica, California 90403

The Radix Institute is directed by Charles Kelley, a neo-Reichian working with Reich's concepts of energy and breathing as a way of releasing deep emotion. Kelley also makes use of the Bates method, in the belief that clarity of vision is intimately related to one's emotional state.

SAN ANDREAS HEALTH COUNCIL
530 Cowper Street
Palo Alto, California 94301
(415) 324-9350

The San Andreas Health Council is an educational center concerned with helping people discover how they can play a greater role in their own health care. To this end, they offer a variety of programs aimed at fostering the concept of holistic health care and furthering interdisciplinary education in the fields of health. Services and activities are divided into two major areas: (1) for health professionals: interdisciplinary seminars and discussions on significant health care themes; workshops on innovative techniques which may be of professional help; the use of a center where health professionals may initiate or sponsor educational programs they feel would benefit the community; (2) for the general public: classes and workshops in areas of health maintenance including nutrition, pregnancy, relaxation and meditation, body care and movement, and emotional well-being; weekly lecture-demonstrations; ongoing groups for senior citizens; blood pressure screening; information and resource center; marriage and family counseling. In addition, a new Integrated Health Skills program has been developed, welcoming participants from all areas, both professional and nonprofessional. This program is aimed at creating a comprehensive and individualized approach to health care education, especially concerned with helping individuals learn how to reduce stress through such techniques as biofeedback, journal work, Yoga, hypnotherapy, assertiveness training, and nutritional counseling.

SANDSTONE
21400 Saddle Peak Road
Topanga, California 90290
(213) 455-2530

Sandstone offers social and recreational options which emphasize the potentialities and values of human existence. The possibility of exploring new approaches to education, philosophy, religion, behavioral sciences, and human sexuality is provided by means of seminars and workshops, residential programs, consulting and training, a private membership club, and an alternative lifestyle research community. The regular weekly social calendar includes the following: potpourri dinner for Sandstone members and guests on Wednesday; feature-length films relevant to the human potential movement on Thursday; ongoing men's and women's consciousness raising and awareness groups on Friday; sports, swimming, sauna, jacuzzi, and evening dinner party on Saturday; three-hour evening massage class on Sunday. Workshops and seminars are usually scheduled on weekends, with a major focus on realization of the dignity and value of human intimacy and sensuality. For individuals interested in a more intensive Sandstone experience, residential-experiental training programs are available on a 14- or 28-day basis. Programs include numerous options and courses of study, such as: alcohol and drug abuse; human sexuality; open relationships; Gestalt training; bioenergetics and other forms of body work; alternative lifestyles; and community living.

SIVANANDA YOGA CENTER
115 North Larchmont Boulevard
Los Angeles, California 90004
(213) 464-1276

Organized in 1967, the purpose of the Sivananda Yoga Center is to advance the teachings of Yoga, and to further the physical, moral and spiritual development of all people. The methods employed are those of Sri Swami Sivananda. The Center offers a full program in all aspects of Yoga and related subjects, with complete courses in Hatha Yoga, meditations, satsangs, and lectures. Programs are periodically presented by direct disciples of Swami Sivananda and other notable speakers, and tours and guided spiritual pilgrimages to India are arranged.

INTERNATIONAL COMMUNITY DEVELOPMENT AND LIAISON ORGANIZATIONS

ARTISTS EMBASSY
2622 Jackson Street
San Francisco, California 94115

Artists Embassy views art as a universal language, and artists as natural ambassadors of good will and understanding. The pilot project of the group was an artists' good will tour of the Orient, from 1947 to 1950; by 1955 it had received nongovernmental organization status with the United Nations. Its primary function during the last two decades has been to serve as a liaison and information center for international understanding through the arts. The group's goal in ensuing years is to establish Embassies of the Arts in all countries throughout the world. In addition to valuing the worldwide contact possible through the arts, Artists Embassy is very aware of the inner aspects of creative art, whereby the artists lead us to the realization of the unique, essential spirit embodied in all of mankind.

**CENTER FOR THE STUDY
OF DEMOCRATIC INSTITUTIONS**
P.O. Box 4068
Santa Barbara, California 93103
(805) 969-2281

The Center for the Study of Democratic Institutions fosters continued examination of crucial issues facing mankind, in the hope that a civilization based on reason and understanding may develop. It stresses the necessity of free dialogue between individuals of different persuasions, and to this end it has been instrumental in bringing together prominent spokesmen from throughout the world. The Center has sponsored three international convocations to discuss possible means of achieving lasting peace in the world, and plans are underway for future conferences. In "The Center Magazine" and a booklet entitled "A Constitution for the World," the Center puts forth a proposal for a new United States constitution. Anyone interested in applying for membership (and thus receiving "The Center Magazine," "Center Report," and invitations to participate in periodic meetings) may write or call the Center for further information.

**CENTER FOR THE STUDY
OF DEMOCRATIC SOCIETIES**
P.O. Box 475
Manhattan Beach, California 90266

The work of the Center for the Study of Democratic Societies is directed at the examination and explanation of the basics of democratic societies. Through continuous research and education, it seeks to arrive at rational, humanistic solutions to societal problems and means of democratically improving societal systems. Results of the Center's investigations are presented through books, magazines, and newspapers, as well as conferences and lecture courses.

CENTRE MONCHANIN
4917 St. Urbain
Montreal, Quebec, Canada

Created to further the ideas and beliefs of Jules Monchanin, the Centre Monchanin attempts to help individuals fully realize their deep interconnections with all other people, regardless of race, culture, ideology, or religion. They hope that through this essential understanding, a worldwide sense of compassion and unity will develop amongst all men. "The Monchanin Review," a publication discussing the center's ideas and activities, is issued five times a year.

**CULTURAL INTEGRATION
FELLOWSHIP, ASHRAM**
2650 Fulton Street
San Francisco, California 94118
(415) 752-9890 or 648-1489

The Cultural Integration Fellowship is a religious and educational corporation concerned with the development of universal religion, cultural harmony, and creative self-unfoldment. Awareness of being is stressed as the foundation of unification of all people. Classes and lecture series are conducted on such topics as Yoga, Hindu dance and music, psychology, religion and nonverbal communication. Religious non-sectarian services are also held every Sunday. In addition, the Fellowship has a graduate school in San Francisco, the California Institute of Asian Studies.

ENCOMPASS
P.O. Box 145
Mercer Island, Washington 98040
(206) 232-8553

The Encompass Institute attempts to further the development of New Age religion through extensive study of religious material based on psychological and scientific data.

**ESPERANTO LEAGUE
FOR NORTH AMERICA**
P.O. Box 508
Burlingame, California 94010

The Esperanto League is an international organization with chapters throughout the United States and the world. Its aim is to acquaint the public with the value of Esperanto as a universal second language which would enable direct communication between people throughout the world. The League believes that the ease with which Esperanto is learned makes it ideal for teaching to elementary school children, broadening their cultural horizons and facilitating the later study of other languages. As of now nearly 10 million people have learned to speak Esperanto, and the Esperanto League is recognized by UNESCO for its contribution to international understanding. Books, periodicals, tapes, and international pen pals are available through the League.

INNER-SPACE INTERPRETERS SERVICES
P.O. Box 1133, Magnolia Park Station
Burbank, California 91507
(213) 843-0476

The aim of the Inner-Space Interpreters Services is to provide a service for the disbursement of information on activities and developments in psychic, metaphysical, astrological, parapsychological, and other related fields. By the Services' definition, an inner-space interpreter is one who, "through the development of extrasensory perceptions, may be able to assist an individual in understanding thoughts, feelings, emotions and desires which do not respond to traditional outer-world methods." ISIS was founded in the hope of not only providing information to the general public, but also working as a liaison between organizations which offer "inner-space interpreter" services. No charge is made for any of the functions of ISIS, but donations are gratefully accepted. An important part of the Services' work is the compilation of annual directories, providing information on inner growth organizations in existence, and listing magazines, newspapers, and newsletters concerned with inner exploration.

INTERNATIONAL COOPERATION COUNCIL
World Headquarters
17819 Roscoe Boulevard
Northridge, California 91324
(213) 345-8325 or 881-9755

The International Cooperation Council is a body of educational, scientific, cultural, and religious organizations which use the disciplines of modern science coupled with the insights of religion, philosophy, and the arts in an attempt to bring about a new world civilization. The Council makes constant efforts to contact organizations throughout the country and throughout the world which share its goals. Its principal concern is to disseminate the work and ideas of these groups and facilitate the exchange of information between organizations to help bring about greater cooperation. ICC activities include the following:

(1) The creation of Area Councils throughout the country and overseas, with a program of experiential Sunday services, weekend work-

shops, and classes at the various sites; (2) International Cooperation Festivals held annually on a January weekend, in or near Los Angeles. Cooperating organizations participate in the event through displays, dialogue sessions, interest groups, etc.; (3) Action Projects, where the Council serves as a facilitator for intergroup efforts between new consciousness organizations. Areas of cooperative discussion and action have included: New Age education, healing the whole person, the media, and spiritual convergence; (4) The New Age Institute, putting together plans for classes and workshops and attempting to introduce New Age understandings into public and private educational programs; (5) Worldview Exploration Seminar, composed of individuals with diverse backgrounds in science, religion, art, education, and philosophy, who meet to discuss concepts of the new universal person and world civilization; (6) "Spectrum," a free monthly newsletter which contains information on New Age activities and resources; (7) "The Cooperator" magazine, which lists ICC cooperating organizations and publishes articles, art work, and poetry of special interest; (8) the annual ICC Directory, listing a wide variety of New Age organizations and describing their motivating beliefs and activities.

NEW YORK CENTRE NUCLEUS
131 West 75th Street
New York, New York 10023

The Centre encourages all peoples, of whatever tradition and background, to join together to form a world community based upon universal love. In this sense it considers itself to be a spiritual United Nations. Members of the Centre believe it possible for an individual to surrender his ego and become part of the master intelligence of the universe, and that a network of such egoless individuals can use their energy to restructure society and govern-

ment. The Centre's headquarters in London hopes to serve as an example of a community devoted to egoless consciousness. It offers assistance and encouragement to others throughout the world who wish to set up similar centers. The Centre's founder, Christopher Hills, teaches techniques for self-growth, meditation, ESP, Yoga, and spiritual healing.

TECHNOCRACY INC.
(Science Applied to the Social Order)
6237 Lankershim Boulevard
North Hollywood, California 91606

Technocracy Inc. has a three-pronged plan aimed at solving problems produced by the present governmental system: "(1) Total mobilization of the resources, technology, energy, and know-how; (2) Energy Certificate — a means of distribution — a mandate each citizen holds upon the government for an equal share of the physical goods produced; (3) Completing the technology for operating a coordinated functional control of: (a) transportation systems, (b) collecting produce from farms, fisheries, etc., (c) clean up of air, soil, and water, (d) housing, (e) health, (f) education, (g) judiciary," and so on. Technocracy believes that an objective, efficient scientific administration can enable all citizens to reap the benefits of America's productivity. Those interested in pursuing this goal may attend classes and lectures and read literature available in centers throughout the United States and Canada.

TEMPLE OF UNDERSTANDING
1436 Connecticut Avenue, N.W.
Washington, D.C. 20036

Founded in 1960 by Mrs. Dickerman Hollister with the encouragement of Eleanor Roosevelt, the Temple of Understanding seeks to increase public understanding of the great world reli-

gions (including Buddhism, Christianity, Confucianism, Hinduism, Islam, and Judaism), and facilitate improved communications between all religions. The Temple is located in a wooded area overlooking the Potomac River, and plans are underway for the establishment of an interfaith Meditation Garden with shrines of the various religious faiths. Thus far the Temple's activities have included participation in two Spiritual Summit Conferences, the first in India and the second in Switzerland, and the creation of a series of high-level interreligious meetings at Harvard Divinity School, Princeton Theological Seminary, and Sarah Lawrence College, among others. Future plans call for more such conferences, focused on better interreligious communication and increased understanding.

THEOSOPHICAL ORDER OF SERVICE
P.O. Box 1862
Tucson, Arizona 85717

The primary objective of the Theosophical Order of Service is to work toward a realization of the brotherhood of all mankind, and expression of this brotherhood through various forms of service to our fellow man. The Order is divided into several different departments, including: (1) Department of Ecological Research, working toward the development of a healthier living environment in harmony with natural laws, and carrying out various projects to provide answers to pollution problems; (2) Peace Department, working to spread good will through meditations and suggestions for harmonious actions; (3) Healing Department, providing a healing ritual for group or individual use, accompanied by explanations of healing principles; (4) Social Service Department, engaging in various projects aimed at alleviating in practical ways some of the ills besetting mankind.

ALTERNATIVE COLLEGES AND EDUCATIONAL AND RESEARCH ORGANIZATIONS

ACADEMY OF PARAPSYCHOLOGY AND MEDICINE
314 Second Street
Los Altos, California 94022
(415) 941-0444

The Academy of Parapsychology and Medicine undertakes the study of all forms of paranormal and unorthodox healing. The intent of its members — scientists and physicians — is to shed further light on the common foundation underlying all healing experiences and thus discover the conditions which make healing possible. Symposia, workshops, and publications are the means by which new information on paranormal and unorthodox healing is brought to the attention of laymen and medical practitioners. The Academy makes available transcripts of symposia and cassette tapes of lectures.

ACADEMY OF WORLD STUDIES
2820 Van Ness Avenue
San Francisco, California 94109
(415) 441-1404 or 441-1405

The central concern of the Academy is to present a global (as opposed to national or ethnocentric) approach to the study of world affairs. Three major programs are offered: (1) a wide variety of language courses in classes of one, two, or three students; (2) quarterly courses in such areas as current world issues and events, culture and the arts, economics and international politics, philosophy, history and education; (3) a special training program consisting of an individualized course of study on

world problems. Arrangements can be made for transferable college credit for Academy courses.

ALI AKBAR COLLEGE OF MUSIC
Box 956
San Rafael, California 94902
(415) 454-6264

The tradition of Indian classical music, one of the most spiritual forms of music, is carried on by the Ali Akbar College of Music. The college, which provides some of the finest Indian musicians as teachers, offers four nine-week sessions during which the student learns hundreds of compositions from which he develops his own individualized musicianship.

ANDERSON RESEARCH FOUNDATION
3960 Ingraham Street
Los Angeles, California 90005
(213) 387-9164

The Anderson Research Foundation is dedicated to research, testing, and evaluation of possible means of life enhancement. All areas of study — physical, nutritional, emotional, esoteric, etc. — are explored to this end. An important recent project is the development of a comprehensive prison reform plan, presently being worked upon by a group of graduates of mind expansion training. Assistance of any kind, whether it be volunteerism or work toward an advanced degree, is welcome on the project. Other ongoing projects include the study of energy forms, holograms, kinesiology, and biofeedback. Lecture-discussions for the

public are given most Friday and Saturday evenings, and training in precision psychodrama is offered.

AQUARIAN ARCANE COLLEGE
(Mankind Centre Australia)
P.O. Box 23
Bondi Beach, 2026, N.S.W.
Australia

The purpose of the Aquarian Arcane College is to study the mysteries of the natural and spiritual laws of the universe, leading to a revelation of the true meaning of man's destiny. Anyone who sincerely seeks to further the concept of the New Universal Man and Civilization, based on unity, recognition of the oneness of life, and the principle of cooperation, may be admitted to the college. Each student follows an individualized course of instruction, based on a teacher-pupil dialogue. No fees of any kind are required. The College's next major project is to establish a course in Dialogues on the New Aquarian Age Civilization.

AQUARIAN RADIO TEACHING
P.O. Box 30127
Santa Barbara, California 93105
(805) 966-6906

Aquarian Radio Teaching seeks to bridge the gap which exists between men in important areas of thought and relationship. For this purpose, A.R.T. offers a catalogue of five-, 10- and 15-minute tapes on a variety of subjects, authored by international writers, philosophers, and speakers. The purpose of these tapes, to be broadcast on AM and FM radio stations, is to acquaint the general public with New Age concepts. Selected titles include: Full Moon Meditation; Energy; Man's Future Hope; Meditation: A Group Process; and Bhagavad Gita Lessons. In addition to individual talks, the tape library also contains intergroup discussions on various topics. Aquarian Radio Teaching will provide information and assistance to anyone wishing to initiate a local radio program designed to deal with subjects related to the emergence of a New World order.

ASSOCIATION FOR HUMAN DEVELOPMENT
P.O. Box 75175
Los Angeles, California 90075
(213) 466-2042

Research, study, and instruction in the fields of science, religion, and the arts is carried out by the Association for Human Development. It is hoped that these efforts will lead to a fuller understanding of all fields of human endeavor, improved communication facilities and abilities of men, and increased energy sources — solar, thermal, cosmic, and human. The Association believes that man can increase his spiritual awareness and learn to make full use of the powers available to him through understanding the basic laws of life and their universal scope. For those who wish to follow this path, the Association offers classes, lectures, experimentation, research and publications in such areas as metaphysics, meditation, occult sciences, health, and nutrition.

ASSOCIATION FOR HUMANISTIC PSYCHOLOGY
325 Ninth Street
San Francisco, California 94103
(415) 626-2375

The Association for Humanistic Psychology, founded in 1962, focuses on the development of the human sciences with special regard to human qualities and capacities. It seeks to include a wide range of disciplines dealing with human experience and behavior. The Association defines humanistic psychology in the following ways: "Humanistic Psychology ... (1) centers attention on the experiencing person and thus on experience as primary to the understanding of people; (2) affirms the fundamental uniqueness and importance of human life; (3) tries to develop methods to enlarge and expand human experience; (4) believes that intentionality and values are crucial in determining human action; (5) encourages attention to topics having little place in most systems, such as choice, self-realization, spontaneity, creativity, authenticity, transcendental experience, and courage; (6) emphasizes the integration of the whole person; (7) is concerned with the individual ... rather than seeking to study only the universal; (8) encourages research based on the significance of the phenomena studied; (9) explores synergistic relationships in groups, communities and institutions; (10) has a fundamental commitment to psychology as an art and a science ...." AHP issues a quarterly publication, "Journal of Humanistic Psychology," and a monthly newsletter. It conducts an annual meeting concerned with the theory and practice of humanistic psychology, and also organizes a variety of domestic and international meetings and conferences. It has local chapters and groups throughout the world, and it has established a network to facilitate communication between individuals attempting to humanize their respective professions. A listing of colleges offering humanistically oriented programs has been compiled, and information about growth centers is also available. Members can make use of an extensive bibliography, a discount book ordering service, and, through the "Paper Dragon," may

obtain copies (at cost) of current papers of special interest. Another important adjunct of the Association is the Humanistic Psychology Institute, an experimental departure in graduate education in psychology.

ASSOCIATION FOR TRANSPERSONAL PSYCHOLOGY
P.O. Box 3049
Stanford, California 94305

The Association for Transpersonal Psychology consists of individuals from a variety of disciplines involved in the area of transpersonal research and teaching. Subjects of exploration include biofeedback, personality theory, spiritual studies, and transpersonal therapies. Although most of its members are professionals, ATP considers itself a special interest group rather than a professional association. It attempts to maintain a degree of informality and appreciates the fact that its membership is still relatively small. Its activities during the past years have included the sponsoring of seminars and small conferences and the co-sponsoring of larger meetings, such as the first International Conference on Psychobiology and Transpersonal Psychology in Iceland in 1972, and the Summer School on the Psychology of Human Consciousness in association with Esalen in the same year. ATP is also closely aligned with the Association for Humanistic Psychology and is active in providing speakers and presentations at their annual meeting.

AUM ESOTERIC STUDY CENTER
2405 Ruscombe Lane
Baltimore, Maryland 21209

The AUM Esoteric Center, approved by the Maryland State Department of Education, grants certification in the Occult Sciences, Mystic Arts, and Religious Metaphysics. Courses include Yoga, Tarot, astrology, symbology and esoteric Christianity. A school system, based on the Ageless Wisdom Teachings, is also being developed.

COLLEGE OF ORIENTAL STUDIES
939 South New Hampshire Avenue
Los Angeles, California 90006
(213) 487-1235 or 384-0850

The College of Oriental Studies was created to increase understanding of Oriental culture and religion and to improve East/West intercultural relations. The College offers B.A., M.A., and Ph.D. programs designed to produce scholars in Oriental arts, culture, languages, philosophy, psychology, and religion. All courses of study incorporate both theory and practice.

CREATIVE EDUCATION FOUNDATION
State University College at Buffalo
Chase Hall
1300 Elmwood Avenue
Buffalo, New York 14222

Alex F. Osborn founded the Creative Education Foundation in 1954 in the hope that it could assist individuals in more fully realizing their innate creativity and problem-solving ability. To this end, it has been disseminating relevant information for the past two decades. In addition to its own official publication, "Journal of Creative Behavior," it has mailed out tens of thousands of important reprints and visual aids dealing with the development of creativity. It also sponsors annual Creative Problem-Solving Institutes, open to anyone who sincerely wishes to strengthen his own creative processes and awaken them in others. Although the Foundation is centered in Buffalo, programs are offered both nationally and internationally.

DEER CREEK INSTITUTE
Boulder, Utah 84716
(801) 335-2220

Deer Creek is a synergetic growth community which has developed innovative approaches and methods of counseling and self-help practices aimed at facilitating personal growth. It offers a residential psychotherapeutic program, a resident fellow program, and professional training and consultation programs. In addition, in its function as an adjunct of Antioch/West, it has a fully accredited academic curriculum leading to B.A. and M.A. degrees in psychology. The degree programs emphasize intensive self-exploration, in the belief that only when a person is in tune with himself can he hope to help others achieve psychological wholeness. The Institute also conducts workshops in communications and self-awareness training in several western states.

DENA FOUNDATION
4117 Northwest Willow Drive
Kansas City, Missouri 64116
(816) 452-8285

The Dena Founcation takes its name from the ancient werd for "balance," believing that balance is synonymous with peace, harmony, and truth. It is an international organization which supports and encourages educational activities in the humanities, creative arts, and sciences. It sponsors scholarships in these fields and publishes a variety of books and papers on topics of New Age research. It also sponsors an international group of women known as the Sisters of the Amber, whose creed is that of mutual love, respect, and cooperation as expressed in service to others.

ELECTRONIC UNIVERSITY
P.O. Box 361
Mill Valley, California 94941

The aim of the Electronic University is to disseminate the teachings of the late Alan Watts through audio and video cassettes made by him just prior to his death. Lecture subjects include: Essence of Buddhism; Introduction to Meditation; Religion and Sexuality; Eastern Philosophy; Psychology; Mythology of Hinduism; Introduction to Zen Practice; Jesus: His Religion, or the Religion About Him. A full listing of available cassettes can be obtained on request. The talks were designed to be used by individuals and in college and university settings in conjunction with Watts' books.

ENTROPY
1914 Polk Street
San Francisco, California 94109

Entropy describes itself as an "all-but-free university," offering courses in such areas as psychology, philosophy, meditation and movement, and music.

FORUM OF COSMIC AWARENESS
4200-B Silver S.E.
Albuquerque, New Mexico 87108
(505) 255-5252

The Forum of Cosmic Awareness is dedicated to conducting research and providing training in the areas of parapsychology, psychology, philosophy, religion, and the healing arts. Its educational program aims at developing man's awareness of his inner self and his relationship to the universe, and bringing to public attention the teachings of some little known but highly important persons in the field of spiritual enlightenment. The immediate goals of the Forum are to work on the development of a full curriculum; maintain a counseling center with highly qualified personnel, open to the public; and acquire a comprehensive library for research and general study.

HUMAN DIMENSIONS INSTITUTE
4380 Main Street
Buffalo, New York 14226
(716) 839-2336

The Human Dimensions Institute is an educational organization which avails itself of both the most modern research and the most ancient wisdom in a continuous attempt to understand and meet the needs of the "whole" person. It engages in scientific research and offers public lectures, in-depth seminars, experience groups, and continuous courses for all age groups. The Institute holds intensive seminars at Swen-i-o, their retreat center in Canandaigua, New York, and conducts special seminar-tours throughout the United States and in foreign countries. HDI has done significant research on the physiological effects of "laying-on-of-hands," precognition, and differences between natural and synthetic foods. Research results and a wide range of professional papers are published in their quarterly magazine, "Human Dimensions," available for $6 a year.

HUMANISTIC PSYCHOLOGY CENTER OF NEW YORK
25 Central Park West
New York, New York 10024
(212) 873-3668

The Humanistic Psychology Center is an interdisciplinary educational institute offering a program of classes and seminars for professionals in all fields who would like to learn how to apply the principles of humanistic psychology to their particular disciplines. The Center also provides consultation services for organizations and institutions, issues publications, and is involved in community education through public lectures and films.

HUMAN RESOURCES CENTER OF CONNECTICUT
210 Prospect Street
New Haven, Connecticut 06511

The Center's primary goal is to provide a comprehensive educational training program focused on the study of group dynamics and the interrelationship of group process and individual influences. It is committed to the development of skills in social, professional, and community interaction.

INSTITUTE OF HUMAN-POTENTIAL PSYCHOLOGY
580 College Avenue
Palo Alto, California 94306
(415) 326-6413

Founded in 1971 as an educational organization, I.H.P. offers various degree programs in psychology. The central focus of the Institute is to develop an integrative humanistic psychology, in the belief that an integrative approach will foster self-understanding and full actualization of human potentialities. The following degree programs are presently available: (1) residential Ph.D. degree program in Clinical-Counseling Psychology, under the Psychological Studies Institute division; and (2) external Ph.D. degree program in Integrative Humanistic Psychology, under the Continuing Education division. Programs of graduate study are all-embracing — they include Humanistic Studies, Eastern Psychology, and Phenomenology, in addition to the study of Psychoanalysis and Behavior Psychology. The Continuing Education Division also offers a variety of growth seminars for professionals and the general public.

INSTITUTE OF MYSTICAL AND PARA-PSYCHOLOGICAL STUDIES
JFK University
Martinez, California 94553

College courses in philosophy and psychology of mysticism, Yoga, comparative religions, and parapsychology are offered by the Institute as part of the John F. Kennedy University. Programs are aimed at meeting the needs of a wide spectrum of individuals.

INSTITUTE OF PSYCHIC SCIENCE
2015 South Broadway
Little Rock, Arkansas 72206
(501) 372-4278

Incorporated in 1971, the Institute of Psychic Science undertakes research and education in the area of personal psychic development. It is Arkansas' largest metaphysical school with courses of instruction embracing both teachings of ancient masters and contemporary psychological concepts. Through a synthesis of many techniques and teachings, it hopes to develop new methods of practical application of psychic abilities. A certificate of Personal Psychic Development is awarded after completion of three nine-week courses: Develop Your Own ESP, Self-Hypnosis, and Wisdom of the Mystic Masters. A certification program for metaphysical teachers has also been established. Members of the Institute receive full information on all activities at the Institute, its bi-monthly publication, "BREAKTHROUGH!," a discount on study group sessions, and use of the lending library.

INTERNATIONAL I CHING STUDIES INSTITUTE
10985 Bluffside Drive
Studio City, California 91604
(213) 761-3334

The International I Ching Studies Institute offers lectures, seminars, and workshops on the significance and use of the I Ching, an ancient Chinese source for inspiration and guidance. The Institute also teaches T'ai Chi Ch'uan and a variety of other Chinese health disciplines.

INTERNATIONAL UNIVERSITY
501 East Armour Boulevard
Kansas City, Missouri 64109

The International University offers over 50 programs of study in the arts, humanities, and sciences, leading to degrees from the A.A. through the Ph.D. It also has a wide range of technical and vocational preparatory studies. Legally incorporated in 1973, it grants provisional admission to all applicants, though a high school equivalency is usually expected. No uniform course requirements exist. Instead, each student works with an advisor to develop a study course appropriate to his own needs and interests. Programs usually include tutorials, small groups, and lecture and lab experiences, in addition to regional seminars, study abroad, and intensive training sessions. The University attempts to make a high quality, personalized education available to everyone, regardless of their socioeconomic status. Those in financial need may apply for a large number of existing financial aids and scholarships. At the present time, the University is working to create mini-campus sites throughout the United States which will serve as regional centers for its activities. Plans are also being developed for the establishment of campus locations in the Caribbean, Great Britain, Japan and Mexico.

LINDISFARNE
Fish Cove Road
Southampton, Long Island
New York, New York 11968
(516) 283-8210

Founded by William Irwin Thompson, Lindisfarne presents a holistic approach to education, incorporating mysticism along with contemporary arts, letters, and sciences. It is a community in constant flux, believing that self-discovery is an essential part of the learning process. The school follows the pattern of a medieval monastic community.

NAROPA INSTITUTE
1441 Broadway
Boulder, Colorado 80302

The Naropa Institute attempts to provide an environment in which the Eastern and Western traditions can interact, and in which these disciplines can be grounded in the personal experience and practice of staff and students. The Institute hopes to develop into a year-round, accredited learning institution, though it is not designed solely for the undergraduate or graduate community. It welcomes teachers, professionals, and all interested individuals. A copy of the Institute's catalogue may be obtained on request.

NATIONAL HUMANISTIC EDUCATION CENTER
Springfield Road
Upper Jay, New York 12987

The National Humanistic Education Center is an educational conference and resource center dedicated to the furthering of theory, research and practice in humanistic education. Its headquarters is located on 188 acres of wooded land in the Adirondack Mountains in northern New York. Sleeping accommodations are available for 45, and meeting and dining facilities for 70. The Center offers spring and fall workshops around the country, and summer workshops at its headquarters. It also sponsors a humanistic educators communication network and sends educational materials throughout the world.

PENDLE HILL
Wallingford, Pennsylvania 19086
(215) 566-4507

Pendle Hill is self-described as "a Quaker center for study and contemplation." It has aspects of both commune and college. It serves as a community for students of all ages, faiths, and nationalities, and is purposely restricted in size to about 40 students per year-long program. Students devote a certain part of each week to work essential for community upkeep. Courses change from year to year in response to the desires of the students, but they generally cluster around four major areas: (1) religion, both Occidental and Oriental, with special emphasis on mystical aspects of religion; (2) the Bible and Christian philosophy; (3) Quakerism; and (4) social problems, both domestic and international. The curriculum has been expanded to also include psychology, creative arts, and crafts. The particular course of study is individually charted by each student, with the aid of a staff consultant. Emphasis is placed on inward growth as facilitated by meditation, interaction with others in small seminar groups, and private reading and creative projects. Although most students enroll for a tri-quarter September-through-June study year, Pendle Hill also offers the options of a non-residency extension program and several week-long summer sessions covering a wide variety of topics. In addition, free public lectures are given every Monday evening. These lectures, plus other lectures of interest, are taped and sold to the public at a nominal price. The center also puts out many publications, foremost of which is a pamphlet series dealing with a wide range of subjects in the areas of religion, philosophy, psychology, race relations, social problems, literature, and the arts.

PSYCHE RESEARCH INSTITUTE
10701 Lomas N.E., Suite 210
Albuquerque, New Mexico 87112
(505) 292-0370

Created in 1971 as an extension of the Center for Hypnosis Training and Consultation, the Psyche Research Institute functions as a center for the study of consciousness through such disciplines as hypnosis, meditation, biofeedback, self-regulation exercises, sensory awareness-isolation and other altered states of consciousness. By encouraging scientific verification of subjective phenomena, the Institute hopes to create a better understanding of the nature of the human psyche and the possibilities of human consciousness. Seminars and workshops are conducted for both professional and lay persons in Albuquerque, where the center is located, or by invitation in other cities throughout the country. Instructional tapes on hypnosis, meditation, and altered states of consciousness are also available, and Certificate Courses are taught for those with a genuine interest. Free information will be mailed on request.

THOMAS JEFFERSON RESEARCH CENTER
1143 North Lake Avenue
Pasadena, California 91104
(213) 798-0791

The Thomas Jefferson Research Center exists for the purpose of research and education in the behavioral disciplines. It seeks to demonstrate that an understanding of human nature is essential for the success of individuals, organizations, and governments. It has undertaken multidisciplinary research which indicates that one of the most effective means of dealing with human problems is through an increase in both the quantity and quality of behavioral education for all age groups. The Center believes that there is a serious lag between discovery and application of important behavioral science information, and it seeks to assist schools, churches, corporations, and all other interested organizations in the effective utilization of information of vital importance in the development of human relations.

CLINICS

CLEVELAND CLINIC
Cleveland, Ohio

Led by outstanding surgeons such as the now-retired Dr. George Crile, Cleveland Clinic is known for innovative surgical procedures. The coronary bypass operation, total hip and knee joint replacement, and new procedures in mastectomy were all developed here. The Cleveland Clinic performs extensive health examinations for early diagnosis and prevention of disease and handles annual checkups for executives.

HEALTH MAINTENANCE CENTER
1370 Avenue of the Americas
New York, New York

This outstanding Center specializes in examination by computer, technically described as "automated multiphasic testing." By combining all testing facilities in one place and mechanizing them as much as possible, a thorough checkup, including a manual examination by a doctor, is completed in a surprisingly short time. Emphasis is placed on preventive medicine, and the Center not only diagnoses any existing malfunctions but points out areas that might give cause for future concern and ways to avoid potential problems. The institute maintains health care centers in New York City, San Francisco, San Diego and Los Angeles and is connected with more than 750 medical examiners throughout the country.

LAHEY CLINIC
Boston, Massachusetts

Well-known for cancer therapy and abdominal and neurosurgery as well as treatment of gastrointestinal ailments, the Lahey Clinic will soon move to a multimillion-dollar complex in Burlington, Massachusetts.

MAYO CLINIC
Rochester, Minnesota

The largest and probably best-known medical center in the world, the Mayo Clinic was founded by Dr. William Mayo and his sons William and Charles. From the joint practice of these three gifted surgeons, the facility has grown to its present staff of 600 doctors who treat 250,000 people a year. Highly regarded by the medical profession as well as the general public, the Mayo Clinic handles every aspect of health care, from routine checkups for 300 top corporate executives to unusual medical problems that have baffled physicians in regular practice.

OCHSNER CLINIC
New Orleans, Louisiana

Ochsner is another facility noted for pioneer work in surgical procedures, such as the umbrella-patch used to close holes in the walls between chambers of the heart, a procedure developed by Drs. Terry King and Noel Mills. The Clinic is also well-known for work in pediatrics, particularly with children who have brain damage and psychiatric problems.

PALO ALTO CLINIC
Palo Alto, California

Especially successful in treatment of retina diseases is a Palo Alto Clinic department headed by Dr. Edwin Boldrey. The Clinic is also noted for the thoracic surgery performed by Dr. Robert Jamplis.

SCOTT-WHITE CLINIC
Temple, Texas

Scott-White Clinic also has a cooperative arrangement with the Mayo Clinic and is known for work in gastrointestinal treatment.

SCRIPPS CLINIC
La Jolla, California

With elaborate diagnostic facilities, Scripps specializes in allergies, dermatology and heart-lung disease. The Clinic also maintains an exchange program with Mayo for West Coast-based executives.

TAVISTOCK INSTITUTE
OF HUMAN RELATIONS
Tavistock Centre, Belsize Lane
London NWS 5BA, England

The Tavistock Institute was founded in 1946 to study human relations in conditions of well-being, conflict or breakdown, in the family, the work group and the larger organization, and to promote the health and effectiveness of individuals and organizations. It is one of the few bodies in Europe that sets out to combine research in the social and psychological sciences with professional practice. It is in touch with theorists and practitioners in many countries. Members of the staff have been trained in different disciplines but share a belief that their integration will yield fresh insights into human relations. The inclusion within the Institute of a broad spectrum of disciplines ranging from psychological medicine to operational research, as well as a concern with theory and practice, sets a distinctive imprint on its activities. Its service and research activities, which are problem-centered rather than discipline-centered, involve collaboration with individuals, families and institutions — public and private, industrial and nonindustrial. The postgraduate training that the Institute provides in some spheres gives priority to practical work, with the learner becoming a temporary member of a project team. In this way, both with postgraduate students and with visiting scientists, considerable opportunity arises for mutual learning and facilitating the Tavistock aim of breaking new ground in theory and practice. The Institute seeks to maintain a forum where theory and practice, research and development can be subjected to critical appraisal from the full range of disciplines represented within it.

INTERNATIONAL INDEX

ALINE MANTEL GRAF
79 Avenue de la Republique
Paris 11, France

ANANDA CENTRE
Eisley Court
20/22 Gt. Titchfield Street
London, W. 1, England

ASSOCIATION "THE HEART
OPEN TO THE WORLD"
35 Rue du Marche
5200 Huy, Belgium

ASSOCIAZIONE ARCHEOSOFICA
Viale Regina Margherita, 244/7
00198 Roma, Italy

ATMA
72a Wake Green Road
Birmingham 13, England

AUSTRALIAN INSTITUTE
OF HUMAN RELATIONS
Royal Parade, Parkville 3052
Melbourne, Victoria, Australia

L'ASSOCIATION POUR LA
PROTECTION DE LA VIE
12.100 Compregnac, France

AVALON GROUP
Castle House
Keinton Mandeville
Somerton, Somerset 6DX, England

BRISTOL ENCOUNTER CENTRE
28 Drakes Way
Portishead, Bristol, England

BUDDHIST PUBLICATION SOCIETY
P.O. Box 61
Kandy, Sri Lanka, Ceylon

CANADIAN INSTITUTE
OF PSYCHOSYNTHESIS
(Quebec Center for Psychosynthesis)
3496 Marlowe Avenue
Montreal H4A-3L7, Quebec, Canada

CENTENNIAL ACRES
Box 960
Bracebridge Muskoka
Ontario, Canada

CENTER
Kromme Waal 14
Amsterdam 1001, Netherlands

CENTER FOR THE WHOLE PERSON
76 Dupont Street
Toronto, Ontario, Canada

CENTRAL ASIAN RESEARCH CENTRE
1B Parkfield Street
London NI OPR, England

C.E.N.T.R.E.
52, Rue de Verneuil
Paris 7, France

CENTRE DE DEVELOPPEMENT
DU POTENTIEL HUMAIN
25 Rue de la Bienfaisance
Paris 8, France

CENTRE DE PSYCHOLOGIE
EXPERIENTIELLE
105 Rue des Poissonniers
Paris 18, France

CENTRE DE PSYCHOLOGIE
CONJUGALE ET FAMILIALE
1256 Sherbrooke est
Montreal 133, Quebec, Canada

CENTRE DE PSYCHOSYNTHESE
EDUCATIVE
CH 1844 Villeneuve, Switzerland

CENTRE FOR ENVIRONMENTAL STUDIES
62 Chandos Place
London WC2, England

CENTRE FOR GROUP WORK
7 Chesham Terrace
Ealing W13, England

CENTRE FOR HUMAN COMMUNICATION
63 Abbey Road
Torquay, Devon, England

CENTRE FOR HUMANISTIC STUDIES
18a Allingham Court
Haverstock Hill
London, NW3, England

CENTRE FOR SAMPLE SURVEYS
16 Duncan Terrace
London NI 8B2, England

CENTRE FOR STUDIES IN SOCIAL POLICY
62 Doughty Street
London WC1 N2LS, England

CENTRE FOR THERAPEUTIC
COMMUNICATION
46 Antrim Mansions
Antrim Road
London NW3, England

CENTRE FRANCAIS DE PSYCHOSYNTHESE
61 Rue de la Verrerie
75004 Paris, France

CENTRE OF MOVEMENT
121 Avenue Road
Toronto, Ontario, Canada

CENTRE OF THE WORLD BEAUTIFUL
Box 56
Kootenay Bay
British Columbia, Canada

CENTRO STUDI UMANOLOGIA
135 Via Anassagora
00124 Rome, Italy

THE CHURCHILL CENTRE
22 Montagu Street
London W1, England

COLD MOUNTAIN INSTITUTE
2527 West 37th Avenue
Vancouver 13, British Columbia, Canada

COLLEGE OF RICHMOND FELLOWSHIP
8 Addison Road
London W14, England

COMMUNITY
6 Harley Road
London, NW3, England

CONSULTANTS IN HUMANISTIC
PSYCHOLOGY
18a Allingham Court
Haverstock Hill
London, NW3, England

COONARDOO CENTRE
6 Oaks Avenue
Cremorne N.S.W.
Sidney 2090, Australia

COSMIC INITIATION CENTER
900 Sherbrooke Street West
Suite 71
Montreal, Quebec, Canada

COSMIC RESEARCH GROUP
13, Highfield Road, Ensbury Park
Bournemouth, Hants, England

DARTINGTON SOCIAL RESEARCH UNIT
The Courtyard
Dartington Hall, Totnes
Devon TQ9 6ES, England

DARTINGTON SOLAR QUEST
Apple Green Court
Dartington, Totnes, Devonshire
England

DRAMA THERAPY CENTRE
c/o PCL
104-8 Bolsover Street
London W1, England

DUTCH GESTALT INSTITUTE
Kralingse Plaslaan 22
Rotterdam 3016, The Netherlands

ECONOMIC AND SOCIAL
RESEARCH INSTITUTE
4 Burlington Road
Dublin 4, Ireland

EDUCATIONAL COMMUNITY
19 Dunollie Road
London NW5, England

EDUCATIONAL RESEARCH CENTRE
St. Patrick's College
Dublin, Ireland

E.G.O. PROGRAMME
(Education and Growth Opportunities)
York University
Downsview 463, Ontario, Canada

ENCUENTRO
Apartado 51855
Caracas 105, Venezuela

ENTROPY
Flat 8, 11 Lindfield Gardens
London NW3, England

EQUALS ONE
Pondicherry 2, India

ERNEST-HOLMES-GESELLSCHAFT
Institut fur Humanpsychologie
und Sozialpsychiatrie Ev
Gemmeinnutziger Verein
896 Kempten/Sankt Mang
Sonnenstrasse 16, Germany

FOUNDATION OF TRUTH
3 Holcome Road
Ilford, Essex IGI 4XF, England

FUTURES
IPC House
32 High Street
Guildford, Surrey, England

GESTALT CENTRE
58A Longridge Road
London SW5, England

GESTALT INSTITUTE OF CANADA
Box 779
Chemainus, British Columbia, Canada

GESTALT INSTITUTE OF QUEBEC
5208 Ponsard
Montreal, Quebec, Canada

GESTALT STUDIOS/CENTRE
FOR HOLISTIC STUDIES
139 Water Street
Vancouver, British Columbia, Canada

GODIAN RELIGION
P.M. Box 1107
Enugu, Nigeria

GREEK CENTER OF PSYCHOSYNTHESIS
Kafkassou 50
Kipseli, Athens 810, Greece

GROUPE FRANCAIS
D'ETUDES DE SOCIOMETRIE
Centre Montsouris, 8
Villa Montsouris
75014 Paris, France

GROUPES DE RENCONTRE RUBAUD
C2, 12R. Dr. Kurzenne
F78350 Jouy en Josas
Paris, France

GROUP RELATIONS
TRAINING ASSOCIATION
Grubb Institute
1 Whitehall Place
London SW1, England

GRUBB INSTITUTE
OF BEHAVIOURAL STUDIES
EWR Centre
Cloudesley Street
London NI OHU, England

HALLAM CENTRE
Weston House, West Bar Green
Sheffield S1 2L, England

HESBJERG PEACE
Research College
5573 Holmstrup
Fyn, Denmark

HUMAN DEVELOPMENT CENTRE
P.O. Box 179
St. Ives, NSW, Australia

HUMAN INTERACTION SEMINARS
Box 4984 GPO
Sydney 2001, NSW, Australia

HUMAN POTENTIAL
RESEARCH PROJECT
Centre for Adult Education
University of Surrey
Guildford, Surrey, England

I.F.G.: CROISSANCE PERSONNELLE
831 Rockland
Montreal, Quebec, Canada

INDIAN INSTITUTE
OF WORLD CULTURE
6 Sri B.P. Wadia Road
P.O. Box 402
Basavangudi, Bangalore-4, India

INDO-AMERICAN SOCIETY
Kitab Mahal, 5, Raveline Street
Fort, Bombay 400 001 India

INSIGHT
64 Rue de Condorcet
Paris 9, France

INSTITUT DE DEVELOPPEMENT HUMAIN
3125 Joncas
Quebec, GIE 1S2, Canada

INSTITUT DES RELATIONS HUMAINES
2120 Sherbrooke est., Suite 208
Montreal, Quebec, Canada

INSTITUTE FOR BIO-ENERGY
22 Montagu Street
London, W1, England

INSTITUTE FOR COMMUNITY STUDIES
18 Victoria Park Square
London E2 9PF, England

INSTITUTE FOR CONSCIOUSNESS
RESEARCH
Laufdsvegur 6, Reykjavik, Iceland

INSTITUTE FOR FISCAL STUDIES
62 Chandos Place
London WC2N 4HH, England

INSTITUTE FOR FUTURES
RESEARCH AND EDUCATION
6, Via Paisiello
00198 Roma, Italy

INSTITUTE FOR RELIGIOUS PSYCHOLOGY
4-11-1 Inokashira, Mitaka
Tokyo, Japan 181

INSTITUTE FOR SOCIAL STUDIES
IN MEDICAL CARE
18 Victoria Park Square
London E2 9PF, England

INSTITUTE FOR STUDIES IN
PSYCHO-PHYSICAL SCIENCE
14 Medici Court
Scarborough 702, Ontario, Canada

INSTITUTE FOR THE
COMMUNICATION OF RELIGIONS
Weena Pavilijoen 9 Postbus 52005
Rotterdam, Netherlands

INSTITUTE FOR THE STUDY
OF DRUG DEPENDENCE
Kingsbury House
3 Blackburn Road
London NW6 1XA, England

INSTITUTE OF DEVELOPMENT STUDIES
University of Sussex
Andrew Cohen Building
Palmer
Brighton BN1 9RE, England

INSTITUTE OF FAMILY
AND ENVIRONMENTAL RESEARCH
7a Kidderpore Avenue
London NW3 7SX, England

INSTITUTE OF GROUP ANALYSIS
1 Bickenhall Mansions
Bickenhall Street
London W1, England

INSTITUTE OF PSYCHOPHYSICAL
RESEARCH
118 Banbury Road
Oxford, England

INSTITUTE OF PSYCHOSYNTHESIS
Highwood Park
London NW7 4HD, England

INSTITUTE OF UNITIVE PSYCHOLOGY
Ewijkshoeve, Soestdijkerweg 12
Lage Vuursche, Netherlands

INSTITUTO DI PSICOSINTESI
Via San Domenico 16
50133 Florence, Italy

INTERAKTIE-ACADEMIE
Mortselsesteenweg 78
2540 Hove, Belgium

INTERCOSMIC CENTRE
FOR SPIRITUAL ASSOCIATION
P.O. Box 246
Nsawam, Ghana

INTERCULTURAL WORLD MOVEMENT
OF COMMUNITIES
Via A. Cantele, 3F
35100 Padova, Italy

INTERFACE
P.O. Box 28
Wilmslow, Cheshire, England

INTERNATIONAL ACADEMY
FOR CONTINUOUS EDUCATION
Sherborne House, Sherborne, Cheltenham
Gloucestershire GL54 3DZ, England

INTERNATIONAL ASSOCIATION
FOR PSYCHOTRONIC RESEARCH
Suite 803, 43 Eglinton Avenue East
Toronto, Ontario, Canada M4P 1A2

INTERNATIONAL ASSOCIATION
FOR RELIGIOUS FREEDOM
The Hague
Laan Copes Van Cattenburch 40, Netherlands

INTERNATIONAL CENTER OF
METHODOLOGY FOR FUTURE
AND DEVELOPMENT STUDIES
3-5 Bucharest 8, Romania

INTERNATIONAL CREATIVE
CENTER — R.C.I.
20, ch. Colladon, 1211 Geneve 28
Switzerland

INTERNATIONAL HUMANIST AND
ETHICAL UNION
P.O. Box 114
Utrecht, Holland

INTERNATIONAL SOCIETY FOR
RELIGION AND PARAPSYCHOLOGY
No. 181, 4-11-7 Inokashira
Mitaka-shi
Tokyo, Japan

LIFE SKILLS INSTITUTE
4459 52A Street
Delta, British Columbia V4K 2Y3, Canada

LONDON CENTRE FOR PSYCHOTHERAPY
19 Fitzjohn's Avenue
London NW3, England

MISSION OF PEACE
Sri Santi Ashram
P.O. (via) Sankhavara
Totapalli Hills, South India

MITRE PRESS
52 Lincoln's Inn Fields
London WC2A 3NW, England

MONDCIVITAN
27 Delancey Street
London NW1, England

MUMAIHE MISSION
15, Olowojeunjeje Street
Ajegunle-Apapa, Lagos, Nigeria

NATIONAL CHILDREN'S BUREAU
8 Wakley Street
Islington, London ECIV 7QE, England

NATIONAL FEDERATION
OF SPIRITUAL HEALERS
Shortacres, Church Hill
Loughton, Essex, England

NATIONAL FOUNDATION
FOR EDUCATIONAL RESEARCH
The Mere
Upton Park, Slough
Berks SL1 2DQ, England

NATIONAL INSTITUTE
FOR SOCIAL WORK
Mary Ward House
5-7 Tavistock Place
London WC1H 9SS, England

NATIONAL INSTITUTE OF
ECONOMIC AND SOCIAL RESEARCH
2 Dean Trench Street
Smith Square
London SW1P 3HE, England

NEMAYA
543 St. Clements Avenue
Toronto M5N 1M3, Canada

NEW UNIVERSAL UNION
P.O. Box 335
Teheran, Iran

NEW VALUES ASSOCIATION
27 Prince Charles Drive
Toronto, Ontario M6A 2H1, Canada

ONTOLOGY-CREATIVITY
21, Quai de la Tournelle
75005 Paris, France

OPEN CIRCLE
20 Dingwall Gardens
London NW11, England

OVERSEAS DEVELOPMENT INSTITUTE
10-11 Percy Street
London W1P OJB, England

POLITICAL AND ECONOMIC PLANNING
12 Upper Belgrave Street
London SW1X 8BB, England

PROD
P.O. Box 65
Horison, Transvaal, Republic of South Africa

QUAESITOR
187 Walm Lane
London NW2, England

ROYAL INSTITUTE
OF INTERNATIONAL AFFAIRS
Chatham House
10 James's Square
London SW1, England

RUHANI SATSANG
Sawan Ashram
Delhi 7, India

SCOTTISH COUNCIL FOR
RESEARCH IN EDUCATION
16 Moray Place
Edinburgh 3, Scotland

SHALAL INSTITUTE
P.O. Box 2196
Vancouver, British Columbia, Canada

SIVANANDA ASHRAM YOGA CAMP
8th Avenue
Val Morin, Quebec, Canada

SOCIAL AND COMMUNITY
PLANNING RESEARCH
16 Duncan Terrace
London N1, England

SON (ZEN) LOTUS SOCIETY
378 Markham Street, B1
Toronto, Ontario, Canada M6G 2K9

SPIRITUAL UNITY OF NATIONS
Liewiet Laan, Land en zeezicht
Somerset West C.P., South Africa

STRATHMERE
RR3, North Gower
Ontario, Canada

SUFI WORKCAMPS
Kanhah Abadan, Abad Dockenfield
Farnham, Surrey, England

SYNERGIA
P.O. Box 1685
Station B
Montreal, Quebec, Canada

TAVISTOCK INSTITUTE
OF HUMAN RELATIONS
Tavistock Centre
120 Belsize Lane
London NW3 5BA, England

TIVYON GROWTH CENTRE
P.O. Box 808
Kfar Shmaryahu, Israel

UNITARIA
Karlova 8/186
Prague 1, Stare Mesto, Czechoslovakia

UNITED WORLD
Post Box 908
Oslo 1, Norway

UNIVERSAL FOUNDATION
71, Princess House
Kensington Park Road
London, W. 11, England

UNIVERSAL GREAT BROTHERHOOD
Consejo Supremo de la Gfu
Apt. 3987
Caracas 101, Venezuela

UNIVERSAL LINK
P.O. Box 13
Borup, Denmark

UNIVERSAL LOVE AND
BROTHERHOOD ASSOCIATION
Kameoka
Kyoto-fu, Japan

UNIVERSAL PEACE MISSION
Purple Heather Farm
Cholesbury Nr. Tring
Herts, England

UNIVERSITY OF THE NEW WORLD
1961 Haute-Nendaz
Valais, Switzerland

UVANNIK
451 Daly Avenue
Ottawa, Ontario, K1N 6H6, Canada

VACANCES 2000
18, Avenue de l'Opera
Paris 1, France

WORLD CONGRESS OF FAITHS
23, Norfolk Square
London W2 1RU, England

WORLD FELLOWSHIP OF BUDDHISTS
41, Phra Atnit Street
Bangkok, Thailand

WORLD UNION FELLOWSHIP
c/o British Monomark/V.S.A.
London W.C.1, England

WREKIN TRUST
1 Shrewsbury Road, Bomere Heath
Salop, England

YASODHARA ASHRAM
Box 9
Kootenay Bay, British Columbia, Canada

YOGA CENTRE TORONTO
27 Valley Woods Road, Unit 11
Don Mills, Ontario, Canada

ZAGT
Keilberger Schulweg
D 84 Regensburg, Germany

ZIST: ZENTRUM FUR INDIVIDUAL
UND SOZIAL THERAPIE
8122 Penzberg, Zist 3
Wolf Buntig, Germany

BIBLIOGRAPHY

ATCHESON, RICHARD. The Bearded Lady. New York: John Day, 1971.

BABA, MEHER. God Speaks. New York: Dodd Mead, 1973.

BARLOW, WILFRED. The Alexander Technique. New York: Knopf, 1973.

BENSON, HERBERT. The Relaxation Response. New York: William Morrow, 1975.

BERNE, ERIC. Games People Play: The Psychology of Human Relationships. New York: Grove, 1964.

BOSTON WOMEN'S HEALTH COLLECTIVE. Our Bodies Our Selves. New York: Simon & Schuster, 1973.

BOURGUIGNON, ERIKA (Ed). Religion, Altered States of Consciousness and Social Change. Columbus, Ohio: Ohio State Univ. Press, 1973.

BRAUN, SAUL (Ed). A Catalog of Sexual Consciousness. New York: Grove.

BRECHER, EDWARD M., et al (Eds). Licit and Illicit Drugs: The Consumers' Union Report. Boston: Little, Brown, 1972.

BROWN, BARBARA B. New Mind, New Body. New York: Harper & Row, 1974.

BRY, ADELAIDE. est: 76 Hours That Transform Your Life. New York: Harper & Row, 1976.

CAMUS, ALBERT. The Stranger. New York: Random House, 1954.

CASTANEDA, CARLOS. The Teachings of Don Juan: A Yaqui Way of Knowledge. New York: Ballantine, 1968.

CASTANEDA, CARLOS. A Separate Reality. New York: Simon & Schuster, 1971.

CASTANEDA, CARLOS. Journey to Ixtlan. New York: Simon & Schuster, 1973.

CASTANEDA, CARLOS. Tales of Power. New York: Simon & Schuster, 1974.

THE CATALOGUE: An Index of Possibilities. New York: Pantheon, 1974.

CHRISTOPHER, MILBOURNE. Mediums, Mystics & the Occult. New York: T. Y. Crowell, 1975.

THE COEVOLUTION QUARTERLY: Supplement to the Whole Earth Catalog. Published quarterly by POINT, Box 428, Sausalito, Ca. 94965, @ $6 per year.

COHEN, SIDNEY. The Beyond Within: The LSD Story. New York: Atheneum, 1967.

COHEN, SIDNEY. The Drug Dilemma. New York: McGraw Hill, 1975.

COOPER, DAVID and LAING, R. D. Reason and Violence: A Decade of Sartre's Philosophy. New York: Pantheon, 1971.

COOPER, PAULETTE. The Scandal of Scientology. New York: Belmont-Tower, 1972.

CORSINI, RAYMOND (Ed). Current Psychotherapies. Itaska, Il.: F. E. Peacock, 1973.

DALLETT, KENT. It's All in Your Mind. Palo Alto, Ca.: Mayfield Publishers, 1973.

DE LANGRE, JACQUES. The First Book of Do'In. The Second Book of Do'In. Magalia, Ca.: Happiness Press, 1971.

DELGADO, JOSE. The Physical Control of the Mind. New York: Harper & Row, 1971.

DENNISTON, DENISE and PETER McWILLIAMS. The TM Book. Los Angeles: Price/Stern/Sloan, 1975.

DEVI, INDRA. Yoga for Americans. New York: NAL, 1959.

DOWNING, GEORGE. The Massage Book. New York: Random House, 1972.

DOWNING, GEORGE. Massage & Meditation. New York: Random House, 1974.

DUBOS, RENE. A God Within. New York: Scribners, 1972.

ELLIS, ALBERT. Growth Through Reason. Palo Alto, Ca.: Science & Behavior Books, 1971.

ELLIS, ALBERT and ROBERT A. HARPER. A Guide to Rational Living. Hollywood, Ca.: Wilshire Books, 1971.

ELLWOOD, ROBERT S., JR. Religious and Spiritual Groups in Modern America. Englewood Cliffs, N.J.: Prentice Hall, 1972.

ERIKSON, ERIK H. Childhood and Society. New York: Norton, 1964.

FARRAR, STEWART. What Witches Do. New York: Coward McCann, 1971.

FELDENKRAIS, MOSHE. Awareness Through Movement. New York: Harper & Row, 1972.

FERGUSON, MARILYN. The Brain Revolution. New York: Taplinger, 1973.

FREUD, SIGMUND. The Interpretation of Dreams. New York: Avon, 1967.

FREUD, SIGMUND. Three Essays on the Theory of Sexuality. New York: Basic Books, 1975.

FULLER, R. BUCKMINSTER. Nine Chains to the Moon. New York: Anchor Books, 1971.

FULLER, R. BUCKMINSTER. Synergetics. New York: Macmillan, 1975.

GALLAGHER, CHUCK, S. J. The Marriage Encounter. New York: Doubleday, 1975.

GALLWEY, TIMOTHY. The Inner Game of Tennis. New York: Random House, 1974.

GASTON, E. THAYER. Music in Therapy. New York: Macmillan, 1968.

GLASSER, WILLIAM, M.D. Reality Therapy. New York: Harper & Row, 1965.

GOLAS, THADDEUS. The Lazy Man's Guide to Enlightenment. Palo Alto, Ca.: The Seed Center, 1972.

GOLEMBIEWSKI, ROBERT and ARTHUR BLUMBERG (Eds). Sensitivity Training. Itaska, Il.: F. E. Peacock, 1973.

GOODE, ERICH. The Drug Phenomenon: Social Aspects of Drug Taking. New York: Bobbs Merrill, 1973.

THE GRAY PANTHERS. Citizen's Action Guide to Nursing Home Reform. Gray Panthers, 3700 Chestnut Street, Philadelphia, 1975.

HARTMAN, WILLIAM E. and MARILYN A. FITHIAN. The Treatment of Sexual Dysfunction: A Bio-Psycho-Social Approach. New York: Aronson, 1974.

HERRIGEL, EUGEN. Zen in the Art of Archery. New York: Vintage, 1953.

HOLZER, HANS. ESP and You. New York: Ace Books, 1972.

HOLZER, HANS. The Directory of the Occult. Chicago: Regnery, 1974.

HORNEY, KAREN. New Ways in Psychoanalysis. New York: Norton, 1939.

HUBBARD, L. RON. Dianetics: The Modern Science of Mental Health. Los Angeles: Publications Organization, 1950.

HUBBARD, L. RON. Scientology: The Fundamentals of Thought. Los Angeles: Publications Organization, 1956.

HURWOOD, BERNHARDT J. (Ed). The Whole Sex Catalogue. New York: Pinnacle, 1975.

ILLICH, IVAN. Deschooling Society. New York: Harper & Row, 1970.

ILLICH, IVAN. After Deschooling — What? New York: Harper & Row, 1973.

JACKINS, HARVEY. Guidebook to Re-evaluation Counseling. Seattle: Rational Island, 1975.

JANOV, ARTHUR. The Primal Scream. New York: Putnam, 1970.

JOHNSON, CLIVE (Ed). Vedanta: An Anthology of Hindu Scripture, Commentary & Poetry. New York: Bantam, 1974.

JUNG, CARL GUSTAV. The Basic Writings of C. G. Jung. New York: Modern Library, 1959.

JUNG, CARL GUSTAV. Man and His Symbols. New York: Doubleday, 1964.

KEYES, KEN, JR. Handbook to a Higher Consciousness. Berkeley, Ca.: Living Love Center, 1974.

KEYES, KEN, JR. and BRUCE T. BURKAN. How to Make Your Life Work. Berkeley, Ca.: Living Love Center, 1974.

KIERNAN, THOMAS. Shrinks, Etc. New York: Dial, 1975.

KLINE, NATHAN S. From Sad to Glad. New York: Ballantine, 1974.

KRISHNAMURTI, JIDDU. Freedom from the Known. New York: Harper & Row, 1975.

KRISHNAMURTI, JIDDU. The Awakening of Intelligence. New York: Avon, 1976.

KROGER, WILLIAM S. Clinical and Experimental Hypnosis. Philadelphia: Lippincott, 1963.

LAING, R. D. The Divided Self. New York: Pantheon, 1969.

LEBOYER, FREDERICK. Birth Without Violence. New York: Knopf, 1975.

LEONARD, GEORGE. Education and Ecstasy. New York: Dell, 1968.

LEONARD, GEORGE B. The Ultimate Athlete. New York: Viking Press, 1975.

LEVI-STRAUSS, CLAUDE. The Savage Mind. Chicago: Univ. of Chicago Press, 1966.

LILLY, JOHN C. The Center of the Cyclone. New York: Bantam, 1973.

LILLY, JOHN C. Programming & Metaprogramming in the Human Biocomputer. New York: Bantam, 1974.

LILLY, JOHN C. Lilly on Dolphins. New York: Doubleday, 1975.

LILLY, JOHN C. and ANTONIETTA LILLY. The Dyadic Cyclone. New York: Simon & Schuster, 1976.

LORENZ, KONRAD. On Aggression. New York: Bantam, 1967.

LOWEN, ALEXANDER. The Betrayal of the Body. New York: Collier Books, 1969.

LUCE, GAY GAER and JULIUS SEGAL. Sleep. New York: Coward McCann, 1966.

LUSCHER, MAX. The Luscher Color Test. New York: Pocket Books, 1971.

MASLOW, ABRAHAM. The Farther Reaches of Human Nature. New York: Viking, 1971.

MASTERS, ROBERT E. L. and JEAN HOUSTON. The Varieties of Psychedelic Experience. New York: Dell, 1967.

MASTERS, ROBERT E. L. and JEAN HOUSTON. Mind Games. New York: Dell, 1973.

MASTERS, WILLIAM and VIRGINIA JOHNSON. Human Sexual Response. Boston: Little, Brown, 1970.

MASTERS, WILLIAM and VIRGINIA JOHNSON. Human Sexual Inadequacy. Boston: Little, Brown, 1966.

MASTERS, WILLIAM H. and VIRGINIA E. JOHNSON. The Pleasure Bond. New York: Bantam, 1976.

MAY, ROLLO. The Courage to Create. New York: Norton, 1975.

MAY, ROLLO. Love and Will. New York: Dell, 1973.

McLUHAN, MARSHALL. Understanding Media. New York: Signet, 1964.

MEARES, AINSLIE. A System of Medical Hypnosis. New York: Julian, 1972.

METZNER, RALPH. Maps of Consciousness. New York: Collier/Macmillan, 1971.

MORGAN, MARABEL. The Total Woman. New York: Pocket Books, 1975.

MOSS, THELMA. The Probability of the Impossible. New York: NAL, 1975.

NAMIKOSHI, TOKUJIRO. Shiatsu Therapy: Its Theory & Practice. San Francisco: Japan Publications, 1974.

THE NEW WOMAN'S SURVIVAL CATALOG. New York: Coward McCann, 1973.

ORAGE, ALFRED. Psychological Exercises & Essays. New York: Weiser.

ORNSTEIN, ROBERT E. Psychology of Consciousness. Baltimore, Md.: Penguin, 1975.

ORNSTEIN, ROBERT E. (Ed). Symposium on Consciousness. New York: Viking Press, 1976.

OSTRANDER, SHEILA and LYNN SCHROEDER. Natural Birth Control. New York: Bantam, 1973.

OSTRANDER, SHEILA and LYNN SCHROEDER. Psychic Discoveries Behind the Iron Curtain. Englewood Cliffs, N.J.: Prentice Hall, 1970.

OSWALD, IAN. Sleep. Baltimore, Md.: Penguin, 1966.

PARKER, ADRIAN. States of Mind: ESP and Alternate States of Consciousness. New York: Taplinger, 1975.

PEARCE, JOSEPH C. Exploring the Crack in the Cosmic Egg. New York: Julian Press, 1974.

PERLS, FREDERICK S. In and Out the Garbage Pail. New York: Bantam, 1972.

PERLS, FREDERICK S. Gestalt Therapy Verbatim. New York: Bantam, 1971.

PETERSON, SEVERIN. A Catalogue of the Ways People Grow. New York: Ballantine, 1971.

A PILGRIM'S GUIDE TO PLANET EARTH. San Rafael, Ca.: Spiritual Community, 1974.

PIRSIG, ROBERT M. Zen and the Art of Motorcycle Maintenance: An Inquiry into Values. New York: William Morrow, 1974.

PONCE, CHARLES. The Game of Wizards. Baltimore, Md.: Penguin, 1975.

RAM DASS, BABA. Be Here Now. New York: Harmony, 1971.

RANDALL, JOHN. Parapsychology and the Nature of Life. New York: Harper & Row, 1976.

REICH, WILHELM. Character Analysis. New York: Farrar, Straus, 1970.

REIK, THEODORE. The Search Within: The Inner Experiences of a Psychoanalyst. Chicago: Funk & Wagnall, 1968.

RHINE, LOUISA E. PSI, What Is It? New York: Harper & Row, 1975.

RIMMER, ROBERT. The Harrad Experiment. New York: Bantam, 1973.

ROGERS, CARL. Client-Centered Therapy. New York: Houghton Mifflin, 1951.

ROGERS, CARL. On Becoming a Person. New York: Houghton Mifflin, 1970.

ROSENFELD, EDWARD. The Book of Highs. New York: Quadrangle/N.Y. Times, 1973.

RUBINSTEIN, MOSHE F. Patterns of Problem Solving. Englewood Cliffs, N.J.: Prentice-Hall, 1975.

RUGG, HAROLD. Imagination. New York: Harper & Row, 1963.

RUITENBECK, HENDRIK M. (Ed). Going Crazy. New York: Bantam, 1972.

RUSSELL, BERTRAND. Autobiography. Boston: Little, Brown, 1967.

SAMUELS, MIKE and HAL BENNETT. The Well Body Book. New York: Random House, 1973.

SAMUELS, MIKE and NANCY SAMUELS. Seeing with the Mind's Eye. New York: Random House, 1975.

SARTRE, JEAN PAUL. Existentialism & Human Emotions. Secaucus, N.J.: Citadel, 1971.

SELYE, HANS, M.D. Stress Without Distress. New York: NAL, 1975.

SHAH, IDRIES. The Way of the Sufi. New York: Dutton, 1970.

SHAPIRO, EVELYN (Ed). Psychosources. New York: Bantam, 1972.

SKINNER, B. F. Walden Two. New York: Macmillan, 1960.

SKINNER, B. F. Beyond Freedom and Dignity. New York: Knopf, 1971.

SPENCE, LEWIS. An Encyclopaedia of Occultism. Secaucus, N.J.: Citadel, 1974.

A SPIRITUAL COMMUNITY GUIDE, 1975-76. San Rafael, Ca.: Spiritual Community, 1975.

STEINBRECHER, EDWIN. The Guide Meditation. Santa Fe: DOME Foundation.

SUZUKI, SHUNRYU. Zen Mind, Beginner's Mind. New York: Weatherhill, 1970.

THIE, JOHN F., et al. Touch for Health. Santa Monica, Ca.: DeVorss & Co.

THOMMEN, GEORGE S. Is This Your Day? New York: Crown, 1973.

THOMPSON, WILLIAM J. At the Edge of History. New York: Harper & Row, 1971.

TOBEN, BOB, JACK SARFATTI and FRED WOLF. Space-Time and Beyond. New York: Dutton, 1975.

TOTH, MAX and GREG NIELSEN. Pyramid Power. New York: Warner, 1976.

TRIPP, C. A. The Homosexual Matrix. New York: McGraw Hill, 1975.

VON NEUMANN, JOHN. The Computer and the Brain. New Haven, Cn.: Yale Univ. Press, 1958.

WALLECHINSKY, DAVID and IRVING WALLACE. The People's Almanac. New York: Doubleday, 1975.

WATTS, ALAN. The Book. New York: Vintage, 1972.

WATTS, ALAN W. The Way of Zen. New York: Vintage, 1957.

WEIL, ANDREW. The Natural Mind: Another Way of Looking at the Higher Consciousness. New York: Houghton Mifflin, 1972.

WHEELER, JOHN A. Geometrodynamics. New York: Academic Press, 1962.

WILHELM, R. and C. F. BAYNES (Eds). The I Ching or Book of Changes. Princeton, N.J.: Princeton Univ. Press, 1967.

YEE, MIN S. and DONALD K. WRIGHT (Eds). The Great Escape. New York: Bantam, 1974.

YOGANANDA, PARAMAHANSA. Autobiography of a Yogi. Los Angeles: Self-Realization Fellowship, 1971.

ALPHABETICAL LISTING / contents

It's not
where
you're
going —

it's
where
you're
coming
from

N.L.

Corita